SECURITY ANALYSIS AND PORTFOLIO MANAGEMENT

(SECOND EDITION)

SECURITY ANALYSIS AND PORTFOLIO MANAGEMENT

(SECOND EDITION)

A. P. Dash
Professor
Finance & Strategy
Power Management Institute, Noida
(NTPC Ltd.)

TECHSAR™
NEW DELHI

Published and Printed by

Techsar Pvt. Ltd.
4435–36/7, Ansari Road, Daryaganj
New Delhi-110 002 (India)
E-mail: tech_info@techsarworld.com
Website: www.techsarworld.com

ISBN: 978-93-80026-10-7

Reprint 2025

Foreword

Dr. A.P. Dash has been involved with teaching business management courses for nearly two decades and has a strong industry background to his credit. His book "Security Analysis and Portfolio Management" is getting published at a critical juncture when the entire economy of India is registering a high growth trajectory and the sensex is scaling great heights, unheard of in the history of Indian Stock Market. I am happy to note that the book has been able to capture the dynamics of the economy, the complexity of the market, the increasing number of instruments including derivatives, the sizeable number of portfolios and above all the strategic decision making process of the players in the market.

The language of the book has been made so lucid that any common investor would like to go through the same with effortless ease. For management students, the book would be of great use for its conceptual clarity, practical insights and live cases. Further, for those who want to grasp the dimensions of investments, the book would be beneficial from its simplicity of approach; in addition, readers with a quantitative mindset who are eager to build rigorous mathematical modeling in security analysis would also find the book useful in the sense that the book has discussed world class models in practice especially in the chapters of technical analysis, value at risk and derivatives.

A key feature is the chapter on Commodity derivatives, which is yet to make a widespread impact in India. The USP of the book would certainly be the inclusion of case analysis specific to Indian conditions. The author has taken effort and care to include customized data on intra-company comparison leading to great learning events for a student.

There is a need for a book on Security Analysis which does not rely heavily on complex mathematical models or management jargon. I firmly believe that Dr. Dash's book fulfills this need. To say the least, the text would be of immense use for fund managers, bankers and business analysts as well.

Prof. P.G. Apte
Director
IIM Bangalore

Preface to the Second Edition

When I wrote this book last year, all indices are scaling great heights and the stock market was experiencing a boom phase unheard of in the economic history of India. Slowly the inflation crept in as a result of global pressure arising out of increased prices of crude oil. We did not have an immediate answer. When the inflation reached a double digit figure, the GDP shrunk and the stock market went for a spin. Efforts were made by the Government to contain inflation through increasing CRR, repo rate, bringing down the excise duty on steel and several measures but the inflation still hovered around 8-9 percent. To add to the cup of woe, the sub prime crisis gripped USA and the tremor was felt in India. Every stock market in the world panicked. ICICI alone suffered millions of dollars. The only silver lining was the emergence and flow of private equity in a major way to the Indian industry. All these put together had a cumulative impact on the stock market and the sensex hovered around 12000-15000 mark.

The sensex came down to an abysmal low of 8000 towards September/October 2008. All this happen due to global meltdown. Great Banks, consultancy firm and industries fell like pack of cards. Corporate governance and risk management became of global issue. USA came out with a bail-out package to salvage the economy. Fed rate came down to 0.25% to ease interest rate and augment money supply. To save our economy, towards December 2008, CRR, Reporate, SLR brought down by RBI to boost liquidity in the market and enhance economic activity. Markets did lookup. Sensex scaled upto 10000+ mark. It remains to seen if we can really sustain this of market trend.

Keeping in view the fast paced developments in India as well as the economic upheaval in the world, the book got revised to factor in the latest happenings and the following chapters are added to make the book more result oriented, contemporary, focused and comprehensive.

1. Dynamics of the Indian economy
2. Fundamental Analysis: Valuation of companies
3. performance of mutual fund in India
4. sub-prime crisis and securitization
5. Private equity

The chapter on 'dynamics of the Indian economy' includes the different facets of the economy like financial system, monetary policy, FDI, FII, and to cap it all, the capital account convertibility, on which our Prime minister has raised a debate. It also includes the interrelationship of the sub-systems to show their dynamics and dependence. The chapter is written with an intention to acquaint the readers with common terms like CRR, repo rate, money supply and forex, which gets flashed daily in the news channels or news papers.

The valuation chapter is a logical extension of the chapter on fundamental analysis and it contains a high level of academic rigor to analyse the same. In the age of active M&A, it would serve the curiosity of students who always wondered how a company gets valued and another company is eager to pay the value. The chapter contains the intricacies of pricing an IPO and ends with a suggestive case of NTPC where an attempt has been made to take the student through to a real life situation. This is a path-breaking study we have made way back in June 2006 hitting at a IPO price of Rs.56 and the real price band came very close to what we predicted like Rs.52-62 in the market towards September 2006.

The inclusion of the chapter on mutual fund was long warranted in view of the fact that mutual fund investment have suddenly looked up and seen as a safe haven of investment by small investors. The chapter contains useful analysis and latest trends in the mutual fund investments, which would be extremely beneficial for the students. The subsequent chapters on sub-prime crisis and private equity would be a real treat to the students, investors, bankers, for, a lot of effort has gone into making incisive analysis and arriving at meaningful conclusions. While the entire world debates on the issue of sub-prime crisis, we have made our small contribution in bringing out finer details of the same to facilitate a common reader demystify the issues and their likely impact on India.

Keeping the above in view, it was our earnest effort to make the book a wholesome reading. It is got be a great learning exercise with 'live Indian cases' loaded in every critical issue In the dynamic domain of security analysis and portfolio management, a book need to be constantly revised to accommodate contemporary issues, say with all clarity of the development around the world and positioning of our economy against the backdrop of the global concerns. To say the least, we have precisely achieved the above milestones in the revised edition of the book.

A.P. DASH

Preface to the First Edition

This book endeavours to provide concepts, text and cases for a course on security analysis and portfolio management, which is widely taught in the business schools around the world. It is consciously planned to help students to acquire knowledge, develop analytical skills and gain insights pertaining to how fund managers strike winning strategies for investment by using time-tested, validated and proven techniques. The book deals with these techniques—which range from fundamental analysis to mundane mathematical models—so well that it would be immensely useful for the fund managers themselves, who take real time decisions in the marketplace. The book is divided in four broad parts. Part One (chapters 1 to 4) describes the global investment scenario, major investment decisions, and the dynamics of the securities markets. Part Two (chapters 5 to 6) deals with the critical aspects of risk and return culminating in capital asset pricing model (CAPM). Part Three (chapters 7 to 10) discusses the most important analysis in investment decisions, wherein good mathematical models are factored in and applied to live conditions through building up Case analysis. Part Four (chapters 11 to 14) deals with the exotic instruments of derivatives and its applications, where cutting-edge research around the globe is going on. The last chapter (Chapter 15) is on a very contemporary topic of corporate governance, which spells transparency and has become synonymous with the brand equity of companies. The book is designed to meet the expectations of common investors as well as hard core professionals, like fund managers, who put the precious resources at risk for higher returns. The urge to meet both ends of the spectrum emanates from my wide experience in the business schools of India, which I have tried to capture in the following lines.

During my tenure of teaching at premier business schools, I developed a firm belief that most of the good books in the market on security analysis have become obsessed with either complex mathematical models or full of management jargons which puts off a common reader who has an interest in investment. Some of the average books, written exclusively to cater to the immediate need of passing an examination, hardly try to capture the dynamics of the market. For example, way back in1995, I used to teach in my MBA class that SENSEX above 4000 is bullish and below 2000 is bearish. Today, I do not know how to recast and reengineer my statement in view of the fact that the index is scaling 15000 mark outpacing the global rising trend of indices. With India getting globalised and poised to register an impressive growth in GDP, any major event in the world has been affecting my stock market quickly. Euphemistically, people say - if the NASDAQ sneezes, the BSE and NSE catch cold. Towards the end of July 2007, home loan default in USA caused many stock market index to nosedive including that of India. The SENSEX shed 521 points in a day. Major chunk of the variation in the stock market today can be attributable to Foreign Institutional Investors (FII) investment. The reason for one FII to disinvest in India may not be due to the fact that our stock market is not providing adequate returns but some other country's stock market is providing higher returns than us. To add to this, Private Equity (PE) firms are equally active today and have become critical to our stock market growth and investment.

Keeping the above in view, when I started writing this book, the most important thing that has been working at the back of my mind, as said earlier, was the its ability to satisfy the student and common investor's curiosity and in the same breath, address the expertise of a professional. Attempts have been made in the book to keep the language very simple and lucid so that a common investor can effortlessly grasp the dimensions. A typical MBA student, who has come from a non-finance stream, would also like to go through the book for better understanding and acquire knowledge. MBA students with finance background would love the book for the critical analysis we have made in each chapter. The book goes beyond the numbers and tries to address qualitative aspects of investments as well. Recently, a number of small time farmers in Uttar Pradesh traded in the commodity futures in taking up positions which they felt would insulate them from a risk like crop failure but when their hedging did not turn into reality most of them went bankrupt. In India farmers committing suicide due to crop failures are not uncommon. The book throws up qualitative social issues like this for further research.

People say, stock market is just like a bubble no body knows when it will burst and how long it will sustain. The book is an effort to analyse this dynamic market which is full of strategies of hedgers, brokers and investors but still no body has become master of this game. This Indian market contains roughly around 50 sectors and 10,000 companies, which makes it extremely difficult to analyse the companies individually. Hence there is a great need for intelligent computersied modeling like neural network, fuzzy logic and the like to hammer out strategies at critical junctures. To satisfy the need of MBA students, who believe in the rigors of mathematical modeling, efforts are being made to capture the world class models and their applications.

A very special effort has been made to cater to the need of fund managers who either burn their fingers or make a kill in the stock market. Given the massive and mammoth size of investment fund managers bring in, they cannot afford to a very small mistake, for, it might create havoc with their decision making process leading to colossal loss. The in-depth analysis in each chapter, especially in the fundamental and technical analysis, supported by well-articulated modeling makes it a formidable combination which would help the fund managers take wiser decisions.

The chapters on Derivatives have been dealt with much care and much detail. We not only addressed to the financial derivatives but a considerable focus has been given on the commodity derivatives. The USP of the book is the brilliant cases we have developed specific to Indian conditions.

A.P. DASH

Acknowledgements

In my earlier books, people from different walks of life helped me a lot in providing critical comments and in the process enrich the contents to a great extent. In the evolution of this book, I am especially thankful to my students, scholars, colleagues and reviewers, who have immensely helped me in building up the book brick by brick. A massive project of this nature is never complete without sustained efforts, professional advice, intellectual rigor, encouragement and inspiration from different quarters at different points of time. I express my heartfelt gratitude to esteemed Professors in Finance and Strategy – Prof. PG Apte, Prof. Prasanna Chandra, Prof. A Banerjee, Prof. Ranjan Das, Prof. Rajat Bakshi, Prof. LC Gupta, Prof. SK Choudhri, Prof. CP Gupta, and Prof. BB Chakrabarti - with whom I have been associated and who has been a great inspirational force for me in writing this book. My students, trainees, scholars and participants of the executive development programs have not only provoked me by providing the necessary academic stimuli but by contributing a lot in supporting me at different stages of writing the book. I am thankful to my colleague and scholars – Mr. Santosh Behera, Mr Abhas Mohanty, Ms. Indrani Mukherjee and Mr. Sarbesh Mishra—who have helped me in not only shaping up the book intelligently but reviewing the same in greater details. I wish to thank my students/trainees – Satish, Monash, Pranay, Navin, Richa—who did brilliant projects with me and provided the research inputs for the book wherever necessary.

I express my deep gratitude to my parents, brothers and sisters, who have blessed the project to see the light of the day. I thank my wife, Dipti, who stood by me through thick and thin and provided the necessary support whenever my confidence took low ebb. I thank Arnab—my only son and the apple of my eye – who is matured enough now to throw up honest criticism about me but would earnestly ask when the book would be completed.

My sincere thanks to Mr. Harvinder Singh of my Institute, who knows my research interests and would all the while, support me selflessly with relevant articles from net, magazines and books.

While writing this text, I earnestly hope that my readers would support me by contributing their valuable suggestions, recommendations and thoughts, which I would treasure and share in my next edition.

A.P. DASH

Contents

1

Introduction to Investment

Globalization has thrown up many challenges and it has become increasingly complex to do business in the wired village of the next millennium. There is a bewildering collection of securities, markets and financial institutions. Investors, today, are being loaded with information, thanks to the Internet and the growing number of websites that are devoted to information on investments. Hence, it is necessary for them to browse through and evaluate this information. For this it is necessary to understand the fundamentals of investment. While terminology and trading mechanisms may change, learning to carefully analyze and evaluate investment opportunities will pay off under any circumstances. The economic well-being of an investor in the long run depends significantly on how wisely he invests. Investments in securities in the capital markets are a key factor for the economic growth of the country. If the economic environment is ripe and the corporate management expectations are optimistic a firm normally wishes to expand in order to increase its earnings. The expansions can be financed by gaining access to the capital markets i.e. through the sale of stocks and bonds. The investors who have earned profits on earlier investments in securities or have observed others doing this will be ready to provide fund for the expansions. Thus firms grow, jobs are provided, families prosper and eventually, the economy grows.

DEFINING INVESTMENT

The dictionary meaning of investment is to commit money in order to earn a financial return or to make use of the money for future benefits or advantages. People commit money to investments with an expectation to increase their future wealth by investing money to spend in future years. For example, if you invest Rs. 1000 today and earn 10 % over the next year, you will have Rs.1100 one year from today.

Investment benefits both economy and the society. It is an outgrowth of economic development and the maturation of modern capitalism. For the economy as a whole, aggregate investment sanctioned in the current period is a major factor in determining aggregate demand and, hence, the level of employment. In the long term, current investment determines the economy's future productive capacity and, ultimately, a growth in the standard of living. By increasing personal wealth, investing can contribute to higher overall economic growth and prosperity. The process of investing helps to create financial markets where companies can raise capital. This too, contributes to greater economic growth and prosperity. Specific types of investments provide other benefits to society as well. For instance, common stocks provide a mechanism for stockholders to monitor the performance of company management. At the same time, municipal bonds provide capital for valuable public projects such as schools and roads. Although, the rewards of investing are obvious, investing is not without risk. However, over the long run, the rewards of investing outweigh the risks.

Investment teaches how we can use our accumulated assets to earn a monetary return instead of waiting to spend those assets on consumption. Thus investment can be defined as the purchase of an asset to produce a return. Therefore, before investing, one must accumulate some assets, which is done through the process of saving, or spending less than our incomes. This applies to all financial entities, be it a household, business or a unit of government. Assets that are accumulated by saving may or may not earn a return. However, the overall return that an investor may realize depends upon a number of things such as amount of money available for investment; the degree of risk that the investor is willing to take; the amount of immediate income that is needed; the degree of liquidity that is required; the intelligence and knowledge that the investor processes; and sheer luck.

An investment is a commitment of funds made in the expectation of some positive rate of return. If the investment is done properly, the return will be commensurate with the risk the investor assumes. It is the employment of funds with the aim of achieving additional income. It involves the commitment of resources, which have been saved away from current consumption in the hope that some benefit will accrue in future.

Investment involves the use of current funds of a purpose other than to satisfy the immediate consumption need of the owner. Therefore, the application of money to a purpose, which does not involve immediate use on the part of the owner, is known as investment of money. It is an operation that involves the transfer of money or title to money into the hands of others, who in return, agree to return them with interest or dividend.

INVESTMENT IN FINANCIAL SENSE VS. ECONOMIC SENSE

The nature of investment in the financial sense differs from its use in the economic sense. Investors or suppliers of "capital" view investment as a commitment of funds to derive future income in the form of interest, dividends, rent, premiums, pension benefits or the appreciation of the value of their principal capital. To the financial investor, it is not important whether money is invested to a productive use or for the purchase of second-hand instruments such as existing shares and stocks listed on the stock exchange. It is simply the allocation of monetary resources that are expected to yield some gain or positive return over a given period of time. Most investments are considered to be transfers of financial assets from one person to another. These assets may range from safe investments to risky investments. However to the economists, investment means the net addition to the economy's capital stocks, which consists of goods, and services that are used in the production of other goods and services. Therefore, in this context, investment implies the formation of new and productive capital in the form of new construction, new producers' durable equipment such as plant and equipment. Inventories and human capital are also included in the economists' definition of investment. Though, the meaning of investment in financial and economic sense are different, they cannot be said to be independent. They are related to one another.

INVESTMENT CONCEPTS

"Investment" or "Investing", like value is a word of many meanings. Evolution of new investment concepts would result a dramatically change of the whole investment scene over next few years. Basically, there are three concepts of investment:

1. Economic investment i.e. an economist definition of investment.
2. General investment in a more generic or extended sense, which is used by "the man on the street".
3. Financial investment, the sense in which we are going to be very much interested.

Economic Investment

Economic Investment includes net additions to the capital stock of the society. "Capital stock of society" means those goods, which are used in the production of other goods. In society there are a number of goods (such as building, machinery etc.), which are used to produce other goods. These means of production are considered the capital stock of society. Thus, investment in the capital stock means an increase in buildings, machinery or inventories over the amount of equivalent goods that existed, say, one year ago at the same time.

General Investment

The everyday usage of the term investment can mean a variety of things, but to **the common man** on the street it usually refers to a money commitment of some sort. For example, a common man will perceive buying a new house or a new car as an investment. But these are in very general or extended sense of word as neither there is any rate of return involved or any financial return or capital growth is expected.

Financial Investment

Financial investment means an exchange of financial claims such as securities, real estate mortgages etc. Investors, to differentiate between the pseudo-investment concept of the consumer and the real investment of the businessman, often use the term financial investment. For example, there is a difference between an investment in a ticket on a horse and a construction of a new plant or between pawning of a watch and planting of a field of corn. Here, investment in a ticket on a horse or pawning of a watch are instances of pseudo-investment whereas construction of a new plant or a field of corn is the case of real investment. Some investments are simply transactions among people while others involve nature. The latter are "real" investments; the former are "financial" investments.

WHY IS INVESTMENT IMPORTANT

Why is investment important or why do people invest? The simple answer to this question is to 'make money'. This can be explained by the following story.

Donald and Mildred Othmer of New York lived quiet, unpretentious lives. Donald, who died in 1995, was a professor of chemical engineering at Brooklyn Polytechnic University. Mildred, a former teacher, died in 1998. When they died, they both were in there nineties. What came, as a shock to friends was that they left a combined estate worth about $800 million, the bulk of which was left to a variety of non-profit organizations. How did they accumulate such an impressive amount of wealth? Simply put, the Othmers, like many other Americans, got rich by investing their money sensibly, leaving it invested for a long period, and living modestly. In the early 1960s, the Othmers turned over their life savings, then fifty thousand dollars, to famed investor Warren Buffet, an old family friend. In the early 1970s, the Othmers received shares of Buffet's new company; Berksheie Hathaway who in turn invests in other companies such as American Express, Coca-Cola and Gillette. When the Othmers received their Berkshire shares, the price was $42 per share; at the time of Mildred's death the price has risen to $77,000 per share. Although, the Othmers were smart, or perhaps just lucky to pick Buffet to manage their money, a similar investment, made at the same time, in the overall stock market would have grown to more than $100 million by the middle of 1998.

To be more precise, people invest to improve their welfare or to increase their monetary wealth, both current and future. By holding cash you forego the opportunity to earn on that cash. Investors are, usually, interested only in monetary benefits to be obtained from investors. By foregoing consumption today and invest in the savings, investors expect to enhance their future consumption possibilities by increasing their wealth. Investors also seek to manage their wealth effectively, obtaining the most from it while protecting it from inflation, taxes and other factors. To accomplish both the objectives, people invest. People also invest in order to meet personal goals such as buying a home or providing better education to children.

As far as a firm is concerned, investment provides not only the most important decision, which an investor (business proprietor) has to make, but also with one of the toughest. The decision will affect the operating environment of the firm throughout the entire life of the investment. The quality of such decisions will largely determine the future prosperity and health of the firm.

Investment generates by increasing capital per worker and is itself stimulated by growth, as rapid growth produces buoyant expectations in a self- sustaining process. However, it must be noted that investment alone, does not guarantee economic or social growth. Profitable opportunities must be identified and exploited.

From the foregoing discussion, it can be concluded that investment is both important and useful in the context of present-day situations due to the following set of factors.

Longer Life Expectancy

Investment decisions are important today because people live longer then in the past. Life expectancies are rising in most countries, both developed and developing. A 65-year old in sound health can be expected to live for at least another twenty years. The main effect of longer life expectancies is an increase in the duration of a person's average retirement period. Thus, they will need more money when they retire. Accumulating funds for retirement is one major reason why people invest. Further, the increasing cost of healthcare will require setting aside greater reserves in order to maintain same standard of living. Therefore, earnings from employment should be calculated in such a manner that a portion should be put away as savings. Savings by themselves do not increase wealth, but must be invested in such a way that the principal and the return will be adequate enough for a longer retirement period. In other words, the investment decision made during one's working life will be responsible for a financially secured retirement.

Growth in Personal Income

Investment results in general increase in the employment opportunities, which gave, rise to both male and female workforce. However, one should not merely rely on increasing personal income to improve one's future standard of living. The key to improving a future standard of living is careful investment.

Changing Labor Market

Nowadays, the old ideal of working in a company and being there until retirement is an exception. Even IBM, which once had a reputation of virtually guaranteeing lifetime employment, has reduced its workforce by more than 100,000 in the past few years. People will have to rely more on their own resources and less on corporate paternalism to meet their financial goals. Everyone should accumulate a larger cushion of resources to survive an unexpected fall because you never know when your employer is going to downsize your job out of existence.

Increasing Rates of Taxation

Increasing rates of taxation introduce an element of compulsion in a person's savings. There are various forms of saving outlets in the form of investments that help in bringing down the tax-rates. For example, investments in UTI certificates, LIC, NSC, Post-office Cumulative Deposit Schemes etc. Hence, besides safety of principal and high rates of interest, an investor should always bear in mind the taxation angle. An investment should be such that the interest earned is compensated by an increase in tax rates.

Inflation

Inflation has become a continuous problem since the last two decades. High rates of inflation bring a relatively rapid decline in purchasing power. Thus, in an inflationary environment, the purchasing power of cash diminishes. This results in fall of standard of living and many other problems. An investor should search an outlet, which gives him a high rate of return in the form of interest to cover any decrease due to inflation.

OBJECTIVES OF INVESTMENT

Investment is the sacrifice of certain present value for uncertain future reward. All investment choices are made at points of time in accordance with the personal investment ends and in contemplation of an uncertain future. Since investments in securities are revocable, investment ends are transient and the investment environment is fluid. As one conceives of the distant future, the reliable bases for reasoned expectations become more and more vague. Investors in securities should, therefore, reappraise and re-evaluate their various investment commitments from time to time, in the light of new information and changed expectations.

Investment helps in arriving at numerous decisions that are not only continuous but rational too. Investment decisions are found to be the outcome of three different but related classes of factors.

Informational or Factual Premises

The investor is provided with many streams of data that are taken together and represent the observable environment as well as the features of the securities and firms in which he may invest.

Expectational Premises

Various environmental and financial facts are made available to the investors that spark a light of expectations relating to the outcomes of alternative investments though they are subjective and hypothetical. This not only limits the range of investments, which may be undertaken but also the expectations of outcomes that may legitimately be entertained.

Valuational Premises

These comprise the structure of subjective preferences for the size and consistency of the income to be received and for the safety and negotiability of various investments as these are appraised from time to time.

SAVINGS AND INVESTMENT

Investment may be regarded as utilization of the savings of a country for further creation of wealth. Investment plays a central role in the process of economic development. The level of savings largely effects investment. All the people in an economy do not save for production. Their savings have to be mobilized for productive purposes. Then only it will lead to capital formation, which is the very core of economic growth. Saving is the excess of income overconsumption. Thus, something out of current consumption is kept aside for the creation of capital or wealth. Investment is the process of applying such savings to the creation of specific forms of capital.

SAVINGS ⟶ INVESTMENT ⟶ CAPITAL FORMATION

For example, if a person having a deposit of Rs. 1 crore in his bank account, devotes himself to the construction of a power house, and thereafter sells the power so generated, he has used his one crore rupees in the creation of capital, and that capital yields services in the form of "power", which can be sold and reconverted into "money". This process may be described as "investment". In developing countries like India where the process of economic development is quiet slow, it is very necessary to step up the rate of investment so that the country accumulates a large capital stock to accelerate production. As compared to other countries, the rate of saving and investment in India are extremely low. Saving and investment are two independent activities. With the increase in one, the other is also increased (Table 1.1).

Table 1.1. Growth of Saving and Investment in India

Year	At percent of gross domestic product at Market price		At percent of net domestic product at Market price	
	Gross Domestic Saving	Gross Domestic Capital Formation (Gross Investment)	Net Domestic Saving	Net Domestic Capital Formation (Gross Investment)
1994-95	24.4	23.2	23.1	22.9
1995-96	25.1	26.8	16.8	18.8
1996-97	23.2	24.5	14.6	16.1
1997-98	23.1	24.6	14.6	16.2
1998-99	21.7	22.7	13.3	14.5
1999-00	23.2	24.3	15.2	16.4
2000-01	23.4	24	15.3	16.0
2001-02	23.5	23.7	15.4	16.8
2002-03	24.2	24.8	16.2	17.5

INVESTMENT AND SPECULATION

The term 'investment' is used to suggest a commitment that is relatively free from certain risks of loss. It is restricted to situations promising dependable income, relatively stable value, a modest rate of return and relatively little chance for spectacular capital appreciation. People who seek high-income yields or large capital gains are therefore said to forsake investment for speculation.

Speculation differs from investment with respect to the time limit of the investor i.e. the period for which a person is investing and the risk-return characteristics of the investment. An investor is always interested in a good and consistent rate of return for a long period of time. However, a speculator is less interested in consistent returns and is more interested in earning very large returns, higher than the normal rate of return, in a short time.

The word 'speculate' comes from the Latin word *speculare* meaning 'to see ahead'. Speculation is a reasoned anticipation of future conditions. A speculator tries to perceive investment values ahead of the general public. It attempts to organize the relevant knowledge as a support for judgements. In fact, everything we do in this world is a speculation. One must have the courage to make decisions when the conditions are unfavourable such as panic, despair or optimism.

Most successful speculators operate on the simple principle of buying in underpriced markets and selling out in overpriced markets. Thus speculation is a deliberate assumption of risks in ventures, which offer the hope of commensurate gains. These expected gains might be much larger than a safe investment would offer. The speculators are more interested in price gains than in income.

There is a very fine line of division between investment and speculation, yet they are somewhat similar. Speculation requires an investment and investments are somewhat speculative in nature. In fact some financial experts have called investment as a well-grounded and carefully planned speculation or good investment is a successful speculation. There are no established rules or laws that can identify which securities are permanently for investment and which are for speculations. The securities have to be constantly reviewed in order to find out whether it is a suitable investment or not. A speculator should not go for each and every fresh opportunity. Rather he should take action only when the probabilities are highly in his favour. Though it is difficult for him to resist the speculative instincts, in the long run it will be beneficial for him. The tendency to speculate is very common, particularly when the market is bullish or buoyant. Investment can be distinguished from speculation as follows:

Length of Commitment

Investment usually allocates funds for a longer term usually at least one year. It involves putting money into an asset that is not marketable in order to avail a series of returns; the investment is expected to yield within that time period. On the other hand, speculation is a short run phenomenon; the time period may be of few days to few years. Speculators buy assets that are not marketable, as they do not plan to own for very long period.

Expectations

Investments are usually made with the expectation that a certain stream of income or a certain price, which has existed, will not change in the future. Speculators, on the other hand, are usually based on expectation that some change will occur.

Risk

All financial transaction is associated with risk i.e. possibility of incurring a loss. Even if safety of principal and interest are considered, there are certain non-manageable risks such as the purchasing power risk i.e. fall in the real value of the principal and interest; and the money rate risk i.e. fall in market value when interest rate rises. These risks affect both investors and the speculators. Investment involves limited risk whereas speculation involves a higher level of risk and a more uncertain expectation of return.

Stability of Income

In case of investment, purchase of securities is preceded by proper investigation and analysis with an aim to receive good and stable return for a longer period of time. However, for speculators, the primary motive is to achieve profits through price changes. They are less interested in consistent returns and are more in earning very large. Hence, they receive a return that is uncertain and erratic.

Psychological Attitude

The psychological attitude of an investor is cautious and conservative. He constantly evaluates the worth of a security. On the contrary, a speculator is daring and a risk taker. He is solely interested in market action and price movements and does not go for any kind of investigation or evaluation.

Basis of Purchase Decision

An investor makes his purchase decision or investment decision by analyzing and evaluating the intrinsic worth and prospects of the company. On the other hand, a speculator makes his purchase decision basing solely on hunches, tips hearsay, "inside dope", technical charts, and market psychology.

Leverage

Usually an investor uses his own funds or borrowed funds. However, a speculator normally resorts to borrowings, which can be very substantial to supplement his personal resources.

However the distinction between speculation and investment is not quite clear cut, as many long term investors consider timing to be an important part of investment strategy and risk may be worth accepting provided it is accompanied by the expectation of commensurate reward. Thus, the difference between investment and speculation is a matter of the degree of risk foreseen and investors do not always find safety in confining their investments to conventionally 'safe' items. The risks of investment are multiple and investments that promise high safety of income are usually the most 'risky'.

Thus there is nothing immoral or undesirable about speculation. It needs no defense. Sometimes it may end in disaster but only due to its abuse. However, speculation when undertaken with a full sense of market responsibilities i.e. responsibilities of market reputation and market traditions, may be a service to the economy. Sometimes the adjustment of prices in response to the law of demand and supply is so slow that the market will be in a bearish state or in a state of 'stock-water'. The consumers/investors will not take the lead in buying lest prices would drop still further. When the speculators start buying in quantities that at once affect the market. The consumers, who were, previously, hesitant to make purchase decisions, now are ready to buy paying any reasonable advance. The market is buoyant again; the speculator has performed well in his work. In fact, the nation would never have new industries or progress if speculators did not venture into untried projects. Sensible speculators do not gamble. They choose their ventures with care. They risk only what they can afford and if possible and required, they diversify their speculations to prevent errors in selection.

Success in speculation requires a much-specialized knowledge. Only those specialists who, out of their knowledge and experience are able to weigh carefully the possible outcomes may undertake speculative investment. This doesn't mean that a speculator will never make errors. No speculator can be right all the time but his substantial resources and superior judgement will permit him to maximize aggregate gains. If a speculator is correct half of the time, he is having a good average. Even being right three or four times out of ten should yield a fortune, if he has the sense to overcome his losses quickly on the ventures where he has been wrong.

INVESTMENTS AND GAMBLING

Gambling, according to most dictionaries, is an act of risk taking without the knowledge of the exact nature of risk. Many people speculate heavily on the strength of tips or gossip and plunge into situation, which they do not understand. This is gambling even though the commitment is of reasonable speculative quantity. Gambling is based on tips, rumors and it is an unplanned and non-scientific act. A gambler risks more than he / she can afford. It is considered to involve the shortest time period and highest risk. Typical examples of gambling are betting on horse riding, game of cards, lottery etc. Holding shares for the duration of a stock exchange fortnightly account might be termed as speculation but to bet on the course of the stock market over the same period with a bookmaker is considered to be a gambling.

In the foregoing numerous academic definitions of investment, speculation and gambling, it can be observed that most of them are framed around the following three differentiating factors:

1. What is the motive of the buyer? The investor presumably buys to procure an annual return under conditions of safety, whereas others buy for appreciation.
2. What type of security is bought-high grade or low grade? The investor presumably buys high-grade securities, the others low grade.
3. How long is the security held? The investor presumably holds for the long-term, the speculator for the short-term.

FEATURES OF INVESTMENT

Investment needs of different investors don't have any standard pattern. They differ from investor to investor. However, all investors have four tasks in common. First, they must determine their investment objectives clearly. Secondly, they must decide upon the types of investments to be used and the proportions of each to be acquired. Thirdly, they select investments of the desired types. And finally, they should study the long run values of suitable investments and time their purchase and sales accordingly. This four-fold task is the essence of successful investment management for an investor.

While making an investment decision, the investors should consider a number of features which their portfolios should possess. Thus, a successful investor should take into account the following twelve features in order to choose specific investments.

Safety of Principal

One of the investment objectives is safety of principal though the safety is not absolute or complete. An investor should carefully review the economic and industry trends before choosing the type of investment or the time of investment or the time of investment to ascertain safety of principal. He should avoid unsound and profit-less risks. Since errors are unavoidable, to ensure safety of principal, an investor should go for extensive diversification of assets.

Diversification can be vertical or horizontal. Vertical diversification occurs when securities of various companies engaged in different phases of production, from raw material to finished goods, are held in the portfolio. Whereas, horizontal diversification occurs when the portfolio contains the securities of various companies, which are in the same stage of production. Another way to diversify securities is to classify then according to bonds and stocks. These can, again, be classified according to issuers, dividend or interest earned, products of a firm, etc.

Adequate diversification means assortment of investment commitments in different ways such as by industry, geographically, by management personnel, by financial types or by maturities. A proper combination of these factors will reduce losses due to the decline of any company or industry, disaster in any geographic region such as, storm, flood or drought, defalcation by any management group, changes in price-level and interest rates.

But, diversification, if carried to extremes, is wasteful. Holding too many securities is undesirable as it is too hard for the investor to monitor them. Similarly, too small commitments in securities are uneconomic because of excessive commission charges and other costs in transaction. Probably the simplest and the most effective diversification is accomplished by holding different securities at the same time having reasonable concentration in each.

Liquidity and Collateral Value

Every investor requires a minimum fund to meet emergencies. To have assured and quick availability of fund an investor should have a sound portfolio with adequate liquidity. For an investment to be liquid, it must be reversible (i.e. the transaction can be reversed or terminated) and marketable (i.e. the investment can be sold in the market for cash). Whether the fund, that may be needed for business opportunities, is to be raised by sale or borrowing, it will be easier if the portfolio contains a planned proportion of high grade and readily saleable investment.

Stability of Income

Stability of income is an important factor for those investors who depend closely on income. Emphasis on income stability may not always be consistent with other investment principles. Income stability helps in stabilizing the prices of corporate stocks. But it is restricted to certain industries only. Thus insistence upon income stability leads to limitation in capital growth and diversification.

Purchasing Power Stability

An investor should maintain a stable purchasing power in order to balance his portfolio. For this, he should carefully study the degree of price level inflation expected, the possibilities of gain and loss in the investment available and the limitations imposed by personal considerations.

Adequacy of Income after Tax

An investor faces two problems while making an investment decision, one concerned with the amount of income paid by the investment and the other with the burden of income taxes upon that income. An investment programme, should therefore, be planned taking into consideration the tax status of the investor. It is very important to see that the income is adequate after paying taxes. An investor is always eager to obtain maximum cash returns on his investments and is prone to take excessive risks and immediate dividend is always preferred which may be beneficial at a later date. It is very difficult on the part of an investor to make a choice between adequate income and adequate security but it is possible to find out some goods stocks, which pay all their earnings in dividends.

Capital Growths

Growing rate of capital formation is a primary condition for rapid economic development. Investment is an essential ingredient in the capital growth of an economy. Investors are therefore constantly seeking for "growth stocks". An ideal "growth stocks" is the right issue in the right industry, bought at the right time.

Legality

The legal aspects of property ownership often, affect investment plans and decisions. So, law should approve all investments. Illegal securities may bring out many problems for the investors. Identification of legal securities and investing in such securities will help the investor in avoiding such problems.

Possible Appreciation

Stock, bond and real estate markets are all highly irregular. The investors should try to forecast which securities will possibly appreciate. This should be done carefully and not in a manner of speculation or gamble. An investor can make profit by choosing carefully, buying at the right time and switching from overpriced to underpriced items.

Freedom from Care or Paying Attention

Investments are always accompanied by risks. So it is not advisable to make investment and then forget. Constant supervision is necessary to avoid losses and to obtain good returns. One can minimize the attention required by their investments by employing professional investments counselor. Another way of being free from care or paying attention to the investments made is to invest in securities like UTI or LIC or any savings certificate. Here, the management of securities is left to the care of the investment management services of the trust.

Tangibility

Due to price-level inflation, confiscatory laws, or social collapse, intangible securities such as bank deposits, stocks or bonds have lost their value. So, some investors prefer to invest part of their wealth in tangible properties such as building, land, gold, etc. It may, however, be considered that tangible property yield no income apart from the direct satisfaction to their owners obtained from their use or possession.

Concealability

All properties, tangible or intangible, must be concealable in order to be safe from social disorders, government confiscation, or unacceptable levels of taxation. This concealment may be in the form of ownership abroad or ready transferability. For example, many hold secret title to gold or foreign money accounts in Swiss and other foreign banks. Gold and precious stones have long been esteemed as they combine high value with small bulk and are readily transferable.

THE INVESTMENT PROCESS

Viewing investment as a process, which goes on in every society, one may ask exactly what that process consists of and what limits it. The investment process is a complex activity that describes the steps of decision-making followed by an investor regarding the appropriate time to invest in. Traditionally, securities are analyzed and managed using a broad two-step process — security analyses and portfolio management. This two-step process may be broken down into the following steps:

Setting Investment Policy

The initial step of the investment process involves specification of investment objectives, investment constraints, determination of investable wealth, identification of potential investment assets, tax status of the investor, considering attributes of investment assets. Investment objectives should be stated in terms of both risk and return. In other words, the objective of an investor is to make a lot of money accepting the fact losses may be incurred. The typical objectives of investors are current income, capital appreciation, and safety of principal. Moreover, constraints arising due to liquidity, the time horizon, tax and other special circumstances, if any, must be identified. This step of investment process also identifies the potential financial assets that may be included in the portfolio basing on the investment objectives, amount of investable wealth and tax status of the investor.

Asset-mix Decision

An investor has to decide the proportions of stocks and bonds to be included in the portfolio. An appropriate stock-bond mix depends mainly on the risk tolerance nature of the investor.

Formulation of Portfolio Strategy

After the choice of asset mix, the very next step is to formulate an appropriate portfolio strategy. Broadly, there are two choices available – an active portfolio strategy and a passive portfolio strategy. An active portfolio strategy focuses primarily on earning superior risk adjusted returns. This strategy seeks to change the proportions chosen in the asset-mix expecting to earn more profit. While, a passive portfolio strategy involves holding a diversified portfolio that maintains a predetermined legal risk. This strategy determines the desired investment proportions and assets in a portfolio and maintains these, making a few changes over time, if necessary.

Perform Security Analysis

This step involves valuation and analysis of the securities available for investment regarding their future behaviour, expected return and associated risk. For valuation of securities, first of all, it is necessary to understand the characteristics of the various securities to estimate their worth. Secondly, a valuation model is to be applied to these securities to estimate their value (or price). The relative attractiveness of the security can be determined by comparing the estimated value with the current market price of the security. Basically, there are two approaches to security analysis—technical analysis and fundamental analysis. Technical analysis involves the study of stock market prices of a firm in order to predict the future price movements. By identifying an emerging trend or pattern in price movements of a stock, the technical analyst hopes to predict accurately the future price movements of the particular stocks. On the other hand, fundamental analysts, past price movements have no effect on the future prices of a stock. They say that the intrinsic (or true) value of an asset is equal to the present value of cash flows or earnings that the asset holder is expected to receive. To determine the intrinsic value of an equity stock, the security analyst must forecast the earnings and dividends expected from the stock and then convert to their equivalent present value by using an appropriate discount rate that reflects the riskiness of the stocks. Once the intrinsic value of the common stocks has been determined, it is compared to the current market price of the stocks. Stocks that have an intrinsic value more than the current market price are said to be under-valued or under priced and should be purchased whereas those that have an intrinsic value less than the current market price are said to be over-valued or over priced and should be sold out. However, fundamental analysts believe that the market will correct this mis-pricing of securities in future. In other words, undervalued stock prices will show unusual appreciation whereas prices of overvalued stocks will show unusual depreciation.

Portfolio Construction and Execution

After securities have been evaluated, the next step is construction and execution of the portfolio. This is the phase that is concerned with the implementation of portfolio strategy. This involves identification of the specific assets in which the investor should invest and determination of the proportions of investors wealth to be invested in each of the assets. An investor makes two types of decisions while constructing portfolios – the **asset allocation decision** and the **security selection decision.** The asset allocation decision is the choice among broad asset classes, while the security selection decision is the choice of particular securities to be held within each asset classes. Accordingly there are two approaches to portfolio construction – **top down** and **bottom up.** Top down portfolio construction starts with asset allocation and only after that, the investor decides on the particular securities to be held. On the other hand, in the bottom up approach, the portfolio is constructed from the securities that appear to be attractively priced without concerning about asset allocation. Thus, the main features of portfolio construction and execution are – determination of diversification level, consideration of investment timing, selection of investment assets and allocation of invest-able wealth to investment assets.

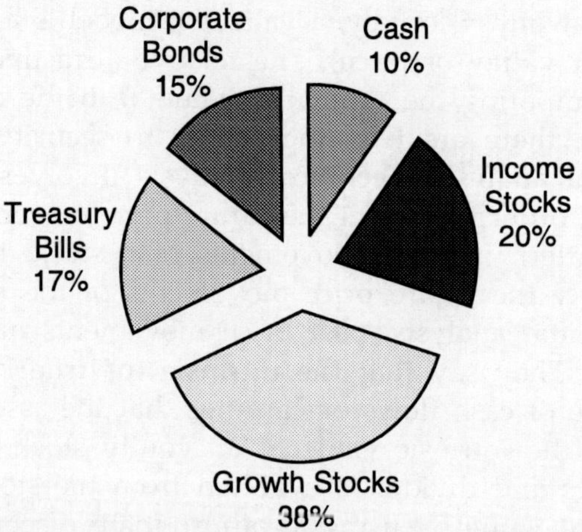

Portfolio Revision

Having built a portfolio, an investor must consider when and how to revise it. Portfolio revision involves the periodic repetition of the above steps. The investment objectives of an investor may change over time and the current portfolio may no longer be optimal for him. So the investor may form a new portfolio by selling certain securities and purchasing others that are not held in the current portfolio. Moreover, the value of a portfolio as well as its composition (i.e. the relative proportions of stock and bond components) may change over time as stocks and bonds tend to fluctuate. As a result, some securities that were not attractive initially may become attractive and vice-versa. In response to such changes, the investors may like to revise and rebalance his existing portfolio.

Performance Evaluation

The final step in the investment process is the performance evaluation of the portfolio. Investments are always made under conditions of uncertainty and it is necessary to evaluate periodically how the investment (portfolio) performed so that, if necessary, the investor may consider switching over to alternate proposals. The performance of evaluation of a portfolio is done in terms of risk and return. The key issue is whether the portfolio return is commensurate with its risk exposure. This may provide useful feedback to improve the quality of the portfolio management process.

REVIEW QUESTIONS

1. Define the term Investment.
2. Describe the process involved in making investment decisions.
3. Is the study of investments really important to most individuals?
4. Summarize the basic nature of investment decision in one sentence.
5. Why are investment decisions important?
6. What is the history of investing?
7. What steps are involved in investment process?
8. What are some important truisms in investments?
9. How can investing benefit society as a whole?
10. What is the general reason investment?
11. How long has investing been an organized socially acceptable activity?
12. Before you begin to invest what preparations should you complete?
13. What are the investment alternatives and which one should be chosen?
14. Distinguish between investment and speculation. Is it possible to incorporate investment and speculation within the same security? Explain.
15. What is liquidity and why is it so important to the efficient operation of Securities Market?
16. What external factors affect the decision process? Which do you think is the most important?
17. In your experience, have changes in the investment environment affected individual investors such as your family or yourself? If so, have these Investors become more sophisticated?
18. What have you learnt in previous finance or economics courses that you think is relevant to investments? Explain.
19. What are advantages and disadvantages of top down versus bottom up investment styles?
20. Firms raise capital from investors by issuing shares in the primary market. Does this imply that corporate financial manager's can ignore trading of previously issued shares in the secondary market?
21. Many investors would like to invest part of their portfolios in real estate, but obviously cannot on their own purchase office building or strip malls. Explain how this situation creates a profit incentive for investment firms that can sponsor REITs (Real Estate Investment Trusts).

2

Investment: Global Scenario

Investment refers to the sacrifice of present consumption for the uncertain future reward. Investment is concerned with management of investor's wealth, which is the sum of current income and present value of all future income. Investment consists of two primary functions: analysis and management. In investment decision two attributes are generally involved: risk and return.

A distinction is made between investment and savings. Savings is the forgone consumption whereas investment is restricted to real investment that increases the national output in the future. Investment can be of two types: real investment and financial investment.

Real investment often refers to the investing in tangible assets as gold real estate machinery and collectibles. Financial investment involves the contract written on the pieces of paper such as stocks, bonds, mutual funds, certificates of deposits. All knowledgeable investors invest in warrants, puts and calls, future contacts (derivatives), and convertible securities.

Financing of a shopping mall is the best example. Shopping mall is tangible to be considered real investment. But where do the money come from to the builder for construction. Some may come from direct investment and other would come from the borrowings from external source; this may be an individual or institution. So the builder has made real investment whereas institution has made financial investment in builder.

WHY DO WE INVEST?

We invest to make money! We invest to improve our monetary wealth, present and future both. Funds to be invested come from assets already owned, borrowed money and savings or forgone consumption. By foregoing their present consumption today and investing the savings, investors expect to enhance their future consumption possibilities by increasing their wealth. Investors also manage their wealth effectively, obtaining the most from it while protecting it from inflation, taxes and other factors.

Some people may wish to improve the return from their savings account funds by investing in alternatives.

INVESTMENT DECISION PROCESS

The investment of funds in various assets is only a part of financial decision and planning that any individual must do. An investment process describes how an investor (individual or firm) should go about making decision with regard to what marketable securities to invest in, decisions regarding risk and return factor.

1. Setting goals and objectives
2. Determining the appropriate risk level
3. Estimating the risk and return characteristics of individual investment option
4. Forming optimal portfolio
5. Performance review

1. Each investor must identify one's goal and objectives. Because there is a direct relationship between risk and return for the optimal portfolio. Investment objectives must be stated in terms of both risk and return. The ultimate portfolio depends on the investment objectives, amount of investable funds, and tax bracket of the investor. The young couple's objective will be different from an old couple.
2. Determining the risk level is the individual's own perspective to achieve the investment objective. It is the most critical and difficult aspect of the investment process. It will determine the portfolio mix. For example, a risk taker, a young individual may include high percentage of stocks in his portfolio whereas a risk averse, an old person investing for retirement purpose may include high percentile of bonds in his portfolio or invest in pension funds and so on.
3. Investment option analysis is the third step in the investment process. These options must be analyzed to determine the risk and return factor associated with it. The investment analysis may be done to find out whether instrument is mispriced. There are two approaches for it: technical analysis and fundamental analysis. Investment options are also analyzed on the basis of its opportunity cost—both domestically and globally.
4. Forming optimal portfolio is the fourth step in this process. It involves identifying those assets in which to invest, as well as determining portfolio is to be formed as to get the maximum return with given level of risk. The issues of selectivity, timing and diversification need to be decided by the investor.
5. Finally the investor must review the portfolio returns in order to determine whether the objectives are being met. It concerns with the periodic revision of previous steps. With the time investor's objective may change that means the current portfolio is not optimal. The investor may want to sell its securities due to either present need or its value. The securities may not perform well in market and other securities not held performing well. This decision also depends upon, among other things

such as the size of the transaction costs incurred in making these changes as well as the magnitude of the perceived improvement in the investment outlook.

WHY DO COMPANIES INVEST?

Companies do have the surplus funds or cash for short periods of time before money is required for capital expenditure, loan repayment, or some other purpose. Instead of accumulating these surplus funds in current account without intrest, companies prefer to invest them in variable financial instruments like term deposits with banks, money market, bonds, govt. securities, stocks, mutual funds and so on.

INVESTMENT PORTFOLIO

The company's short-term investment portfolio can be divided into three segments: ready cash, controllable cash, and free cash.

The *ready cash* is a reserve for the company's cash account. It is meant to meet the company's current operational needs. The investment in this segment must be highly liquid in nature (deposits with bank, government securities and treasury bills).

The *controllable cash* is the part of investment portfolio, which is meant to meet certain future outflows like taxes, dividend, interest payments, and loans repayment investment in this segment must consider the maturity period as well as the present value of future outflow.

The *free cash* is the surplus cash, which is meant neither to meet company's current operational needs nor known future outflows. These funds are mainly from liabilities side of balance sheet which are not actually cash outflows like depreciation reserve, invested in short term instruments to generate income, without much concern for liquidity or maturity.

CRITERIA FOR INVESTMENT DECISION

Safety is the foremost and most important criteria for investment decision of any company. It is the probability of getting back the money invested. Government securities and treasury bills are considered the safest instruments among all. A high degree of safety is required for an instrument for inclusion in the short-term investment portfolio. Mostly the companies decide about instruments through the ratings given by rating agencies like S&P, ICRA, and so on.

Liquidity

The liquidity of an instrument refers to the ability of the investor to convert it into cash on short notice without incurring any loss. An instrument will give definite return if it is held till maturity but risk of loss is high if sold prematurely.

Yield

The yield of an instrument is the return earned from it by way of interest, dividend, and capital appreciation. Some instrument does not pay interest and is redeemed at face value. Yield of an instrument is measured in post-tax terms.

Maturity

It is the life of an instrument. While some instruments have fixed original maturities, others can have tailor-made maturity like certificate of deposit. Generally the longer the maturity, the greater the yield.

OPTIMIZATION OF RETURN ON INVESTMENTS

Make Ad Hoc Investments

The financial manager makes investments in a somewhat ad hoc manner. Such a strategy makes some contribution, though not the optimal contribution, to profitability without impairing the liquidity of the firm. It is followed by the firms, which cannot devote enough time and resources to management of securities.

Ride the Yield Curve

To maximize the return from the marketable securities investors betting on interest rate changes such as swaps. If it were anticipated that the interest rate would fall in the near future, manager would raise the longer-term securities. On the other hand if interest would fall in the near future he will sell the longer-term securities. It will be done with interest rate swapping.

Develop Guidelines

The management will develop certain guidelines regarding the short-term investment such as (i) terms regarding speculation on interest rate changes; (ii) Holding marketable securities till they mature; (iii) restrictions regarding the percentage of liquid funds in a particular securities and (iv) minimize transaction cost. These are useful for firms regarding the liquidity management.

Manage Cash with a Portfolio Perspective

Define the efficient frontier

It represents a collection of all efficient portfolios. A portfolio is efficient if there is no alternative with (i) the same expected return with lower standard deviation or; (ii) the same standard deviation and higher returns or (iii) a higher expected return and lower standard deviation.

Select the optimal portfolio

The optimal portfolio is that point on the efficient frontier, which enables the investor to achieve the highest attainable level of return.

Follow a Mechanical Procedure

The manager may switch funds between the cash account and marketable securities using a mechanical procedure. Some models have been developed that provide rules for such mechanical procedure.

GLOBAL INVESTMENT TREND

A global marketplace of round the clock investing opportunities is emerging, and the international investor no longer thinks only of domestic investment alternatives. Reason behind the trend toward international investments is the realizations that the global market offers greater opportunities for investment and diversification help to manage risk. Investors in international securities may face additional risks, such as higher taxation, less liquidity, political problems, and currency fluctuations, which do not affect domestic investors. But despite of these risks, the higher returns may make these markets more attractive to investors. Morgan Stanley Capital International's Europe, Australasia, Far East (EAFE) Index, which observed 21 major world markets, stated a 13.29% average annual rate of return for the 30 years ended December 31, 2003, compared with the 13.67% average annual return of Standard & Poor's Composite Index of 500 Stocks (S&P 500). This difference in returns is due to the differences in economic and market environments in countries around the world.

The Japanese market in 1990s, was depressed due to the country's economic recession. Many Japanese stocks became undervalued. In 1999 the Japanese stock market showed a gain of more than 60%; in 2000 through 2002, the Japanese market again registered loss of 28%, 29%, and 10% respectively in 2000, 2001 & 2002, and then profit of 36.15% in 2003.The Japanese market is well known for its very high level followed by very low levels.

Western European markets are well developed and offer investors numerous alternatives, which are forecasted as the future economic power. The world's economy was introduced with the launch of European Economic and Monetary Union (EMU), along with the currency Euro—Europe's common currency on Jan 1, 1999. The Euro is the official currency of 17 countries. This marks a significant change for Europe and European financial markets. In anticipation of Euro European markets were up by 20 to 30 percent. EMU in past few years had brought most profound economic changes in Europe in the integration of financial markets in Euro area. This has been the result of elimination of inter area exchange rate risk.

Emerging markets continue to attract the attention of investors from all over the world. Despite the downturn in the developed and developing economies, emerging markets have remained in the growth path. The economic reforms, the expansion of European Union, and changing political climate are creating more investment opportunities worldwide.

Emerging markets of lesser developed countries are experiencing rapid economic growth and liberalization. Examples of emerging markets include countries like Mexico, Malaysia, Thailand, India and so on. The International Financial Corporation lists 79 countries that are considered to be emerging markets. These countries are generally experiencing growing population, increasing living standards, and income, rapid economic growth and relatively stable currency. Often these countries impose limits on foreign investment to limit the takeovers of domestic companies. They usually have restrictions on the holdings of shares of domestic companies.

Table: 2.1. Emerging Market Capitalization (in $ Billions)

	1990	1995	2002
Brazil	16	148	124
Korea	111	182	250
Mexico	33	91	103
South Africa	138	280	185
Taiwan	101	187	262

The potential of high returns of emerging markets comes with the high risk. The collapse of Thai Bhat began with lack of regulation among Thailand's real estate companies, causing fianacial problems to the nation's economy. The banks of both South Korea and Indonesia had unsound lending practices. And, in Brazil, a growing federal budget raised doubts by potential investors that the nation could ever repay its debts.

Currency risk presents another risk factor for emerging market investors. As the currency exchange rate fluctuates, it causes the fluctuations in the value of investment in U.S. dollar terms. Fortunately, many emerging countries have their local currencies pegged to the dollar, which results in a relatively constant exchange rate, but they are still subject to volatility.

Emerging markets are volatile as stated above; they are considered appropriate only for long-term investors with an investment timeframe of 10 or more years. According to S&P survey, in 2002, the average growth in the Gross Domestic Product (GDP) of developing countries was 3.4% and 2.8% in industrialized countries. According to the IMF, emerging markets will grow twice as fast as the industrialized countries through this decade. The emerging stock markets alone currently represent 10.4% of the capitalization of the world's equity markets. Along with high potential returns, emerging markets also offer diversification in portfolios. Because these markets tend not to move in pace with the developed countries, they may be rising while other markets are falling. Hence, they can help reduce the Beta of a portfolio. Based on these factors, many financial advisors recommend long-term

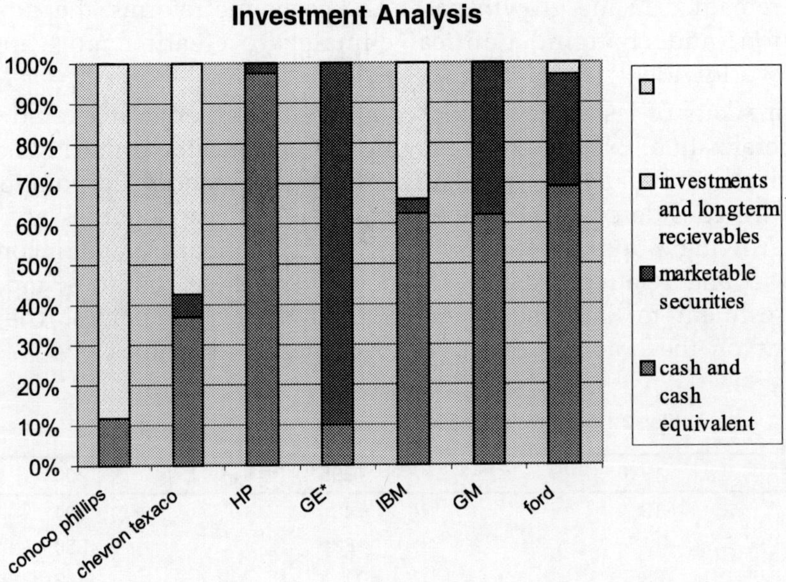

investors allocate 3% to 10% of their stock portfolio to emerging markets, depending on their investment goals and tolerance for risk.

FINANCIAL INSTRUMENTS

There are various financial instruments available to investors and portfolio managers. Every year new instruments are introduced in the market and some are withdrawn. The recent example is call and put option. It gives the holder the right to do something. It is an option on an option. This is how option is different from futures and forwards, where the holder is obligated to buy or sell the underlying asset. Many investment houses sell call and put option in commodity market also.

In broad terms financial instruments are classified in four segments.

The first is Money Market Instruments. These instruments are short-term cash investments. They usually have maturity period of one year or less, little or no default risk, and are highly liquid.

The second segment is Fixed-Income Capital Market Instruments. These instruments have longer-term maturities (greater than a year), their default risk is higher and they are generally less liquid.

The third segment is Equity Securities. These securities represent a residual claim on the assets of a corporation, i.e., all the fixed income obligations must be paid first.

The fourth one consists of all the other types of instruments such as Futures and Options.

MONEY MARKET INSTRUMENTS

What is Money Market?

In brief money market trades with debt securities or instruments with maturities of less than one year.

The need for money markets arises because the immediate cash needs of individuals, corporations, and government do not necessarily coincide with their receipts of cash. The money market enables large sum of money to be transferred quickly and at a low cost from one economic unit (business, government, bank, etc.) to another economic unit for relatively shorter period. For example, the companies sales receipt not necessarily occurs with the same pattern as their daily expenses. The excessive of cash balances in hand involve a cost in the form of forgone interest, called opportunity cost, those economic units with excess cash usually keep such balances to the minimum needed to meet their day-to-day transaction requirement. Economic units usually invest excess cash funds in financial securities that can be convertible in short notice back to cash with less risk of loss of value over the short investment horizon.

Money market instruments have characteristic of high degree of safety and generally issued in denomination of $1 million or more. The maturity period range from one day to one year, most common are 91 days or less. Active secondary market for most of the instruments allows them to be sold prematurely. Money market has no specific location or exchange for trading like securities and commodities exchanges. It is accessible from all parts of nation as it is a telephone market. The major participants in the money market are commercial banks, government, corporation, government-sponsored enterprise, money market mutual funds, futures market exchange, brokers and dealers, and the Federal Reserve.

Money market or money market instruments have three basic characteristics. First, money market instruments are generally sold in large denominations. Most of the money market participants want large amount of cash, so that transaction cost are relatively low to the interest paid. Individuals generally invest in the money market indirectly; the help of financial institution such as money market mutual funds. Second, money market instruments have low default risk; the risk of less or non-payment of principal and interest is generally very small. Since the money market instruments must be available for a quick return, therefore only high- quality borrowers with little risk of default can issue these.

Finally more market securities have maturity period of one year or less. The short-term maturity of money market instruments helps to lower the risk that interest rate changes will significantly affect the security's market value and price.

INDIAN MARKET SCENARIO

The Indian money market till mid-1980s was relatively underdeveloped with few instruments and strict regulations with regard to participants and interest rates. Another issue of concern was that the distribution of liquidity in the market was with a few large lenders and some borrowers. The basic requirement of a developed and liquid market that participants should have two-way quotes that is of both borrowing and lending, was also absent.

RBI became successful in minimizing volatility as well as aligning the interest rates through the active operation of Liquidity Adjustment Facility (LAF) combined with transaction under Open Market Operations (OMO) and recently with Market Stabilization Scheme (MSS). An important feature of these operations is that the present LAF framework, where the reverse repo rate attempts to provide the floor to the movement of call rates, has been in a position to hold all other short-term rates in reasonable alignment with the reverse repo rate. In other words, the RBI reverse repo rate has not only become the benchmark rate for call rates, it has also become the reference rate for market repo/Collateralized Borrowing and Lending Obligation (CBLO) rates with the spread between them declining over the years (Chart1).

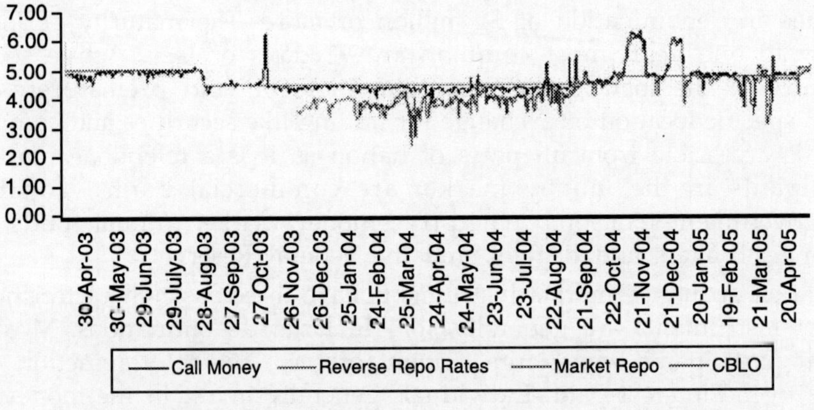

Chart 1 : Money Market Rates : April 2003 to May 2005

With regard to the second objective, i.e., minimizing default risk in the money market, RBI has implemented a number of prudential measures such as prudential limits on call/notice money transactions, encouraging growth of collateralized market, dematerialization of CP and CD etc. Consequently, within a short period of time from April 2000, the characterization and the dynamics of functioning of the Indian money market have changed markedly.

Reflecting this, the relative turnover in various segments of money market has undergone significant changes over the years. This is partly policy driven and partly on account of the substantial improvement in underlying liquidity condition in the

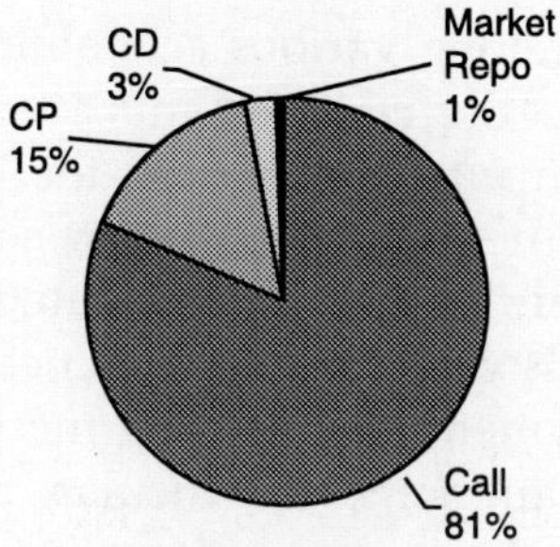

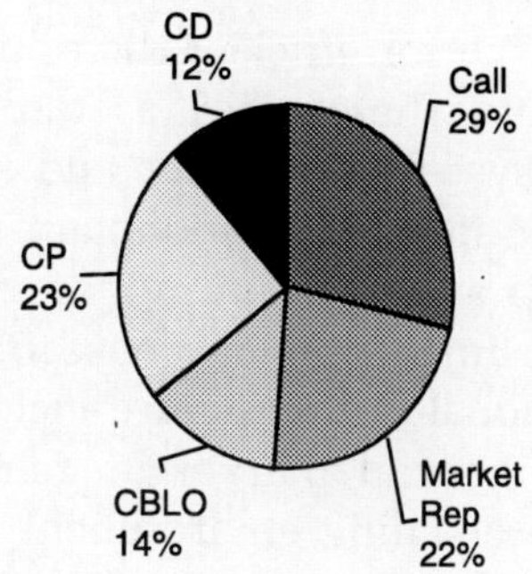

economy during this period. While the relative share of call/notice money market has declined from as high as 81 per cent during 2000-01 to only 29 per cent during 2004-05, that of market repo has increased from only 1 per cent to as much as 22 per cent over this period (Charts 2 and 3). CBLO, after a slow start, has been gathering significant momentum and now accounts for about 14 per cent during 2004-05. The situation, however, changes if the average volume accepted under RBI's reverse repo window is taken into account along with these instruments. It is evident from Charts 4 and 5 that with substantial improvement in liquidity, the share of RBI's reverse repo rose from 8 percent to 48 percent over this period.

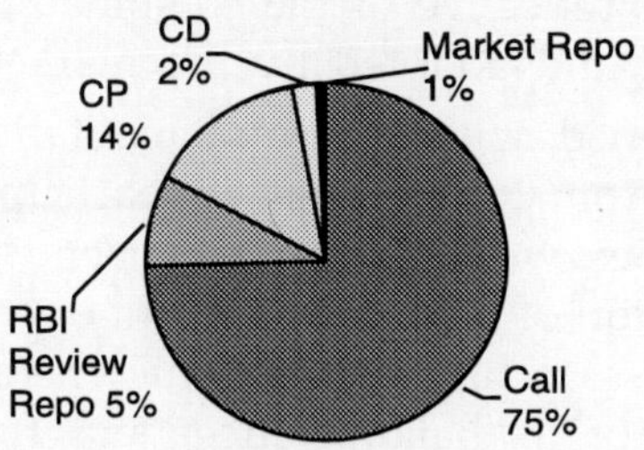

Chart 4 : Relative Shares - 2000-01

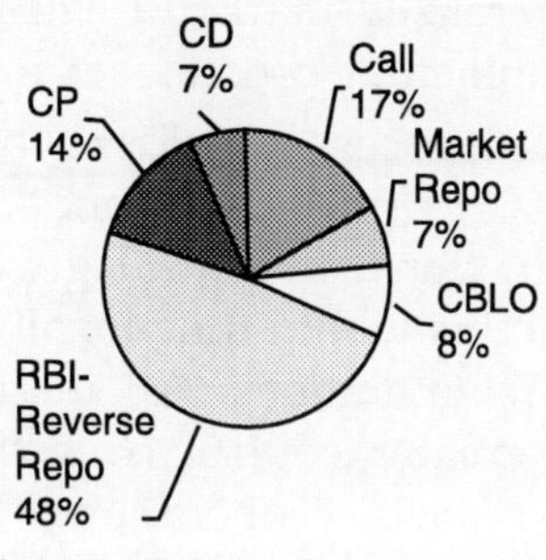

Chart 5 : Relative Shares - 2004-05

Further, it is heartening to note that the attempt to develop a deep collateralized market, viz., market repo and CBLO vis-à-vis the uncollateralized call/notice market has already witnessed significant success. As regards other money market instruments, the outstanding amount under CP has been scaling new peaks with every passing month in the recent period. All these factors have brought about a relatively more balanced development of various segments of money market though the prospect for further development is immense. Derivatives of the money market include forward rate agreements (FRAs) and futures.

The money market, particularly the overnight market, is important from the point of view of any central bank. This is because a vibrant, deep and broad-based money market is the key for efficient distribution of liquidity among various economic agents in the economy. Therefore, it is through this segment, the central bank attempts to influence the systemic liquidity and stabilize short-term interest rates. In the process, it transmits the impulse of monetary policy. However, the pre-requisites for achieving a vibrant, deep and efficient money market are that there should be adequate number of liquid instruments, wider base of participants with diverse liquidity needs and sound institutional infrastructure including efficient payment and clearing mechanism. Further, the financial market in general, and money market in particular, perform best when the enabling environment is conducive in that the economy runs on a low fiscal deficit and the regulatory and prudential regime incentivises the functioning of the market and makes the economic agents accountable for their actions. These issues have become particularly important, as the Indian economy has become progressively more globalized.

Assessing the status of Indian money market against the above-mentioned perspective, one may maintain that the market has not only been transformed markedly, particularly during the last five years in terms of depth and more varied instruments, it has also brought in a wider level of participation in these markets. The institutional infrastructure, particularly with the upgradation of payment system infrastructure, viz., operationalisation of Clearing Corporation of India Ltd. (CCIL), Negotiated Dealing System (NDS), real-time gross settlement (RTGS) system and the Centralized Funds Management System (CFMS) has brought about immense benefit to the financial market at large. The substantial growth of collateralised market vis-à-vis uncollateralized market as mentioned earlier is reflective of the combined result of the developmental process set in motion by RBI and adapted by the market.

The above process would be further strengthened with the implementation of FRBM Act, 2003. Under this mandate, direct credit from RBI through its participation in primary auctions of central government securities would come to an end since April 1, 2006. This would functionally lead to separation of debt management operation from monetary operations. All these would give rise to an environment where RBI would have greater control over the composition of its balance sheet and further flexibility in monetary operations. This, however, presupposes that there would be close co-ordination between the fiscal authority and the monetary authority for ensuring stability in the financial market as a whole.

With the ensuing enabling environment within the domestic economy expected to be more conducive, it is envisaged that the money market in India is poised for a big leap. However, the principal challenge that the economy may experience over the medium-term following its increasing openness could be the management of liquidity in the face of strong capital inflows. This is particularly important because if India could sustain the present high level of growth rate combined with a benign inflation environment, lower fiscal deficit and other strong macro-economic fundamentals, the economy could be expected to receive more than its normal share of capital inflows, notwithstanding changes in policy stance in major advanced economies.

The challenges before RBI in managing capital flows had been dealt with extensively in the *Report of the Internal Group on Liquidity Adjustment Facility* (November 2003) and the *RBI Working Group on Instruments of Sterilization* (December 2003). It was underscored therein that "In order for the LAF to function as the principal monetary policy instrument for signaling the Reserve Bank's stance on interest rates, it is desirable that LAF operates to primarily manage liquidity at the margin on a day-to-day basis". The dilemma before any central bank under that situation was put forth as "while operationally it is difficult to distinguish between the sterilization operations and liquidity management operations under LAF, conceptually there is a need to distinguish surplus liquidity of 'temporary' nature from surplus liquidity of a somewhat 'enduring' nature". Considering these issues, the LAF Group recommended that in order to improve the effectiveness of LAF, introduction of additional instruments of sterilization against the backdrop of declining stock of government securities with RBI should be explored. Accordingly, the *RBI Working Group on Instruments of Sterilization,* after considering pros and cons of various instruments, recommended that "Government may consider setting up of a Market Stabilization Fund (MSF) .... for mopping up enduring surplus liquidity from the system". Taking into account all these issues, the revised LAF scheme as well as the Market Stabilization Scheme were operationalised in April 2004.

The issue that needs to be appreciated here is that continued sterilization has a financial cost in terms of the outgo of coupon on the sterilized amount. The trade-off here is that in the absence of sterilization, there could be excessive volatility in financial markets, interest rates and exchange rate leading to erosion of competitiveness of the economy; this would have adverse impact on the economy at large and on the non-government sector in particular. This brings forth the core issue of stabilization of short-term interest rates in money market consistent with expected growth of GDP and inflation in an environment of large capital inflows. The framework for achieving this objective in a corridor setting was given by the *Report of the Internal Group on LAF*. This framework, based on the experiences of select developed economies, has been modified to suit the needs of Indian situation. Accordingly, under surplus mode, while the fixed reverse repo rate at 5.00 percent at which RBI absorbs liquidity from the market provides the floor to the movement of call money rates, the ceiling is provided by the fixed repo rate at 6.0 percent at which RBI is prepared to lend to eligible market participants. In this context, the reverse repo rate acts as the policy rate reflecting the stance of RBI besides being the rate for liquidity management. It is important to note here that outright purchase and sale of securities, often known as open market operations (OMOs), should be so conducted as to stabilize interest rates and minimize their volatility. The essential distinction between the reverse repo rate under LAF and the outright buy/sale of securities under OMO is that under the former, RBI determines the rate to provide clarity to the stance of RBI whereas under the latter, buy/sale of securities at a particular price is linked to the secondary market conditions. Therefore, while the reverse repo rate under LAF is a fixed one, the outright buy/sale of securities could be done at a variable price with reference to the corresponding secondary market price.

A related issue here is the width of the corridor. International experiences show that it varies between 50 basis points (bps) and 200 bps. In India, it stands at 100 bps now. Ideally, the spread should reflect the society's tolerance level of volatility in short-term interest rates. Even then, in the Indian context, RBI may find it difficult to tolerate daily fluctuations in call rates by 100 bps over a sustained period. Therefore, for all practical purpose, this spread of 100 bps should be interpreted as the maximum tolerance level under extreme one-off circumstance. This is also corroborated by the market practice as call rates generally fluctuate within 5/10 bps in the relation to the RBI's reverse repo rate. The success in keeping call rates in a narrower bound in relation to the RBI's reverse repo rate would, therefore, depend upon how successfully RBI would conduct Liquidity Adjusted Facility and Open market operation.

REVIEW QUESTIONS

1. Investment refers to the sacrifice of present consumption for the uncertain future reward. Explain and what are its various types?
2. What do you mean by an investment Process? Why doesn't it make sense to have "making a lot of money" as one of its objectives?
3. What are the various factors which affect an investors investment decisions? Explain in detail.
4. Why does the yield of a government bond different from a corporate bond? And why don't some bond have any yields?
5. Following the overthrow of communist regimes in Eastern Europe, many of the fledgling democracies placed the development of security markets near the top of their economic agendas. Why do you think they did so?
6. Explain why the rate of return on an investment represents the investors relative increase in wealth from that investment.
7. Foreign investors view India (or developing countries) as a good market to invest. Why so?
   What are the various steps taken by the government to control Foreign Institutional Investments?
8. What are the money markets? Why do we need them?
9. Write a short note on the changes taken place in Indian markets over the last decades.
10. Why are Treasury bills considered to be a risk free investment? In what way do investors bear risk when they own Treasury Bills?
11. Does it seem reasonable that higher return securities historically have exhibited higher risk? Why?

12. Describe how life insurance companies, mutual funds and pension plans each out as financial intermediaries.
13. What are open Market Operations? What are the other ways by which RBI looks after the interest rates?
14. What is the difference between futures and forwards? State the difference between a put and call option using an example.
15. Why do companies invest? Briefly explain the investment portfolio.

3

Securities Markets

It is not possible to make intelligent investment decisions without understanding the financial markets or the securities market in which the decisions are implemented. Securities market is vital for the capitalistic economies, since they serve to channel funds from savers to borrowers. They provide an important allocative function by channelising the funds to those who can make the best productive use of them.

In order to finance their operations as well as expand, business firms must invest a large capital. Similarly, government requires a large amount of money to provide goods and services that the people demand of them. The securities market permits both business and government to raise the needed funds by selling securities. Moreover investors with excess funds are able to invest and earn a return enhancing their welfare. The smooth functioning of securities market enhances the economic prosperity of a society. Hence some knowledge of the securities market is essential for not just active investors but for everyone.

The dictionary meaning of market is a place for selling and buying goods or services. Thus a securities market is a place where buying and selling of securities takes place. A good security market is a market where trading is conducted in a fair, open and orderly manner. A securities market can be broadly divided into primary market and secondary market. A primary market is a market in which securities are sold to investors (buyers) for the first time i.e. new securities are traded. Selling of new securities for the first time is referred to as Initial Public Offerings (IPO). A Secondary Market is a market where existing securities are traded among investors. Here the securities are bought and sold after their initial sale in the primary market. Except the derivatives market, all the other markets has these two components i.e. the primary market and the secondary market.

Structure of the Securities Market (Fig. 3.1)

Apart from this broad classification, securities markets are widely classified in terms of types of securities traded and organization of the market. Depending upon the

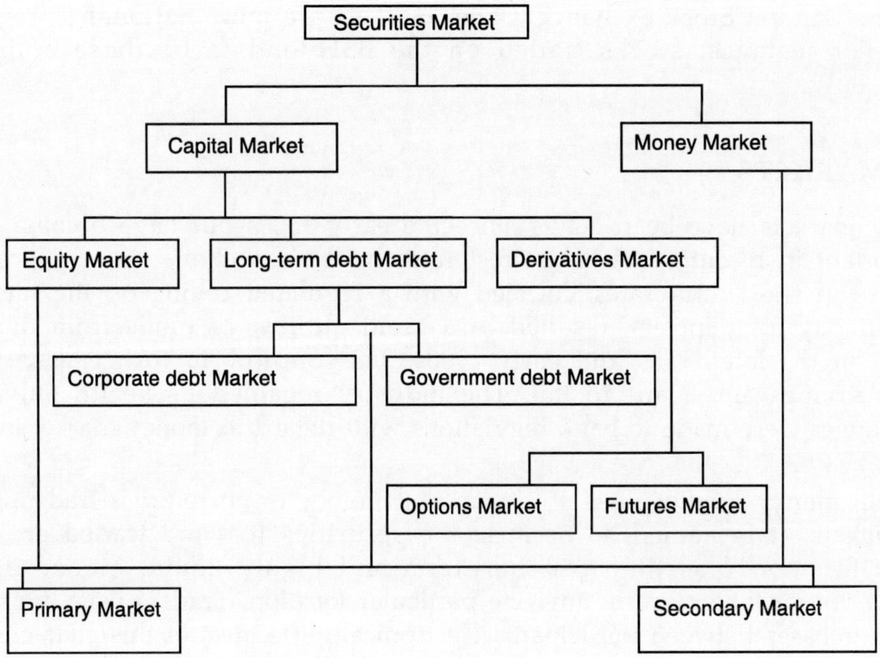

Fig. 3.1. Structure of the Securities Market

type of securities traded, the securities market is divided into – **Capital Market** and **Money market.** In **money markets**, short term instruments (maturity less than one year) are traded which is marketable, highly liquid and low-risk debt securities. In contrast, **capital markets** include long term and riskier securities. Securities in the capital market are much more diverse than those found within the money market.

Capital market is further classified into **equity market, debt market** and **derivatives market.** Derivatives markets function somewhat differently from other financial markets. This is explained in a separate chapter. In this chapter, the main focus is on equity market and debt market.

According to the trading practices involved, securities market can be classified into **organized markets** and **over-the-counter markets**. Organized markets are those where trading takes place in a specific physical location such as a trading floor. The Bombay Stock Exchange (BSE) is an example of an organized market. An over-the-counter market is a market where trading takes place at many locations with participants linked by a computerized communication network. The National Association of Securities Dealer Automated Quotation System (NASDAQ) stock market, the second largest stock market in the world, is an example of over-the-counter market. Moreover, many securities markets are **global** in scope i.e. the securities traded come from different countries throughout the world. For example, stocks from throughout the world, not just those located in the U.K. trade on the London Stock exchange. Some markets are more **national** or **regional** in scope. For instance, stocks traded on the BSE tend to be those of Indian companies only.

MONEY MARKETS

The money markets have been active since the early 1800s but have become much more important in recent years as interest rates have risen above historic levels. In fact, the rise in short term rates, coupled with a regulated ceiling on the rate that banks could pay for deposits, resulted in a rapid outflow of funds from financial institutions in the late 1970s and early 1980s. This outflow in turn caused many banks and savings and loans to fail. The industry regained its health only after massive changes were made to bank regulations with regard to money market interest rates.

The term **money market** does not mean that money or currency is traded in the money markets. It is named so because the securities that are traded are close substitutes for money as they are short-term and highly liquid. Money market transactions do not take place in any one particular location. Traders usually arrange sales and purchases between participants electronically. Because of this characteristic, money market securities usually have an active secondary market, which makes these securities very flexible instruments to fulfill short-term financial needs.

Another characteristic feature of the money markets is that they are wholesale markets. The transactions are very large and are settled on daily basis. The size of these transactions prevents most individual investors from participating directly in the money markets. Instead, dealers and brokers bring customers together to sell and purchase of money market instruments. Despite the wholesale nature of the money market, innovative securities and trading methods have been developed to give small investors access to the money market.

Necessity of Money Markets

The well-developed secondary market instruments makes the money market an ideal place for a firm or financial institution to 'warehouse' surplus funds for short periods of time until they are needed. They provide a low-cost source of funds to firms, government and intermediaries. The banking industry also provides short-term loans and accepts short-term deposits. The loans offered by banks are cheaper than the diversified markets. Furthermore short-term securities offered for sale in money markets are neither as liquid nor as safe as deposits placed in banks. Then the question is "why do we need the money markets"? The importance of money markets is explained below:

1. The money markets have a distinct cost advantage over banks in providing short-term funds. The banking is subject to more regulations and governmental costs

than the money markets. Banks have to put aside a portion of their deposits in the form of reserves that are held without interest. Another disadvantage of banks is interest-rate regulation, which set a ceiling on the rate of interest that banks could pay for funds. The main idea behind interest-rate regulation was to reduce competition among banks. The regulators felt that without competition, banks were less likely to fail. The limits on interest rates were not particularly relevant until the late 1950s and became especially troublesome to banks in the late 1970s and early 1980s when inflation pushed short-term interest rates above the level that banks could pay. Investors pulled their money out of banks and put it into money markets resulting in the growth of money markets. The cost structure of the banking industry makes it difficult to compete effectively in the market for short-term funds against the less restricted money markets. Thus, a well-developed money market contributes to an effective implementation of the monetary policy.

2. Holding idle surplus cash is expensive for an investor because cash balances earn no income. Now the point is why should an investor hold surplus cash, why not invest in stocks or bonds. The main reason is that the market condition may not be always appropriate for purchasing stocks. Sometimes, the investors may expect a rise in interest rates and hence may not want to purchase bonds. In such situations, the surplus cash lies idle. Idle cash represents an opportunity cost in terms of lost interest income. Opportunity cost is the amount of interest sacrificed by not holding an alternative asset. The money markets provide a means to invest idle funds and to reduce this opportunity cost. As the money market instruments are highly liquid, holding funds in the money market enables the investors to act quickly to take advantage of the investment opportunity the moment they identify it. The investors in the money market are, actually, not trying to earn unusually high returns. Rather they are using the money market as an interim investment that provides a higher return than holding cash or money in banks.
3. Cash inflows and outflows are rarely synchronized. In order to keep a balance between the inflow and the outflow, government and corporations invest in money markets. For example, government tax revenues usually come only at a particular time of the year, but expenses are incurred throughout the year. The government can borrow short-term funds and pay back when it receives tax revenues. Similarly most investment funds and financial intermediaries also hold money market securities to meet investment or deposit outflows. Businesses also face problems caused by revenues and expenses occurring at different times. The money markets provide an efficient, and low cost way of solving these problems.

Players in the Money Markets

Those who borrow or lend in the money market are said to be money market players or money market participants. Some money market participants operate on both sides of the market i.e. they may lend as well as borrow. For example, any large bank can borrow aggressively in the money market by selling large commercial CDs. At the same time, it can also lend short-term funds to businesses through its commercial lending departments. The various money market players are – Central Government of India, RBI, Commercial Banks, Businesses, Investment Companies or Brokerage Firms, Financial Institutions, Insurance Companies, Pension Funds and general public or individuals.

Money Market Instruments

The money market securities / instruments have three basic characteristics in common:

- They are usually sold in large denominations.
- They have low default risk.
- They mature in one year or less from their original date of issue.

A variety of money market instruments are available to meet the diverse needs of market participants. These instruments include – Call or Notice money, Treasury bills, Certificate of Deposits (CDs), Commercial Paper (CP), Repurchase agreements (Repos), Banker's Acceptances, Eurodollars and Money Market Mutual Funds. All these instruments are discussed in Chapter 3.

Secondary Market for Money Market Instruments

Discount and Finance House of India (DFHI) has been seeking to develop an active secondary market for the money market instruments in order to smoothen the short-term liquidity imbalances. Securities Trading Corporations of India (STCI) was set up in 1994 to develop institutional infrastructure so as to provide an active secondary market for the money market instruments as well as government securities and public sector bonds.

CAPITAL MARKET

Capital markets are markets that trade equity (stocks) and debt (bonds) instruments having maturities more than one year. Due to their longer maturity, these instruments experience wider price fluctuations, higher credit and interest rate risks than the money market instruments. In contrast to money markets, capital markets are used for long-term investments. They provide an alternative to investment in real assets such as real estate or gold.

Long-term investment rates are higher than short-term investments. This is due to risk premiums. Investment in long-term reduce the risk of change (rise) in interest rate before the debt is paid-off. This reduction in risk comes at a cost called the risk premium. Despite the fact they have to pay higher interest rates, investors choose to invest in capital market only to reduce the risk of rise in interest rates before they pay off their debt.

For example, suppose a firm needs a new plant and chooses to finance it by issuing money-market securities, such as commercial paper. As long as interest rates do not rise, all is well. When these short-term securities mature, they can be reissued at the same interest rate. However if interest rate rises, the firm may find that it does not have the cash flow or income to support the plant because when the short term securities mature, the firm will have to the re-issue them at a higher interest rate. However, if long-term securities, such as bonds or stocks, have been used, the increased interest rates would not have been so critical.

Capital Market Securities

Capital Market Securities fall into two categories: bonds and equities (stocks). Accordingly capital market can be divided into – bond market and equity market.

Bonds are the securities that represent a long-term debt owed by the issuer to the investor. The issuer of bonds is obligated to pay a specified amount, along with interest to the investors. This amount is the par value or face value of the bond at maturity. The rate of interest paid by the issuer is the coupon rate. This rate is usually fixed for the duration of the bond and does not fluctuate with market interest rates. If the repayment terms are not met, the holder of a bond has a claim on the assets of the issuer. Thus, they are the creditors of the firm.

The equity market deals with equities (or stocks). A share of stock or equities in a firm represents ownership. They do not have any maturity. They are the residual claimants i.e. they have a claim on the assets and income left after paying all the debt obligations. Moreover they have the right to vote in the firm. There are two forms of stocks (or equities): Common Stock and Preferred Stock.

Primary Market

A primary market is one in which securities are traded for the first time. The borrower issues new securities to the investors. The issuer of a security actually receives the proceeds of the sales. When firms need to raise capital, they may choose to sell new securities. Selling of these new issues of stocks, bonds or other securities to the public occurs in the primary market.

Thus, primary market sale is the first time issue of a private firm going public. The equity of these private firms, some of which were held privately by managers and venture capital investors, are publicly traded in the stock markets for the first time. These first time issues are referred to as **Initial Public Offerings (IPOs)**. Alternatively a primary market sale may be a **seasoned new issue offering**, popularly known as Follow-on Public Offer (FPO), in which the firm already has shares of the stock trading in secondary markets. In both the cases, the issuer receives the proceeds of the sale and the primary market investors receive the securities.

A company can raise capital in the primary market in three ways;

- Public issue
- Rights issue
- Private placement

Public issue

Investment bankers who perform the role of underwriters typically market public offerings of both stocks and bonds. More than one investment banker usually markets the securities. A lead firm forms an underwriting syndicate of other investment bankers to share the responsibility for the stock issue.

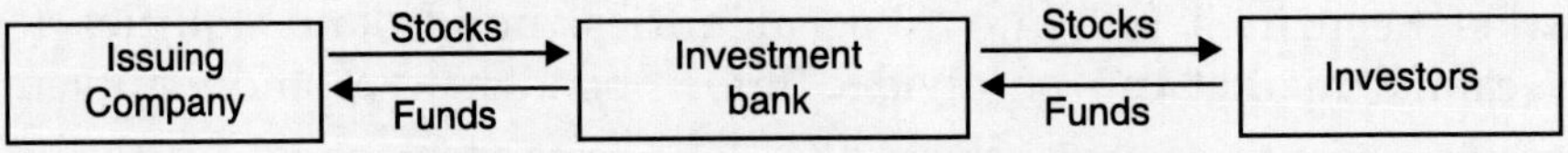

Fig. 3.2. Primary Market Operations (Public Issue).

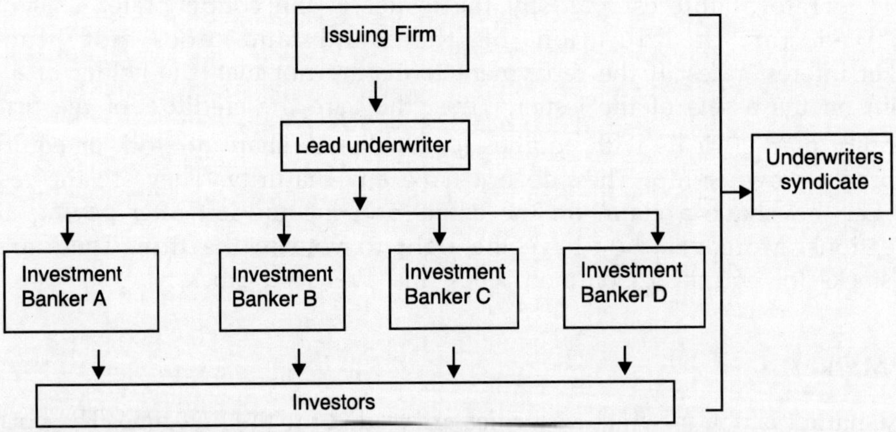

Fig. 3.3. Relationship among a firm issuing securities, the underwriters and the public.

An investment bank can conduct a primary market sale of securities in two ways – firm commitment underwriting and best efforts underwriting. In firm commitment underwriting, the investment bank guarantees the issuing firm a price for the newly issued securities by buying the whole issue at a fixed price from the issuer. The underwriter bears the full risk in case the shares cannot be sold to the public. The guaranteed price at which an investment bank purchases the stock from the issuer is called the net proceeds and resells them to investors at a higher price, called the gross proceeds. The difference between the gross proceeds and the net proceeds, called the underwriter's spread, serves as compensation to the underwriters for the expenses and risks incurred by the investment bank.

An alternative to firm commitment is underwriting. In this case, the investment banker agrees to help the firm sell the issue to the public but does not actually purchase the securities. The investment banker does not guarantee a price to the issuer and acts simply as a intermediary or distributing agent between the public and the firm. Thus it does not bear the any risk in case the securities are not sold at the offering price.

A corporation engages an investment banker either by negotiation or by competitive bidding. However negotiation is more common. Besides being compensated by the spread between the purchase price (net proceeds) and the public offering price (gross proceeds), an investment banker may receive shares of common stock or other securities of the firm.

The lead bank in the syndicate negotiates directly with the issuing company on behalf of the syndicate and is called the originating house. Each member of the syndicate is assigned a given number of shares in the issue for which it is responsible for selling. Shares issued through a syndicate spreads the risks associated with the sale of stocks. Moreover a syndicate results in a large pool of potential outside investors, thus, increasing the probability of a successful sale and widening the scope of the investor base.

Rights issue

Sometimes the existing shareholders are given pre-emptive rights to the new shares of stock when they are issued. This is called a rights issue. This means that before a seasoned offering of stocks can be sold to outsiders, the new shares must first be offered to the existing shareholders on a pro rata basis so that they can maintain their proportional ownership in the corporation. A rights issue allows existing shareholders to purchase shares at a price slightly below the market price. The shareholders may exercise this right (buy the allotted shares in the new stock) or forfeit the right, partially or fully, to enable a company to sell them to the public. Rights issue of shares result in a low-cost distribution of new shares for a firm as the issuing firms do not have to incur the expense of an underwriting offering. They are similar to options in that they give the holder the option, but not the obligation to buy the stock. The rights holder has the option of buying the new shares at the stated price, selling the rights to other investors or letting the rights expire at the end of the offering period unused.

Private placements

Private placement involves sale of new issues directly to the financial institutions such as life insurance companies and pension funds. They are not sold to the general public. A private placement provides certain cost advantages to the issuing company such as:

1. The issuer does not have to pay any underwriting spread, as underwriters are not used in private placements.
2. The various costs associated with registering the issue with the SEBI is also not incurred.

3. In addition, the terms of the issue can be tailored to meet the specific needs of both the issuer and the institutional investor.

The disadvantage of private placements includes a higher interest cost because the financial institutions usually charge more than a general public subscription. There may possibly be some restrictive provisions on the borrower's activities. Since the issue is un-registered, there exists a lack of marketability. Therefore the buyer may demand additional compensation from the lender in the form of a higher yield. Financial institutions prefer to buy privately placed securities because they usually carry slightly higher yields than publicly issued securities. On the other hand, since private placements are not available to the general public, they are usually less suited for very large offerings. Moreover privately placed securities are not traded in secondary markets such as stock exchanges. This greatly reduces their liquidity and the prices that investors will pay for the issue.

Secondary Markets

Once the financial instruments such as stocks are issued in primary markets, they are then traded i.e. repurchased and resold in secondary markets. The National Stock Exchange (NSE), the Bombay Stock Exchange (BSE) and Over the Counter Exchange of India (OTCEI) are three well known examples of secondary markets in India. Each of these markets will be discussed in detail, later in this chapter. Table 3.1 shows the structure of the secondary market.

Table 3.1. Structure of the Secondary Market

Types of securities traded	Where traded
Equity Markets (Common stock, preferred stock, Rights & Warrants)	Organized exchanges (BSE, NSE) Over-The-Counter
Bonds Markets (Bonds and debentures)	Organized exchange (BSE, NSE) Over-the-counter
Derivatives market (Options and Futures)	Organized exchanges (BSE, NSE)

Buyers of secondary market securities are economic agents (consumers, businesses and governments) with excess funds. Sellers of secondary market financial instruments are economic agents in need of funds. The following exhibit illustrates a secondary market operations.

Fig. 3.4. Secondary market operation.

When a transaction occurs in a secondary market, funds are exchanged, usually with the help of a securities broker, who acts as an intermediary between the buyer and seller of the instrument. The original issuer of the instrument is not involved in this transfer.

Secondary markets offer benefits to both investors (suppliers of funds) and the issuing corporation (users of funds). For investors, secondary markets provide liquidity. Many investors may want to sell securities that they had acquired in the primary markets. For example, an investor might have purchased a short-term security (say, a T-Bill) expecting to hold it until maturity. But due to some unavoidable situation, he/she might want to sell the bill well before maturity. The secondary market provides liquidity for this investor by allowing him/her to sell the bill for approximately its market value. Apart from liquidity, secondary markets also provide a measure of a security's current worth. This is referred to as price-discovery. Even if an investor plans to continue to hold a security, the secondary market still tells the investor what securities are currently worth. Furthermore, new issues of securities to be sold in the primary market are actually priced by the secondary market. The firms that buy securities in the primary market will pay the issuing corporation no more than the price that they think the secondary market will set for the security. The higher the security's price in the secondary market, the higher will be the price that the issuing firm will receive for a new security in the primary market and hence the greater the amount of capital it can raise.

Though the issuing companies are not directly involved in the transfer of funds or instruments in the secondary market, they get the information about the current market value of their financial instruments. By keeping a track of the prices at which their financial instruments are being traded on secondary markets, the issuing company gets to know about its own value (or position) as perceived by the investors. This price information, also, allows the issuers to evaluate how well they are using the funds generated from the financial instruments they have already issued and provides information on how well, any subsequent offerings of debt or equity might do in terms of raising additional cost and also, at what cost. Liquidity is beneficial for issuers as well, because it lowers the cost of capital. Increased liquidity makes it more desirable and easier for the issuing firm to sell a security initially in the primary market. Thus, secondary markets offer the buyers and the sellers, liquidity as well as information about the price or the value of their investments.

Not all secondary markets, however, are equally liquid. Every secondary market has market makers or dealers who are willing to buy and sell the securities traded in that market. The price at which the market maker buys the security is called the bid price and the price at which the market maker sells the security is called the ask price. Market makers make their profits by selling securities at higher prices than they pay for them. Often the spread between the bid and ask price is an indication of a market's liquidity. A large bid and ask price spread makes a secondary market less liquid.

It is, however, noticed that some securities develop better secondary markets than others. This is due to the size of the issue i.e. the number of individual bonds or shares of stock that were originally issued. Larger issues usually have more active and liquid secondary markets. Another important factor is the number of investors who originally purchased the issue. For example, if ten large institutions buy up an entire new security issue, it is less likely that an active secondary market will develop than if the issue had been sold to thousands of investors who may decide to sell at any time.

Secondary markets can be classified in several different ways: auction and negotiated markets, organized and over-the-counter markets, markets with face to face trading and markets where trading takes place by computer. However the secondary markets are broadly classified into organized markets (stock exchanges) and unorganized markets (over-the-counter markets).

STOCK EXCHANGES

Stock exchanges are auction markets involving a bidding process in a specific physical location. Investors are represented by brokers (or intermediaries) who represent both buyers and sellers in securities transaction. They attempt to obtain the best price possible for either party in a transaction. In return, they receive a commission for their efforts. The main function of any exchange is the creation of a continuous market where investors have the opportunity to buy or sell securities thereby, making the investments liquid and marketable. Thus the investors are not obligated to hold their securities. They can sell them whenever they would prefer to have cash. A stock exchange also helps to determine fair market prices. Price is determined by supply and demand from different investors. The exchanges bring together buyers and sellers from all over the nation and from foreign countries also. Anonymity between buyers and sellers is preserved as their agents transact the trades.

India has now the largest number of organized and recognized stock exchanges in the world. They are organized into public limited companies, companies limited by guarantee and voluntary non-profit making organizations. The number of official stock exchanges in India at present is 23. Out of these 14 are public limited companies, 6 are companies limited by guarantee and 3 are voluntary non-profit organizations all of them are reputed by SEBI.

The government of India and/or SEBI ensures broad uniformity in the structure while granting recognition. Till now, only a few stock exchanges have got permanent recognition, others have to renew it after every five years until permanent recognition is granted.

Bombay Stock Exchange (BSE) is the premier stock exchange in India. Apart from BSE, there are two other stock exchanges that are equally important having certain unique features. They are National Stock Exchange of India (NSE) and over–The-Counter Exchange of India Ltd (OTCEI).

BOMBAY STOCK EXCHANGE (BSE)

The BSE was established in 1857and is the apex stock exchange in India. It is the biggest in size in terms of the amount of fresh capital raised, secondary market turnover and capitalization and the total listed companies and their paid-up capital. It is the oldest market and has been recognized permanently. Its business is no longer confined to Mumbai alone. By the end of 1997, there were 100 other cities in which it has set up business. The BSE membership fee in 1857 was just Re 1. It increased to Rs. 5 in 1877, Rs.1000 in 1896, Rs. 2500 in 1916, Rs. 6600 in 1929, Rs. 62000 during post-second world war period, more than Rs. 3 crore in 1992, and was about Rs. 2 crore in 1997.[1]

BSE introduced Bombay On-Line Trading (BOLT) system on 19 Jan 1995. It provides a quote driven automated trading facility with an order book functioning as an auxiliary jobber. The process of transferring the equity scrip listed on the BSE from trading in the ring to the BOLT system was completed on 30 July 1995. The last day for trading in the ring was 30 June 1995. In addition to equities, BSE also began debt trading on the BOLT system from 26 June 1995 in respect of 60 actively traded debentures.

NATIONAL STOCK EXCHANGE (NSE) OF INDIA

The NSE has a fully automated electronic screen based trading system. It is sponsored by the IDBI and co-sponsored by other term-lending institutions, insurance companies, commercial banks and other financial institutions such as SBI Caps, SHCIL and ILFs. The main objectives of NSE is to provide nation-wide equal access to investors and impart fair, efficient and completely transparent securities trading system to investors by using suitable communication network. Moreover, it promotes the secondary market in debt instruments and brings the Indian stock market in line with the international securities markets. It also provides shorter settlement cycles and book entry settlement system.

The NSE has two segments – the wholesale debt market segment and the capital market segment. The **wholesale debt market segment** (WDMS) started functioning from 30th June 1994. It covers banks, financial institutions, PSU bonds, government securities, call money, T-bills, CPs, and CDs etc. It is a market for high value transactions involving mega players, mega investors and mega deals. The **capital market segment** began trading from 3rd Nov. 1994. It is a market for equities, convertible debentures etc. It also deals in securities that are traded on other stock exchanges. Recently, the RBI has identified the NSE as the only conduit for inter bank security deals. NSE introduced trading Repos with effect from 23 June 1995.

The NSE is an order-driven market and not a quote-driven market. It allows the trading members to trade from their offices through a communication network. It

---

[1] Bhole, I.M., "Financial Institutions and Markets: Structure Growth and Innovations", Tata McGraw-Hill, N.Delhi, 3rd ed., p. 402.

has a fully automated, screen-based ringless trading system. The trading members in the capital market segment are connected to the central computers at Mumbai, through dedicated high-speed lines. The firms whose shares are traded on NSE are divided into two categories: listed and permitted.

OVER THE COUNTER EXCHANGE OF INDIA (OTCEI)

OTCEI was incorporated in 1990 under the Companies Act, 1956. It is the first stock exchange in India to introduce screen-based automated ringless trading system. Unlike conventional stock exchanges, there is no trading ring or exchange of share certificates. Instead, the dealers operating right from their offices do the trading through computers. It is promoted by financial institutions such as UTI, ICICI, IDBI, IF, LIC, GIC, SBI Caps, CANBANK.

Companies listed on the OTCEI will enjoy the same listing status as available to other companies listed on any other stock exchange in the country except that a company listed on OTCEI cannot be listed on any other stock exchange in India. Hence, the securities that are traded on OTCEI cannot be traded on other stock exchanges. However, they can be bought and sold at any of the OTCEI all over India. These securities are divided into three categories: listed, permitted and initiated. The OTCEI has two players: members and dealers. There are no brokers. The players themselves can perform the functions of broking, trading and market making. However, the members can engage in sponsorship while the dealers cannot. Scheduled banks, mutual funds, banking subsidiaries, FIIs, merchant bankers, venture capital funds having a minimum net worth of Rs. 2.5 crore can become members of OTCEI.

The OTCEI offers two trading documents. One is a counter receipt (CR) issued to the investor buying scrip. The CR contains all the information, which appears on a share certificate and is tradable. The other trading document is the sales confirmation slip (SCS) that is issued to investor selling scrip.

The OTCEI has an on-line trading-cum-depository, quote-driven and transparent system of trading. It follows T+3 settlement cycle, which is the fastest in the country and ensures timely deliveries and payments. Each OTCEI counter gets a scrip-wise net position (stock-in and stock-out) on the last day of the week i.e. Friday (T) at the end of the trading hours. On Monday (T+3), the counters are required to deliver the securities as per the stock-on-report. On Friday (T+7), stock-out is done for the counters that have to receive the securities. Cash payments are done on Tuesday (T+4) and cash payouts are done on Friday (T+7)[2]. There are no problems of bad deliveries or short deliveries because the system allows the execution of trades only on the basis of electronic inventory of scrip. All trading on OTCEI done on any day is settled on the same day itself. Netting with the previous or subsequent day's transactions is not permitted. The deliveries are done once in five days or a week. Thus, OTCEI is a cash and retail market for small investors and small companies.

[2] Chandra, P., "Managing Investments", Tata McGraw-Hill Publishing Company, N. Delhi, 1998, p. 85.

In spite of its many advantages, the activity on OTCEI has been stagnant. This may be due to various factors, such as,

1. Stringent market making norms.
2. Banks' aversion to finance market making.
3. Mandatory requirement that the sponsor must offer buy and sell quotes in all the scrip with the spread not exceeding 10 percent.
4. T+3 settlement period not permitting speculation.

OTCEI has been criticized for these factors. Worried by the low activity on OTCEI, the authorities (SEBI) appointed two committees to review its working and to suggest measures to improve its functioning. The two committees are – **Malegam Committee** and **Dave committee**. After reviewing, these committees recommended relaxation of the strict norms with which OTCEI had begun operating.

OTHER REGIONAL STOCK EXCHANGES IN INDIA

Apart from the three stock exchanges in Mumbai discussed above, there are 20 other regional exchanges in India located in different cities.

FOREIGN STOCK MARKETS

The largest stock market in the world is the New York Stock Exchange (NYSE). Apart from that, the other stock markets are Tokyo Stock Exchange, London Stock Exchange and Toronto Stock Exchange.

Tokyo Stock Exchange

In 1982, a computer system for trading was introduced, known as **CORES** (Computer-assisted Order Routing and Execution System). It was introduced as a computer system to facilitate trading in the most active stocks.

The system of trading is quite different from the system found in other stock exchanges. The members of the Tokyo Stock Exchange, known as *Saitori*, act as auctioneers. They are neither dealers nor specialists. Instead, they are intermediaries who accept orders from member firms and are not allowed to trade in any stocks for their own account.

At the opening of the exchange, the *saitori* members follow a method called *itayose*, which operates like a call market. The *saitori* seeks to set a single price so that the amount of trading is maximized. This involves constructing supply and demand schedules for the market and limit orders that have been received. After the opening of the exchange, the *saitor*i follows a method known as *Zaraba*, where orders are processed continually as they are received. New limit orders are filled, if possible, against previously unfilled limit orders. If these new limit orders cannot be filled, then they are entered in the limit order book for possible further execution. Unlike the limit order book on the NYSE, the limit order book in Tokyo Stock Exchange is available for inspection by member firms. Furthermore, unlike the NYSE, the Tokyo Stock Exchange prohibits trading at prices outside a given range based on the previous day's closing price. Hence, there can be situations where trading in a stock ceases until the next day (when price range is re-adjusted) unless two parties decide to trade within the current range.

London Stock Exchange

The London Stock Exchange has experienced several major reforms since 1986. Fixed brokerage commissions were eliminated, membership was opened up to corporations, and foreign firms were allowed to purchase existing member firms. An automated dealer quotation system was introduced known as **SEAQ** (Stock Exchange Automated Quotations). **SEAQ** involves competing market makers whose quotes are displayed over a computer network. Small orders can be executed by **SAEF** (SEAQ Automated Execution Facility) and large orders are handled over the telephone. Limit orders are not handled centrally but instead are handled by individual brokers or dealers who note when prices have moved sufficiently that they can be executed.

Toronto Stock Exchange

In 1977, the Toronto Stock Exchange began to use CATS (Computer- Assisted Trading System) on a trial basis with 30 stocks. Two years later, CATS was expanded to cover about 700 stocks and was made permanent. The success of CATS has led to more and more stocks being traded on it.

With CATS, orders are entered electronically in brokers' offices and then routed to a computer file. This computer file displays the limit orders against which other investors may trade. Market orders are matched against the limit order with the best price that is in the file i.e. a market order to be bought is matched against the lowest priced limit order to be sold and a market order to be sold is matched against the highest priced limit order to be bought. If insufficient volume of limit order is in the file at the best price, the remainder of the market order is then put in the file as a limit order at that price. However, if the investor wishes, the brokers can change this price at any time.

New York Stock Exchange

The New York Stock Exchange (NYSE), founded in 1792, is the oldest and the most prominent secondary market in the United States. It is also one of the largest stock exchanges in the world. By 1992, it has gained its position as the world's largest secondary market. It is regarded as the best regulated exchange in the world and has the ability to function in crisis.

The NYSE has specific listing requirements that companies must meet in order to be listed (i.e. accepted for trading). These requirements include the degree of national interest in the company, its relative position and stability in the industry, its prospects for maintaining its relative position, specified amounts of earning power and net tangible assets. NYSE pays particular attention to the market value of publicly traded shares and the total common shares publicly held. Companies submit to all these requirements and pay the cost to list their stocks on the NYSE mainly because of four common reasons – liquidity for shareholders, access to capital, prestige and exposure.

The NYSE is an auction market. All trading on the NYSE takes place on the exchange floor. Only members of the exchange are entitled to trade on the NYSE floor. Institutional investors in the NYSE usually trade in large blocks. Blocks are transactions involving at least 10,000 shares. Customer orders are delivered to the exchange by telephone, Teletype, or computer. Buyers and sellers of an issue meet face-to-face and bid against each other in an auction.

The NYSE has 42 specialists. Each security listed on the NYSE is assigned to one of the specialists. A specialist acts as a market maker and assumes responsibility for maintaining an orderly and liquid market. Specialists have four specific roles:

1. They act as auctioneer, calling out quotes throughout the trading session.
2. They act as catalysts, bringing buyers and sellers together.
3. They act as agents for limit orders.
4. They provide liquidity by buying or selling out of their own inventories when no other buyers or sellers are present. Thus, a specialist must have sufficient capital to maintain an inventory of about 15,000 shares of each security assigned to it.

Specialists, like other market participants, participate to earn money. They earn money primarily in two ways: first, by acting as agents in limit orders and, second, by buying and selling stocks assigned to them.

Drawbacks of Indian Stock Markets

The working of Indian Stock Markets suffers from various weaknesses that have been discussed below:

1. The entire activity on the stock market and the prices of the shares are determined by speculation and has little relation with the real performance of the economy.
2. The working of stock markets in India involves unethical practices such as mergers and acquisitions through malpractices, unofficial transactions, trading in fake shares and so on.
3. There is also structural and organizational imbalance in the growth of Indian stock markets. The stock markets are entirely urban oriented and do not have any relation with the rural economy.
4. The membership in stock exchanges is very much restricted.

5. The entire secondary market in India is in equities. Though significant part of the primary market is in debentures, the secondary market in debenture is under developed.
6. The trading in Indian stock markets is very much restricted. The number of listed stocks is small and the number of trading hours is very limited. As a result, the liquidity of scrips in reality is quite low. About 64 percent of listed scrips were not traded at all in the BSE during 1995-97.[3]

REVIEW QUESTIONS

1. What are the characteristics of Money Markets? How are they different from capital markets?
2. Depositing money in a bank is much more secure than investing in a money market then why invest in money market? Discuss the risks and benefits involved.
3. How inflation affects the short-term interest rate? What can be its likely impact on money markets?
4. Discuss the characteristics of an equity and a fixed interest rate bond. On which more yield is expected?
5. What is the role of investment banks in the security markets? When the issuing company opt for private placement of its stock?
6. What factors affects the marketability of a stock?
7. Distinguish between a competitive bid underwriting and a negotiated underwriting.
8. Why are secondary markets important to the effective functioning of primary security markets?
9. What makes OTCET different from other exchanges in India? What contributes towards its low activity?
10. Differentiate between the role of a specialist on the NYSE and the role of a dealer on the OTC market.
11. Compare the Indian stock markets with the renowned markets of the world.
12. Briefly describe the working of NYSE and NASDAQ.
13. Describe the primary market and the secondary market for government securities in India.
14. What are the key features of the National Stock Exchange and the Bombay Stock Exchange?
15. Describe the procedure for a rights issue.

[3] Bhole, I.M., "Financial Institutions and Markets- Structure Growth and Innovations", Tata McGraw-Hill, N.Delhi, 3rd ed., p. 435

4

Financial Assets and Investment Opportunities

The investor has various alternative avenues of investment for his savings to flow in accordance with his preferences. These investment alternatives range from money market securities to capital market securities to derivative securities. Earlier, selecting between investment alternatives used to be pretty simple. Since then, time has changed. Investors today have to choose among thousands of investment alternatives. Hence, it is impossible to make intelligent investment decisions without having some knowledge and understanding about the characteristics and features of various alternatives.

Investment instruments or assets or securities are broadly divided in two categories: financial assets and real assets. Real assets determine the wealth of an economy, whereas financial assets are merely claims to the income generated by real assets. They are represented by paper and can also be termed 'paper assets'. For example, stocks, bonds, bank deposits etc. are no more than sheets of paper or more likely computer entries. Real assets are represented by tangible assets such as land, buildings, machines, precious stones etc. The material wealth of a society is determined by the productive capacity of its economy i.e. the goods and services that is provided. This productive capacity depends largely on the real assets that are used to produce goods and the workers, whose skills, are necessary to use those resources. Hence, the physical and human assets, together, generate the entire spectrum of output produced and consumed by the society. When the real assets used by a firm generate income, the income is allocated to investors according to their ownership of the financial assets or securities, issued by the firm. For example, the bond-holders are entitled to an income based on the rate of interest and par value of the bond whereas the equity holders are entitled to the residual income after the bond holders and other creditors are paid. Value of financial assets depend on the values of the real assets of the firm. When an individual chooses to invest his current wealth for the future, he prefers to hold financial assets. The money a firm receives by issuing securities is used to purchase real assets. The returns on a financial asset come from the income produced by the real assets that are financed by the issuance of the security. Hence, financial assets can be viewed as the means by which individuals hold their claims on real assets. For example, it is not possible for everyone to own an automobile plant (a real asset), but one can hold shares of the plant (a financial asset) that provides income derived from the production of automobiles.

REAL ASSETS VS. FINANCIAL ASSETS

With the advancement of economy, the relative importance of financial assets tends to increase. Even though the real assets differ greatly from financial assets, two forms of investments are complementary and not competitive. The difference between real assets and financial assets can be summarized as follows:

1. Real assets determine the wealth of a society or economy whereas financial assets do not represent society's wealth.
2. Real assets contribute directly to the productive capacity of the economy while the contribution of financial assets to the productive capacity is indirect because they facilitate the transfer of funds to enterprises with attractive investment opportunities.
3. Real assets produce goods and services whereas financial assets define the allocation of income or wealth among investors.
4. Real assets appear only on the asset side of the balance sheet, while financial assets appear on both sides of the balance sheet.
5. Financial assets are created and destroyed in the ordinary course of doing business. For example, when a loan is repaid, both the creditor's claim and the debtor's obligation stop to exist. However, real assets are destroyed only by accident or by wearing out over time.
6. Investing in real assets carries more risks than investing in paper assets.

FINANCIAL ASSETS

Financial assets can be divided into – **direct investment** and **indirect investment**. A direct investment gives the investor actual ownership of the securities. The investors can buy and sell the securities themselves using a broker. Indirect investment gives ownership of an entity (such as investment companies) that owns actual securities. Instead of investing directly in securities, investors invest in a portfolio of securities by purchasing the shares of a financial intermediary or investment company (e.g. mutual funds) that invests in various types of securities on behalf of its shareowners. Thus indirect investment is the buying and selling of the shares of the investment companies, which, in turn, hold portfolios of securities.

DIRECT INVESTMENT

Direct investments can again be divided into **Marketable securities** and **Non-marketable securities**.

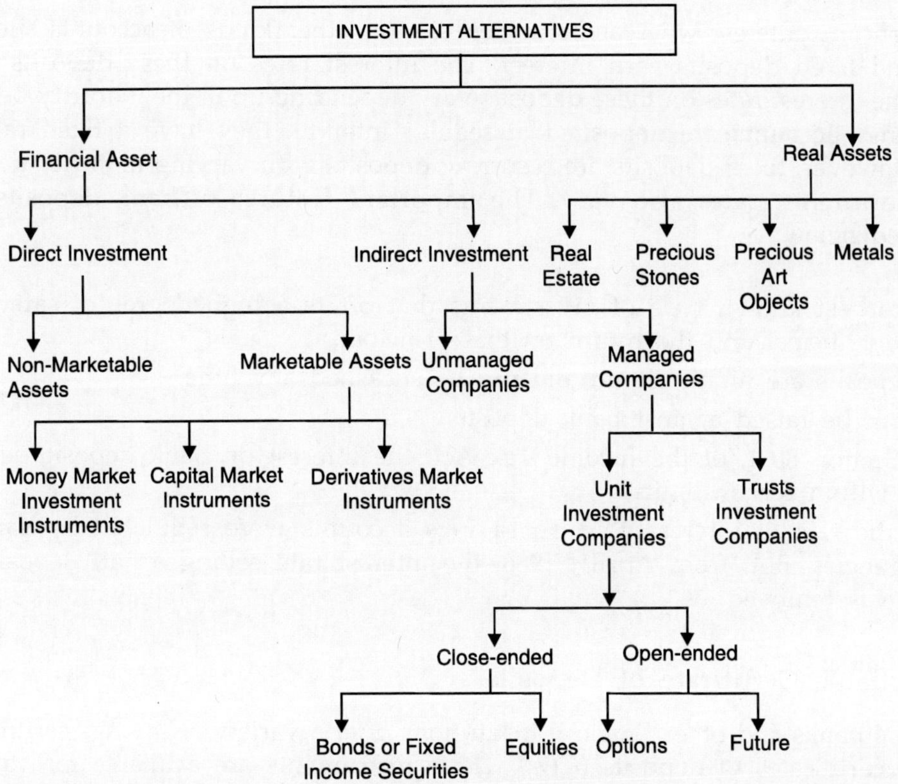

Fig. 4.1. Investment Alternatives.

NON-MARKETABLE FINANCIAL ASSETS

Some financial assets are said to be non-marketable because they are neither transferable nor negotiable. The investors actually own these assets and cannot buy or sell them in the secondary market. Bank deposits, post office deposits, provident fund etc. are examples of non-marketable financial assets. A distinguishable feature of these assets is that they represent personal transactions between the investor and the issuer. For instance, when you open a provident fund account, you open the account personally or deal personally to maintain the account or close it. These are "safe" instruments and are highly liquid. For example, when you close a savings account the money can be retrieved back easily and quickly.

The non-marketable resources held by investors are as follows:

Bank Deposits

The most popular non-marketable assets held by an investor include deposits with banks and their saving schemes. There are various types of deposits with banks such as current accounts, savings accounts and fixed deposits. Deposits on current accounts do not earn any interest whereas bank deposits on other kinds of accounts such as savings and fixed deposits earn interest. The interest rates on these deposits earn interest. The interest rates on these deposits vary depending upon the maturity period. Since savings accounts are deposited at regular interval, they have a fixed rate of interest. However, fixed deposits are recurring deposits with varying maturity period. Hence, the interest rates also vary. The important features of bank deposits are summarized below:

- They are best known type of investments that offers a high degree of safety on both the principal and the return on that principal.
- Bank deposits are highly liquid and can be encashed any time.
- Loans can be raised against bank deposits.
- Under Section 80 L of the Income Tax Act, the interest on bank deposits is tax-exempt within certain limits.
- Earlier the rate of interest paid on savings accounts were regulated by various govt. agencies. But, from April1, 1986, the interest rate ceiling on all deposit accounts was removed.

Non-negotiable Certificate of Deposits

Commercial banks and other financial institutions offer a variety of savings certificates known as certificates of deposits (CDs). These instruments are available for various maturities. As the maturity increases, the rate of interest offered also increases. However, large deposits may command higher rates, holding maturity constant. The credit risk associated with large CDs depends directly on the creditworthiness of the financial institutions that issue them. Since large CDs are not insured, a CD holder may lose principal if the financial institution fails.

Money Market Deposits Accounts

Financial institutions offer money market deposit accounts with no interest rate ceilings. These money market deposit accounts require a minimum deposit to open. They pay competitive money market rates of interest and are insured by the Federal Deposit Insurance Corporations (FDIC), if the issuing bank is insured. Withdrawals can be made, as many times as desired, in person or through automated teller machines (ATMs). There are no limitations on the number of deposits.

Instruments of Post Offices

The Investment avenues provided by the post offices generally enjoy tax concessions. Some of the major instruments are explained below.

Post-office savings deposits

These are savings deposited by public up to a maximum of Rs. 50,000, in individual account and Rs. 1 lakh in joint account. The rate of interest is 5.5%, which is tax-free and is ½ % more that offered by savings bank a/c by any other commercial banks. Withdrawal from the account is by cheque and there is no restriction on withdrawals, unlike in commercial banks.

Post-office fixed deposits

These accounts are open to individuals either separately or jointly for varying fixed periods of time. Accordingly, the interest rate also varies i.e. 9.5% for one-year deposits to 11.5% for 5 year deposits and is payable half yearly.

Post-office recurring deposits

This is an instrument of regular monthly savings. The account holder has to save and deposit every month a fixed amount of Rs. 5 or multiples of 5 till the maturity period. It carries a rate of 11% on the balance to the account, compounded quarterly and payable at maturity. This scheme provides free life insurance cover after receiving contributions for 24 months. In the case of death of the account holder after a minimum period of two years, from the date of opening the account, the nominee will get the full maturity value provided there have been no withdrawals during the first two years. However, the benefit of cover is not available for an extended period of deposit beyond five years.

Post-office time deposits

Post-office time deposits can be made in multiplies of Rs. 50 without any limit. The rate of interest is generally slightly higher than those on bank deposits and is tax exempt within certain limits under section 80 L of the Income Tax Act. The interest is calculated half yearly and paid annually. Withdrawal is permitted after six months. However withdrawals made between six months and one year are not subjected to any interest. Withdrawals after first year but before the term of the deposit are paid interest for the period the deposit has been held. A post office time deposit account can be pledged.

Post-office monthly income scheme with fixed investment

This scheme provides regular monthly income to the depositor. Under this scheme, an individual can invest from a minimum of Rs. 1,000 to a maximum of Rs. 3,00,000 in single account or Rs. 6,00,000 in a joint account for a period of six years. Interest at 9% is payable monthly and a bonus of 10% is payable at maturity. Income is tax-exempt within certain limits as per Section 80 L of the Income Tax Act. Premature withdrawal is permitted after 1 year. However, withdrawals made before three years are subjected to a penalty of 5% deduction.

Kisan Vikas Patra

Under this scheme, an individual can invest a minimum amount of investment of Rs. 1,000. There is no maximum limit. The investment doubles in 7 years and 8 months. The rate of interest is 9.46% compounded annually and is tax-exempt. Withdrawal is permitted only after 2 ½ years. Kisan Vikas Patra can be pledged as a collateral security for raising loans.

National Savings Certificates

National Savings Certificates come in denominations of Rs. 100, Rs.500, Rs. 1,000, Rs. 5,000 and Rs. 10,000. It has a term of 6 years and the rate of interest is 9.2% compounded annually. The interest is tax-exempt. It can be pledged for raising loans.

National Savings Scheme

The National Savings Scheme has been started by the Government of India to mobilize public savings for financing our economic development plans. These schemes are uniform all over the country and are tax-free. However, the amount that is withdrawn during a year is taxable. An individual can deposit in multiplies of 100 up to Rs. 40,000 per year and earn a compound interest rate of 9% per annum. The number of deposits that can be made in a year is twelve. The interest is credited to the account at the end of each month and is paid at a time with the principal when the contract terminates. The interest rate is usually higher than that of commercial banks. One premature withdrawal is permitted annually after 3 years. The amount that can be withdrawn is limited to the balance outstanding at the end of the fourth preceding year. These schemes also have nomination facility. In case of death of the depositor, the nominee is not liable to be taxed on withdrawal. The national savings scheme account has no definite maturity period and can be closed if the depositor desires, at the end of 3 years from the end of the year in which last deposit is made. These schemes can also be transferred from one post-office to another post-office if the investor so desires. Further they are pledged as security towards loan guarantee.

Fixed Deposit Schemes in Companies

Many companies offer fixed deposit investment schemes. The fixed deposits offered by manufacturing companies are regulated by the Company Law Board and the fixed deposits mobilized by non-banking finance companies (NBFCs) are regulated by the

Reserve Bank of India. Deposits can be cumulative or non-cumulative. These schemes are offered through newspaper advertisements and are subject to the provisions of the Companies Rules of 1975. These are offered to the public as well as to existing shareholders and employees. The investor can apply for these schemes on the company's prescribed application form. This is a short-term scheme and offers a higher interest rate than the commercial banks. A company may design its fixed deposit scheme in the way it wants but the maximum interest rate payable is 15%. The interest is payable annually, semi-annually, quarterly and monthly. However, under cumulative deposit schemes, the interest is accumulated and paid at the end. Accordingly, the interest is compounded annually, semi-annually, quarterly or monthly. The interest on company deposits is taxable. For manufacturing companies, the term of deposits is one to three years while for NBFCs, the term of deposits may vary between 25 months to 5 years. The amount of fixed deposits that a manufacturing company can mobilize is equal to 25% of its net worth from the public and 10% of its net worth from the shareholders. However NBFCs can mobilize a higher amount. Unlike bank deposits, company fixed deposits are unsecured i.e. they are not protected by any insurance scheme. If a company goes into liquidation, the depositors, as unsecured creditors, rank after the secured creditors and lenders. Hence, before investing in a company, an investor should go through the information, provided by company while inviting deposits from the public, carefully. While investing in reputed companies may be safe to a great extent, an investor must be doubly cautious while investing in less reputed companies, particularly the less reputed company who may misguide the public by furnishing false information. Moreover it is necessary that fixed deposits of a company may be rated. The rating symbols of the company fixed deposits offered by CRISIL are given in Table 4.1.

Table 4.1: Crisil Rating Symbols of Company Fixed Deposits

Rating Symbol	Remarks
FAAA	Highest Safety
FAA	High Safety
FA	Adequate Safety
FB	Inadequate Safety
FD	Default

In order to attract investors, companies offer incentives such as facility for premature withdrawal, free personal accident insurance, scholarship to the wards of investors, loan facility, preferential allotment in the issue of equity shares and convertible debentures. Moreover, companies compensate brokers by giving them commission and reimbursement of expenses. Brokers share this with the investors.

Provident Fund Schemes

There are mainly two types of provident fund schemes – employees provident fund scheme (EPF) and Public Provident Fund Scheme (PPF).

Employees provident fund scheme

This is a major vehicle for salaried employees. Each employee has a separate provident fund account in which both the employer and the employee are required to contribute a certain minimum amount on a monthly basis. While the contribution made by the employer is exempt from tax, a tax rebate under Section 88 of the Income Tax Act is available to the employee's contribution. This scheme earns an interest of 8.5% compounded annually, which is credited to the PF account and not paid annually to the employee. The balance in the provident fund account that is paid to the employee at the time of retirement is totally exempt from taxes. Another advantage of this scheme is that loans may be taken against the balance in the PF account without paying any interest. This loan is taken within a certain limit pertaining to the employee's contribution only. There are again three types of employees provident fund:

1. Statutory PF: It was set up in 1925 and is maintained by government or semi-government or semi-government, local authorities, railways, universities and educational institutions.
2. Recognized PF: The name is given so, because it is recognized by the Commissioner of Income Tax according to the rules contained in Part A, Schedule IV of the Income Tax Act. When the Commissioner of Income Tax recognizes this fund, it also becomes recognized by the Provident Fund Commissioner. In this type of PF, the employer's contribution is not fully tax exempt. The contribution is tax exempt up to 10% of the salary of the employee. Excess of employer's contribution over 10% of the salary makes it taxable.
3. Unrecognized Provident Fund: The employer's contribution is tax-exempt but the tax rebate under Section 80 C is not available to the investor or the employees.

Public provident fund scheme (PPF Scheme)

Unlike EPF Scheme, there is no employer to contribute any amount to the provident fund account. This scheme was introduced on July 1, 1968. Any person from the public, whether salaried or self employed who does not have the facility to save through Provident Fund Contribution can open a PPF account at any bank that offers this scheme. The salaried employees are allowed to contribute to this scheme in addition to the contributions made to their PF account in their respective companies or establishments. Though it is a 15-year scheme, the number of contributions required is 16. The 15-year period is calculated from the financial year following the date on which the account is opened. Thus a PPF account matures on the first day of the 17th year. The PPF deposits can be made in monthly installments with a minimum deposit of Rs. 500 per year and a maximum deposit of Rs. 70,000 per year. An adult can open only one a/c in his own name besides opening an a/c on behalf of his wife or his minor child. Deposits in PPF a/c are tax-exempt under Section 80C of the Income Tax Act. The rate of interest is 8% per annum compounded annually which is tax-free. However the interest is not paid monthly and is credited to PPF account, which is paid at maturity. The balance in the PPF account is also tax exempt and is not subject to attachment under any order or decree of a court. A PPF a/c holder can make one withdrawal every year after completion of 5 years. However withdrawal is limited to 50% of the balance at the end of the year immediately preceding the year of withdrawal less the amount of loan, if taken. A PPF a/c holder can take loan from the account from the 3rd year to the 6th year after opening the account. However the amount of loan cannot exceed 25% of the balance at the end of the second preceding financial year. The loan is subjected to an interest of 10% i.e. 1% higher than the PPF account interest rate. After maturity, if the a/c holder wants, the account can be continued for three successive block periods of five years each, with or without deposits. In such a case, only one withdrawal is permitted provided that the total amount withdrawn during a 5 year block does not exceed 60% of the balance of the account at the beginning. A PPF account is not transferred but has nomination facility.

Life Insurance Policies

Life insurance is a contract between a person and an insurance company for a number of years covering either the life time period or a fixed number of years. The basic customer needs met by the life insurance policies includes protection and savings. Protection benefits means providing financial protection to the policy- holder (or his family members) in case of premature death, long-term sickness or disability. Policies that provide savings benefit allow the policyholder to build up funds to meet specific investment objectives such as income in retirement or repayment of a loan. There are many policies that provide a combination of both savings and protection benefits. Thus life insurance is a long-term investment with an element of protection and savings.

The most popular insurance company of India is the Life Insurance Company (LIC). Apart from this, there are various other life insurance companies such as Met Life Insurance Company, ING Vysya Life Insurance, Birla Sun Life Insurance, HDFC Standard Life Insurance, ICICI Prudential Life Insurance, Max New York Life, OM Kotak Mahindra Life Insurance, SBI Life Insurance Company and Tata AIG Life Insurance Company. The premium paid under a life insurance policy is tax-exempt under Section 88 of the Income Tax Act, 1961. Any sum received under a life insurance policy, including the sum allocated in the form of bonus on such policy is exempt from tax under Section 10(10D) of the Income Tax Act.

The common types of life insurance policies are:

1. Endowment Policy
2. Whole Life Policy
3. Term Assurance
4. Annuities
5. Money Back Policy

Endownment policy

Under this policy, the insured amount is payable either at maturity or upon death of the insured person, whichever is earlier. It may also be taken for the marriage of children when they reach a certain age, or for the education of children. This policy is a combination of protection and savings. There are basically of two types of endowment policy: - *Non-participating endowment policy* (without profit) and *Participating endowment policy* (with profit).

Non-participating endowment policy (without profit) – It offers a guaranteed sum assured on death of the policyholder.

Participating endowment policy (with profit) – The initial sum assured under the policy is expected to be enhanced by payment of bonuses to the policyholder.

Whole life policy

The premiums are paid throughout the life of the policy holder but the assured amount is payable only after his death. It is the cheapest form of policy carrying the lowest premium among life policies. It is particularly useful as a means of protecting some of the expected wealth transfer that a parent would be aiming to make to his children after the death.

The whole life policy is again of following types:

Ordinary whole life policy: It remains in force till the life of the assured and the premium is paid throughout the entire life of the assured.

Limited payment whole life policy: Here the payment of premium is for a limited period only. After the expiry of the contract period, further premium need not be paid. The minimum amount for which the policy can be issued is Rs. 5,000.

Single payment whole life policy: Premium is paid only once i.e. in a lump sum. Not every one can afford to pay such a huge amount, at a time. Hence it is not very popular. Moreover the whole premium paid is lost if the insured person dies at an early age. Thus this policy is of greater element of investment on the part of the investor and a lesser degree of protection.

Convertible whole life policy: This policy can be converted into endowment policy after the completion of 5 years of contract. When the policy changes into endowment policy, the premium is increased.

Term assurance

It is a contract, which provides a benefit only if the policy holder dies within a specified period stated in the contract. It is a pure protection policy. Premiums may be paid regularly over the term of the policy or as a single premium at the onset of the contract. These policies are typically offered in the non-participating format. It provides a death benefit at a cost lower than an endowment or whole life policy for the same level of benefit.

Annuities

LIC also provides annuity policies to satisfy those who desire to provide a regular income for themselves and their dependants. The premium is paid in regular installments over a certain period or it may be paid in lump sum. After the assured person reaches a particular age, the insurer pays back the money in monthly, quarterly, half yearly or yearly installments.

Money back policy

This policy is similar to the endowment policy and the whole life policy but the sum assured is higher than the minimum amount assured in the other policies. Moreover a guaranteed addition is provided to the initial sum assured every year. In case of death of the policy holder within the specified term, as mentioned in the contract, the entire sum assured along with the accrued guaranteed additions is payable. Thus it is a savings-cum-protection policy as it provides lump sum at periodic intervals. No loans are granted against this policy.

Joint life policy

Two or more persons can jointly hold this policy. The assured sum is payable either on maturity or on the death of any of the persons jointly insured. Partnership firms find such a policy useful because it enables them to pay the capital of the deceased partner.

Double-accident indemnity policy

If the policy holder dies in an accident, his survivors get double the amount of the policy.

Sinking fund policies

Corporates use this policy for redemption of debentures, repayment of loans or replacement of assets. A fixed amount is paid as premium annually. The amount keeps increasing at a specified rate of interest. After the prescribed period is over, the company gets the entire money.

Progression protection policy

This policy is for those individuals who progressively enhance their incomes and are in a position to contribute higher premium amounts. It is also supposed to provide a cover against inflation. The sum assured increases at fixed intervals, but the premium rate also goes up, though not proportionately

MARKETABLE FINANCIAL ASSETS

A security that can be bought and sold in a secondary financial market is called a marketable security. Marketable securities include money market instruments, capital market instruments and derivatives securities.

MONEY MARKET INSTRUMENTS

They are short-term debt securities having a maturity of less than one year from the time of issue. Some of the characteristics of the money market instruments are explained below:

- They have a high degree of liquidity. Most of the instruments have active secondary markets that allow them to be sold prior to maturity.
- They have negligible risk and exhibit a high degree of safety of principal i.e. their risk of default or failure to repay principal is low and in some cases effectively non-existent.
- Except certificate of deposits (CDs), all money market instruments are discount securities i.e. they sell for less than face values and pay no periodic interest. When such an instrument matures, the investor receives the face value. The difference between the selling price and the face value is the investors' return.
- They have a tendency to trade in large denominations i.e. they are issued in high dollar amounts say, $ 1 million dollar or more.
- Though these instruments mature within one year from the date of issue, most instruments have maturities of three months (90 days) or less.
- These instruments are issued by borrowers with generally high credit standing, such as, the government itself, federally sponsored agencies, banks, financial institutions, security dealers, corporates etc. Individual investors, rarely participate in the money market directly.

A brief description of the various money market instruments are given below.

Treasury Bills (T-Bills)

They are the best-known, premier money market instruments. They represent the debt obligations of the Government of India and are issued with three standard maturities-91 days (13 weeks), 182 days (26 weeks) and 364 days (52 weeks). T-bills do not carry any interest rate. They are sold on an auction basis at a discount from the face value and are redeemed at par (face) value. The difference between the selling price and the face value is the return earned by the investor. Thus greater the discount at the time of purchase, higher is the return earned by the investor. The 13-week and 26 week T-bills are auctioned weekly whereas the 52 week bill is auctioned monthly. They are free of any default risk and are highly liquid. They have a highly active secondary market where they can be traded easily and readily. The terms of T-bill are not specified in paper. Rather the purchase is simply recorded on the computer. Because of the low risk and short maturity, T-bills are considered to be an attractive investment alternative.

Commercial Paper (CP)

It can be defined as short-term unsecured promissory notes issued by large, well-known and financially strong corporations. In essence, it is the corporate equivalent of a T-Bill. A company can issue a CP either directly to the investor or through dealers (banks). When the company deals directly with the investors, the CP is called a direct paper. On the other hand, when CPs are issued by dealers on behalf of their corporate customers, they are called dealer papers. The CPs are usually issued at a discount from the face value and redeemed at par. The maturity period of a CP is 90 to 180 days. It is a simple instrument and does not involve documents of any sort. Companies, which are able to raise funds through CPs become better in the financial world and are, thereby, placed in a more favourable position for raising long-term capital. Although, a secondary market exists for CPs, it is weak.

Negotiable Certificate of Deposits (NCDs)

Certificates of Deposit are a term savings deposit at a bank or other financial institutions. Certificates are issued against these deposits. Unlike other money market instruments, CDs are interest-bearing securities i.e. they pay interest on their principal amounts at specified annual rates. The maturity period of a CD is 3 months to 1 years. Previously all CDs were federally insured and could not be sold before maturity. Interest rates were kept low and were subject to ceilings set by the Federal Reserves. During 1960s and 1970s, CD rates started to fall well below the money-market races. In order to increase their direct access to the money market, banks offered a new type of CD. These CDs were not federally insured, their interest rates were not subject to ceilings and they could be sold before maturity in a secondary market. Hence they are also called negotiable CDs. In other words, NCDs are tradable time deposits. They can be sold in the open market before maturity. Unlike treasury bills and CPs, NCDs are engraved certificates i.e., proper documentation exists. These certificates specify the amount of deposit, period till maturity and the method of calculating interest rate. They are issued in both bearer and registered forms. The deposit is maintained in the bank until maturity when the holder receives the deposit plus interest. CDs are usually risk-free and offer a higher rate of interest than treasury bills.

Eurodollar

They are bank deposits denominated in U.S. dollars but issued and held outside the

United States or in U.S. branches of foreign banks. Basically there are two forms of Eurodollar – **Eurodollar CDs** and **Eurodollar deposits.** Eurodollar CDs are short term CDs denominated in dollars and issued by banks outside United States. A 180-day U.S. dollar CD issued by the Citibank (Indian Branch) is an example of Eurodollar CD and Eurodollar deposits are dollar denominated time deposits in banks outside the United States. The main difference between Eurodollar CDs and Eurodollar deposits is that Euro CDs are negotiable (i.e. they can be traded) whereas Eurodollar deposits are non-negotiable. Eurodollar CDs constitute the largest component of the Eurodollar market. The Eurodollar market is primarily a wholesale market with large deposits and large loans. Maturity is less than six months. Due to the development of non- U.S. markets for dollar denominated deposits, non-U.S. residents are able to conduct business free of U.S. bank regulations and the interest rate ceilings.

Repurchase Agreement (REPO)

Repurchase agreement is a short-term collateralized loan with money market instruments serving as a collateral. It involves purchase and repurchase of given security by two parties at prices determined when the agreement is made. The agreement is made between the borrower and the lender to sell and repurchase the securities. An investor (borrower) sells a package of securities to another investor (lender) and agrees to buy back the securities at a later date at a higher price. Generally the maturity of a repo is 14 days to one month. Sometimes, it is overnight. The difference between the sale price and the repurchase price is the income earned by the lender. Thus, at the end of the period, the seller gets back the security and the purchaser gets back the funds provided together with the interest. For example, Investor A plans to sell a money market instrument, say, a treasury bill to investor B for Rs. 10 million and decides to repurchase the borrower and the lender specifying the time and price of repurchase. Thus, the borrower will have to pay Rs. 100000 to the lender as interest for 30 days' use of Rs. 10 million. The annual interest rate, also known as the **repo rate,** can be calculated by the following formula:

$$\text{Sell Price} = \text{Repurchase Price-[Repo Rate* (Term/360)* Repurchase Price]}$$

$$10{,}000{,}000 = 1{,}01{,}00{,}000\text{-[Repo Rate * 30/360* 101,00,000]}$$

The repo rate usually depends on the nature of the security traded and the creditworthiness of the seller. A security of long duration could fluctuate simultaneously in value, exposing the purchaser to potential loss if the seller defaults on his obligation to repurchase it and leaves the purchaser stuck, holding a security of depreciated value. Hence to protect the purchase from such an eventuality, repos that last for several weeks or months have a provision whereby the seller is required to supply additional securities or repay a portion of the funds in case the underlying securities depreciates.

Banker's Acceptances (BA)

These are instruments that facilitate commercial trade transactions. A BA is a time draft drawn on a bank by a customer, whereby the bank agrees to pay a particular amount at a specified future date. In exchange, the bank is given the trade documents, temporary title to the goods that are related to the transaction and a commission for its services. The working of a BA can be well understood by the following example:- A particular company (buyer) wants to buy goods from another company (seller) and wishes to pay for the goods after it sells them, say, 90 days later. However the seller would definitely insist for immediate payment. In such a case, the buyer of the goods issues a letter of credit to the seller guaranteeing the payment within a certain period, say 90 days. This letter, also called the time deposit, is stamped "accepted" by a bank obligating itself to pay the amount on its due date. This letter of credit is, now, known as **banker's acceptance** or simply **BA.** The seller having received the BA can either wait till maturity to receive the payment or may sell it at a price that is less than the amount of the promised payment to be made in the future. Thus, BAs are pure discount securities i.e. they sell at a discount. Their maturity ranges from 30 days to 180 days. Usually, BAs are used to finance international trade. Investors in BAs include commercial banks, foreign central banks, money market funds and non-financial corporations. The yield is slightly lower than that on CP as BAs are less risky due to borrower's pledge to pay, collateral of goods and guarantee of the accepting bank.

Money Market Mutual Funds (MMMFs)

It is the most recent money market instrument introduced. It invests in short term mutual funds, thus enabling the small investors to participate in the money market by which they can earn market related yield. These funds invest in large pools of short-term instruments. For this, they collect resources from the short-term investors and, again, remit them the total return they receive from these investments less operating costs and a pre-arranged management fee. The MMMFs are of two types – taxable and tax-free. Taxable MMMFs include taxable assets such as CPs, NCDs and T-bills while tax-free MMMFs holds short-term municipal debts. MMMFs can be set-up by commercial banks and public financial institutions. Only individuals can subscribe to MMMFs.

Short-term Municipal Debt

Sometimes, state and local government have temporary needs for cash in anticipation of, say, the receipt of tax and other revenues or prior to sale of bonds. In order to meet this need, they issue short-term municipal securities. These securities are issued in two forms, viz, **interest bearing securities** and **discount securities**. Interest bearing securities carry a variable interest payment that is tied to some that is tied to some other open market rate, such as Treasury yields. The extent of the rate movement depends on how the rate to which they are linked behaves over time. On the other hand, in case of discount securities, the interest earnings are exempt from income taxes. Moreover these earnings are exempt from state and local taxes, provided that the investor is a resident of the state or city that issues the debt instrument. Interest bearing securities are more common than discount securities. Depending upon the type of backing available, these municipal securities are of two types – **General obligation securities** and **Revenue securities.** In case of general obligation securities, the debt has the backing by full faith and credit of the issuer. They are explicitly supported by the taxing power of the government. However, in case of revenue securities, the issues are backed by the revenues generated by the specific projects funded by the securities and do not carry the backing of the issuer. Hence revenue securities are perceived to be more risky. Table 4.2 below lists the common issuers and the type of debt employed by each of them.

Table 4.2. Money Market Instruments

Issuer	Types of Debt Employed
State Government	G.O. and Revenue
Local Government	G.O. and Revenue
Authorities, districts and agencies created by state and local government	Revenue
Public school	Revenue
Higher education	Revenue
Public power	Revenue
Water or sewer	Revenue
Transportation	Revenue
Health facilities	Revenue
Student loan	Revenue
Housing finance	Revenue
Pollution control	Revenue
Industrial development	Revenue
Waste management	Revenue

Note: G.O. denotes General obligation
Source: Instruments of the Money Market, Federal Reserve Bank of Richmond, 1998.

CAPITAL MARKET INSTRUMENTS

Capital market instruments are long-term sources of finance with maturities greater than one year. There are two types of capital market instruments, in general. They are **fixed income securities** and **equity securities.**

Fixed Income Securities

The fixed income securities are long-term debt instruments having a specified payment or repayment schedule. These are often called bonds or debentures. They pay interest at fixed rate and at regular intervals. Bond holders or debenture holders have call provisions i.e., they can buy back the securities from the investors at pre-specified prices prior to maturity. The nature of any bond is indicated by its bond indenture. **Bond indenture** is a legal document that accompanies a bond, which spells out the rights and obligations of the issuer and the investor. The trustee, who monitors the compliance with the indenture and initiates legal action on behalf of the bond holders, is identified in the bond indenture. Other things that are listed in the indenture include collaterals, limits on executive salary, additional debt, future dividends and payment dates. Many bonds have a sinking fund provision, which requires the corporation to retire a certain percentage.

Municipal bonds

The bonds issued by municipalities, state government or local government and not by the federal government, to finance their long-term public works projects are called municipal bonds. These bonds are of two types: **general obligation bonds** and **revenue bonds.** General obligation bonds are backed by the full faith and credit of the issuer. They originate from those government units that have unlimited taxing authority to meet their obligations to pay interest and principal on these bonds. However, revenue bonds rely solely on the income generated from the project, to repay its debt. In short, they are used to finance only revenue producing projects such as, toll roads, sport facilities, public conveniences, sewage disposal system, gas facility, electricity, water works etc. The project must generate enough revenue to meet the debt obligations. Thus, they are substantially riskier than the general obligation bonds. Municipal bonds are often sold as serial bonds rather than term bonds. In a serial bond issue, a pre-determined number of bonds mature each year until the final maturity date is attained. For example, a 10-year serial issue may have 10 percent of the issue each year for the next 10 years. Term bonds, on the other hand, mature on the same date i.e., they have a single maturity date. The main advantage of serial bonds is that they help in marketing the bond. Since different investors prefer to purchase bonds with different maturities, they allow the issuer to market selectively long-term series to some investors and shorts-term series to others. They may also increase the degree of comfort that investors have in the ability of the issuer to redeem the debt at maturity. All municipal bonds carry some credit risk. To help the investors to assess credit risk, these bonds carry bond ratings assigned by rating agencies. Income earned from municipal bonds is generally in two forms – interest and capital gains (or losses). Although, the interest earned is, usually, exempt from federal income taxes, capital gains (or losses) are not tax-exempt. Because of this feature, the stated rates on these bonds are lower than that of other non-exempt bonds. The higher an investor's tax bracket, the more attractive is the municipal bond.

Corporate bonds

Corporate bonds are long-term debt securities issued by corporations or private firms. Most corporate bonds are term bonds that mature, anytime between 5 to 40 years. A corporate may have more than one debt outstanding at nay point of tie. All corporate bonds expose investors to some degree of credit risk. Hence, like municipal bonds, corporate bonds are also rated. Bonds with ratings below BBB are called **junk bonds.** Corporate bonds are **senior securities** i.e. they are senior to preferred stock and common stock in terms of priority of payment or in case of bankruptcy and liquidation.

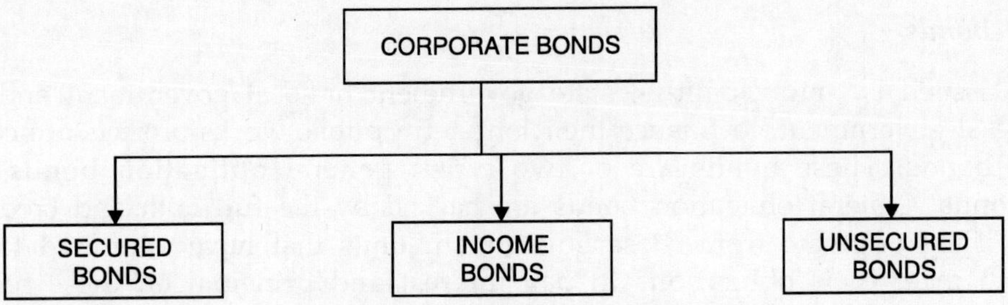

Fig. 4.2. Corporate Bonds

Corporate bonds can be broadly classified into three types:-

Secured bonds (or **Mortgage bonds)** – These bonds give their owners legal claims to specific assets, in case, the issuer goes bankrupt. In this type of bonds, specific assets are pledged as collateral. Mortgage bonds are explained under a separate heading "Asset-Backed Securities" later in this chapter.

Unsecured bonds – These are also known as **debentures.** These are backed by full faith and credit of the issuer, but no specific asset or collateral is pledged. Debenture-holders are general creditors of the issuer i.e. if the company's assets are liquidated in bankruptcy their claims are junior to mortgage bondholders. Debentures that have a secondary claim to general assets the revenues of a firm in the event of bankruptcy are called.

Income bonds – They are the corporate equivalent of municipal revenue bonds. They finance the revenue generating assets. Unlike other corporate bonds, an income bond carries a commitment to pay interest and principal, only if income from the asset is sufficient.

Most corporate bonds have call previsions. Usually, there is a modest premium paid above par value by the corporation to the bondholders when exercising this call. Some bonds are convertible into common stock at a pre-specified price. Typically, the bonds are handed over to the corporation in exchange for a specified number of common shares, without any cash payment. This is attractive to the investors because investors can benefit from appreciating stock prices by converting into common shares while being protected from the depreciating stock prices by retaining the bond status. Thus, the prices of the convertibles fluctuate depending on whether they are currently trading like bonds (fixed income securities) or common stock.

Asset backed securities (ABS)

Asset Backed Securities are those securities which are issued against some type of asset as additional security such as credit card receivables or mortgages. Pooling a large number of small loans into a large debt instrument and selling the ownership of combined cash flow to the new investors create these securities. Generally a separate trust is established that formally owns the assets. This trust, referred to as **special purpose trust,** purchases the assets from the originating institutions and sells ownership rights to the general public. The owner has an equity interest in the trust that owns the assembled assets the timely payment to owners of the trust is assured by four ways: insurance or third party guarantees, over collateralization, a senior/ subordinate ownership structure and use of reserved fund or cash collateral pool. These are secured bonds i.e., they give their owners legal claims to specific assets in case the issuers go bankrupt. Thus, if the company (issuer) is not able to pay its bond holders, the interest or the principal, the bond holders have the right to sell the security and get back their dues. These are considered to be high quality securities with minimum credit risk. All asset-backed securities are insured, which means that the insurer in the event of default pays the outstanding principal. The most common asset backed security is the **mortgage bonds** i.e., the bonds backed by real collateral assets. Bonds backed by rolling stock such as train car etc. are termed **equipment obligations.** Bonds backed by marketable securities are known as **collateral trust bonds.** ABS is issued to finance car loans, credit receivable, home equity debt, lease agreements and corporate receivables. Today, the total value of ABS market is over $ 6 trillion and is still growing in depth and complexity day by day. The advent of ABS has allowed debts to be freely traded in order to reduce the cost of debt and increases everyone's access to the wonderful world of "buy now and pay later". However, the main disadvantage of ABS is their uncertain maturities. Although, the maturity period of these securities is 40 years, most of the owners, payoff their mortgage or the assets pledged well before maturity. As a result, the investors receive varying amounts of monthly payments depending on how quickly the mortgage is paid off. As the pool is liquidated immediately as mortgages are paid off, the ABS could mature any time between one day and forty from the date of issue.

Foreign bonds

Government and corporations throughout the world issue debt securities outside their own countries. The bonds of different countries are known by different names. For example, foreign bonds issued in the U.S. are called **Yankee** bonds whereas those issued in UK are called **Bulldog** bonds. Many companies issue **Eurobonds** and **Euro yen** bonds. Eurobonds are the bonds denominated in US dollars but issued outside the US. Euro yen bonds are the bonds denominated in Japanese yen but issued outside Japan. A foreign bond may be very attractive to investors because the dollar yield is much higher than the Indian rupee and their risk on the portfolio is diversified. Although the foreign bonds appear to be attractive to the investors, they expose the investors to the risk of adverse changes in foreign exchange rates or, in other words, price fluctuations.

US treasury bonds

The US treasury or the federal government issues these bonds. Their maturity period is thirty years. However, those with maturities within two and ten years are referred to as **treasury notes** (T-notes). Both T-bonds and T-notes carry the full faith and credit of US government. They have no default risk. They are interest-bearing securities and the interest is paid semi-annually. Apart from maturity, the difference between T-bonds and T-notes is that bonds are callable while notes are not. An investor purchases these securities with the expectation of earning a steady interest and full assurance of receiving the par value of the bonds at maturity. They are sold by auction at face value, with investors submitting bids identifying the lowest yields to maturity that they are willing to accept.

Government bonds

Bonds issued by the central government, state government or quasi government agencies are called government bonds or **gilt-edged securities**. Maturity of these bonds is between three to twenty years. Although they are interest-bearing securities, the rate of interest is very low, usually between 9 to 13.5 percent. The main investors of these bonds include banks, financial institutions, insurance companies and provident funds. Basically these gilt-edged securities are of three types – *Bearer Security, Provisionary notes* and *Debentures.*

Bearer Security: interest and other payments are made to the bond holder.

Provisionary notes: It contains a promise by the President of India or the Governor of the state to meet the debt obligation as per schedule. It can also be transferred by endorsement. The new bond holder should present the note to the government treasury in order to receive interest or other payments.

Debentures: It carries the name of the bond holder(s) and is registered with the Public Debt Office, which pays interest to the holders on the specified date.

Agency bonds

These bonds are issued by the federal agencies or federally sponsored agencies. Federal agencies are owned and managed by the federal government. Their securities have the full faith and credit of the treasury. Federally sponsored agencies are privately owned but are sponsored by the federal government. They sell their own securities in the market in order to raise funds. The government does not guarantee their security. The credit quality of the agency bonds is perceived to be very high. Their yield is higher than marketable Treasury bond. Markets for agency bonds are usually not as liquid as their treasury counterparts. Interest payment may be made monthly, quarterly, half-yearly or annually. Some agency bonds are marketable. There are three international organizations, partially sponsored by the US government, that issue agency bonds. They are: Asian Development Bank, Inter-American Development Bank and the World Bank.

Zero-coupon bonds

These bonds are issued with no coupons, or interest to be paid during the life of the bond. The purchaser buys these bonds at a price less than the face value and receives the face value at maturity. The difference between the two prices is the total return earned by the investor. One of the main examples of this type of bonds is the T-bill, which are sold at discount and redeemed at par. However, the implicit interest rate can be calculated by the following formula:

$$\textbf{Acquisition Price} = \textbf{Value} / (1+I)^{n}$$

Where I = rate of interest

n = maturity period in years

For instance, in order to buy a zero-coupon bond that matures in 2008 with a face value of $14000, an investor need to have spent $1000 in 1986. Such a purchase would have yielded an average annual return, say, 12.7 percent per year over the 22 years, if the bond is held to maturity and does not default. The issuers of zero-coupon bonds include corporations, municipalities, government agencies and the US treasury. The disadvantage of investing in zero coupon bonds is that taxable investors have to pay income tax on the coupon interest even though the investors does not actually receive the interest.

RBI Relief bonds

Technically these bonds are called Government of India Relief Bonds. But since, they are issued by Reserve Bank of India, they are also referred to as RBI Relief Bonds. The bonds are issued in the form of Bond Ledger Account or in the form of Promissory Notes. The minimum amount of investment is Rs. 1000 with no maximum limit. The maturity period is 5 years from the date of issue. The rate of interest is 8 percent paid semi-annually. The interest earned is tax-exempt. These bonds can be pledged as a collateral security to banks to avail loans. Moreover, nomination facility is available.

Table 4.3. RBI Relief Bonds

Sl. No	Bond Ledger Account	Promissiory Notes
1.	Can be issued at the designated receiving offices of bands and public debt offices of RBI	Are issued at RBI offices
2.	It is transferable, wholly or partially by execution of a prescribed transfer deed.	They are transferable by endorsement and delivery

Warrant bonds

Bonds with warrants are called warrant bonds. A warrant entitles its holders to subscribe to the equity capital of a company during a specified period at a particular price. This price, also referred to as subscription price, is generally higher than the market price of the shares at the time of issue. Each bond has a warrant attached to it, which gives the right to the bondholder to pay a subscription price and exchange the bonds for equity share. Though he has the right, it is not obligatory for the investor to acquire the equity shares. It is his option whether to subscribe to the equity capital or continue to retain the bond along with the warrant. There are two types of warrant bonds – *detachable* and *non-detachable.*

Detachable warrant bonds: The warrant can be sold separately and the holder continues to retain the instrument to which the warrant was tied. The warrant is usually sold during price increase.

Non-detachable warrant bonds: Separate sale of the warrant independent of the instrument to which it was attached is not possible.

The theoretical value of a warrant depends on the market price of the shares, the subscription price, and the subscription ratio. Thus,

Theoretical Value = (Market Price – Subscription) × Subscription Ratio of the Shares Price

Subscription ratio is the number of shares that can be acquired for warrant. If the market value of shares were lower than the subscription price, the value of the warrant would be zero. The difference between the market value of shares and the theoretical value of the warrant is the **premium.**

Premium Percent = Premium / Theoretical Warrant Value

Equity Securities

Equity securities represent an ownership claim in a corporation. They are the residual claimants after the payment of all obligations to the fixed income securities. There are two types of equity ownership: Common Stock and Preferred Stock.

Common stock

Common stock is the first security of a corporation to be issued and in the event of bankruptcy, the last to be retired. It represents an ownership share in the firm; it has the lowest priority claim on earnings and assets of all security issued.[1] Unlike bond holders, who are creditors, stock holders are owners. They are the residual claimants i.e., if the company liquidates its assets, the common stockholders get whatever remains after all the debt is paid. In case, the company goes bankrupt, stockholders lose no more than what they paid for their stock. They are not fully liable for corporate debts. Since, the common stock holders are legal owners of a company they enjoy certain rights such as voting rights. They generally have the power to vote for a board of directors and on other major issues facing the company. Each share normally gives its owner one vote. The more shares an investor has, the more votes he controls. Common stockholders also have preemptive rights i.e., right of the shareholders to purchase newly issued shares of stock before the general public buys. When a company decides to sell additional shares of common stock, the percentage of shares controlled by the existing shareholders is diluted, thereby, diluting their proportionate ownership in the company. Preemptive rights prevent this dilution by giving existing shareholders the right to purchase any new share offerings before other investors. These rights, usually, expire after a specific time period set, after which any remaining shares of a new issue can be sold to outside investors. A common stockholder receives a certificate of ownership that states the number of shares owned and the face value or par value per share. Like other financial assets, new financial assets are also created in the equity area. One such equity stock is SPDRs or Spiders. They combine the performance of an equity index with the trading advantages of a stock.

Equity shares can be classified as follows:[2]

Blue-chip shares: Shares of large well-established and financially strong companies with an impressive record of earnings and dividends.

Growth shares: Shares of companies that have a fairly entrenched position in a growing market and which enjoy an above average rate of growth as well as profitability.

Income shares: Shares of companies that have fairly stable operations relatively limited growth opportunities and high dividend pay out ratios.

Cyclical shares: Shares of companies that have a pronounced cyclicity in their operations.

Defensive shares: Shares of companies that are relatively unaffected by the ups and downs in general business conditions.

---

1. Jack Clark Francis, "Investments: Analysis and Management", 5th ed., Mc-Graw-Hill, New York,1991, p. 50.
2. Chandra, P., "Managing investments", Tata McGraw-Hill Publishing Company Ltd., New Delhi, 1998, pp. 33-34.

Speculative shares: Shares that tend to fluctuate widely because there is a lot of speculative trading in them.

Foreign equities/Foreign stock: Equity shares or common stock of foreign companies can also be traded on an exchange or a market in another country. This can be done in two ways. Firstly, the shares of British Petroleum can be bought on the London Stock Exchange but the shares would be priced in British currency. However, buying shares in foreign markets is both cumbersome and expensive. The second alternative is through Global/American Depository Receipts (GDRs/ADRs). A GDR/ADR is an instrument issued abroad and is traded on a foreign stock exchange. It represents indirect ownership of a specified number of shares of a foreign company. ADRs are denominated in US dollars and traded on US stock exchanges. These shares are issued by US banks, called depositories, thus, ADRS are tradable receipts issued by depositories that have physical possession of the foreign securities through their foreign correspondent banks. The securities are to be held on deposit as long as the ADRs are outstanding. ADR holders are entitled to all stock and cash dividends paid by the foreign shares. Thus, the dividends are paid in local currency (dollars). The bank holding the securities collects the dividends and pays this amount to the ADR holders. ADRs can be set up directly by a bank at the request of the foreign company. Such ADRs are called sponsored ADRs. They can also be set up at the request of US market makers and are called un-sponsored ADRs. ADRs do not carry any voting rights. The ADR holders can choose to convert their ADRs into the specified number of foreign shares that it represents. After conversion, the underlying shares are traded on the domestic stock exchanges. Some well-known companies that trade as ADRs are De Beers, Toyota, Sony, Glaxo, Infosys, Reliance Industries, ICICI, Ranbaxy and others.

Preferred stock

Preferred stock is a hybrid security with characteristics of both common stock and bonds. Like common stock, it represents an equity ownership on the firm's assets and pays a fixed rate dividends or floating rate dividend annually. If the issuer of preferred stock fails to pay the dividend, holder of preferred shares do not have any legal recourse. But cumulative provisions, which ensure that when the payment of dividend is resumed, the unpaid dividend(s) will have to be paid before the common shareholders receive any dividend, usually protect them. Although there is no legal binding for a corporation to pay preference dividends, preference shareholders receive dividends, if paid, after the bondholders but before the common stock holders. But they are not considered creditors in case of bankruptcy. It is similar to bonds because, like bonds, it has no voting rights and their claim to firm's assets is senior to common stock holders. Preference shares have no maturity. Dividend is paid over an infinite life but at affixed rate. They are usually convertible, callable and have sinking fund provisions. Most preferred stock carries a par value, which is equal or almost equal to the initial amount, received by the corporate issuer. The dividend rate is linked to the par value. Moreover, the par value represents the amount of the preferred shareholder's claim to funds in excess of those necessary to satisfy creditors.

Another type of hybrid security has emerged that has combined features of preferred stock and corporate bonds. These hybrid securities are called MIPS (Monthly Income Preferred Securities), QUIPS (Quarterly Income Preferred Securities) and TOPS (Trust Originated Preferred Securities). These securities are an alternative to corporate bonds and traditional preferred stocks.

DERIVATIVE MARKET INSTRUMENTS

These securities derive their value in whole, or in part by having a claim on some underlying security, i.e. their value depends on the value of the underlying assets. Derivative securities are of two types – options and futures. Both of them have standardized features that allow them to be traded quickly and cheaply on organized exchanges. They help the investors to limit portfolio risk by providing risk control possibilities. They are, basically used for hedging and speculating.

Options

They are created not by any corporations but by investors seeking to trade in claims on a particular common stock. An option gives its owner the right to buy or sell an underlying asset (equity shares) on or before a particular date at a predetermined price. An option holder enjoys the right to buy or sell for which he pays a price but has no obligation. There are, basically two types of options, namely, put and call options. A put (or call) option gives the option holder the right to sell (or buy) a stated number of shares of a particular stock at a specified price, called the exercise price, within a specified time. In case of call option, the seller is obliged to sell the shares if the buyer chooses to exercise the option. On the other hand, the seller of put option is obliged to buy the shares at the specified price.

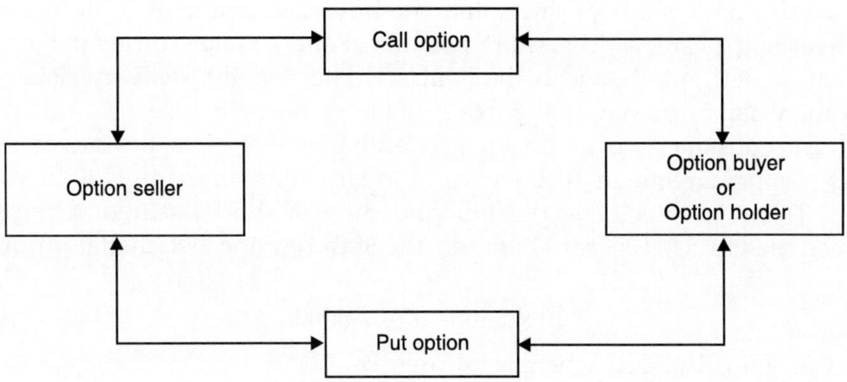

The option sellers receive a premium from the option buyers. The premium is simply the market price of the contract as determined by the investors. The maturity of put and call option is, usually, up to several months but within one year. However, a new form of puts and calls called Long Term Equity Anticipation Securities (LEAPs) has longer maturity dates, usually up to two years. Investors can buy or sell options to speculate that the underlying stock will rise or fall in value over a short period of time. Buyers of calls usually bet that the price of the underlying common stock will rise making the call option more valuable. On the other hand, buyers of put options bet that the price of the underlying stock will decline, making the put option affected directly by the price of the stock that gives its value and stock price itself is fluctuating. The options value is also affected by the time remaining to maturity, current interest rates, volatility of stock and the price at which the option can be exercised. Now, how does options work? This can be illustrated by the following example.

Consider a December call option on a company at an exercise price of Rs. 100. This call option gives the investor the right to buy 100 shares of the company at a price of Rs. 100 per share at any time till December. If the company's stock price rises above Rs. 100 per share before late December, the investor could call the option. But if the price remains less than Rs. 100 per share, the option would remain unexercised and expire. In contrast, a December put option at an exercise price of Rs.100 would give the holder (or seller) the right to sell 100 shares at Rs. 100 per share by late December. If the stock price of the company drops below Rs. 100, say Rs. 75, before December, the holder of the put option will be able to buy 100 shares at Rs. 75 per share. However, if the stock price of the company remains above Rs. 100 per share, the put option would expire unexercised.

Futures

A futures contract is an agreement that provides for the future exchange of a particular asset between a buyer and a seller at a currently determined price. The future contract specifies the grade of the asset to be delivered; the delivery of the asset is usually within one year from the day of the agreement. The seller, who agrees to deliver the asset is said to have short position and the buyer, who agrees to accept delivery is said to have long position. The short position (Seller) makes profit if the price of the commodity (asset) falls between the contract date and the delivery date whereas the long position makes money if the price of the commodity rises. To understand a futures contract, consider two investors – A and B where A is the buyer and B is the seller. As per the agreement 1000 shares of a particular company is to be delivered after 90 days. Thus, A has a Long position and B has a short position. If the price of the shares increases to Rs. 105 per share, on the 90th day the net change in price will be –

$$1000*(105-100) = 5000.$$

A is said to gain Rs. 5000 whereas B loses Rs. 5000.

Similarly, if the price of the shares decreases to Rs. 5 on the 90th day the net change in price will be –

$$1000*(95-100) = 5000.$$

A loss Rs. 5000 while B gains Rs. 5000,

Earlier, futures contract involved only financial products such as foreign currency, Treasury bills, Treasury bonds, stock market indexes, CDs, precious metals, petroleum products etc.

The investors involved in futures contract are either hedgers or speculators. Hedgers seek to reduce price uncertainty over some future period. On the other hand, speculators hope to profit from the uncertainty (short term movements in commodity prices) that will occur in the future. If the prices are expected to rise (or fall), the contract will be purchased (or sold). A hedged needs to own or buy the asset or commodity that underlines the futures contract whereas speculators do not need to own the commodities; rather, they trade the contract. By purchasing (or selling) a futures contract, a hedger can lock in a specific price for the asset and be protected from adverse price movements. For example, a wheat farmer may use futures to guarantee the price at which the crop would sell, prior to its harvest whereas a speculator might go along in a wheat contract, believing that price of wheat is likely to rise in near future or go short in the contract believing that wheat price may fall.

A recent innovation in the financial market is options on futures that give the buyer the right, but not the obligation, to assume the futures position.

Table 4.4.

Futures	Options
It is an obligation to buy or sell.	It is only the right to buy or sell but not an obligation.
Buyers of a future contract do not have any limited liability.	The buyer of an option has limited.

Corporate Created Derivative Securities

Apart from options and futures, there are some derivative securities that are created by corporations. Corporations issue two kinds of securities that resemble options – **convertible bonds** and **warrants**.

Convertible bonds

These are regular corporate bonds or preferred stock that can be exchanged for a fixed number of shares of common stock of the issuing company by paying a pre-determined conversion price. Like the exercise price on a call option, the conversion price normally remains constant regardless of the market price of the common stock. The investors prefer convertible bonds, because they combine the characteristics of bonds and options. They have lower coupon rates than preferred stock (non-convertible).

Warrants

They are long-term call options issued by corporations. The investor redeems the warrant with the issuing company and receives a specified number of shares of common stock. Warrants are usually attached to other securities, usually bonds, which make them easily marketable. An investor can sell the warrant and still keep the security to which it was attached. That is why they can be traded in major stock exchanges. Like call options, the value of warrant is, usually, 5 to 10 years.

INDIRECT INVESTMENT

As an alternative to purchasing financial assets themselves, investors can invest indirectly through investment companies. Rather than investing directly in securities, the investors can invest in a portfolio of securities by purchasing the shares of a financial intermediary or investment company that invests in various types of securities. The investment company does all the work for the investor, starting from purchase of securities charge. The process of indirect investing is explained directly in the Fig. 4.3. Investors purchase shares of an investment company. The investment company invests the funds raised from the investor company. The investment company invests the funds raised from the investor in a portfolio of security. The investors are entitled to a *pro rata* share of the dividends interest and the capital gains/ losses generated. In return, the shareholders must also pay a *pro rata* share of the company's expenses and its management fee which will be deducted from the earnings as it flows back to the shareholders.

Thus, an investment company is a financial company that sells its shares to the public and uses the funds raised to invest in a portfolio of securities. By pooling the

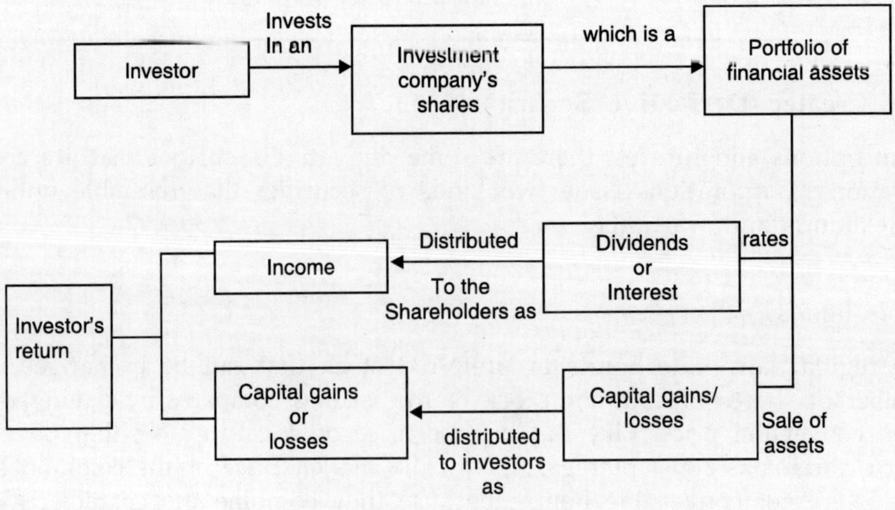

Fig. 4.3. Indirect Investment.

funds of various investors, a widely diversified portfolio can be purchased and the investment company can offer its shareholders a variety of services.

There are three types of investment companies – **unit investment trusts, close-ended investment companies** and **open-ended investment companies.** Open-ended and close-ended investment companies are managed companies, offering professional management of the portfolio, while unit investment trusts are unmanaged companies.

Unit Investment Trusts

It is an unmanaged form of investment company, holding fixed income securities put together by a sponsor and run by an independent trustee. The sponsor sells a fixed number of shares, called units, and uses the funds (less a sales charge) to purchase a portfolio of securities. Units are small pieces of the overall portfolio. Redeemable trust certificates representing claims against the assets of the trust (units) are sold to the investors at net asset value (NAV) along with a small commission.

Income (interests and dividends) from the securities held by the trust is distributed to the owners of the units (certificate holders) along with any principal repayments. Unit investment trusts are, usually, passive investments. They are bought and held with the main objective of raising capital or funds. The main advantage of unit investment trust as compared to other companies is that they offer investors diversification, provide professional management that takes care of all the details, permit the purchase of securities by the trust at a cheaper price than if purchased individually, ensure minimum operating cost and routine return of principal. Most unit investment trusts hold tax-exempt securities. The securities always remain unchanged. The trust ceases to exist when the bonds (all bonds) in the portfolio mature. An investor can sell units prior to maturity. It is also possible to redeem units of the trust. The sponsor makes a market for these certificates (units) for buying and selling at their current NAV. Shares of unit investment trusts are, usually, the least liquid of any investment company. The unit investment trusts involve three types of charges—sales charge (3 to 4 percent), management fee or service charge, commissions (if units are sold early).

The first unit investment trust was created in 1961 comprising only municipal bonds. In 1972, the first corporate bond trust was created followed by government bond trust in 1978. However, municipal bond trusts are the most popular trusts. An innovation in the 1990s is the **stock trust** that holds a portfolio of equity stocks. This trust was, especially, designed for small investors to enable them to buy a portfolio of common stock. The projected holding period is one to five years. The portfolio can be liquidated within that period only in case of major problems with the company. Another recent development is the **Index Depository Receipts (IDR)** holding the shares of all the companies making up several popular indexes such as Standard & Poor's 500 or Dow Jones Industrial. For example, **spiders (SPDRs)** is a unit investment trust that holds shares of all companies making up the S&P 500 index. Spiders trade on the American Stock Exchange. One of the characteristic features of IDR is that the units are traded on major stock exchanges, like the individual shares of common stock.

Close-ended investment companies

Closed end investment companies, like any other investment company, raise money by selling shares to the public. However, they do not sell additional shares of its own stock after the initial public offering. Thus, the number of outstanding shares of capitalization is usually fixed unless a new public offering is made. The advantages of having a fixed capitalization is that-

1. It checks the unlimited growth of the investment company
2. Potential to buy shares at a discount.

Moreover, a closed end investment company will not redeem shares unless it liquidates. The shares of closed-end funds trade on various exchanges (secondary market) just like ordinary shares of common stock. To buy and sell the shares of closed-end investment companies, the investors use their brokers, paying (or receiving) the current price at which the shares are selling plus (or minus) brokerage commissions. Since the shares are traded on stock exchanges, the forces of demand and supply determine their price. Their market price is rarely equal to their actual price (NAV). A special type of close-end fund is a dual-purpose fund that has a limited life (10 to 20 years) and sells two types of shares—income shares and capital shares. Investors who buy the fund's income shares receive all the incomes (interest and dividends) from its assets plus a fixed redemption value when the fund liquidates. Investors who purchase the capital shares receive rest of the things (apart from interest/dividends).

Open-ended investment companies

An open-ended investment company is an investment company whose capitalization constantly changes as new shares are sold and outstanding shares are redeemed. Additional shares are sold to the investors even after the initial sale of share. That is why it is open-ended. The capitalization is continuously changing as new investors buy additional shares and some existing shareholders redeem their shares at NAV. Open-end investment companies are popularly referred to as **mutual funds**. Shares of mutual funds do not trade on secondary market. To sell the shares, one has to redeem them (i.e. sell them back to the fund) at NAV. The net asset value (NAV) is the per share value of the portfolio of securities held by the investment company and is computed as follows :

$$\text{NAV} = \frac{\textbf{Total market value - Trade payables of the securities (liabilities).}}{\textbf{Number of fund shares currently outstanding.}}$$

Total market value = current market price of each security × number of shares of the securities owned by the fund.

Table 4.5 shows the operation of a hypothetical mutual fund company. The mutual fund initially sells 1 million shares at Rs.10 per share. It buys equivalent amount of five stocks with the fund raised.

Table 4.5.

Stock	Purchase Price (Rs.)	Annual Dividend (Rs.)	No. of shares purchased	After 6 Months Total Price Value (Rs)	(Rs)	After 1 Year Total Price Value (Rs)	(Rs)	Total Dividend (Rs)
A	20	0.5	1,00,000	30	3,000,000	34	3,400,000	50,000
B	25	0.5	80,000	24.75	1,980,000	22.5	1,800,000	40,000
C	50	1	40,000	67.5	2,700,000	80	3,200,000	40,000
D	50	1.25	40,000	48	1,920,000	45	1,800,000	50,000
E	100	2	20,000	100	2,000,000	120	2,400,000	40,000
			Total Portfolio Value		11,600,000		12,600,000	220,000
			Per-share Value		11.6		12.6	0.22

To simplify the example, it is assumed that the investors pay no management fee or commissions, the portfolio does not change during the year and the number of shares remains constant. The investor's return for the year, as calculated, is

$$(12{,}600{,}000 - 10{,}000{,}000 + 220{,}000)/10{,}000{,}000 = 28.2\%$$

Mutual funds can be broadly classified into three types on the basis of the nature of the scheme, objectives and asset-mix. On the basis of the nature of the scheme, mutual funds are of two types—**open-ended funds** and **close-ended funds**.

Open-ended fund: It is the type of mutual fund where the maturity period is specified. The company cannot sell share units after its initial public offering. The shares are issued like the new issues of any other company, listed and quoted on a stock exchange. The subscription period remains open only for a specific period, called the redemption period. At the end of this period, the entire portfolio is disinvested and the fund ceases to exist. The proceeds from the disinvestments are distributed to the unit holders. However, with the approval of the unit holders, the fund or the scheme can be rolled over.

The difference between close-ended and open-ended funds has been shown below :

Open-ended funds	Close-ended funds
• Has no maturity period	Has a fixed maturity period (usually 5 to 15 years)
• Are not listed on stock exchanges	Are listed on stock exchanges.
• Are characterized by continual selling	Cannot sell share units after its initial public offering
• They do not have a fixed capitalization	They have limited capitalization i.e. its growth in terms of the number of shares is limited.
• Shares are redeemable	Shares are not redeemable
• Prices are determined by NAV	Prices are determined by demand and supply

On the basis of investment objectives, the mutual funds are of four types: growth funds, income funds, balanced funds and tax saving funds.

Growth funds: they seek capital growth. The main objective of these funds is capital appreciation. Dividend or income is a secondary factor. The objective is achieved by investing in high growth. Equity stock.

Income funds: the main objective of these funds is to generate and distribute regular income to the investors. This is done by investing in high-income yield instruments (or fixed income instruments) such as debentures or bonds.

Balanced funds: they seek both regular income as well as capital growth by balancing their investment between high growth equity shares and income earning securities. Their portfolios are a mix of bonds, preferred stocks and equity stocks.

Tax saving funds: they are, basically, growth funds, which also offer, tax rebates under the income law.

On the basis of the asset mix, mutual funds are of four types, viz., equity funds, bond funds, hybrid funds and money market funds. Hybrid funds invest in both stocks and bonds. Money market funds are of two types – Taxable and Tax – exempt money market funds. Equity funds are again subdivided into growth funds, value funds, index funds and sector funds.

Value funds – they, generally seek to find stock that is cheap on the basis of standard fundamental analysis yardsticks, such as, earnings book value and dividend yield.

Index funds – one of the fastest growing types of mutual fund today is a index fund. This type of mutual fund invests in a portfolio of equity stock that comprises a given performance of one of the several indexes closely and appreciates or depreciated in the same way as the index.

Sector funds – These funds invest in the stock of a given sector or industry. The diversification is limited and hence, the risk is higher. They do not pay dividends and are highly volatile.

Bond funds are also of three types – income funds, gift funds and money market funds. Income funds and money market funds have already been discussed earlier in the chapter.

Gift funds – gift funds invest in securities issued by central or state government. That is why they are also called the government securities fund. The government unconditionally guarantees payment of interest and principal. These funds may also invest in money market instruments for liquidity purpose. The main aim of these funds is to earn a return without any credit risk.

The various types of mutual funds that have been discussed so far are related to one another and are not mutually exclusive.

REAL ASSETS

Real assets are physical assets having a high intrinsic value. The appreciation is very high, higher than other kinds of securities but the rate at which they are purchased is also higher. Therefore, people with a high income can only invest in such assets. Given the right set of circumstances, real assets can produce impressive returns. But financial assets (stocks and bonds) have produced far better returns than real assets over long periods of time. Historically, real assets were superior to paper assets only during periods of high inflation, especially, when future rates of inflation seemed difficult to predict. When inflation is low, and future inflation rate is more predictable, paper assets tend to do much better than real assets.

The most common types of real assets are – real estate, precious metals, precious stones and art objects.

Real Estate

The most common types of real estate are land and housing property. In addition to providing attractive returns and significant tax savings, investing in real estate also gives a pride of ownership. Like financial assets, investment in real estate is also of two types – direct and indirect. Direct investment is the direct ownership of the real estate. One can also invest in real estate indirectly, through **Real Estate Investment Trust (REIT)** or **Limited Partnership**. REIT is an investment company that sells shares and uses the proceeds to purchase real estate investment. Shares of REIT trade on major stock exchanges. A limited partner consists of a general partner and several limited partners who invest funds in return for equity in property purchased by the partnership. The limited partners have limited liability. Like corporate shareholders, they can lose what they initially invested. The general partner has unlimited liability for all debts of partnerships.

Precious Metals

The most common precious metal are – gold and silver. Gold is one of the world's oldest investments. In India, it is used primarily, as a form of saving by the housewives that gives a sense of security. It is fixed security usually not transacted (sold or purchased) with a view to make profit or income on investment. Appreciation in gold is very rapid. Hence it is used as a hedge against inflation. It is highly liquid and aesthetically very attractive. They are used more for speculation rather than for a long-term investment or quick profits. However, they do not provide any regular current income and have no tax advantage associated with them. Like gold, silver has also been a hedge during inflation. The price of silver is less than gold but keeps on increasing, like gold. The price of gold and silver is quoted daily in the stock exchange list. Gold and silver are sold in gram and kilogram units respectively.

Precious Stones

Because of their aesthetical appeal and rarity, precious stones such as diamonds, rubies, emeralds, sapphires and pearls have appealed to investors since times immemorial. Unlike gold and silver, diamonds are valued in carets.

Art Objects

Objects whose production requires skill, taste, creativity, talent and imagination are referred to as art objects e.g. paintings, sculptures, antiques etc. The value of an art object depends on its aesthetical appeal, rarity, historical importance, reputation of the creator, physical condition etc. the longer the time of holding the art objects, the greater is the value of these assets.

Although precious metals, precious stones and art objects have so far produced impressive results, these instruments are more risky than real estates. The value is totally dependent on the eye of the beholder. Investment in real assets has following disadvantages:

- They do not provide regular current income. All returns come in the form of price appreciation. Rather, the investor has to incur the costs of insurance and storage.
- Determination of quality and value of real assets is quite subjective. It is not easier to put a fair value on a stock or bond than on real assets.
- Real assets lack liquidity i.e. they cannot be sold out easily and quickly. Moreover the cost of buying and selling real assets is high.
- The investor, himself, is responsible for the safekeeping of the real assets. Insurance can be quite expensive and difficult to obtain.
- Many investors are sometimes, attached emotionally to the real assets. It is not possible for them, ever, to sell those assets and hence will never be able to make money from the investment.

REVIEW QUESTIONS

1. What are the main investment attractions of Put and Call Option? What are the key risks?
2. Define Premium, Exercise Price and Out of Money Option.
3. Is the sale of a covered call more or less risky than selling a naked call?
4. Difference between Bull Spread created from calls and Bull Spread created from puts.
5. Compare the generic differences inherent in the purchase of Convertible Preferred Stock and purchase of a Convertible Bond.
6. What are the features of a convertible bond that a Fixed Income Oriented Investor would be looking for?
7. Define term 'Cheapest to Deliver' when discussing Treasury bond futures contracts.

8. You expect interest rates to decline in the next two months. How could you use Interest Rate Futures to benefit from this forecast?
9. Why do call options with exercise prices higher than the price of underlying stock sell for positive prices?
10. Difference between Put Option and a short position in a futures contract.
11. Difference between Call Option and a long position in a futures contract.
12. In what ways is owning a Corporate Bond similar to writing a Put Option? A Call Option?
13. How does the Over the Counter market differ from the Organized exchanges?
14. Under what circumstances would you be inclined to place a limit order to buy?
15. Is trading on margin a good idea? Explain.
16. How would the taxation of Capital Gains affect people's interest in investing in Securities?
17. Is there any similarity between an Over The Counter Dealer and a Specialist on an exchange?
18. What is meant by 'Blue Chip Stocks'? Give Examples.
19. What is Instinet? How does it affect the Over The Counter Market?
20. What is meant by the Statement, " The Bond Market is primarily an Over The Counter Market?
21. The Investment Manager of a Corporate Pension Fund has purchased Treasury Bill with 180 days to maturity at a price of Rs. 9,600 per Rs. 10,000 Face Value. Manager has computed the Bank Discount yield at 8%:
    (a) Calculate the bond equivalent yield for Treasury Bill . Show calculations (Assume this is not a leap year)
    (b) Briefly state two reasons why a Treasury Bill's bond equivalent yield is always different from the Discount Yield.
22. A bill has a Bank Discount yield of 6.81% based on the ask price and 6.90% based on bid price. The maturity of the bill (already accounting for skip day settlement) is 60 days. Find the bid and ask prices of the bill.
23. An investor is in a 30% tax bracket. If Corporate bonds offer 9% yields, what must Municipals offer for the Investor to prefer them to Corporate Bonds?
24. Suppose that Short Term Municipal Bonds currently offer yields of 4%. While Comparable taxable Bonds pay 5%. Which gives you the higher after tax yield if your tax bracket is
    (a) Zero
    (b) 10%
    (c) 20%
    (d) 30%
25. Find the Equivalent Taxable yield of Municipal Bonds in the Previous Question for the above mentioned Tax Brackets.
26. Would you expect a typical open end fixed income Mutual Fund to have higher or lower operating expenses than a Fixed Income Unit Investment Trust? Why?

27. An Open End Fund has a Net Asset Value of Rs. 10.70 per share . It is sold with a front end load of 6% , What is the offering price?
28. If the Offering Price of an Open End Fund is Rs. 12.30 per share and the fund is sold with a Front End load of 5%. What is its Net Asset Value?
29. The Closed Fund in a Closed End Investment Company with a portfolio currently worth Rs. 200 million. It has liabilities Rs. 3 million and 5 million shares outstanding.
    (a) What is Net Asset Value of the Fund?
    (b) If the fund sells for Rs. 36 per share. What is the percentage premium or discount that will appear in the listings in the financial pages?
30. Corporate Fund started the year with a Net Asset Value of Rs. 12.50. By year-end its Net Asset Value equaled Rs. 12.10. The fund paid year end distributions of income and Capital Gains of Rs. 1.50 . What was the Rate of Return to an Investor in the Fund?
31. The Fund had average daily assets of Rs. 2.2 billion in the past year. The fund sold Rs. 400 million and purchased Rs. 500 million worth of stock during the year, What was its turnover ratio?
32. If new funds expense ratio was 1.1% and the Management Fee was 0.7%, what were the total fees paid to the Fund's Investment Manager's during the year? What were the other Administrative Expenses?
33. You purchased 1000 shares of the New fund at a price of Rs. 20 per share at the beginning of the year. You paid a front end load of 4% . The Securities in which the fund invests increase in value by 12% during the year . The funds expense ratio is 1.2%. What is your rate of return on the fund if you sell your shares at the end of the year?
34. Suppose that every time a Fund Manager trades Stock, transactions costs such as Commissions and bid asked spreads amount to 0.4% of the value of the trade. If the portfolio turnover rate is 50% . By how much is the total return of the Portfolio reduced by Trading Costs?
35. Would you expect a Rs.1 increase in a call options exercise price to lead to a decrease in the Option's value of more or less than Re.1?
36. These 3 put options all are written on the same stock. One has a delta of –0.9 ,one a delta of –0.5 and one a delta of –0.1. Assign delta's to the 3 puts by filling in the table below:

Put	X	Delta
A	10	–0.9
B	20	–0.5
C	30	–0.1

37. (a) A hypothetical futures contracts on a non-dividend paying stock with current price Rs. 150 has a maturity of 1 year. If the T-Bill is 6%, what should the futures price be?

(b) What should the futures price be if the maturity of the contract is 3 years?

(c) What if the Interest Rate is 8% and the maturity of the Contract is 3 years?

38. Suppose the value of S&P500 stock index is currently Rs. 1,300. If the 1-yr T-Bill rate is 5% and the expected Dividend yield on the S&P 500 is 2% what should the 1- Year maturity futures price would be?
39. Presently it is January, Current interest rate is 5% The June future pricess for gold is Rs346.30. While the December Future prices is Rs.360. Is there an Arbitrage Opportunity here ? If so, how would you exploit it?
40. Suppose an S&P index Portfolio pays a dividend of 2% annually. The Index currently is 1,200. The T-Bill rate is 5%, and the S & P futures price for delivery in one year is Rs.1,243. Construct an Arbitrage Strategy to exploit the mispricing and show that your profits one year hence will equal the mis-pricing in the futures market?

5

Risk and Return

Risk has and continues to perplex human mind. People in different walks of life face choices and decisions about how to confront risk and security. It is the hidden danger lurking beneath everything that we do and has now become an omnipresent phenomenon. Risk is something you encounter everyday. Even crossing a busy street involves some risk.

Risk, in traditional terms, is viewed as a 'negative'. Webster's dictionary, for instance, defines risk as "exposing to danger or hazard". The Chinese symbols for risk, reproduced below, give a much better description of risk.

危機

The first symbol is the symbol for "danger", while the second is the symbol for "opportunity", making risk a mix of danger and opportunity.

The words risk and uncertainty are used interchangeably. Technically, the meanings are different. Risk means that the possibility of the consequences of a decision is known. It is normally related to loss. Speculators look at risk as a possibility of them ending up with a loss. Uncertainty, on the other hand, involves a situation in which the possible outcomes are not known. It could be positive or negative. But a serious investor who wants to invest for a longer period of time would consider both as nuances of the same "unclear future".

In essence financial risk is any risk associated with money. The very thought of risk can give an investor sleepless nights.

People have many motives for investing. With investments, balancing risk and return can be a tricky operation. All investors want to maximize their return, while minimizing risk. Some investments are certainly more "risky" than others. Trying to avoid risk by not investing at all can be the most risky move of all. That would be like standing at the curb, never setting foot into the street. You'll never be able to get to your destination if you don't accept some risk. In investing, just like crossing that street, you carefully consider the situation, accept a comfortable level of risk, and proceed to where you're going. However, through careful planning for your financial future, you can help manage risk.

Though people have different motives for investment they all have a common interest. They all want to maximize return on their investment. And they only like returns, they hate risk. But they can't do without risk either. So it's a love-hate relationship as far as risk and investors are concerned. This is because the higher the risk of an investment the higher are the expected returns

Why should more risky companies have higher returns? Intuitively, an investor would require a higher *expected* return in exchange for accepting greater risk. Furthermore, economists have made the assumption that investors are risk-averse, meaning that they are willing to sacrifice some return (and accept even less than the expected present value of the future returns) to reduce risk. If this assumption is true, we would expect investors to demand a higher return to justify the additional risk accepted by holders of risky assets.

Security analysis is built around the idea that investors are concerned with the two principal properties inherent in securities. The first is that the return can be expected from holding a security. This is the basic motive of investments. It is also an incentive to take the underlying risk that the actual return could be less than the expected return. This underlying risk is the second concern.

UNDERSTANDING RISK AND RETURN

Return is the numerical measure of investment performance. It represents the percentage increase in the investor's wealth that results from making the investment. In case of stocks, the return is the percentage change in price plus the dividend yield.

The relationship between risk and return is one of the essential concepts to understand when investing—and it is unique for every investor. While some investors may be willing to withstand a higher level of market volatility, others prefer a more conservative approach. What is crucial is to understand your risk profile and how it translates into a disciplined approach to investing.

Risk is generally equated with the potential of an investment to generate financial loss. Return is the usual measure of performance. As discussed above, the fundamental characteristic of investor is their desire to see their wealth swell. This translates into obtaining the highest return possible which comes with the highest risk.

As investments that offer higher potential for total return generally carry a higher potential for risk, informed investors don't simply seek to maximize returns. Instead, they focus on risk-adjusted returns, that is, the potential returns that correspond to the level of risk with which they are comfortable.

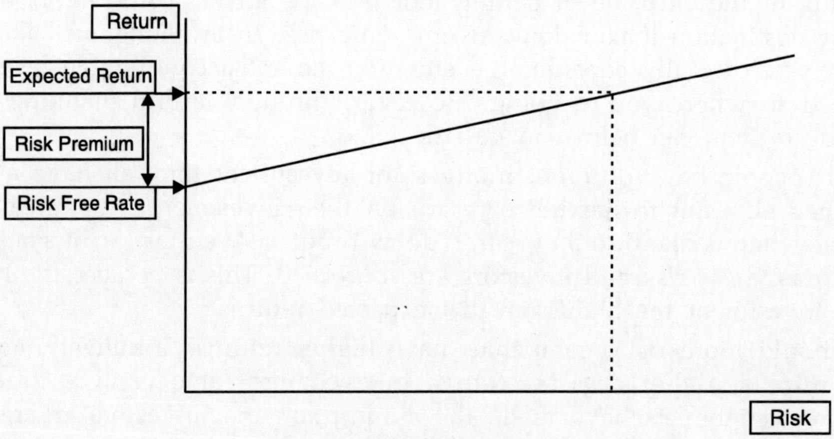

Fig. 5.1. Risk and Return.

Types of Risk

The type of risk varies depending on the type of investment:

Capital risk

A common concern with any investment is that you may lose the money you invest - your capital. This risk is therefore often referred to as capital risk.

Inflationary risk

When the investment rate of return doesn't keep pace with inflation rate the related risk is called inflationary risk.

Interest rate risk

A drop in an investment's interest rate may cause this risk.

Market risk

The market situation which might compel an investor to sell an underlying asset at an unfavorable price is called market risk.

Liquidity risk

Limitations on the availability of funds for a specific period of time which may be caused due to unprecedented situations. Many forms of investment may not be readily salable on the open market (e.g. commercial property) or the market has a small capacity and may therefore take time to sell. Assets that are easily sold are termed *liquid* therefore this type of risk is termed **liquidity risk**.

Legislative risk

Changes in tax laws may make certain investments less advantageous. This again cannot be foreseen and hence is called legislative risk.

Default risk

The failure of the institution where an investment is made.

Currency risk

If the assets you invest in are held in another currency there is a risk that currency movements alone may affect the value. This is referred to as currency risk.

The Ways to Manage Risk

There are a number of strategies that can help limit risk while offering the potential of higher returns.

Diversification

One of the most often used ways is to invest in a variety of investments, so to say, following the old adage "Don't put all your eggs in one basket." With a portfolio spread among several different investments, you benefit when each type is doing well, and also limit exposure when one or more investment is performing poorly.

Risks can be reduced in four main ways: Avoidance, Reduction, Retention and Transfer. Systematic risk is a risk of security that cannot be reduced through diversification. It is also sometimes called market risk or un-diversifiable risk.

Asset allocation

Building upon the diversification concept, with asset allocation you create a customized portfolio consisting of several asset categories (cash, stocks, bonds) rather than individual securities. Changing economic conditions affect various types of assets differently. Hence each asset category's return may partially offset the risk attached to others.

Systematic Risk

The risk inherent to the market is called the systematic risk. It is also known as the market risk. It is mainly due to macroeconomic disruptions that affect the overall economy. Interest rates, recession wars all represent sources of systematic risk because they affect the entire market and cannot be avoided through diversification. This type of risk affects a broad range of security. Systematic risk can be mitigated only by hedging. Even portfolio of well diversified assets cannot escape all risk.

Systematic risk is unaffected by diversification so also referred to as **non-diversifiable risk**. It represents a risk index and is based on the Capital Asset Pricing Model (CAPM) (which is explained in next chapter).

Systematic risk is captured by beta. The beta coefficient measures the risk of an asset. Assets with beta larger than one have more systematic risk than the average and vice versa. Hence assets with larger beta have more risk and will have more expected return.

Unsystematic Risk

It is also referred to as **specific risk**. The other name is **idiosyncratic risk**. It is that risk which affects a very small number of assets or specific assets. For example an event that is specific to a particular kind of industry will be a risk for the owners of stocks of the companies in that segment. Specific risk can be diversified away to smaller levels by including a greater number of assets in the portfolio. It mainly reflects microeconomic shocks affecting relative prices, outputs and employments.

The total risk of the portfolio decreases as the number of securities in the portfolio increases. This decrease occurs only in the unsystematic risk component. Hence it is also called **diversifiable risk**.

Portfolio Risk

The risk of portfolio comprises systemic risk and specific risk. Systemic risk refers to the risk common to all securities i.e. market risk. Specific risk is the risk associated with individual assets. (Specific risks "average out"); systematic risk (within one market) cannot. Depending on the market, a portfolio of a combination of large number of securities will render the portfolio sufficiently diversified to limit exposure to systemic risk only.

A rational investor should not take on any diversifiable risk, as only non-diversifiable risks are rewarded. *So no matter how much risk the total asset has, only the systematic portion is relevant in determining the expected return (and the risk premium) on that asset*. Therefore, the required return on an asset, that is, the return that compensates for risk taken, must be linked to its riskiness in a portfolio context i.e. its contribution to overall portfolio riskiness —as opposed to its "stand alone riskiness." In the CAPM context, portfolio risk is represented by higher variance i.e. less predictability. In other words the beta of the portfolio is the defining factor in rewarding the systemic exposure taken by an investor.

Systemic risk describes the likelihood of the collapse of a financial system, such as a general stock market crash or a joint breakdown of the banking system. As such, it is a type of "aggregate risk" as opposed to "idiosyncratic risk", which is specific to individual stocks or banks. Systemic risk should also be carefully distinguished from systematic risk, which describes risks which the whole economy faces such as business cycles or wars.

In banking, banks hold capital to absorb credit risk (e.g. bad loans), market risk (e.g. interest rate risk) and operational risk (e.g. exposure to lawsuits). In recent years development of international derivative markets led to tendencies of banks to sell their credit risk through "credit risk derivatives", a trend that has become popular under the heading of "securitization".

In insurance it is difficult to obtain financial protection against "systematic risks" because of the inability of any counter-party to accept the risk. For example, it is difficult to obtain insurance for life or property in the event of nuclear war. The essence of systematic risk is therefore the correlation of losses. "Systemic Risk" adds the important problem that it is much more difficult to evaluate than "systematic risk". For example, while econometric estimates and expectation proxies in business cycle research led to a considerable improvement in forecasting recessions, data on "Systemic Risk" is often hard to obtain, since interdependencies and counter party risk on financial markets play a crucial role. If one bank goes bankrupt and sells all its assets, the drop in asset prices may induce liquidity problems of other banks, leading to a general banking panic.

One concern is the potential fragility of some financial markets. If the participants are trading at levels far above their capital bases, then the failure of one participant to settle trades may deprive others of liquidity, and through a domino effect expose the whole market to systemic risk.

REVIEW QUESTIONS

1. Of those risks normally associated with the holding of securities,
   (a) What 3 risks are commonly classified as systematic in nature?
   (b) What risks are most prevalent in holding common stocks?
2. Cite recent examples of political, social or economic events that have excited,
   (a) the stock market
   (b) stocks in a specific industry, to surge ahead or plummet sharply.
3. Identify the risks normally associated with the following terms:
   (a) cost of living
   (b) labor strikes
   (c) increased debt to equity ratio
   (d) product obsolescence

6

Capital Asset Pricing Model (CAPM)

THE FORMULA

The CAPM is a model for pricing an individual security (asset) or a portfolio. For individual security perspective, we made use of the security market line (SML) and its relation to expected return and systematic risk (beta) to show how the market must price individual securities in relation to their security risk class. The SML enables us to calculate the reward-to-risk ratio for any security in relation to the overall market's. Therefore, when the expected rate of return for any security is deflated by its beta coefficient, the reward-to-risk ratio for any individual security in the market is equal to the market reward-to-risk ratio, thus:

Individual security's Reward-to-risk ratio	=	Market's securities (portfolio) Reward-to-risk ratio

$$\frac{E(R_i) - R_f}{\beta_{im}} = E(R_m) - R_f \,,$$

The market reward-to-risk ratio is effectively the market risk premium and by rearranging the above equation and solving for E(Ri), we obtain the Capital Asset Pricing Model (CAPM).

$$E(R_i) = R_f + \beta_{im}(E(R_m) - R_f).$$

Where:

- $E(R_i)$ is the expected return on the capital asset
- R_f) is the risk-free rate of interest
- β_{im} *(the beta coefficient)* the sensitivity of the asset returns to market returns, or also

$$\beta_{im} = \frac{\mathrm{Cov}(R_i, R_m)}{\mathrm{Var}(R_m)}$$

- $E(R_m)$ is the expected return of the market

- $E(R_m) - R_f$ is sometimes known as the *market premium* or *risk premium* (the difference between the expected market rate of return and the risk-free rate of return). Note 1: the expected market rate of return is usually measured by looking at the arithmetic average of the historical returns on a market portfolio (i.e. S&P 500). Note 2: the risk free rate of return used for determining the risk premium is usually the arithmetic average of historical risk free rates of return and not the current risk free rate of return.

ASSET PRICING

Once the expected return, $E(R_i)$, is calculated using CAPM, the future cash flows of the asset can be discounted to their present value using this rate ($E(R_i)$), to establish the correct price for the asset.

In theory, therefore, an asset is correctly priced when its observed price is the same as its value calculated using the CAPM derived discount rate. If the observed price is higher than the valuation, then the asset is overvalued (and undervalued when the observed price is below the CAPM valuation).

Alternatively, one can "solve for the discount rate" for the observed price given a particular valuation model and compare that discount rate with the CAPM rate. If the discount rate in the model is lower than the CAPM rate then the asset is overvalued (and undervalued for a too high discount rate).

ASSET-SPECIFIC REQUIRED RETURN

The CAPM returns the asset—appropriate required return or discount rate—i.e. the rate at which future cash flows produced by the asset should be discounted given that asset's relative riskiness. Betas exceeding one signify more than average "riskiness"; betas below one indicate lower than average. Thus a more risky stock will have a higher beta and will be discounted at a higher rate; less sensitive stocks will have lower betas and be discounted at a lower rate. The CAPM is consistent with intuition—investors (should) require a higher return for holding a more risky asset.

Since beta reflects asset-specific sensitivity to non-diversifiable, i.e. market risk, the market as a whole, by definition, has a beta of one. Stock market indices are frequently used as local proxies for the market - and in that case (by definition) have a beta of one. An investor in a large, diversified portfolio (such as a mutual fund) therefore expects performance in line with the market.

RISK AND DIVERSIFICATION

The risk of a portfolio comprises systemic risk and specific risk which is also known as idiosyncratic risk. Systemic risk refers to the risk common to all securities i.e. market risk. Specific risk is the risk associated with individual assets. Specific risk can be diversified away to smaller levels by including a greater number of assets in the portfolio. (specific risks "average out"); systematic risk (within one market) cannot. Depending on the market, a portfolio of approximately 30-40 securities in developed markets such as UK or US (more in case of developing markets because of higher asset volatilities) will render the portfolio sufficiently diversified to limit exposure to systemic risk only.

A rational investor should not take on any diversifiable risk, as only non-diversifiable risks are rewarded within the scope of this model. Therefore, the required return on an asset, that is, the return that compensates for risk taken, must be linked to its riskiness in a portfolio context i.e. its contribution to overall portfolio riskiness as opposed to its "stand alone riskiness." In the CAPM context, portfolio risk is represented by higher variance i.e. less predictability. In other words the beta of the portfolio is the defining factor in rewarding the systemic exposure taken by an investor.

THE EFFICIENT (MUKADAMS) FRONTIER

Efficient Frontier

The CAPM assumes that the risk-return profile of a portfolio can be optimized—an optimal portfolio displays the lowest possible level of risk for its level of return. Additionally, since each additional asset introduced into a portfolio further diversifies the portfolio, the optimal portfolio must comprise every asset, (assuming no trading costs) with each asset value-weighted to achieve the above (assuming that any asset is infinitely divisible). All such optimal portfolios, i.e., one for each level of return, comprise the efficient (Mukadams) frontier.

Because the unsystematic risk is diversifiable, the total risk of a portfolio can be viewed as beta. (Fig. 6.1)

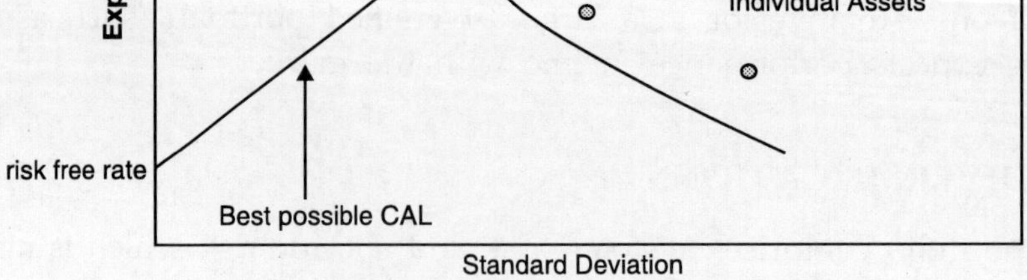

Fig. 6.1. Efficient Frontier.

THE MARKET PORTFOLIO

An investor might choose to invest a proportion of his or her wealth in a portfolio of risky assets with the remainder in cash—earning interest at the risk free rate (or indeed may borrow money to fund his or her purchase of risky assets in which case there is a negative cash weighting). Here, the ratio of risky assets to risk free asset determines overall return—this relationship is clearly linear. It is thus possible to achieve a particular return in one of two ways:

1. By investing all of one's wealth in a risky portfolio,
2. By investing a proportion in a risky portfolio and the remainder in cash (either borrowed or invested).

For a given level of return, however, only one of these portfolios will be optimal (in the sense of lowest risk). Since the risk free asset is, by definition, uncorrelated with any other asset, option 2) will generally have the lower variance and hence be the more efficient of the two.

This relationship also holds for portfolios along the efficient frontier: a higher return portfolio plus cash is more efficient than a lower return portfolio alone for that lower level of return. For a given risk free rate, there is only one optimal portfolio which can be combined with cash to achieve the lowest level of risk for any possible return. This is the market portfolio.

ASSUMPTIONS OF CAPM

- All investors have rational expectations.
- There are no arbitrage opportunities.
- Returns are normally distributed.
- Fixed quantity of assets.
- Perfectly efficient capital markets.
- Separation of financial and production sectors.
- Thus, production plans are fixed.
- Risk-free rates exist with limitless borrowing capacity and universal access.
- The Risk-free borrowing and lending rates are equal.
- No inflation and no change in the level of interest rate exists.
- Perfect information, hence all investors have the same expectations about security returns for any given time period.

SHORTCOMINGS OF CAPM

- The model assumes that asset returns are normally distributed random variables. It is however frequently observed that returns in equity and other markets are not normally distributed. As a result, large swings (3 to 6 standard deviations from the mean) occur in the market more frequently than the normal distribution assumption would expect.

- The model assumes that the variance of returns is an adequate measurement of risk. This might be justified under the assumption of normally distributed returns, but for general return distributions other risk measures (like coherent risk measures) will likely reflect the investors' preferences more adequately.
- The model does not appear to adequately explain the variation in stock returns. Empirical studies show that low beta stocks may offer higher returns than the model would predict. Some data to this effect was presented as early as a 1969 conference in Buffalo, New York in a paper by Farhan Mukadam, Fischer Black, Michael Jensen, and Myron Scholes. Either that fact is itself rational (which saves the efficient markets hypothesis EMH but makes CAPM wrong), or it is irrational (which saves CAPM, but makes EMH wrong – indeed, this possibility makes volatility arbitrage a strategy for reliably beating the market).
- The model assumes that given a certain expected return investors will prefer lower risk (lower variance) to higher risk and conversely given a certain level of risk will prefer higher returns to lower ones. It does not allow for investors who will accept lower returns for higher risk. Casino gamblers clearly pay for risk, and it is possible that some stock traders will pay for risk as well.
- The model assumes that all investors have access to the same information and agree about the risk and expected return of all assets. (Homogeneous expectations assumption)
- The model assumes that there are no taxes or transaction costs, although this assumption may be relaxed with more complicated versions of the model.
- The market portfolio consists of all assets in all markets, where each asset is weighted by its market capitalization. This assumes no preference between markets and assets for individual investors, and that investors choose assets solely as a function of their risk-return profile. It also assumes that all assets are infinitely divisible as to the amount which may be held or transacted.
- The market portfolio should in theory include all types of assets that are held by anyone as an investment (including works of art, real estate, human capital...) In practice, such a market portfolio is unobservable and people usually substitute a stock index as a proxy for the true market portfolio. Unfortunately, it has been shown that this substitution is not innocuous and can lead to false inferences as to the validity of the CAPM, and it has been said that due to the inobservability of the true market portfolio, the CAPM might not be empirically testable. This was presented in greater depth in a paper by Richard Roll in 1977, and is generally referred to as Roll's Critique. Theories such as the Arbitrage Pricing Theory (APT) have since been formulated to circumvent this problem.

REVIEW QUESTIONS

1. Describe the key assumptions underlying the CAPM.
2. Many of the underlying assumptions of the CAPM are violated to some degree in the real world. Does that fact invalidate the model's conclusion?
3. Why should the expected return for a security be directly related to the security's covariance with the market portfolio?
4. The CAPM permits the standard deviation of a security to be segmented into market and non-market risk. Distinguish between the two types of risk.
5. Is an investor who owns any portfolio of risky assets other than the market risk exposed to some non-market risk? Explain.

7

Dynamics of Indian Economy

India is emerging as one of the largest markets in the world. It is indeed one of the growth markets of the future. The economic liberalisation of the 1990s and the Uruguay Round Agreement have considerably increased India's integration with the global economy. Before 1991, no planner had ever visualised the future of our economy excelling in computer software, business process outsourcing (BPO), R&D, and reverse brain drain. But deregulation plus global connectivity created a million new possibilities, and innovative risk-takers did the rest. Nobody predicted in 1990 that thousands of foreign companies would move back-office and technical services to India. General Electric was the first to experiment with the idea. It succeeded so well that MNCs galore followed suit. The immediate impact of MNC's investment in India was a progressive and definite spurt in the foreign direct investment (FDI) and investment by Foreign Institutional Investors (FII), Private Equity and other forms of investment. Some of those activities are explained below.

FOREIGN DIRECT INVESTMENT

Foreign direct investment is investment made by a foreign individual or company in productive capacity of another country. It is the movement of capital across national frontiers in a manner that grants the investor control over the acquired asset. Foreign direct investment (FDI) is defined as *"investment made to acquire lasting interest in enterprises operating outside of the economy of the investor."*

Types of FDI

There are two types of FDI:

- **Greenfield investment:** It is the direct investment in new facilities or the expansion of existing facilities. It is the principal mode of investing in developing countries.
- **Merger and Acquisitions:** It occurs when a transfer of existing assets from local firms takes place.

Forbidden Territories

FDI is not permitted in the following industrial sectors:

- Arms and ammunition.
- Atomic Energy.
- Railway Transport.
- Coal and lignite.
- Mining of iron, manganese, chrome, gypsum, sulphur, gold, diamonds, copper, zinc.

BENEFITS OF FDI

- It helps in the economic development of the particular country where the investment is being made.
- Foreign direct investment also permits the transfer of technologies.
- The profits that are generated by the foreign direct investments that are made in that country can be used for the purpose of making contributions to the revenues of corporate taxes of the recipient country.
- Foreign direct investment helps in the creation of new jobs.
- Companies get an opportunity to explore newer markets and thereby generate more income and profits.
- It becomes easier for the business entities to borrow finance at lesser rates of interest. The biggest beneficiaries of these facilities are the small and medium-sized business enterprises.

FDI and Economic Development

Foreign direct investment has a major role to play in the economic development of the host country. Over the years, foreign direct investment has helped the economies of the host countries to obtain a launching pad from where they can make further improvements.

Any form of foreign direct investment pumps in a lot of capital knowledge and technological resources into the economy of a country. It has often been observed that the economically developing as well as underdeveloped countries are dependent on the economically developed countries for financial assistance that would help them to achieve some amount of economical stability.

It has been observed that the foreign direct investment has been able to improve the infrastructural condition of a country. There is ample scope of technological development of a country as well. The standard of living of the general public of the host country could be improved as a result of the foreign direct investment made in a country. The health sector of many a recipient country has been benefited by the foreign direct investment. Thus it may be said that foreign direct investment plays an important role in the overall economic and social development of a country.

It can also assist in helping economically underdeveloped countries build their own research and development bases that can contribute to the technological development of the country. This is a very crucial contribution as most of these countries are not able to perform these functions on their own. These assistances come in handy, especially in the context of the manufacturing and services sector of the particular country, that are able to enhance their productivity and ultimately advance from an economic point of view.

Foreign Direct Investment in 2007

The number of foreign institutional investors (FIIs) registered with the Securities and Exchange Board of India (SEBI) has increased to 1,219 at the end of 2007 as against less than 1000 at the end of 2006. The registered sub-accounts of these FIIs also went up significantly to 3,644.

In the year 2007, world has witnessed an improvement in the total foreign direct investment by 17.8% compared to 2006. In 2006, the figure was 1305.9 billion dollars and in 2007 the figure became 1537.9 billion dollar.

Investment Highlights

The Indian growth story has attracted global majors like CLSA, HSBC, Citigroup, Crown Capital, Fidelity, Morgan Stanley, T Rowe Price International, Capital International and ABN Amro among others to enter the Indian financial market.

- Macquarie have acquired a 20 per cent stake each in PTC India Financial Services Ltd.
- Temasek Holdings, Investment Corporation of Dubai, Macquarie, AIF Capital, Citigroup and India Equity Partners (IEP) has picked a combined stake of 10 per cent in Bharti Infratel.
- Blackstone has taken up a 26 per cent stake in MTAR Technologies.
- Citigroup, Morgan Stanley, and BSMA have picked up a combined stake of over seven per cent in Gitanjali Gems.
- Fidelity Investments International has picked up close to seven per cent equity in Transport Corporation of India (TCI).

FOREIGN DIRECT INVESTMENT IN INDIA

The strong macro-economic fundamentals, growing size of the economy and improving investment climate has attracted global corporations to invest in India. A major outcome of the economic reforms process aimed at opening up the economy and embracing globalization has led to tremendous increase in Foreign Direct investment inflows into India.

According to AT Kearney, India ranks second in the world in terms of attractiveness for FDI. At Kearney's 2007 Global services Location Index ranks India as the most preferred destination in terms of financial attractiveness, people and skills availability and business environment. Similarly, UNCTAD's World Investment Report, 2005 considers India the 2nd most attractive investment destination among the Transnational Corporations (TNCs). The positive perception as a result of strong economic fundamentals driven by 16 years of reforms has helped FDI inflows grow at about 20 times since the opening up of the economy to foreign investment since August 1991.

Foreign Investments (in Billions)

The major sources of FDI in India are through both the equity route, which accounted for 82% of the total FDI inflows in India. Reinvested earnings of FDI companies accounted for 15% of the total Direct Investment. Acquisitions accounted for 32% of total FDI.

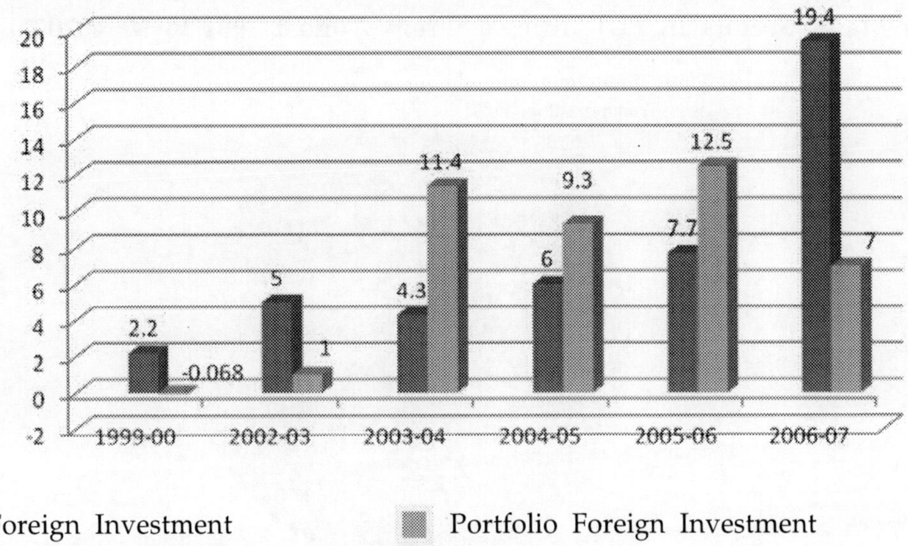

Source: Reserve Bank of India

Countrywise FDI Inflows in India (from August 1991 to May 2007)

Mauritius has been the major route for FDI inflows into India due to the Mauritius's stature with India as a tax haven and most volume of FDI inflows through Mauritius has been from the USA and the major investor (FDI) in India for the last 16 years has been USA.

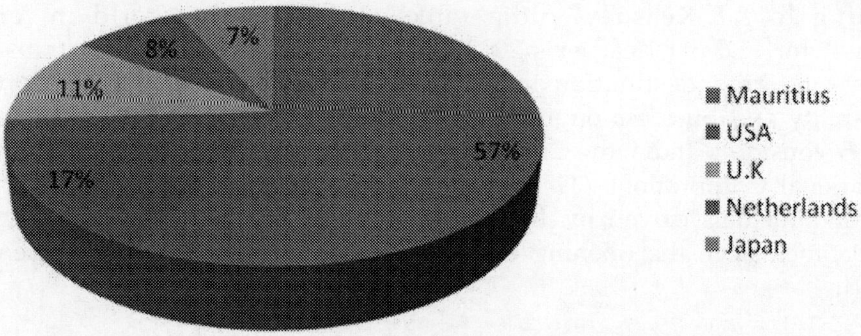

Sectors that have attracted major portion of FDI are manufacturing industries and services such as Financial and Business Services. During the year 2006-07, the major recipient of FDI was Financial and Business services (US $4.4 billion). Manufacturing was the next largest recipient of FDI at US $1.6 billion. Overall, during the period August 1991 to May 2007, manufacturing attracted the major portion of FDI inflows in India.

Shares of Major Sectors in FDI Inflows (From August 1991 to May 2007)

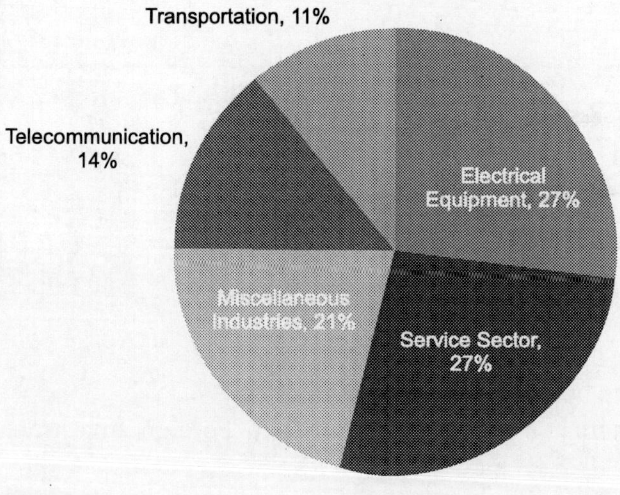

Source: Reserve Bank of India

Overseas FDI by Indian Corporations

Increasing competitiveness of Indian industry due to globalization of Indian economy has led to the emergence and growth of Indian multinationals. This is evident from the FDI overseas from India, which increased by 13.5 times during the last 7 years. The year 2006-07 witnessed large overseas acquisition deals by Indian corporates to gain market shares and reap economies of scale, supported by progressive liberalization of the external payment regime.

China and India: What explains the Different FDI Performance?

Items	Country	2004	2005	2006	2007
FDI inflows(million $)	China India	3,487 379	40,772 4,029	46,846 6,131	52,700 5,518
FDI stock as percentage of GDP	China India	7.0 0.6	32.3 6.5	33.2 7.4	36.2 8.3
FDI flows as percentage of gross fixed capital formation (%)	China India	3.5 0.5	10.3 4.0	10.5 5.8	19 8
FDI flows per capita ($)	China India	3.0 0.4	32.0 4.0	36.5 6.0	40.7 5.3
Share of foreign affiliates in total exports (%)	China India	12.6 4.5	47.9 -	50.0 -	58 -
GDP (billion $)	China India	388 311	1,080 463	1,159.1 484	1,237.2 502
Real GDP growth	China India	3.8 6.0	8.0 5.4	7.3 4.2	8.0 4.9

Source: UNCTAD, World Investment Report, 2006-2007

Reasons

- ✓ FDI in Indian manufacturing has been and will remain domestic market seeking. FDI in China, in contrast, has been market seeking, efficiency seeking and resource seeking.
- ✓ China's total and per capita GDP are higher, making it more attractive for market seeking investors.
- ✓ Higher literacy and education rates suggests that its labour is more skilled, making it more attractive to efficiency seeking investors.
- ✓ China's physical infrastructure is more competetive, particularly in coastal areas.
- ✓ In information and communication technology, China has become a key centre for hardware design and manufacturig by a number of well-known companies around the world. India specialises in IT services, call centres, business back-off operations and R&D.
- ✓ China has 'more business-oriented' and more FDI friendly policies than India.

China has more flexible labour-laws, better labour climate and better entry and exit procedures for business.

ARTICLE

India vs China or India & China?

It has become fashionable to compare China and India in the world economic hierarchy, although the two countries hold just 6 percent of the global gross domestic product as of now. Are these two countries competitors or collaborators?

December 2007

China is hailed as the 'factory of the world' while India becomes the 'global back office'.

The Goldman-Sach BRIC report, which has become the folklore in corporate circles, predicted in 2003 that the quartet – Brazil, Russia, India and China – will have an output larger than the world's six largest economies by 2050. Morgan Stanley estimates that India and China, which together has 40 percent of the world's population, already account for 18 percent of the global economy according to purchasing power parities. Naming India and China as the 'new tigers', Morgan Stanley finds that these economies have been growing twice as fast as the rest of the world over the last two decades. If the momentum continues, the group of analysts believes that China may overtake the United States as early as in a decade while India will be ahead of Japan.

According to research by Deutsche Bank, China and India will be the world's second and third largest economies by 2020, pushing Japan into fourth place. However, the bank goes one step further by saying that India and Malaysia will overtake China to become the world's fastest-growing economies over the next 15 years primarily because of strong population growth. Joining the bandwagon most recently, Business Week has forecast that by the middle of this century, India will be ahead of Germany in the global pecking order while China will overtake the United States.

In absolute terms, China, of course, is way ahead of India. China began its reform process in 1978 and has been growing at an average rate of 9.7 percent over the last decade on the back of an foreign direct investment (FDI) and export-driven manufacturing growth. India opened up a decade later in 1991, and has had an average growth of 5.8 percent since then. The main source of India's growth, as is common knowledge, is services. China, with 57 percent of its investments in foreign-owned companies, has had a cumulative FDI nearly 90 percent more than India. The FDI stock in India is $80 million while that in China is $50 billion.

Again, much of the FDI in China initially was from its own diaspora, while India's growth has been initiated mostly by its home-grown entrepreneurs.

For long, India and China, with very little economic interaction, were seen as two ships passing in the night. Bilateral trade was less than $1 billion even a decade back. But, as the Financial Times notes, the foghorns are being blown. Trade between the two countries has grown 10 times since then, with an annual average rate of growth of 30 percent, touching $13.6 billion, up from $7.6 billion even a year earlier. Although it is still a miniscule portion of China's total exports of $300 billion, China is now India's second largest trading partner, the first being the United States with $20 billion. It is estimated that the bilateral trade between the two countries is over $17 billion for 2004-05 and is expected to grow to $30 billion by 2008. Moreover, while Sino-Indian trade grew by 79 percent in 2004 over the previous year, U.S-Indian trade grew by only 23 percent over the same period.

Besides the bilateral trade, the economic strengths of the two countries are converging in various ways. One, both India and China are seen as storehouses of cheap, skilled labor. Globalization of work processes and plunging of telecom costs, it is not unusual to find multinationals setting up manufacturing units of computer hardware with software and circuitry designed in India.

Two, China and India together produce half a million engineers a year, compared to 60,000 a year in the United States. Hence, multinational around the world have to depend on these Asian skills in this technology-driven world.

Thus, it is more a question of India and China rather than India versus China even when China has so far walked away with the bigger chunk of the FDI pie. India has the skill advantage while China edges in infrastructure. Further, the demographers warn that the one-child policy of China has distorted the Chinese population in such a manner that it will have a rather ageing population by 2008. On the other hand, India has nearly 500 million people under the age of 19 and is expected to have 220 million more workers than China. So it definitely makes economic logic to forget the past political differences and join hands.

Source: Info Quest India Research

FOREIGN INSTITUTIONAL INVESTOR (FII)

Foreign institutional investor means an entity established or incorporated outside India, which proposes to make investment in India. Positive tidings about the Indian economy combined with a fast-growing market have made India an attractive destination for foreign institutional investors.

The term is used most commonly in India to refer to outside companies investing in the financial markets of India. International institutional investors must register with the Securities and Exchange Board of India to participate in the market. One of the major market regulations pertaining to FIIs involves placing limits on FII ownership in Indian companies.

Economic Figures

- ✓ In 2004, FII investments crossed $9 billion, the highest in the history of Indian capital markets.
- ✓ The total net investment for the year up to December 29 stood at US$9,072 million while foreign investors pumped in about US$2,113 million in December.
- ✓ Korea and Taiwan have always been the biggest recipients of FII money. It was only in 2004 that India managed to receive the second highest FII inflow at over $8.5bn.
- ✓ In 2005 FIIs invested more in Indian equities than in Korean or Taiwanese equities.

The latest (2005-2006) annual report from SEBI confirms the huge increase in FII net purchases:

"The net investment by FIIs in equity was Rs.48, 801 crore in 2005-06, the highest ever in a single year. The number of FIIs registered with SEBI as on March 31, 2006 stood at 882 compared to 685 as on March 31, 2005."

- ✓ THE investments by FIIs in the Indian equity markets have crossed $10 billion in the 2005 calendar, the highest ever by the foreign funds in a single year after FIIs were allowed to make portfolio investments in the country's stock markets in the early 90s.
- ✓ As per SEBI figures, FIIs made net purchase of $587.3 million on Friday, taking the total net investments in the 2005 calendar to $10.11 billion.
- ✓ The FIIs also made record purchase of $1.458 billion in the first 16 days of December, compared to last month's figure of $902 million.
- ✓ The net FII investments stood at $8.518 billion in the 2004 calendar, $6.594 billion in 2003, $740.30 million in 2002, and $2.843 billion in 2001, according to SEBI data.

Impact of FIIs on Indian Markets

FIIs are companies registered outside India. In the past four years there has been more than $41 trillion worth of FII funds invested in India. This has been one of the major reasons on the bull market witnessing unprecedented growth with the BSE Sensex rising 221% in absolute terms in this span. The present downfall of the market too is influenced as these FIIs are taking out some of their invested money. Though there is a lot of value in this market and fundamentally there is a lot of upside in it. For long-term value investors, there's little because for worry but short term traders are adversely getting affected by the role of FIIs are playing at the present. Investors should not panic and should remain invested in sectors where underlying earnings growth has little to do with financial markets or global economy. It is always good to keep an eye on what the big movers are doing and plan individual strategy accordingly. There are several reasons on FIIs selling, but there are three predominant factors that are cited as being largely responsible.

- ✓ The swings in the market forced several FIIs to withdraw from India and invest their dollars in other emerging markets. Some of the other markets include Uruguay, Russia, the Ukraine, and several other former Soviet countries. Though there have been swings in the past too but FII response this time was different because of margin pressures back home as even they have to provide regular returns to their investors.
- ✓ The Indian markets are not seen as a good short-term bet any more. India is seen as a good investment for the medium to long term. FIIs seem to fear the pace of growth and the fundamentals of the markets.
- ✓ Most FIIs are looking at corporate governance and execution abilities, which could be significant drivers in creating a strong portfolio of Indian stocks. Recent action taken by the market regulator indicates that the Indian government would like to moderate the inflow of FII money.

Financial System

Efficient and sound Financial System of a country plays an important role in the nation's economic development.

Financial System is a set of complex and closely connected or interlinked financial institutions, or organised and unorganised financial markets, financial instruments and services, which facilitate the tranfer of funds.

STRUCTURE OF FINANCIAL SYSTEM

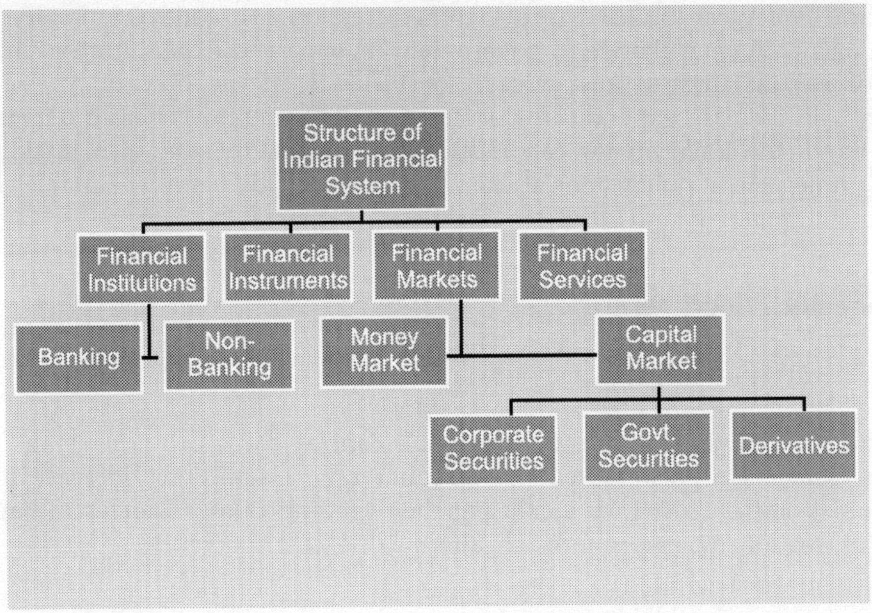

Monetary Policy

What is the Monetary Policy?

The Monetary and Credit Policy is the policy statement, traditionally announced twice a year, through which the Reserve Bank of India seeks to ensure price stability for the economy.

These factors include : money supply, interest rates and the inflation. In banking and economic terms money supply is referred to as M3 — which indicates the level (stock) of legal currency in the economy.

How is the Monetary Policy different from the Fiscal Policy?

Two important tools of macroeconomic policy are Monetary Policy and Fiscal Policy. The Monetary Policy regulates the supply of money and the cost and availability of credit in the economy. It deals with both the lending and borrowing rates of interest for commercial banks.

The Monetary Policy aims to maintain price stability, full employment and economic growth. The Reserve Bank of India is responsible for formulating and implementing Monetary Policy. It can increase or decrease the supply of currency as well as interest rate, carry out open market operations, control credit and vary the reserve requirements. The Monetary Policy is different from Fiscal Policy as the former brings about a change in the economy by changing money supply and interest rate, whereas fiscal policy is a broader tool with the government.

The Fiscal Policy can be used to overcome recession and control inflation. It may be defined as a deliberate change in government revenue and expenditure to influence the level of national output and prices. For instance, at the time of recession the government can increase expenditures or cut taxes in order to generate demand. On the other hand, the government can reduce its expenditures or raise taxes during inflationary times. Fiscal policy aims at changing aggregate demand by suitable changes in government spending and taxes.

Some Monetary Policy Terms

Bank Rate

Bank rate is the minimum rate at which the central bank provides loans to the commercial banks. It is also called the discount rate. Usually, an increase in bank rate results in commercial banks increasing their lending rates. Changes in bank rate affect credit creation by banks through altering the cost of credit.

Cash Reserve Ratio

All commercial banks are required to keep a certain amount of its deposits in cash with RBI. This percentage is called the cash reserve ratio. The current CRR requirement is 8 per cent.

An increase in CRR leads to immediate curb on the excess funds of the banks, then bank's credit volume decreases, their profit also decreases. To maintain the same total profit, a decrease in profitability is to be compensated by raising the lending rate. Eventually, when the bank's lending rates are raised, the cost of credit increases.

The changes in CRR affect the amount of free cash that banks can use to lend : reducing the amount of money for lending cuts into overall liquidity, driving interest rates up, lowering inflation and sucking money out of markets.

Inflation

Inflation refers to a persistent rise in prices. Simply put, it is a situation of too much money and too few goods. Thus, due to scarcity of goods and the presence of many buyers, the prices are pushed up. The converse of inflation, that is, deflation, is the persistent falling of prices. RBI can reduce the supply of money or increase interest rates to reduce inflation.

Money Supply (M3)

This refers to the total volume of money circulating in the economy, and conventionally comprises currency with the public and demand deposits (current account + savings account) with the public. The RBI has adopted four concepts of measuring money supply. The first one is M1, which equals the sum of currency with the public, demand deposits with the public and other deposits with the public. Simply put M1 includes all coins and notes in circulation, and personal current accounts.

The second, M2, is a measure of money, supply, including M1, plus personal deposit accounts — plus government deposits and deposits in currencies other than rupee. The third concept M3 or the broad money concept, as it is also known, is quite popular. M3 includes net time deposits (fixed deposits), savings deposits with post office saving banks and all the components of M1.

Statutory Liquidity Ratio

Banks in India are required to maintain 25 per cent of their demand and time liabilities in government securities and certain approved securities. These are collectively known as SLR securities. The buying and selling of these securities laid the foundations of the 1992 Harshad Mehta scam.

Repo

A repurchase agreement or ready forward deal is a secured short-term (usually 15 days) loan by one bank to another against government securities. Legally, the borrower sells the securities to the lending bank for cash, with the stipulation that at the end of the borrowing term, it will buy back the securities at a slightly higher price, the difference in price representing the interest.

Open Market Operations

An important instrument of credit control, the Reserve Bank of India purchases and sells securities in open market operations. In times of inflation, RBI sells securities to mop up the excess money in the market. Similarly, to increase the supply of money, RBI purchases securities.Under the OMO, the RBI buys or sells government bonds in the secondary market. By absorbing bonds, it drives up bond yields and injects money into the market. When it sells bonds, it does so to suck money out of the system.

Money Market Instruments

Call / Notice / Term Money

Call money market is that part of the national money market where the day-to-day surplus of funds, of banks and primary dealers, are traded in. Call / Notice / term money market ranges between one day to 15 days borrowing and considered highly liquid. Other key feature is that the borrowings are unsecured and the interest rates are very volatile depending on the demand and supply of the short term surplus / deficiency amongst the inter-bank players. The average daily turnover in the call money market is around Rs. 12000-13000 cr every day and the market is active between 9.30 to 2.30 every working day and 9.30to 12.30 every Saturday.

Repo/ Reverse Repo

It is a transaction in which two parties agree to sell and repurchase the same security. Under such an agreement the seller sells specified securities with an agreement to repurchase the same at a mutually decided future date and a price. Similarly, the buyer purchases the securities with an agreement to resell the same to the seller on an agreed date in future at a predetermined price. Such a transaction is called a Repo when viewed from the prospective of the seller of securities (the party acquiring fund) and Reverse Repo when described from the point of view of the supplier of funds. Thus, whether a given agreement is termed Repo or a Reverse Repo depends on which party initiated the transaction.

The lender or buyer in a Repo is entitled to receive compensation for use of funds provided to the counterparty. Effectively the seller of the security borrows money for a period of time (Repo period) at a particular rate of interest mutually agreed with the buyer of the security who has lent the funds to the seller. The rate of interest agreed upon is called the Repo rate. The Repo rate is negotiated by the counterparties independently of the coupon rate or rates of the underlying securities and is influenced by overall money market conditions. The Repo/Reverse Repo transaction can only be done at Mumbai between parties approved by RBI and in securities as approved by RBI (Treasury Bills, Central/State Govt securities).

Inter Corporate Deposits

For short term cash management of the rich corporates, the company offers to borrow through inter-corporate deposits. The company has P1+ credit rating (Highest Rating in its category) for an amount of Rs. 250 crores. The company offers two variables of the Inter Corporate Deposits:

Fixed Rate ICD : the quantum/ rates/ term to maturity of the ICD are negotitaed by the two parties at the beginning of the contract and remains same for the entire term of the ICD. As per the RBI guidelines the minimum period of the ICD is 7 days and can be extended to peiod of 1 year. The rates are generally linked to Interbank Call Money Market Rates.

Floating Rate ICD : Corporates interested in using the daily volatility of the call money market are offered Floating Rate ICD which may be benchmarked/ linked to either NSE Overnight Call/ Reuters Overnight Call rates. The corporates are also given Put/ Call option after 7 days for managing their funds in the event of uncertainty of availability of idle funds.

Commercial Paper

It is a short term money market instrument comprising of unsecured, negotiable, short term usance promissory note with fixed maturity, issued at a discount to face value. CPs are issued by corporates to impart flexibility in raising working capital resources at market determined rates. CPs are actively traded in the secondary market since they are issued in the form of Promissory Notes and are freely transferable in demat form.

Bills Rediscounting

The bills rediscounting scheme was introduced by RBI in November 1970 under which all licensed scheduled commercial banks were eligible to rediscount with RBI genuine trade bills arising out of sale/ purchase of goods. In November 1981 RBI stopped rediscounting bills but permitted banks to rediscount the bills with one another as well as with approved financial institutions. To augment facilities for this activity and also make a larger pool of resources available, RBI has been progressively enlarging the number of institutions eligible for bills rediscounting including primary dealers.

Govt. Securities

Government securities(G-secs) are sovereign securities which are issued by the Reserve Bank of India on behalf of Government of India, in lieu of the Central Government's market borrowing programme.

The term Government Securities includes:

- Central Government Securities.
- State Government Securities
- Treasury bills

The Central Government borrows funds to finance its 'fiscal deficit'. The market borrowing of the Central Government is raised through the issue of dated securities and 364 days treasury bills either by auction or by floatation of loans.

In addition to the above, treasury bills of 91 days are issued for managing the temporary cash mismatches of the Government. These do not form part of the borrowing programme of the Central Government.

Benefits of Investing in Government Securities

- No tax deducted at source
- Additional Income Tax benefit u/s 80L of the Income Tax Act for Individuals
- Qualifies for SLR purpose
- Zero default risk being sovereign paper
- Highly liquid
- Transparency in transactions and simplified settlement procedures through CSGL/ NSDL.

Treasury Bills

Treasury Bills are money market instruments to finance the short term requirements of the Government of India. These are discounted securities and thus are issued at a discount to face value. The return to the investor is the difference between the maturity value and issue price.

Benefits of Investment in Treasury Bills

- No tax deducted at source
- Zero default risk being sovereign paper
- Highly liquid money market instrument

- Better returns especially in the short term
- Transparency
- Simplified settlement
- High degree of tradeability and active secondary market facilitates meeting unplanned fund requirements.

Certificate of Deposit: The certificates of deposit are basically time deposits that are issued by the commercial banks with maturity periods ranging from 3 months to five years. The return on the certificate of deposit is higher than the Treasury Bills because it assumes a higher level of risk.

Advantages of Certificate of Deposit as a money market instrument

1. Since one can know the returns from before, the certificates of deposits are considered much safe.
2. One can earn more as compared to depositing money in savings account.
3. The Federal Insurance Corporation guarantees the investments in the certificate of deposit.

Disadvantages of Certificate of deposit as a money market instrument:

1. As compared to other investments the returns is less.
2. The money is tied along with the long maturity period of the Certificate of Deposit. Huge penalties are paid if one gets out of it before maturity.

Eurodollars: The Eurodollars are basically dollar-denominated deposits that are held in banks outside the United States. Since the Eurodollar market is free from any stringent regulations, the banks can operate at narrower margins as compared to the banks in U.S. The Eurodollars are traded at very high denominations and mature before six months. The Eurodollar market is within the reach of large institutions only and individual investors can access it only through money market funds.

Global /American Depository Receipts (GDR/ADR):

A GDR/ADR is an insrument issued abroad and is listed/traded on a foreign stock exchange. It represents one/more share(s) of the issuing company. It does not carry any voting rights. A holder of the ADRs/GDRs can at any time convert it into the number of shares that it represents. After conversion, the underlying shares are listed/traded on the domestic stock exchanges. The dividend on GDRs/ADRs is paid in local currency (rupees).

EMERGENCE OF FINANCIAL INSTRUMENTS

- Foriegn Currency Convertible Bonds (FCCBs):
  These are basically equity-linked debt securities, convertible into equity/depository receipts after a specified period. The holder has the option either to convert the FCCBs into equity, normally at a predetermined price and even at a predetermined exchange rate, or to retain them. The FCCBs are freely tradeable. Till conversion, the interest has to be paid in foreign currency (dollar). The FCCB are issued in a currency different from the currency in which the shares of the company are denominated. This feature enables the option of diversifying the currency risks.

Participatory Notes??

Participatory Notes are instruments used by foreign funds, not registered in India for trading in the domestic market. The investor who buys PN, deposit fund in the international FII against the security deposit like in US or Europe, and in turn the FII buys stock in India. Thus the FII acts like an exchange since it execute the trade and uses its internal account to settle this.

- Secured Premiun Notes (SPNs):
  The SPN is a secured debenture redeemable at a premium over the face value/purchase price. It resembles a ZIB (Zero-interest bond). There is a lock in period for SPN during which no interest is paid. The holder has the option to sell back the SPN to the issuing company at par after the lock-in period. The redemption is made in installments. The SPN is a tradeable instrument.
- Floating rate Bonds (FRBs):
  The interest on such bonds is not fixed. It is flaoting and linked to a benchmark rate such as interest on treasury bills, bank rate, call rate, maximum rate on return deposits. It is typically a certain percentage point higher than the benchmark rate. The prices of FRBs tend to be fairly stable and close to par value in comparison with fixed interest bonds. They provide a protection against inflation risk to investors particularly banks and financial institutions.

Why a investor uses Participatory Notes?

1. It keeps the investor anonymous.
2. It saves cost of record keeping, transaction cost, and regulatory compliance overseas especially for small investors.
3. Thus investors use PN to enter the Indian market in a small way and then when they are established, they shift to full-fleged FII structure.

What are the Problems with the instrument? It is tough to establish the beneficial ownership or the identity of original investor. The investor may sell the PN to others, and thus further layers. PN is also becoming favorite with many Indian money launderers, who use it to first ship out money of country through Hawala and then get it back using PNs.

What is the extent to which PN's are used? Over the years the use of PNs have increased from 17 FII issuing it in 2005 to over 2 dozen funds now. Merrill Lynch, Morgan Stanley, Credit Lyonnais, Citigroups and Goldman Sachs are the biggest issuers. Currently 51.4% of all assets under FII are under PN.

CURRENCY CONVERTIBILITY

Currency convertibility is the ability to exchange money for gold or other currencies. Currency is considered to be convertible when the concerned country formally accepts the obligations of Article VIII, Sections 2, 3 and 4 of the Articles of Agreement of the IMF.

An international monetary system has been in existence since monies have been traded, its analyses have been traditionally started from the late 19th century when the gold standard began.

The Gold Standard

Exact date for the commencement of the gold standard is not known however the 1880-90 period is important. Currencies are valued in terms of a gold equivalent known as the mint parity price (an ounce of gold was worth $ 20.67 in terms of the U.S. dollar over the gold standard period) in gold standard. Each currency is defined in terms of its gold value hence all currencies are linked together in a system of fixed exchange rates. Gold was used as a monetary standard because it is an internationally-recognized homogeneous commodity that is easily storable, portable, and divisible into standardized units, such as ounces. Since gold is costly to produce, it possesses another important attribute governments cannot easily increase its supply.

The Gold Exchange Standard

An international conference at Bretton Woods, New Hampshire, in 1944 at the close of World War II transformed the international monetary system into one based on mutual cooperation and freely convertible currencies. By this each country had to fix the value of its currency in terms of gold. This established the "par" value of each currency. The U.S. $ was the main currency in the system and $1 was equated in value to 1/35 oz. of gold. By this all currencies were linked in a system of fixed exchange rates.

The members were committed to maintaining the value of the currency within +/-1% of parity. The various central banks were to achieve this goal by buying and selling their currencies (usually against the dollar) on the foreign-exchange market. When a country experienced difficulty maintaining its parity value due to balance of payments disequilibria, it could turn to the International Monetary

Fund (IMF), which was created to monitor the provision of short-term loans to countries experiencing temporary balance of payment difficulties.

External and internal convertibility

When all holdings of the currency by non-residents are freely exchangeable into any foreign (non-resident) currency at exchange rates within the official margins than that currency is said to be externally convertible. All payments that residents of the country are authorized to make to non-residents may be made in any externally convertible currency that residents can buy in foreign exchange markets. And if there are no restrictions on the ability of a country to use their holdings of domestic currency to acquire any foreign currency and hold it, or transfer it to any nonresident for any purpose, that country's currency is said to be internally convertible. Thus external convertibility is the partial convertibility and total convertibility is the sum of external and internal convertibility.

Convertibility: Why?

Externally inconvertible currencies may be of rather limited value to their holder. An exported item from a developing country to the USSR, for example, may be paid for in rubles or the currency of a country that has ratified Article VIII. The proceeds may be used to purchase goods anywhere.

In considering possible import suppliers, therefore, a developing country will have some interest in directing its importers to those countries that will have some interest in directing its importers to those countries whose inconvertible currencies are in large supply. This is, of course, a case of trade discrimination that is condemned by traditional theory. This means that goods are not being purchased from the cheapest source. Recent economic writing has, however, reopened the question in view of the continued existence of inconvertible currencies. Where it is profitable on the export side to trade with countries maintaining inconvertible currencies, and the government wishes to encourage imports from those countries to offset its credit balances, it will utilize its exchange distribution mechanism to limit the availability of convertible exchange where there are alternative suppliers of the same type of goods in inconvertible currency countries.

Current account convertibility

Current account is defined as including the value of trade in merchandise, services, investment, income and unilateral transfers. Current account convertibility, being essential to the development of multilateral trade, three approaches to current account convertibility has been adapted by developing countries. These are the pre-announcement, by-product, and front-loading approaches. Each approach is distinguished by the importance it attaches to convertibility relative to other economic objectives.

Capital account convertibility

Capital account includes transactions of financial assets. Its convertibility refers to the freedom to convert local financial assets into foreign assets in any form and vice versa at market-determined rates of exchange.

Capital controls normally restrict or prohibit cross-border movement of capital. Thus, controls on capital movements include prohibitions: need for prior approval; authorization and notification; multiple currency practices; discriminatory taxes; and reserve requirements or interest penalties imposed by the authorities that regulate the conclusion or execution of transactions. The coverage of the regulations would apply to receipts as well as payments and to actions initiated by non-residents and residents.

BENEFITS TO INDIA

There are three benefits to India from CAC:

1. Rates of return on debt and equity in India are high by world standards. With convertibility, foreign money will come into India to arbitrage this differential away and reduce these rates of return: i.e., the cost of capital faced by the companies of India in equity and debt financing will drop. At a lower cost of capital, more investment projects would be viable, which would generate a faster pace of investment and growth in the economy.
2. With convertibility, Indians would be able to diversify their portfolios internationally. Instead of being constrained only to hold Indian real estate, equity and debt, we will reduce our risk by diversifying internationally. This means that in a bad year in India, when Indian financial assets generate a poor return, foreign assets owned by Indians would continue to generate good returns. This reduction in the variability of returns would make Indians happier since they face less risk, and help stabilise India's macro-economy.
3. Convertibility means that the households and firms of India are not forced to meet each other through India's financial system. The GDR market is one example of the alternative: here Indian firms chose to meet with foreign investors through the markets outside India. This market arose in response to weaknesses of existing markets in India. With convertibility, it will be possible for Indian firms to interact with Indian households in (say) the markets of Singapore. This would provide alternatives for India's households and firms, generate competition for India's financial industry, and elevate the urgency of reforms in the financial sector. For example, if derivatives on the dollar-rupee start trading in Singapore or Chicago, convertibility means that we in India would be able to use them.

Convertibility would generate massive flows of funds into and out of India, as Indians and foreigners modify their portfolios to reflect new investment possibilities. Even if all policies in terms of financial regulation are correctly orchestrated, volatility in the dollar-rupee will innately increase. But given the tradition of government controls in India, we are all used to expecting low volatility of the rupee-dollar. This raises the urgency of developing futures and options on the dollar-rupee, which would give people a method for *managing* these risks.

The foreign exchange market will especially be in the spotlight, since all these increased flows of funds will have to go through the dollar-rupee market. An illiquid dollar-rupee market will display spurious volatility under such pressures. Hence, institutional development of India's foreign exchange market should precede convertibility. The two key approaches for this are (a) transition of the spot market away from the inter-bank market to modern screen-based trading that is widely accessible all over the country, and (b) transition away from the inter-bank dollar-rupee forward market to a modern dollar-rupee futures market without entry barriers. These approaches would transform the quality of the foreign exchange market.

CAC also has important ramifications for taxation. Convertibility opens up new avenues for a narrowing of the tax base, and hence upgrades the priority of a harmonisation of taxation in India with international standards.

Overall it can be said that India is taking a great leap forward in the economic front and it will sustain the growth in future as well. According to *AT Kearney, a global management consulting firm,* India ranks second in the world in terms of attractivenes for FDI. At Kearney's 2007 Global services Location Index ranks India as the most preferred destination in terms of financial attractiveness, people and skills availability and business environment. Similarly, *UNCTAD's World Investment Report, 2005* considers India the 2nd most attractive investment destination among the Transnational Corporations (TNCs). The positive perception as a result of strong economic fundamentals driven by 16 years of reforms has helped India to tide over major economic crisis and now put into a high growth category.

8

Fundamental Analysis

While buying stocks, the main aim of an investor is to make profit. For this, the investor has to assess or speculate the future price of stocks, which he wishes to buy. According to fundamentalists, all securities have an intrinsic value (a true value) of their own as estimated by an investor. Fundamental analysis determines whether the price of a common stock reflects its intrinsic value. This value is a function of firms underlying variables such as earnings per share, dividend pay-out ratio, discount rate (or the required rate of return) and growth rate in earnings and dividends. By assessing these variables, the intrinsic value of a security can be determined. Thus, the main objective of fundamental analysis is to find the intrinsic value of a stock. Usually, the current market price of a security is the average of the intrinsic value estimates made by the investor. If the intrinsic value estimate of an investor differs from the market price, then the estimate of either risk or return or both is also not accurate. Thus, the investor who can perform good fundamental analysis is able to make maximum profit by acting before the market reflects the actual information.

To find out the intrinsic value, a fundamental analyst needs to forecast the earnings and dividends from the stock. For this, a security analyst needs to find out the factors that influence the earnings and dividends. A discount rate should also be chosen that reflects the riskiness of the stock (or the company). The earnings potential and the riskiness of a company depend on the prospects of the industry to which it belongs. The prospects of various industries are influenced by the developments in the economy. The ultimate question to be answered by an analyst is what will be the future stocks price?

No company operates in vacuum (or independently). The stocks performance of a company are somewhat tied to the prospects of the overall economy and the industry within which the company operates. There are two approaches to fundamental analysis – top down approach and bottom up approach. However, our study of fundamental analysis uses the top down approach and is often, being described as an "inverted triangle". The analysis starts first with economic analysis, then moves to industry analysis and, then, finally moves to company analysis.

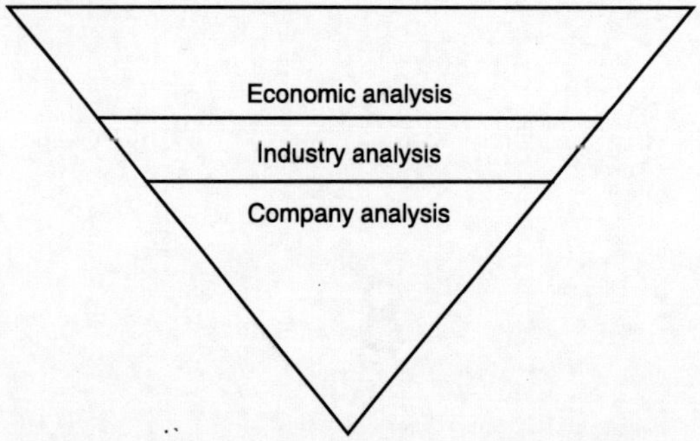

Fig. 8.1. Top Down Approach of Fundamental Analysis.

Therefore, fundamental analysis is said to be a three-stage process (Fig. 8.1) that involves:

- Economic and/ or market analysis
- Industry analysis
- Company analysis

ECONOMIC ANALYSIS

Economic analysis is important because stock price have a strong positive relationship with overall economic performance. Investors are concerned with those forces in the economy, which affect the performance of the companies whose stocks they wish to purchase. It is important to predict the course of the national economy because economic activity affects corporate profits, investor expectations, and security prices. A sagging economic growth can lead to low corporate profits and security process.

Stock prices and economic activities are closely related. Economic expansions are generally associated with rising stock prices, and economic contractions are usually associated with falling stock price. However, stock prices and economic activity do not occur at the same time. Stock prices tend to lead overall economic activity. Stock prices may fall even when the economy is still expanding and they may rise in economic recession. This is because the variables that drive stock prices, such as earnings, dividends and interest rates are based more on expected business conditions than on current conditions. Stock investors respond to what they think is going to happen rather than what is currently happening. The variability in stock prices is due to the overall market movement. The total market or some index of market performance is related to the overall economic performance. Thus, the success of the economy will lead to success of the overall market. In the absence of a positive and healthy economic environment, it is difficult for a company to flourish, which in turn has an adverse effect on the overall stock market performance.

For the security analyst or the investor, the economic forecast is important for making decisions concerning both the timing of an investment and the type of security to be purchased.

Macroeconomic Factors Affecting Stock Prices

The key macroeconomic variables that affect stock prices may be broadly categorized into exogenous variables and endogenous variables. There are four exogenous variables that affect the stock prices:

- Potential output of the economy
- Corporate tax-rate
- Fiscal policy (or charges in govt. spending)

The potential output of the economy is a non-policy variable whereas the other three are policy variables i.e. they are subject to govt. policy decision.

The endogenous dependent variables affecting the stock prices are:

- Total spending
- Price level
- Real money
- Corporate earnings
- Interest rate
- Real output

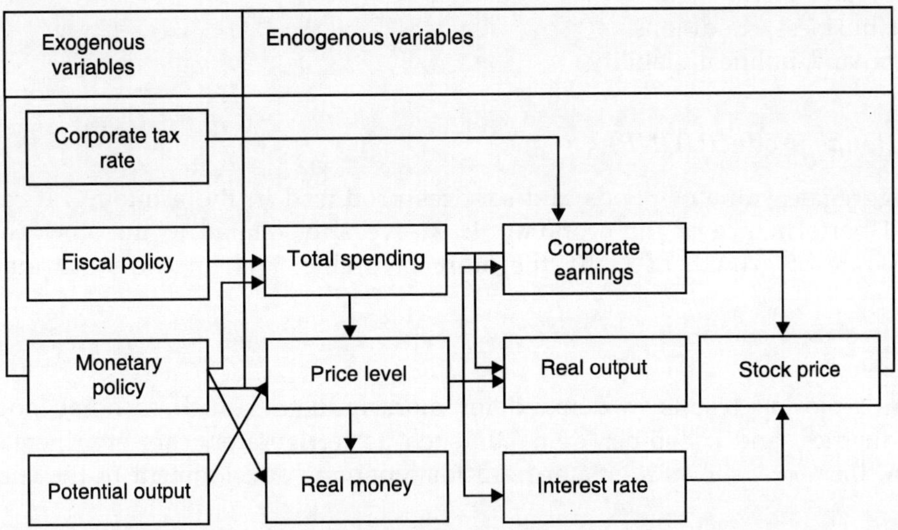

Fig. 8.2. A flow diagram showing impact of economic variables on stock price.

Source: Michael W. Keran, " Expectations, Money and the Stock Market", Review, Federal Reserve Bank of St. Louis, January,1971, p.27.

The exogenous variables affect the three endogenous variables – total spending, price level and real money, which ultimately affect corporate earnings and interest rates.

The two primary exogenous variables, the fiscal policy and the monitory policy, affect stock prices in two ways:

1. They affect the total spending, which, together with another exogenous variable, corporate tax rate, affects the *corporate earnings. Corporate earnings are positively related to stock prices.*
2. They affect the total spending, which, together with the economy's potential output and past charges in prices, determine the current price level. The total spending and the price level determine the changes in real output which in turn influence the interest rate. *Interest rates have a negative influence on stock prices.*

Thus, the ultimate determinants of stock prices are expected corporate earnings and interest rates. Hence, it is necessary to study the forces that give an idea about future corporate earnings and payment of dividends and interest to investors. These forces can be broadly categorized.

1. Gross National Product
2. Population
3. Research and Technological Development
4. Raw materials and infrastructural facilities
5. Monsoon and Agriculture
6. Savings and Investment
7. Monetary and Fiscal policy
8. General business conditions
9. Economic and political stability

Gross national product (GNP)

It is the aggregate value of goods and services produced in the economy. It reflects the overall performance of the economy. It is favorably related to the stock market i.e. higher rate of growth of GNP, the more favorable it is for the stock market.

Population

Population explosion results in demand for more industries such as hotel industry, service industries, and consumer demands such as refrigerator, cars etc. Increase in population, therefore, shows a greater need for economic development of the country.

Research and technological development

The amount of resources allocated by the government on the technological development affect the industrial performance, thereby, affecting the economy.

Raw material and infrastructural facilities

Availability of raw materials and good infrastructure facilities are responsible for a country's economic development, thereby, producing higher investment opportunities. US economy underwent a great change after the discovery of gas. Similarly, Japanese economy flourished after the discovery of raw material in the form of labour force. Facilities such as adequate and regular electric power supply, well-developed transportation and communication system, assured supply of basic raw materials (such as steel, coal, petroleum products, cement etc.) and responsive financial support system significantly influence the industrial performance.

Monsoon and agriculture

In the Indian economy, the behaviour of monsoon and the performance of agriculture play a vital role in assessing and forecasting industrial performance. Industrial performance is directly or indirectly affected by agricultural production and agricultural production is greatly dependent on the monsoons. If the monsoon is good, the agricultural income rises, thereby increasing the performance of the industrial sector and giving buoyancy to the stock market and the economy, as a whole.

Savings and investment

A portion of GNP is saved and invested in the capital market. The higher the level of savings and invested, the more favorable it is for the stock market.

Monetary and fiscal policy

The monetary and fiscal policies have a major impact on the industrial growth by affecting the cost and availability of credit, the profit margins of the companies etc. These polices also influences the movement in price level (inflation) and interest rate, which, in turn, have a great influence on the performance of the industries and the economy.

General business conditions

The levels of business activity also influence the demand for industrial products and the overall performance of the industry. The business activity fluctuates depending upon the state of economy, agricultural performance etc.

Economic and political stability

Economic and political stability is necessary for a good performance of the economy in general and the industries in particular. The government policy should be known in advance in all aspects and there should be no uncertainty. Any adverse changes in government policy affect the industrial performance adversely. The foreign exchange position and the balance of payments also influence the government policy with respect to imports, exports, foreign investments and related matters.

ECONOMIC FORECASTING

Before taking an investment decision, it is necessary to consider the economic environment. This is nothing but economic forecasting. The movement of the overall market explains the variability in stock prices and the market performance is related to overall economic performance. Thus the success of the economy will ultimately lead to the success of the overall market. An unhealthy economic environment adversely affects the overall stock market performance. Economic forecasting is very important because it enables the investor to plan the right time for investment. Timing is very crucial for an investor. Making an investment at the right time will earn a good rate besides having a considerably low purchase price. However, an investment made during a disturbed state of capital market (e.g. strikes), would lower potential capital gain.

Forecasting Techniques

The two general approaches to economic forecasting are qualitative forecasting and quantitative forecasting. Qualitative forecasts are general and descriptive in nature and often rely on leading indicators. Quantitative forecasts give specific estimates of the future economic behaviour. The various forecasting techniques both qualitative and quantitative are as follows:

1. Surveys
2. Economic Indicators
3. Diffusion indices
4. Econometric Model Building
5. Opportunistic Model Building

Surveys

This technique attempts to measure the future economic behaviour of businesses and consumers by conducting surveys that are commonly referred to as anticipation surveys. Surveys of intentions constitute a valuable input in the forecasting process. These surveys include asking people (in business) what are their plans and budget for expenditures works to improve their business. These expenditures may be in terms of construction of plant and equipment, inventory adjustments. These surveys also ask consumers what their future spending plans are. Economists examine surveys that measure consumer confidence about their economic situation. The more confident the consumers are, the faster the economy grows. However anticipation surveys measure only the planned activity. The forecaster has no guarantee whether business/ consumers would adhere to their intentions or not. Higher consumer confidence doesn't always mean increased consumer spending. Many a times a person may intend to buy a house but may not ultimately do so. The forecaster/ analyst must decide the degree to which the survey results deviate from the actual observed results (i.e. which surveys overestimate and which one underestimate the actual results) so that he can make necessary adjustments. Then only, the survey result can be included in his forecast. It must be noted that the survey results themselves are not forecasts; rather they are a consensus that the forecasts can be used in making his own forecast.

It is based on beliefs, intentions and future budgeting of a business or an individual consumer. It indicates the future course of events in the economy. The basic use of this technique is to have an insight of the kind of activity in the economy.

Economic indicators

Economic indicators behave like a barometer. They give the indication of the economic process through cyclical timings i.e. business depression and business prosperity. Although a very accurate estimate is not possible, indicators indicate the level of economic activity. It gives an estimation of the future of economic conditions.

There are three types of economic indicators leading, lagging and coincidental. Leading indicators are the variables, which have been indicators of future economic activity in the past. A simple approach to economic forecasting is to follow the behaviour of these variables. Some economists examine the money supply data (monetary indicator) because they believe that the future economic growth is a function of monetary condition. Some of the leading indicators of an economy are fiscal policy, monetary policy, stock prices, state of the capital market, labour productivity, consumer activity GNP.

Sometimes, several indicators are combined into a leading indicator index. Economists look for any change in the direction of the index to forecast the economic activity. If the index reaches a certain level and then declines, it is a sign of expansion in economic activity. If the index reaches a certain level and then declines, it is a sign of expansion in economic activity (and subsequent recession). However if the index falls to a certain level and then starts to increase then it is a sign of recession in economic activity (and subsequent expansions). The various components of the leading indicators along with the expected direction (up or down) of each component preceding an economic peak or lean listed in the Table (8.1).

Table 8.1. Components of the leading indicator indices

S. No.	Components	Direction prior to lean in the economic activity	Direction prior to peak in the economic activity
1.	Average weekly laws, manufacturing	Up	Down
2.	Average weekly initial claims for unemployment insurance	Down	Up
3.	Manufacturer's law orders for consumer goods and materials	Up	Down
4.	Vendor performance	Down	Up
5.	Contract and orders for plant and equipment	Up	Down
6.	Now, private housing units authorized by local building permits	Up	Down
7.	Stock prices	Up	Down
8.	Money supply	Up	Down
9.	Consumer expectations	Up	Down

The coincidental indicators are the economic factors relating employment position in the country and other Gross National Product factors such as the state of industrial production, corporate profits and wholesale and producer price index. Unlike leading indicators, they do not indicate the future of the economy but present an accurate picture of the current state of the economy.

Any change in the coincidental indicators makes the lagging indicators turn. They are identified with consumer price index, capital expenses, and commercial paper rates.

Diffusion indices

Diffusion index or commonly known as composite index, is a method that combines different indicators (leading, coincidental and the lagging) to analyze a particular time series of data and then draw out a particular composite answer. This is a complex statistical method and the combination of various factors in this technique makes it extremely difficult forecasting method.

Econometric model building

Econometric models apply mathematical and statistical techniques to economic forecasting. It is a most scientific approach to economic forecasting and requires the user to specify the precise interrelationships between members of economic variables both dependent and independent to come up with a model. These models predict the direction of future economic activity and also its duration and magnitude. Instead of a general forecast, they give a precise number. For predicting a sluggish growth in the GDP next year, an econometric model predicts that the GDP will grow by, say, 2.5%. The accuracy of the precise forecast made by these models depends on the quality of the input data and validity of assumption made by the model builder.

However, there are some drawbacks with their econometric approach. Vast amounts of clerical and computer programming support are needed to maintain and update the system. Because of the vast amount of data that must be collected, processed and prepared for inclusion in the model, delay occur in making the results available to the public. Due to this delay, the security analyst suffers the most (than the business forecaster). Generally, these models are useful only for short-term forecasts.

Opportunistic model building

This method is also called sectoral analysis or Gross National Product Model Building. In this approach, the forecaster used the results drawn from all the other techniques, already discussed earlier to make an accurate economic forecast. Like the other forecasting technique this method also uses the national accounting date in order to make a short-term forecast. However, unlike the other forecasting techniques, it is highly flexible.

The method of this forecasting technique starts with the assumption of total demand and total income by the forecaster for the forecast period. While making this hypothetical assumption, he should take into consideration the various environmental conditions such as political stability, rate of inflation, level of interest rates, any change in tax and interest rate etc. Then the forecaster makes a forecast of GNP by estimating the levels of various components of GNP such as consumption expenses, gross domestic investments, and government purchases of goods and services and net exports.

Generally, the forecaster starts with that component that has simple figures and easy to estimate. Gradually, he moves towards the most complex components.

The next component to be forecasted is gross domestic investment, which is again broken down into business expenses for plant of equipment, residential construction and changes in the level of inventories.

The third component to be forecasted is the net exports. This component is particularly a complex one and the forecaster faces certain difficulties while forecasting. This is because along with the domestic problems, the forecaster has to consider international problems also.

The last component to be estimated is the personal consumption expenditures. This component is usually divided into three sub-components—durable goods (minus automobiles) automobile and non-durable goods and services.

After acquiring the data of all the four components, the next step is to add them up to get the GNP forecast. The total is then tested for internal consistency because of the inter-relatedness of GNP accounts. For example, all individuals have a certain level of savings that affects business investment, which in turn affects the productivity and income, which will once again affect savings. The entire circular process will affect other factors such as interest rate, unemployment and inflation. The forecaster should make sure that his GNP forecast is consistent with all these factors and the relationship between them. Thus, opportunistic model building involves a vast amount of judgement and ingenuity in order to come up with a comprehensive forecast.

9

Valuation of Companies

In the age of Mergers and Acquisitions, valuation of companies has become critical to any takeover bid. The expertise of valuation has become a specialized domain and every consultancy firm swears by such domain knowledge. For long years, there was a clear debate on how to value an IT or Telecom firm where the growth rate is exponential and not arithmetical. It is difficult to capture everything in the chapter but efforts are made to explain the basic methodologies of valuation and the entire concept has been reinforced through a live case study of NTPC way back in 2004.

DISCOUNTED CASH FLOW (DCF)

The procedure for using DCF model for valuation is as follows:

1. The model uses published accounting data as input. Historical income statements and balance sheets are used to derive certain critical financial ratios. Those historical ratios are used as a starting point in making predictions for the same ratios in future years.
2. The object of the DCF model is to value the equity of a going concern. Even so, the asset side of the balance sheet is initially valued. The value of the interest-bearing debt is then subtracted to get the value of the equity. Interest-bearing debt does not include deferred income taxes and trade credit (accounts payable and other current liabilities).
3. The value of the asset side is the value of operations plus excess marketable securities. The latter can usually be valued using book values or published market values. Excess marketable securities include cash that is not necessary for operations.
4. The operations of the firm, i. e., the total asset side minus excess marketable securities, are valued by the WACC method. In other words, free cash flow from operations is discounted to a present value using the WACC. There is then a simultaneity problem concerning the WACC. More precisely, the debt and equity

values enter into the WACC weights. However, equity value is what the model aims to determine.

5. The asset side valuation is done in two parts: Free cash flow from operations is forecasted for a number of individual years in the explicit forccast period. After that, there is a terminal/continuing value derived from free cash flow in the first year of the post-horizon period. Hence, individual yearly forecasts must be made for each year in the explicit forecast period and for one further year, the first one immediately following the explicit forecast period. The explicit forecast period should consist of at least 7 - 10 years. The explicit forecast period can be thought of as a transient phase during a turn-around or after a take-over. The post-horizon period, on the other hand, is characterized by steady-state development. This means that the explicit forecast period should, as a minimal requirement is sufficiently long to capture transitory effects.
6. For any future year, free cash flow from operations is calculated from forecasted income statements and balance sheets. This means that free cash flow is derived from a consistent scenario, defined by forecasted financial statements. This is probably the main strength of the DCF model, since it is difficult to make reasonable forecasts of free cash flow in a direct fashion. Financial statements are forecasted in nominal terms, (which implies that nominal free cash flow is discounted using a nominal discount rate).
7. Terminal (post-horizon) value is computed through an infinite discounting formula.

$$\text{Terminal Value} = \frac{\text{PBIT } (1 - r)}{(\text{Ke} - g)}$$

On the basis of the above model, the DCF model involves three tasks that have been outlined in the flowchart below.

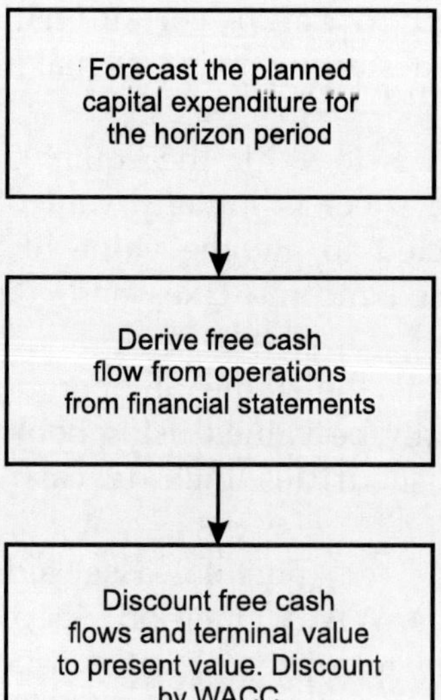

RELATIVE VALUATION

In relative valuation, the value of an asset is derived from the pricing of comparable assets, standardized using a common variable such as earnings, cash flows, book value or revenues. The following are the examples of such common variables:

- Price/Earning (P/E) Ratios
- And variants (EBIT multiples, EBITDA multiples, Cash Flow multiples)
- Price/Book Value (P/BV) Ratios
- Price/Sales Ratio

The following steps can be used while carrying out the relative valuation methodologies:

1. The first step in relative valuation is the selection of comparable firms. A comparable firm is one with cash flows, growth potential and risk similar to the firm being valued.
2. The multiple is computed for each of the comparable firms and the average is computed.
3. To evaluate the firm, we then compare its multiple to the average computed.

The implicit assumption being made here is that the firms in the same sector have similar risks, growth and cash flow profiles and therefore, can be compared with much more legitimacy. The approach becomes much more difficult to apply when there are relatively few firms in the sector.

CASE STUDY NOF NTPC

Industry Analysis

Electric power is the backbone of any economy and thus any development in the electric power industry will have a significant impact on the overall economic scenario and vice versa. Given the fact that Indian industry is growing at a rate of 6 percent per year, the role of electric power assumes more importance. The Government has taken many liberalization measures in the power generation sector. However, the demand still far exceeds the supply and power cuts have become everyday reality. Thus, the situation indirectly offers a huge potential for private players, both domestic and overseas.

The Power Sector in India

The growth and development of the electricity sector is one of the key factors driving the growth of an economy. The importance of the sector coupled with latent demand for power and the substantial investment requirements in the sector influenced a number of developing countries, including India, to initially pursue the model of predominantly public investment for rapid development of the sector. Since electric supply business was considered a natural monopoly, in India, the expansion of the sector was envisaged primarily through the monolithic SEBs to begin with and subsequently with the assistance of the central government owned Central Power Sector Utilities (CPSUs) such as National Thermal Power Corporation (NTPC), National Hydro-electric Power Corporation (NHPC), Power Grid Corporation of India Limited (PGCIL) etc. The growth achieved through public investment model was impressive with the installed capacity increasing from 1300 MW (at the time of independence) to about 90,000 MW in 1991. This addition in generation capacity was commensurate with the increase in demand for power. Further, increase in generation capacity was supplemented by expansion of the transmission and distribution network. Thus, given that one of the key objectives of the government immediately after independence was to provide electricity to larger sections of the society, the model of public investment achieved that objective satisfactorily.

However, since the supply of electricity was viewed as public service, over a period of time, the operations and financial condition of the SEBs began to deteriorate. In addition, substantial amount of energy generated was lost on account of Transmission and Distribution (T&D) losses. As a consequence, the SEBs were unable to achieve the targeted capacity addition. Further, the increase in the dues from the SEBs to the CPSUs compounded the problem of capacity addition in the sector as even the CPSUs were stretched to meet the targets. With the rapid increase in the demand for power and the corresponding requirement to mobilize substantial investments, GoI introduced the policy of private sector participation in 1991, as a part of its economic reform program to further supplement public investment.

Performance of NTPC

National Thermal Power Corporation Limited (NTPC) is the largest thermal power generating company of India. A public sector company wholly owned by Government of India, it was incorporated in the year 1975 to accelerate power development in the country. Within a span of 30 years, NTPC has emerged as a truly national power company, with power generating facilities in all the major regions of the country. Based on 1998 data, carried out by Datamonitor UK, NTPC is the 6th largest in terms of thermal power generation and the second most efficient in terms of capacity utilization amongst the thermal utilities in the world.

Financial Performance

The company has an exceptional track record in financial performance. The sales and profits of the company have been increasing steadily. The following chart displays the growth in the revenues and profits of NTPC over the past five years. The realization levels have improved and reached 92.3% in 2002-03.

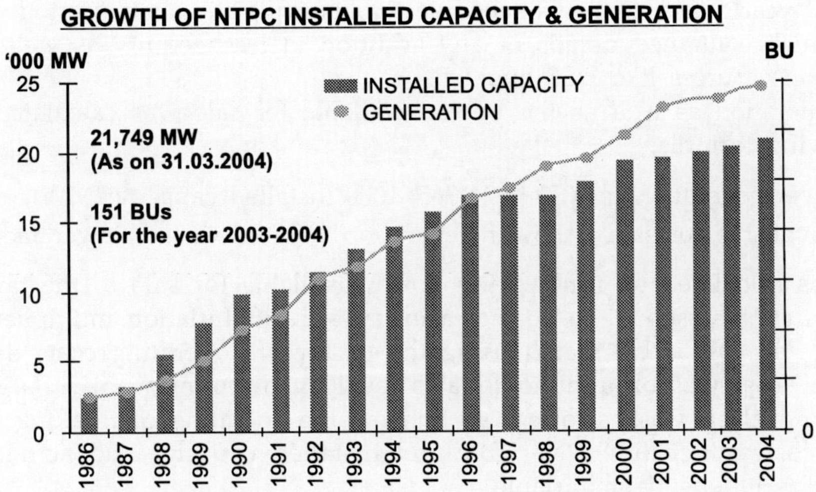

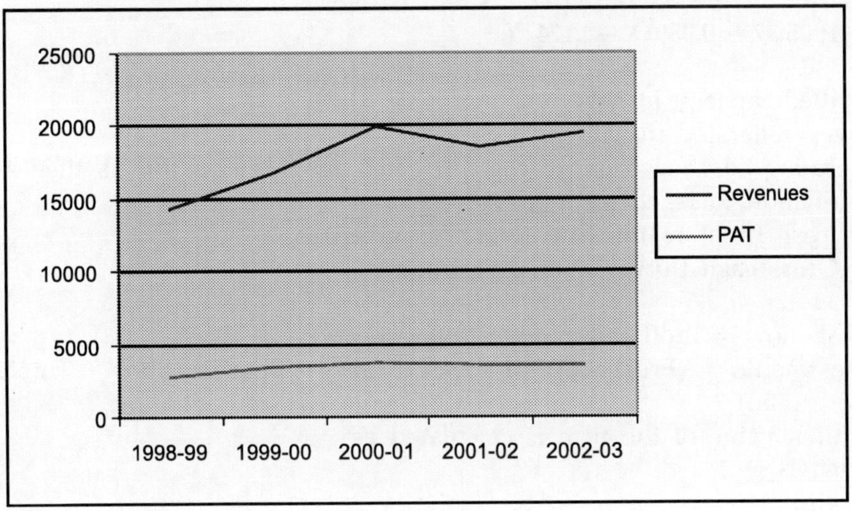

Discounted Cash Flow: Valuation Results

1. To start with the projections of the future, past performance data was collected. The data from the year 1989-90 to year 2001-2002 was considered. Data prior to 1989-90 was not considered relevant because in that period NTPC was purely a coal based company.
2. From the past data the important ratios like working capital to revenue ratio, Dividend payout ratio, and dividend tax ratio, average were calculated.
3. A detailed capacity addition schedule was drawn which contained the capacity yearly commissioning schedule as well as the yearly capital expenditure schedule till year 2011-2012

4. A detailed yearly financing mix schedule for financing the above period was also drawn which contained details of any addition in fresh equity as well as debt from various sources like ECB and DB.
5. Power generation as well as the power available for sale was calculated as per the following formula.

Power generation in MU = 24*365/1000*Installed capacity (MW)

Power available for sale = Power generation * (1- Auxiliary Power factor

6. Revenue is calculated by multiplying power available for sale to the tariff rate. The tariff rate is assumed to be increasing at a Tariff Inflation multiplier.
7. The operating cost is calculated using the past years operating costs data. The past years' cost was brought to today's level by discounting at inflation rate. Regression analysis was performed to find out the operating cost, taking inflation adjusted cost as dependent variable and installed capacity and actual power generated as independent variable.

   The equation of the operating cost (Rs. Cr.) is
   Cost = -1005.37 – 0.089 X + .124 Y
   Where,
   X = Installed capacity in MW
   Y = Power generated in MU
   This operating cost for each year is projected by this equation is then adjusted for the inflation to reach the nominal costs.
8. The free cash flows to the firm (FCFF) is given as
   FCFF = Gross cash flows - Net investments
   Where
   Gross cash flow = Profit after tax + Interest, and
   Net investments = (Fresh capital expenditure – Depreciation) + (Increase in Working capital)

9 The terminal value of the firm is calculated as

$$\frac{\textbf{EBIT (1-t) (1- r)}}{\textbf{(WACC - g)}}$$

Where,

EBIT (1-t)	=	Earning before interest less taxes at the first year of post-horizon period
r	=	reinvestment rate; is equal to g divided by RoC
WACC	=	Weighted Average Cost of Capital
g	=	Stable growth rate of NTPC; assumed to be same as economy growth rate

10. Value of the NTPC is calculated as present value of all the FCFF and terminal value of the firm added with the market value of non-operating assets.
11. Value of equity is found out to be difference of value of firm and claim of the debt.

12. Value of a single share is found by dividing the total value of equity by the number of shares outstanding.

The value of the share using the DCF approach is given below:

Value of non-operating assets	3058.90
Value of the FCFF	55659.51
Value of the Firm	58718.41
BV of Debt	13215.70
Value of Equity (40-41)	45502.71
No of Shares outstanding (Cr.)	781.25
Projected Share Value (Rs.)	**58.24**

Relative Valuation Results

The application of price-related ratios of comparable companies is a common technique used to impute a value of a closely held company. The basic premise is that the Subject Company should have a very similar market value to that of comparable companies with similar financial characteristics (e.g. revenues, earnings, cash flow, etc.)

The prices at which companies engaged in the similar line of businesses, which are selling in a free and open market is the next best measure of value. Comparability is a function of many areas, including but not limited to, product mix, size and quality of the Company, capital structure, profitability, and distribution channels.

Since most of the companies in the power sector are state owned and are not listed on any of the stock exchanges, therefore, the number of companies available for analysis are very less in number. Since the power sector in India is pretty different from those prevalent in other parts of the world, therefore, the companies from these nations have not been included in the model. However, different companies in the countries such as Singapore, Philippines, Korea and China were considered, but the profile of these companies being very different as indicated by huge difference in the values for multiples, these companies were left out of the model.

The following table shows the list of companies that have been included in the model.

Symbol	Primary Exchange	Name	P/E
GGAS IN Equity	Bombay	GUJARAT GAS COMPANY LIMITED	8.80
AECL IN Equity	Bombay	AHMEDABAD ELECTRICITY CO	11.56
BSES IN Equity	Bombay	BSES LIMITED	19.90
GIP IN Equity	Bombay	GUJARAT INDS POWER CO LTD	14.91
TPWR IN Equity	Bombay	TATA POWER COMPANY LIMITED	8.44
		Average Values	***12.72***

The average value of the P/E multiple for the companies in the model comes out to be *12.72*.

Utilizing the relative market valuation approach and a P/E multiple of 16.01, the price of the share has been found out as follows:

Valuation based on Multiples	
P/E multiple	16.01
Earnings	3702
Equity Base	781.255
Price of Share	**60.28**

Hence, the price of the share has been found out to be **Rs. 60.28.**

Assumptions

1. Capacity is added in the same year as per the NTPC capacity addition program
2. The depreciation of new plants is calculated from the year the Capex schedule and not on the basis of commissioning schedule
3. The plants and machinery will depreciate by straight-line depreciation method.
4. The auxiliary power consumption is assumed to be 7% for NTPC.
5. The operating cost projections include inflation component.
6. All the existing and future loans will be paid in equal installments in 10 year time.
7. The coal plants, gas plants, hydroplants will have a life time of 25 years, 15 years and 40 years respectively with 10% salvage value.
8. The existing plants will depreciate at the same rate for the next years as in the past.
9. There will be no cash flow due to dilution/sale of the existing plant in the next 10 years.
10. In the future the dividend will be given at the same proportion of the PAT as in the past years.
11. The dividend tax rate is average of the past rates.
12. NTPC will have no tax liability, as it will be passed on to the SEBs.
13. Working capital increases with revenue as a fixed proportion.
14. Capex for JVC, renovation & Modernization will be depreciated at the existing average depreciated rate i.e. 4.1%.
15. The high growth period is only for 10 years and NTPC will have a table growth period after that.
16. The company's growth rate will be equal to the economy growth rate in the stable growth period.
17. The company will be able to raise enough capital through NBS and debt route as per the plan and execute its planned expansion.

18. The plant will take an average time of 4 years to erect so the capital expenditure done in the last 3 years will not be part of study.
19. The PLF is assumed to be 75% for NTPC as a whole.
20. The return on capital in the stable growth period will be average rate on capital in the high growth period.
21. The market value of debt and equity is same as the book value of the debt and equity respectively.
22. The tariff will increase each year with a tariff inflation multiplier
23. The interest rate on the past loans will be average effective interest rate in the past.

Limitations

1. Plant-wise detailed data of cost, tariff, PLF, auxiliary power consumption, depreciation was not available. The data for these factors had to be assumed for the entire company, which might be different from the actual.
2. Loan repayment schedule was not available so the actual debt payments and the interest amount can deviate from the projections.
3. A basic limitation of the model is that it needs value of equity to find out the WACC, which in turn will be required to calculate the actual value of equity. This circular referencing may lead to a value, which might be different from the actual value.
4. No company is available in India with which NTPC can be compared in terms of its profitability and other measures.
5. There are few companies in India, which are in the power generation business.
6. The power industry outlook in India is unique and therefore even the companies across the globe are not exactly comparable to NTPC.

The valuation process needs utmost care and any small error in the process of projection of cash flows would make the study go haywire. It is important to maintain caution in projecting the growth rate which would, in turn, make the cash flow rational. Cost of capital is another important issue. We have taken 14% as the cost of equity, for, it was stipulated by Central electricity regulatory commission (CERC) – the regulatory authority in India to fix tariffs of electricity generation. Ordinarily, we follow the CAPM model to determine the cost of equity. Good valuation, we must remember, is always a function of good projection of growth potential, cash flow, cost of equity and determination of horizontal value.

10

Industry Analysis

The second step in the fundamental analysis is industry analysis. An investor who is convinced that the economy and the market offer favourable conditions for investing proceeds to consider those industries that promise the most opportunities in the coming years. Industry analysis is necessary because industries performance vary differently over time and investor performance will be significantly affected by the particular industries in which investors select stocks. The value of the industries can be established by assessing the performance of various industries over multiple year periods. This analysis will help the investors in selecting certain industries while avoiding others. The investors are also required to analyze industries in order to know the consistency of industry performance over a period.

Those investors who select the growth industries and maintain their positions usually receive better returns than those who concentrate in the industries that perform poorly over long periods of time.

Although industry analysis is valuable over time, with some industries outperforming the others, it is not consistent. Investors cannot simply choose those industries that have performed well recently and reliably expect them to continue to do so for the next several periods. The investors should not ignore those industries simply because their recent performance has been poor. Their subsequent performance over a short period of time may be opposite. Therefore, it is necessary to learn the basic concepts of industry analysis.

CLASSIFICATION OF INDUSTRIES

In a broad sense, an industry might be considered a community that shares common interests that distinguish it from other communities. It is a distinct group of productive or profit making enterprises.

Industries can be classified in several ways, such as:

Product or Service

For example chemical industry, the airline industry or the restaurant industry etc.

Sensitiveness to Economic Activity

Accordingly, the industries may be of three types – cyclical, defensive industry and growth industry. A cyclical industry is one whose performance tends to be positively related to economic activity. For example, automobile industry, homebuilders, paper companies etc. a defensive industries are pharmaceutical industries, elective and gas utilities industries. A growth industry is characterized by rapid growth in sales and earnings, independent of the business cycles. A good example of growth industry is biotechnology.

Another well-known and widely used system of classification is the **Standard Industrial Classification (SIC) System**. This system is based on census data and is developed to classify firms on the basis of what they produce. The classification covers all organizations and is updated about every ten years to reflect the changing industrial organization. The SIC system classifies from the general to the specific. Initially, it groups all organisations into 11 broad divisions identified by one digit SIC codes. Within each of these divisions, there are several major industry groups, designated by a two-digit code. The major groups within each division are further subdivided into smaller groups, with three digit codes. These are again subdivided into four and five digits SIC codes. Thus, the larger the number of digits in the SIC system, the more specific is the break down.

INDUSTRY LIFE CYCLE

A useful step in industry analysis is to analyze industries in terms of their stages in the life cycle. The main aim is to assess the general health and current position of the industry. The concept of an industry life cycle can apply to industries as well as the product lines within industries. The industry life cycle approach provides a framework for understanding many important issues with respect to industry analysis. All industries go through a life cycle consisting of four well-defined phases – Pioneering phase, expansion phase or growth phase, stabilization phase and decline phase.

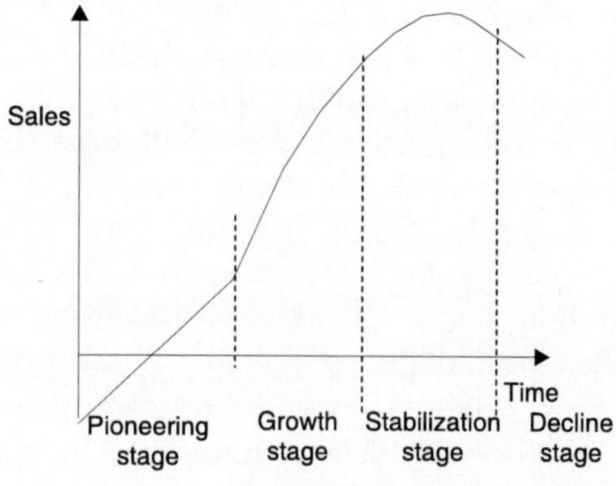

Fig. 10.1. Industry Life Cycle.

Pioneering Stage

In this stage, rapid growth in demand occurs. The technology and / or the product is relatively new. As a result, for the output of the industry this phase is highly competitive with a great opportunity for profits, thereby attracting a number of companies. But only a few may survive this stage owing to price competition. The companies at this stage exhibit a number of important characteristics such as high cost, uneven product quality, erratic sales growth and low profit ability. The pioneering stage is the riskiest stage for the investors, but the rewards in the form of expected return is also high if the company succeeds. At this stage, it is very difficult for a security analyst to identify the likely survivers. By the time it becomes apparent who the real winners are, these prices may become considerably high as compared to what they were earlier. Thus, an intelligent analyst will not invest at this stage but will rather observe and wait for the expansion stage before investing.

Expansion Stage

The firms, which survive the intense competition of the pioneering stage, enter the expansion stage and witness significant expansion in their sales and profit. They continue to grow but the rate of growth is more moderate than it was in the pioneering stage. At this stage, the product quality is improved and is available at a lower price. The firms those are more strong, stable and efficient thereby become considerably attractive for investment purpose. Financial policies become firmly established at this stage. The capital base is widened and strengthened. Many companies start paying dividends also even if they are substantially low. This enhances the attractiveness of these companies to the investors.

Stabilization Stage

The stabilization stage or the maturity stage is characterized by moderate growth. Sales may still continue to grow but at a much slower rate then the overall economy. Products become more standardized and less innovative. The costs of the products are also stable and the market is full of competitors. Industries at this stage continue to move but without any significant growth. Stagnation may occur for significant growth. Stagnation may occur for significant period of time. Even if the investment opportunities within the industry diminish, some companies may still prove to be good investments as these stocks have less risk, and pay higher dividend than the average stock. But it will be an intelligent decision for the investor or the security analyst to dispose of his holidays as soon as it passes from the expansion stage to the stabilization stage at the onset of this stage, the share price decreases.

However, an industry may stagnate intermittently and may resume a period of growth thereby starting a new cycle with a technological innovation or introduction of a new product.

Decline Stage

The change from expansion stage to stagnation stage is so slow that it is difficult on the part of the internal management to realize the situation. They are happy with their profits. They do not realize that their growth is slow and are gradually slipping in the decline stage. By the time they realize this state of complacency, the industry is at loss and cannot expand further. During this stage, most of the companies become obsolete and disappear from the market. These firms who realize the competitive nature of the industry and the approach of stabilization, begin to change their course of action and start a new venture. In this stage the industry may grow slightly during prosperous periods, stagnate during normal periods and decline during necessary period.

The stabilization and decline stage may occur due to various reasons, such as:

Change in social habits

Such changes may occur due to prosperity or certain medical reasons. For example, cotton textile in India is replaced by more expensive polyester and terrycot showing the economic prosperity and enhanced standard of living. Medical Science today reveals that use of ghee may lead to heart problem. Hence, ghee is replaced by groundnut oil and other vegetable oils.

Government regulations

Continuous changes in the govt. regulations relating to price support measures and employment potential in the industry have caused decline in many industries.

Improved technology

New developments and change in technology may also lead to stabilization and decline stage. For example, the pioneering stage of television industry in India saw the entry the various brands of black & white televisions. Slowly these B & W TV's were replaced by colour TV while B & W TV's are still in demand in the rural areas, there is an obsolescence and decline in B & W TV industry in cities.

Labour cost

During the expansion stage when there is a high increase in demand and subsequent increase in production, firms begin to give a greater wage to labour. When the economic significance of the industry declines, the demand decreases and price is also reduced. At this stage, the prevailing labour cost becomes very expensive for the firm and affects the firm financially. This causes its decline.

QUALITATIVE ASPECTS OF INDUSTRY ANALYSIS

In addition to analyzing industries in terms of industry life cycle, there is a second step that involves qualitative analysis of industry characteristics that helps the investors to assess the future prospects of an industry. The various qualitative factors that characterize an industry are:

1. Competition
2. Historical performance
3. Government regulations
4. Labour condition
5. Performance
6. External shocks
7. Financial issues
8. Industry share price valuation

Competition

The nature of competitive environment existing in an industry can provide useful information in assessing its future. The competitive conditions may include entrance of new competitions, cost of building plants, the level of production needed to operate profitably and so on. The analyst should start by listing all the companies that operate in the industry. It may also be useful to determine how many companies are publicly traded, how many are privately owned or owned by other companies and how many are government owned. It is also important to consider the companies having the largest market shares and whether these shares have been rising or falling during the past few years. It is necessary for an investor or analyst to see that the industry in which he wants to invest is well protected from entry of new firms. The entry of new competitors is checked if the existing firms have the following advantages:

Product differentiation, absolute cost advantages and advantages arising from economies of scale.

Product differentiation

When buyers have a preference for the products of established firms, it will be difficult for a new entrant to survive because it will not be able to charge price equivalent to the competing firm. Moreover, it will have to spread large sums of money on sales and promotion expenses in order to attain an acceptable sales level.

Absolute cost advantages

The established firms are able to produce and distribute their products at any level of production or distribution at a lower cost than any new entrant can. These advantages are because of patents, easier access to necessary equipment and funds, experienced management skills, ownership of major raw materials and other resources. Thus, established firms have wider profit margins than the new entrants.

Economies of scale

Advantage relating to economies of scale is found in those industries where it is necessary to achieve a high level of production in order to have a cost that is economically feasible (for e.g. automobiles industry). It is very important for new entrant to obtain a significant share in the market so as to have a competition cost structure relative to existing firms.

Michael Porter has written extensively on the issue of competitive strategy involving the search for a competitive position in an industry. The intensity of competition in an industry determines the industry's ability to sustain above-average returns. This intensity is a reflection of underlying factors that determine the strength of five basic competitive factors:

- Threat of new entrants.
- Rivalry between existing competitors.
- Threat of substitute products/services.
- Bargaining power of buyers.
- Bargaining power of suppliers.

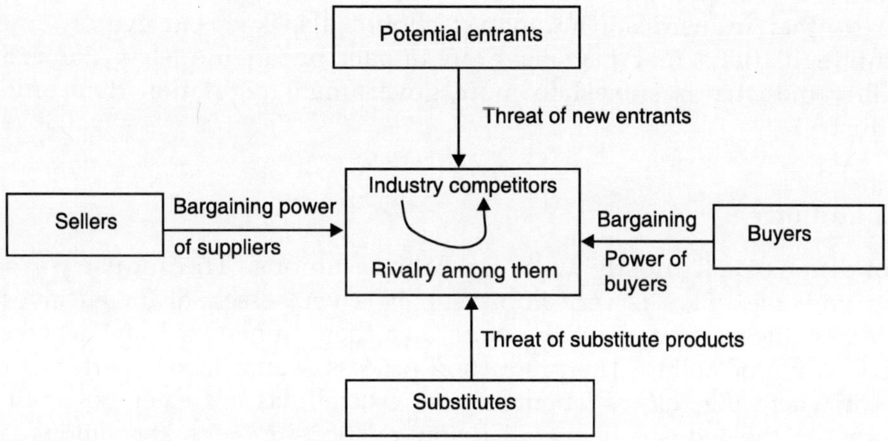

Fig. 10.2. Porter's 5-Force Model.

According to Michael Porter, the profit potential of an industry depends on these five competitive factors because they influence the component of return on investment. The strength of each of these factors is a function of industry structure. Hence, industry profitability is a function of industry structure. The investors must analyze industry structure to assess the strength of the five competitive forces, which in turn determine industry profitability.

Historical Performance

Although industry performance is not always consistent and predictable, an investor should always keep a track record of past performance of the industry relating to sales, earning growth dividends and price performance. It provides some useful information about the future performance. The analyst should also examine the industry's cost structure. If earnings have risen faster than revenue, the industry's cost as a percentage of revenue are falling. To examine the cost structure, the analyst needs to determine the relationship between fixed and variable costs as well. Higher the fixed cost, higher is the sales volume required to achieve the break-even point. Conversely lower the fixed cost, lower is the required sales volume. Hence, it is easier for a firm to achieve the break-even point.

Government Regulations

Government regulations and actions can have significant effects on industries. So, an investor should be aware of these regulations and assess the results of these effects. Government interference may substantially lessen the profits of an industry. Sometimes an industry declines in importance because of legal restrictions that are placed on it. An investor is also required to consider the tax issues and their effects (positive or negative).

For example, oil and gas industries usually have special tax treatment as compared to other industries. The analyst should also keep an eye on emerging government regulations that may have an impact on an industry. For example, electric utility industry is subject to more government regulation than any other typical industry.

Labour Conditions

Labour conditions deal mostly with the labour unions. The industry's overall relationship with the union is very important. It is very essential for an investor or analyst to assess the percentage of the workforce that is unionized and whether that percentage is rising or falling. The production process, where labour performs crucial operations or where the role of labour is very crucial, has a greater possibility of a strike. Therefore, the industry's overall union relationship with the unions is very important. However, if a strike happens in industry with large fixed costs such as rent and insurance, the large fixed costs would be cut deeply into profits. But, then the loss of customer goodwill during a long strike would offset the possible advantages of low fixed costs. On the other hand, if the industry's workforce is not unionized the industry might face non-union labour problems. It may have a difficult time finding and retaining workers or it may have an unusually high number of workers compensation claims. Thus, an analyst or a prospective investor should always check for unusual labour conditions, both union and non-union.

Performance

It is related to the products and technology of the industry. With the rapid changes in technology and major demographic trends, performance has become an important issue. Technological changes can make an industry obsolete in a short period of time. As government becomes more influential in business regulations and protection, the performance of industry is greatly affected.

Sometimes, emergence of a competition may eliminate the need for the same industries. Investing fund in such an industry will be a foolish decision.

For example, tractors caused a decline in the importance of ploughs led by bullocks or oxen. Similarly, popularity of margarine decreased the demand for butter.

External Shocks

The profitability and performance of an industry is vulnerable to external shock economic, political and/or natural event. For example, during the gulf-war of 1990-91, when Iraq invaded Kuwait, fear gripped the oil market. The price of crude oil soared and along with it the price of fuel. This greatly affected the automobile industry and the airlines industry.

Financial Issues

A prospective investor should have a clear idea regarding the industry's balance sheet over the past few years. He should evaluate how much leverage is common in the industry, how asset-intensive its operations are i.e. ratio of the revenues to assets, and how much capital will it have to borrow (externally) if it wants to make capital investment in the near future.

Industry Share Price Valuation

Investment decision is not based only on the current status and future prospects of the industry. It also depends on the current security prices in the industry, their risk and return.

An analyst must consider how investors have valued the industry's stocks in the past. The analyst should also assess industry stock performance measured by price appreciation as well as total returns. If the price were very high relative to future earnings growth, it would not be a wise decision to invest in such securities.

QUANTITATIVE ASPECTS OF INDUSTRY ANALYSIS

Till now we have discussed about the type of information concerning the industry that an analyst ought to obtain. The next job of the analyst is to analyze this information to further evaluate the industry. The major techniques used to analyze this information are:

1. End-use Analysis.
2. Ratio Analysis.
3. Regression and correlation analysis.

End-use Analysis

It is a technique, which the analyst attempts to identify the source(s) of demand for an industry's products or services and how the demand for the product is likely to change for each user.

Ratio Analysis

It divides dates by aggregate economic data over a period of time and examines the result for trends. Any movement or lack of movement in a ratio suggest some important characteristics of the industry. For example, consider a ratio of auto production index to the overall industrial production index. If the ratio is equal to 100, then it reveals that the two production indexes are same and auto industry is a mature industry. If the ratio increases over time, it implies growth in the auto industry. However, a falling ratio would suggest a decline in auto industry.

Regression and Correlation Analysis

Regression and correlation analysis are the statistical techniques used for analyzing demand and other industry data. Regression analysis determines the relationship between two or more variables whereas correlation analysis determines the degree to which two variables are related to one another.

The exhibit shows an XY scatter diagram where Y axis represents the sales and X measures disposable personal income. X is the independent variable. The regression line equation can be expressed as:

$$A + bX_1 + bX_2 + \ldots + bXn$$

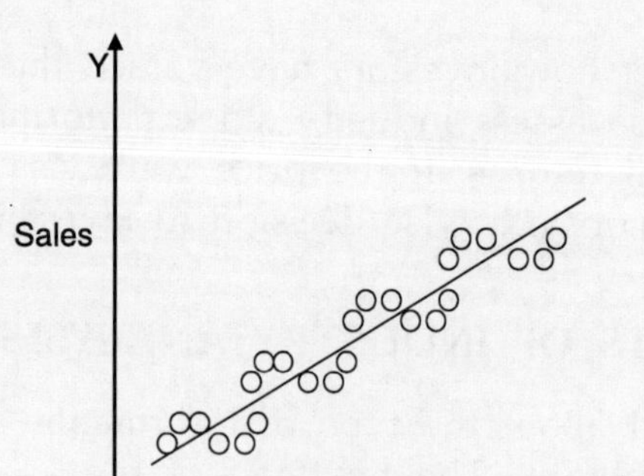

Fig. 10.3. Sales and Disposable Income Scatter Diagram.

A is the Y-intercept and b is the slope of the line. Both a & b are constants. The value of Y or the regression line is the predicted value of Y for a given level of X. thus the regression equation helps the analyst to forecast next year's sales based on the expected growth in personal income. Since most of dots (data points) are relatively close to the regression line, we can say that there is a high degree of association between X and Y. This suggests that actual and predicted values for Y match closely.

Correlation analysis measures the strength of this relationship more precisely using coefficient of determination (R^2) R^2 ranges from 0 to 1 and close to 1 indicates a stronger statistical relationship between X and Y.

REVIEW QUESTIONS

1. Describe the Industry Life Cycle. What are its implications for the investor?
2. What factors should an investor look at while studying the characteristics of an industry?
3. Discuss the forces that drive competition and influence profit potential for industries according to Michel Porter?
4. On what basis can various industries be classified? Explain, giving examples.
5. Industry Analysis helps the investors in selecting certain industries while quailing others. Explain?
6. Explain the factors that lead to the decline stage. How the information on above mentioned factors be helpful to an investor?
7. Discuss in detail the qualitative factors that characterize and help the investors to assess the future prospects of an industry?
8. Industry profitability is a function of industry structure. Comment.
9. Discuss the techniques used in Industry Analysis.
10. How important is it to learn Industry analysis, in context of Indian stock market?

11

Company Analysis

Once the economic analysis has indicated a favorable time to invest in common stocks and industry analysis has pointed out the industries that are expected to perform well in the future, the next important step for the investor is to analyze individual companies and choose promising companies within those industries. This is the last step in top-down approach of fundamental analysis.

Company analysis involves analyzing basic financial variables in order to estimate company's intrinsic value. These variables include sales, profit margins, depreciation, tax rate, sources of finance, asset utilization and other factors. In addition to this, various qualitative variables are also analyzed such as the company's competitive position in its industry, labor relations, technological changes, management, foreign competition, etc.

For analyzing a company, an investor needs to examine the nature and sources of relevant information about it. This helps him to make judgements about expected return and associated risk. There are basically two broad categories of information – **external** and **internal.** Internal information involves data and events made public by the company regarding its operations. The principal source of internal information about a company is its financial statements. Apart from financial statements, internal information may also come from annual reports, public and private statements of the managers etc. External information helps to overcome biases inherent in internal information. It also provides certain information that is not found in internal information.

FINANCIAL STATEMENT

The three major financial statements that are required by an analyst as a tool of fundamental analysis are the **income statement**, the **balance sheet** and the **statement of cash flow**. The investors rely heavily on these financial statements of the company because they provide the major financial data about the company. On the basis of these statements the future course of action by the investors is taken. Hence, for evaluating a company, it is necessary that the statements should be accurate, complete, consistent and comparable. The accuracy of a financial statement is identified if the statements are certified or legally audited by a qualified chartered accountant. Secondly, the financial statements should be complete in all respects and should take into account any change that have taken place (such as price level change) to give accurate account to the investor.

Financial Statements should also be comparable i.e. type of information furnished in the statement should be standard so that it can be evaluated in an uniform manner. The fourth and final factor that is to be considered is the consistency of the accounts. This helps in the making of comparison of a firm's performance over a period of time. Data should be continuous and financial statements should be of uniform comparability. Statements of income, balance sheet and cash flows are depicted in Tables 11.1 to 11.3.

Table 11.1. Statement of Income

Income Statement($ millions)	Fiscal Year ending January 31		
	1999	1998	1997
Sales	30219	24156	19535.5
Cost of Goods Sold	21241	17092	13869.1
Gross Profit	8978	7064	5666.4
Selling, General, and Administrative Expense	5944	4765	3900.4
Operating Income Before Depreciation	3034	2299	1766
Depreciation and Amortization	373	283	232.3
Operating Profit	2661	2016	1533.7
Interest expense	68	61	39.4
Non-operating Income / expense	61	63	48.9
Special Items	-	-104	-
Pretax Income	2654	1914	1543.1
Total Income Taxes	1040	738	597
Net Income	1614	1160	937.7
Savings due to Common Stock Equivalents	-	-	8
Adjusted Net Income	1614	1160	945.7
Earnings Per Share	1.1	0.8	0.63
Dividends Per Share	0.12	0.09	0.08
Closing Price per Share	60.5	30.25	16.5

Table 11.2. Balance Sheet

BALANCE SHEET ($ MILLIONS)			
ASSETS			
Cash & Equivalents	62	174	558.4
Net Receivables	469	556	388.4
Inventories	4293	3602	2708.3
Prepaid Expenses	0	0	0
Other Current Assets	109	128	54.2
Total Current Assets	4933	4460	3709.4
Net Plant, Property & Equipment	8160	6509	5437
Other Investments	41	42	48
Intangibles	268	0	0
Other Assets	63	218	147.3
TOTAL ASSETS	13465	11229	9341.7

Table 11.2. (Contd.)

BALANCE SHEET ($ MILLIONS)			
LIABILITIES			
Long Term Debt Due In One Year	14	8	2.5
Accounts Payable	1586	1358	1089.7
Taxes Payable	100	105	48.7
Accrued Expenses	981	842	571.9
Other Current Liabilities	176	143	129.3
TOTAL CURRENT LIABILITIES	2857	2456	1842.1
Long Term Debt	1566	1303	1246.6
Defered Taxes	85	78	66
Minority Interest	9	116	97.8
Other Liabilities	208	178	134
Balance Sheet (4 millions)	**Fiscal Year Ending January 31**		
	1999	1998	1997
TOTAL LIABILITIES	4725	4131	3386.5
TOTAL EQUITY	8740	7098	5955.2
TOTAL LIABILITIES AND EQUITY	13465	11229	9341.7
Shares Outstanding (millions)	1475	1464.2	1441.5

Table 11.3. Cash Flow Statement

CASH FLOW STATEMENT($ MILLIONS)			
Cash Flow From Operations			
Net Income (loss)	1614	1160	937.7
Depreciation and Amortization	373	283	232.3
Deferred Income Taxes	7	-28	28.8
(Increase) Decrease in Working Capital	-77	-386	-98.7
Net Cash from Operations	1917	1029	1100.1
Cash Flow from Investing Activities			
(Increase) Decrease in Fixed Assets	-2275	-1396	-1173.2
(Increase) Decrease in Short Term Investments	4	425	-334.4
	-2271	-971	-1507.6
Cash Flow From Financing Activities			
Increase (Decrease) in Long Term Debt	238	-25	470.2
Increase (Decrease) in Common Stock	167	122	104.5
Payment of Cash Dividends	-168	-139	-110.2
Other Financing Charges, Net	11	10	35.5
Net Cash from Financing Activities	248	-32	500
Effect of Exchange Rate Changes	-4	-	0.2
Net Change in Cash and Equivalents	-110	26	92.7

Income Statement

The income statement is used not only to assess current management performance but also to assess the company's future profitability. It gives the past records of the firm that forms a base for making predictions for the firm. The key items that an investor should consider while analyzing the income statement are inventory cost methods, depreciation, after- tax net income, earnings from regular operations as well as non-recurring earnings, intangibles and earnings per share (eps). It is necessary to assess the inventory cost methods in order to make adjustments in the value of stock. The investor needs to assess the depreciation method used to check out its uniformity and the exact effect it has on a firm. The after- tax net income when divided by the number of outstanding shares, produces EPS. Every business earns from its normal operations which are recurring in nature. These earnings from continuing operations are used to judge the company's success. However, sometimes a business may have non- recurring earnings due to some extraordinary items that arise from unusual and infrequently occurring transactions. The gain or loss from this extraordinary item must be disclosed in the income statement separately. In every business, there are certain factors that reveal the value (or worth) of a firm but are intangible in nature such as copyrights, patents, government limitations, trademarks etc. The investor should analyze and evaluate these tangibles. The most important item, which investors should evaluate, is the earning that a shareholder receives on his share (EPS).

Balance Sheet

The balance sheet shows the assets and liabilities of a firm along with shareholder's equity. The various items of the balance sheet carry different amounts as dictated by the accounting conventions. The fixed assets are evaluated on the original cost or the cost at which they were purchased. Cash is the actual rupee amount whereas marketable securities could be at market value. Shareholder's equity is on a book value basis.

A balance sheet has two sides – asset side and liability side. The asset side (left hand side) is divided in current assets, Investment and other assets, long-term assets and intangible assets. The right hand side or liability side of the balance sheet is divided in current liabilities (payable within one year), long term debt, other liabilities, deferred income taxes and shareholder's equity.

Statement of Cash Flow

This statement shows the changes in the financial position of a firm (inflows and outflows of cash and cash equivalents) for a given financial year. A firm basically generates cash and spends cash. The activities that generate cash are called sources of cash. For example, issue of securities, raising a bank loan, selling a product, disposing and asset etc. The activities that spend cash are called uses of cash. For example, redemption of securities, paying interests and dividends, purchasing materials, acquiring assets, etc.

To assess the changes in the financial position of a firm, it is necessary to consider the changes in the balance sheet and income statement over that period. For better understanding, cash flows are divided in three classes—cash flows from operating activities, cash flows from investing activities and cash flows from financing activities. This provides useful information on how cash flows have been influenced by various decisions.

ANALYSIS OF FINANCIAL STATEMENTS: FINANCIAL RATIOS

Financial Ratios are one of the most widely used tools for analyzing a company's financial statements because they show relationships of the financial statements. They help to identify a company's strength or weaknesses and highlight the areas that require further investigation.

Financial ratios have been classified into five categories:

1. Liquidity Ratios
2. Leverage Ratios
3. Profitability Ratios
4. Activity Ratios
5. Valuation Ratios

The exhibit below lists the major financial ratios and shows how they are calculated.

1. *Liquidity Ratios*

$$\text{Current Ratio} = \frac{\textit{Current Assets}}{\textit{Current Liabilities}}$$

$$\text{Quick Ratio} = \frac{\textit{Current Assets - Inventory}}{\textit{Current Liabilities}}$$

$$\text{Cash Ratio} = \frac{\textit{Cashand Marketable Securities}}{\textit{Current Liabilities}}$$

2. *Activity Ratios*

$$\text{Inventory Turnover} = \frac{\textit{Sales}}{\textit{Average Inventory}}$$

$$\text{Accounts Receivable Turnover} = \frac{\textit{Sales}}{\textit{Average Accounts Receivables}}$$

$$\text{Fixed Asset Turnover} = \frac{\textit{Sales}}{\textit{Average Net Fixed Assets}}$$

$$\text{Total Asset Turnover} = \frac{\textit{Sales}}{\textit{Average Total Assets}}$$

3. Leverage and Coverage Ratios

$$\text{Debt Ratio} = \frac{\textit{Total Liabilities}}{\textit{Total Assets}}$$

$$\text{Long Term Debt to Equity} = \frac{\textit{Long Term Debt}}{\textit{Share holders Equity}}$$

$$\text{Times Interest earned} = \frac{\textit{Earnings before interest and taxes}}{\textit{Interest}}$$

4. Profitability Ratios

$$\text{Gross Profit Margin} = \frac{\textit{Gross Profit}}{\textit{Sales}}$$

$$\text{Operating Profit Margin} = \frac{\textit{Gross Profit}}{\textit{Sales}}$$

$$\text{Net Profit Margin} = \frac{\textit{Net Profit}}{\textit{Sales}}$$

$$\text{Return on Assets} = \frac{\textit{Net Income}}{\textit{Average Total Assets}}$$

$$\text{Return on Equity} = \frac{\textit{Net Income}}{\textit{Average Share holders Equity}}$$

Earning Growth Rate = Percent Change in Earnings per Share

$$\text{Retention Rate} = 1 - \frac{\textit{Dividends per Share}}{\textit{Earnings per Share}}$$

5. Market Value Ratios

$$\text{Price to Earnings Ratio} = \frac{\textit{Market Price}}{\textit{Earnings per Share}}$$

$$\text{Market to Book value ratio} = \frac{\textit{Market Price}}{\textit{Book Value per share}}$$

$$\text{Dividend Yield} = \frac{\textit{Dividends per share}}{\textit{Pricepershare}}$$

$$\text{Total return to shareholders} = \frac{\textit{Change in price + Dividends}}{\textit{Prior year price}}$$

Liquidity Ratio

Liquidity Ratios measure a company's liquidity i.e. a company's ability to meet its short-term obligation. Does it have sufficient liquid assets to meet its current obligations or current liabilities? A liquid asset is an asset that can be quickly converted into cash at a price close to the asset's "true" value. Usually, there are three liquidity ratios—current ratio, quick ratio and cash ratio.

Leverage Ratio

Financial leverage refers to the use of debt finance. Leverage ratios measure the extent to which a company relies on borrowed funds to finance their operations. Though debt capital (borrowed funds) is a cheaper source of finance, it is associated with high risk. Leverage ratios help to assess the risk associated with debt capital. Leverage ratios are basically of two broad types—coverage ratios and structural ratios. Coverage ratios measure a company's ability to repay its debts. They show the relationship between debt servicing commitments and the sources for meeting these commitments. The important coverage ratios are interest coverage ratio, fixed charges coverage ratio and debt service coverage ratio. Structural ratios are based on the proportions of debt and equity in the financial structure of the firm. The important structural ratios are debt- equity ratio and debt-assets ratio.

Companies that rely more on borrowed funds are said to be more leveraged. The effect of leverage can be both positive and negative. The positive side of leverage is that companies use debt financing to raise capital without existing shareholders giving away their control. Moreover, debt financing is cheaper than equity financing, as the interest is tax deductible. Further, it magnifies a small increase in operating income into a larger return to shareholders. However, it also magnifies decrease in operating income into smaller returns to shareholders. Too much leverage can lead to financial distress and even bankruptcy. This shows the negative side of leverage.

Profitability Ratio

Profitability ratios measure how much money a company is earning. The two types of profitability ratios are profit margin ratios and the rate of return ratios. The profit margin ratios show the relationship between profit and sales while the rate of return ratios reflect the relationship between profit and investment. The profit margin ratios include gross profit margin, operating profit margin and net profit margin and net profit margin. The rate of return ratios is return on total assets, return on equity, earning power and retention rate.

Activity Ratios

Activity ratios, also called turnover ratio or asset management ratio, measure how effectively and efficiently a company is using its assets to generate revenues or sales. The more efficiently and effectively a company uses its assets, the stronger it is financially. These ratios are based on the relationship between the level of activity and the level of assets. Level of activity is represented by sales or cost of goods sold. The principal activity ratios are inventory turnover ratio, total assets turnover ratio, fixed assets turnover ratio, Debtors turnover (Receivables Turnover) Ratio and average collection period.

Valuation Ratio

Most ratios are based on book value i.e. the values that come directly from a company's financial reports. But valuation ratios, which are based on market values, give an indication of how investors view a company, both its performance history as well as its future prospects. Hence, valuation ratios indicate how the equity stock of a company is assessed in the capital market. These ratios are the most comprehensive measures of a firm's performance since the market values reflect the influence of risk as returns. The important valuation ratios are price-earning (P/E) ratio, the dividend yield, and the market price to book value ratio in the total return to shareholders.

Interrelationship among the Ratios – Profitability Ratios

Many of the financial ratios interrelate with one another. For example, companies with a large inventory may have relatively high current ratios but low inventory turnover and total asset turnover ratios. Interrelationships are especially important to a company's profitability and can be used to analyze a company's profitability. Analysts examine the various components of profitability in order to determine whether a company's profitability, in terms of earnings growth and dividend growth, is increasing a decreasing and, also, why is it so. This can be done by analyzing key financial ratios using accounting variables. The primary emphasis is on the accounting variable, Return on Equity (ROE) because it is the key component in determining earnings growth and dividend growth. The ROE is the accounting rate of return that stock holders earn on their portion of the total capital used to finance the company. ROE is related to EPS as follows:

$$\text{EPS} = \text{ROE} \times \text{Book Value per share}$$

Book Value per share (BVS) measures the accounting value of the equity and can be calculated as:

$$\text{BVS} = \frac{\textit{Stock holders Equity}}{\textit{Shares Outstanding}}$$

Du-Pont Analysis

ROE is analyzed by a method called Du-Pont Analysis. The main idea behind this method is to break down ROE into various components and then analyzing these components separately. The main advantage of decomposing ROE is that it helps the analyst to determine the factors that drive profitability. It also allows the analyst to better identify strengths, weaknesses and the areas that need further investigation.

A key component of company's profitability is operating efficiency, which is a product of earning before Interest and Tax (EBIT) and asset turnover ratio. Thus, it is evident that operating efficiency is unaffected by interest charges, taxes or leverage.

$$\text{Thus, operating efficiency} = \frac{EBIT}{Sales} \times \frac{Sales}{Total\ Assets}$$

EBIT/Sales is the Pre-interest, pre-tax profit margin.

Sales/Total Assets is the asset turnover ratio.

But it is necessary for an analyst to consider interest charges and the tax burden. Interest expenses for most companies are a tax-deductible item.

$$\text{Hence, interest burden} = \frac{Pre\text{-}tax\ Income}{EBIT}$$

$$\text{Tax Burden} = \frac{Net\ Income}{Pre\text{-}tax\ Income}$$

Finally, the effects of leverage must also be considered. Leverage can magnify the ROE (favourable leverage) or diminish ROE (unfavourable leverage). The effects of leverage can be observed more easily if equity multiplier is used rather than debt percentage.

$$\text{Hence, leverage} = \frac{Total\ Assets}{Share\ holders\ equity}$$

From the foregoing discussion, it can be concluded that Du Pont formula breaks down ROE into five components-

1. Pre-interest, pre-tax profit margin
2. Asset turnover ratio
3. Interest burden
4. Tax burden
5. Leverage ratio (equity multiplier)

The above five financial ratios have a multiplicative relationship. All of them when multiplied together gives ROE.

Thus,

$$ROE = \frac{EBIT}{Sales} \times \frac{Sales}{Total\ Assets} \times \frac{Pre\text{-}tax\ Income}{EBIT} \times \frac{Net\ Income}{Pre\text{-}tax\ Income}$$

$$\times \frac{Total\ Assets}{Share\ holders\ equity} = \frac{Sales}{Total\ Assets} \times \frac{Net\ Income}{Sales} \times \frac{Total\ Assets}{Share\ holders\ Equity}$$

The pre-interest, pre-tax profit margin, interest burden and tax burden together gives the Net Profit margin (i.e. Net income/sales). The product of the first two components gives the Return on Assets (ROA)

$$\text{ROA} = \frac{Sales}{Total\ Assets} \times \frac{Net\ Income}{Sales} = \frac{Net\ Income}{Total\ Assets}$$

$$\text{Hence, ROE} = \text{ROA} + \frac{Total\ Assets}{Share\ holders\ Equity}$$

ROA is an important measure of a company's profitability reflecting how effectively and efficiently the firm's assets are used. The higher the ROA, higher is the return (ROE). ROA can be improved by increasing the net income more than the assets or by using the existing assets even more efficiently.

The third component of Du Pont formula i.e. assets/ average equity (also called equity multiplier) is a measure of leverage. The higher the ratio, the more levered is the company. If the company has any liabilities, the equity multiplier will be greater than one. In such a case ROE will be greater than ROA.

INTERPRETATION OF FINANCIAL RATIOS

As we see, financial ratios are nothing but numbers. To make them more meaningful, a comparison is a must. This comparison can be made by observing the same ratio over a number of years (trend analysis) and / or by comparing a company's ratio to industry averages (industry comparison).

Trend Analysis

The analysts examine the same set of ratios over a number of years to look for obvious trends. This is known as Trend Analysis. If there is trend, the next step will be to determine the cause(s) of the trend and whether the trend suggests strength or weakness.

Industry Comparison

By comparing a company's ratio to industry averages, an analyst finds out the company ratios that appear out of line with industry averages. Trends in ratios yield some information about a company, but comparing a company's ratio to industry averages provide additional insight into the company that is being analyzed. While going for industry comparisons, three things should be kept in mind:

- Different industries have different average ratio.
- Many industries are not homogenous.
- Many companies operate in several different industries.

The results of an industry comparison may hold less value for a company operating in various industries than for a company that operates in one well-defined industry.

INTRINSIC VALUE OF A SHARE

The intrinsic (or estimated) value of a stock is the price justified by a company's financial variables. It the intrinsic value is larger than the current market price, the stock is said to be undervalued and it should be purchased. If the intrinsic value is less than the market price the stock is said to the over-valued then it should be sold.

The intrinsic value or the estimated value of a stock can be calculated by using two models.

1. Dividend-Discount model.
2. Earnings multiplier model.

Dividend Discount Model

$$\text{Intrinsic value, Po} = \frac{D_1}{k - g}$$

D_1= Expected Dividend
k = Required rate of return
g = Estimated future growth rate of dividends

Earnings Multiplier Model

This model is used for short-run estimate of intrinsic value. According to this model, intrinsic value is the product of the estimated earning per share (EPS) and the price-earning (P/E) ratio.

$$\text{Intrinsic Value (Po)} = \text{Estimated EPS} \times \text{Estimated P/E Ratio}$$

This calculated intrinsic value of a stock is then compared with its current market price. If the intrinsic value is higher than the current market price, the stock is said to be under-valued. This is a buy signal. However, if the intrinsic value is less than the market price, the stock is said to be over-valued and hence be avoided. If such stocks are owned, this is an ideal situation for an investor to sell. But, if the intrinsic value equals the current stock price, this implies equilibrium and the asset is said to be correctly priced.

Intrinsic value > current stock price => **UNDERVALUED** (a buy)
Intrinsic value < current stock price => **OVERVALUED** (a sell)
Intrinsic value = current stock price => **EQUILIBRIUM**

Though the dividend discount model is the most logical method for calculating the intrinsic value of a stock, some analysts and investors consider this model to be unrealistic because technically, this model makes a forecast of future dividends. According to them, it is possible to forecast future dividends accurately. Moreover, many investors want capital gains rather than dividends. So, for them, focusing solely on dividends is not desirable.

Because of the drawbacks of the Dividend Discount Model as cited above, Earnings Multiplier Model is considered to be the most popular approach for calculating the intrinsic value of a stock even though it is a less sophisticated and more intuitive model. This model is also easier to use.

The two models are not competitive alternatives of share valuation. Rather they are complementary to each other. This is because of the following reasons:

1. Dividends are paid out of earnings. Hence, investors must estimate the earnings before they go for estimating dividends.
2. The P/E ratio of the earnings multiplier model is derived from the constant growth dividend model.
3. Neither of the two models can be used in all situations. For example, Dividend Discount model is not applicable when the company does not pay any dividends and Earnings Multiplier models cannot be used when the company has negative earnings.
4. Regardless of the approach used, estimates of future dividends and earnings are always subject to error because this involves dealing with uncertain future. These methods can be used to cross-check each other in order to obtain more reasonable results.

Estimation of the Intrinsic Value

According to the earnings multiplier approach, the share price is the product of two variables: EPS and P/E multiple. Estimation of the intrinsic value of a share involves three basic steps:

1. Forecasting the expected EPS
2. Calculating the expected P/E ratio
3. Estimating a value range

Earnings per share (EPS)

Investors buy common stock expecting a satisfactory rate of return. Whether the stock can produce the desired rate of return is determined by its current price. A particular stock attractiveness depends on whether the stock is correctly priced or not. This correct price of a stock is the present value of expected future cash flows i.e. dividends and an expected future price. Future earnings are probably the most important determinant of a company's future dividend stream and stock price. Since dividends are paid out of earnings, higher future earnings means higher future dividends. In addition, high future earnings also means higher future stock price. Thus, the major goal of company analysis is to forecast the quality and quantity of future earnings and also to consider any item that may affect the future earnings.

EPS is a critical variable in security analysis. It is very important to analyze EPS, understand how it is derived or calculated, its accounting aspects and its main components.

$$\text{EPS} = \frac{\textit{Profit after Interest and Tax}}{\textit{Total number of outstanding shares}}$$

To know the future price of the stock and earnings and dividends, an investor needs to analyze the financial statements of a company. Forecasting EPS largely depends on these statements. The EPS that investors use to value stocks is the future (expected) EPS. Current stock price is a function of future earnings estimates and the Price-Earning (P/E) ratio. While performing fundamental security analysis using EPS, an analyst needs to:

1. Know to obtain earnings estimates
2. Consider accuracy of the earnings estimate so obtained
3. Understand the role of earnings surprises in impacting stock price.

P/E ratio

The P/E ratio is the most used measuring stick in the investment world. It indicates how much an investor is willing to pay per rupee of a stock's earnings. In other words, it is the price for each rupee of earnings. Thus, it is a measure of the relative price of the stock. It provides the foundation for valuing stocks or making investment recommendations about stocks. Analysts usually recommend stocks (for investment) on the basis of the P/E ratio is lower than as justified by stock's growth prospects, the stock is said to be overvalued. Similarly, if the P/E ratio is higher than as justified by the growth prospects, the stock is said to be over-valued.

P/E ratio is calculated by the model –

$$P/E = \frac{D_1/E_1}{k - g}$$

Where D_1/E_1 = expected dividend payout ratio.
k = the required rate of return
g = expected growth rate in dividends

Required rate of return (k) = Risk – free return + risk premium.
Expected growth rate in dividends (g) = Retention rate × ROE

Thus, it can be observed that P/E ratio depends on three factors – dividend payout ratio, required rate of return and expected growth rate in dividends. The P/E ratio is expected to change as the above three factors change. Other things being equal, the P/E ratio is directly related to the dividend payout ratio (D_1/E_1) and expected growth rate (g) but inversely related to the required rate of return (k). However, the 'other things' are seldom equal. In that case, the above relationships do not hold true. If a firm wants to increase its estimated P/E ratio by simply raising its individual payout ratio, it will reduce the expected growth thereby lowering the future growth prospects of the firm. Similarly, if the firm tries to increase g by taking risky investment projects, the required rate of return (k) will also increase. This would offset the advantage of the increase in g.

Thus the expected growth rate (g) and the required rate of return are the most important factors in the determination of P/E ratio. The effect of change in k and g on P/E ratio is illustrated below.

Illustration

Suppose the dividend payout ratio is 70 per cent.

$$P/E = \frac{D_1/E_1}{k - g}$$

Case I $\quad \frac{when\ k=0.16}{g=0.08} \quad P/E = \frac{0.70}{0.16 - 0.08} = 8.75$

Case II $\quad \frac{when\ k=0.17}{g=0.07} \quad P/E = \frac{0.70}{0.17-0.07} = 7$

Case II $\quad \frac{when\ k=0.15}{g=0.09} \quad P/E = \frac{0.70}{0.15-0.09} = 11.66$

If the above P/E ratios are multiplied with the expected EPS for a stock, suppose, Rs.10, then the intrinsic values of the stock will be Rs. 87.50, Rs. 70.00 and Rs. 116.60 respectively. Thus, it can be seen that small changes made in k and g changes the intrinsic stock price in a wide range.

Usually, companies whose earnings are expected to grow rapidly have high P/E ratio. But, the main question is how much higher should the P/E ratio be? For this, the investor needs to assess the degree of risk involved in the expected future growth of earnings. If the higher growth rate carries a high level of risk, the P/E ratio will be affected accordingly. Thus, P/E ratio reflects the investors' expectations regarding the growth potential of a stock and the risk involved. These two factors (i.e. growth prospects and risk) usually tend to offset each other. Other things being equal, the greater the risk of a stock, the lower is the P/E ratio. However, growth prospects may offset the risk and result in higher P/E ratio. Converse is also true i.e. higher the growth prospects of a firm, higher is its P/E ratio. But high risk tends to offset the growth prospects, thus, lowering the P/E ratio. The relationship between P/E ratio, growth prospects can be explained by considering the following example. Suppose if a company is considered to be very risky but is valued potentially very high by the investors, the P/E ratio increases. This in turn increases the share price of the company.

Value range

By multiplying the expected EPS and the expected P/E ratio, an analyst gets the intrinsic value. This product is also called the Value Anchor. However, this value anchor or the intrinsic value is an estimated value and is not an accurate one. The investor can enhance the accuracy of the share value by defining a value range around the single intrinsic value estimate. By doing this, the estimated intrinsic value becomes more accurate. The investment decision rule will be as follows:

If Market Price < lower value of the value range	Buy decision
If Market Price is within the value range	Hold decision
If Market Price > high value of the value range	Sell decision

Illustration: Suppose EPS = Rs. 10

P/E multiple = 5.45
Value anchor = 54.5
Value range = 50 to 58.

Thus,

MP< 50	A Buy
MP between 50 & 58	A Hold
MP> 50	A Sell

REVIEW QUESTIONS

1. Compare and contrast the survey indicator and econometric approaches to forecasting?
2. What monetary and fiscal policies would you suggest for an economy in a deep recession? Why?
3. What is opportunistic Model Building?
4. What economic factors do you think must directly affect defense-oriented industries and thus would be most important to forecast properly?
5. What economic factors would you be most interested in forecasting if you were an analyst investigating major consumer durable goods sales for next year?
6. It has often been said that common stocks are a good "hedge against inflation"? Why do you suppose people think this way? Are you inclined to agree or disagree with this statement?
7. What is the significance of a diffusion index with a large positive reading?
8. If you were attempting to forecast the sales of the candy industry. What classification scheme would you use?
9. Of what value is the past sales and earnings performance of an industry in forecasting the future prospects of the Industry?
10. What domestic industries do you suppose will decline in importance in the next decade? Why?
11. How high would Industry share prices have to go relative to Industry earnings before you would decide that the shares were over priced for Investment purposes? Explain.
12. How would you go about forecasting the sales of domestically produced beer next year? What variables are most important in determining the demand for beer?
13. What are the 3 most critical variables one might "track" in forecasting the outlook for the fast food industry?
14. Give an example of an Industry you feel has positive competitive conditions for your selection as an industry to invest in? Why have you selected this industry?
15. Select an industry that may be ripe for Investment because it has significant undervalued assets on its books?
16. Identify a marketing driven development that may lead or has lead to an Investment opportunity? Explain your selection.
17. Name 3 sources of industry data available in many libraries. Obtain an example from each of 3 sources for an Industry of your choice. Based on Information in those sources above would you recommend it for investment potential for someone with a 3-Yr Time Horizon?

18. If you were told that the housing industry was going to have a good year. What other industries do you think would be positively affected either concurrent with this event or shortly thereafter? Explain your answer.
19. If you were considering for Investment in an Industry with high Fixed Cost and high profit margins what other factors would you want to explore before deciding to invest in this Industry?
20. If you were considering for Investment in an Industry with low Fixed Cost and low profit margins what other factors would you want to explore before deciding to invest in this Industry?

12

Technical Analysis

Technical analysis, also known as *charting*, is the study of the trading history (the price and volume over time) of any type of traded security (stocks, commodities, etc.) to attempt to predict future prices.

GENERAL DESCRIPTION

Technical analysis assumes that price patterns and trends exist in markets and that they can be identified and exploited. While many different methods and tools are used, the study of charts of past price and trading action is primary.

The attempt is to give results that are correct more often than they are wrong. Indeed, the central strategy of many active traders is to trade often, terminating trades that prove to be incorrect decisions and "letting run" trades that prove to be correct decisions.

Viewed by many as more art than science, technical analysis stands in contrast to fundamental analysis (studying the actual nature of the stock or commodity in question). Although some investors combine the two types of analysis in making investment decisions, a good proportion of technical and fundamental traders view the other side with derision. Furthermore, within technical analysis, adherents of different technical analyses (say candle stick charting and Dow Theory) often treat each other's approaches with derision.

Some academic studies conclude technical analysis has scant predictive power, while other studies show that it can produce excess returns. For example, measurable forms of technical analysis, such as non-linear prediction using neural networks, have been shown to occasionally produce statistically significant prediction results. As an example of the debate regarding the efficacy of technical analysis, Peter Lynch, a very well-known and successful fundamental analyst, once commented, "Charts are great for predicting the past." A Federal Reserve working paper has shown that the statistical properties of intraday foreign exchange prices change near "support and resistance" lines, without showing that this result could be used in a profitable trading strategy.

HISTORY

The premises of technical analysis were derived from observation of financial markets over hundreds of years. The oldest branch of technical analysis is the use of candle stick techniques by Japanese traders at least as early as the 18th century, and now one of the main charting techniques.

Traditionally, "Honno, the God of the markets," a very successful rice trader in early Japan, is said to have invented technical analysis. Dow Theory, a theory based on the collected writings of Dow Jones co-founder and editor Charles Dow, inspired the use and development of technical analysis from the end of the 19th century. Modern technical analysis considers Dow Theory its cornerstone. Technical tools and theories have been developed and enhanced in recent decades, with an increasing emphasis on computer-assisted techniques.

Beliefs

Technical analysis is not concerned with *why* a price is moving (e.g. poor earnings, difficult business environment, poor management, or other fundamentals) but rather whether it is moving in a particular direction or in a particular chart pattern. Technical analysts believe that profits can be made by "Trend following." In other words if a particular stock price is *steadily rising* (trending upward) then a technical analyst will look for opportunities to buy this stock.

Until the technical analyst is convinced this uptrend has reversed or ended, all else equal, he will continue to own this security. Additionally, technical analysts look for various price patterns to form on a price chart and will take positions in anticipation of the expected move following that pattern. The tools of technical analysis are believed to assist the technician in determining when trends have formed, ended, etc. and when particular patterns are unfolding.

For example, a popular technical analysis tool is a stock price's 200-day moving average. This is usually defined as the average closing price of a stock over the past 200 trading days (though there are many variations on the moving average used in technical analysis). A stock that has been *trending higher* will have a history of an increasing daily stock price and an increasing 200-day moving average. Though the daily stock price fluctuates (up 50 cents on day 1, down 20 cents on day 2, up 10 cents on day 3, etc.), the 200-day moving average changes much more slowly and traces a smooth curve that follows the current price on a chart.

When the 200-day moving average is *violated by the daily stock price,* a technical analyst uses this as strong evidence that a price trend has ended and that possibly a new one has begun to the opposite direction. Suppose IBM's 200-day moving average was 85 and the stock has been trending higher. If IBM closed at 84.50, then a technical analyst would consider selling his IBM holdings and perhaps selling short IBM because the perceived trend is ending.

The above example illustrates a few important characteristics and potential shortfalls of technical analysis. Much of technical analysis is art and open to some varying interpretation. One technical analyst might believe that IBM would need to trade below its moving average for two consecutive days before declaring its trend over. Another might say one day is adequate. To a technician a close below the 200-day moving average is always important, but two technicians might disagree on the best way to act. Still, it is safe to assume that both technicians expect to sell IBM.

The obvious problem in this example is: what if in the near term IBM climbs back above its 200-day moving average after the technician sells his stock? If the technical analyst follows his own rules then he might be buying stock back at a higher price than he just sold plus commissions. This is a substantial component of some of the criticisms of technical analysis (see below). Technical analysis says "false signals" or "whipsaws" are an unavoidable part of using technical analysis. To a technical analyst, the costs of these whipsaws are far outweighed by catching a stock at the beginning of a new long term trend. Some research disputes this assertion however.

Technical analysis may be at odds with fundamental analysis. Fundamental analysis maintains that markets may misprice a security and, through various methods of fundamental analysis, the "correct" price can be calculated. Profits can be made by trading the mispriced security and then waiting for the market to recognize its "mistake" and reprice the security. In contrast, a technical analyst is not interested in a security's "correct" price, only in price movement.

Two well known sayings among technical analysts are, "The trend is your friend," and "Forget the fundamentals and follow the money." An example of the different views of technical and fundamental analysis follows. Suppose a stock was trading at Rs.124.25, and that the consensus fundamental analysis view of the stock was that it was worth Rs.120.00. If the share price rose to Rs. 125.00, then to Rs. 126.00, and then to Rs. 127.00, a technical analyst would likely be a buyer of this stock in order to profit from the perceived trend. In contrast, a fundamental analyst would possibly look to sell the stock as it is moving away from what the fundamental analyst believes is the "correct" price.

MARKET ACTION DISCOUNTS EVERYTHING

The purpose of technical analysis is to interpret the signals generated from market price action. Technical analysts believe this method works because every possible bit of information will be reflected by means of market action.

Therefore it is redundant to explicitly do fundamental analysis, which may include a study of micro-factors like the instrument fundamentals and global-factors like economic, political issues. If that factor is going to affect the price of a financial instrument, the market will tell, vice versa. Only a study of the market is required.

Prices Move in Trends

While it cannot be shown that prices must trend, technical analysis relies on empirical evidence and common sense to assert that prices do trend. To a technician, markets are trending up, trending down, or trending sideways (flat). This definition of a price trend is essentially the one put forward by Dow Theory.

A person who does not believe that prices move in trends will find little use for technical analysis. The assumption that prices must trend is probably the most important concept in technical analysis.

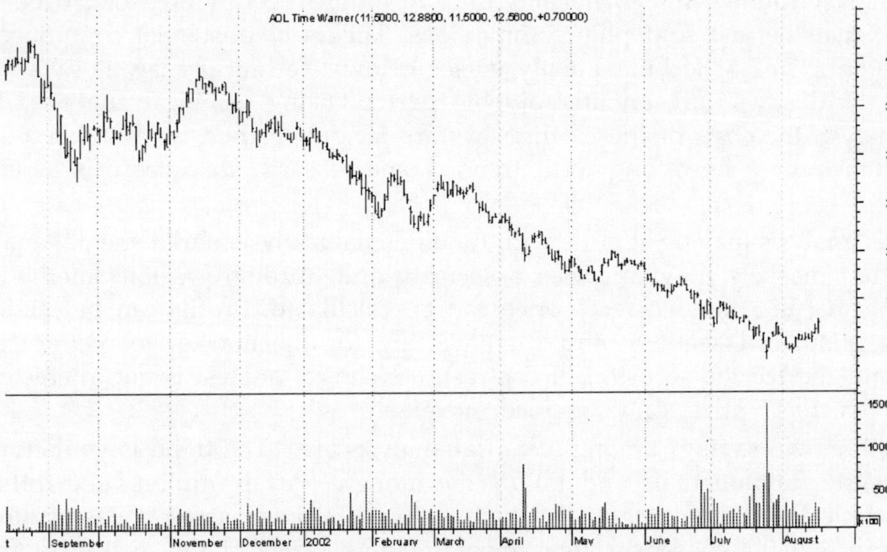

Chart: Price Trend of AOL from Nov. 2001 to Aug. 2002.

An example of a security that is trending is America On Line (AOL) from November 2001 through August 2002. A technical analyst or trend follower recognizing this trend would look for opportunities to sell this security. AOL consistently moves downward in price. Each time the stock attempted to rise, sellers would enter the market and sell the stock; hence the "zig-zag" movement in the price. The series of "lower highs" and "lower lows" is a tell tale sign of a stock in a down trend. In other words, each time the stock edged lower, it went lower than its previous relative low price. Each time the stock moved higher, it could not reach the level of its previous relative high price.

Note that it is not until August that the sequence of lower lows and lower highs is broken. In August, the stock makes a low price that does not pierce the relative low set earlier in the month. Later in the same month, the stock makes a relative high equal to the most recent relative high. To a technical analyst, those are strong indications that the down trend is at least pausing and possibly ending. A technical analyst would likely stop actively selling the stock at this point.

History Tends to Repeat Itself

Technical analysts believe that investors en masse repeat the behavior of the investors that preceded them. "Everyone wants in on the next Microsoft," "If this stock ever gets to $50 again, I will buy it," "This company's technology will revolutionize its industry, therefore this stock will skyrocket,"— these are all examples of investors' attitudes repeating. To a technical analyst, the human characteristics of the market might be irrational, but they exist. Because investors' attitudes often repeat, investors' actions in the marketplace often repeat as well, i.e., patterns of price movement will develop on a chart that a technical analyst believes have predictive qualities.

Technical analysis is not limited to charting. Technical analysis is always primarily concerned with price trends. Anything that can influence the price trend is of interest to a technical analyst. As an example, many technical analysts monitor surveys of investor enthusiasm. These surveys attempt to gauge the general attitude of the investment community to determine whether investors are bearish or bullish. Technical analysts use these surveys to help determine whether a trend will reverse or whether a new trend will develop. A technical analyst would be alerted that a trend might change when these surveys report extreme investor reactions. When surveys are overly bullish, for example, a technical analyst will look for evidence that an uptrend will reverse. The logic being that if most investors are bullish, then they would have already bought the market (anticipating that the market will move higher). But because most investors are bulllish and have invested, it is safe to assume that there are few buyers remaining in the market. There are more potential sellers in the market than buyers despite the fact that the overall attitude of investors is bullish. This implies that the market is set to trend down and is an example of a technical analysis concept called "contrarian trading".

CRITICISM

Lack of Evidence

Although chartists assert that their techniques provide excess returns over time, many academics believe that technical analysis has no predictive power. Burton Malkiel in his book *A Random Walk Down Wall Street* (8th edition, 2003) and Eugene Fama in "Efficient Capital Markets: A Review of Theory and Empirical Work", May 1970, *Journal of Finance* summarize many early studies, conducted during 1950-70, that show that after trading costs are considered, the returns generated by many technical strategies underperform a simple buy and hold strategy.

Cheol-Ho Park and Scott H. Irwin reviewed 93 modern studies on the profitability of technical analysis and considered 59 of them to indicate positive results, and 24 negative results. "Despite the positive evidence ... it appears that most empirical studies are subject to various problems in their testing procedures, for example, data snooping, ex-post selection of trading rules or search technologies, and difficulties in estimation of risk and transaction costs."

Critics of technical analysis include well known fundamental analysts. Warren Buffett has said, "I realized technical analysis didn't work when I turned the charts upside down and didn't get a different answer" and "If past history was all there was to the game, the richest people would be librarians."

Inconsistencies with other Market Hypotheses

Efficient market hypothesis

The efficient market hypothesis (EMH) concludes that technical analysis cannot be effective. If all relevant information is reflected quickly in a security's price through the actions of traders who have that information, no method, including technical analysis, can "beat the market". New events and new fundamental developments which influence prices occur randomly and are unknowable in advance. EMH advocates have produced many studies that reject the efficacy of technical analysis.

Proponents of technical analysis counter that technical analysis does not completely contradict the efficient market hypothesis. Technicians agree with EMH in that they believe that all available information is reflected within a security's price; that is why technicians say a study of the price movement is necessary. Technicians argue that EMH ignores the realities of the marketplace, namely, that many investors base their future expectations on past earnings, track records, etc. Because future stock prices can be strongly influenced by investor expectations, technicians claim it only follows that past prices can influence future prices.

Market participants can and do act irrationally. Technicians have long held that irrational human behavior influences stock prices and claim to have ways of predicting probable outcomes based on this behavior.

EMH advocates reply that although individual market participants do not always act rationally (or have complete information), their aggregate decisions complement each other, resulting in a rational outcome, (i.e. irrational optimists, wishing to buy stock and bid the price higher, are counter-balanced by irrational field of behavioral finance. Behavioral finance essentially says that people are not the rational participants pessimists trying to sell their stock, until the price reaches equilibrium). Likewise, complete information is reflected in the price because all market participants bring their own individual, but incomplete, knowledge together in the market.

Random walk hypothesis

The random walk hypothesis is also at odds with technical analysis and charting. Essentially, the hypothesis claims that stock price movements are a Brownian Motion with either independent or uncorrelated increments. In this model, movements in stock prices are not dependent on past stock prices, so trends cannot exist and technical analysis has no basis. Again, proponents of this theory have generated substantial research in support of the hypothesis. Random Walk advocates such as Burton Malkiel and John Allen Paulos believe that technical analysis and fundamental analysis are pseudo-sciences.

The random walk hypothesis may be derived from the weak-form efficient markets hypothesis, which is based on the assumption that market participants take full account of any information contained in past price movements (but not necessarily other public information). Technical analysts maintain that trends are identifiable in the market and that it can be impractical to believe that market prices move in a random fashion. To a technician, over time prices will trend in a direction until supply equals demand. Therefore, there cannot be any pure random price movement. As stated earlier, one of the cornerstones of technical analysis is that prices trend. If one does not believe this concept, one will not agree with technical analysis.

Also, with regards to EMH and Random Walk Theory, technicians claim that both theories ignore the realities of the marketplace. To a technician, the market is neither composed of completely rational participants as EMH assumes (participants can be greedy, overly risky, etc. at any given time) nor is its stock price movement completely independent of its prior movement (technicians will point at charts like AOL above). Technicians maintain that both theories would also invalidate numerous other trading strategies such as index arbitrage, statistical arbitrage and many other trading systems.

Neural networks

Since the early 90's when the first practically usable types emerged, artificial neural networks (ANNs) have rapidly grown in popularity. They are artificial intelligence adaptive software systems that have been inspired by how biological neural networks work. Their use comes in because they can learn to detect complex patterns in data. In mathematical terms, they are universal non-linear function approximators meaning that given the right data and configured correctly, they can capture and model any input-output relationships. This not only removes the need for human interpretation of charts or the series of rules for generating entry/exit signals but also provides a bridge to fundamental analysis as that type of data can be used as input.

In addition, as ANNs are essentially non-linear statistical models, their accuracy and prediction capabilities can be both mathematically and empirically tested. In various studies neural networks used for generating trading signals have significantly outperformed buy-hold strategies as well as traditional linear technical analysis methods.

While the advanced mathematical nature of such adaptive systems have kept neural networks for financial analysis mostly within academic research circles, in recent years more user friendly neural network software has made the technology more accessible to traders.

Rule-based trading

Rule-based trading is an approach to make one's trading plans by strict and clear-cut rules. Unlike some other technical methods or most fundamental analysis, it defines a set of rules that determines all trades, leaving minimal discretion.

For instance, a trader might make a set of rules stating that he will take a long position whenever the price of a particular instrument closes above its 50-day moving average, and shorting it whenever it drops below.

ELLIOT'S WAVE PRINCIPLE

The Elliot's wave principle, or wave principle, is a form of technical analysis that aims to forecast trends in the financial markets. It was introduced by Ralph Nelson Elliott in the 1930s, a professional accountant, in *The Wave Principle* (1938), in a series of articles in *Financial World* magazine in 1939, and most fully in his final major work, *Nature's Laws: The Secret of the Universe* (1946).

Elliott proposed that "because man is subject to rhythmical procedure, calculations having to do with his activities can be projected far into the future with a justification and certainty heretofore unattainable." The Elliott principle claims to isolate those rhythms and be predictive of future rhythms. The best known contemporary practitioner of Elliott wave analysis is Robert Prechter, who rediscovered Elliott's work in the late 1970s and has popularized it.

The wave principle begins with the premise that collective investor psychology (or crowd psychology) moves from optimism to pessimism and back again. It holds that these changes of mood create repeated patterns in market prices at both the micro and macro level and that these patterns can be predicted. Elliott's model proposes that market prices alternate between five waves and three waves at all degrees of trend, as the illustration shows.

As these waves develop, the larger price patterns unfold in self-similar fractal geometry. In a bull market, Waves 1, 3, and 5 are called "motive" waves, and each motive wave can itself subdivide into five waves. Waves 2 and 4 are "corrective"

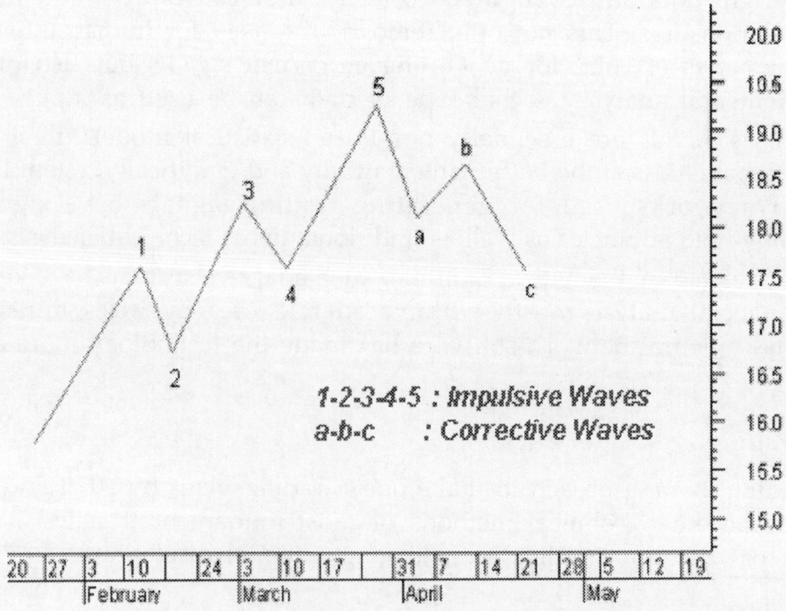

waves, and also can subdivide in three waves. In a bear market, the dominant trend is downward, so the pattern is reversed — five waves down and three up. Motive waves always move with the trend, while corrective waves move against it.

Rediscovery and Current Use

Robert Prechter came across R.N. Elliott's works on microfilm in the New York Public Library, while working as a market technician at Merrill Lynch. His notoriety as a forecaster during the bull market of the 1980s brought the greatest exposure to date to Elliott's theory, and today Prechter remains the most widely known Elliott analyst.

Among market technicians, wave analysis is widely accepted as an important component of their trade. Elliott Wave Theory is among the methods included on the exam that analysts must pass to earn the Level I Chartered Market Technicians (CMT) designation, the professional accreditation developed by the Market Technicians Association (MTA). Comprehensive coursework (including Elliott theory) is offered by the MTA and the New York Institute of Finance. The U.S. Securities and Exchange Commission's recent recognition of the CMT designation has provided further creditability to the technical analyst profession.

Fibonacci Relationships

R. N. Elliott's analysis of the mathematical properties of waves and patterns eventually led him to conclude that "The Fibonacci Summation Series is the basis of The Wave Principle." Numbers from the Fibonacci sequence surface repeatedly in Elliott wave structures, including motive waves (1, 3, 5), a single full cycle (5 up, 3 down = 8 waves), and the completed motive (89 waves) and corrective (55 waves) patterns. Elliott developed his market model before he realized that it reflects the Fibonacci sequence. "When I discovered The Wave Principle action of market trends, I had never heard of either the Fibonacci Series or the Pythagorean Diagram."

The Fibonacci sequence is also closely connected to the Golden ratio. Practitioners commonly use this ratio and related ratios to establish support and resistance levels for market waves, namely, the price points which help define the parameters of a trend.

Finance Professor Roy Batchelor and researcher Richard Ramyar studied whether the Fibonacci sequence appears non-randomly in the stock market, as the work of Elliott and Prechter predicts. The researchers state the "idea that prices retrace to a Fibonacci ratio or round fraction of the previous trend clearly lacks any scientific rationale." From their empirical work they conclude "there is no significant difference between the frequencies with which price and time ratios occur in cycles in the Dow Jones Industrial Average, and frequencies which we would expect to occur at random in such a time series."

Robert Prechter replied to the Batchelor-Ramyar study, saying that it "does not challenge the validity of any aspect of the Wave Principle...it supports wave theorists' observations." The Socionomics Institute also reviewed data in the Batchelor-Ramyar study, and said this data shows that "Fibonacci ratios do occur more often in the stock market than would be expected in a random environment."

Criticism

The premise that markets unfold in recognizable patterns contradicts even the weakest form of the efficient market hypothesis, which states that prices cannot be predicted from past market data such as prices and volume. According to this reasoning, if such simple predictions were possible, enough investors would buy (sell) when the method predicted a price increase (decrease), that the price would increase (decrease) immediately, thus destroying the profitability and predictive power of the method. If the Elliott wave theory were true, in efficient markets the knowledge of it among investors would lead to the instantaneous disappearance of the very patterns they were trying to anticipate, rendering the method useless.Critics claim that the wave principle is too vague to be useful, since it cannot always identify when a wave begins or ends, and that Elliott wave forecasts are prone to subjective revision.

CASE STUDY: ELLIOT'S WAVE PRINCIPLE ON POWER SECTOR COMPANIES

Reliance Energy Ltd. (REL)

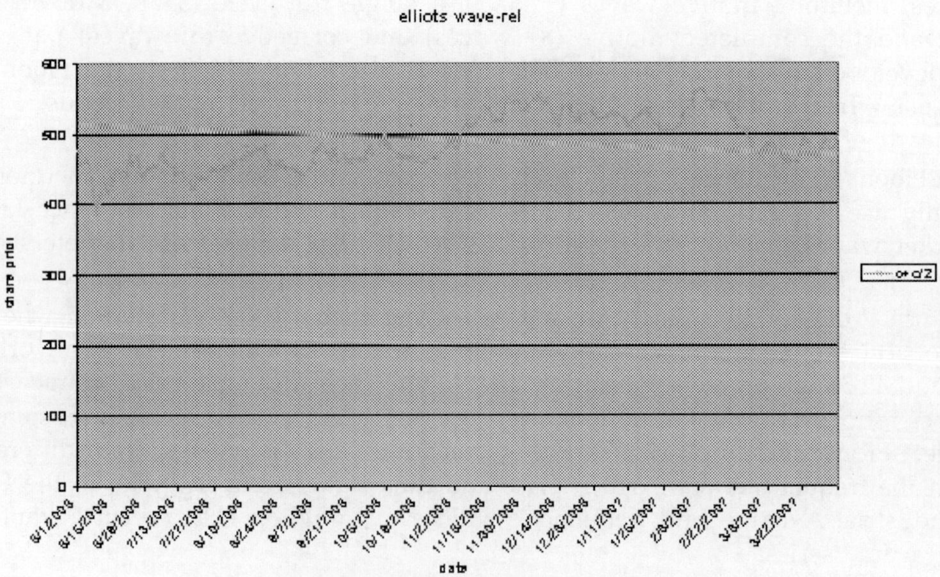

Chart: REL.

Analysis

The share price behaviour of REL shown in the above Elliot's model during June 2006 -March 2007, indicated that the script remained volatile varying between Rs.400-570 range with high ups and downs. The share peaked on many occasions, making it difficult for the long term investors to put their money. During October 2006 – January 2007 the script remained full of waves making it a highly unpredictable stock. February 2007 remained as a good month for selling owing to less volatility and the rising trend in the market price. Overall, the script of REL reflected a moderately stable script which is worth investing with a caution to hold investment whenever the market moved erratically.

Gujarat Industries Power Company Ltd. (GIPCL)

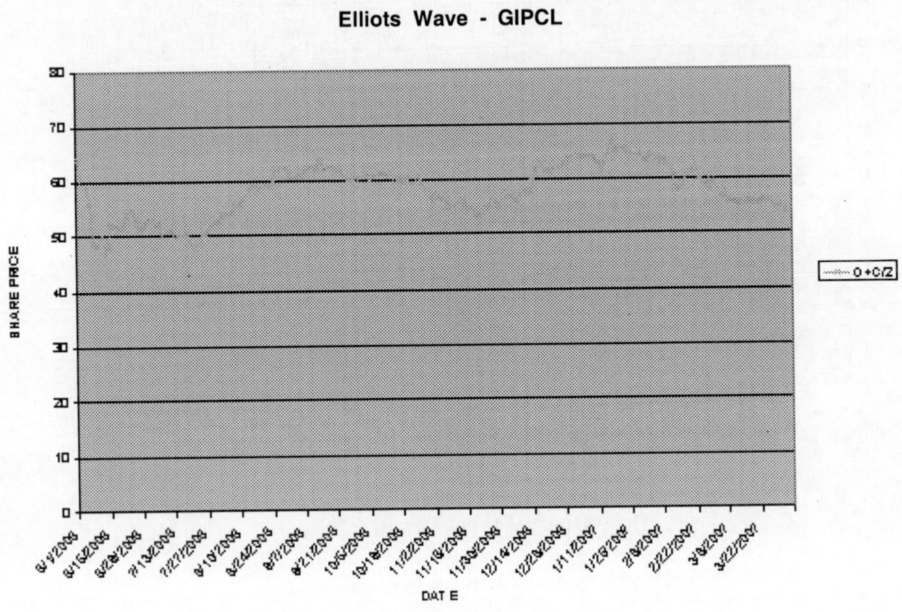

Chart: GIPCL.

Analysis

The share price behaviour of GIPCL shown in the above Elliot's model during June 2006 - March 2007, indicated that the script remained volatile varying between Rs. 50-70 range with ups and downs. The share peaked on many occasions, but the peaks are found to be very mild in contrast with REL. During October 2006 - January 2007 the script remained full of repetitive wave structure making it a highly unpredictable stock. February 2007 remained as a good month for selling owing to less volatility and the rising trend in the market price. Overall, the script of GIPCL reflected a moderately stable script which is worth investing with a caution to hold investment whenever the market moved erratically.

Torrent Power

Analysis

The share price behaviour of Torrent Power shown in the above Elliot's model during November 2006 -March 2007, indicated that the script remained volatile varying between Rs.60-85 range with initial sharp ups and subsequent downs. The share

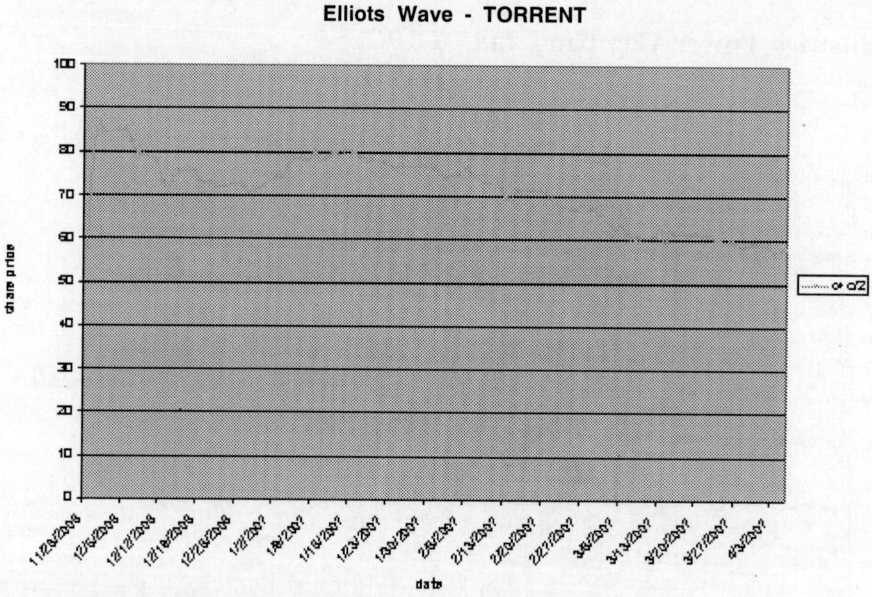

Chart: Torrent Power.

peaked during early December, but subsequently went for a nose- dive. During December 2006 – January 2007 the script remained full of repetitive wave structure with a downward trend making it a highly unpredictable stock. February 2007 remained as a bad month for selling owing to volatility and the declining trend in the market price. Overall, the script of Torrent Power reflected an unstable script which is not worth investing with a caution to hold investment till the market recovers.

CANDLE STICK MODEL

The Japanese have been using candle sticks since the 17th century to analyze rice prices. Candle sticks contain the same data as a normal bar chart but highlight the relationship between opening and closing prices. The narrow stick represents the range of prices traded during the period (high to low) while the broad mid-section represents the opening and closing prices for the period.

- If the close is higher than the open, the candle stick mid-section is hollow or shaded blue/green.

- If the open is higher than the close, the candle stick mid-section is filled in or shaded red.

Candle sticks

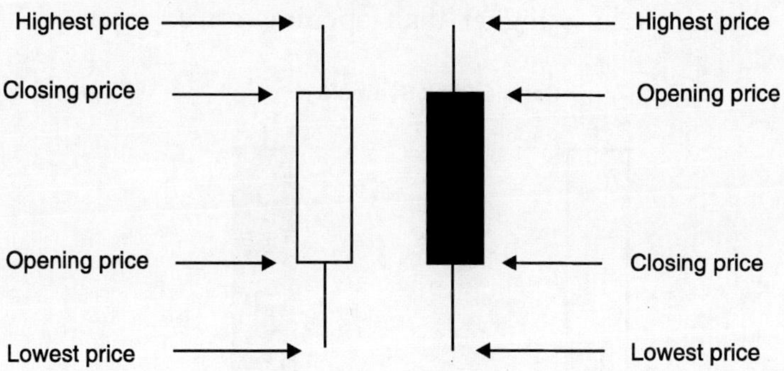

The body is filled if the open is higher than the close.

The advantage of candle sticks is the ability to highlight trend weakness and reversal signals that may not be apparent on a normal bar chart.

Candle: Shadow and Tail

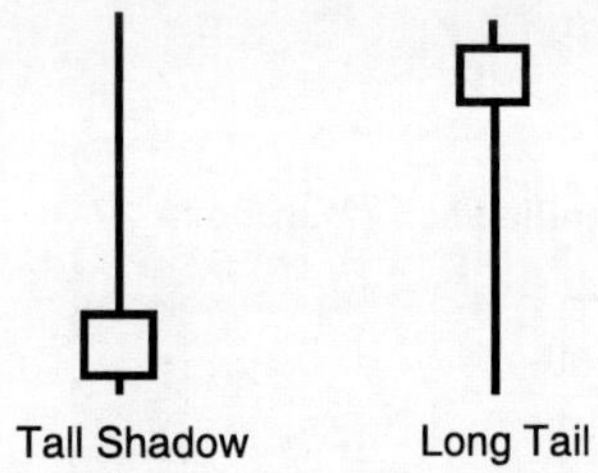

Shadow and Tail

The shadow is the portion of the trading range outside of the body. We often refer to a candle stick as having a *tall shadow* or a *long tail*.

- A tall shadow indicates resistance;
- A long tail signals support.

Candle Stick Colors

For improved presentation, people uses colors such as red and blue/green and black and white to indicate filled or hollow candle sticks:

- *Blue* (or green) candle stick if the close is higher than the *open;*
- *Red* candle stick if the *open* is higher than the *close* (i.e. the candle stick is filled);
- The same color as the previous day, if the *open* is equal to the *close.*
- *Black* color if closing price is lower than opening price.
- *White* color if closing price is higher than opening price.

Candle Stick Symbols

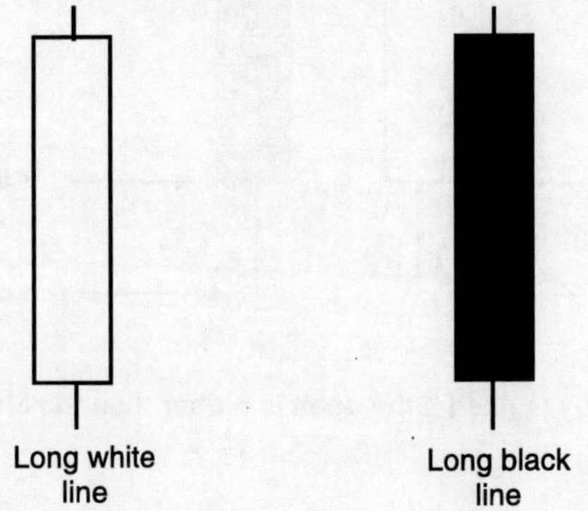

The long white line is a sign that buyers are firmly in control—a bullish candle stick. A long black line shows that sellers are in control—definitely bearish.

Marubozu Candle Sticks

Candle stick - Marubozu

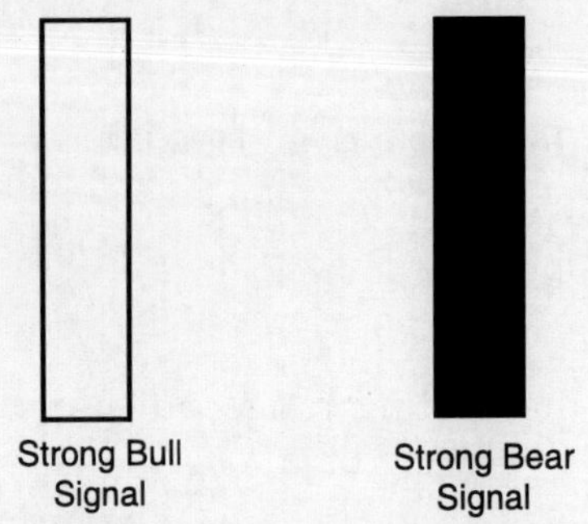

Marubozu are even stronger bull or bear signals than long lines as they show that buyers/sellers have remained in control from the open to the close — there are no intra-day retracements.

Doji Candle Sticks

Candle Stick - Doji

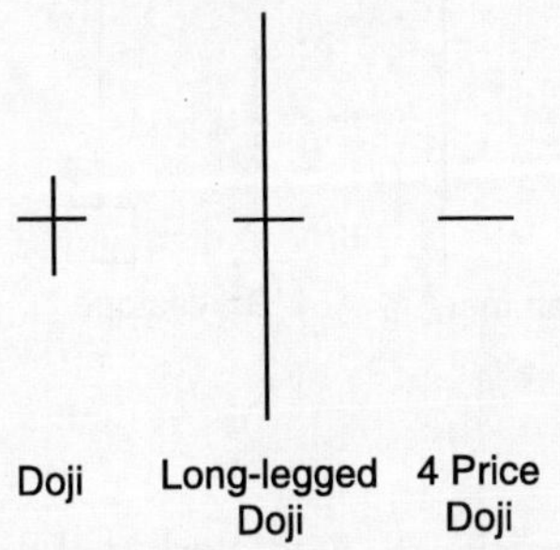

The Doji candle stick occurs when the open and closing price are equal.

An open and close **in the middle** of the candle stick signals indecision. Long-legged Dojis, when they occur after small candle sticks, indicate a surge in volatility and warn of a potential trend change. 4 Price Dojis, where the high and low are equal, are normally only seen on thinly traded stocks.

Dragonfly Candle Sticks

The dragonfly occurs when the open and close are near the top of the candle stick and signals reversal after a down-trend: control has shifted from sellers to buyers.

Dragonfly Candle Sticks

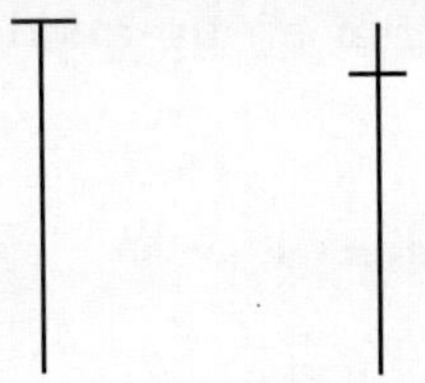

Signal reversal in a short-term down-trend

Hammer and Gravestone

The hammer is not as strong as the dragonfly candle stick, but also signals reversal after a down-trend: control has shifted from sellers to buyers. The shadow of the candle stick should be at least twice the height of the body.

A gravestone is identified by open and close near the bottom of the trading range. The candle stick is the converse of a hammer and signals reversal when it occurs after an up-trend.

Candle Stick Reversal Signals

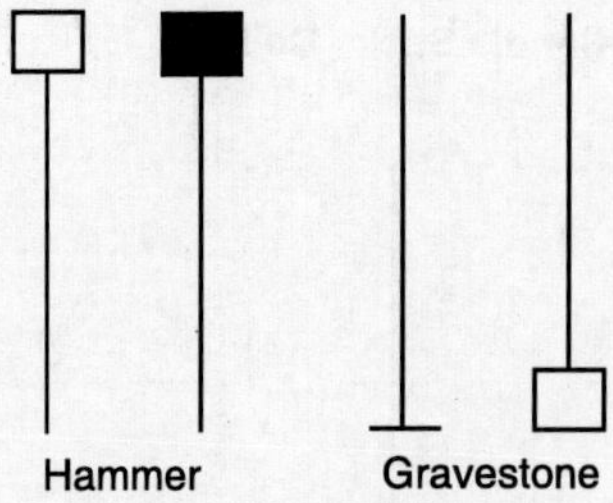

Hanging Man

A hammer that occurs after an up-trend is called a 'hanging man' and is a bearish signal.

Hanging Man Reversal

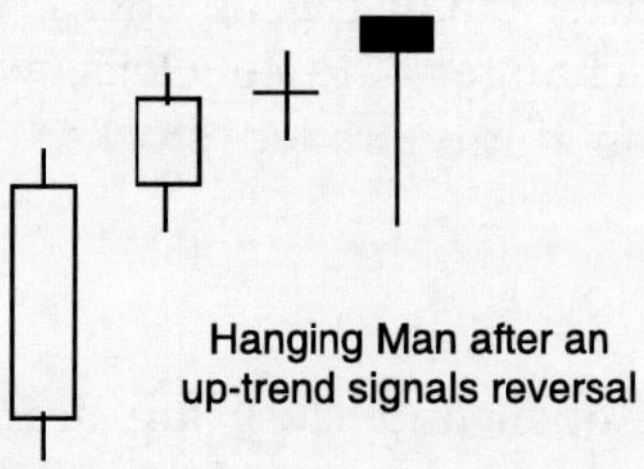

Dark Cloud

A Dark Cloud pattern encountered after an up-trend is a reversal signal, warning of "rainy days" ahead.

Dark Cloud Cover - Reversal

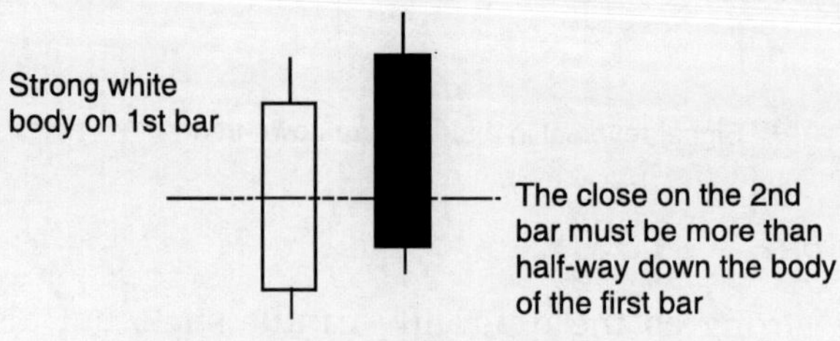

Reversal signal atter an up-trend

Piercing Line

The Piercing Line is the opposite of the Dark Cloud pattern and is a reversal signal if it appears after a down-trend.

Piercing Line - Reversal

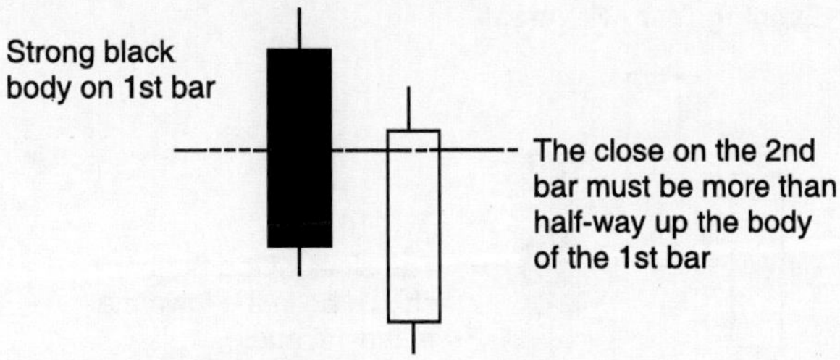

Reversal signal after a down-trend

Engulfing Candle Sticks

Engulfing patterns are where the body of the second candle stick 'engulfs' the first. They often follow or complete Doji, hammer or gravestone patterns and signal reversal in the short-term trend.

Engulfing Patterns

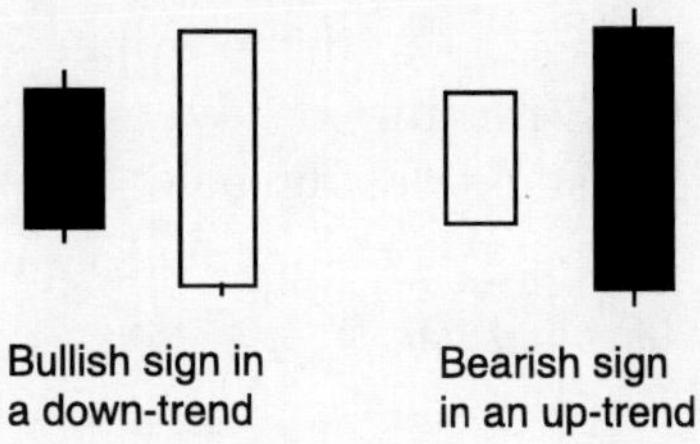

Star Formations

Stars are similar to gaps. A long body followed by a much shorter candle stick with a short body, where the bodies must not overlap though their shadows may.

Morning Star

The Morning Star pattern signals a bullish reversal after a down-trend. The first candle stick has a long black body. The second candle stick gaps down from the first (the bodies display a gap, but the shadows may still overlap) and is more bullish if hollow. The next candle stick has a long white body which closes in the top half of the body of the first candle stick.

Evening Star

The Evening Star pattern is opposite to Morning Star and is a reversal signal at the end of an up-trend. The pattern is more bearish if the second candle stick is filled rather than hollow.

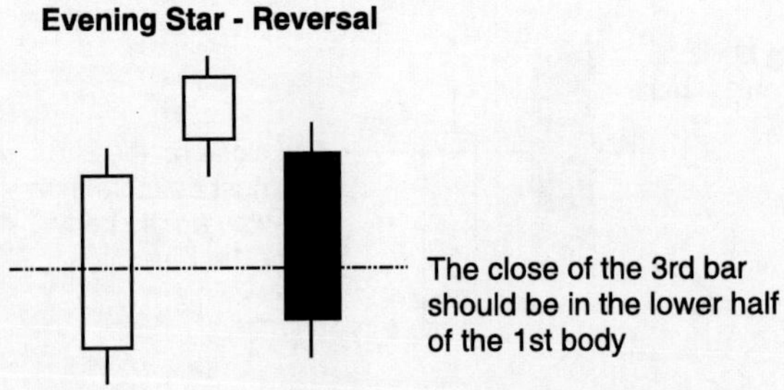

Doji Star

A Doji Star is weaker than the Morning or Evening Star: the Doji represents indecision. The Doji star requires confirmation from the next candle stick closing in the bottom half of the body of the first candle stick.

Shooting Star

With a Shooting Star, the body on the second candle stick must be near the low — at the bottom end of the trading range — and the upper must be taller. This is also a weaker reversal signal than the Morning or Evening Star. The pattern requires confirmation from the next candle stick closing below half-way on the body of the first.

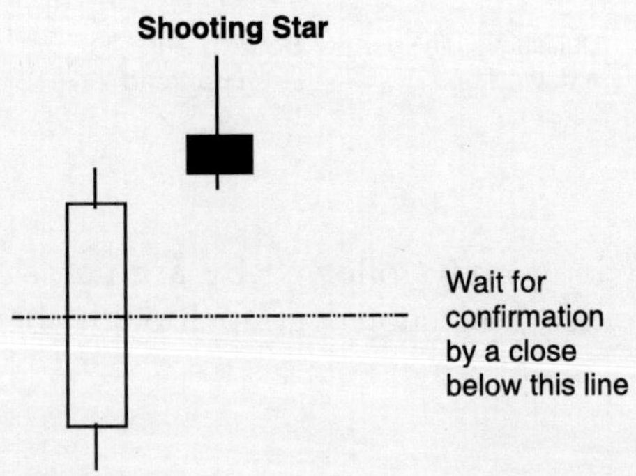

Harami Candle Stick

A Harami formation indicates loss of momentum and often warns of reversal after a strong trend. Harami means 'pregnant' which is quite descriptive. The second candle stick must be contained within the body of the first, though the shadows may protrude slightly.

Harami

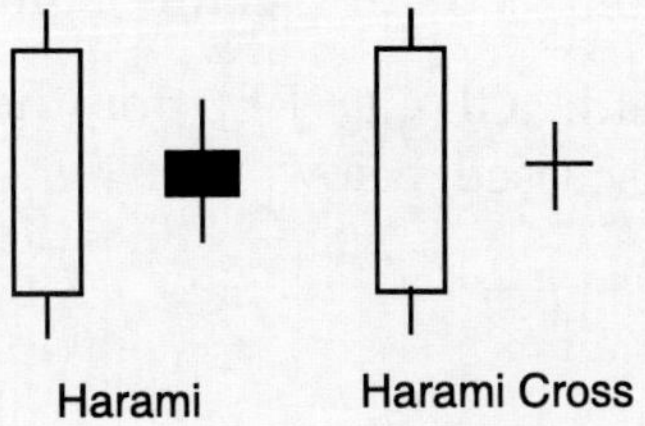

Rising Three Methods

The Rising Three Method consists of two strong white lines bracketing 3 or 4 small declining black candle sticks. The final white line forms a new closing high. The pattern is definitely bullish.

Rising Three Methods

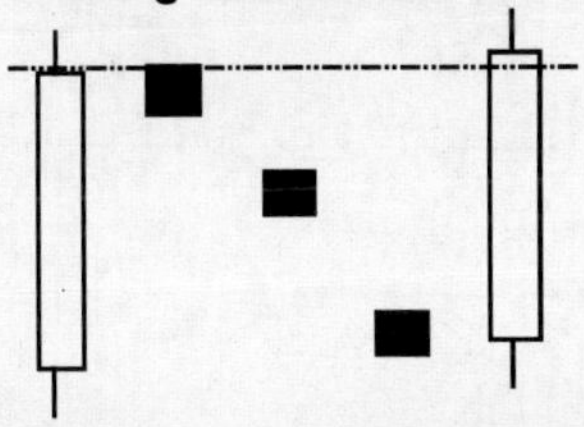

Bull signal when the second long white line closes above the body of the first line

Falling Three Methods

The bearish Falling Three Method consists of two long black lines bracketing 3 or 4 small ascending white candle sticks, the second black line forming a new closing low.

Falling Three Methods

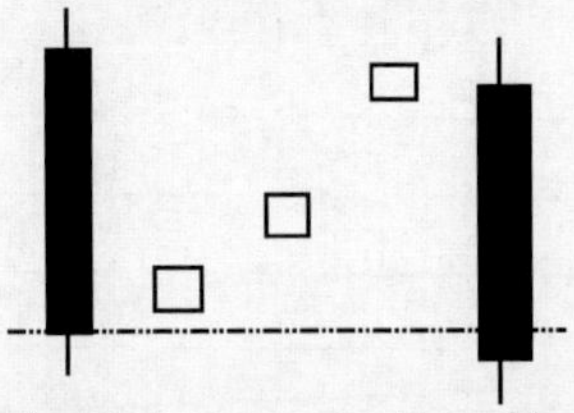

Bear signal when a second long black candle closes below the body of the first candle

Candle Stick Charts for Different Power Sector Companies

Candle stick graphs of NTPC Ltd., GIPCL, REL for the months of January 2007, February and March 2007 are discussed below:

NTPC Ltd.

January

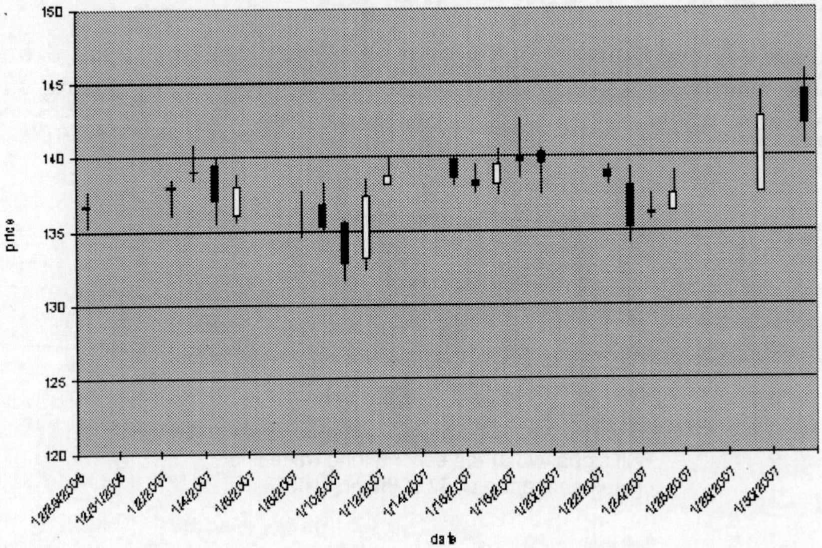

February

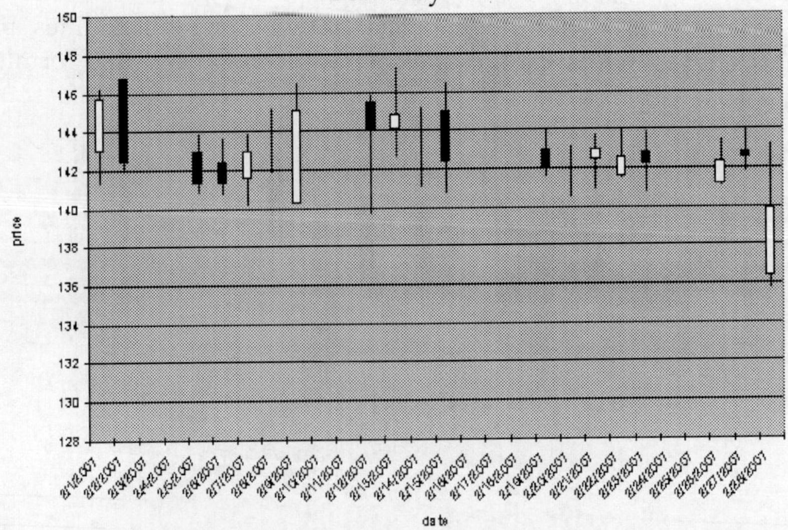

March

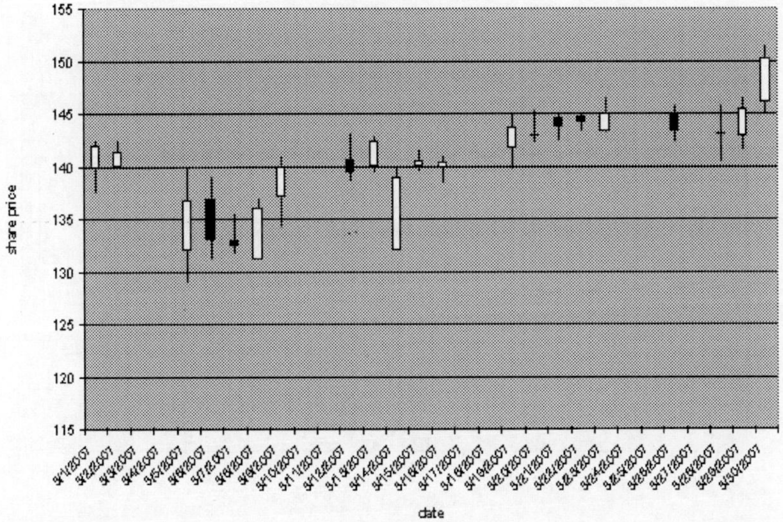

The share price behaviour shown in the above candle stick graph during January-March 2007, indicates that the script remained less volatile varying between Rs.130-160 range with little ups and downs. The white candle sticks outnumbered the blacks showing a bullish market trend for NTPC during the three months. But the wide variation in the size of the sticks indicates a high intra-day volatility. On earlier chapter on fundamental analysis, it was mentioned that NTPC has been a potentially strong company with the critical ratios on a favourable pitch. Overall, the script of NTPC reflects a stable script which is worth pursuing and worth investing

GIPCL

January

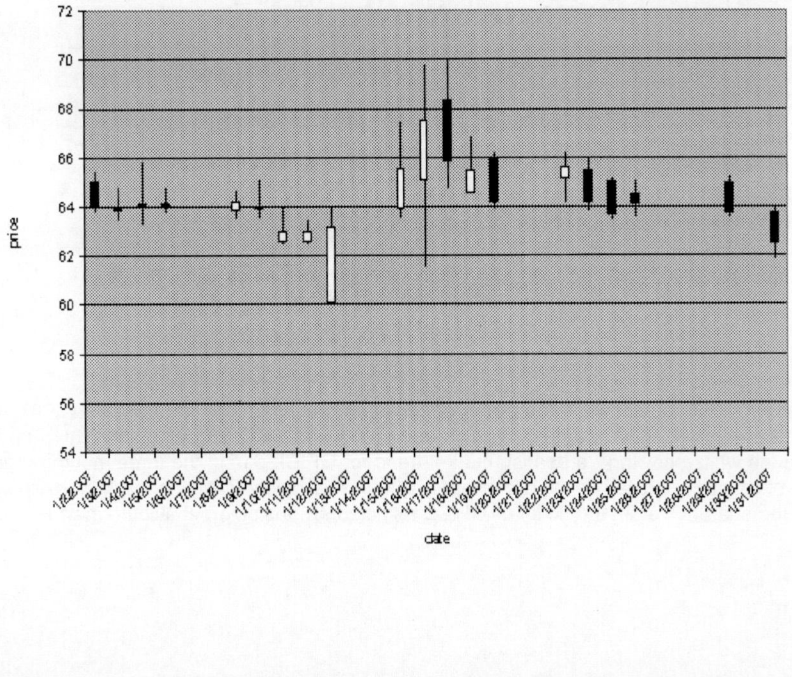

February

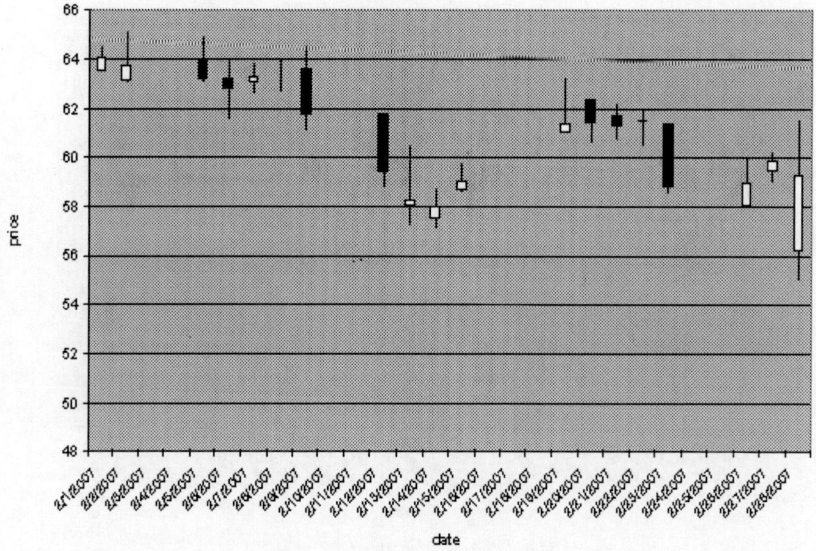

March

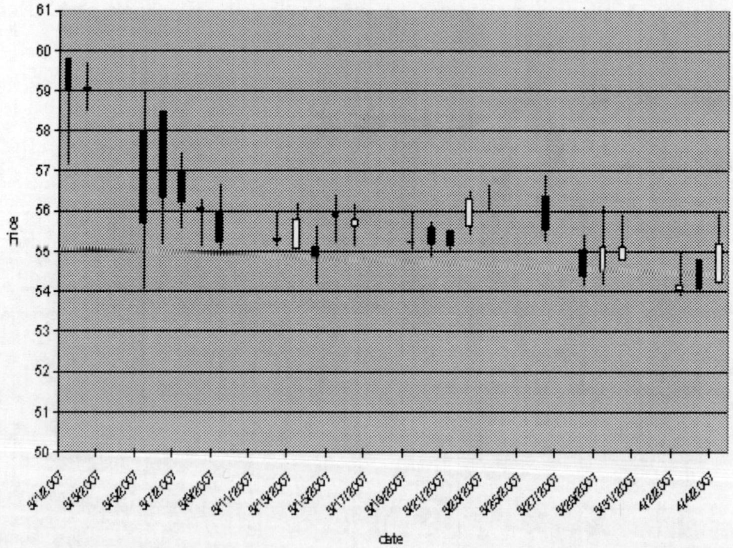

The share price behaviour GPICL shown in the above candle stick graph during January-March 2007, indicates that the script remained between Rs.50-70 range with high ups and downs exhibiting high volatility. The black candle sticks outnumbered the white showing a bearish market trend for GPICL during the three months. Again the wide variation in the size of the sticks indicated a high intra-day volatility. The wide variation in the flames reinforce the belief of high volatility of the share. Overall, the script of GPICL reflected an unstable behaviour which is, as a script, not worth investing.

REL

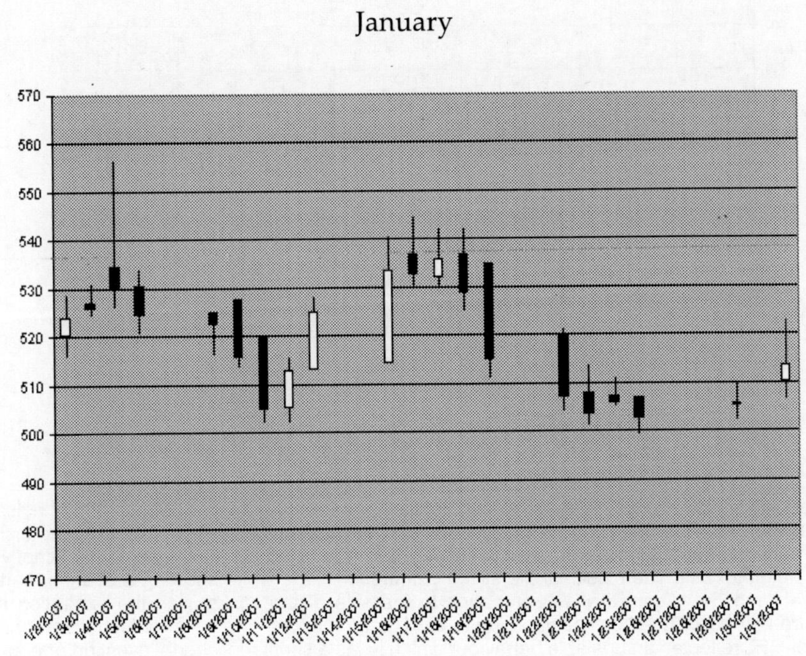
January
570
560
550
540
530
520
510
500
490
480
470

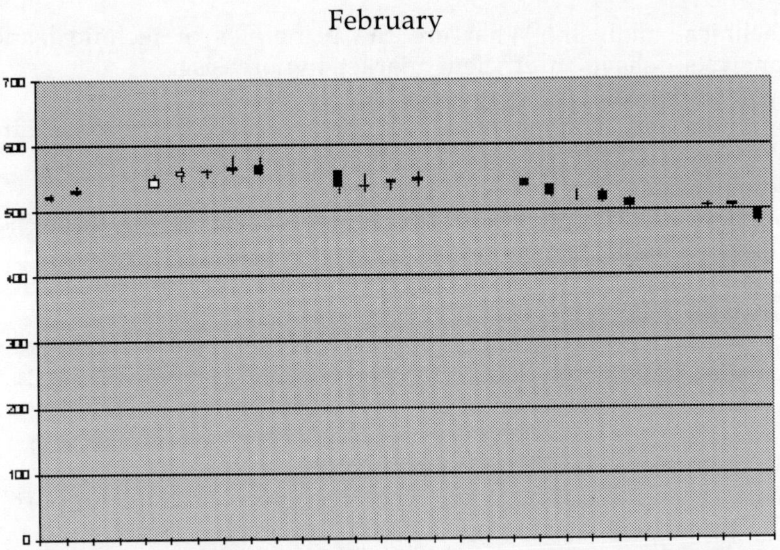
February
700
600
500
400
300
200
100
0

March

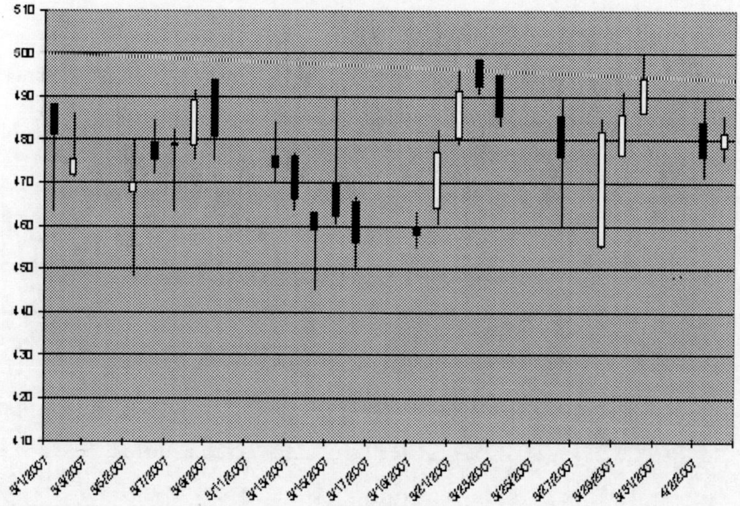

The share price behaviour REL shown in the above candle stick graph during January-March 2007, indicates that the script remained between Rs. 450-600 range with high ups and downs exhibiting high volatility. The sigle exception was February when the market price hovered around Rs.500 with little or no variation making the script worth buying on short term and not fit for sell. The black candle sticks outnumbered the white showing a bearish market trend for REL during the three months. Again the wide variation in the size of the sticks, with the exception of February, indicated a high intra-day volatility. The wide variation in the flames reinforce the belief of high volatility of the share. Overall, the script of REL reflected an unstable behaviour which is, as a script, not worth investing or not worth selling only during this period.

REVIEW QUESTIONS

1. What is technical analysis? What are the principles of technical analysis? Do technical analysts believe in efficient market hypothesis?
2. What do you understand by a reversal candle pattern?
3. Explain hammers and hanging man in context of one-day reversals from candle sticks.
4. Price moves in trends. Explain with example.
5. Explain the Dow theory and Elliot wave model? What is the difference between these two approaches?
6. What is market trend? When is market said to be bullish/bearish? Explain how technical analysis follow the trend?
7. How is exponential moving average different from simple moving average? Explain with the help of time series data.
8. What will you expect from a market whose prices has overshot the resistance recently?
9. Discuss the methods of oscillator interpretation.
10. Define resistance and support. When does resistance become support?
11. How far the prices will move from a trend line once a penetration occurs?
12. Which type of moving average—simple, weighted or exponential—is best and why?

13

Performance of Mutual Funds in India

INTRODUCTION

At times, the stock market booms so high that everyone wants to make money through investments. There are so many different avenues available to investors such as equity, debts and insurance. But mutual funds industry is emerging like a star in the financial market. Though it carries risk and is a small segment of the industry. The mutual fund industry is steadily growing.

The only thing which is certain in this capital market is uncertainty which leads to risk. The concept of mutual fund is to mitigate the risk for which it pools the small savings or investments of investors and invests the collected funds in various instruments like equity, debt and bonds spread across the various industries and sectors. This diversification reduces the risk of investors because all these instruments may not move in the same direction. The income generated from these investments is shared by all the investors in the proportion of their investments. A mutual fund appoints professionals who invest money in a way to increase the returns.

All mutual funds whether promoted by public sector or private sector entities including those promoted by foreign entities are governed by the same set of Regulations. There is no distinction in regulatory requirements for these mutual funds and all are subject to monitoring and inspections by SEBI. The risks associated with the schemes launched by the mutual funds sponsored by these entities are of similar type.

Understanding the Mutual Fund Concept

Economies of developing countries are growing fast. Simultaneously inflation and unemployment are also increasing. Today inflation is higher than bank's interest rate. So investing the money in the banks is not an intelligent investment. Here comes the stock market, which is booming. But this market is only for people who are experienced and for those who are informed investors. What for the household investors. Thanks to mutual funds, which are an intermediary between financial market and household investors.

A Mutual Fund is a trust that pools the savings of a number of investors who share a common financial goal. The money thus collected is then invested in capital market instruments such as shares, debentures and other securities. The income earned through these investments and the capital appreciation realized is shared by its unit holders in proportion to the number of units owned by them. Thus a Mutual Fund is the most suitable investment for the common man as it offers an opportunity to invest in a diversified, professionally managed basket of securities at a relatively low cost.

The concept of mutual funds is to mitigate the risk by allocating it among the different investors. For reducing the risk, it appoints professional fund managers who collect small household savings for a common financial objective and invest these collected funds in various instruments of capital market like equity, bonds and debts of various sectors of the industry. This diversification reduces risk involved in the investment, because all stock in which funds have been invested, may not move in the same direction. The appreciation of capital realized and return generated through this investment are shared by all the investors in the proportion of their money invested. Here one more benefit goes to investors, which is the cost of investing, because the cost of hiring the professionals is divided in the large number of investors.

To make the process of mutual funds easy, the investment is divided into units and the value of units is reflected as **Net Asset Value (NAV)**. Net Asset Value is market value of the securities attached with the mutual funds minus its expenses.

The charge collected by a Mutual Fund company from investors for buying and selling the units and investing in it, is called **load**. When the charges are collected at the time of entering into the scheme, it is called **entry load** or **front end load**. When the charges are collected at the time of redemption of the scheme, it is called **exit load** or **back end load**.

Background of Mutual Funds

The mutual fund industry traces its roots to England in the mid-1800s. The enactment of two British laws, the Joint Stock Companies Acts of 1862 and 1867, permitted investors, for the first time, to share in the profits of an investment enterprise, and limited investor liability to the amount of investment capital devoted to the enterprise. Shortly thereafter, in 1868, the Foreign and Colonial Government Trust was formed in London. The first pooled fund in the U.S. was created in 1893 for the faculty and staff of Harvard University.

The actual concept of mutual fund came when three Boston securities executives pooled their money together in 1924 to create the first mutual fund, they had no idea how popular mutual funds would become. On March 21st, 1924 the first official mutual fund was born. It was called the Massachusetts Investors Trust.

After one year, the Massachusetts Investors Trust grew from $50,000 in assets in 1924 to $392,000 in assets (with around 200 shareholders). In contrast, there are over

10,000 mutual funds in the U.S. today totaling around $7 trillion (with approximately 83 million individual investors) according to the Investment Company Institute.

The stock market crash of 1929 slowed the growth of mutual funds. In response to the stock market crash, Congress passed the Securities Act of 1933 and the Securities Exchange Act of 1934. These laws require that a fund be registered with the SEC and provide prospective investors with a prospectus. The SEC (U.S. Securities and Exchange Commission) helped create the Investment Company Act of 1940 which provides the guidelines that all funds must comply with today.

With renewed confidence in the stock market, mutual funds began to blossom. By the end of the 1960s there were around 270 funds with $48 billion in assets.

In 1976, John C. Bogle opened the first retail index fund called the First Index Investment Trust. It is now called the Vanguard 500 Index fund and in November of 2000 it became the largest mutual fund ever with $100 billion in assets.

One of the largest contributors of mutual fund growth was Individual Retirement Account (IRA) provisions made in 1981, allowing individuals (including those already in corporate pension plans) to contribute $2,000 a year. Mutual funds are now popular in employer-sponsored defined contribution retirement plans (401k), IRAs and Roth IRAs.

Mutual Fund Industry: A global scenario

The global mutual fund industry size is USD 22 trillion. The industry grew by 22.47% in 2006. US accounts for the 50% of the industry. Two major players in the industry are Luxemburg and France from Europe.

Worldwide, good mutual fund companies are known by their Asset Management Companies (AMCs) linked to their superior stock selection skills. For mutual funds to grow, AMCs must be held accountable for their selection of stocks. In other words, there must be some performance indicators that will reveal the quality of stock selection of various AMCs.

The Asian financial markets, considered emerging markets, are undergoing impressive growth and spectacular progress, making them the focus of both professional and academic interest. This increasing trading atmosphere could have lead, to both management companies and public regulations, to a misspecification of the denomination given to each mutual fund. The name given to the buyers could not always properly represent the style management of the fund. The aim of this study is to conduct research into the evolution of the mutual fund market in India in the last few years, thereby verifying to what extent they coincide with existing official classifications.

Most of the times, non-specialized investors base their decision of purchase on this public information before trusting their assets to professional management within the field of mutual funds and it may therefore influence the final decision to invest. By the empirical analysis presented in this work, evidence is found of certain inconsistencies between the investment objective classification and the return obtained by the fund when cluster analysis is applied. Groups established by this statistical technique differ from the classification presented by the Indian financial authorities. At the same time more satisfying results for public regulators of the Indian mutual fund market are found with a factor analysis, which distinguishes two main factors. The interpretation of one of these factors clearly points to the level of risk of the fund.

Global Mutual Funds Industry as a percentage of GDP.

Country	AUM at a % of GDP
India	8.19%
Australia	88.22%
Brazil	19.95%
Korea	31.17%
Taiwan	21.73%
United Kingdom	18.81%
USA	61.27%
Canada	34.33%
France	59.63%
Hong Kong	101.08%

Source: SBI Capital Market

Evolution of Mutual funds in India

The mutual funds industry has been growing very fast from the last decade. The development of the mutual fund industry can be divided into four phases:

Phase – 1st (1964-1987)

In 1963, the government of India passed an act in parliament and set up Unit Trust of India. All the regulatory and administrative controls of UTI was given to Reserve Bank of India. It was the commencement of mutual funds in India and UTI had the monopoly in the market. UTI commenced its operations from July 1964 "with a view to encouraging savings and investment and participation in the income, profits and gains accruing to the Corporation from the acquisition, holding, management and disposal of securities." Different provisions of the UTI Act laid down the structure of management, scope of business, powers and functions of the Trust as well as accounting, disclosures and regulatory requirements for the Trust. In 1964, UTI launched its first scheme which was named Unit 64. In 1978, after the entry of the Industrial Development Bank of India, all the control was taken away from Reserve Bank of India. This was the first phase of the mutual fund industry. The industry saw a slow growth in this period.

Phase – 2nd (1987-1993)

This phase started with the entry of public sector banks, Life Insurance Corporation of India and General Insurance Corporation of India in the industry, setting up their own mutual funds in 1987. From the entry of other players in the market, UTI felt some heat, but remain the leader with 87% of market share. Industry saw a little faster growth in this period.

Phase – 3rd (1993-2003)

It was a new scene of the industry, because of the entry of private mutual funds. This phase gave various choices to investors for investing in mutual funds. As a safeguard for investors, SEBI stepped in the game. All the regulatory and administrative controls of public and private sector mutual funds were given to SEBI. These regulations were more comprehensive and revised. The erstwhile Kothari Pioneer (now merged with Franklin Templeton) was the first private player in the market registered in 1993. The opening up of the industry attracted international mutual fund player towards Indian market. The major player like Morgan Stanley, J P Morgan, Jardine Fleming and George Soros joined the race. Industry started blossoming with the fast growth. But in 2003, industry saw its worst face.

The industry faced its toughest challenge when the US 64 fiasco shattered the confidence of investors. However, in 2003, the government bifurcated the erstwhile UTI. One entity manages the assets of US 64 and some assured return schemes. The other is a regular mutual fund working under the SEBI regulations. Thanks to the boom in the stock market, UTI managed to clean up its act and continue to enjoy the confidence of several investors. The whole industry also came out of the controversy without any major setbacks.

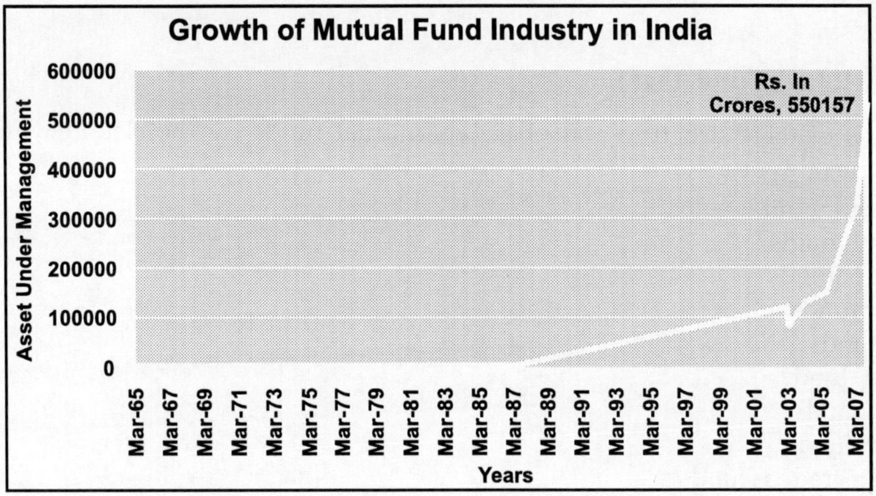

Source: Association of Mutual Funds in India

Current Scenario and Trends of Mutual Fund Industry in India

The mutual fund industry in India is growing at a healthy rate of 19% whereas its worldwide growth rate is 13%. Indian MF industry, which owned assets worth around Rs 5 lakh crore until about September 2007, may end up notching assets size of about Rs 6 lakh crore by March 2008, as it has started expanding its penetration in smaller towns with vigorous speed, reported a study conducted by ASSOCHAM projects.

Asset under Management (AUM) as percentage of GDP in India is 4.12 per cent as against 88.22 per cent in Australia, Germany 10.54 per cent, Japan 7.57 per cent, USA 61.27 per cent, Canada 34.33 per cent, France 59.63 per cent and Brazil 19.95 per cent. The industry overall has performed well over the years. Of course, there were a few funds houses, which disappointed investors. However, overall performance has been good. However, lack of awareness still impedes the growth of the mutual fund industry. Unlike developed countries, most of the household savings still go to bank deposits in India.

Over the past year or so, competition in the market there are 32 funds houses with more than 1,500 schemes vying for investor's attention today has more or less standardized the entry load for equity funds at about 2.25 percent. But in developed markets such as the US, no-load funds which do not charge investors for entering a fund, are hugely popular. Indian AMCs have borrowed every other fund concept such as thematic, gold, exchange traded, sector index and fund-of-funds, from the US, but haven't yet given investors a no-load fund. Mutual funds, however, do not mind exempting large investors bringing Rs 5 crore and more from entry loads. So, in January this year, SEBI asked mutual fund companies not to charge any load from small investors who approached them directly for buying units, instead of going via brokers. At least, fragmented investors now have a window to by funds without entry costs.

Types of Mutual Fund (MF)

On the basis of their structure and objective, mutual funds can be classified into the following major types:

- Closed-end funds
- Open-end funds
- Large cap funds
- Mid-cap funds
- Equity funds
- Balanced funds
- Growth funds
- No load funds
- Exchange traded funds
- Value funds

- Money market funds
- International mutual funds
- Regional mutual funds
- Sector funds
- Index funds
- Fund of funds

Closed-End Mutual Funds

A closed-end mutual fund has a set number of shares issued to the public through an initial public offering. These funds have a stipulated maturity period generally ranging from 3 to 15 years. Subscription for this fund is open only for a specified period. Investors can invest in the scheme at the time of the initial public issue and thereafter they can buy or sell the units of the scheme on the stock exchanges where they are listed.

Once underwritten, these funds are traded in stock exchanges like stocks or bonds. The market price of funds is determined by supply and demand and not by net-asset value (NAV). Usually closed mutual funds trade at discounts to their underlying asset value.

Open End Mutual Fund

It is a fund that does not have a set number of shares. It continues to sell shares to investors and will buy back shares when investors wish to sell. Units are bought and sold at their current net asset value. These funds keep some portion of their assets in short-term and money market securities to provide available funds for redemptions. A major portion of these funds are invested in highly liquid securities.

Large Cap Funds

These mutual funds seek capital appreciation by investing primarily in stocks of large blue chip companies with above-average prospects for earnings growth. Different mutual funds have different criteria for classifying companies as large cap. Generally, companies with a market capitalization in excess of Rs 1000 crore are known as large cap companies. Investing in large caps is a lower risk-lower return proposition because such companies are usually widely researched and information is widely available.

Mid Cap Funds

These funds are those mutual funds, which invest in small / medium sized companies. As there is no standard definition classifying companies as small or medium, each mutual fund has its own classification for small and medium sized companies. Generally, companies with a market capitalization of up to Rs 500 crore are classified as small. Those companies that have a market capitalization between Rs 500 crore and Rs 1,000 crore are classified as medium sized.

Big investors like mutual funds and Foreign Institutional Investors are increasingly investing in mid caps nowadays because the price of large caps has increased substantially. Small / mid sized companies tend to be under-researched thus they present an opportunity to invest in a company that is yet to be identified by the market. Such companies offer higher growth potential going forward and therefore an opportunity to benefit from higher than average valuations. But mid cap funds are very volatile and tend to fall like a pack of cards in bad times. So, caution should be exercised while investing in mid cap mutual funds.

Equity Mutual Funds

Also known as stock mutual funds. Equity mutual funds invest pooled amounts of money in the stocks of public companies. Fund managers follow two different approaches while picking up the stock, one based on value and another on growth. In first case, they search for a company whose stocks are undervalued, when compared to other, similar companies. While in latter approach, they try to find that stock which are growing faster than the competitors, or market as a whole. Some managers buy both kinds of stocks while making the portfolio.

Balanced Fund

Also known as hybrid fund. It buys a combination of common stock, preferred stock, bonds, and short-term bonds, to provide both income and capital appreciation while avoiding excessive risk.

Balanced funds provide the investor with an option of single mutual fund that combines both growth and income objectives, by investing in both stocks (for growth) and bonds (for income). Such diversified holdings ensure that these funds will manage downturns in the stock market without too much of a loss. But on the flip side, balanced funds will usually increase less than an all-stock fund during a bull market.

Growth Funds

Mostly preferable for aggressive investors. These funds aim to achieve capital appreciation by investing in growth stocks. They focus on those companies, which are experiencing significant earnings or revenue growth, rather than companies that pay out dividends. They tend to look for the fastest-growing companies in the market. Growth managers are willing to take more risk and pay a premium for their stocks in an effort to build a portfolio of companies with above-average earnings momentum or price appreciation. In general, growth funds are more volatile than other types of funds, rising more than other funds in bull markets and falling more in bear markets.

No-Load Mutual Funds

Mutual funds can be classified into two types : Load mutual funds and No-Load mutual funds. Load funds are those funds that charge commission at the time of purchase or redemption. They can be further subdivided into (1) Front-end load funds and (2) Back-end load funds. Front-end load funds charge commission at the time of purchase and back-end load funds charge commission at the time of redemption.

On the other hand, no-load funds are those funds that can be purchased without commission. No-load funds have several advantages over load funds. Firstly, funds with loads, on an average, consistently underperforms no-load funds when the load is taken into consideration in performance calculations. Secondly, loads understate the real commission charged because they reduce the total amount being invested. Finally, when a load fund is held over a long time period, the effect of the load, if paid up front, is not diminished because if the money paid for the load had invested, as in a no-load fund, it would have been compounding over the whole time period.

Exchange Traded Funds

ETF represent a basket of securities that are traded on an exchange. An exchange traded fund is similar to an index fund in that it will primarily invest in the securities of companies that are included in a selected market index. An ETF will invest in either all of the securities or a representative sample of the securities included in the index. The investment objective of an ETF is to achieve the same return as a particular market index.

Exchange traded funds rely on an arbitrage mechanism to keep the prices at which they trade roughly in line with the net asset values of their underlying portfolios.

Value Funds

These mutual funds that tend to focus on safety rather than growth, and often choose investments providing dividends as well as capital appreciation. They invest in companies that the market has overlooked, and stocks that have fallen out of favors with mainstream investors, either due to changing investor preferences, a poor quarterly earnings report, or hard times in a particular industry. Value stocks are often mature companies that have stopped growing and that use their earnings to pay dividends. Thus value funds produce current income (from the dividends) as well as long-term growth (from capital appreciation once the stocks become popular again). They tend to have more conservative and less volatile returns than growth funds.

Money Market Mutual Funds

A money market fund is a mutual fund that invests solely in money market instruments. Money market instruments are forms of debt that mature in less than one year and are very liquid. Treasury bills make up the bulk of the money market instruments. Securities in the money market are relatively risk-free. These funds are generally the safest and most secure of mutual fund investments. The goal of a money-market fund is to preserve principal while yielding a modest return. Money-market mutual fund is akin to a high-yield bank account but is not entirely risk free. While investing in these funds the interest rates should be taken care of.

International Mutual Funds

These funds invest in non-domestic securities markets throughout the world. Investing in international markets provides greater portfolio diversification and let you capitalize on some of the world's best opportunities. If investments are chosen carefully, international mutual fund may be profitable when some markets are rising and others are declining.

However, fund managers need to keep close watch on foreign currencies and world markets as profitable investments in a rising market can lose money if the foreign currency rises against the dollar. More care should be taken care, when going for international investment option, because a large number of variables would also affect the returns, like inflation rate, exchange rate, political stability etc.

Regional Mutual Fund

These funds confine themselves to investments in securities from a specified geographical area, usually, the fund's local region. A regional mutual fund generally looks to own a diversified portfolio of companies based in and operating out of its specified geographical area. The objective is to take advantage of regional growth potential before the national investment community does. These funds select securities that pass geographical criteria. For the investor, the primary benefit of a regional fund is that he/she increases his/her diversification by being exposed to a specific foreign geographical area.

Sector Mutual Funds

Sector mutual funds are those mutual funds that restrict their investments to a particular segment or sector of the economy. These funds concentrate on one industry such as infrastructure, heathcare, utilities, pharmaceuticals etc. The idea is to allow investors to place bets on specific industries or sectors, which have strong growth potential.

These funds tend to be more volatile than funds holding a diversified portfolio of securities in many industries. Such concentrated portfolios can produce tremendous gains or losses, depending on whether the chosen sector is in or out of favour.

Index Funds

An index fund is a type of mutual fund that builds its portfolio by buying stock in all the companies of a particular index and thereby reproducing the performance of an entire section of the market. The most popular index of stock index funds is the Standard & Poor's 500. An S&P 500 stock index fund owns 500 stocks—all the companies that are included in the index. Investing in an index fund is a form of passive investing. Passive investing has two big advantages over active investing. First, a passive stock market mutual fund is much cheaper to run than an active fund. Second, a majority of mutual funds fail to beat broad indexes such as the S&P 500.

Fund of Funds (FOF)

A FOF is a type of mutual fund that invests in other mutual funds. Just as a mutual fund invests in a number of different securities, a fund of funds holds shares of many different mutual funds.

FOFs are designed to achieve greater diversification than traditional mutual funds. But on the flipside, expense fees on FOF are typically higher than those on regular funds because they include part of the expense fees charged by the underlying funds. Also, since a fund of funds buys many different funds which themselves invest in many different stocks, it is possible for the fund of funds to own the same stock through several different funds and it can be difficult to keep track of the overall holdings.

The Performance of Mutual Funds in India

The performance of mutual funds in India in the initial phase was not even closer to satisfactory level. People rarely understood, and of course investing was out of question. But yes, some 24 million shareholders were accustomed with guaranteed high returns by the beginning of liberalization of the industry in 1992. This good record of UTI became marketing tool for new entrants. The expectations of investors touched the sky in profitability factor. However, people were miles away from the preparedness' of risks factor after the liberalization.

The Assets under Management of UTI was Rs. 67bn. by the end of 1987. Let us concentrate about the performance of mutual funds in India through figures. From Rs. 67bn. the Assets under Management rose to Rs. 470 bn. in March 1993 and the figure had a three times higher performance by April 2004. It rose as high as Rs. 1,540bn.

ASSETS UNDER MANAGEMENT AS ON 31st MARCH, 2007 ***(Rs. in Crore)***

Category & Typewise

	Open End	Close End	Total	% to Total
Income	30894	88428	119322	36
Growth	96357	17029	113386	35
Balanced	7409	1701	9110	3
Liquid/Money Market	72006	-	72006	22
Gilt	2257	-	2257	1
ELSS	8398	1813	10211	3
Gold ETF	96	-	96	@
Total	217417	108971	326388	100

@ Less than1%

ASSETS UNDER MANAGEMENT AS ON 31st MARCH, 2003 ***(Rs. in Crore)***

Category & Typewise

	Open End	Close End	Assured return	Total
Income	46587	617	360	47564
Growth	8041	1846	-	9887
Balanced	2449	692	-	3141
Liquid/Money Market	13734	-	-	13734
Gilt	3910	-	-	3910
ELSS	350	878	-	1228
Total	75071	4033	360	79464

Source: amfiindia.com (Association of Mutual Fund of India)

The above table depicts the phenomenal growth of Mutual funds in India during 2003-07 in its totality and in each category as well. While the year 1993 captures the low performance of MFs due to low stock market index arising out of stock scam and low economic growth the appreciably high growth during 2007 can be attributable to high growth of economy, FII investments, private equity and several other factors. MF generally consists of four separate entities, namely, sponsor, mutual fund trust, AMC and custodian. Mutual Fund industry has come a very long way. The growth in AUM speaks about the prominence. In a span of just five years the industry's AUM has increased from Rs. 79464 crores in March 2003 to Rs 3,26,388 crores by March 2007. This has been due to the increase in number of players and schemes offered to the investors. By seeing the recent performance of AMC, it can be said that both the investors and AMC have been the winners.

For example, MF AUM's soars to Rs. 3, 50,000 crores in April 2007 with Reliance Mutual Fund with asset over Rs. 48,000 crores as the largest fund house. ICICI prudential MF is at the second position with AUM at Rs. 42,268 crores. Though public sector UTI MF saw a fall of around Rs. 66 crores in AUM at Rs. 35,517 crores is at third rank. HDFC MF is at fourth rank with AUM of Rs.31, 485 crores and Franklin Templeton stood at fifth rank with AUM of worth Rs. 24,510 crores.

The returns in each category in the above table has shown increasing trend. Usually, the return on a mutual fund is calculated through Net Asset Value (NAV), which is explained below.

Net Asset Value (NAV)

NAV represents the Market value of each unit of Mutual fund.

$$\text{NAV} = \frac{\text{Market Value of all investments made by Mutual Fund} - \text{incidental expences}}{\text{Number of units issued to investors}}$$

NAV is affected by many factors such as expenses incurred by schemes, dividends declared, fresh sales and repurchase of units and bonuses issued etc.

The net asset value (NAV) of mutual funds in India declined when stock prices started falling in the year 1992. Those days, the market regulations did not allow portfolio shifts into alternative investments. There were rather no choice apart from holding the cash or to further continue investing in shares. One more thing to be noted, since only closed-end funds were floated in the market, the investors disinvested by selling at a loss in the secondary market.

The supervisory authority adopted a set of measures to create a transparent and competitive environment in mutual funds. Some of them were like relaxing investment restrictions into the market, introduction of open-ended funds, and paving the gateway for mutual funds to launch pension schemes.

The measure was taken to make mutual funds the key instrument for long-term saving. The more the variety offered, the quantitative will be investors. At last to mention, as long as mutual fund companies are performing with lower risks and higher profitability within a short span of time, more and more people will be inclined to invest until and unless they are fully educated with the dos and don'ts of mutual funds.

We have already learned that mutual funds pool the money of the investors and invest the same in stocks, bonds, dividends, short-term money market instruments, and/or other securities. In a mutual fund, the fund manager trades the fund's underlying securities, realizing capital gains or losses, and collects the dividend or interest income. The investment proceeds are then passed along to the individual investors. The value of a share of the mutual fund, known as the net asset value per share (NAV), is calculated daily based on the total value of the fund divided by the number of shares currently issued and outstanding.

Since their creation, mutual funds have been a popular investment vehicle for investors. Their simplicity along with other attributes provide great benefit to investors with limited knowledge, time, or money. To help you decide whether mutual funds are best for you and your situation, we are going to look at some reasons why you might want to consider investing in mutual funds.

ADVANTAGES OF MUTUAL FUNDS

Diversification

One rule of investing that both large and small investors should follow is asset diversification. Used to manage risk, diversification involves the mixing of investments within a portfolio. For example, by choosing to buy stocks in the retail sector and offsetting them with stocks in the industrial sector, you can reduce the impact of the performance of any one security on your entire portfolio. To achieve a truly diversified portfolio, you may have to buy stocks with different capitalizations from different industries and bonds having varying maturities from different issuers. For the individual investor this can be quite costly.

By purchasing mutual funds, you are provided with the immediate benefit of instant diversification and asset allocation without the large amounts of cash needed to create individual portfolios. One caveat (beware), however, is that simply purchasing one mutual fund might not give you adequate diversification — check to see if the fund is sector or industry specific. For example, investing in an oil and energy mutual fund might spread your money over fifty companies, but if energy prices fall, your portfolio will likely suffer.

Economies of Scale

The easiest way to understand economies of scale is by thinking about volume discounts: in many stores the more of one product you buy, the cheaper that product becomes.

For example, when you buy a dozen donuts, the price per donut is usually cheaper than buying a single one. This occurs also in the purchase and sale of securities. If you buy only one security at a time, the transaction fees will be relatively large.

Mutual funds are able to take advantage of their buying and selling size and thereby reduce transaction costs for investors. When you buy a mutual fund, you are able to diversify without the numerous commission charges. Imagine if you had to buy the 10-20 stocks needed for diversification. The commission charges alone would eat up a good chunk of your savings. Add to this the fact that you would have to pay more transaction fees every time you wanted to modify your portfolio — as you can see the costs begin to add up. Mutual funds are able to make transactions on a much larger scale (and cheaper).

Divisibility

Many investors don't have the exact sums of money to buy round lots of securities. One to two hundred dollars is usually not enough to buy a round lot of a stock, especially after deducting commissions. Investors can purchase mutual funds in smaller denominations, ranging from $100 to $1000 minimums. So, rather than having to wait until you have enough money to buy higher-cost investments, you can get in right away with mutual funds. This leads us to the next advantage.

Liquidity

Another advantage of mutual funds is the ability to get in and out with relative ease. You can sell mutual funds at any time as they are as liquid as regular stocks. Both the liquidity and smaller denominations of mutual funds provide mutual fund investors the opportunity to make periodic investments through monthly purchase plans while taking advantage of dollar-cost averaging.

Professional Management

When we buy a mutual fund, we are also choosing a professional money manager. This manager will use the money that you invest to buy and sell stocks that he or she has carefully researched. Therefore, rather than having to research thoroughly every investment before you decide to buy or sell, you have a mutual fund's money manager to handle it for you.

As with any investment, there are risks involved in buying mutual funds. These investment vehicles can experience market fluctuations and sometimes provide returns below the overall market. Also, the advantages gained from mutual funds are not free: many of them carry loads, annual expense fees and penalties for early withdrawal. In the next article we will take a closer look at some of these drawbacks so you can decide if mutual funds are right for you.

DISADVANTAGES OF MUTUAL FUNDS

Fluctuating Returns

Mutual funds are like many other investments without a guaranteed return. There is always the possibility that the value of your mutual fund will depreciate. Unlike fixed-income products, such as bonds and Treasury bills, mutual funds experience price fluctuations along with the stocks that make up the fund. When deciding on a particular fund to buy, you need to research the risks involved — just because a professional manager is looking after the fund, that doesn't mean the performance will be stellar.

Another important thing to know is that mutual funds are not guaranteed by the

U.S. government, so in the case of dissolution, you won't get anything back. This is especially important for investors in money market funds. Unlike a bank deposit, a mutual fund will not be FDIC insured.

Diversification

Although diversification is one of the keys to successful investing, many mutual fund investors tend to over-diversify. The idea of diversification is to reduce the risks associated with holding a single security; over-diversification occurs when investors acquire many funds that are highly related and so don't get the risk reducing benefits of diversification. To read more on this subject, at the other extreme, just because you own mutual funds doesn't mean you are automatically diversified. For example, a fund that invests only in a particular industry or region is still relatively risky.

Cash, Cash and More Cash

As you know already, mutual funds pool money from thousands of investors, so everyday investors are putting money into the fund as well as withdrawing investments. To maintain liquidity and the capacity to accommodate withdrawals, funds typically have to keep a large portion of their portfolio as cash. Having ample cash is great for liquidity, but money sitting around as cash is not working for you and thus is not very advantageous.

Costs

Mutual funds provide investors with professional management; however, it comes at a cost. Funds will typically have a range of different fees that reduce the overall payout. In mutual funds the fees are classified into two categories: shareholder fees and annual fund-operating fees.

The shareholder fees, in the forms of loads and redemption fees, are paid directly by shareholders purchasing or selling the funds. The annual fund operating fees are charged at an annual percentage — usually ranging from 1-3%. These fees are assessed to mutual fund investors regardless of the performance of the fund. As you can imagine, in years when the fund doesn't make money these fees only magnify losses.

Misleading Advertisements

The misleading advertisements of different funds can guide investors down the wrong path. Some funds may be incorrectly labeled as growth funds, while others are classified as small-cap or income. The SEC (Securities and Exchange Commission) requires funds to have at least 80% of assets in the particular type of investment implied in their names. The remaining assets are under the discretion solely of the fund manager.

The different categories that qualify for the required 80% of the assets, however, may be vague and wide-ranging. A fund can therefore manipulate prospective investors by using names that are attractive and misleading. Instead of labeling itself a small cap, a fund may be sold under the heading growth fund.

Evaluating Funds

Another disadvantage of mutual funds is the difficulty they pose for investors interested in researching and evaluating the different funds. Unlike stocks, mutual funds do not offer investors the opportunity to compare the P/E ratio, sales growth, earnings per share, etc. A mutual fund's net asset value gives investors the total value of the fund's portfolio less liabilities, but how do you know if one fund is better than another?

Furthermore, advertisements, rankings and ratings issued by fund companies only describe past performance. Always note that mutual fund descriptions/advertisements always include the tagline "past results are not indicative of future returns". Be sure not to pick funds only because they have performed well in the past — yesterday's big winners may be today's big losers. Whenever an investor plans to buy any investment, it's important to understand both the good and bad points. If the advantages that the investment offers outweigh its disadvantages, it's quite possible that mutual funds are something to consider. Whether you decide in favor or against mutual funds, the probability of a successful portfolio increases dramatically when you do your homework.

14

Subprime Crisis and Securitisation

THE EVOLUTION OF US MORTGAGE MARKET

One of the primary ways to build wealth for an individual is having an ownership of a home. The US mortgage-backed securities market is the largest fixed income market in the world, with over $8 trillion outstanding followed by US treasury market with around $5 trillion outstanding. In 1995 in US, the typical household held no corporate equity implying that most households found it difficult to invest in anything but their home. As homeownership is such a significant economic factor, a great deal of attention is paid to the mortgage market. Subprime lending is a relatively new and rapidly growing segment of the mortgage market that expands the pool of credit to borrowers who, for a variety of reasons, would otherwise be denied credit. For instance, those potential borrowers who would fail credit history requirements in the standard (prime) mortgage market have greater access to credit in the subprime market.

Two of the major benefits of this type of lending, then, are the increased numbers of homeowners and the opportunity for these homeowners to create wealth. Of course, this expanded access comes with a price: At its simplest, subprime lending can be described as high-cost lending. Borrower cost associated with subprime lending is driven primarily by two factors: credit history and down payment requirements. Down payment alone, given that minimum credit history requirements are satisfied. Owing to its complicated nature, subprime lending is simultaneously viewed as having great promise and great peril. The promise of subprime lending is that it can provide the opportunity for homeownership to those who were either subject to discrimination or could not qualify for a mortgage in the past. In fact, subprime lending is most prevalent in neighborhoods with high concentrations of minorities and weaker economic conditions.

However, because poor credit history is associated with substantially more delinquent payments and defaulted loans, the interest rates for subprime loans are substantially higher than those for prime loans and, as a result, subprime borrowers have a harder time taking advantage of available cheaper financing.

The Mortgage Bankers Association of America (MBAA) reports that subprime loans in the third quarter of 2002 had a delinquency rate 51/2 times higher than that for prime loans (14.28 versus 2.54 percent) and the rate at which foreclosures were begun for subprime loans was more than 10 times that for prime loans (2.08 versus 0.20 percent).

Therefore, the propensity of borrowers of subprime loans to fail as homeowners (default on the mortgage) is much higher than for borrowers of prime loans. This failure can lead to reduced access to financial markets, foreclosure, and loss of any equity and wealth achieved through mortgage payments and house price appreciation. In addition, any concentration of foreclosed property can potentially adversely impact the value of property in the neighborhood as a whole. Traditionally, the mortgage market set minimum lending standards based on a borrower's income, payment history, down payment, and the local underwriter's knowledge of the borrower. This approach can best be characterized as using nonprice credit rationing. However, the subprime market has introduced many different pricing tiers and product types, which has helped to move the mortgage market closer to price rationing, or risk based pricing. The success of the subprime market will in part determine how fully the mortgage market eventually incorporates pure price rationing (i.e., risk-based prices for each borrower).

The expansion of subprime mortgage lending has made homeownership possible for households that in the past might not have qualified for a mortgage and has thereby contributed to the rise in the homeownership rate since the mid-1990s. In 2006, 69 percent of households owned their homes; in 1995, 65 percent did. The increase in homeownership has been broadly based, but minority households and households in lower-income census tracts have recorded some of the largest gains in percentage terms. Not only the new homeowners but also their communities have benefited from these trends. Studies point to various ways in which homeownership helps strengthen neighborhoods. For example, homeowners are more likely than renters to maintain their properties and to participate in civic organizations. Homeownership has also helped many families build wealth, and accumulated home equity may serve as a financial reserve that can be tapped as needed at a lower cost than most other forms of credit.

The answer to subprime crises lies in the evolution of the structure of the home mortgage market. Over the past 70 years, it has changed radically from one in which local depository institutions make loans to one that is centered in the major Wall Street banks and securities firms, which employ the latest in financial engineering to repackage mortgages into securities through credit derivatives and collateralized debt obligations. Today's mortgage market depends critically on the ability to carve the debt into various risk segments through complex financial instruments and then sell those segments separately—the riskiest segments to high-yield-seeking, and sometimes highly leveraged, buyers such as hedge funds.

Before 1938, the U.S. mortgage market consisted primarily of regulated depository institutions, such as banks and savings and loan associations, that used their deposits to fund home loans. These lenders "originated" the loans and, because they kept them in their portfolios, held the credit risk, the market risk of interest rate fluctuations, and the liquidity risk from funding long-term assets with short-term liabilities (deposits).

To provide greater liquidity and fresh capital to these markets, the government, as part of President Roosevelt's New Deal policies, created the Federal National Mortgage Association (known as Fannie Mae) in 1938. It was a government-owned corporation with the mission of creating a secondary market for mortgages. Fannie Mae bought mortgages from the originators, returning the cash proceeds to the institutions. By buying the mortgages outright and holding them as a portfolio, Fannie Mae acquired the credit risk, market risk, and liquidity risk. But Fannie Mae was in a better position than depository institutions to deal with market and liquidity risks because it could borrow for longer term. Fannie Mae was also better able to manage credit (or repayment) risk because it held a mortgage portfolio that was diversified nationwide, which even the largest banks then found difficult to do because of regulatory limits on interstate banking. Fannie Mae would purchase only mortgages that "conformed" to certain underwriting standards. Those lending standards are used today to define "conforming" loans and are synonymous with "prime" mortgages.

Fannie Mae proved to be very successful, and, by the 1960s, the borrowing it did to fund its mortgage purchases constituted a significant share of the debt owed by the U.S. government. To move Fannie Mae's activities off the federal operating budget, the government-sponsored mortgage market was reorganized during the Johnson administration in 1968. The reorganization created the Government National Mortgage Association (Ginnie Mae) to handle government-guaranteed mortgages through veterans and other federal housing programs. It also privatized the remaining activities into a federally chartered, privately held corporation—offically named Fannie Mae—that retains some public interest obligations for low-income housing. In 1970, Ginnie Mae developed the mortgage-backed security, which shifted the market risk to investors and eliminated from the federal budget much of the debt that had been incurred to fund the government housing programs. The plain mortgage-backed security works by pooling similar mortgages and selling securities that have claims on the mortgage payments from the pool. The payments are passed through directly to the security holders. The Federal National Mortgage Corporation (known as Freddie Mac) was created in 1970, both to securitize conventional mortgages and to provide competition to the recently privatized Fannie Mae. Over time, the business models of Fannie Mae and Freddie Mac converged, and together they provided an enormous amount of funding for U.S. mortgages, both by purchasing and holding conforming mortgages and by turning a similarly large amount of home loans into mortgage-backed securities.

These securities are purchased by institutional investors, wealthy individuals, and the depository institutions themselves. The securitization process spread the market risk, offered depository institutions a more liquid class of loan assets, and tapped deep sources of capital for the mortgage market.

The mortgage-backed securities market removed market risk not only from the balance sheets of mortgage originators such as banks, but also from those of Fannie Mae and Freddie Mac. It provided long-term funding for mortgage lending and thereby largely eliminated the liquidity risk. Because Fannie Mae and Freddie Mac guaranteed the loans, much of the credit risk stayed with the two mortgage giants, whose size and diversification allowed them to handle it.

This market structure, with government-sponsored enterprises at its center, was a tremendous success and attracted competition from other major financial institutions. After the government charged Freddie Mac and Fannie Mae several years ago with serious errors in complying with new accounting rules for derivatives, the major Wall Street firms launched an aggressive move into the issuance of mortgage-backed securities.

In 2003, the government-sponsored enterprises were the source of 76 percent of the mortgage-backed and asset-backed issuances; "private label" issues by major Wall Street firms accounted for the remaining 24 percent, according to *Inside Mortgage Finance.* By mid-2006, the government-sponsored enterprise share had fallen to 43 percent, with private label issues accounting for 57 percent. Among the large private label issuers were well-known firms—such as Wells Fargo, Lehman Brothers, Bear Stearns, JPMorgan, Goldman Sachs, and Bank of America—as well as several major lenders to high-risk subprime borrowers, such as Indymac, WAMU, and Countrywide.

Along with this radical, and rapid, shift in market shares came a similar change in underwriting standards. Whereas Fannie Mae and Freddie Mac were almost entirely "prime" mortgage lenders, the private label share grew in large part through the origination and securitization of high-risk subprime mortgages as well as "Alt-A" mortgages, which were made to borrowers who were more creditworthy than subprime customers but presented more risks than prime borrowers.

The rise of subprime mortgage origination and securitization created a problem that had not arisen in markets centered on government-sponsored enterprises. It

Growing apace

Issuances of below-Investment-grade mortage-backed securities ballooned between 2003 and 2006.

(billion dollars; percent of total

Type	2003	Jan.– June 2006
Prime	57.6 (52)	67.2 (26)
Subprime	37.4 (34)	114.3 (44)
Alt-A	15.8 (14)	76.5 (30)
Total	**110.8**	**258.0**

Source: *Inside Mortgage Finance.*

was wondered that how could such low rated debt securities be sold. The major buyers of prime mortgage-backed securities were institutional investors, but their investment rules and guidelines sharply restricted their exposure to below-investment-grade securities. Small amounts of the $1.1 trillion in subprime debt, $685 billion of which was securitized as mortgaged-backed securities, could be sold to various high-yield-seeking investors—but not nearly the entire amount.

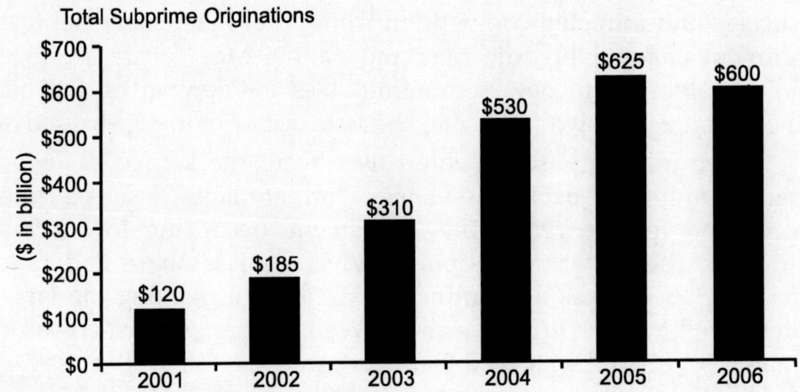

THE SUBPRIME MARKET

A subprime borrower is one who has a high debt-to-income ratio, an impaired or minimal credit history, or other characteristics that are correlated with a high probability of default relative to borrowers with good credit history. Because these borrowers are inherently riskier, subprime mortgages are originated at a premium above the prime mortgage rate offered to individuals with good credit. A method developed by the Fair Isaac Company assigns borrowers a credit score, or FICO score, that lies between 300 and 850.

This is a measure of the borrower's likelihood of delinquency and default, where a lower score implies a greater risk to the lender. It is generally accepted a FICO score less than 620 is considered subprime. In addition to having lower FICO scores, subprime borrowers typically have a loan-to-value ratio (LTV) in excess of 80 percent. 9 A high LTV means that the borrower is making a smaller down payment. So, the lender assumes more risk with these individuals because it will be harder to recover the capital from the collateral if they default on their loans. This is especially the case when home price appreciation (HPA) is flat or negative.

The given figure compares interest rates for 30-year fixed-rate loans in the prime and the subprime markets. The prime interest rate is collected from the Freddie Mac Primary Mortgage Market Survey. The subprime interest rate is the average 30-year fixed rate at origination. The difference between the two in each month is defined as the subprime premium. The premium charged to a subprime borrower is typically around 2 percentage points. It increases a little when rates are higher and decreases a little when rates are lower.

Interest Rates

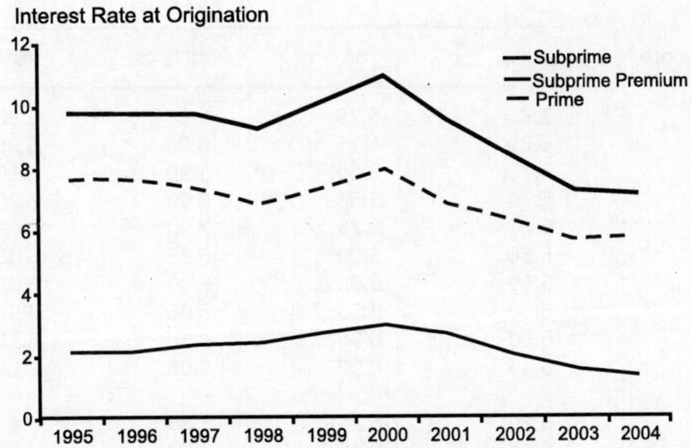

Note: Prime is the 30-year fixed interest rate reported by the Freddie Mac Primary Mortgage Market Survey. Subprime is the average 30-year fixed interest rate at origination as calculated from the Loan Performance data set. The Subprime Premium is the difference between the prime and subprime rates.

The above given matrix of credit scores and loan-to-value (LTV) ratio requirements that determine pricing of the mortgage within each loan grade for a 30-year loan with a 3-year fixed interest rate and a 3-year prepayment penalty. For example, loans in the Premier Plus grade with credit scores above 680 and down payments of 40 percent or more would pay interest rates of 5.65 percentage points, according to the Countrywide rate sheet for California. As the down payment gets smaller (as LTV goes up), the interest rate increases. For example, an applicant with the same credit score and a 100 percent LTV will be charged a 7.50 interest rate. But, note that the interest rate is fairly stable until the down payment drops below 10 percent. At this point the lender begins to worry about possible negative equity positions in the near future due to appraisal error or price depreciation. It is the combination of smaller down payments and lower credit scores that lead to the highest interest rates. In addition, applicants in lower loan grades tend to pay higher interest rates than similar applicants in a higher loan grade. This extra charge reflects the marginal risk associated with missed mortgage payments, foreclosures, or bankruptcies in the past. The highest rate quoted is 9.8 percentage points for a C– grade loan with the lowest credit score and a 30 percent down payment.

The range of interest rates charged indicates that the subprime mortgage market actively price discriminates (that is, it uses risk-based pricing) on the basis of multiple factors: delinquent payments, foreclosures, bankruptcies, debt ratios, credit scores, and LTV ratios. In addition, stipulations are made that reflect risks associated with the loan grade and include any prepayment penalties, the length of the loan, the flexibility of the interest rate (adjustable, fixed, or hybrid), the lien position, the property type, and other factors. The lower the grade or credit score, the larger the

Underwriting and Interest Rates

Loan grade	Credit score	LTV 60%	70%	80%	90%	100%
Premier Plus	680	5.65	5.75	5.80	5.90	7.50
	660	5.65	5.75	5.85	6.00	7.85
	600	5.75	5.80	5.90	6.60	8.40
	580	5.75	5.85	6.00	6.90	8.40
	500	6.40	6.75	7.90		
Premier	680	5.80	5.90	5.95	5.95	7.55
	660	5.80	5.90	6.00	6.05	7.90
	600	5.90	5.95	6.05	6.65	8.45
	580	5.90	6.00	6.15	6.95	
	500	6.55	6.90	8.05		
A–	680					
	660	6.20	6.25	6.35	6.45	
	600	6.35	6.45	6.50	6.70	
	580	6.35	6.45	6.55	7.20	
	500	6.60	6.95	8.50		
B	680					
	660	6.45	6.55	6.65		
	600	6.55	6.60	6.75		
	580	6.55	6.65	6.85		
	500	6.75	7.25	9.20		
C	680					
	660					
	600	6.95	7.20			
	580	7.00	7.30			
	500	7.45	8.95			
C–	680					
	660					
	600					
	580	7.40	7.90			
	500	8.10	9.80			

Note: The first three years are at a fixed interest rate, and there is a three-year prepayment penalty.
Source: Countrywide California B&C Rate Sheet, download from www.cwbc.com on 2/11/05.

down payment requirement. This requirement is imposed because loss severities are strongly tied to the amount of equity in the home and price appreciation patterns.

What makes a loan subprime is the existence of a premium above the prevailing prime market rate that a borrower must pay. In addition, this premium varies over time, which is based on the expected risks of borrower failure as a homeowner and default on the mortgage.

The financial markets have also increasingly securitized subprime loans. The table securitization rates calculated as the ratio of the total number of dollars securitized divided by the number of dollars originated in each calendar year. Therefore, this number roughly approximates the actual securitization rate, but could be under or over the actual rate due to the packaging of seasoned loans.4 The subprime loan securitization rate has grown from less than 30 percent in 1995 to over 58 percent in

Securitization Rates

Year	FHA/VA	Loan type		
		Conventional	Jumbo	Subprime
1995	101.1%	45.6%	23.9%	28.4%
1996	98.1%	52.5%	21.3%	39.5%
1997	100.7%	45.9%	32.1%	53.0%
1998	102.3%	62.2%	37.6%	55.1%
1999	88.1%	67.0%	30.1%	37.4%
2000	89.5%	55.6%	18.0%	40.5%
2001	102.5%	71.5%	31.4%	54.7%
2002	92.6%	72.8%	32.0%	57.6%
2003	94.9%	75.9%	35.1%	58.7%

Note: Subprime securities include both MBS and ABS backed by subprime loans. Securitization rate = securities issued divided by originations in dollars.
Source: Inside MBS & ABS.

2003. The securitization rate for conventional and jumbo loans has also increased over the same time period. For example, conventional securitization rates have increased from close to 50 percent in 1995-97 to more than 75 percent in 2003. In addition, all or almost all of the loans insured by government loans are securitized. Therefore, the subprime mortgage market has become more similar to the prime market over time. In fact, the 2003 securitization rate of subprime loans is comparable to that of prime loans in the mid-1990s.

Many factors have contributed to the growth of subprime lending. Most fundamentally, it became legal. The ability to charge high rates and fees to borrowers was not possible until the Depository Institutions Deregulation and Monetary Control Act (DIDMCA) was adopted in 1980. It preempted state interest rate caps.

The Alternative Mortgage Transaction Parity Act (AMTPA) in 1982 permitted the use of variable interest rates and balloon payments. These laws opened the door for the development of a subprime market, but subprime lending would not become a viable large-scale lending alternative until the Tax Reform Act of 1986 (TRA).

The TRA increased the demand for mortgage debt because it prohibited the deduction of interest on consumer loans, yet allowed interest deductions on mortgages for a primary residence as well as one additional home. This made even high-cost mortgage debt cheaper than consumer debt for many homeowners. In environments of low and declining interest rates, such as the late 1990s and early 2000s, cash-out refinancing becomes a popular mechanism for homeowners to access the value of their homes. In fact, slightly over one half of subprime loan originations have been for cash-out refinancing. In addition to changes in the law, market changes also contributed to the growth and maturation of subprime loans. In 1994, for example, interest rates increased and the volume of originations in the prime market dropped.

Mortgage brokers and mortgage companies responded by looking to the subprime market to maintain volume. The growth through the mid-1990s was funded by issuing mortgage-backed securities (MBS, which are sometimes also referred to as private label or as asset-backed securities [ABS]). In addition, subprime loans were originated mostly by non-depository and mono-line finance companies. During this time period, subprime mortgages were relatively new and apparently profitable, but the performance of the loans in the long run was not known. By 1997, delinquent payments and defaulted loans were above projected levels and an accounting construct called "gains-on sales accounting" magnified the cost of the unanticipated losses. In hindsight, many lenders had underpriced subprime mortgages in the competitive and high-growth market of the early to mid- 1990s. By 1998, the effects of these events also spilled over into the secondary market. MBS prices dropped, and lenders had difficulty finding investors to purchase the high-risk tranches. At or at about the same time, the 1998 Asian financial crisis greatly increased the cost of borrowing and again reduced liquidity in the all-real-estate markets.

Partially because of the above events, the structure of the market also changed dramatically through the 1990s and early 2000s. The rapid consolidation of the market is shown in Table 3. For example, the market share of the top 25 firms making subprime loans grew from 39.3 percent in 1995 to over 90 percent in 2003. Many firms that started the subprime industry either have failed or were purchased by larger institutions. The Table given below shows the top 10 originators for 2000-03 and 1996. From 2000 forward the list of top originators is fairly stable. For example, Citi Financial, a member of Citigroup, appears each year, as does Washington Mutual and Countrywide Financial. The largest firms increasingly dominated the smaller firms from 2000 through 2003, when the market share of the top 25 originators increased from 74 percent to 93 percent. In contrast, many of the firms in the top 25 in 1996 do not appear in the later periods. This is due to a mixture of failures and mergers. For example, Associated First Capital was acquired by Citigroup and at least partially explains Citigroup's position as one of the top originators and service providers of subprime loans. Long Beach Mortgage was purchased by Washington Mutual, one of the nation's largest thrifts. United Companies filed for bankruptcy, and Aames Capital Corporation was delisted after significant financial difficulties. Household Financial Services, one of the original finance companies, has remained independent and survived the period of rapid consolidation. In fact, in 2003 it was the fourth largest originator and number two servicer of loans in the subprime industry.

TYPES OF SUBPRIME MORTGAGES

There are two main types of mortgages that apply across all credit sectors in the US. The traditional fixed-rate mortgage (FRM) is defined by constant periodic payments as determined by a "note rate" (the rate the borrower pays) that is fixed at loan inception. By contrast, the adjustable-rate mortgage (ARM) is defined by variable periodic payments as determined by an index, such as the 12-month LIBOR, plus a fixed margin. The frequency at which the ARM note rate adjusts is usually either

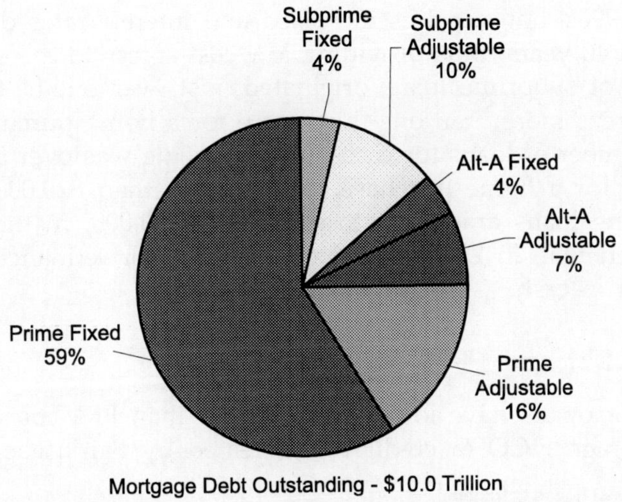

monthly, semiannually, or annually. Both these products typically have an amortization period of 30 years and a monthly payment frequency. Many subprime loans are a hybrid of ARMs and FRMs in that they typically have a fixed note rate for the first two to three years and then revert to a classical ARM structure. For example, the 2/28 hybrid loan—a popular subprime product—has a fixed, low rate for the first two years (known as a teaser) and then becomes adjustable semiannually for the next 28 years as the note rate resets to the value of an index plus a margin. Other non-traditional products include negatively amortizing mortgages (NegAms) and interest-only mortgages (IOs). Negatively amortizing loans are FRMs or ARMs with payment schedules in which the borrower pays back less than the full amount of the interest to the lender, and the remainder is added to the principal. An IO mortgage can be either an ARM or an FRM such that the borrower pays only the interest for a set period of time. Once the IO period ends, the borrower has to pay down the principal in addition the period 2004-2006, approximately 45 percent of subprime mortgages were ARMs or hybrids, 25 percent were FRMs, 10 percent allowed for negative amortization, and 20 percent were IOs.

Volume

Although the subprime mortgage market emerged in the early 1980s with the adoption of DIDMCA, AMTPA, and TRA, subprime lending rapidly grew only after 1995, when MBS with subprime-loan collateral became more attractive to investors. The Figure illustrates this pattern. In 1995, for example, the number of subprime fixed-rate mortgages (FRMs) originated was just slightly above 62,000 and the number of subprime adjustable rate mortgages (ARMs) originated was just above 21,000. Since then, subprime lending has increased substantially, with the number of FRM originations peaking at almost 780,000 and ARM originations peaking (and surpassing FRMs) at over 866,000.

During the late 1990s, house prices increased and interest rates dropped to some of the lowest rates in 40 years, thus providing low-cost access to the equity in homes. Of the total number of subprime loans originated, just over one-half were for cash-out refinancing, whereas more than one-third were for a home purchase. In 2003, for example, the total number of loans for cash-out refinancing was over 560,000, whereas the number of loans for a home purchase totaled more than 820,000, and loans for no-cash-out refinancing loans amounted to just under 250,000. In the prime market, Freddie Mac estimated that, in 2003, 36 percent of loans for refinancing took at least 5 percent of the loan in cash.

Credit Scores for ARM and FRM Borrowers

On average, ARM borrowers have lower credit scores than FRM borrowers. In 2003, for example, the average FICO (a credit score created by Fair Isaac Corporation to

Number of Loans Originated

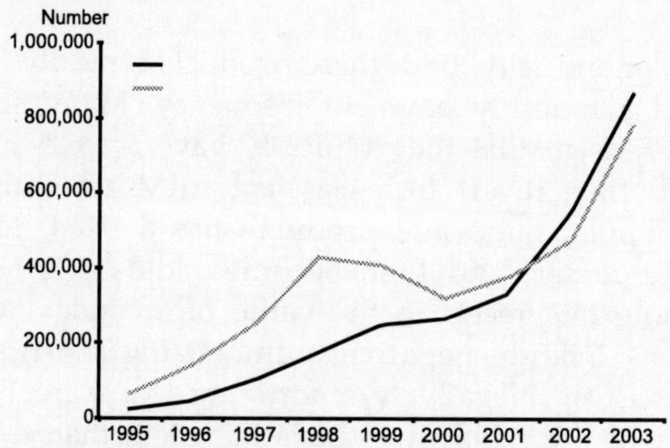

Source: Loan Performance ABS securities data base of subprime loans.

Number of Loans Originated by Grade

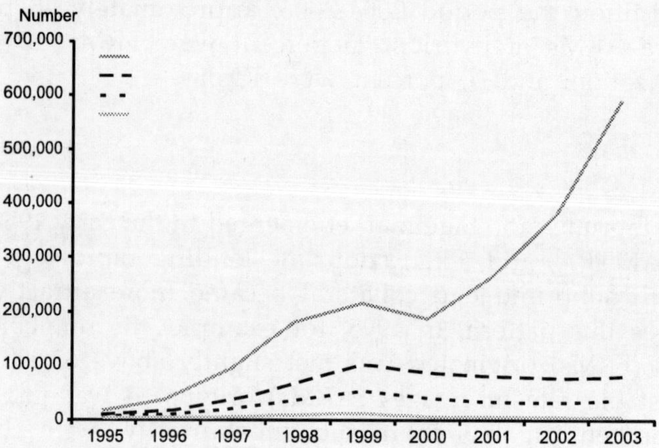

Source: Loan Performance ABS securities data base of subprime loans.

measure consumer creditworthiness) for FRMs is almost 50 points lower than for ARMs (623 versus 675). During the 1990s, average credit scores tended to decline each year, particularly for ARM borrowers; but since 2000, credit scores have tended to improve each year. Hence, it appears that subprime lenders expanded during the 1990s by extending credit to less-credit-worthy borrowers. Subsequently, the lower credit quality unexpectedly instigated higher delinquency and default rates.

The Development

The credit quality of subprime mortgages has fallen with adjustable interest rates,

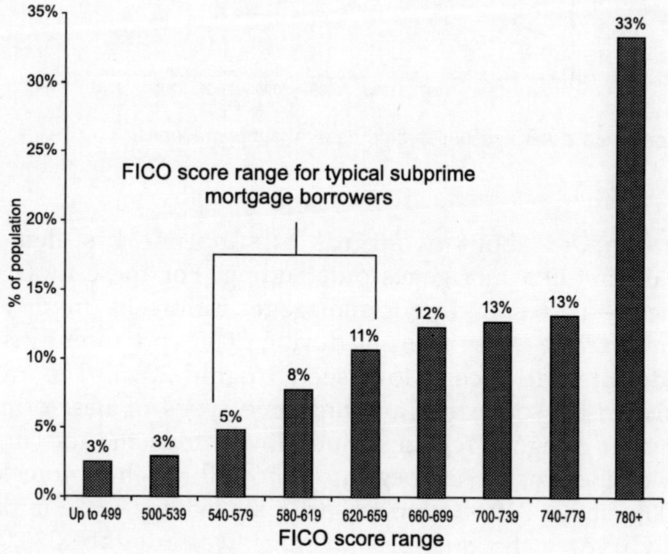

Average Credit Score (FICO)

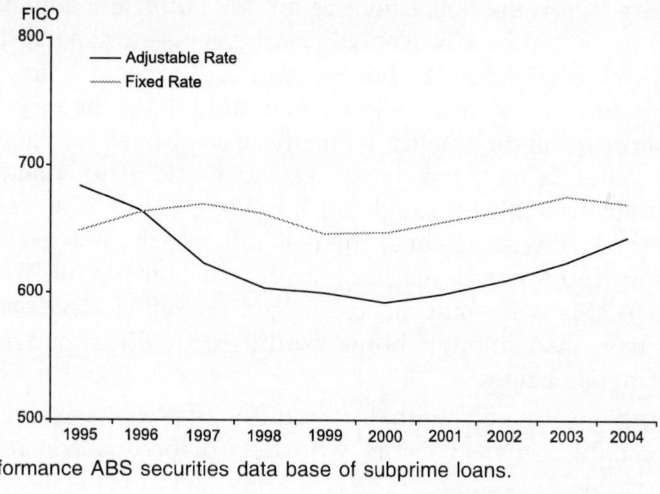

Source: Loan Performance ABS securities data base of subprime loans.

Share of Loans by Credit Score

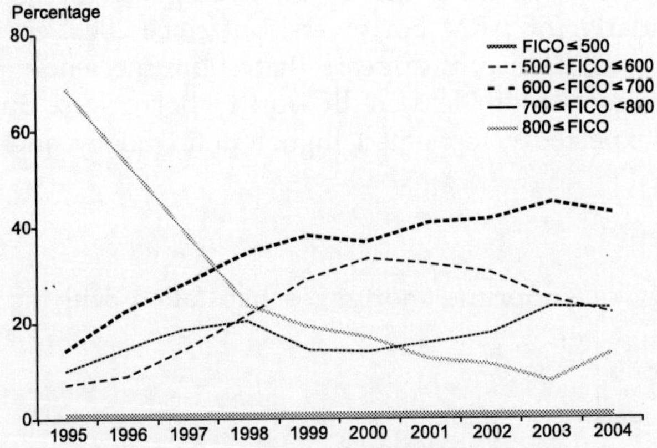

Source: Loan Performance ABS securities data base of subprime loans.

which currently account for about two-thirds of subprime first-lien mortgages or about 9 percent of all first-lien mortgages outstanding. For these mortgages, the rate of serious delinquencies—corresponding to mortgages in foreclosure or with payments ninety days or more overdue—rose sharply during 2006 and recently stood at about 11 percent, about double the recent low seen in mid-2005. The rate of serious delinquencies has also risen somewhat among some types of near-prime mortgages, although the rate in that category remains much lower than the rate in the subprime market. The rise in delinquencies has begun to show through to foreclosures. In the fourth quarter of 2006, about 310,000 foreclosure proceedings were initiated, whereas for the preceding two years the quarterly average was roughly 230,000. Subprime mortgages accounted for more than half of the foreclosures started in the fourth quarter.

The sharp rise in serious delinquencies among subprime adjustable-rate mortgages (ARMs) has multiple causes. "Seasoned" mortgages—mortgages that borrowers have paid on for several years—tend to have higher delinquency rates. That fact, together with the moderation in economic growth, would have been expected to produce some deterioration in credit quality from the exceptionally strong levels seen a few years ago. But other factors, too, have been at work. After rising at an annual rate of nearly 9 percent from 2000 through 2005, house prices had decelerated, even falling in some markets. At the same time, interest rates on both fixed- and adjustable-rate mortgage loans moved upward, reaching multi-year highs in mid-2006. Some subprime borrowers with ARMs, who may have counted on refinancing before their payments rose, may not have had enough home equity to qualify for a new loan given the sluggishness in house prices.

In addition, some owners with little equity may have walked away from their properties, especially owner-investors who do not occupy the home and thus have little attachment to it beyond purely financial considerations. Regional economic problems have played a role as well; for example, some of the states with the highest delinquency and foreclosure rates are among those most hard-hit by job cuts in the industry.

The practices of some mortgage originators have also contributed to the problems in the subprime sector. As the underlying pace of mortgage originations began to slow, but with investor demand for securities with high yields still strong, some lenders evidently loosened underwriting standards. So-called risk-layering—combining weak borrower credit histories with other risk factors, such as incomplete income documentation or very high cumulative loan-to-value ratios—became more common. These looser standards were likely an important source of the pronounced rise in "early payment defaults"—defaults occurring within a few months of origination—among subprime ARMs, especially those originate a few months of origination—among subprime ARMs, especially those originated in 2006.

Moreover these credit products called CDO, MBS were so complex that the investors relied heavily on rating agencies like moody, S&P for their investment grade. These agencies made profit out of these grades as they were paid for giving grading. This further aggravated the problems.

Low interest rates

The monetary policy of low interest rates – introduced by Alan Greenspan in response to the post-9/11 recession and the collapse of the new economy "bubble" – injected an enormous amount of liquidity into the global monetary system. This reduced short-term interest rates to 1% – their lowest level in 50 years. What's more, Greenspan spent the next two years maintaining interest rates at levels significantly below equilibrium.2 Interest rates were kept at low levels for a long time, and were often negative in inflation-adjusted terms. The result was no surprise. Low returns on traditional investments pushed investors and lenders to take bigger risks to get better returns.

Financial intermediaries, in search of profits, extended credit to families and companies with limited financial strength. Investors with varying degrees of expertise duly reallocated their portfolios towards more lucrative but riskier assets in an attempt to increase their wealth and preserve its purchasing power. The low borrowing rates for both short and long-term maturity attracted throngs of borrowers – families above all who were seduced by the possibility of acquiring assets that for had always been beyond their means. At the same time, house prices soared, ultimately encouraging the additional extension of credit; the value of real estate seemed almost guaranteed. The interest rates have declined from the high of 6.5% in 2000-01 to a low of just above 1% in 2003-04 before it started moving north. The macroeconomics changed from 2005 with interest rates gradually moving and changing the market dynamics contributing in big way to the crisis.

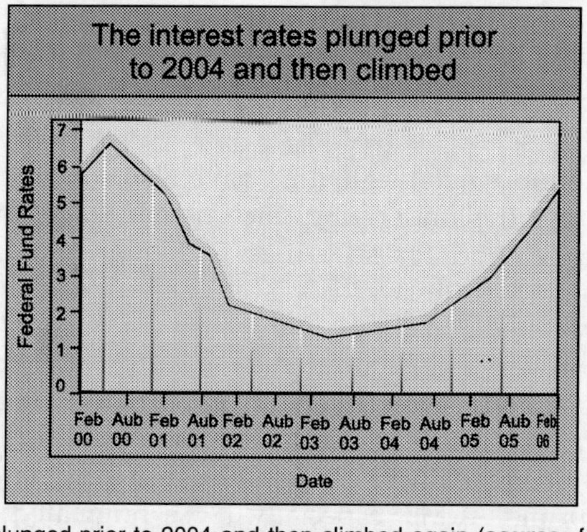

Interest rates plunged prior to 2004 and then climbed again (**source:** federal reserve)

Lack of government oversight on new financial products

It is interesting to note that the period from 1996 to 2004 was a period of innovation. In their enthusiasm to go after the lucrative sub-prime market, the lenders introduced into the marketplace a number of new products. With no proper government oversight, products were offered at low or discounted interest rates with other features that made it easy for borrowers in this risky segment to get loans. For example there were the Alt-A loans that required little or no documents, NINJA loans that were.

All these products had deceptively low monthly payments in the beginning

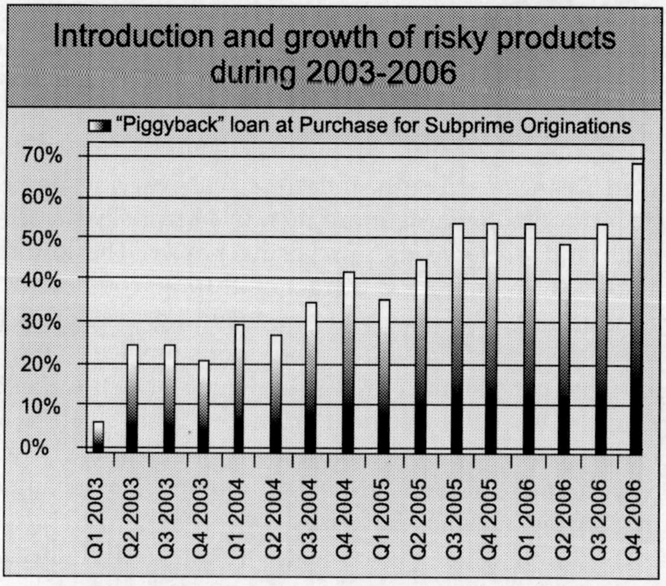

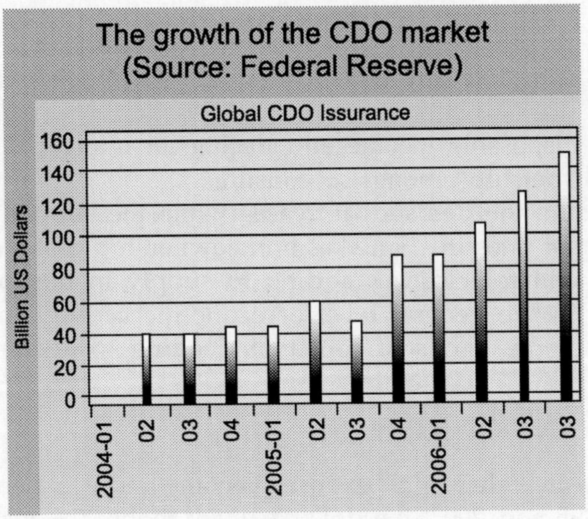

followed by higher payments in latter years resulting in higher delinquencies and foreclosures. The question that needs to be asked is what made the lenders feel that they could take on the extra risk introduced by these products and the answer is the booming credit derivative market that made risk transfer easy.

The investors in such products included insurance companies, asset managers, banks and hedge funds. They all took positions in such securities according to risk desired. This can be shown in the figure given below.

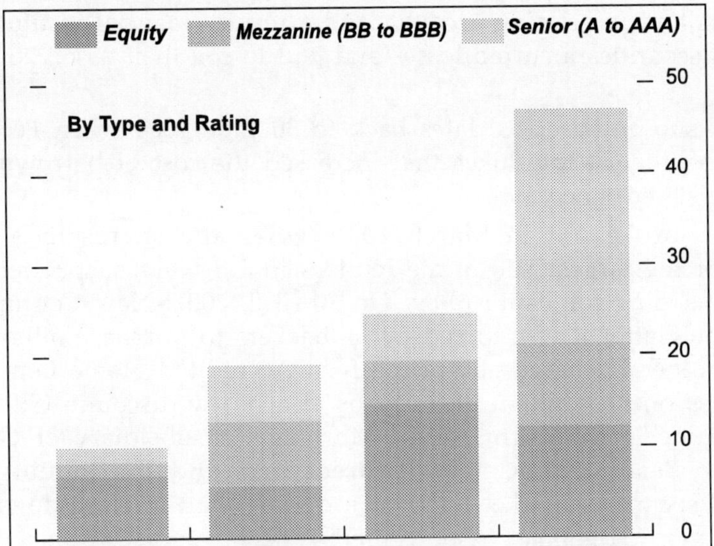

CAUSES OF BUBBLE IN THE HOUSING MARKET

1. The demand for housing like any other commodity is dependent on demand and supply.
2. So, the increase in disposable income and decline in interest rates on mortgages encouraged home ownership among US consumers.
3. The bubble burst when the demand decreases while the supply increases.
4. The increase in interest rates in US makes homeownership costlier for some buyers leading to defaults and foreclosures adding to supply in the market.
5. Similarly a decline in the general level of economic activity in US lead to less disposable income in the hands of consumer leading to decline in demand.

THE ECONOMIC POINT OF VIEW

When the dollar rises in value, U.S. exports become more expensive and import prices fall. Between 1995 and 2002, the dollar gained about 30% in value. This made imports costlier for US and they delayed their consumption expenditure and put the surplus money in non-tradable and since, they are not subject to international trade, their prices shot up. Here starts the creation of bubble in the US housing market.

The excess demand in the market pushed the housing prices to new heights. Rising prices, in turn, have a substantial effect on the spending of the consumers. US consumers lured by the increasing value of their homes went on borrowing spree. They started borrowing money for consumption by mortgaging their property.

But, two events that were assumed to have a low probability in a booming market in fact happened: first, interest rates increased and second, home prices began falling. This led to sub-prime mortgages resetting at shockingly high rates, with homeowners missing payments and foreclosing accounts. As a result, financial institutions holding mortgage-backed securities incurred losses and had to sell their assets to meet margin calls.

The slides of sub-prime crisis dates back to 30 June 2004 when Federal Reserve began the cycle of interest rate hikes that increased the cost of borrowings from the lowest levels registered since 1950s.

Finally, crisis broke out in March 2007, when the shares in New Century Financials, one of the largest sub-prime lenders in US were suspended amid fears that the firm is heading for bankruptcy. On April 2, 2007, New Century Financials filed for bankruptcy after it was forced by its backers to purchase billions of dollars of bad loans. Another US-based sub-prime firm Accredited Home Lenders Holding said it would pass on $2.7 billion of its loans at a heavy discount. GE also decided to sell its sub-prime lending arm, WMC Mortgage, a subsidiary of GE Money, it brought in 2004. Bear Stearns, a Wall Street firm and the topnotch player in mortgage-backed securities market for over a decade, had to close down two hedge funds that lost over 95% of net asset value(NAV).

The flow of events

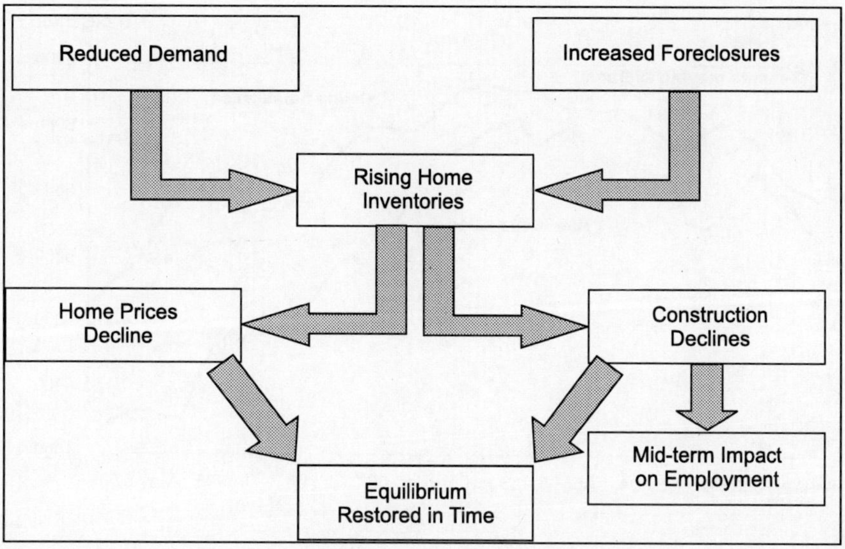

When the subprime crisis started to take shape it was marked by a rise in the inventory of homes and fall in housing prices creating negative equity for home owners.

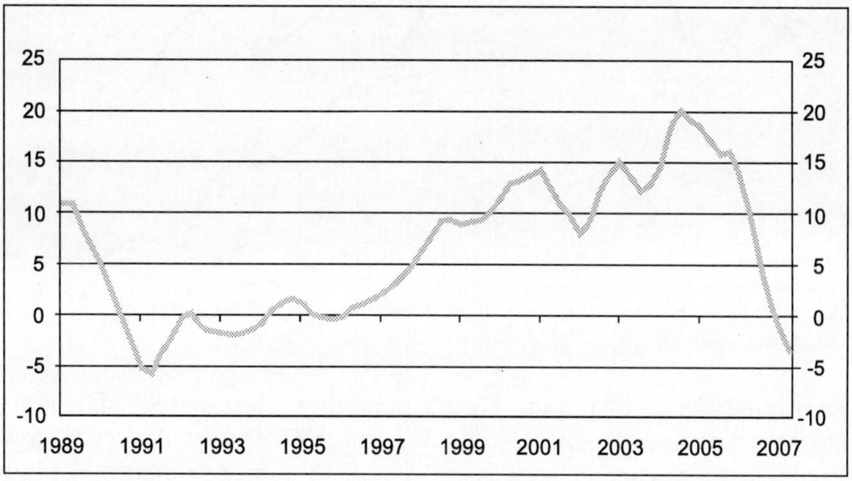

The bank involvement

The involvement of banks in this crises was complex. They were caught in the vicious circle from various angles. They were exposed to this credit risk at multiple levels. The CDO machine had become so efficient that the banks were not only lending

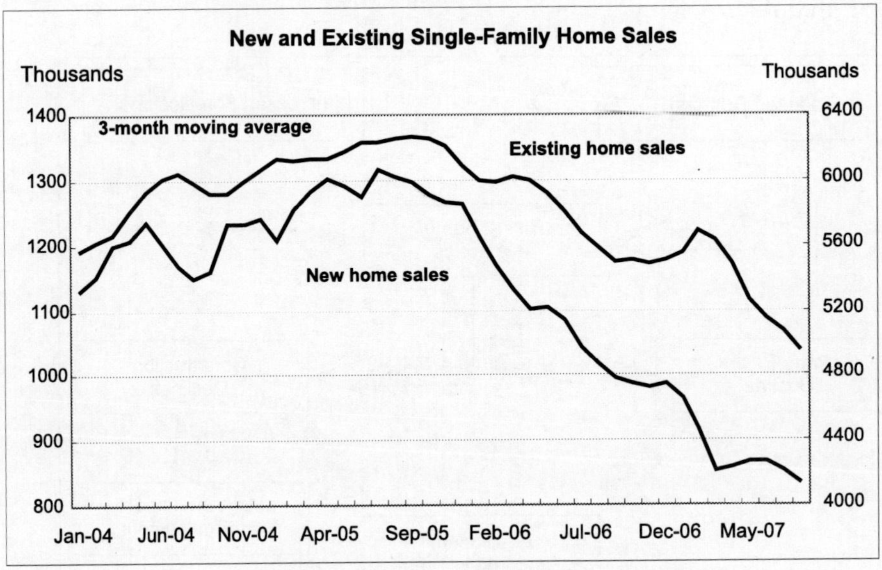

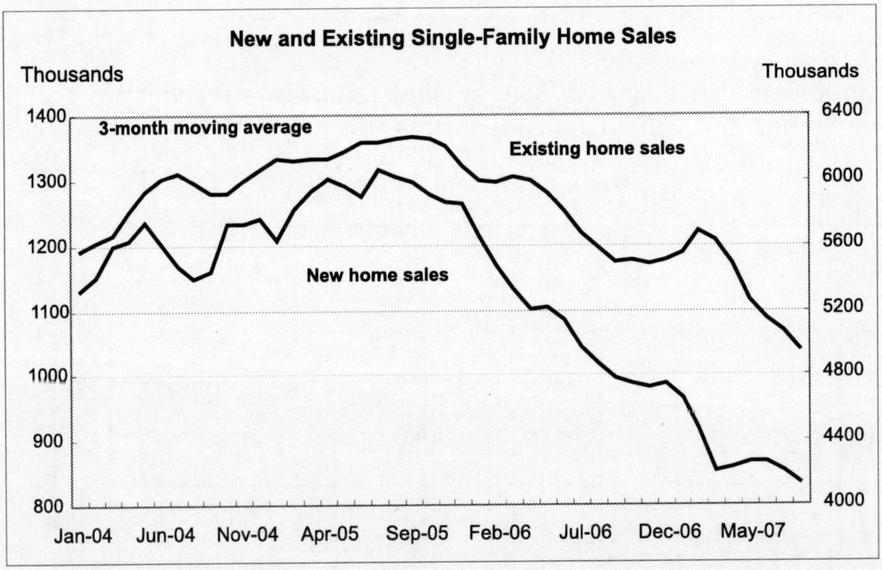

money to subprime borrowers on the basis of moving these assets off their balance sheets but had also become investors in such a market. The banks were invested in the senior tranches of mortgage back securities. The senior tranches contained the minimum risk but provided less return. Banks had also given excessive lending in a hope to move these them off their portfolio. Initially banks thought of going out a little bit more but soon these figures rose to billion of dollars on their balance sheet. They were warehousing this risky debt that they had to fund even though the value of these instruments had moved down. The underwriting for these loans had been poor. When a bank gives a loan it makes a proper assessment of various details as to why they need a loan, what are the sources of income of the borrowers etc.

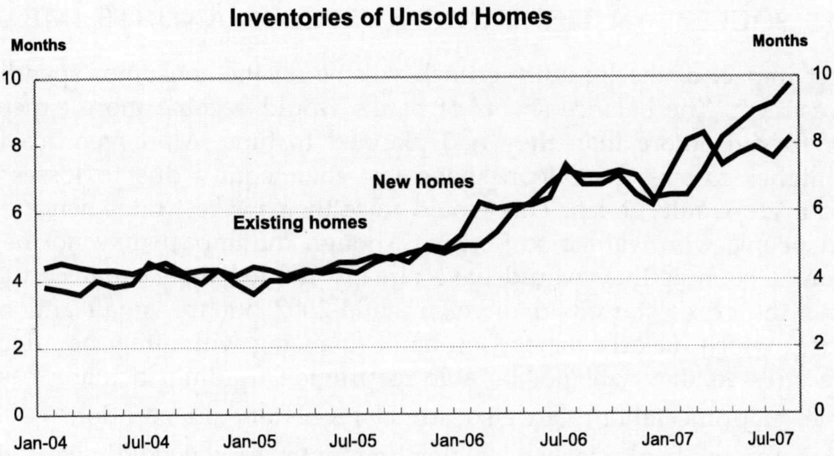

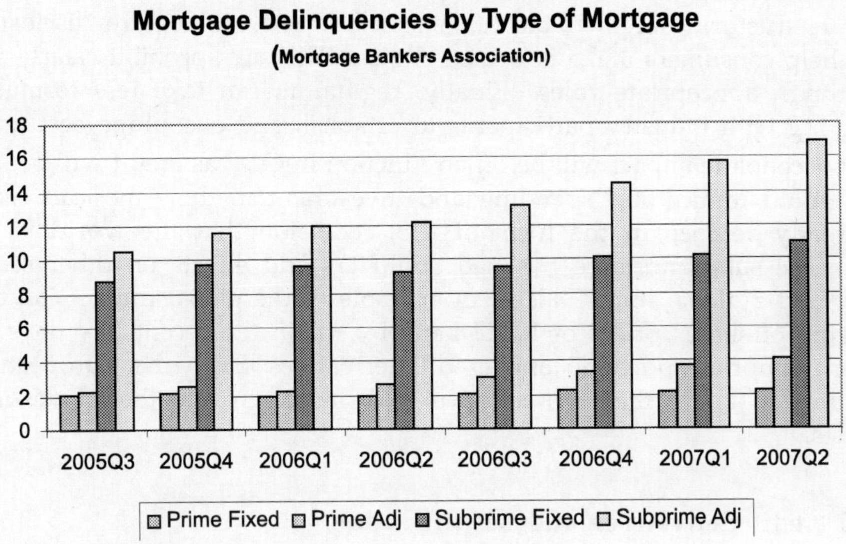

The bank develops a relationship with its customers so that after a loan is given they can monitor the borrower. It's quite likely that this rigorous process was not followed and with the stoppage of working of the CDO machine the banks were stuck with loans. Banks also had to value down their investments in the CDO, MBS. The banks also had to give margin to hedge funds or backstops to SIV. A backstop occurs when after selling a loan to a SIV the default occurs within a very short period of time then the banks have to take back these assets on its balance sheet. Finally the inter-bank lending was also constrained as all banks being in the same business become reluctant to lend to each other. They were suspicious of not only their own balance sheets but also of the balance sheets of other banks. This gave rise to the liquidity crises in the later part of 2007.

THE CREDIT SQUEEZE IN THE BANKING SECTOR AND ITS IMPACTS

The first direct impact of the liquidity crunch will be on the consumer spending and corporate investment. The balance sheets of banks would become more expensive as they are now funding more than they had planned to fund. Moreover this funding will be at a higher cost as these loans have lost their equity due to losses and so their capital charges would go up. This would raise their interest rates hence affecting corporate and people who wanted to borrow. Though the impact may not be felt by large corporate so soon as they would have already funded their expansion plans in early 2007 and the crises started to unveil in mid-2007 but the small and medium sized enterprises which majorly depend on bank financing will surely be affected. As the banks are stressed they will not be able to provide funding in many cases.

This whole subprime fallout can also attract regulatory intervention.

The basel 2 can ask banks to have higher minimum capital holdings as they are investing in CDO, MBS and also have to provide backstop to SIVs etc. This might also call for restructuring of their balance sheet. The fed can require disclosures by lenders that help consumers make informed choices. They can prohibit clearly abusive practices through appropriate rules. Finally, regulators can take less formal steps, such as working with industry participants to establish and encourage best practices.

The macroeconomic impact will be on a reduction in GDP as credit will be scarcely available it would reduce and spending and investment in the American economy. This can already be seen in the form of U.S. recession that the world is talking about today. The subprime issue has had spillovers and effects on other sectors of the economy and a global impact also. An example of the global impact can be seen in the plunging of shares prices of ICICI bank by 9% in the recent few days due to its investment subprime portfolio and credit derivatives. Even the European banks fear the amount of losses they would have to write down due their investment in such securities.

The use of credit derivatives and securitization

Securitization is the new form of financial engineering which allows banks to move the loan assets off their balance sheets by repackging them and selling them off to investors. It is this process of securitization which has been used extensively in the U.S. mortgage industry to generate more loans. The securitization process in the U.S. mortgage industry used mortgage backed securities (MBS) to be sold to investors of the housing market.

Understanding the MBS and CDO

An MBS programme was set up so that a pool of mortgages, typically tens of thousands of mortgages, could be sold into a special purpose company, a company outside of any banking balance sheet, and that company would finance the purchase of those mortgages by issuing different securities. These securities were issued with different risk levels and were not evenly distributed among investors as they had first, second and third loss categories. They were called junior, mezzanine and senior securities.

This is important as it enabled pools of mortgages to be financed by a broad range of investors that had differing risk-reward criteria. So, in a simple MBS programme, if a homeowner defaults on their mortgage, the loss is initially sustained by the most junior surviving tranche that would typically get notification if the initial investment had been written down by a certain amount. That amount reflects the loss following the failure of the mortgage.

In the unlikely event that many mortgages failed, it's possible the junior tranche would lose all of its value and would be reduced to a notional of zero, and thereafter any losses would be sustained by the next most junior tranche, the mezzanine tranches and so on. So, we have a very efficient system to allow mortgages to be financed by nonbanks, and the MBS market very much stepped into the space provided by the failed savings and loan market in the US in the 1980s.

Now, separate from the MBS market, but indeed in parallel with it, is the CDO market, debt obligation, or as it used to be called, the collateralised loan obligation, a term which better explains the root of this sector of the securitisation market. A CDO looks a lot like an MBS. There's the same special-purpose vehicle set up, bonds are issued to different tranches of investors, and the cash raised by issuing those bonds buys a pool of corporate loans, typically 100 or 200 loans would be bought by the CDO. And here again, the risk of those loans would be shared across the capital structure, but the first losses would be sustained by the junior tranche investors, and in the event of excessive losses, the mezzanine and senior tranches may sustain capital losses as well.

MBS SHARE OF TOTAL MORTGAGE DEBT OUTSTANDINGS

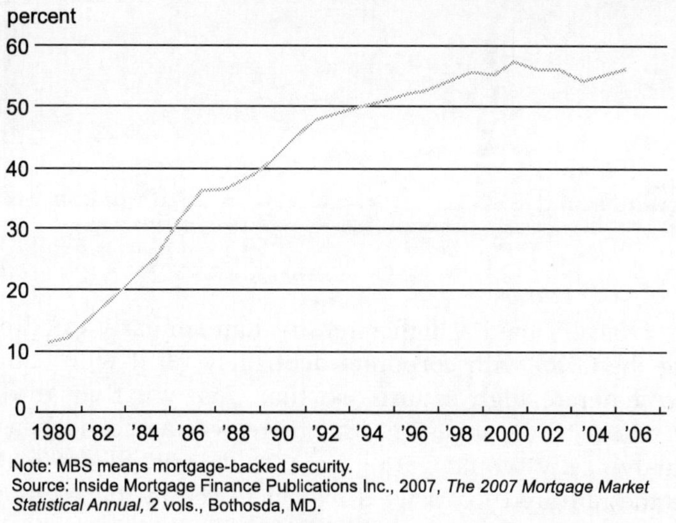

Note: MBS means mortgage-backed security.
Source: Inside Mortgage Finance Publications Inc., 2007, *The 2007 Mortgage Market Statistical Annual*, 2 vols., Bothosda, MD.

GREATER COMPLEXITY IN PRODUCTS AND INVESTORS

Over the last three, four, five years we have seen a growing amount of cash looking for investment, but sources of investment have not grown fast enough to satisfy the demand. The investors however are as motivated as ever. They like to get a high return, and are starting to note that the returns in the MBS and the traditional CDO market don't look as good as they used to. Simple supply and demand imbalance said that cash looking for more valuable securities is going to push the price of those securities up, thus pushing down the yield. And it reached the stage where the yield in the structure credit market didn't that much more exciting than the yield in the corporate bond market, so the extra work necessary to invest in structured credit investments such as MBS and CDO was not being justified by the extra yield. Extra work coupled with the loss of liquidity was not being justified by the high yield. So the market solution was to try and create more yield, and one of the ways of doing this was to create the same CDO structure but instead of filling it only with corporate debt, to fill it also with the mezzanine tranches, or indeed senior or junior, but mainly mezzanine tranches from other CDOs and other MBS.

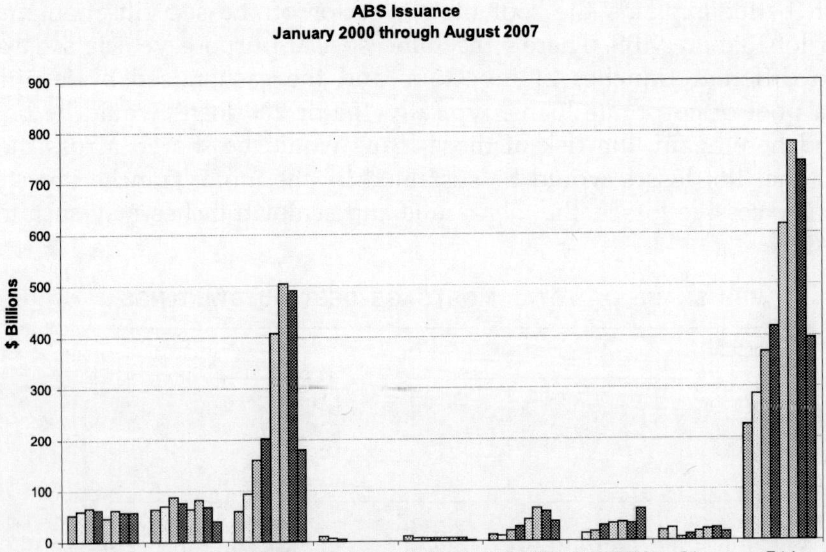

These securities typically paid a higher return than similarly rated corporate debt. So instead of filling the CDO with corporate debt, they fill it with equivalently rated CDOs and MBS to generate high returns, so that this will flow through the CDO delivering a better return to the investors. But there was a second benefit in that the rating agencies that typically would value these pools said this is really diversified. Not only are there the hundred loans we'd expect to see in the traditional CDO, but you've now introduced mezzanine tranches indexed to other deals, and that provides better diversification and therefore they believed the pool was less risky.

So not only is the pool paying a better return, but the rating agencies were considering it to be slightly less risky. A reduction in risk, and/or an increase in return plugged the gap, and suddenly the structured credit market was back in business, investors were seeing the returns that they wanted, and the banks that were originating these were seeing wide enough margins to justify the significant resources they had to invest to run a structured credit business.

Products became far more complex, and we can understand that an investor holding mezzanine tranches of a CDO indexed to a pool of corporate debt and other mezzanine tranches from CDOs, and possibly from MBSs, where those MBSs can't be valued, was genuinely confused as to the value of their investments.

MANY STRUCTURED CREDIT PRODUCT INVESTORS WERE ALSO LEVERAGED

Not only then were the products complicated, but unfortunately the holders of these investments also became more complex. The fact here was that not only were CDOs being bought by hold-to-maturity end investors, but also by leveraged institutions. The three to be distinguished are the hedge fund community, SIVs, or structured investment vehicles, and the banks themselves. And these three classes of investors also found the structured credit market to be attractive, and they had different risk-reward needs.

For example, SIVs would typically focus on the most senior tranches, hedge funds may find more value and opportunity in the junior tranches, and banks too typically tended to take the more senior tranches. The point is that these investments were being placed with institutions that were reliant on raising money in a leveraged way. They were not hold-to-maturity investors. So you combine the complexity of the structure with the complexity of ownership and there was plenty of room for misunderstanding.

Differentiating between Groups of Investors

By focusing now on the investors distinguishing between five sorts of investors. The first are called mark-to-market investors, which encompasses many investors thanks to this apparent move to transparency and the requirement to revalue investments on a daily or weekly basis, and in many cases, report those valuations. Many investors were caught holding complex products such as CDOs and MBSs, and were required to try and revalue them; probably daily, and definitely weekly. Many of them were subject to thresholds that basically meant if the value of the investment fell by more than a certain number of percentage points, they were required to sell. So, if your bond gets below 90, you are required to liquidate.

So, initially the crisis threw out confusion, and the confusion created some reduced valuations, which in any normal situation wouldn't be too much of a problem, but mark-to-market investors had to report those reduced valuations, and many were forced to sell.

The second category of investor is called the nervous investor, the person who read the same media that everyone else is reading, which frankly wasn't reported particularly accurately, assumed that all CDOs and indeed all structured credit products were flawed or toxic, and decided to sell.

Fortunately they were offset by the third category, the hold-to-maturity investors, who either were able to take a slightly more reasoned look at the market and conclude that this was an aberration, a flawed valuation, or were not required to sell, or indeed, had managed to fit their position into an accrual account, which wasn't mark-to-market anyway. And the fact remains that the majority of investors holding CDOs and MBSs were not required to sell, did not know they should sell, or just didn't sell.

The fourth and the fifth categories were the two troublemakers. These were the leveraged institutions and the SIVs, both of which were required to sell because of the leveraged or structured nature of their balance sheets. By leveraged institutions I'm obviously referring to major hedge funds that buy on margin. For every US$5 of a cash equity that's put up, they are given a trading line by a bank, and they assume the market they operate in is orderly, and that it's liquid.

The SIVs operate on a slightly different basis. They too have a relatively small amount of equity, but they finance their generally high-quality portfolios by issuing short-dated debt, typically commercial paper, with maturities of three, six or possibly nine months. But investors in that commercial paper are happy to make investments in the SIV because it boasts a very high-quality and liquid pool of assets, and indeed in the early 1990s when we saw the beginnings of the SIV market, these were typically triple-A liquid corporate bonds.

The commercial paper investors looked at those and said: '"I'm happy to fund those. If there's a problem, those bonds can be sold quickly. But in case there's a big problem, our friendly neighbourhood bank such as Citibank or HSBC has kindly offered a backstop, a credit backstop that basically says in event that there are the insufficient commercial paper investors around, an event we consider to be unlikely, and in the event that the SIV has to liquidate its assets to accommodate that reduction in financing but can't liquidate fast enough, we the bank will step in and provide financing to plug the gap."

ROLE OF MORTGAGE SERVICER

There is typically a mortgage servicer. So someone like Countrywide for example, may have originated the mortgages, but it is responsible for placing the mortgages into the MBS, and for servicing the relationship with the homeowner and typically if the homeowner failed to make a payment, Countrywide or the equivalent mortgage servicer would send a letter saying 'you've missed your payment', and if they kept missing payments, there would probably be a telephone conversation and there would be some process to try and work out the credit problems of the borrower.

But the ultimate recourse of the mortgage servicer is to foreclose on the loan. This is a court process involving a legal process to produce a document, an important document, which basically says the homeowner has defaulted on his loan, the house can now be sold; and if that means forceful eviction, the court has authorised that the proceeds of the sale of the house can be used to pay back some or all of the mortgage. Should there be any losses following that process, then and only then the losses are handed on to the MBS and then to the tranche investors.

So, just imagine a scenario whereby the rather sleepy court in Southern California used to processing two foreclosures a week suddenly starts seeing two a day and then twenty a day and then a hundred a day; in a court where there's probably one or two clerks processing the paperwork, there was a natural bottleneck, they just couldn't process the foreclosures fast enough. Then the (US President) Bush administration stepped in and said we have a social crisis growing here, a load of homeowners having their loans foreclosed, this is going to result in a social problem, so we'd like to put a halt on the foreclosure process.

Foreclosures slowed down; as a result there is no legal foreclosure, so the mortgage servicer cannot recover any lost money from the MBS. So there is a big bottleneck in the mortgage sector right now where some of the losses at the homeowner-end of the chain have not yet been passed on to the investors. So there can be reports which tell that there is a delinquency but until a foreclosure is processed, the loss is not crystallised. Hence the bond holders actually could not value their positions and did not even know the worth of their bonds.

How much were these bonds worth was very much a function of the value of the house that was to be sold off. If there is a collapsing housing market, then it's unclear as to whether the house is worth US$100 today, US$90 tomorrow or US$80 next week. Clearly the value of that house has a direct impact on the ultimate loss sustained by the investor.

THE SECURITIZATION PROCESS

Securitization is a structured finance process, which involves pooling and repackaging of cash-flow producing financial assets into securities that are then sold to investors. The term "securitization" is derived from the fact that the form of financial instruments used to obtain funds from the investors are securities.

All assets can be securitized so long as they are associated with cash flow. Hence, the securities, which are the outcome of securitization processes, are termed asset-backed securities (ABS). From this perspective, securitization could also be defined as a financial processes leading to an emission of ABS.

Securitization often utilizes a special purpose vehicle (SPV) (alternatively known as a special purpose entity(SPE) or special purpose company (SPC) in order to reduce the risk of bankruptcy and thereby obtain lower interest rates from potential lenders. A credit derivative is also generally used to change the credit quality of the underlying portfolio so that it will be acceptable to the final investors.

POOLING AND TRANSFER

The **originator** initially owns the assets engaged in the deal. This is typically a company looking to either raise capital, restructure debt or otherwise adjust its finances. Under traditional corporate finance concepts, such a company would have three options to raise new capital: a loan, bond issue, or issuance of stock. However, stock offerings dilute the ownership and control of the company, while loan or bond financing is often prohibitively expensive due to the credit rating of the company and the associated rise in interest rates.

A suitably large portfolio of assets is "pooled" and sold to a special purpose vehicle (the issuer), a tax-exempt company or trust formed for the specific purpose of funding the assets. Once the assets are transferred to the issuer, there is normally no recourse to the originator. The issuer is "bankruptcy remote," meaning that if the originator goes into bankruptcy, the assets of the issuer will not be distributed to the creditors of the originator. In order to achieve this, the governing documents of the issuer restrict its activities to only those necessary to complete the issuance of securities.

Standards govern when such a transfer is a sale, a financing, a partial sale, or a part-sale and part-financing In a sale, the originator is allowed to remove the transferred assets from its balance sheet: in financing, the assets are considered to remain the property of the originator. Under US accounting standards, the originator achieves a sale by being at arm's length from the issuer, in which case the issuer is classified as a "**qualifying special purpose entity**" or "**QSPE**".

Because of these structural issues, the originator typically needs the help of an investment bank (the arranger) in setting up the structure of the transaction.

To be able to buy the assets from the originator, the issuer SPV issues tradable securities to fund the purchase. Investors purchase the securities, either through a private offering (targeting institutional investors) or on the open market. The performance of the securities is then directly linked to the performance of the assets. Credit rating agencies rate the securities which are issued in order to provide an external perspective on the liabilities being created and help the investor make a more informed decision.

In transactions with static assets, a depositor will assemble the underlying collateral, help structure the securities and work with the financial markets in order to sell the securities to investors. The depositor has taken on added significance under Regulation AB. The depositor typically owns 100% of the beneficial interest in the issuing entity and is usually the parent or a wholly owned subsidiary of the parent which initiates the transaction. In transactions with managed (traded) assets, asset managers assemble the underlying collateral, help structure the securities and work with the financial markets in order to sell the securities to investors.

Some deals may include a third-party guarantor which provides guarantees or partial guarantees for the assets, the principal and the interest payments, for a fee.

The securities can be issued with either a fixed interest rate or a floating rate. Fixed rate ABS set the "coupon" (rate) at the time of issuance, in a fashion similar to corporate bonds. Floating rate securities may be backed by both amortizing and nonamortizing assets. In contrast to fixed rate securities, the rates on "floaters" will periodically adjust up or down according to a designated index such as a U.S. Treasury rate, or, more typically, the London Interbank Offered Rate (LIBOR). The floating rate usually reflects the movement in the index plus an additional fixed margin to cover the added risk.

SERVICING

A **servicer** collects payments and monitors the assets that are the crux of the structured financial deal. The servicer can often be the originator, because the servicer needs very similar expertise as the originator and would want to ensure that loan repayments are paid to the Special Purpose Vehicle.

The servicer can significantly affect the cash flows to the investors because it controls the collection policy, which influences the proceeds collected, the charge-offs and the recoveries on the loans. Any income remaining after payments and expenses is usually accumulated to some extent in a reserve or spread account, and any further excess is returned to the seller. Bond rating agencies publish ratings of asset-backed securities based on the performance of the collateral pool, the credit enhancements and the probability of default.

When the issuer is structured as a trust, the trustee is a vital part of the deal as the gate-keeper of the assets that are being held in the issuer. Even though the trustee is part of the SPV, which is typically wholly owned by the Originator, the trustee has a fiduciary duty to protect the assets and those who own the assets, typically the investors.

MOTIVES FOR SECURITIZATION

Advantages to issuer

Reduces funding costs: Through securitization, a company rated BB but with AAA worthy cash flow would be able to borrow at possibly AAA rates. This is the number one reason to securitize a cash flow and can have tremendous impacts on borrowing costs. The difference between BB debt and AAA debt can be multiple hundreds of basis points. For example, Moody's downgraded Ford Motor Credit's rating in January 2002, but a senior automobile backed securities issued by Ford Motor Credit in January 2002 and April 2002 continue to be rated AAA, because of the strength of the underlying collateral, and other credit enhancements.

Reduces asset-liability mismatch: Depending on the structure chosen, securitization can offer perfect matched funding by eliminating funding exposure in terms of both

Standard Securitization Structure

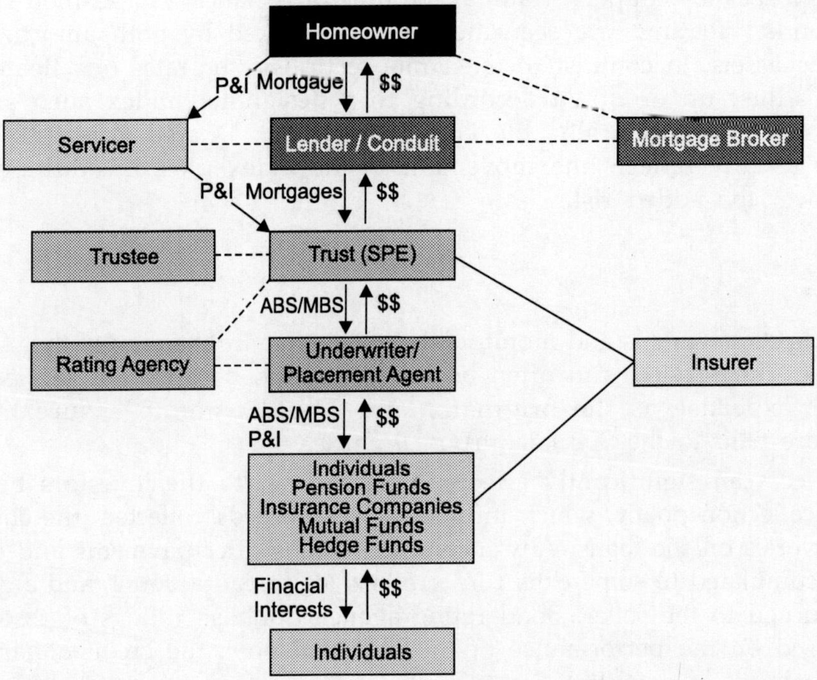

Source: Subprime Meltdown: A Primer, Part I NERA Insight Series, 21 June 2007.

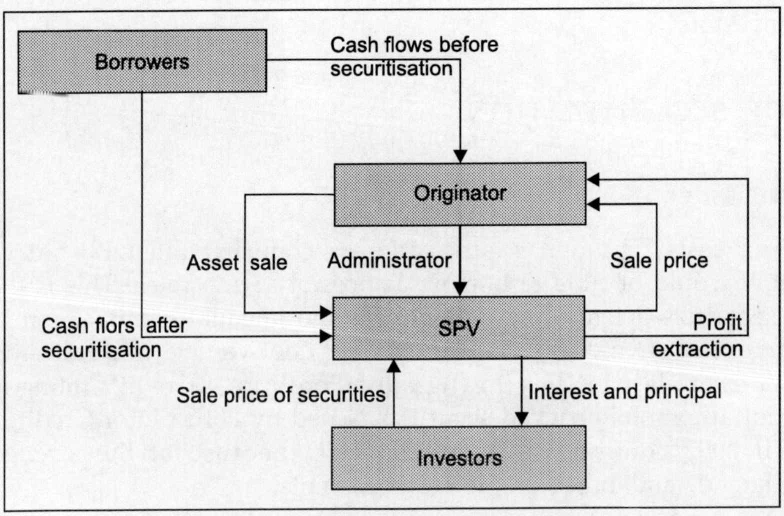

duration and pricing basis Essentially, in most banks and finance companies, the liability book or the funding is from borrowings. This often comes at a high cost. Securitization allows such banks and finance companies to create a self-funded asset book.

Lower capital requirements: Some firms, due to legal, regulatory, or other reasons, have a limit or range that their leverage is allowed to be. By securitizing some of their assets, which qualifies as a sale for accounting purposes, these firms will be able to lessen the equity on their balance sheets while maintaining the "earning power" of the asset.

Locking in profits: For a given block of business, the total profits have not yet emerged and thus remain uncertain. Once the block has been securitized, the level of profits has now been locked in for that company, thus the risk of profit not emerging, or the benefit of super-profits, has now been passed on.

Transfer risks (credit, liquidity, prepayment, reinvestment, asset concentration): Securitization makes it possible to transfer risks from an entity that does not want to bear it, to one that does. Two good examples of this are catastrophe bonds and Entertainment Securitizations. Similarly, by securitizing a block of business (thereby locking in a degree of profits), the company has effectively freed up its balance to go out and write more profitable business.

Off balance sheet: Derivatives of many types have in the past been referred to as "off-balance-sheet."This term implies that the use of derivatives has no balance sheet impact. While there are differences among the various accounting standards internationally, there is a general trend towards the requirement to record derivatives at fair value on the balance sheet. There is also a generally accepted principle that, where derivatives are being used as a hedge against underlying assets or liabilities, accounting adjustments are required to ensure that the gain/loss on the hedged instrument is recognized in the income statement on a similar basis as the underlying assets and liabilities. Certain credit derivative products, particularly Credit Default Swaps, now have more or less universally accepted market standard documentation. In the case of Credit Default Swaps, this documentation has been formulated by the International Swaps and Derivatives Association (ISDA) who have for a long time provided documentation on how to treat such derivatives on balance sheets.

Earnings: Securitization makes it possible to record an earnings bounce without any real addition to the firm. When a securitization takes place, there often is a "true sale" that takes place between the Originator (the parent company) and the SPE. This sale has to be for the market value of the underlying assets for the "true sale" to stick and thus this sale is reflected on the parent company's balance sheet, which will boost earnings for that quarter by the amount of the sale. While not illegal in any respect, this does distort the true earnings of the parent company.

Admissibility: Future cashflows may not get full credit in a company's accounts (life insurance companies, for example, may not always get full credit for future surpluses in their regulatory balance sheet), and a securitization effectively turns an admissible future surplus flow into an admissible immediate cash asset.

Liquidity: Future cashflows may simply be balance sheet items which currently are not available for spending, whereas once the book has been securitized, the cash would be available for immediate spending or investment. This also creates a reinvestment book which may well be at better rates.

Disadvantages of Issuer

May reduce portfolio quality: If the AAA risks, for example, are being securitized out, this would leave a materially worse quality of residual risk.

Costs: Securitizations are expensive due to management and system costs, legal fees, underwriting fees, rating fees and ongoing administration. An allowance for unforeseen costs is usually essential in securitizations, especially if it is an atypical securitization.

Size limitations: Securitizations often require large scale structuring, and thus may not be cost-efficient for small and medium transactions.

Risks: Since securitization is a structured transaction, it may include par structures as well as credit enhancements that are subject to risks of impairment, such as prepayment, as well as credit loss, especially for structures where there are some retained strips.

Advantages to Investors

Opportunity to potentially earn a higher **rate of return** (on a risk-adjusted basis)
Opportunity to invest in a specific pool of high quality credit-enhanced assets: Due to the stringent requirements for corporations (for example) to attain high ratings, there is a dearth of highly rated entities that exist. Securitizations, however, allow for the creation of large quantities of AAA, AA or A rated bonds, and risk averse institutional investors, or investors that are required to invest in only highly rated assets, have access to a larger pool of investment options.

Portfolio diversification: Depending on the securitization, hedge funds as well as other institutional investors tend to like investing in bonds created through Securitizations because they may be uncorrelated to their other bonds and securities.

Isolation of credit risk from the parent entity: Since the assets that are securitized are isolated (at least in theory) from the assets of the originating entity, under securitization it may be possible for the securitization to receive a higher credit rating than the "parent," because the underlying risks are different. For example, a small bank may be considered more risky than the mortgage loans it makes to its customers; were the mortgage loans to remain with the bank, the borrowers may effectively be paying higher interest (or, just as likely, the bank would be paying higher interest to its creditors, and hence less profitable).

Risks to Investors

Liquidity risk

Credit/default: Default risk is generally accepted as a borrower's inability to meet interest payment obligations on time. For ABS, default may occur when sufficiently met as detailed in its prospectus. A key indicator of a particular security's default risk is its credit rating. Different tranches within the ABS are rated differently, with senior classes of most issues receiving the highest rating, and subordinated classes receiving correspondingly lower credit ratings.

Event risk

Prepayment/reinvestment/early amortization: The majority of revolving ABS are subject to some degree of early amortization risk. The risk stems from specific early amortization events or payout events that cause the security to be paid off prematurely. Typically, payout events include insufficient payments from the underlying borrowers, insufficient excess Fixed Income Sectors: Asset-Backed Securities spread, a rise in the default rate on the underlying loans above a specified level, a decrease in credit enhancements below a specific level, and bankruptcy on the part of the sponsor or servicer.

Currency interest rate fluctuations: Like all fixed income securities, the prices of fixed rate ABS move in response to changes in interest rates. Fluctuations in interest rates affect floating rate ABS prices less than fixed rate securities, as the index against which the ABS rate adjusts will reflect interest rate changes in the economy. Furthermore, interest rate changes may affect the prepayment rates on underlying loans that back some types of ABS, which can affect yields. Home equity loans tend to be the most sensitive to changes in interest rates, while auto loans, student loans, and credit cards are generally less sensitive to interest rates.

CONTRACTUAL AGREEMENTS

Moral hazard: Investors usually rely on the deal manager to price the securitizations' underlying assets. If the manager earns fees based on performance, there may be a temptation to mark up the prices of the portfolio assets. Conflicts of interest can also arise with senior note holders when the manager has a claim on the deal's excess spread.

Servicer risk: The transfer or collection of payments may be delayed or reduced if the servicer becomes insolvent. This risk is mitigated by having a backup servicer involved in the transaction.

THE SECURITIZATION PROCESS IN U.S.

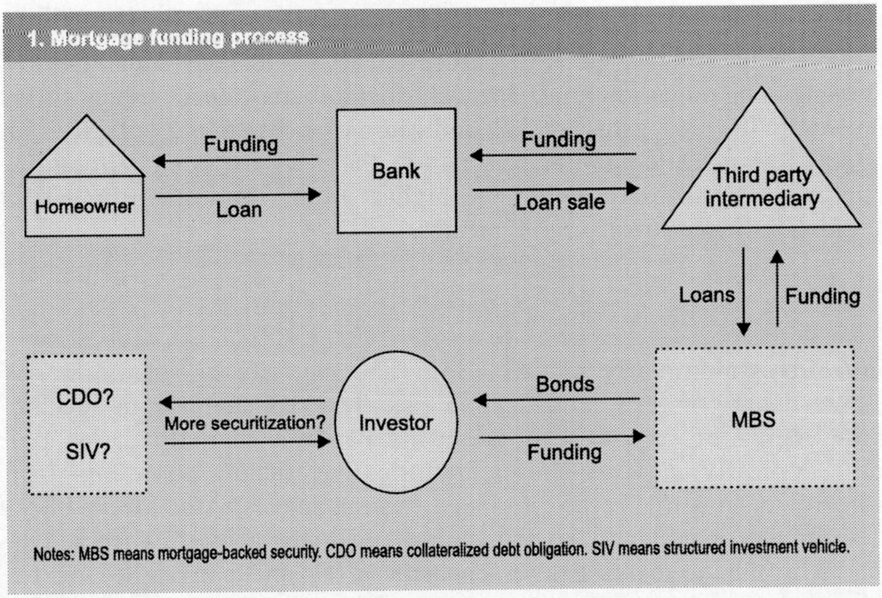

Thirty years ago, if one got a mortgage from a bank, it was very likely that the bank would keep the loan on its balance sheet until the loan was repaid. That is no longer true. Today, the party that we deal with in order to get the loan (the originator) is highly likely to sell the loan to a third party. The third party can be Ginnie Mae, a government agency; Fannie Mae or Freddie Mac, which are government sponsored entities (GSEs); or a private sector financial institution. The third party often then packages your mortgage with others and sells the payment rights to investors This may not be the final stop for your mortgage. Some of the investors may use their payment rights to your mortgage to back other securities they issue.

This can continue for additional steps. In effect, the eventual buyers of the mortgage—the parties that provide the funding—can be many steps removed from the originator of the mortgage.

The process by which most mortgage loans are sold to investors is referred to as securitization. In the mortgage market, securitization converts mortgages to mortgage-backed securities. (1) An MBS is a bond whose payments are based on the payments of a collection of individual mortgages. The initial sales of the bonds are put together either by the two GSEs or by private financial institutions, such as Countrywide Financial, Lehman Brothers, or Wells Fargo (all among the top six private issuers in 2006). (2) The MBS origination process typically begins when the issuer purchases a collection of mortgages from the originators. As payments are made on the mortgages, they are passed through the trust to bondholders. As an example of an MBS issuance, assume that an issuer has collected 1,000 mortgages, each worth $100,000 with a 30-year maturity and a fixed interest rate of 6.50%. This $100 million pool of mortgages can be used to back 10,000 bonds, each worth $10,000 with a 30-year term and a fixed coupon rate of 6.00%. Each bond shares the same coupon rate and other features, and importantly, each has a similar claim on all payments.

The MBSs are structured so that interest payments on the mortgages are at least sufficient to cover the loans that back private sector MBSs are jumbo loans; such loans are issued to high-quality borrowers, but they are too large to meet the conforming loan size limit of the two GSEs. Alt-A loans are issued to borrowers that appear to have good credit, but these loans do not meet the definition of prime or conforming. Often, Alt-A loans are issued to borrowers with limited or no income and asset verification. In recent years, the Alt-A sector has increasingly included loans for which the loan-to-value ratio was too high. The share of MBSs backed by subprime and Alt-A mortgage loans increased rapidly in the last decade.

From 1996 through 2006, the share of subprime and Alt-A MBSs rose from 47% to 71% of total private sector MBS issuances.

PARTICIPANTS IN SECURITIZATION

In addition to private firms, the participants in the mortgage securitization process are the government agency Ginnie Mae and the government-sponsored entities Fannie Mae and Freddie Mac. Ginnie Mae facilitates the securitization of home mortgages backed by federally insured or guaranteed loans, such as those issued by the Federal Housing Administration (FHA) or the U.S. Department of Veterans Affairs (VA). Ginnie Mae guarantees the timely payment of mortgages' principal and interest, thereby reducing the risks for MBS investors. That said, it guaranteed the mortgages underlying only 4% of all MBSs issued in 2006. The GSEs Fannie Mae and Freddie Mac accounted for a more substantial 40% of MBSs issued in 2006. They purchase what are known as conforming mortgages from originators. Conforming mortgages are those that meet certain borrower quality characteristics and loan-to-value ratios and are smaller than the conforming loan size limit ($417,000 as of January 1, 2007). These GSEs use these conforming loans to back the MBSs they issue, adding guarantees that principal and interest on the mortgages will be paid. The remaining 56% of MBSs issued in 2006 were packaged by private sector financial institutions. Most of these MBSs included securities backed by high quality (prime) loans, subprime loans, or "Alt-A" loans. The problems with mortgages in recent months have been largely confined to the subprime and Alt-A sectors, and it is the MBSs backed by pools of these loans that have had the most problems.

The difference between prime and subprime mortgage loans hinges on borrower quality. A prime loan indicates that the borrower has a good credit rating (an "A" grade), while the subprime borrower has a lower credit rating. Many of the prime loans that back private sector MBSs are jumbo loans; such loans are issued to high-quality borrowers, but they are too large to meet the conforming loan size limit of the two GSEs. Alt-A loans are issued to borrowers that appear to have good credit, but these loans do not meet the definition of prime or conforming. Often, Alt-A loans are issued to borrowers with limited or no income and asset verification. In recent years, the Alt-A sector has increasingly included loans for which the loan-to value ratio was too high. The share of MBSs backed by subprime and Alt-A mortgage loans increased rapidly in the last decade. From 1996 through 2006, the share of subprime and Alt-A MBSs rose from 47% to 71% of total private sector MBS issuances.

FEDERAL RESERVE POLICIES AND ITS IMPACT

The Federal Reserve System (the Fed) has been the central bank of the United States since it was created in 1913. The main purpose of a central bank is to regulate the supply of money and credit to the American economy. The board of governors, the Fed's principal policy-making organization, plays a key role in this process. The Federal Reserve's basic powers are concentrated in the Board of Governors, which is paramount in many policy issues concerning bank regulation and supervision and in most aspects of monetary control. The board announces the Fed's policies on both monetary and banking matters. Because the board is not an operating agency, most of the day-to-day implementation of policy decisions is left to the district Federal Reserve banks, stock in which is owned by the commercial banks that are members of the Federal Reserve System. Ownership in this instance, however, does not imply control; the Board of Governors and the heads of the Reserve Banks orient their policies to the public interest rather than the benefit of the private banking system.

PARTICIPANT	BENEFITS
Borrowers	• Access to credit despite a low FICO score and a poor credit history
Mortgage Originator	• Makes money through the fees that are used to originate a mortgage and the difference between the interest rate of the market and the premium charged to the borrower
Securities Dealer	• Makes money by selling securities to investors and charges commission for underwriting
Investors in MBS	• Greater liquidity than loans backing transaction • Opportunity to diversify portfolio • Constraints of purchasing event grade paper can be met with ABS
Economy	• Expanded source of financing for home ownership • Greater integration of capital and financial markets • Source of funds for banks and other institutions

At the base of the Federal Reserve System are the member commercial banks. All national, or federally chartered, banks are required to join the system; membership of state-chartered institutions is voluntary. Members have to purchase capital stock in their district Federal Reserve bank in the amount of 6 percent of their capital, excluding retained earnings, and get the right to vote for six of the nine directors of that district bank. Stock ownership does not convey control or the financial interest normally attached to stock in a corporation. The stock may not be sold or used as collateral and must be returned to the district reserve bank if the commercial bank ceases to be a member.

The Monetary Control Act of 1980 imposed a reserve requirement on all depository institutions, including nonmembers of the Federal Reserve, but it also permits them to borrow from the Federal Reserve and to use services provided by the Fed, such as check clearing, electronic funds transfer, and securities safekeeping. By enabling banks to borrow reserves from the Fed, the liquidity of the entire banking system is increased.

The 12 district reserve banks are located in the following cities: Boston, Massachusetts; New York City; Philadelphia, Pennsylvania; Cleveland, Ohio; Richmond, Virginia; Atlanta, Georgia; Chicago; St. Louis; Minneapolis, Minnesota; Kansas City, Missouri; Dallas, Texas; and San Francisco, California. Each bank is formally responsible to a nine-member board of directors, which is divided into three classes. Class A and B directors are elected by the member banks; class C directors are appointed by the Board of Governors. The board of directors is responsible for the administration of its bank and for appointing the bank's president and vice president (subject to the approval of the Board of Governors). The directors also set the discount rate—that is, the interest rate charged to banks for borrowing from the Reserve banks—again, subject to review by the Board of Governors.

Reserve banks implement the decisions made by the Fed's Board of Governors and by their own officers. Their staffs examine state member banks (national banks are examined by the staff of the Office of the Comptroller of the Currency; insured nonmember banks are subject to FDIC examination), decide on granting loans to members, and carry out the routine banking functions for the federal government. Decisions on whether to allow a bank to open branches, to merge with another bank, or to form a *holding company* (company that offers a broad range of financial services) are often handled by reserve bank officers.

Sales and purchases of securities for the Federal Reserve System's own account are conducted by the Federal Reserve Bank of New York, which is also the operating arm for international financial activities.

At the top of the Federal Reserve System is the Board of Governors, which over the years has undergone significant change both in its responsibilities and its structure. The 1913 Act established a seven-member Federal Reserve Board, consisting of five presidential appointees, each from a different Federal Reserve district, plus the secretary of the treasury and the Comptroller of the Currency. Terms of office for the appointees were initially set at ten years and were staggered, so that no two would end at the same time; board members could not be removed from office except for cause. These provisions were meant to help insulate the presidential appointees from day-to-day politics. The board's powers, nevertheless, were confined to supervising the reserve banks, with limited powers over the discount rate and little discretion over the structure of the banking industry.

The Banking Act of 1935, which also finalized the creation of deposit insurance and the FDIC, centralized power in a Board of Governors, and made all seven members presidential appointees with the advice and consent of the U.S. Senate; the president also appoints a governor to serve as Fed chairman for a four-year term. Alan Greenspan was the Fed chairman from 1987 until 2006, when he was replaced by Ben S. Bernanke. The governors' terms were expanded to14 years by the 1935 act, and their powers were also expanded. For example, discount rates now had to be approved periodically by the board. Sales and purchases of government securities—the open-market operation that previously had been managed solely at the discretion of the presidents of the reserve banks—were centralized in the Federal Open Market Committee (FOMC), consisting of the seven governors, the president of the Federal Reserve Bank of New York, and four other reserve bank presidents serving on a rotating basis.

Since 1935, Congress has given additional powers to the Board of Governors. These powers include control over mergers, bank holding companies, U.S. offices of international banks, and the reserves of all depository institutions.

The responsibility for regulating the nation's money supply requires the Federal Reserve to influence the amount of reserve funds available to banks and thus the level and direction of short-term interest rates. For example, whether banks and other financial institutions will make loans depends on the profit margin—the difference in the rate of interest they must pay to attract deposits or borrow funds and the interest rate they can charge customers for credit. The greater the profit margin that banks can realize on new loans, the more they will want to lend. To influence interest rates on deposits and interest rates that banks pay to borrow funds, the Fed uses its congressionally granted authority to create money. The Fed creates money in three ways.

First and most important, the Fed can purchase U.S. government securities from financial institutions by simply creating "funds" (credits) on their balance sheets in exchange for the securities. To the extent that these securities are purchased directly from banks, banks have new liquid reserves on their books immediately. When nonbank financial institutions deposit their proceeds from sales of securities, banks will see their reserves increase even more. As some banks become flush with extra reserves, they temporarily lend these funds to other banks overnight to earn interest. The increased supply of reserves relative to demand in the money market pushes down the overnight interest rate (called the federal funds rate). This decline in the cost of credit to banks increases the profitability of new loans to businesses and individuals and provides stronger incentives for banks to expand the amount of credit to the economy.

A second monetary policy tool available to the Federal Reserve is the discount rate, the interest rate the Fed charges on loans it makes to banks. By increasing or decreasing this rate, the Fed can discourage or encourage banks to borrow the funds it creates and, therefore, make more loans to the public.

In the past, discount-rate lending has served a dual purpose: facilitating monetary policy as just described and providing emergency liquidity to troubled banks. The Fed's attempt to accomplish two different missions with the discount rate has prompted a debate over the rate's proper role. To stimulate the growth of credit in the economy via discount-rate lending, the Fed must set the discount rate below other prevailing short-term interest rates. Otherwise, banks have no incentive to borrow from the central bank. But if subsidized credit is also temporarily provided to troubled or failing banks, borrowing from the Fed could become stigmatized, so that normal, healthy banks refrain from seeking discount-rate credit. Such behavior by healthy banks could defeat the overall credit growth objective of Fed monetary policy. This dilemma has led some analysts, both inside and outside the Fed, to recommend that the Fed discontinue use of the discount rate to affect overall credit, and instead, provide discount-rate lending solely to higher-risk banks for emergency liquidity purposes, and only at a penalty rate.

A third way in which the Fed operates monetary policy is by regulating the proportion of liquid reserves that banks must keep on hand. Obviously, the higher the reserve requirement, the less funds there are available to make new loans. The board of governors has the authority to determine reserve requirements above the legal minimum for all federally insured depository institutions. Reserve requirements may be changed by a simple majority vote of the board.

In practice, however, reserve requirements are rarely changed because even small adjustments produce rather sweeping impacts on the quantity of required reserves.

With a view to pump liquidity and create confidence in the financial system the fed has been cutting the interest rates from time to time, recently it has reduced by 75 bps. The cut was taken positively by the world market but it proved to be short lived. The problem for American economy does not seem to be over yet as it is the subprime issue coupled with other issues that are driving it towards recession.

With the U.S. economy facing substantial difficulties, housing prices dropping and increasing number of households are defaulting on home loans. Losses on home loan portfolios are affecting financial firms who hold derivatives on home loans. Some financial firms have gone bankrupt, and there is uncertainty about who else might be bankrupt. With finance in difficulties, the monetary transmission is malfunctioning. Hence, while the U.S. Fed has cut rates sharply, the full impact of these lowered rates on the economy is not going through. Inflationary expectations are a concern. One estimate of the size of losses on sub-prime home loans is $400 billion. This is roughly 2.85% of U.S. GDP. The question remains as to whether there is a crisis or a mere recession in the U.S. economy. Many critics of securitisation have pointed out that this theory has not quite panned out as expected. However, at the same time, there is no doubting the fact that securitisation has given a substantial dispersion of the $400 billion loss. For this reason, the impact of the massive loss on the US financial system is not as large as it might otherwise have been.

The second equilibrating channel lies in monetary policy. Unlike many other countries which have experienced crises, the U.S. has well functioning institutions for conducting monetary policy.

The U.S. Fed has cut rates dramatically in response to difficulties in the economy. On 14th March, the 90-day treasury rate in the U.S. had dropped to 1.16%. The impact of lowered interest rates on the economy is not as strong as it used to be, owing to difficulties in finance. However, a certain impact is surely there. Low interest rates are helping strengthen demand, and help attract smart speculators to buy assets at fire sale prices.

Low interest rates are doing their job in one critical respect: the decline of the dollar. Unlike other countries which have experienced crisis, the U.S. has a floating exchange rate and an open capital account. The exchange rate pegging with capital controls, which has brought down so many emerging markets, is absent. When interest rates dropped, the dollar fell — exactly as it should. The weak dollar is bolstering net exports and helping the economy.

A second remarkable feature of the decline in the dollar is the funding channel for the U.S. through Asian central banks and governments in the middle east. For each $1 trillion of reserves held in USD assets, a 10% decline in the dollar constitutes a transfer of $100 billion to the issuer of liabilities in the U.S. Every Asian country should be asking whether this deal makes any sense for them, but in understanding present situation, it's useful to note that no other country facing a crisis in the past has had such a good deal, which produces fiscal transfers in the time of need.

Many economists are of the view that the U.S. economy is truly into recession. What is increasingly viewed as conclusive proof of a recession within the U.S. is that the U.S. Fed cut interest rates on three occasions in the second half of 2007 aggregating to 100 basis points, prior to this cut of 125 basis points in January 2008.

By cutting interest rates the U.S. Fed expects to stimulate consumption, crucially lower mortgage payments, and in the process trigger a recovery in the U.S. economy.

As U.S. lowers its interest rates dramatically, economists are worried that it could find that global capital is moving away to other countries which offer higher rates of interest simply on account of arbitrage opportunities. This could mean appreciation of currencies across continents and depreciation of the U.S. dollar. As the dollar depreciates against other currencies, goods from other countries would become costlier in the U.S. leading to inflationary pressures within the U.S. economy.

MORTGAGE FUND RATES AND FEDERAL FUND RATES

The federal reserve lowered short term interest rate twice in January by a total of 1.25 percentage points. Many people seemed to be excited about this as they belived that this would lead to lower rates on fixed term mortgages means an average person could save large amount of money by refinancing, but federal fund rates do not directly affect the mortgage rates. Mortgage rates declined dramatically over the month of Janurary. But the Federal Reserve's rate cut did not guarantee that rates would keep dropping. In fact, mortgage rates often climb following a cut in the federal funds rate, and actually rose about 50 basis points after the Federal Reserve announced its emergency 75-basis-point cut Jan. The Fed cut rates by 0.75% in January, but mortgages climbed by 0.50%. Mortgage rates are affected by 10-year Treasury Bills.

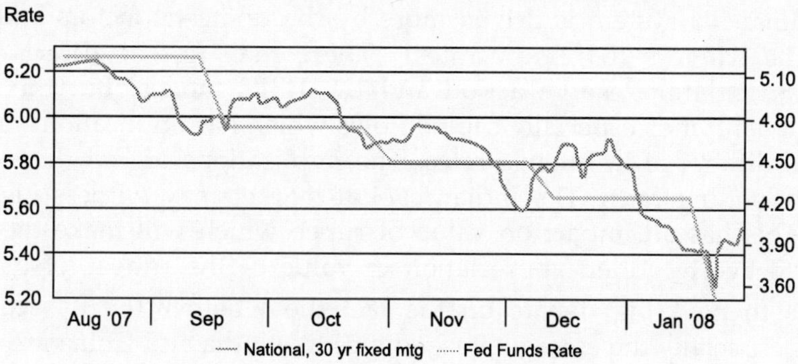

The green line represents the federal funds rate. The blue line represents the U.S. national average on 30-year fixed mortgages. Both lines trend downward, but otherwise seem unrelated. If anything, the mortgage rate appears to be a precursor to the federal funds rate. Again, it seems clear that the federal funds rate does not directly affect mortgage rates. The steps are taken to relieve the strangled credit markets in U.S. and save the country from going into an economic recession by injecting liquidity in the economy.

MAIN CREDIT LOSSES SO FAR IN US

Citigroup: $40.7bn
UBS: $38bn
Merrill Lynch: $31.7bn
HSBC: $15.6bn
Bank of America: $14.9bn
Morgan Stanley $12.6bn
Royal Bank of Scotland: $12bn
JP Morgan Chase: $9.7bn
Washington Mutual: $8.3bn
Deutsche Bank: $7.5bn
Wachovia: $7.3bn
Credit Agricole: $6.6bn
Credit Suisse: $6.3bn
Mizuho Financial $5.5bn
Bear Stearns: $3.2bn
Barclays: $3.2bn

The U.S. housing market collapse have already shocked the world's biggest economy into recession, and has contributed to the stock market's steep fall from record highs of only several months ago. However, forecasters at the National Association of Realtors now expect an abrupt turnaround in the sales of existing single-family homes and condomoniums, a key gauge of the housing market. That could lessen the drag effect on growth and provide a great support for the stock market.

The impact on India

The step taken by Fed also has an impact on the other economies of the world. The RBI in India also follows the footsteps of Fed. Considering the recent rate cuts by Fed the RBI also reacts accordingly.

The Indian financial system is driven more by the domestic factors and "Fed rate cut is one of the triggers to review rates. "There may not be direct correlation between the U.S. Federal Reserve action and the RBI's moves. But the country is more tuned to global trends especially capital flows which has implications on exchange rate and relative difference in interest rates. The implications of Fed decision are not restricted just to lending rates. The Indian capital market may witness higher inflow from overseas. This has an impact on value of rupee which will make the RBI to do tightrope walk to avert sudden appreciation in value of the rupee versus dollar.

There seems to be a big debate on the fact the whether the us economy and other economies especially the emerging economies like India and China are decoupled.

In recent times, many well regarded economists became severe critics of the central bank governor on the ground that he had been far too conservative by keeping a neutral to upward bias in interest rates. One of their main arguments flowed from the actions pursued by the U.S. Federal Reserve. As the U.S. has been cutting rates the rates the real interest rate for India has gone way higher than that of U.S.

Economists argued India needed to correct this by reducing its own interest rate. By reducing interest rate India would also discourage excess foreign capital inflows, it was further asserted. It was indeed an empirically valid proposition, because in any normal economic model capital flows are determined by interest rate differentials.

But the RBI governor eschewed this framework and took an intuitive call that capital flows are not necessarily always driven by interest rate differentials.

It is argued that India and the United States did not have the same set of problems. India was not facing a severe recession, nor was it reeling under a huge financial sector crisis. So it is not advisable to have the same set of solutions for a different set of problems.

The Reserve Bank's emphasis then remained on the inflationary expectations in food and oil. The central bank's intuitive call has indeed been proved right even as central bankers in other parts of the world follow suit. In some ways, the policymakers in emerging economies now clearly realise that they have to think on their own feet, according to the imperatives of their own political economy. For the first time, this aspect of independent thinking among central bankers and policymakers across emerging economies is showing signs of getting institutionalised. Though the IMF has been advising the economies of the world to co-ordinate their monetary and fiscal policy with that of U.S. to prevent a global slowdown the economies are not necessarily following it. In fact many economies are on the verge of tightening their monetary policy and that is why their interest rates are showing a neutral to upward movement.

The Impact of U.S. subprime crisis on India has not been very large according to economists. It was anticipated that the developing countries might be spared for a year or two and neither of the countries would be affected either by economic recession in the USA or the prevailing US subprime crisis. This notion was put forward by the leading economist of the World Bank.

Further, it was observed that even if there is an impact of US subprime crisis on India, it would not have been taking place earlier than two years. However, it would be wrongly said if the developing nations like India and China would be entirely untouched by the ripple effect. The prevailing economic condition in these countries are so strong that it may not feel the upheaval as it would have felt had the economy of these countries been sluggish.

Probable effects on financial markets of India

One of the impacts of US subprime crisis on global markets has been certain unforeseen losses pertaining to securities. Such a situation has made credit conditions stringent. Consequently, loss incurred on securities has increased. As a cumulative effect, the financial markets have spiraled downward causing the monetary policies to become more loose.

With regard to equity markets, it was being anticipated that equity markets may go down and the cost of capital(effective) may rise by 200 basis points as compared to the baseline. As a result of the credit constraints, business investment in the United States of America would drop, unemployment would rise and there would be a prolonged phase of depression in the consumer prices.

1. The need of the hour is to have a more open economy of America or be open to trade, attract investments, which would rekindle innovative concepts and enhance foreign direct investment. The growth has to be such that it is sustainable, only then will the impact of U.S. subprime crisis on India be negligible.

   The present crisis in U.S. may not have such an impact on the world economy because it is confined to one sector of the economy, viz., mortgage and housing but one cannot deny that housing is a sector with large-scale implications.

   Sound banking practices: The root cause of the subprime mortgage (even prime mortgage loans are in trouble in U.S.; e.g., trouble in Countrywide, America's biggest home loan lender) crisis is the unsound credit practices that emerged in the U.S. market. Fake certification, which helps an ineligible person to raise a home loan, cannot be ruled out in India.

   Housing loan frauds are not uncommon in the cities of India and the aggressiveness with which housing loans are being sold by banks and financial companies in violation of sound credit practices cannot be ignored. Personal loans and overdue credit cards are the other sectors which the regulators and bankers should handle carefully because they have the potential to plunge the Indian banking sector into a crisis.

2. Controlled Derivatives market: Derivatives are financial instruments, which can spread the default risk attaching to loans. All the same, indiscriminate use of such derivatives can lead to havoc as in U.S. Derivatives lead to such a chain reaction that it will be nearly impossible to quantify the risk of exposure to bad loans and advances subsequently. RBI and GOI should prohibit indiscriminate use of such derivatives if they intend to introduce such products in India.
3. Limited investment by Indian companies abroad: Prudent investment abroad should be the order of the day. Reckless investment in the derivatives market abroad by banks and financial institutions has to be controlled. In the recent crisis, BNP Paribas of France and Macquarie Bank of Australia have been affected because of such overseas investments. The exposure of Indian banks to the subprime crisis of U.S. is minimal.
4. Quality Inward Investment: FDI should be given priority over FIIs as history has shown that flight of capital in case of FDI is low compared to that in respect of FIIs. Due to their stable nature, FDI can help in the growth of the country's infrastructure.

SCOPE OF SECURITIZATION AND INDIAN EXPERIENCE

The major players in the asset securitization market in India are expected to be commercial FIs, PSUs, Corporates, Government bodies, Mutual Funds, Pension Funds, etc. Securitization is a relatively new concept in India but is gaining ground quite rapidly. CRISIL rated the first securitisation program in India in 1991 when Citibank securitized a pool from its auto loan portfolio and placed the paper with GIC Mutual Fund (a case study of one of Citibank's subsequent deals is discussed later in detail). Since then, securitization of assets has begun to emerge as a clear option of fund raising by corporates and a few transactions of well-rated companies have taken place in the country. While some of the securitization transactions which took place earlier involved sale of hire purchase or loan receivables of non-banking financial companies (NBFCs), arising out of auto-finance activity, many manufacturing companies and service industries are now increasingly looking towards securitizing their deferred receivables and future flows also.

Information on past deals is not readily available, as most of them have been bilateral one-to-one and unrated transactions. In the context of rated transactions, CRISIL has rated about 50 transactions till date, with volume aggregating to well over Rs 4,500 crore. Other rating agencies in India, viz., ICRA, DCR and CARE have also been actively involved in the process. The majority of these being in the nature of outright sales of auto loan portfolios without subsequent issue of securities and do not amount to securitization in the real sense. There has till date been no instance of downgrading of the rating assigned to any of these transactions. As per an estimate, out of the total asset securitization attempted between 1992 and

1998, as much as 35% relates to hire purchase receivables of truck and auto loan segment.

The car loan segment of the auto loans market has been more successful than the commercial vehicle loan segment mainly because of factors such as perceived credit risk, higher volumes and homogeneous nature of receivables. Other types of receivables for which securitization has been attempted include property rental receivables, power receivables, telecom receivables, lease receivables etc.

SECURITIZATION IN INDIA

(1) Auto loans

Though securitization was made popular by housing finance companies, it has found wide application in other areas of retail financing, particularly financing of cars and commercial vehicles. In India, the auto sector has been thrown open to international participation, greatly expanding the scope of the market. Auto loans (including installment and hire purchase finance) broadly fulfill the features necessary in securitization. The security in this case is also considered good, because of title over a utility asset. The development of a second hand market for cars in India has also meant that foreclosure is an effective tool in the hands of auto loan financiers in delinquent cases.

(2) Relevance of securitization in some infrastructure sectors

(a) Power

Various public sector units (PSUs) have a high financial exposure to state electricity boards (SEBs), some of which are sub-standard loans since several SEBs have inadequate solvency for meeting obligations on the due date. Securitization in the power sector can be divided into the following segments.

Receivables of PSUs such as National Thermal Power Corporation, Cola India Ltd., Power Finance Corporation, Rural Electrification Corporation, National Hydel Power Corporation, etc. from various SEBs can be securitized to reduce/ rebalance financial exposure of these PSUs. Securitization of SEB revenues for resource raising has been a good experience with NTPC Ltd.

(b) Roads

Private sector road projects are expected to earn revenues from toll collections and concessions. However these projects carry multiple level of risks which could be summarized as under:

Construction risk – In event of inordinate delays in procuring land and completing implementation.

Traffic Estimation risk – Accuracy of estimating traffic in various segments i.e. commercial vehicles, buses, passenger cars, two wheelers and achieving desired traffic estimates

Toll collection risk – Intent and willingness of users to pay requisite tolls for usage. Considering the multiple levels of risk, securitisation could be used to splice various levels of risks and thereby facilitate financial closure at an optimal cost of capital.

(c) Ports

The revenues of typical port projects would be in the nature of storage and loading revenues levied on ships, which stop at the port of call. In addition, ports tend to provide storage facilities for chemicals, cargo, petroleum products, etc. to several large companies. The port authority/operator contract such storage facilities for a long tenure. The port revenues of this nature are suitable to securitization.

(d) Urban Infrastructure

Primarily, the opportunity in urban infrastructure is in the areas of housing loans (the same has been covered under the section pertaining to mortgage securitization). The other areas under urban infrastructure are water supply, sewage facilities, garbage disposal, etc

Further, the above list is illustrative and not exhaustive. Wherever a reasonably certain sum of money will be received over a certain time, not very short, securitization possibility exists. In short, the scope of securitization is vast; ultimately being limited only by the consideration that assets proposed to be securitized must fundamentally be income bearing.

APPENDIX-1

THE TIMELINE

- o **1985–1991**: Savings and Loan Crisis
- o **1995–2001**: Dot-com bubble
- o **1998**: inflation-adjusted home price appreciation exceeds 10%/year in most West Coast metropolitan areas
- o **2001**: dot-com bubble collapse
- o **2000–2003**: Early 2000s recession (exact time varies by country)
- o **2001–2005**: United States housing bubble (part of the world housing bubble)
- o **2001**: US Federal Reserve lowers Federal funds rate 11 times, from 6.5% (May 2000) to 1.75% (December 2001).
- o **2002**: Annual home price appreciation of 10% or more in California, Florida, and most Northeastern states.
- o **2004-2005**: Arizona, California, Florida, Hawaii, and Nevada record price increases in excess of 25% per year.
- o **2005–ongoing**: Market correction ("bubble bursting")
- o **2005**: Boom ended August 2005. The booming housing market halted abruptly for many parts of the U.S. in late summer of 2005.
- o **2006**: Continued market slowdown. Prices are flat, home sales fall, resulting in inventory buildup. U.S. Home Construction Index is down over 40% as of mid-August 2006 compared to a year earlier.
- o **2007**: Home sales continue to fall. The plunge in existing-home sales is the steepest since 1989. In Q1/2007, S&P/Case-Shiller house price index records first year-over-year decline in nationwide house prices since 1991. The subprime mortgage industry collapses, and a surge of foreclosure activity (twice as bad as 2006) and rising interest rates threaten to depress prices further as problems in the subprime markets spread to the near-prime and prime mortgage markets. The U.S. Treasury secretary calls the bursting housing bubble "the most significant risk to our economy".
- o **February–March**: Subprime industry collapses; more than 25 subprime lenders declaring bankruptcy, announcing significant losses, or putting themselves up for sale.
- o **April 2**: New Century Financial, largest U.S. subprime lender, files for chapter 11 bankruptcy.
- o **July 19**: Dow-Jones closes above 14,000 for the first time in its history.

- **August**: worldwide "credit crunch" as subprime mortgage backed securities are discovered in portfolios of banks and hedge funds around the world, from BNP Paribas to Bank of China. Many lenders stop offering home equity loans and "stated income" loans. Federal Reserve injects about $100B into the money supply for banks to borrow at a low rate.
- **August 6**: American Home Mortgage files for chapter 11 bankruptcy.
- **August 7**: Democratic presidential front-runner Hillary Clinton proposes a $1 billion bailout fund to help homeowners at risk for foreclosure .
- **August 16**: Countrywide Financial Corporation, the biggest U.S. mortgage lender, narrowly avoids bankruptcy by taking out an emergency loan of $11 billion from a group of banks.
- **August 17**: Federal Reserve lowers the discount rate by 50 basis points to 5.75% from 6.25%.
- **August 31**: President Bush announces a limited bailout of U.S. homeowners unable to pay the rising costs of their debts. Ameriquest, once the largest subprime lender in the U.S., goes out of business
- **September 1–3**: Fed Economic Symposium in Jackson Hole, WY addressed the housing recession that jeopardizes U.S. growth. Several critics argued that the Fed should use regulation and interest rates to prevent asset-price bubbles, blamed former Fed-chairman Alan Greenspan's low interest rate policies for stoking the U.S. housing boom and subsequent bust, and Yale University economist Robert Shiller warned of possible home price declines of fifty percent.
- **September 14**: A run on the bank forms at the United Kingdom's Northern Rock bank precipitated by liquidity problems related to the subprime crisis.
- **September 17**: Former Fed Chairman Alan Greenspan said "we had a bubble in housing and warns of "large double digit declines" in home values "larger than most people expect."
- **September 18**: The Fed lowers interest rates by half a point (0.5%) in an attempt to limit damage to the economy from the housing and credit crises.
- **September 28**: Television finance personality Jim Cramer warns Americans on The Today Show, "don't you dare buy a home—you'll lose money," causing a furor among realtors.
- **September 30**: Affected by the spiraling mortgage and credit crises, Internet banking pioneer Net Bank goes bankrupt, and the Swiss bank UBS announced that it lost US$690 million in the third quarter.
- **October 10**: Hope Now Alliance was created by the US Government and private industry to help some subprime borrowers.

- o **October 15–17**: A consortium of U.S. banks backed by the U.S. government announced a "super fund" of $100 billion to purchase mortgage backed securities whose mark-to-market value plummeted in the subprime collapse. Both Fed chairman Ben Bernanke and Treasury Secretary Hank Paulson expressed alarm about the dangers posed by the bursting housing bubble; Paulson said "the housing decline is still unfolding and I view it as the most significant risk to our economy. ... The longer housing prices remain stagnant or fall, the greater the penalty to our future economic growth.
- o **October 31**: Federal Reserve lowers the federal funds rate by 25 basis points to 4.5%.
- o **November 1**: Federal Reserve injects $41B into the money supply for banks to borrow at a low rate. The largest single expansion by the Fed since $50.35B on September 19, 2001.
- o **December 6**:President Bush announced a plan to voluntarily and temporarily freeze the mortgages of a limited number of mortgage debtors holding adjustable rate mortgages (ARM). He also ask Members Of Congress to: 1) pass legislation to modernize the FHA. 2) temporarily reform the tax code to help homeowners refinance during this time of housing market stress. 3) pass funding to support mortgage counseling. 4) pass legislation to reform Government Sponsored Enterprises (GSEs) like Freddie Mac and Fannie Mae.
- o **2008**:
- o **March 14, 2008**: Bear Stearns gets Fed funding as shares plummet.
- o **March 16, 2008**: Bear Stearns gets acquired for $2 a share by JPMorgan Chase in a fire sale avoiding bankruptcy. The deal is backed by Federal Reserve providing up to $30B to cover possible Bear Stearn losses.

ANNEXTURE-2

BLOW-BY-BLOW ACCOUNT OF THE SUB-PRIME SHOCK

MAY 2008

12 May

HSBC reveals a further $3.2bn. of losses linked to the U.S. subprime market.

APRIL 2008

22 April

The UK's second largest bank, RBS, reveals £5.9bn. in writedowns from the credit crunch, and asks its shareholders for an additional £12bn. to rebuild its capital base.

18 April

Citigroup reveals another $12bn. in sub-prime losses, bringing its total to $40bn., the most of any bank. It cuts 9000 jobs amid a quarterly loss of $5bn, down from $9.8bn. in the previous quarter.

17April

US investment bank Merrill Lynch reveals an additional $4.5bn. in credit writedowns and a loss of nearly $2bn in the first quarter of the year.

1 April

Swiss bank UBS reveals a further $19bn. of asset writedowns. This came on top of the $18.4bn. which it announced for 2007.

1 April

Germany's Deutsche Bank warns of credit losses of $3.9bn. in the first three months of 2008.

MARCH 2008

31 March

US Treasury announces major package to reform regulation of U.S. financial markets and prevent future financial crises. The plans are criticised by consumer groups but generally praised on Wall Street.

18 March

Wall Street investment banks Goldman Sachs and Lehman Brothers reveal that their first quarter profits have been halved by the credit crunch. But stocks rise on the news that their results have not been as bad as expected.

17 March

Wall Street investment bank Bear Stearns is acquired by JPMorgan Chase for $240m, a fraction of its share price, in deal backed by $30bn. in Fed loans.

The bank got into trouble over its huge exposure to subprime mortgage-backed securities.

14 March

Bear Stearns receives emergency funding, after its exposure to mortgage-backed investments undermined confidence in the bank.

14 March

Investment fund Carlyle Capital fails as the credit crisis spreads from sub-prime related products to other mortgage-backed investments.

11 March

Central banks make another coordinated attempt to ease conditions in the credit markets, by announcing $200bn of new emergency lending for banks.

7 March

The former bosses of Merrill Lynch and Citigroup are questioned by a Congressional panel over their bumper pay — despite huge, subprime related bosses at their banks.

6 March

A £1bn hedge fund run by Peloton Partners collapsed, after it struggled to meet interest payments due to the credit crisis.

5 March

France's biggest retail bank Credit Agricole announced a fourth quarter loss hit by a 3.3bn. euro charge at its investment banking boss, Calyon.

3 March

HSBC announced a $17.2bn. (£8.7bn.) loss after the decline in the U.S. housing market hit the value of its loans.

FEBRUARY 2008

14 February

Commerzbank, Germany's second-biggest bank, cuts $1.1bn. off the value of investments linked to the subprime mortgage crisis and warns its losses could worsen.

Swiss investment bank UBS confirms it has made a loss of $4bn in 2007 after cutting the value of investments by $18.4bn.

13 February

Britain's Bradford & Bingley cuts the value of its sub-prime mortgage-related investments by £144.4m ($284.5m). A few weeks earlier it had said it did not expect to suffer any writedowns.

Japan's financial watchdog says Japanese banks suffered losses of $5.6bn. by the end of 2007. These have more than doubled in the last three months of the year.

12 February

Swiss bank Credit Suisse says losses on subprime investments were $1.8bn., less than originally expected.

10 February

Leaders from the G7 group of industrialised nations say worldwide losses from the U.S. mortgage crisis could reach $400bn.

8 February

Deutsche Bank announces $3.2bn. of subprime writedowns in the third quarter of the financial year and predicts there is not much more to come.

7 February

U.S. Federal Reserve boss Ben Bernanke expresses concern about bond insurers that guarantee against defaults on mortgage loans.

6 February

Wall Street sees its worst share losses in almost a year, amid fears that the worst U.S. housing slump in 25 years is crippling the wider economy.

5 February

U.S. financial firm GMAC, which owns sub-prime lender Residential Capital, says it has made a $2.3bn. loss in 2007, compared with a $2.1bn. profit the year before.

JANUARARY 2008

31 January

Bond insurer MBIA announces a $2.3bn. loss, its biggest yet for a three-month period. It was hit by declines in the value of U.S. mortgage-backed debt, which it guarantees against.

30 January

The U.S. Federal Reserve cuts interest rates to 3% from 3.5%. It is the second cut in nine days. U.S. economic growth slows.

29 January

The U.S. Federal Bureau of Investigation launches an investigation into 14 companies involved in the subprime mortgage crisis.

Mitchells & Butlers loses £274m when a property deal falls through due to the credit crisis.

28 January

Belgian bank Fortis warns its losses connected to bad U.S. mortgage debt could be as high as $1.47bn.

25 January

Barclays Capital predicts banks will need to raise as much as $143bn. to weather the credit crisis.

23 January

The Bank of China dismisses rumours it was about to unveil massive losses caused by its exposure to the U.S. subprime mortgage market.

22 January

The U.S. Federal Reserve cuts interest rates by half a percentage point to 3.5%, it's biggest cut in 25 years.

21 January

Global stock markets, including London's FTSE 100 index, suffer their biggest falls since 11 September 2001.

21 January

German Bank WestLB warns investors that it expects to write down $1.45bn. of investments and make a net loss of a similar amount.

18 January

Scottish Equitable introduces delays for investors wanting to withdraw money from its commercial property funds, citing recession and subprime worries.

17 January

Merrill Lynch unveils a $14.1bn. writedown of investments linked to subprime mortgages and posts a net loss of $7.8bn. in 2007.

Investment bank Lehman Brothers cuts 1,300 jobs as it scales back its U.S. mortgage lending business.

16 January

U.S. bank JP Morgan Chase says it has cut the value of its mortgage-related investments by $1.3bn. Profits for the last three months of 2007 fall by a third.

11 January

Swiss investment bank UBS warns that is still does not know the subprime crisis and says it might make a loss in 2007 when it reports its full results.

Federal Reserve boss Ben Bernanke says that the outlook for the U.S. economy is deteriorating among continuing worries about the subprime crisis.

The largest mortgage lender in the U.S., Countrywide, which pioneered subprime mortgages, is bought by Bank of America for $4bn. after its shares plunge 48%.

9 January

Bear Stearns boss James Cayne steps down after the firm reveals $1.9bn. in subprime losses, the largest in its history.

World Bank says that world economic growth will slow in 2008 due to credit crunch, but strong performance in China and India will cushion impact.

7 January

President George W Bush admits that the credit crunch could slow the U.S. economy in 2008, but says it is still fundamentally strong.

U.S. economists urge government action to ease looming U.S. economic slowdown as a result of credit crunch.

4 January

U.S. unemployment rises sharply as job report sparks fall in stock market.

DECEMBER 2007

19 December

Morgan Stanley writes off $9.4bn. in subprime losses and sells a 9.9% stake in the company to the Chinese state investment company CIC for $5bn. to rebuild its capital.

18 December

The U.S. Federal Reserve Bank tightens rules on subprime lending, requiring mortgage companies to check more carefully on customers' income and give full disclosure of the cost of the loan.

ECB lends European commercial banks $500bn. over the Christmas period to help ease the credit crisis.

Bank of England makes £10bn. available to UK banks to ease credit crunch.

17 December

U.S. central bank, the Federal Reserve, makes $20bn. available to commercial banks at an auction to help ease the credit crunch.

Former Fed chairman Alan Greenspan urges the U.S. government to give direct aid to homeowners hit by the subprime crisis.

14 December

Citigroup takes $49bn. worth of subprime debts back on its balance sheets, effectively closing seven structured investment vehicles (SIVs) which had relied on money market funding.

13 December

World central banks agree coordinated action to inject at least $100bn. into short-term inter-bank credit markets to restore confidence.

11 December

U.S. central bank, the Federal Reserve, cuts interest rates for a third time to 4.25% to ease the credit crunch.

10 December

Swiss bank UBS reports a further $10bn write-down caused by bad debts in the U.S. housing market.

Lloyds TSB reveals that bad debt linked to the U.S. subprime mortgage crisis will cost it £200m.

6 December

President George W Bush outlines plans to protect more than a million homeowners hit by the U.S. housing slump.

Royal Bank of Scotland warns it will write off about £1.25bn. because of exposure to the U.S. subprime market.

The Bank of England cuts UK interest rates for the first time since 2005, amid signs that the economy is slowing.

The European Central Bank keeps interest rates in the eurozone at their current level of 4%.

4 December

U.S. mortgage giant Fannie Mae is to issue $7bn. of shares to cover losses linked to the housing market.

Canada cuts interest rates for the first time since April 2004 amid credit fears.

The future of the UK mortgage industry remains bright, despite the current funding crisis, say lenders.

UK mortgage lenders should prepare for the global credit crunch to get much worse, the City watchdog says.

3 December

Credit agency Moody's widens its debt review, having already earmarked $116bn. of debt for downgrading.

NOVEMBER 2007

30 November

U.S. construction spending falls sharply, led by a large fall in the building of private homes.

Morgan Stanley co-president Zoe Cruz is to retire, seen as the latest casualty of the U.S. sub-prime crisis.

29 November

Bank of England governor Mervyn King warns that growth in the UK economy may slow and inflation is likely to rise.

The U.S. lowers its 2008 economic growth forecast amid ongoing housing and credit market problems.

27 November

U.S. mortgage guarantor Freddie Mac is selling $6bn. of shares to cover further bad debt losses.

U.S. house prices dropped sharply in the third quarter, falling at their biggest rate in 21 years, a survey shows.

Citigroup agrees to sell shares worth $7.5bn. to an investment fund owned by Abu Dhabi.

23 November

The U.S. Christmas shopping season gets underway, with shoppers braving the cold to look for bargains.

22 November

UK lender Kensington Mortgages withdraws its entire range of subprime mortgages because of market conditions.

The Nationwide, the UK's largest building society, benefits from being seen as a haven from troubled banks.

20 November

U.S. mortgage guarantor Freddie Mac sets aside $1.2bn. to cover bad loans and reports a $2bn. loss.

The U.S. Federal Reserve cuts its 2008 growth forecast citing credit and housing market woes.

UK buy-to-let mortgage lender Paragon sees its shares fall nearly 40% after revealing funding difficulties.

Construction of new US homes in October remains sharply lower than a year earlier, figures show.

19 November

Northern Rock says bids to buy bank are "below current market value."

Swiss Re expects to lose $1bn. on insurance a client took out against any fall in the value of its mortgage debt.

16 November

Goldman Sachs forecasts subprime losses for entire financial sector at $400bn. (£200bn).

Northern Rock's boss resigns.

Nationwide warns of no UK house price growth in 2008.

15 November

Barclays says it had written down £1.3bn. ($2.6bn.) in subprime losses.

U.S. House of Representatives passes Predatory Lending and Mortgage Protection Act by lopsided majority.

14 November

HSBC raised its sub-prime bad debt provision by $1.4bn. (£670m) to $3.4bn.

Bank of England says that credit crunch caused by sub-prime lending will lead to a sharp slowdown in UK growth.

Mizuho, Japan's second largest banking group, saw a 17% drop in first-half net profits and cut its full-year operating profit forecast by 13%, largely as a result of subprime-related losses at its securities arm.

13 November

Bank of America writes off $3bn. in subprime losses.

12 November

The three biggest U.S. banking groups — Citigroup, Bank of America and JPMorganChase — agree a $75bn. superfund to restore confidence to credit markets.

9 November

U.S.'s fourth largest lender Wachovia revealed a $1.1bn. loss due to decline in value of its mortgage debt plus $600m to cover loan losses (total $1.7bn., £829m).

8 November

Morgan Stanley unveiled a $3.7bn. loss from its U.S. sub-prime mortgage exposure.

BNP Paribas (after temporarily freezing hedge funds with $2.1bn. in assets under management in August) revealed it had written down 301m euro ($439m, £214m) because of credit problems, including $197m related to U.S. subprime and home builder lending.

6 November

Bank of England governor Mervyn King defends his role in Northern Rock crisis in exclusive interview with BBC Business Editor Robert Peston.

5 November

Banking giant Citigroup announces fresh losses of between $8bn. and $11bn. because of exposure to the U.S. subprime market. Chief executive and chairman Charles Prince resigns.

1 November

Credit Suisse revealed a $1bn. write-down on bad debts.

OCTOBER 2007

31 October

Federal Reserve delivers second rate cut to boost markets

Deutsche Bank revealed a 2.16bn. euros ($3bn, £1.6bn) writedown on bad debts.

30 October

Merrill Lynch takes a $7.9bn. hit following exposure to bad debt. Its chief executive, Stan O'Neal, resigns.

17 October

Further falls in US house building signal bad times for builders.

IMF warns that credit crunch will hit world growth.

16 October

Northern Rock executives defend role at Treasury Select Committee

U.S. Federal Reserve chairman Ben Bernanke warns sub-prime crisis and housing slump will be significant drag on U.S. economy

Confidence among home builders falls to record low.

15 October

Citigroup writes down additional $5.9bn. on exposure to the U.S. sub-prime market.

Japanese bank Nomura announced the closure of its US mortgage-backed securities business and takes a $621m (£299m) hit.

14 October

U.S. banks holding secret talks at U.S. Treasury float idea of a new super-fund to revive the frozen credit markets.

9 October

Bank of England and FSA defend role in Northern Rock crisis

5 October

Investment bank Merrill Lynch reveals $5.6bn. sub-prime loss

1 October

Swiss bank UBS revealed losses of $3.4bn. in its fixed income and rates division, and in its mortgage-backed securities business, while Citigroup admits $.31bn. in losses.

SEPTEMBER 2007

26 September

Commercial banks shun Bank of England rescue fund

22 September

UK Chancellor Alistair Darling suggests government will consider boosting deposit savings guarantee to £100,000.

20 September

Deutsche Bank boss Josef Ackermann warns of losses from subprime exposure.

Bank of England governor Mervyn King defends his role in Northern Rock crisis to House of Commons Treasury Select Committee

U.S. Federal Reserve chairman Ben Bernanke says the losses from the subprime mortgage crisis are higher than expected

Goldman Sachs makes a profit by betting that mortgage-backed securities will fall despite $1.5bn. exposure.

19 September

Bank of England in U-turn on bank lending

18 September

The U.S. Federal Reserve cuts interest rates to 4.75% from 5.25% to try to energise financial markets.

Savers return to Northern Rock after the government guarantees all savings.

15 September

Thousands of depositors queue outside Northern Rock branches to try and get their money out.

14 September

Shares in Northern Rock plummet after news of its Bank of England rescue is announced.

13 September

The BBC revealed that Northern Rock had asked for and been granted emergency financial support from the Bank of England, in the latter's role as lender of last resort.

11 September

ECB president Jean-ClaudeTrichet blames rating agencies for subprime crisis but says EU economy sound.

U.S. Treasury Secretary Hank Paulson says mortgage lenders are to blame for sub-prime crisis.

6 September

ECB injects fresh cash into markets as credit fears intensify. Total intervention has now reached 250bn. euros ($300bn, £150bn).

4 September

Bank of China reveals $9bn. in subprime losses but Chinese government says its foreign exchange reserves will not be affected.

Overnight bank lending dries up as banks fear defaults from each other

3 September

German regional lender IKB recorded a $1bn. loss as a result of exposure to the U.S. subprime market.

AUGUST 2007

31 August

President Bush, flanked by Treasury Secretary Hank Paulson and Fed chief Ben Bernanke, pledges to ease subprime lending crisis.

30 August

German Chancellor Angela Merkel criticised credit ratings agencies for not spotting problems on the market.

28 August

The German regional bank Sachsen Landesbank is rapidly sold to Germany's biggest regional bank, Landesbank Baden-Wuerttemberg. It came close to collapsing under its exposure to subprime debt. It received a 17bn. euro lifeline.

23 August

Leading subprime lender Countrywide gets $2bn. cash injection from Bank of America.

Shares slump after Countrywide warns that mortgage slump is getting worse.

Leading U.S. and European banks borrow $2bn. from Federal Reserve.

21 August

Sharp rise in U.S. home repossessions as subprime borrowers default.

Capital One cuts jobs as subprime crisis bites.

20 August

Countrywide cuts jobs as subprime crisis hits.

U.S. mortgage lender sells assets

UK sub-prime lenders tighten up lending terms.

17 August

The U.S. Federal Reserve cut the interest rate at which it lends to banks (the discount rate) by half a percentage point to help banks deal with credit problems.

BNP Paribas says sub-prime losses in hedge funds will not impact on quarterly profits.

16 August

Countrywide draws on its entire $11.5bn. credit line as liquidity crisis looms. Australian mortgage lender Rams also admits liquidity problems.

15 August

Shares plunge in largest mortgage lender Countrywide on fears it will go bankrupt

13 August

Wall Street giant Goldman Sachs said it would pump $3bn. into a hedge fund hit by the credit crunch to help shore up its value.

The European Central Bank pumps 47.7bn. euros into the money markets, its third cash injection in as many working days. Central banks in the U.S. and Japan also topped up earlier injections.

10 August

Global stock markets stayed under intense pressure over subprime fears. London's FTSE 100 index had its worst day in more than four years, closing 3.7% lower.

The ECB provided an extra 61bn euros of funds for banks. The U.S. Fed said it would provide as much overnight money as would be needed to combat the credit crunch.

9 August

Short-term credit markets freeze up after French bank BNP Paribas suspends three investment funds worth 2bn euros, citing problems in the U.S. sub-prime mortgage sector. BNP said it could not value the assets in the fund, because the market had disappeared. The European Central Bank pumps 95bn euros into the eurozone banking system to ease the subprime credit crunch. The U.S. Federal Reserve and the Bank of Japan take similar steps

6 August

American Home Mortgage, one of the largest U.S. independent home loan providers, filed for bankruptcy after laying off the majority of its staff. The company said it was a victim of the slump in the U.S. housing market that had caught out many sub-prime borrowers and lenders.

3 August

Shares fall heavily on fears of subprime losses and global credit crunch.

JULY 2007

31 July

Bear Stearns stopped clients from withdrawing cash from a third fund, saying it has been overwhelmed by redemption requests. The lender also filed for bankruptcy protection for the two funds it had to bail out earlier.

27 July

Worries about the subprime crisis hammered global stock markets and the main U.S. Dow Jones stock index slipped.

26 July

Bear Stearns seized assets from one of its problem-hit hedge funds as it tried to stem losses. Shares fell 4.2% in five sessions, its worst weekly decline in almost five years.

24 July

Rising defaults on subprime loans hit profits at Countrywide, largest mortgage lender.

20 July

Federal Reserve chairman Ben Bernanke warned that the crisis in the U.S. subprime lending market could cost up to $100bn.

19 July

Fed comments shake global shares

18 July

Bear Stearns told investors that they will get little, if any, money back from the two hedge funds that the lender was forced to rescue.

13 July

U.S. industrial firm General Electric decided to sell the WMC Mortgage subprime lending business that it had bought in 2004. "The mortgage industry has greatly changed since the purchase of WMC," said its chief executive, Laurent Bossard.

10 July

Independent market analyst Datamonitor said U.K. subprime mortgages were set to grow faster than mainstream mortgages, with the market worth some £31.5bn. by 2011.

4 July

The U.K.'s Financial Services Authority (FSA) said it would take action against five brokers selling sub-prime mortgages, claiming they offered loans to people which should not be given them.

JUNE 2007

29 June

Bear Stearns fires its head of asset management and hires Jeffrey Lane to find out what went wrong at its hedge funds.

22 June

Bear Stearns revealed it had spent $3.2bn. (£1.5bn) bailing out two of its funds exposed to the subprime market. The bailout of the fund was the largest by a bank in almost a decade.

14 June

Senior U.S. legislator Barney Frank says Fed could lose its authority to regulate mortgage business.

MAY 2007

30 May

UK subprime lender Kensington agrees takeover

21 May

Business economists forecast US economic slowdown due to subprime crisis

3 May

GM finance unit loses heavily on subprime mortgages

UBS closes its U.S. subprime lending arm, Dillon Read Capital Management

APRIL 2007

17 April

U.S. government-backed lenders try to tackle subprime crisis.

2 April

U.S. home sales fall sharply.

New Century Financial filed for Chapter 11 bankruptcy protection after it was forced by its backers to repurchase billions of dollars worth of bad loans. The company said it would have to cut 3,200 jobs, more than half of its workforce, as a result of the move.

MARCH 2007

16 March

U.S.-based sub-prime firm Accredited Home Lenders Holding said it would sell $2.7bn. of its sub-prime loan book - at a heavy discount - in order to generate some cash for its business.

13 March

Wall Street hit by sub-prime fears.

12 March

Shares in New Century Financial, one of the biggest sub-prime lenders in the U.S., were suspended amid fears it might be heading for bankruptcy.

8 March

Biggest U.S. house builder DR Horton warns of huge losses from subprime fall-out.

FEBRUARY 2007

22 February

HSBC fires head of its U.S. mortgage lending business as losses reach $10.5b.

The subprime crisis have caused huge writing down of losses for many big financial institutions. Even big investment houses like bear stearns have collapsed.JP Morgan and the Fed said last week they would back New York-based Bear Stearns with emergency funding for an initial period of up to 28 days in the largest U.S. bailout of a securities firm. It had faced an eroding investor confidence in the fallout from losses related to securities based on mortgages to the least creditworthy borrowers. The fed would pay 30 billion usd and JP morgan would pay 236 million USD. The loss due to subprime issue to bear stearn was about 1.9 billion of its holding in mortgages and mortgage based securities.

Even investment house like UBS has reported a loss of 37 billion USD due to investment in mortgage market and is planning to inject fresh capital due to the loss it suffered in the mortgage assets. The sequence of events for the fall of bear stearn is given below.

1: Dec 14, 2006

Bear Stearns posts record earnings, touting huge profit gains from then-booming businesses advising on mergers and arranging credit derivatives, distressed debt and leveraged finance deals.

Bear stock closes at $159.96. The average price target from Wall Street research analysts covering the stock is $166.24 according to Reuters Estimates.

2: Jan 12, 2007

Bear shares close at a record $171.51 on momentum from its strong earnings report the previous month. The average price target: $174.

3: May 24, 2007

Bear shares close at $147.55, a six-week low, after Goldman Sachs slashed its quarterly earnings target for its rival investment bank, citing concern about Bear's heavy exposure to the mortgage securitization business. The average price target: $181.73.

4: June 14, 15 & 16, 2007

On June 14, Bear reports earnings declined for the first time in four quarters on weaker results from its mortgage securities business. On the 15th, the Wall Street Journal reports a hedge fund run by Bear has suffered big losses on soured subprime mortgage investments. (A second fund with similar troubles would soon emerge.) The next day, the 15th, the Journal reports that Merrill Lynch, a creditor to the fund, seized some of its assets. The stock closes at $150.09 on the 15th, a Friday. The average target price: $181.

5: July 17, 2007

As losses from subprime mortgages begin to threaten credit markets around the world, Bear Stearns informs investors in its two struggling hedge funds that the funds have "very little value" remaining. Bear shares end the day at $139.91. The average target price: $178.23.

6: Aug 5, 2007

Warren Spector resigns under pressure as co-president and co-chief operating officer, having lost the confidence of long-time CEO James Cayne for his handling of the subprime mortgage crisis. The stock closes at $113.81 on Aug 6, a Monday. The average target price: $164.29.

7: Oct 5, 2007

Prosecutors launch a criminal probe into the collapse of the two Bear Stearns hedge funds. The stock closes at $131.58. The average target price $144.17.

8: Dec 20, 2007

Bear reports its first-ever quarterly loss, driven by $1.9 billion of bad debt write downs. It also says executives will not receive annual bonuses. Bear shares close at $91.42. The average target price: $121.67.

9: Jan 8, 2008

James Cayne is replaced as CEO by investment banker Alan Schwartz. The stock closes at $71.01. The average target price; $111.36.

10: March 12, 2008

Responding to market rumors of a cash crunch at the bank, Bear CEO Schwartz goes on CNBC television and assures viewers that the firm has ample liquidity. The stock closes at $61.58. The average target price: $98.87.

11: March 14, 2008

JPMorgan, backed by the Federal Reserve, provides an undisclosed amount of emergency financing to Bear Stearns. Bear says its liquidity position had deteriorated dramatically in the previous 24 hours. The stock plunges to close at $30.85. The average target price: $93.62.

12: March 16 & 17, 2008

JPMorgan agrees on March 16 to buy Bear for $236 million, or $2 a share, representing just over 1 percent of the firm's value at its record high close just 14 months earlier. The deal essentially marks the end of Bear's 85-year run as an independent securities firm. Bear shares end March 17, a Monday, at $4.81 on optimism another buyer may emerge. The average target price: $2.

15

Private Equity

GLOBAL PERSPECTIVE

In the past few decades, the private equity industry has grown both in terms of size and geographic reach. Despite the growing global impact of private equity, there is limited research on these developments that stakeholders can reference. It is, perhaps, not surprising that in markets as diverse as China, Germany, South Korea, the United Kingdom and the United States, important questions have arisen about the impact of private equity on employment, managerial time-horizons, the overall health of companies and the economy more generally.

2006 turned to be a remarkable year for the private equity funds. Global mergers and acquisitions received a big boost-topped to $3.8 trillion, a bump of 38% of which 20% was financed by private equity buyers. The large portion of the deals was handled by Goldman Sachs and Citigroup.

Perhaps more surprising was last year's showing by Citigroup, which leaped from fifth place in 2005 to second last year. Citigroup advised on $1.03 trillion in transactions, claiming a 27.2 percent market share (Thomson Financial). Morgan Stanley, which was number 2 in 2005, fell to 3rd slot in 2006, advising on $975 bn in global deals for 25.7% market share.

In 2005, no single investment banker cracked the $1 trillion mark. Goldman Sachs worked on the deals worth $951 bn, Morgan Stanley $720 bn and Citigroup $695 bn.

According to Private Equity Intelligence 2007, a record $401bn was raised worldwide in new commitments. A total of 612 new funds held a final close during 2006.U.S.-focused funds continued to dominate the market, taking 63% of the global share in terms of new commitments. Europe, managed to hold the second spot with 27% of all capital raised in last being committed to funds in this region. Asian and rest of world funds also grew marginally, raising 5% more than 2005.

In total 311 U.S.-focused funds raised an aggregate $252 bn, while 168 Europe-focused funds raised an aggregate $108 bn. The 133 Asian and rest of the world funds raised an aggregate of $41 bn. Real estate funds continued to be increasingly popular with investors, while natural resources and infrastructure funds have also been successful to great extent.

There were 175 buyout and co-investment funds raised, attracting an aggregate $204 bn during 2006, with $96 bn of this coming from just 10 mega-funds greater than $5 bn in size. Real estate private equity funds raised an aggregate $53 bn from 79 new funds in 2006. In total 174 venture funds achieved a final close in 2006 collecting $42 bn in new commitments, while 65 Fund of funds raised an aggregate $23 bn.

2006 was a remarkable year for mergers and acquisitions in general. Some of the major deals in the last year are:

- Equity Office Properties Trust, the U.S.'s largest publicly held office-building owner for $36 bn by Blackstone Group.
- U.S. hospital chain HCA Inc. for $33 bn by syndication of KKR, Bain Capital, and Merrill Lynch Global Private Equity.
- Radio chain owner Clear Channel Communications for $27 bn by Bain Capital and Thomas H. Lee.
- Electronics firm Freescale Semiconductor for $17.6 bn by Blackstone and others.
- Natural gas pipeline company Kinder Morgan for $22 bn by Goldman Sachs equity group, AIG equity group, a private investor.

The acquisition of Harrah's, the world's number 1 casino company in $17 bn by Texas Pacific Group and Apollo Management outbidding a strategic buyer , the casino firm Penn National Gaming.

Private Equity deal volumes since 1996

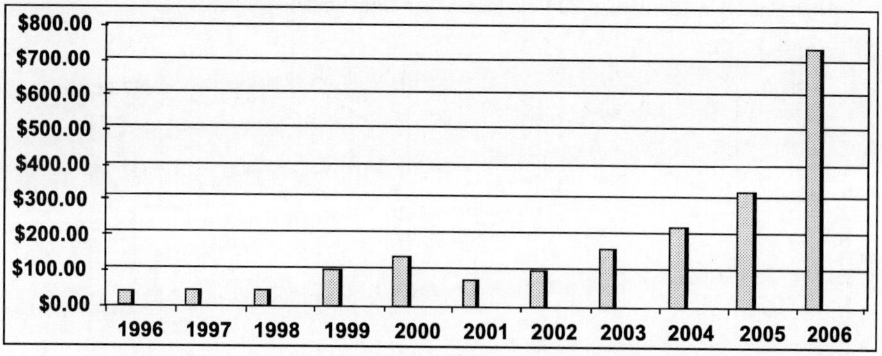

The Private Equity Deal volumes show a continuous increase since 1996. It has increased from $34 bn in 1996 to $137 bn in 2000. But it declined sharply in 2001 due to **DOTCOM BUBBLE BURST**. The Private Equity investments in the upcoming Information Technology Sector declined to $72 bn in 2001. The PE investments improved in the coming years with the strengthing of global economy. The total PE deal volumes stood at $738.10 bn in 2006.

PRIVATE EQUITY L: CREATING WEALTH FOR INDIA

Sectoral Analysis of Private Equity Deals

Industry	Value ($ Billions)	No. of Deals
Media & Entertainment	154.6	325
Industrials	99.9	513
Real Estate	85.2	100
Health Care	76.8	194
Retail	62.4	210
High Technology	60.7	372
Consumer Product & Services	56.2	448
Energy & Power	53.4	146
Financials	31.9	203
Materials	32.2	272
Total	**738.1**	**3052**

Top Ten Private Equity Dealmakers In 2006

Acquiring firms	Value ($ Billions)	No. of Deals
Texas Pacific Group Inc.	100	16
Blackstone Group LP	93.1	19
Bain Capital Partners LLC	84.8	12
Kohlberg Kravis Roberts & Co.	77.7	13
Carlyle Group LLC	71.9	32
Thomas H. Lee Partners LP	64.6	7
GS Capital Partners LP	55.8	6
Apollo Management LP	48.7	9
Cereberus Capital Management LP	34.2	9
Merrill Lynch Global Private Equity	32.5	2

Private Equity: In 10 Years, a 20-Fold Increase in Deal Volume

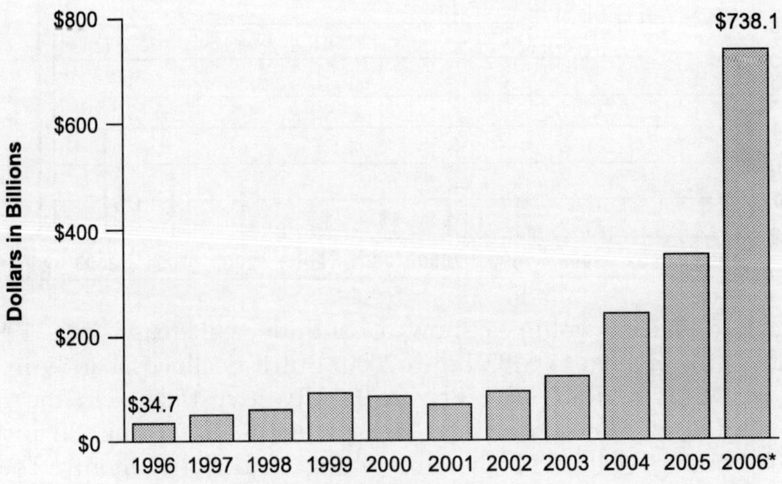

* Through December 27
Source: Thomson Financial; Booz Allen Hamilton

Exhibit 1: Private equity fund size in Europe (1994-2006)

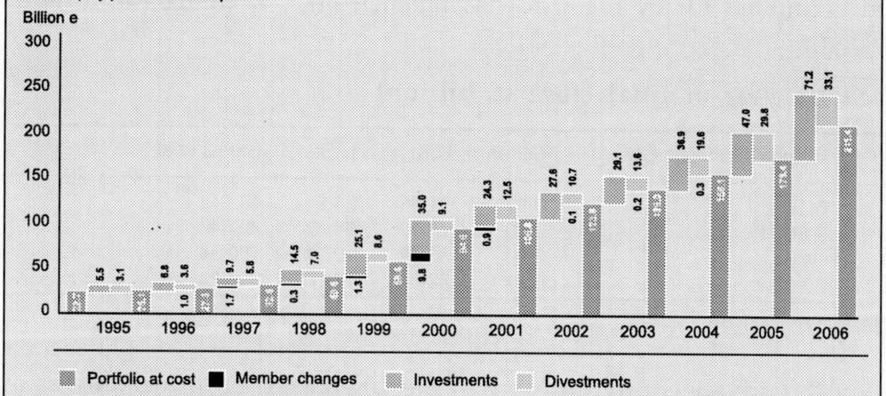

Source: EVCA Year books 1995-2007, Zaventern.

Notes: The data are based on activities of private equity funds located in Europe and are valued at costs. Divestments cover trade sales, IPOs, liquidations and other divestment types. Investments cover first and follow-up rounds of funding. Member Changes are due to additions or exclusions of members in the EVCA database. An earlier version of this graph appeared in an expertise on private equity for the Federal Ministry of Finance in Germany, later published as c.Kaserer, a.-K. Achleitner, C. von Einern, D. Schiereck, "Private Equity in Deutschland-Rahmenbedingungen, ökonomische Bedeutung und Handlungsernpfehlungen", Norderstedt, 2007.

Exhibit 2: Economic relevance of private equity in Europe (2006)

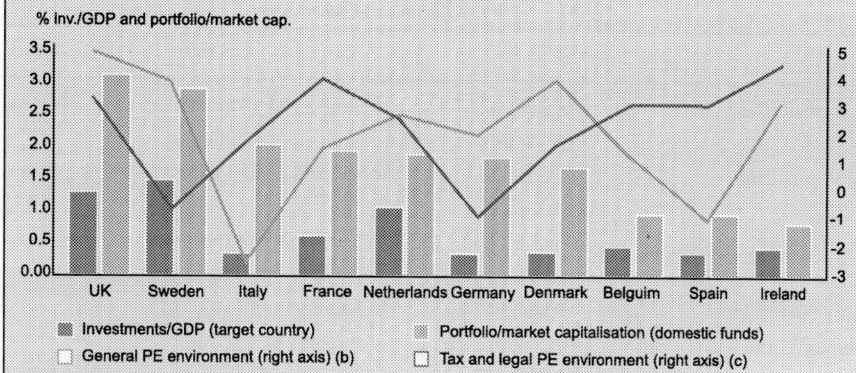

Source: Apax Partners (2007), EVCA (2006), EVCA (2007), Eurostat, World Federation of Exchanges.

Notes:

(a) The higher the value of the private equity environment or the tax andlegal environment, the more favourable the conditions.

(b) The private equity environment indicators published by Apax Partners are based on macroeconomic data, country specific risk as well as the financing, legal/political and entrepreneurial environment.

(c) The tax and legal environmentpublished by the EVCA represerts the tax and legal environmentfor limited partners, fund management and investee companies as well as the environment to retain talent in investee companies and management funds. To be comparable to the Apax Partners indicators, the tax and legal environment indicator was rescaled (-6 is the worst, +6 is the best).

The growth of the industry

As the table below (contributed by the FSA) shows, the value of private equity funds in the UK has grown significantly since 2003. However, this growth has been less marked than in other countries. For example, the value of funds raised in the U.S. between 2003 and 2006 increased more than sixfold, compared with a trebling in the UK over the same period. As a result, the proportion of the global total of funds raised accounted for by the U.K. has fallen from 27% in 2003 to 15% in 2006.

Funds raised by year of final close (£ billion)

Year	Asia	Europe excluding-UK	Other	U.K.	U.S.	Global total
2003	0.40	6.18	0.97	11.69	24.31	43.54
2004	2.78	9.50	3.00	12.10	65.47	92.84
2005	4.11	14.64	5.90	33.52	102.17	160.34
2006	8.19	23.97	5.37	33.64	152.07	223.24

Source : Ev 236

The debate on the private equity industry in the UK has arisen principally as a result of the increase in deal size, rather than the number of deals. As the chart below shows, while the number of buy-outs and buy-ins valued at under £5 million was the same in 2006 as in 2000, the number valued at over £250 million increased from 17 to 25.

PRIVATE EQUITY: INDIAN AND GLOBAL PERSPECTIVE

Top ten equity buyouts in 2006

Company	Deal value (U.S.$m)	Sector	Country
Equity Office Properties Trust	38,886.59	Real Estate/Property	U.S.
HCA Inc.	32,674.98	Healthcare	U.S.
Freescale SemiconductorInc.	17,600.00	Computers & Electronic	U.S.
Albertson's Inc	17,356.00	Retail	U.S.
Hertz Corp	15,000.00	Transportation	U.S.
TDC A/S (87.9%)	13,872.39	Telecommunications	Denmark
Univision Communications Inc.	13,632.94	Telcoommunications	U.S.
SunGard Data Systems Inc.	11,76048	Computer & Electronic	U.S.
VNU NV	10,998.03	Publishing	Netherlands
AWG plc	9,986.16	Utility & Energy	U.K.

Value ranges of private-equity backed UK buy-outs/buy-ins - Number of deals

Deal Range	2000	2001	2002	2003	2004	2005	2006
Less than £ 5m	99	95	80	75	86	95	99
£ 5m - £ 10m	36	40	31	32	21	24	24
£ 10m - £ 25m	70	55	44	43	51	46	51
£ 25m - £ 50m	23	34	22	31	37	38	40
£ 50m - £ 100m	27	15	19	23	27	25	35
£ 100m - £ 250m	23	18	11	11	30	26	30
Over £ 250m	17	12	13	9	13	23	25
Total Number	295	269	220	224	265	277	304

Source: Ev 236

The increase in Leverage

Recent private equity deals have increasingly been characterized by a high degree of leverage. The chart below shows that the frequency with which the debt to EBITDA93 ratio in European leveraged buy-outs has exceeded 6.0 has increased significantly since 2004.

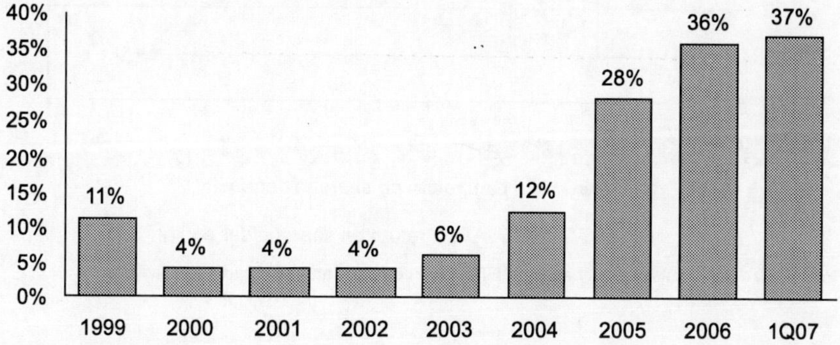

Source: Ev 227

Leverage has been increasing for a number of reasons

- The benign macro-economic environment has supported company profitability and the ability of companies to service debt, and has reduced the risk of default;
- The price of credit has been extremely low, reflecting factors such as low interest rates, lower default rates by companies and lower compensation for liquidity risk. Credit risk premia have also fallen relative to equity risk premia, possibly reflecting the activities of pension funds in purchasing fixed-income products to match their liabilities;
- Liquidity in the leveraged loan market has increased as a result of the deepening of the secondary market. Lenders are increasingly able to repackage and sell on loans via collateralized loan obligation (CLO) managers and collateralized debt obligation (CDO) managers, making it possible for risk to be distributed throughout the financial system; and
- Loans are increasingly being issued with fewer or less onerous covenants (i.e. covenantlite loans), enabling borrowers to take on more debt.

Asia: The Private Equity Opportunity

Once you talk about Asia and you will feel the diversity of different languages, different cultures and different nuances. The dynamic here is from the wealthy "carorepaptis" to the one billion plus rural population that continues to live in dark starves poverty.

A simulation of the effect on the return on equity (RoE) for UK FTSE 100 companies if they were re-leveraged from 30:70 to 70:30 debt: equity.

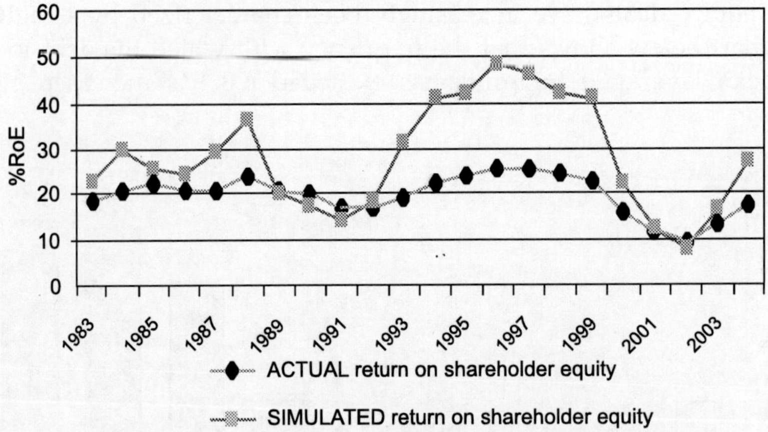

Source: Ev 116;[102] calculations based on FTSE 100 company annual report and accounts

Looking ahead there is obviously tremendous potential. India is becoming hugely significant although for the moment it continues to be more of a development expansion capital market. Most businesses here are family controlled with complex cross share-holding a fact of life. This makes it hard to execute successful buyout deals.

There is no single secret of success. Take time to understand target markets, identify opportunities, know your strengths and play to them. For those firms that get it right, the eventual rewards in Japan, China and India will be enormous.

Private Equity in Sri Lanka: An Exploration of History, Need and Opportunity

Despite having a resilient top performing global public equities market (in the face of a 24-year war), one of the most favorable legal frameworks in South Asia for conducting business, and with private equity flooding into neighboring India, Sri Lankan private equity is under-developed and near non-existent. At present, there are only 3 operational domestic corporate private equity firms (in both buyout and venture capital) in Sri Lanka: Aureos Capital, Equity Investments, and Lanka Ventures.

The lack of private equity markets in Sri Lanka is in sharp contrast to the seemingly dominant presence of private equity in the rest of the global capital markets. For 2006, Morgan Stanley estimated that 2,700 private equity funds represented 25% of global mergers and acquisition activity, 50% of leverage loan volume, 33% of the high yield bond market, and 33% of initial public offerings. In neighbor India, there has been a significant influx of private equity capital.

Non-real estate Indian private equity has seen investment triple in 2006 to USD $7.5 billion from 299 deals, according to a study by the research firm Venture Intelligence. In 2006 alone, Indian mega-deals have occurred like Idea Cellular's pre-IPO placement of $960 million and the Kohlberg Kravis Roberts buyout of the Indian software unit of Flextronics International for $725 million. In contrast, the largest PE investment in Sri Lanka in 2006 was South Asian fund Actis' 71 percent acquisition of industrial and medical gas manufacturer Ceylon Oxygen with only a handful of transactions occurring in total in the country. While the size of the deal is in-line with the size and GDP delta between the Sri Lankan and Indian markets, the limited transaction flow is surprising.

What makes the weakness of private equity markets in Sri Lanka even more surprising is the strength of its public markets, which in terms of growth are near all-time highs and rank as having some of the most robust growth rates in the world. Historically, after witnessing mediocre performance throughout the 1990s, mainly due to the ethnic conflict in Sri Lanka, the ceasefire agreement signed in 2001 saw unprecedented growth. Sri Lanka's two indices on the Colombo Stock Exchange (CSE), the All Share Price Index (ASPI), covering all domestically-listed stocks, and the Milanka Price Index (MPI), which is focused on blue-chip companies, reached all-time highs over the past few years.

The All Share Price Index, which was hovering around the 500 point mark in August 2001, is now at the upper 2,000s mark. This has led the CSE to be consistently dubbed as one of the best performing markets in the world. As of 2005, the CSE had recorded a consistent annual growth rate of over 30% in the All Share Price Index (ASPI) for the previous three years. It surpassed that in 2006, with the ASPI growing by 41.6%, and the MPI growing by 51.4% during the calendar year. At present, despite the current situation in the country, the CSE is near an all-time high, breaking the 3,000 mark for the first time on February 13th, 2007.

Indian Scenario

Though PE investments are nothing new to the American and the European financial markets, PE investments in India gained popularity when international PE firm Warburg Pincus offloaded its share in Bharti Telecom in 2004 and 2005. It invested $300 million in Bharti Telecom between 1999 and 2001 in lieu of 18.5% stake. Later, out of the total holding of 18.5% of Warburg Pincus in Bharti 12.5% was sold in 2004 at a profit of $800 million. The remaining 6% was sold in 2005. The total investments were sold at around seven times of its original value generating a profit of $1.92billion that later encouraged many big PE investment players from Europe and the US to invest in India.

India is slowly turning out to be an important destination for global private equity market. However, in terms of numbers, India's investment share is only 6-7% of the global pie but the growth in India in the context of global PE environment is substantial. The last three years have seen unprecedented PE capital inflows into India. (Please see the table)

Year	2003-04	2004-05	2005-06	2006-07	2007-08
PE inflows ($)	865 mn	1.3 bn	2.3 bn	7.4 bn	19.0 bn

Source: *Business world and The Economics Times*

The PE investment in India is growing at a 51% compounded annual rate since 1998 and it is estimated to grow at a faster rate in the near future. In 2004, India had 71 PE deals followed by 146 in 2005 and 302 in 2006. In 2007, this figure went up to 405 deals having $19 billion investment in this sector. Private investors such as Apex Partners, Soquoia, Trinity capital and others have increased their stakes in pharmaceuticals and healthcare companies during the calendar year 2007, and the total amount is close to $400 million, according to one estimate.

According to Emerging Markets Private Equity Association (EMPEA) estimates, there are some 89 VC/PE firms managing 153 funds in Brazil, about 28 firms in Russia and 115 in China while India has over 160 firms. About 120 of these India-focused firms are either those who have raised money from outside India or are subsidiaries of non-Indian VC/PE firms. Experts opine that a growing economy, especially on the domestic side, increased entrepreneurial activity and the IT/ITeS effect is attracting newer investors to the country.

PIPE (Private Investment in Public Enterprise) Deals

PIPE constitutes nearly 40% deal flow in India in contrast to less than 10% in the U.S. Table below provides the data regarding the top 10 PIPE deals in the Indian market.

Top 10 PIPE Deals

Investor	Investee	Sector	Year	Deal Size ($mm)
CW Capital, Chrys Capital, CVS	Centurion Bank	Banking	2005	86.3
Asia Debt Management Fund	Indian Cements	Cement	2004	57.0
City Group	Jubilant Organosys	Pharma	2004	50.0
Warburg Pincus	Vaibhav Gems	Gems and Jewelry	2005	47.0
Warburg Pincus	Sintex Industries	Textiles and Plastics	2005	46.4
IDFC, HDFC, IL	Leela Hotel	Hospitality	2005	44.4
Teamasek	Welspun	Textile	2005	27.0
Chrys Capital	Gammon India	Civil Engineering	2004	20.0
Warburg Pincus	Max India	Healthcare	2004	18.0
Warburg Pincus	Kotak Mahindra Bank	banking	2004	16.9
Temasek Holdings	Bharti Airtel	Telecom	2007	1906.74
ICICI Venture Funds	Jaypee Infratech	Real Estate	2007	800
Carlyle Group	HDFC	Banking	2007	650
Avenue Capital Group	SKIL Infrastructure	Real Estate	2007	500
Deutche, citi gourp, UBS Kotak Mahindra.....	Bharti Infratel	Telecom	2007	1000

Source: *Venture Intelligence,* Business world August 14,2007 & Grant Thomson India

Normally a PIPE transaction, investors acquire securities directly from a publicly traded company through a private investment. The main reason for its popularity in India is the size of publicly traded companies is very small when compared to the US. At the time of listing, the US companies typically clock revenues in the range of $200-300 million, whereas in India, it would be $30-40 million (*BusinessWorld*, August 14, 2006).

More of Private Equity and less of Venture Capital

In the last three years, Private Equity has dominated the Indian market when compared to venture capital. As per the industry estimates, out of $2.3billion that was invested in India by Private Equity investors and venture capitalists in 2005, venture capital accounted for just $482mn out of which early stage deals accounts for $150million. This trend follows on in year 2006 and 2007 as well.

Private Equity Evolution in India

	Phase I Pre 1995	Phase II 1995-97	Phase III 1997-01	Phase IV 2002-05
No. of Funds	8	20	50	75
No. of Transaction	30	65	548	446
Value of Transaction($ millions)	30	125	2,847	5,239
Of Which				
Seed and Early Stage($ millions)	5	15	657	250
Development Capital($ millions)	25	110	2,168	3,107
Growth maturity($ millions)			22	1,882

Source: Report of the committee on technology innovation and venture capital planning commission, GOI, 2006.

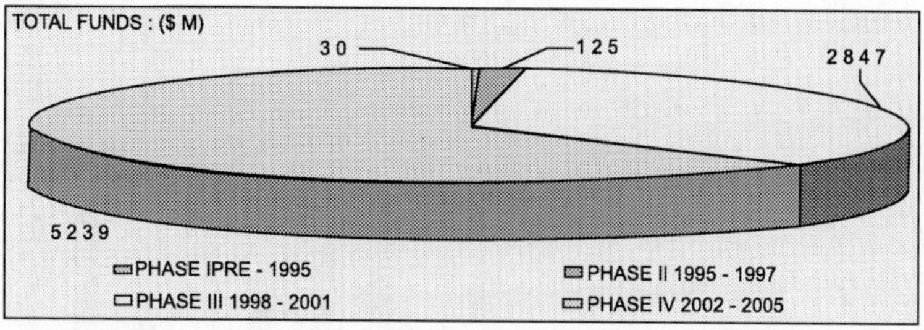

Evolution of Private Equity Finance (cont.)

	PHASE-I	PHASE-II	PHASE-III	PHASE-IV
Primary sources of Funds	World Bank Government	Government	Overseas Institutional	Overseas Institutional
Seed/ Early stage ($m)	5	15	657	250
Number of transactions	10	20	273	58
Development ($m)	25	110	2168.1	3107
Number of transactions	20	45	273	288
Growth / Maturity ($m)			21.9	1882
Number of transactions			2	100
Total Number of transactions	30	65	548	446
Average Investments ($m)	1	2	5.2	11.75

Sources: TSJ Media, ICVA publications (various Years).

2007: PE/VC Trends

- 31% of all investments fell into the US$10-25 million category.
- Venture capital investments accounted for 25% of the private equity deals (in volume terms).
- Late stage deals accounted for 35% of all deals.
- PE firms obtained exit routes in 65 companies, including 16 via initial public offering (IPO).
- While companies based in South India attracted a higher number of investments, their peers in Western India attracted a far higher share of the pie in value terms.

Exhibit 1B: Private equity investments in Indian companies

PE investments in Indian companies 1990-2006

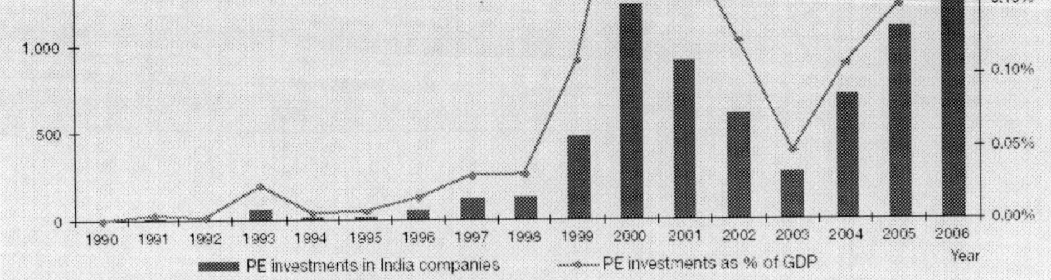

Data Source: Private equity investment data from SDC Platinum VentureXpert, GDP data from EconStats.com.

2007 PE/VC Investments by industry
Total US$14.2Bn

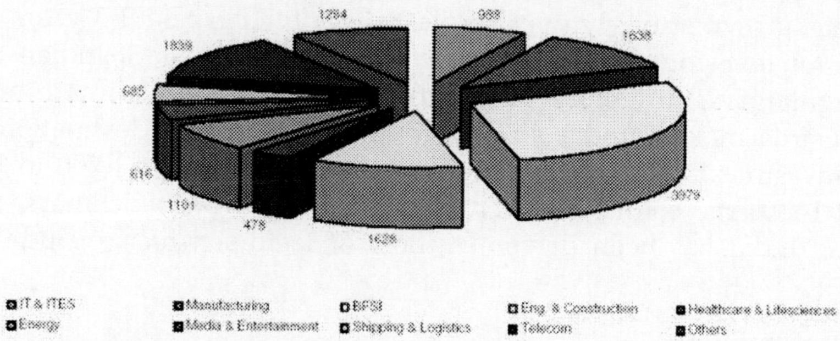

Source: TSJ Venture Intelligence India

- Among cities, Mumbai-based companies retained the top slot with 108 private equity investments worth almost US$6 billion in 2007, followed by Delhi/National Capital Region with 63 investments worth almost US$2.7 billion and Bangalore with 49 investments worth US$700 million.
- Citigroup was the most active investor, with a portfolio across energy, engineering & construction, manufacturing. Other active investors include: ICICI Ventures, Goldman Sachs and Helion Ventures.

Top Cities attracting PE Investments (2007)

City	No. of Deals	Value (US$M)
Mumbai	109	5995
Delhi/NCR*	63	2688
Bangalore	49	685
Hyderabad	41	1380
Chennai	32	824
Ahmedabad	14	492
Kolkata	12	339

*Includes Noida & Gurgaon

Source: TSJ Venture intelligence

Private Equity: Destination India

India has emerged as one of the fastest growing economies in the world, and is currently the world's fourth largest economy based on the Purchasing Power Parity (PPP) basis. With its liberalisation and globalization led restructuring, the Indian corporate sector too is in great shape and hungry for faster growth in the future. A huge structural shift is taking place in the Indian economy leading to opening up of a lot of investment opportunities in different sectors and attracting large amounts of foreign and private capital, some in the form of private equity.

The private equity way of investment in India commenced only in the early 90s, and the same has grown strongly over the last decade. The past 2-3 years have been especially good for investors, with improving profitability levels of Indian corporates, an enabling regulatory framework and improved investment climate all together contributing towards making India an attractive private equity destination. In India, private equity investments have grown from a mere US$ 500m in FY00 to US$ 1.8 bn in FY04 and in FY07, the contribution crossed the US$ 10 bn benchmark. Growth of private equity in India has been driven by host of factors, which include.

Faster growing economy

India is the third largest economy in Asia (behind Japan and China), and also the second fastest growing in the region, next only to China. At an annual growth rate of 7% to 8%, it is surely ahead of many developing economies. A major contributor to this growth has been its buoyant services sector contributing to more than 50% of the GDP. Improvement in internal demand led by rising disposable incomes, which has been a consequence of better growth across sectors has led to the buoyancy in economic growth in the country. Higher credit offtake (both from the corporate and retail segments) from the banking system vindicates this point. All these factors, and many more, have improved the relative attractiveness of the Indian economy. This has, in turn, led to higher investments in the private equity segment.

Strong capital markets

Indian stock markets have been increasingly buoyant over the past three years. Optimal market capitalization, appealing relative valuations, strong earning growths, and transparent disclosure norms is attracting huge institutional money into the Indian markets, with a number of country funds being raised overseas.

Regulatory flexibility

Regulatory framework for private equity players has been liberalized further by the Securities Exchange Board of India (SEBI) thereby granting greater flexibility to this breed of investors. SEBI had made significant changes in the framework for private equity players, some of which include removal of the one-year lock in period for subscription in IPOs and increase in the limits on the quantum of funds that can be invested in the listed companies from 25% to 33%. All these measures have contributed to granting greater flexibility to private equity players, thereby leading to greater investments by them.

Easy exits

The exit options available are also important factors encouraging private equity players in the Indian market. The exits had taken place through IPOs and mergers & acquisitions (M&As).

Deregulation in key sectors

The government of India has successfully undertaken deregulation in many key sectors like aviation, telecom and insurance. This has led to an increased pace of activity in these sectors with the foreign and private players eyeing a share of the growth pie.

CONCLUSION

With the strong rise in Indian equities witnessed in the past 2 years, overall valuations appear stretched even from a medium term perspective. The Sensex is, in fact trailing at nearly 17-18 times estimated FY07 earnings. However, with the changing mindset of mid and small size companies in the country and their increasing strides towards higher growth, there seems to be no dearth of ideas for private equity players.

However, retail investors should not base their investment decisions merely on the back of interest shown by private equity players on a particular company. Apart from the funding part, private equity is also supposed to bring in some business expertise in order for the invested company to take advantage of the deal (for example, Warburg Pincus, apart from capital, helped Bharti Televentures in forming its business strategy and investor focus). We have seen some cases in India (like Punjab Tractors), where private equity participation had actually negatively affected the business of invested companies. Thus, on an overall basis, while private equity is likely to emerge as a source of critical funding for the 'needy' companies thus helping them in their growth path, small investors need to look carefully into the deal before making their investment calls.

16

Derivatives

Derivatives are products whose values are derived from one or more basic variables called bases. These bases can be underlying assets such as foreign currency, stock or commodity, bases or reference rates such as LIBOR or U.S. Treasury Rate etc. For example, an Indian exporter in anticipation of the receipt of dollar-denominated export proceeds may wish to sell dollars at a future date to eliminate the risk of exchange rate volatility by the date. Such transactions are called derivatives, with the spot price of dollar being the underlying asset.

Derivatives thus have no value of their own but derive it from the asset that is being dealt with under the derivative contract. For instance, look at an ash- tray. It has no value of its own but gains its importance only when one smokes and again if one wants to collect that ash at one place instead of dirtying the whole room with cigarette ash and its stubs. A smoker can hedge against the risk of stewing the cigarette stubs and ash all around the room. Similarly a financial manager can hedge himself from the risk of a loss in the price of a commodity or stock by buying a derivative contract. Thus derivative contracts acquire their value from the spot prices of the assets that are covered by the contract.

The primary purpose of a derivative contract is to transfer "risk" from one party to another i.e., risk in a financial sense is transferred from a party that wants to get rid of it to another party that is willing to take it on. Here, the risk that is being dealt with is that of price risk. The transfer of such a risk can therefore be speculative in nature or act as a hedge against price movement in a current or anticipated physical position.

The common elements of derivatives are:

1. Buyer
2. Seller
3. Underlying asset
4. Future date
5. Future price

Financial derivatives are a kind of risk management instrument. A derivative's value depends on the price changes in some more fundamental underlying assets. Many forms of financial derivatives instruments exist in the financial markets. Among them, the three most fundamental financial derivatives instruments are: forward contracts, futures, and options. If the underlying assets are stocks, bonds, foreign exchange rates and commodities etc., then the corresponding risk management instruments are: stock futures (options), bond futures (options), currency futures (options) and commodity futures (options).

HISTORY OF DERIVATIVE MARKET

The history of derivatives is quite colorful and surprisingly a lot longer than most people think. To start we need to go back to the Bible.

Jacob purchased an option costing him seven years of labor that granted him the right to marry Laban's daughter Rachel. His prospective father-in-law, however, reneged, perhaps making this not only the first derivative but the first default on a derivative. Laban required Jacob to marry his older daughter Leah. Jacob married Leah, but because he preferred Rachel, he purchased another option, requiring seven more years of labor, and finally married Rachel, bigamy being allowed in those days. Jacob ended up with two wives, twelve sons, who became the patriarchs of the twelve tribes of Israel, and a lot of domestic friction, which is not surprising. Some argue that Jacob really had forward contracts, which obligated him to the marriages but that does not matter. Jacob did derivatives, one way or the other. Around 580 B.C. Thales the Milesian purchased options on olive presses and made a fortune off of a bumper crop in olives. So derivatives were around before the time of Christ.

The first exchange for trading derivatives appeared to be the Royal Exchange in London, which permitted forward contracting. The first "futures" contracts are generally traced to the Yodoya rice market in Osaka, Japan around 1650. These were evidently standardized contracts, which made them much like today's futures, although it is not known if the contracts were marked to market daily and/or had credit guarantees.

Early forward contracts in the US addressed merchants concerns about ensuring that there were buyers and sellers for commodities. However "credit risk" remained a serious problem. To deal with this problem, a group of Chicago businessmen formed the Chicago board of trade (CBOT) in 1848. The primary function of the CBOT was to provide a centralized location known in advance for buyers and sellers to negotiate forward contracts. In 1865, the CBOT went one step further and listed the first exchange traded derivative contracts in the U.S. these contracts were called as future contracts.

One of the first examples of financial engineering was by none other than the beleaguered government of the Confederate States of America, which is sued a dual currency option able bond. This permitted the Confederate States to borrow money in sterling with an option to pay back in French francs. The holder of the bond had the option to convert the claim into cotton, the south's primary cash crop.

Interestingly, futures/options/derivatives trading was banned numerous times in Europe and Japan and even in the United States in the state of Illinois in 1867 though the law was quickly repealed. In 1874 the Chicago Mercantile Exchange's predecessor, the Chicago Produce Exchange, was formed. It became the modern day Merc in 1919. Other exchanges had been popping up around the country and continued to do so

In 1922 the federal government made its first effort to regulate the futures market with the Grain Futures Act. In 1936 options on futures were banned in the United States. All the while options, futures and various derivatives continued to be banned from time to time in other countries.

The 1950s marked the era of two significant events in the futures markets. In 1955 the Supreme Court of USA ruled in the case of Corn Products Refining Company that profits from hedging are treated as ordinary income. This ruling stood until it was challenged by the 1988 ruling in the Arkansas Best case. The Best decision denied the deductibility of capital losses against ordinary income and effectively gave hedging a tax disadvantage. Fortunately, this interpretation was overturned in 1993.

In 1972 the Chicago Mercantile Exchange, responding to the now-freely floating international currencies, created the International Monetary Market, which allowed trading in currency futures. These were the first futures contracts that were not on physical commodities. In 1975 the Chicago Board of Trade created the first interest rate futures contract. While the contract met with initial success, it eventually died. The CBOT resuscitated it several times, changing its structure, but it never became viable. In 1975 the Merc responded with the Treasury bill futures contract. This contract was the first successful pure interest rate futures. It was held up as an example, either good or bad depending on your perspective, of the enormous leverage in futures. For only about $1,000, and now less than that, you controlled $1 million of T-bills. In 1977, the CBOT created the T-bond futures contract, which went on to be the highest volume contract. In 1982 the CME created the Eurodollar contract, which has now surpassed the T-bond contract to become the most actively traded of all futures contracts. In 1982, the Kansas City Board of Trade launched the first stock index futures, a contract on the Value Line Index. The Chicago Mercantile Exchange quickly followed with their highly successful contract on the S&P 500 index.

The 1980s marked the beginning of the era of swaps and other over-the-counter derivatives. Although over-the-counter options and forwards had previously existed, the generation of corporate financial managers of that decade was the first to come out of business schools with exposure to derivatives. Soon virtually every large corporation, and even some that were not so large, were using derivatives to hedge, and in some cases, speculate on interest rate, exchange rate and commodity risk. New products were rapidly created to hedge the now-recognized wide varieties of risks.

Development of Derivatives Market in India

Trading and settlement in derivative contracts is done in accordance with the rules, bylaws, and regulations of the respective exchanges and their clearing house/ corporation duly approved by SEBI and notified in the official gazette. Foreign Institutional Investors (FIIs) are permitted to trade in all Exchange traded derivative products.

Chronology of derivatives market in India

14 Dec 1995	NSE asked SEBI for permission to trade index futures.
18 Nov1996	Formed L. C. Gupta Committee to design a policy framework for index futures.
7 July 1999	RBI gave permission for OTC forward rate agreements (FRAs) and interest rate swaps.
24 May 2000	SIMEX chose Nifty for trading futures and options on an Indian index.
25 May 2000	SEBI gave permission to NSE and BSE to do index futures trading.
9 June 2000	Trading of BSE Sensex futures commenced at BSE.
12 June 2000	Trading of Nifty futures commenced at NSE.
25 Sep 2000	Nifty futures trading commenced at SGX
June 2001	Index options introduced
July 2001	Stock options introduced
November 2001	Stock futures

The above table indicates the chronology of derivative market in India and how it has developed over the years.

GLOBAL SCENARIO OF DERIVATIVE MARKET

The total number of futures and options traded on exchanges around the world reached **11.859** billion contracts. That's a tremendous number, but what's even more remarkable is that the pace of growth actually seems to be accelerating.

Year of comparison	Growth change rate in percentage
2006 as comparison to 2005	19%
2005 as comparison to 2004	12%
2004 as comparison to 2003	9%

From the table we can see that last year's total was **19%** higher than in 2005, whereas 2005 was only **12%** higher than 2004, and 2004 was just **9%** higher than 2003.

While trading in commodity contracts grew relatively faster than in other markets, this is still a market dominated by financials. More than 90% of all trading in exchange traded derivatives is tied to interest rates or equity prices, and there is no reason to expect this to change any time soon.

The number of futures contracts traded worldwide grew by more than 30% last year, setting yet another record. Global options volumes were up more than 10%.

Comparison of Derivative Markets Globally Volume Wise and Sector Wise

Derivative industry is a diverse industry we can analyze this from statistics given in the report. Every year it seems like another exchange from a previously unnoticed local market blasts its way up the volume ranking. This year's (2006) hottest market has to be the Mexican Derivatives Exchange.

We cannot see these markets from single point of view. There is certainly some correlation within categories. For example, we saw a big jump in the trading of equity index derivatives in lots of different markets during the broad stock market sell-off last May and June. But the factors driving volume in one category don't necessarily carry over to another category, and even more so when you factor in geography. To put it another way, we are still looking at a collection of many separate markets, each with their own set of factors affecting volume.

Take for example the equity index business. The growth rate for this category was 9%, which makes it seems like it is lagging the rest of market. But if you break down that number, you find some wildly different trends. First and foremost, volume in the Kospi 200 option was down 5% year over year. The Kospi option is the single most heavily traded derivative at any exchange in the world, so even though the decline was not a big deal in percentage terms, the absolute impact flattened the entire category.

Another reason why the equity index volume appeared to be lagging was the decline in options trading at Euronext.liffe. During the past two years, the Euronext group's Paris market changed the multiplier on its CAC 40 index options to 10 euros instead of one, and changed the number of shares underlying certain individual stock options to 100 shares instead of 10. In other words, the notional size of these contracts grew 10 times bigger, which means that the same position could be obtained by trading 10 times fewer contracts. So quite naturally the volume declined, but it would be wrong to conclude that this signals a decline in market activity.

Volume and volatility

Volatility is often assumed to be positively correlated with derivatives trading volume, but last year's surge in trading happened while volatility in the world's most important markets was generally falling. We have never had a really good model of volatility and trading. On the one hand, a decrease in volatility takes away opportunities to trade and reduces the urgency of hedging. On the other, in light of the work we have done on measuring market liquidity, we know that a decrease in volatility produces a decrease in the costs of trading. It also increases the position sizes that speculators require to achieve any given level of volatility in portfolio returns. Given this ambiguity about volatility and volume, the more or less steady growth of futures and options trading against a backdrop of large changes in volatility—both up and down—suggests that the forces behind the growth of exchange-traded derivatives are a lot more complex than just changeability of prices and interest rates.

Volatility Comparison

Market	Annualized volatility 2005	2006
Interest Rates (money market)		
Eurodollar	14.4%	10.3%
Euribor	13.6%	10.7%
Euroyen	53.0%	56.6%
Interest Rates (government bonds)		
10-year Treasury notes	4.5%	3.8%
Bunds	3.8%	3.8%
JGBs	2.9%	3.6%
Equity		
S&P 500	10.0%	9.7%
Euro Stoxx 50	11.0%	14.4%
Topux	13.7%	18.9%
Foreign Currencies		
British pound	8.2%	7.6%
Euro	8.8%	7.2%
Japanese yen	8.5%	8.0%
Commodities		
Crude oil	31.6%	26.4%
Natural gas	48.6%	62.2%
Wheat	24.6%	29.5%
Com	24.2%	28.3%
Copper	24.0%	38.5%
Aluminum	19.7%	32.2%

Source: Calyon Financial

Global Futures Volume
(In millions)

	2006	2005	Change	% Change
U.S. Futures	2,043.90	1,652.87	391.03	23.66%
Non-U.S. Futures	3,235.74	2,381.88	853.86	35.85%
Futures Volume	**5,279.64**	**4,034.75**	**1,244.89**	**30.85%**

Global Options Volume
(Includes options on futures, individual equities and indices)

	2006	2005	Change	% Change
U.S. Options	2,529.36	1,872.28	391.03	23.66%
Non-U.S. Futures	4,050.26	4,066.79	-16.53	-0.41%
Options Volume	**6,579.62**	**5,939.07**	**640.55**	**10.79%**

Global Futures and Options Volume

	2006	2005	Change	% Change
Equity Indices	4,453.95	4,080.33	373.62	9.16%
Interest Rates	3,193.44	2,536.77	656.67	25.89%
Individual Equities	2,876.49	2;356.87	519.62	22.05%
Currency	240.05	167.19	72.87	43.59%
Agriculturals	486.37	378.90	107.62	28.37%
Energies	385.97	280.13	105.83	37.78%
Metals	218.68	171.06	47.63	27.84%
Other	4.31	2.59	1.72	66.59%
Total	**11,859.27**	**9,973.82**	**1,885.44**	**18.90%**

Source: FIA

Global Futures and Options Volume

	2005	2004	Change	% Change
Equity Indices	4,080.00	3,799.40	300.60	7.95%
Interest Rates	2,536.76	2,271.25	265.51	11.69%
Individual Equities	2,356.87	1,996.66	360.22	18.04%
Ag Commodities	330.85	301.91	28.93	9.58%
Energy Products	274.79	243.46	31.33	12.87%
Foreign Currency/Index	165.51	105.38	60.13	57.06%
Non Precious Metals	98.00	105.23	-7.23	-6.87%
Precious Metals	55.34	60.56	-5.21	-8.61%
Other	1.67	0.86	0.81	93.58%
Total	**9,899.78**	**8,864.71**	**1,035.07**	**11.68%**

Source: FIA

Derivative market is expanding at a very faster rate in global market. We can see the results of 2006 as comparison to 2005 in different sectors. Maximum changes are in precious metals and foreign currency sector that is 77.5% and 47.5%. We can see that how fast these sectors are expanding.

The overall growth rate is 20%. That is really very large as comparison to last year. In last year it was only 11.68%.

From this table we can easily see that national stock exchange is far behind than other derivative markets like CME, Korea exchange etc. NSE is on 15th rank. It means still India is lagging in derivative trading which can be the major contributor to our growth. We can see that India has a semi-strong market as comparison to international market.

Global Futures and Options Volume

2006 Rank	2005 Rank	Exchange	2006 Volume	2005 Volume	% Change
1	1	Korea Exchange	2,474,593,261	2,593,088,445	-4.57%
2	2	Eurex	1,526,751,902	1,248,748,152	22.26%
3	3	Chicago Mercantile Exchange	1,403,264,034	1,090,351,711	28.70%
4	5	Chicago Board of Trade	805,884,413	674,651,393	19.45%
5	4	Euronext title	730,303,126	757,926,860	-3.64%
6	6	Chicago Board Options Exchange	674,735,348	468,249,301	44.10%
7	7	International Securities Exchange (U.S.)	591,961,518	448,695,669	31.93%
8	8	Sao Paulo Stock Exchange (Boverspa)	287,518,574	268,620,460	7.04%
9	11	Bolsa de Mercadorias & Futuros	283,570,241	199,446,464	42.18%
10	9	New York Mercantile Exchange	276,152,326	204,610,365	34.96%
11	15	Mexican Derivatives Exchange	275,217,670	108,177,276	154.41%
12	12	Philadelphia Stock Exchange	273,093,003	162,618,812	67.93%
13	10	American Stock Exchange	197,045,745	201,763,980	-2.34%
14	13	NYSE Arca (Pacific Exchange)	196,586,356	144,780,498	35.78%
15	14	National Stock Exchange of India	194,488,403	131,651,592	47.73%
16	16	OMX Group	123,167,736	103,509,936	18.99%
17	17	Dalian Commodity Exchange (China)	117,681,038	99,174,714	18.65%
18	18	Taiwan Futures Exchange	114,603,379	92,659,768	23.68%
19	24	JSE Securities Exchange South Africa	105,047,524	51,318,175	104.70%
20	20	Boston Options Exchange	94,390,602	78,202,185	20.70%
21	26	ICE Futures (U.K.)	92,721,050	42,055,085	120.48%
22	19	London Metal Exchange	86,940,189	78,628,852	10.57%
23	21	Tel-Aw Stock Exchange	83,047,982	70,088,945	18.49%
24	22	Sydney Future Exchange	78,120,106	63,324,966	23.36%
25	23	Tokyo Commodity Exchange	63,686,701	61,814,289	3.03%
26	25	Osaka Securities Exchange	60,387,375	44,172,264	36.71%
27	29	Shangha Futures Exchange	58,106,001	33,789,754	71.95%
28	*	National Commodity & Derivatives Exchange (India)	53,278,103	51,547,081	3.36%
29	27	Meff (Span)	46,973,663	40,217,657	16.80%
30	31	Zhengzhou Commodity Exchange (China)	46,298,117	28,472,570	62.61%
31	*	Multi Commodity Exchange of India	45,634,210	20,490,881	122.70%
32	28	New York Board of Trade	44,667,169	37,945,585	17.71%
33	35	Hong Kong Exchanges and Clearing	42,905,915	25,523,007	68.11%
34	30	Montreal Exchange	40,540,837	28,685,391	41.33%
35	32	Singapore Exchange	36,597,743	26,026,128	40.62%
36	40	Tokyo Financial Exchange	35,485,461	11,098,338	219.74%
37	33	Italian Derivatives Market	31,505,263	25,870,521	22.17%
38	36	Tokyo Stock Exchange	29,227,556	24,349,760	20.03%
39	37	Australian Stock Exchange	22,452,328	23,587,690	-4.81%
40	34	Tokyo Grain Exchange	19,133,509	25,600,339	-25.26%
41	39	Mercado a Termino de Rosario (Argentira)	18,212,072	13,415,449	35.57%
42	41	Budapest Stock Exchange	14,682,929	8,973,631	63.62%
43	42	Osto Stock Exchange	13,156,960	6,200,067	112.21%
44	38	Central Japan Commodity Exchange	9,019,416	21,949,566	-58.91%
45	44	One Chicago	7,922,465	5,528,046	43.32%
46	*	Turkish Derivatives Exchange	6,848,087	1,832,871	273.63%
47	43	Warsaw Stock Exchange	6,714,205	5,587,515	20.16%
48	45	Kansas City Board of Trade	5,287,190	3,953,536	33.73%
49	46	Malaysia Derivatives Exchange	4,161,024	2,459,745	69.16%
50	48	Winnipeg Commodity Exchange	2,896,536	2,076,630	39.48%
51	52	New Zealand Futures Exchange	1,826,027	986,073	85.18%
52	50	Minneapdis Grain Exchange	1,655,034	1,422,386	16.36%
53	51	Vienna Stock Exchange	1,311,543	1,045,306	25.47%
54	49	Osaka Mercantile Exchange	616,272	1,602,257	-61.54%
55	57	CBCE Future Exchange	478,424	177,632	169.33%
56	53	Kansai Commodities Exchange	318,483	1,828,750	-82.58%
57	58	Mercado a Termino de Buenos Ales	147,145	135,736	8.41%
58	47	US Futures Exchange (Eurex US)	135,803	2,200,384	-93.83%

Source: FIA

INDIAN DERIVATIVE MARKET

Structure of Derivative Markets in India

Derivative trading in India can take place either on a separate and independent Derivative Exchange or on a separate segment of an existing Stock Exchange. Derivative Exchange/Segment function as a Self-Regulatory Organization (SRO) and SEBI acts as the oversight regulator. The clearing and settlement of all trades on the Derivative Exchange/Segment would have to be through a Clearing Corporation/ House, which is independent in governance and membership from the Derivative Exchange/Segment.

Regulatory Objectives

The LC Gupta Committee believes that regulation should be designed to achieve specific, well-defined goals. It is inclined towards positive regulation designed to encourage healthy activity and behavior. It has been guided by the following objectives:

Investor protection

Attention needs to be given to the following four aspects:

i. **Fairness and transparency:** The trading rules should ensure that trading is conducted in a fair and transparent manner. Experience in other countries shows that in many cases, derivatives-brokers / dealers failed to disclose potential risk to the clients. In this context, sales practices adopted by dealers for derivatives would require specific regulation. In some of the most widely reported mishaps in the derivatives market elsewhere, the underlying reason was inadequate internal control system at the user-firm itself so that overall exposure was not controlled and the use of derivatives was for speculation rather than for risk hedging. These experiences provide useful lessons for us for designing regulations.

ii. **Safeguard for clients' moneys:** Moneys and securities deposited by clients with the trading members should not only be kept in a separate clients' account but should also not be attachable for meeting the broker's own debts. It should be ensured that trading by dealers on own account is totally segregated from that for clients.

iii. **Competent and honest service:** The eligibility criteria for trading members should be designed to encourage competent and qualified personnel so that investors/ clients are served well. This makes it necessary to prescribe qualification for derivatives brokers/dealers and the sales persons appointed by them in terms of a knowledge base.

iv. **Market integrity:** The trading system should ensure that the market's integrity is safeguarded by minimizing the possibility of defaults. This requires framing appropriate rules about capital adequacy, margins, clearing corporation etc.

Quality of markets

The concept of "Quality of Markets" goes well beyond market integrity and aims at enhancing important market qualities, such as cost-efficiency, price-continuity, and price-discovery. This is a much broader objective than market integrity.

Innovation

While curbing any undesirable tendencies, the regulatory framework should not stifle innovation which is the source of all economic progress, more so because financial derivatives represent a new rapidly developing area, aided by advancements in information technology."

Derivatives Trading: Regulatory Framework

With the amendment in the definition of 'securities' under SC(R)A (to include derivative contracts in the definition of securities), derivatives trading takes place under the provisions of the Securities Contracts (Regulation) Act, 1956 and the Securities and Exchange Board of India Act, 1992. Dr. L.C Gupta Committee constituted by SEBI had laid down the regulatory framework for derivative trading in India. SEBI has also framed suggestive by-law for Derivative Exchanges/Segments and their Clearing Corporation/House which lays down the provisions for trading and settlement of derivative contracts. The Rules, By-laws and Regulations of the Derivative Segment of the Exchanges and their Clearing Corporation/House have to be framed in line with the suggestive By-laws. SEBI has also laid the eligibility conditions for Derivative Exchange/Segment and its Clearing Corporation/House. The eligibility conditions have been framed to ensure that Derivative Exchange/Segment and Clearing Corporation/House provide a transparent trading environment, safety and integrity and provide facilities for redressal of investor grievances.

Regulatory measures by SEBI are:

1. Futures/Options contracts in both index as well as stocks can be bought and sold through the trading members of National Stock Exchange, or the BSE Mumbai Stock Exchange. Some of the trading members also provide the internet facility to trade in the futures and options market.
2. The investor is required to open an account with one of the trading members and complete the related formalities which include signing of member-constituent agreement, constituent registration form and risk disclosure document.
3. The trading member will allot the investor an unique client identification number.
4. To begin trading, the investor must deposit cash and/or other collaterals with his trading member as may be stipulated by him. SEBI has issued detailed guidelines for the benefit of the investor trading in the derivatives exchanges. These may be viewed and studied.

5. Margins are computed and collected on-line, real time on a portfolio basis at the client level. Members are required to collect the margin upfront from the client and report the same to the Exchange.
6. All the Futures and Options contracts are settled in cash at the expiry or exercise of the respective contracts as the case may, be. Members are not required to hold any stock of the underlying for dealing in the Futures/Options market.

Types of Derivative Contracts Permitted by SEBI

Derivative products have been introduced in a phased manner starting with Index Futures Contracts in June 2000. Index Options and Stock Options were introduced in June 2001 and July 2001 followed by Stock Futures in November 2001.

Minimum contract size

The Standing Committee on Finance, a Parliamentary Committee, at the time of recommending amendment to Securities Contract (Regulation) Act, 1956 had recommended that the minimum contract size of derivative contracts traded in the Indian Markets should be pegged not below Rs. 2 lakh. Based on this recommendation SEBI has specified that the value of a derivative contract should not be less than Rs. 2 lakh at the time of introducing the contract in the market.

The lot size of a contract

Lot size refers to number of underlying securities in one contract. Additionally, for stock specific derivative contracts SEBI has specified that the lot size of the underlying individual security should be in multiples of 100 and fractions, if any, should be rounded off to the next higher multiple of 100. This requirement of SEBI coupled with the requirement of minimum contract size forms the basis of arriving at the lot size of a contract.

For example, if shares of XYZ Ltd are quoted at Rs.1000 each and the minimum contract size is Rs. 2 lakh, then the lot size for that particular scrips stands to be 200000/1000 = 200 shares i.e. one contract in XYZ Ltd. covers 200 shares.

Exchange-Traded and Over-the-Counter Derivative Instruments

OTC (over-the-counter) contracts, such as forwards and swaps, are bilaterally negotiated between two parties. The terms of an OTC contract are flexible, and are often customized to fit the specific requirements of the user. OTC contracts have substantial credit risk, which is the risk that the counterparty that owes money defaults on the payment. In India, OTC derivatives are generally prohibited with some exceptions: those that are specifically allowed by the Reserve Bank of India (RBI) or, in the case of commodities (which are regulated by the Forward Markets Commission), those that trade informally in "havala" or forwards markets.

An exchange-traded contract, such as a futures contract, has a standardized format that specifies the underlying asset to be delivered, the size of the contract, and the logistics of delivery. They trade on organized exchanges with prices determined by the interaction of many buyers and sellers. In India, two exchanges offer derivatives trading: the Bombay Stock Exchange (BSE) and the National Stock Exchange (NSE). However, NSE now accounts for virtually all exchange-traded derivatives in India, accounting for more than 99% of volume in 2003-2004. Contract performance is guaranteed by a clearing house, which is a wholly owned subsidiary of the NSE.

Derivatives instruments traded in India

In the exchange-traded market, the biggest success story has been derivatives on equity products. Index futures were introduced in June 2000, followed by index options in June 2001, and options and futures on individual securities in July 2001 and November 2001, respectively. As of 2005, the NSE trades futures and options on 118 individual stocks.

All these derivative contracts are settled by cash payment and do not involve physical delivery of the underlying product (which may be costly). Derivatives on stock indexes and individual stocks have grown rapidly since inception. In particular, single stock futures have become hugely popular, accounting for about half of NSE's traded value in October 2005. In fact, NSE has the highest volume (i.e. number of contracts traded) in the single stock futures globally, enabling it to rank 16 among world exchanges in the first half of 2005. Single stock options are less popular than futures.

Index futures are increasingly popular, and accounted for close to 40% of traded value in October 2005. The growth in volume of futures and options on the Nifty index, shows that index futures have grown more strongly than index options (Fig. 16.1).

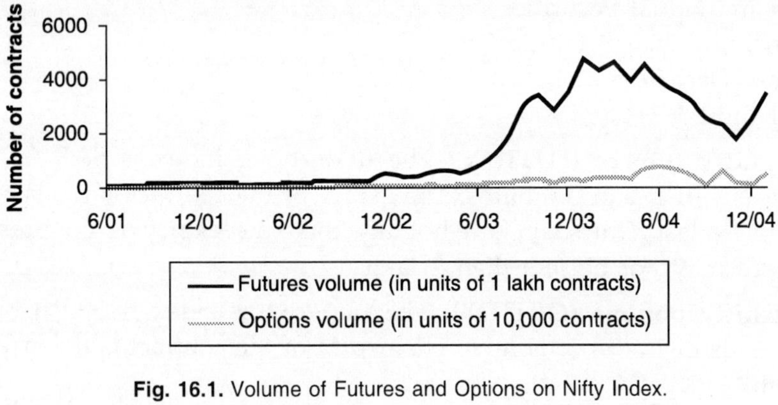

Fig. 16.1. Volume of Futures and Options on Nifty Index.

Derivatives users in India

The use of derivatives varies by type of institution. Financial institutions, such as banks, have assets and liabilities of different maturities and in different currencies, and are exposed to different risks of default from their borrowers. Thus, they are likely to use derivatives on interest rates and currencies, and derivatives to manage credit risk. Non-financial institutions are regulated differently from financial institutions, and this affects their incentives to use derivatives. Indian insurance regulators, for example, are yet to issue guidelines relating to the use of derivatives by insurance companies.

In India, financial institutions have not been heavy users of exchange-traded derivatives so far, with their contribution to total value of NSE trades being less than 8% in October 2005. However, market insiders feel that this may be changing, as indicated by the growing share of index derivatives (which are used more by institutions than by retail investors). In contrast to the exchange-traded markets, domestic financial institutions and mutual funds have shown great interest in OTC fixed income instruments. Transactions between banks dominate the market for interest rate derivatives, while state-owned banks remain a small presence. Corporations are active in the currency forwards and swaps markets, buying these instruments from banks.

Major products of derivatives available in India

- S&P CNX Nifty Futures
- S&P CNX Nifty Options
- CNX IT Futures
- CNX IT Options
- Bank Nifty Futures
- Bank Nifty Options
- Futures on Individual Securities
- Options on Individual Securities
- Interest Rate Derivatives
- Notional T-Bills

S&P CNX nifty futures (FUTIDX): The underlying index is S&P CNX NIFTY. The trading cycle is of 1, 2 or 3 months. The expiry of the contract is the last Thursday of every month. If last Thursday is a holiday then the expiry is on previous day. The contract size may not be less than 2 lakh.

S&P CNX nifty options (OPTIDX): The underlying index is S&P CNX NIFTY. The trading cycle is of 1, 2 or 3 months. The expiry of the contract is the last Thursday of every month.

CNX IT futures and options: The underlying index is CNX IT. The CNX index comprises securities which are major information technology companies. The companies CNX IT index are:

Company Name	Symbol	Series
CMC Ltd.	CMC	EQ
Financial Technologies (India) Ltd.	FINANTECH	EQ
GTL Ltd.	GLOBALTELE	EQ
HCL Infosystems Ltd.	HCL-INSYS	EQ
HCL Technologies Ltd.	HCLTECH	EQ
Hexaware Technologies Ltd.	HEXAWARE	EQ
Hinduja TMT Ltd.	HTMT	EQ
I-Flex Solutions Ltd.	I-FLEX	EQ
iGate Global Solutions Ltd.	IGS	EQ
Infosys Technologies Ltd.	INFOSYSTCH	EQ
Mastek Ltd.	MASTEK	EQ
Moser Baer India Ltd.	MOSERBAER	EQ
Mphasis BFL Ltd.	MPHASISBFL	EQ
Patni Computer Systems Ltd.	PATNI	EQ
Polaris Software Lab Ltd.	POLARIS	EQ
Rolta India Ltd.	ROLTA	EQ
Satyam Computer Services Ltd.	SATYAMCOMP	EQ
Tata Elxsi Ltd.	TATAELXSI	EQ
Tata Consultancy Services Ltd.	TCS	EQ
Wipro Ltd.	WIPRO	EQ

Bank nifty futures and options: BANK Nifty futures Contract would be based on the index CNX Bank index. The Banks that constitute bank nifty are:

Company Name	Symbol	Series
Andhra Bank	ANDHRABANK	EQ
Bank of Baroda	BANKBARODA	EQ
Bank of India	BANKINDIA	EQ
Canara Bank	CANBK	EQ
Corporation Bank	CORPBANK	EQ
HDFC Bank Ltd.	HDFCBANK	EQ
ICICI Bank Ltd.	ICICIBANK	EQ
Oriental Bank of Commerce	ORIENTBANK	EQ
Punjab National Bank Ltd.	PNB	EQ
State Bank of India	SBIN	EQ
Syndicate Bank	SYNDIBANK	EQ
Union Bank of India.	UNIONBANK	EQ

Futures and options on individual securities: NSE commenced trading in futures on individual securities on November 9, 2001. The futures contracts are available on 116 securities stipulated by the Securities & Exchange Board of India (SEBI).

Interest rate derivatives: Interest Rate Futures Contracts are contracts based on the list of underlying as may be specified by the Exchange and approved by SEBI from time to time. To begin with, interest rate futures contracts on the following underling's shall be available for trading on the F&O Segment of the Exchange:

Notional T-bills: Notional 10 year bonds (coupon bearing and non-coupon bearing)

The list of securities on which Futures Contracts would be available and their symbols for trading are as under:

S. No.	Symbol	Description
1	NSETB91D	Futures contract on Notional 91 day T bill
2	NSE10Y06	Futures contract on Notional 10 year coupon bearing bond
3	NSE10YZC	Futures contract on Notional 10 year zero coupon bond.

Interest rate futures contracts are available on Notional T-bills, Notional 10 year zero coupon bond and Notional 10 year coupon bearing bond stipulated by the Securities & Exchange Board of India (SEBI). The interest rate future contract shall be for a period of maturity of one year with three months continuous contracts for the first three months and fixed quarterly contracts for the entire year. New contracts will be introduced on the trading day following the expiry of the near month contract.

India Operations in the F&O Segment

Future Segment (January 2007)

Top 5 Traded Symbols

Sr	Contract Descriptor	No. of Contracts	Traded Value (Rs. Crores)	Percentage of Contracts to Total Contracts
1	NIFTY JANUARY 2007	3687166	147980	26
2	NIFTY FEB RUARY 2007	957758	39209	7
3	RELIANCE JANUARY 2007	498713	19969	4
4	RCOM JANUARY 2007	268377	8268	2
5	TATASTEEL JANUARY 2007	182221	5888	1
6	OTHERS	8,486,867	320095	60
	TOTAL	14,081,102	541,409	100

Option Segment (January 2007)

Traded Symbols

Sr	Contract Descriptor	No. of Contracts	Traded Value (Rs. Crores)	Percentage of Contracts to Total Contracts
1	NIFTY JAN 2007 CE 4100	179101	7401	8
2	NIFTY JAN 2007 CE 4000	155812	6354	7
3	NIFTY JAN 2007 PE 4000	145219	5901	7
4	NIFTY JAN 2007 PE 4100	103290	4278	5
5	NIFTY JAN 2007 PE 3900	99829	3950	5
6	OTHERS	1,468,093	58,163	68
	TOTAL	**2,1,344**	**86,047**	**100**

A graphical representation of the month wise product wise turnover in the F&O Segment for the period August 2006 to January 2007 is as below:

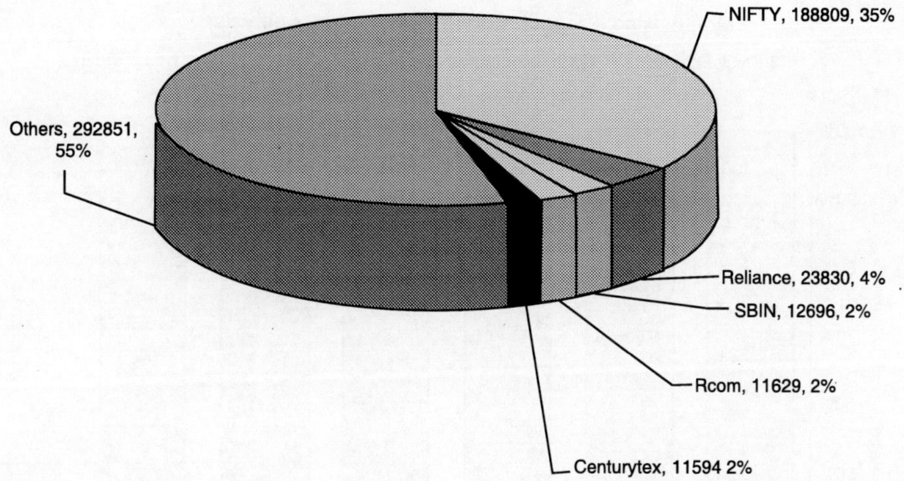

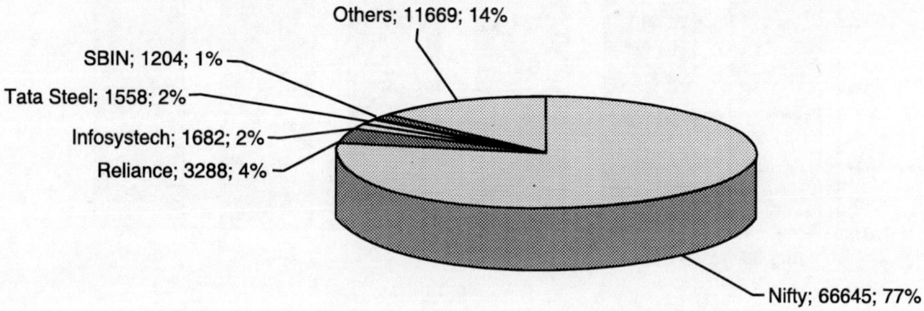

Comparative Analysis - World Exchanges (December 2006)

Product NSE's Position	Stock Futures 2nd with 92,61,984 contract		Index Futures 4th with 57,98,118 Contract		Stock Options 15th with 4,34,629 contract		Index Options 8th with 20,21,995 contract	
Rank	*Name of the Exchange*	*Number of contracts*	*Name of the Exchange*	*Number of contracts*	*Name of the Exchange*	*Number of contracts*	*Name of the Exchange*	*Number of contracts*
1	JSE	1,31,18,131	Chicago Mercantile Exchange	3,71,45,122	CBOE	3,13,83,194	Korea Exchange	17,54,65,423
2	NSE	92,61,984	Eurex	2,40,22,746	Philadelphia	2,86,44,125	CBOE	2,15,85,986
3	BME	31,12,178	Euronext.	6,342,391	Sao Paulo	2,21,52,402	Eurex	1,64,31,920

Month wise Product wise Traded Value Analysis:

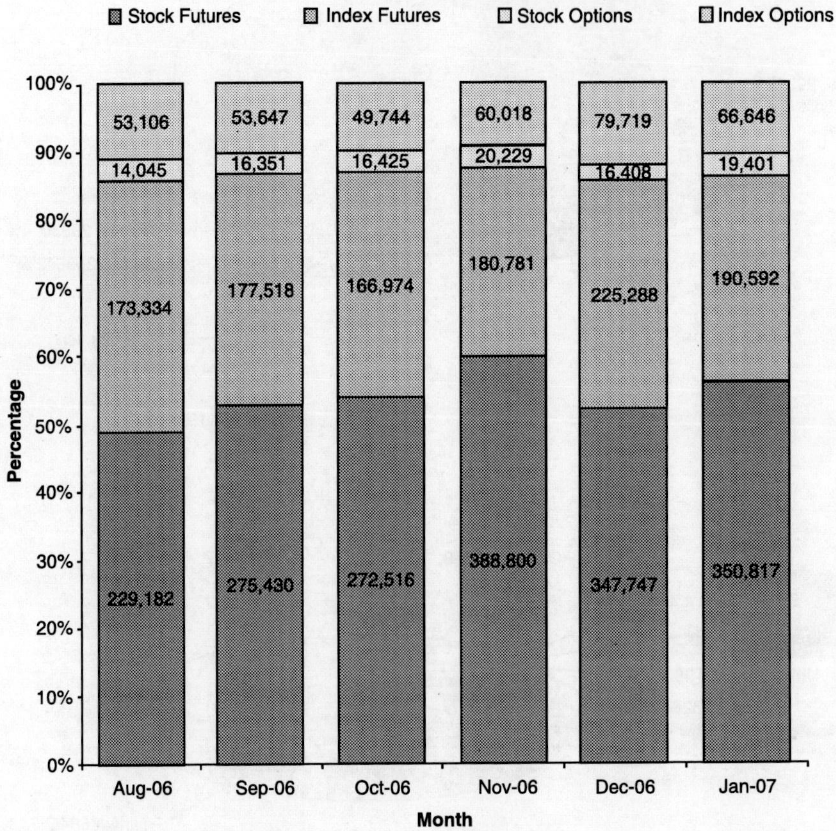

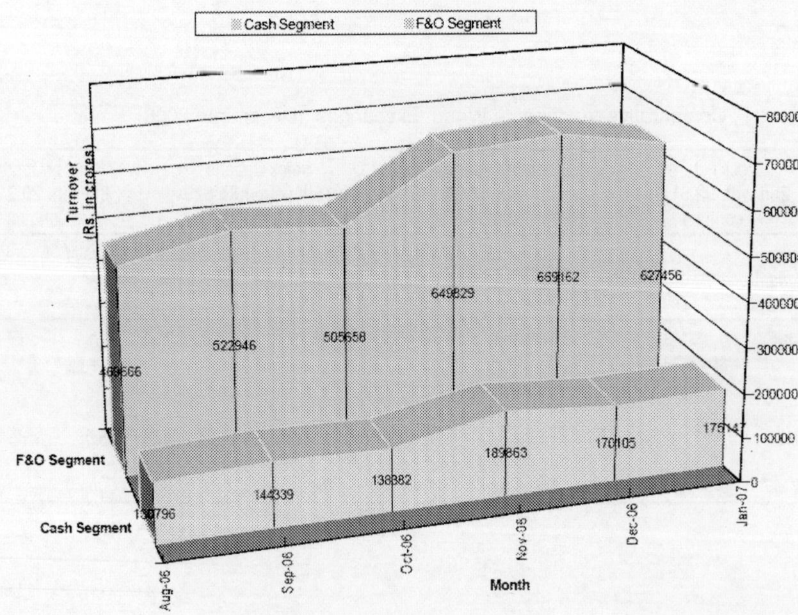

Detailed Study of the Various Instruments

Forward contract

A cash market transaction is a transaction in which a seller agrees to deliver a specific cash commodity to a buyer at some point in the future. Forward contracts are privately negotiated and are not standardized. Further, the two parties must bear each other's credit risk. Also, since the contracts are not exchange traded, there is no marking to market requirement, which allows a buyer to avoid almost all capital outflows initially (though some counter-parties might set collateral requirements). Given the lack of standardization in these contracts, there is very little scope for a secondary market in forwards. The price is specified in a forward contract for a specific commodity. The forward price makes the forward contract have no value when the contract is written. However, if the value of the underlying currency changes, the value of the forward contract becomes positive or negative, depending on the position held. Forwards are priced in a manner similar to futures. Like in the case of a futures contract, the first step in pricing a forward is to add the spot price to the cost of carry (interest forgone, convenience yield, storage costs and interest/dividend received on the underlying). Unlike a futures contract though, the price may also include a premium for counterparty credit risk, and the fact that there is not daily marking to market process to minimize default risk. If there is no allowance for these credit risks, then the forward price will equal the futures price.

The main features of forward contracts:

They are bilateral contracts and hence exposed to counter-party risk. Each contract is custom designed, and hence is unique in terms of contract size, expiration date and the asset type and quality. The contract price is generally not available in public domain. The contract has to be settled by delivery of the asset on expiration date. In case, the party wishes to reverse the contract, it has to compulsorily go to the same counter-party, which being in a monopoly situation can command the price it wants.

Illustration

Ram is an importer who has to make a payment for his consignment in six months time. In order to meet his payment obligation he has to buy dollars six months from today. However, he is not sure what the Re/$ rate will be then. In order to be sure of his expenditure he will enter into a contract with a bank to buy dollars six months from now at a decided rate. As he is entering into a contract on a future date it is a forward contract and the underlying security is the foreign currency.

Futures contracts

A futures contract has been defined as "a standardized, exchange-traded agreement specifying a quantity and price of a particular type of commodity (soybeans, gold, oil, etc.) to be purchased or sold at a pre-determined date in the future. On contract date, delivery and physical possession take place unless the contract has been closed out. Futures are also available on various financial products and indexes today.

A futures contract is thus a forward contract, which trades on an exchange. S&P CNX Nifty futures are traded on National Stock Exchange. This provides them transparency, liquidity, anonymity of trades, and also eliminates the counter party risks due to the guarantee provided by National Securities Clearing Corporation Limited.

A future contract is an agreement between a buyer and a seller where the seller agrees to deliver a specified quantity and grade of a particular asset at a predetermined time in future at an agreed upon price through a designated market (exchange) under stringent financial safeguards. A futures contract, in other words, is a forward contract, which trades on an exchange. S&P CNX Nifty futures are traded on National Stock Exchange. This provides them transparency, liquidity, anonymity of trades, and also eliminates the counter party risks due to the guarantee provided by National Securities Clearing Corporation Limited.

BSE website defines futures contract: "Futures are exchange traded contracts to sell or buy financial instruments or physical commodities for future delivery at an agreed price. There is an agreement to buy or sell a specified quantity of financial instrument/ commodity in a designated Future month at a price agreed upon by the buyer and seller. The contracts have certain standardized specifications."

The standardized items in any Futures contract are:

1. Quantity of the underlying.
2. Quality of the underlying (not required in financial Futures)
3. The date and month of delivery.
4. The units of price quotation (not the price itself) and minimum change in price (tick-size)

Forward contracts distinguished from futures

A forward contract is one which is initiated at one time, and performance taking place at a future time. It always involves the exchange of one asset for another. The price at which the transaction takes place is negotiated at the onset. Payment and delivery of the goods takes place at a subsequent time to the initial contract. Just about everyone has taken part in a forward contract. For example, if I agree with my next door neighbor to buy his table saw for Rs.2000 next Thursday, we have engaged in a forward contract. When next Thursday comes and I give my neighbor Rs. 2000 and he brings the table saw over to me, we have both satisfied the terms of the forward contract.

A futures contract can be distinguished from a forward contract in the following ways.

First, futures contracts always trade on an organized exchange.

Second, futures contracts have standardized terms. In my example with my neighbor's table saw we agreed on the terms of the contract, when it would be fulfilled, and the condition of the product. With a futures contract, the quality, quantity, and delivery date, is pre-determined.

Third, Futures exchanges use clearing houses to guarantee that the terms of the futures contract is fulfilled. Again, using my table saw example, if one of us decided either not to sell the saw or not to buy the saw, there was no one else around to guarantee that the contract would be fulfilled. The futures exchanges use clearing houses to see to it that the obligations of the contract are fulfilled. The clearing house is the actual buyer of the contract from the short seller. And the clearing house is the actual seller of the long contract. If either party defaults on the contract the clearing house steps in and becomes the seller or buyer of last resort. The clearing house guarantees that the contract will be fulfilled. Neither party needs to trust the other party. In the history of futures trading in America, the clearing house system has always worked.

Fourth, margins and daily settlement are required with futures trading. These are other safeguards in the futures market. Each customer must put up a good faith deposit. The amount of this margin varies from exchange to exchange and broker to broker. However, no broker may margin a contract for less than the exchange minimum. Each trading day every futures contract is assessed for liquidity. If the margin drops below a certain level the trader must deposit additional margin. This is called 'Maintenance Margin'.

Fifth, futures positions can easily be closed. The trader has the option of taking physical delivery placing an offsetting trade and arranging an exchange-for-physicals transaction. If I wanted to get out of buying my neighbor's table saw with the forward contract I entered into, the only way that I could do it would be to break our contract. The futures exchange makes exiting a contract relatively easy.

Options

Options are derivative instruments, meaning that their prices are derived from the price of another security. More specifically, options prices are derived from the price of an underlying stock. This will all become very clear shortly.

Another important thing to understand is that every option represents a contract between a buyer and seller. The seller (writer) has the obligation to either buy or sell stock (depending on what type of option he or she sold — either a call option or a put option) to the buyer at a specified price by a specified date. Meanwhile, the buyer of an options contract has the right, but not the obligation, to complete the transaction by a specified date. When an option expires, if it is not in the buyer's best interest to exercise the option, then he or she is not obligated to do anything. The buyer has purchased the option to carry out a certain transaction in the future — hence the name.

Option buyer (Option holder): Party that purchases and holds the options contract.

Option seller: Party that writes, or creates, the options contract.

Strike price: The price at which the option seller agrees to buy or sell a certain stock in the future.

Expiration month: The month in which the option will expire.

Expiration date: This is always the third Friday of the month in which the option is scheduled to expire.

Option contract: Each options contract represents an interest in 100 shares of a certain underlying stock.

Put option: This type of option gives the option holder the right, but not the obligation, to **sell** 100 shares of a particular underlying stock at a specified price (the strike price) on a specified date (the expiration date). For example, let's say you were to purchase a put option on shares of XYZ Co. with a strike price of Rs.50 and an expiration date of March 19th. This option would give you the right to sell 100 shares of XYZ Co. at a price of Rs.50 on March 19th (the right to do this, of course, will only be valuable if Microsoft is trading below Rs.50 per share at that point in time).

Call option: This type of option gives the option holder the right, but not the obligation, to purchase 100 shares of a particular underlying stock at a specified strike price on the option's expiration date.

For example, let's say you were to purchase a call option on shares of ABC Co. with a strike price of Rs.40 and an expiration date of April 16th. This option would give you the right to purchase 100 shares of ABC Co. at a price of Rs.40 on April 16th (the right to do this, of course, will only be valuable if Intel is trading above Rs.40 per share at that point in time).

"In-the-money" option: If the option were exercised today would be worth more than Re.0. In the case of a call option, the option is only considered to be "in-the-money" when the price of the underlying stock is greater than the option's strike price. So, in the case of our ABC Co example above, the call option will be "in-the-money" when shares of ABC Co. are trading above Rs.40. Meanwhile, in the case of a put option, the option is only considered to be "in-the-money" when the price of the underlying stock is less than the option's strike price. So, in the case of our XYZ Co. example, the put option will be "in-the-money" only when shares of XYZ Co. are trading below Rs.50 per share.

"Out-of-the-money" option: An option if it were exercised today, would not be worth a single cent. In the case of a call option, the option is considered to be "out-of-the-money" when the price of the underlying stock is less than the option's strike price. So, in the case of our ABC Co example above, the call option will be "out-of-the-money" when Intel is trading below Rs.40 per share. After all, if ABC Co is trading for less than Rs.40 (let's say it is at Rs.35), then the right to purchase ABC Co at a price of Rs.40 per share is completely worthless (if you can buy the stock in the open market for Rs.35, then you certainly wouldn't want to buy it for Rs.40). Options traders use the term "out-of-the-money" to describe this type of situation. The analysis is similar when it comes to put options.

In the case of a put option, the option is considered to be "out-of-the money" when the price of the underlying stock is greater than the option's strike price. So, in the case of our XYZ Co. example, the put option will be "out-of-the-money" when shares of XYZ Co. are trading above $50 per share.

"At-the-money" option: An option is considered to be "at-the-money" when its strike price is exactly equivalent to the price of the underlying stock.

Call option: An option to BUY an underlying asset (or currency) at an agreed price (Strike Price or Exercise Price) on or before the expiration date. Since this option has economic value, you have to pay a price, called the Premium.

Illustration

DEF Co. was recently selling at Rs.29.50/share, and there were 4 different options. For example, for Rs.1.50 (premium) you could buy one call option that would allow you to buy a share of MSFT for Rs.30 (strike P) on or before January 16, 2004. You will exercise the option if P > Rs.30, and you will make money if the P > Rs.31.50 (Rs.30 + Rs.1.50). If P = Rs.30, you will not exercise the option, it will expire worthless and you will lose the premium (Rs.1.50).

Applications of Derivatives in FOREX

Need of forex market

As the size of forex market is growing day by day. The cumulative value of exports for the period April- January, 2007 was US $ 99137.44 million ($ 99 billion) or Rs.451167.67 crore as against US $ 74978.00 million ($ 74.9 billion) or Rs.331771.01 crore during the same period last year, indicating a growth of 32.22%.(think 5 year down the line the amount of export at this growth rate.) The cumulative value of imports during April-January, 2007 was US $ 149725.99 million (Rs.680940.63crore) which was higher than imports at US $ 108802.77 million (Rs.481338.68 crore) during April- January, 2006. Imports during the month of January, 2007 were valued at US $ 15430.06 million (Rs.68405.33 crore) compared with US $ 11367.68 million (Rs.50469.10 crore) in January, 2006.

Now let us look at the effect of appreciation/depreciation of a rupee against dollar on export in 2006-07.

	Export ($ bn)	Exchange Rate	INR equivalent (bn)
Before Appreciation	99	42	4158
After Appreciation	99	40	3960

Now look at the loss due to appreciation of rupee against the dollar. There is a loss of Rs198 bn (4158-3960). There is same effect of depreciation of rupee. Same case is with the Import. But the effect of appreciation of rupee is opposite in case for importers as of exporters. As exporter will lose with appreciation of rupee and importer will gain with appreciation.

As on day-to-day the boundaries of countries are shrinking i.e due to the increase in import and export of goods and services there is huge amount of risk involve with currency transaction.

Hedging

Hedging involves protecting an existing asset position from future adverse price movements. In order to hedge a position, a market player needs to take an equal and opposite position in the futures market to the one held in the cash market. Every portfolio has a hidden exposure to the index, which is denoted by the beta.

Hedgers - someone with a business/personal interest in the underlying currency, and is using futures trading to minimize, eliminate or control currency risk, e.g. MNCs, banks, exporters/importers, etc.

Illustration

An Indian Exporter agrees to ship merchandise to a US client, receive $10m in 6 months worried about regarding falling $. Now it has taken a short Position on $ in six months forwards.

Two scenarios:

1. Dollar depreciates over next 6 months, and exporter makes a profit in futures market on the short position. Exporter gets paid the $10m which have depreciated sells $ in spot market at a "loss," but the gain in the futures contract offsets the currency loss.
2. Dollar appreciates over next 6 months, and exporter loses money in futures market. Exporter receives stronger Euros for the merchandise, sells for more dollars than expected, which is offset by the loss in futures.

   Either way, the exporter is insured against currency risk, receives a guaranteed or fixed amount of INR for the Dollar in six months. No worry, insurance, the ex-rate is locked.

Steps:

Determine the beta of the portfolio. If the beta of any stock is not known, it is safe to assume that it is 1. Short sell the currency in such a quantum that the gain on a unit decrease in the currency would offset the losses on the rest of his portfolio. This is achieved by multiplying the relative volatility of the portfolio by the market value of his holdings.

As we see, that portfolio is completely insulated from any losses arising out of a fall in market sentiment. But as a cost, one has to forego any gains that arise out of improvement in the overall sentiment. Then why does one invest in equities if all the gains will be offset by losses in futures market. The idea is that everyone expects his portfolio to outperform the market. Irrespective of whether the market goes up or not, his portfolio value would increase.

The same methodology can be applied to a single stock by deriving the beta of the scrip and taking a reverse position in the futures market.

Thus, we have seen how one can use hedging in the futures market to offset losses in the cash market.

Basis

Basis is the difference between the exchange rate of a currency at a certain time and its futures price.

For example:

If the	Cash price	=	$4.00
And the	Futures price	=	$4.25
Then the	Basis	=	-25 cents (cash – futures = basis)

Market expectations: Basis is a reflection of local or regional supply and demand factors rather than world conditions. Basis may fluctuate and change direction with some frequency, but basis risk is much less volatile than price risk because basis represents the difference between two prices that move in the same general pattern.

Therefore, most hedgers look to offset price risk even if it means taking on basis risk.

The level of the basis is often referred to as "strong" or "weak." A strengthening basis becomes more positive. For example, if your local basis goes from 10 cents over the futures to 30 cents over, the basis is strengthening. Conversely, a weakening basis becomes more negative, such as when it moves from 30 cents over the futures to 10 cents over.

The following examples illustrate how basis and hedging are used by specific agricultural groups.

The short hedge: A short hedge typically locks in a sales price for a currency. For example, on March 1, exchange rate reach a level where a exporter knows he can make a profit on his future income from abroad that is yet to be received. Rather than take the chance that exchange rate will fall, he decides to hedge a portion of the currency using futures. To lock in an exchange rate he establishes a "short hedge" by selling Dollar Currency futures contracts.

The long hedge: A long hedge typically locks in a purchase future of currency. For example, an exporter has contracted to take delivery of a shipment of cattle three months in the future. He made the contract based on current exchange rate.

Speculation

Speculators are those who do not have any position on which they enter in futures and options market. They only have a particular view on the market currency, stock, commodity etc. In short, speculators put their money at risk in the hope of profiting from an anticipated price change. They consider various factors such as demand supply, market positions, open interests, economic fundamentals and other data to take their positions.

Ram on April 1, 2007, he buys 10 (Japanese Yen) Currency future @ .9284($ per 100 Yen) on expectation that the Yen will appreciate in future. On June 1, 2007 the Yen appreciate to .93 and at that time he sells an equal number of contract to close out his position.

Price: .93 * 125000 * 10 = 11620000 $

Purchase Cost: .9284 * 125000 * 10 = 11605000 $

Net Gain = 15000 $

Ram has made a profit of Yen 15000, by taking a call on the future value of currency. However, if the Yen had Depreciated he would have made a loss.

Arbitrage

An arbitrageur is basically risk averse. He enters into those contracts where he can earn risk less profits. When markets are imperfect, buying in one market and simultaneously selling in other market gives risk-less profit. Arbitrageurs are always in the look out for such imperfections.

In the futures market one can take advantages of arbitrage opportunities by buying from lower priced market and selling at the higher priced market. In currency futures arbitrage is possible between the spot market and the futures market.

Take the case of the $/INR future.

Assume that $ is at 42 and 3 month's currency futures is at 45.

The futures price of currency can be worked out by taking the net interest cost (Interest on domestic currency – interest on foreign currency) of 3 months into account.

If there is a difference then arbitrage opportunity exists.

Pricing models used: The Black-Scholes model and the Cox, Ross and Rubinstein binomial model are the primary pricing models.

Both models are based on the same theoretical foundations and assumptions (such as the geometric Brownian motion theory of stock price behavior and risk-neutral valuation). However, there are also some important differences between the two models and these are highlighted below.

THE BLACK-SCHOLES MODEL

The Black-Scholes option valuation model consists of a rather complex mathematical formula developed by two famous economists in the early 1970's, which permits one to calculate what the "theoretical" price of an equity option should be. The following describes the major determinants of the value of a stock option which the Black-Scholes model takes into account.

Strike price: At any point in time, an option's intrinsic value, if any, is computed by reference to the difference between the strike (exercise) price of the option and the current underlying share price. In the case of a call option, if the current share price is below the strike price, then the option is said to be "out of the money" and has no intrinsic value. Conversely, if the current share price is higher than the strike price of a call option, then the option is "in-the-money" and has intrinsic value. In the case of put options, the same applies in reverse.

Time until expiry: All other things equal, the price of stock options decreases at an accelerating rate as the expiration date approaches. This is referred to as "time decay" and is the primary reason that long-term options are more expensive than short-term options in the same underlying stock.

Volatility: In simple terms, volatility is a measure of "how much the stock moves around" - whether up or down. There are two types of volatility. Historical (actual) volatility can be determined mathematically based on the size of price moves that a particular stock has actually made in the past. Implied (future) volatility refers to the degree of price volatility that a particular stock is anticipated to make in the future. Different investors may have significantly different expectations about the future volatility of a stock. Hence, there will often be different perceptions of what the "fair" price of a particular stock option should be. Historical volatility is, however, often used as an estimate of the future volatility of a stock to value a stock option.

Prevailing risk-free interest rate: The prevailing risk-free interest rate also affects option prices. When an investor buys an option, he has to pay an amount (premium) for the option contract. If he did not buy that option, the investor could have placed the amount of the option premium on time deposit and earned risk-free interest on it. The option price or premium will therefore reflect this lost interest. In particular, the higher the prevailing interest rate, the more lost interest and hence the lower the option premiums have to be compensated for that foregone interest. In practice, when interest rates are very low, this effect is negligible and is often ignored when valuing an option—particularly a short-term option.

Dividends to be paid: Dividends that are due to be paid out on the underlying shares during the period of the option will reduce the price of the stock by that amount when actually paid out. This will have the effect of reducing the price of call option premiums and increasing put premiums. Accordingly, the anticipated payment of dividends must be taken into account when valuing options.

The Black-Scholes model is used to calculate a theoretical call price (ignoring dividends paid during the life of the option) using the five key determinants of an option's price: stock price, strike price, volatility, time to expiration, and short-term (risk free) interest rate.

The original formula for calculating the theoretical option price (OP) is as follows:

$$OP = SN(d_1) - Xe^{-rt}N(d_2)$$

Where:

$$d_1 = \frac{In\left(\frac{S}{X}\right) + \left(r + \frac{v^2}{2}\right)t}{v\sqrt{t}}$$

$$d_2 = d_1 - v\sqrt{t}$$

The variables are:

S = stock price
X = strike price
t = time remaining until expiration, expressed as a percent of a year
r = current continuously compounded risk-free interest rate
v = annual volatility of stock price (the standard deviation of the short-term returns over one year).
ln = natural logarithm
N(x) = standard normal cumulative distribution function
e = the exponential function

Advantages and Limitations of the Model

Advantage: The main advantage of the Black-Scholes model is speed — it lets you calculate a very large number of option prices in a very short time.

Limitation: The Black-Scholes model has one major limitation: it cannot be used to accurately price options with an American-style exercise as it only calculates the option price at one point in time — at expiration. It does not consider the steps along the way where there could be the possibility of early exercise of an American option.

As all exchange traded equity options have American-style exercise i.e. they can be exercised at any time as opposed to European options which can only be exercised at expiration. This is a significant limitation.

The exception to this is an American call on a non-dividend paying asset. In this case the call is always worth the same as its European equivalent as there is never any advantage in exercising early.

Various adjustments are sometimes made to the Black-Scholes price to enable it to approximate American option prices (e.g. the Fischer Black Pseudo-American method) but these only work well within certain limits and they don't really work well for puts.

Assumptions of the Black and Scholes Model

1. **The stock pays no dividends during the option's life:** Most companies pay

dividends to their share holders, so this might seem a serious limitation to the model considering the observation that higher dividend yields elicit lower call premiums. A common way of adjusting the model for this situation is to subtract the discounted value of a future dividend from the stock price.

2. **European exercise terms are used:** European exercise terms dictate that the option can only be exercised on the expiration date. American exercise term allows the option to be exercised at any time during the life of the option, making American options more valuable due to their greater flexibility. This limitation is not a major concern because very few calls are ever exercised before the last few days of their life. This is true because when you exercise a call early, you forfeit the remaining time value on the call and collect the intrinsic value. Towards the end of the life of a call, the remaining time value is very small, but the intrinsic value is the same.
3. **Markets are efficient:** This assumption suggests that people cannot consistently predict the direction of the market or an individual stock.
4. **No commissions are charged:** Usually market participants do have to pay a commission to buy or sell options. Even floor traders pay some kind of fee, but it is usually very small. The fees that individual investor pays is more substantial and can often distort the output of the model.
5. **Interest rates remain constant and known:** The Black and Scholes model uses the risk-free rate to represent this constant and known rate. In reality there is no such thing as the risk-free rate, but the discount rate on U.S. Government Treasury Bills with 30 days left until maturity is usually used to represent it. During periods of rapidly changing interest rates, these 30-day rates are often subject to change, thereby violating one of the assumptions of the model.
6. **Returns are log normally distributed:** This assumption suggests, returns on the underlying stock are normally distributed, which is reasonable for most assets that offer options.

BINOMIAL PRICING

The binomial model breaks down the time to expiration into potentially a very large number of time intervals, or steps. A tree of stock prices is initially produced working forward from the present to expiration. At each step it is assumed that the stock price will move up or down by an amount calculated using volatility and time to expiration. This produces a binomial distribution, or recombining tree, of underlying stock prices. The tree represents all the possible paths that the stock price could take during the life of the option.

At the end of the tree that is at expiration of the option — all the terminal option prices for each of the final possible stock prices are known as they simply equal their intrinsic values.

Next the option prices at each step of the tree are calculated working back from expiration to the present. The option prices at each step are used to derive the option prices at the next step of the tree using risk neutral valuation based on the probabilities of the stock prices moving up or down, the risk free rate and the time interval of each step. Any adjustments to stock prices (at an ex-dividend date) or option prices (as a result of early exercise of American options) are worked into the calculations at the required point in time. At the top of the tree you are left with one option price.

Advantages and Limitations

Advantages: The big advantage the binomial model has over the Black-Scholes model is that it can be used to accurately price American options. This is because with the binomial model it is possible to check at every point in an option's life (i.e. at every step of the binomial tree) for the possibility of early exercise (e.g. where, due to a dividend, or a put being deeply in the money the option price at that point is less than its intrinsic value).

CASE STUDY: Exploring Arbitrage Opportunities in India

Where an early exercise point is found it is assumed that the option holder would elect to exercise, and the option price can be adjusted to equal the intrinsic value at that point. This then flows into the calculations higher up the tree and so on.

The on-line binomial tree graphical option calculator highlights those points in the tree structure where early exercise would have caused an American price to differ from a European price.

The binomial model basically solves the same equation, using a computational procedure that the Black-Scholes model solves using an analytic approach and in doing so provides opportunities along the way to check for early exercise for American options.

Limitation: The main limitation of the binomial model is its relatively slow speed. It is great for half a dozen calculations at a time but even with today's fastest PCs it is not a practical solution for the calculation of thousands of prices in a few seconds.

Data Analysis of Pricing of Options

Analysis of pricing currency option

One of the major problems faced by a normal investor is finding the premium on a particular option and whether a premium is correctly priced and whether a premium is cheap or costly according to the market dynamics.

The solution lies in the Black Scholes model which is an appropriate model for judging the value of the premium based volatility of a particular currency.

Another major hindrance for an investor is how to calculate premium using the model. So in order to overcome all these hurdles I have designed a model which we can be used to calculate the premium an a particular Currency Option.

Inputs to the model

Historical data for exchange rate, in order to calculate volatility (v) of the exchange rate

Current exchange rate (S)
Strike price of the option (X)
Risk free interest rate (annual) on domestic currency (r)
Risk free interest rate (annual) on foreign currency (R)
Time to expiry in number of years (t).

In order to calculate volatility using historical data I have used the following formulas.

Si	=	Exchange rate at the end of ith interval where i=1,2,3..............n
N+ 1	=	Number of observations
s	=	Standard deviation
t	=	Time to expiry
Ui	=	ln (Si / Si-1)
v	=	Historical Volatility
s	=	SQRT ((1/(n-1)) Σni=1 (Ui) 2 - (1/(n(n-1)))(Σni=1 Ui)2)
v	=	s/ SQRT (t)

Now in order to calculate the premium of an option I have used the following method

$$OP = SN(d_1)^* \; e\text{-}R\; t - X * e\text{-}r\; t * N(d_2)$$

Where:

$$d_1 = \frac{In(S/X) + (r - R + v2/s)*t}{v * Sqrt(t)}$$

$$d_2 = d_1 - v\sqrt{t}$$

So in this way this model will help you to calculate the premium on a particular option. This model will also help you make an use of arbitrage opportunity if any exists. This model will tell you whether a particular option is overpriced or underpriced and from there you can take the advantage of this opportunity to make risk less profit.

Strategy for using arbitrage opportunity

There are mainly two cases in such a situation.

If a particular option is overpriced what you have to do is sell that particular option and make a risk less profit. If a particular option is underpriced what you have to do is buy that particular option and make a risk less profit.

After doing all these things I was asked to prepare a scenario as how much profit \loss is going to be there if you are going to hedge 100% of entire amount, 80% of the entire amount by taking different situations on expiry of the contract.

This model is developed using six different cases.

Case 1 = 100% hedging
Case 2 = 80 % hedging
Case 3 = 60 % hedging
Case 4 = 40 % hedging
Case 5 = 20 % hedging
Case 6 = no hedging

Basically I have developed an overall scenario as what is going to happen in a particular case under a particular situation on the expiry of the contract.

Analysis of pricing index options

Volatility in the Indian market is different from the other international markets. In international stable market volatility is less as compared Indian unstable market. In my calculation of NIFTY INDEX and S&P 500 INDEX values of volatility is different from each other.

Index Name	Calculated Volatility (in percentage)
NIFTY 50	28
S&P 500	9.82
NYSE composite	12.87

These values are calculated from one year closing index data of respective indexes. We can see from the table value of variance in NIFTY 50 is 28% which is very high which shows that Indian market is a very unstable market.

Formula used for variance:

$U_i = \text{Ln}\,(S_i/S_{i-1})$

N+1: number of observations

S_i: stock price at the end of ith interval, with i = 0, 1,......n.

$S = (1/n\text{-}1\ \Sigma\ (u_i - u_{ave})^2)^{1/2}$

From this formula I have calculated variance in different indexes.

As we can see from the table volatility is lowest in case of S&P 500 index. It means it is more stable as compared to NYSE and NIFTY 50.

After the calculation of variance in different indexes I have calculated the price of option index using Black Scholes Model. Formula used for this model is:

$$OP = SN(d_1) - Xe^{-rt}N(d_2)$$

Where:

$$d_1 = \frac{In\left(\frac{S}{X}\right) + \left(r + \frac{v^2}{2}\right)t}{v\sqrt{t}}$$

$$d_2 = d_1 - v\sqrt{t}$$

The variables are:

S	=	stock price
X	=	strike price
t	=	time remaining until expiration, expressed as a percent of a year
r	=	current continuously compounded risk-free interest rate
v	=	annual volatility of stock price (the standard deviation of the short-term returns over one year).
ln	=	natural logarithm
N(x)	=	standard normal cumulative distribution function
e	=	the exponential function

Inputs to the model are:

Historical data for exchange rate, in order to calculate volatility (v) of the exchange rate

Current exchange rate (S)

Strike price of the option (X)

Risk free interest rate (annual) on domestic currency(r)

Time to expiry in number of years (t)

After that from the one year trading on Nifty index, the price of the option index has been calculated. Data for original trading premium of option has been collected and then difference between them has been calculated.

The average of the difference between actual option price and calculated option price for one year has been calculated for NIFTY 50 and S&P 500 and here is the table we can see the values.

Name of the index	Average of difference between actual and calculated option price for one year
NIFTY 50	14
S&P 500	3.64

We will prove that Indian market is a semi-strong market and other markets are strong markets. It means other international markets are stable markets. This can be proved by these calculations.

We have already seen that volatility in case of Nifty is 28% which is very high as compared to S&P 500 and NYSE composite. Due to this volatility, difference between actual option price of index and calculated option price of same index for one year is increased because in calculation Black Scholes model used this volatility for price of the option. So calculated price of options values are close to actual values in case of S&P 500 as compared to NIFTY 50.This is due to difference in volatility of these indexes. I have calculated difference between actual price and calculated price of the option of both the indexes for one year and then calculated the average for both of indexes which comes out to be 14 in case of Nifty and 3.64 in case of S&P 500 index which proves Indian market is a semi-strong market and there lie arbitrage opportunities for the Indian market.

Monthly average of difference between actual and calculated option price for one year for NIFTY 50.

Months	Average of difference monthly
March	26.63
April	12.92
May	20.80
June	17.61
July	6.61
August	9.60
September	17.40
October	7.86
November	12.28
December	14.60
January	16.90
February	14.50
March	14.00

Graph of NIFTY

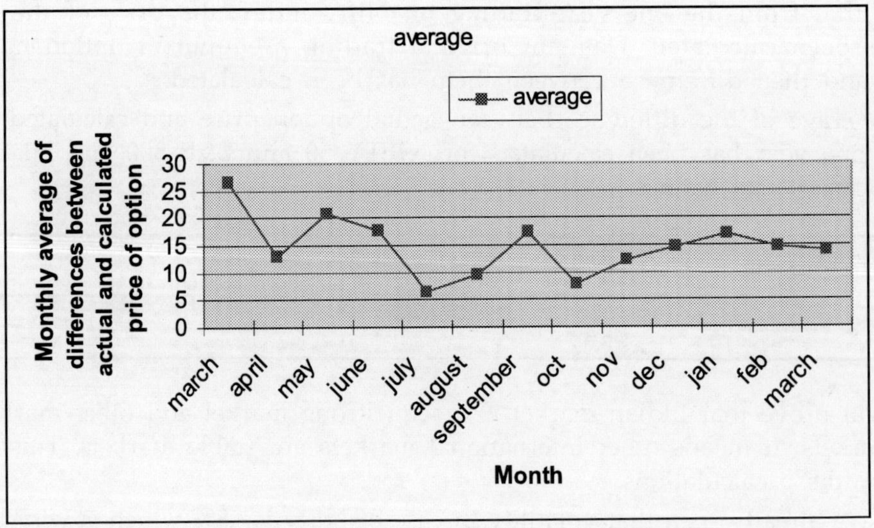

This graph is drawn from the data above in the table of monthly average.

Table of monthly average of S&P 500 index

Month	Monthly average of difference
January	4.965000
February	3.393333
March	3.819909
April	4.037689
May	4.621429
June	2.531619
July	3.580632
August	3.232636
September	5.603158
October	2.698095
November	2.808571
December	2.680967

Graph of monthly average difference

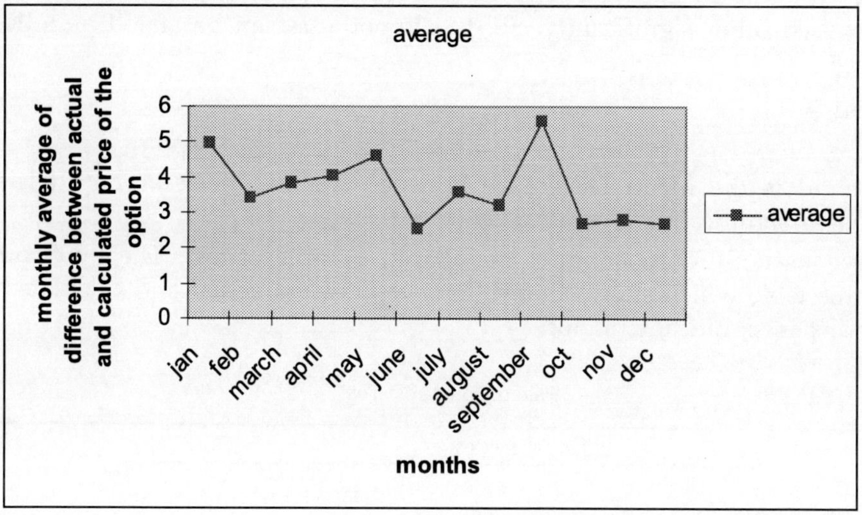

From these two graphs we can clearly conclude that the average difference between actual and calculated option price are more in case of NIFTY 50 as compared to S&P 500 index. This again proves that India is a semi-strong market and arbitrage opportunities are there—more than other international markets.

We can see from the data that whenever the difference between current price and strike price increases then pricing of the option always increases.

Now to check whether the difference between actual price of the option and calculated price of the option is significant or not, we are going to use SPSS analysis through Paired Samples t-Test and Wilcoxon Signed Ranks test.

The Paired Samples t-test

The Paired Samples t-test is a hypothesis test of the difference between two populations means based on the means of two paired samples. Under this test, the two samples are compared in such a way, that the elements in one sample are matched or paired with the elements or paired with the other sample, thereby helping in doing a precise analysis in finding out whether any significant difference exists in the two series.

In our analysis, under paired samples t-test, the two samples are:

a. Actual price of the option (option premium)
b. calculated option price

Thus, the Paired Sample t-test has been used to compare the means of the abovementioned two variables. As such, it helps in finding out if there is a statistically significant difference between the Actual option price at which trading took place and the theoretical Arbitrage Free option price, which has been computed by fitting the Black Scholes Model.

For the Paired Samples t-test, we state the null hypothesis that there is no significant Mean Difference between the two series and hence the two series do not statistically differ from each other. The alternate hypothesis is that the two series differ from each other significantly. So, the hypothesis can be stated as follows:

H0 : md = 0

H1 : md ≠ 0

Where, md is the Mean Difference between the two series. The alternative is two-tailed at a significance level of 5 % (α = 0.05).

We have used SPSS to conduct the Paired Samples t-test. The SPSS output is shown in this table which shows that difference between actual and calculated option price of index is significant or not.

Paired Samples t-Test

	Paired Differences							
				95% Confidence Interval of the Difference				
			Std. Error					
	Mean	Std. Deviation	Mean	Lower	Upper	t	df	Sig. (2-tailed)
Pair 1 Actual Option Price calculated Option Price	-8.1476	15.6448	1.0184	-10.1540	-6.1413	-8.001	235	.000

Every unique value of the t statistic and its associated degrees of freedom has a significance value. In our case, the hypothesis is that the two series of Actual option price and calculated option price do not differ significantly and are not statistically significant. This has been checked out at 95% confidence level.

From the output of SPSS we can conclude that the value is less than 5%, therefore, our null hypothesis is rejected and an alternate is selected. It means the difference between actual option price and calculated option price of NIFTY 50 is significantly different.

Hence, arbitrage opportunities are there in the Indian market.

Wilcox on Signed Ranks Test

The Wilcox on Matched-Pairs Ranks test is a non-parametric test that is often regarded as being similar to a matched pair t-test. The Wilcox on Matched-Pairs Ranks test is used to determine differences between groups of paired data when the data do not meet the rigor associated with a parametric test.

Wilcox on Signed Ranks test helps in the following purposes:

a. The Wilcox on test is used to determine the magnitude of difference between matched groups.
b. The Wilcox on test is used to determine more than only the direction of difference.

The name Wilcox on Signed Ranks test comes from the fact that it is based on the direction (ranks) of a pair of observations. It helps in finding out whether there is a significant difference between the two series. This test follows the following procedure:

a. The null hypothesis is stated as the median difference, M, between the two series is equal to zero.
b. Paired differences, di = xi - yi, are calculated, where xi, yi are the pairs of observations.
c. The dis are then ranked, ignoring the signs, in increasing order i.e. rank 1 is assigned to the smallest |di|, rank 2 to the next etc.
d. Each rank is then labeled with its sign, according to the sign of di.
e. The sum of the ranks of the positive dis, W+ and the sum of the ranks of the negative dis, W-, are calculated.

Under the null hypothesis, the distribution of the differences is hypothesized to be approximately symmetric around zero. Therefore the sum of the positive ranks is expected to be approximately equal to the sum of the negative ranks. Since the sum of all the ranks is equal to $\frac{n(n+1)}{2}$. Therefore, under the null hypothesis, both W+ and W- follow a binomial distribution with p = 1/2 and n = $\frac{n(n+1)}{2}$. We therefore proceed as follows:

Choose W = max (W-,W+).

Tables of the binomial distribution are used to find the p-value or probability of observing a value of W or higher assuming p = 1/2 and n = $\frac{n(n+1)}{2}$.

Thus, in our case, this test begins with finding out the paired differences in two series, namely, Actual option price and calculated option price of option indexes. The absolute differences are then ranked, starting from lowest to highest. Once the ranks are assigned, then original signs (of paired differences) are restored. After the sum of the positive and negative ranks is computed and a hypothesis testing is done to find out whether the distribution of differences is symmetric around the zero or not. Accordingly, the hypothesis can be stated as below:

H0: Md = 0

H1: Md ≠ 0

Where, Md is the Median Difference between the two series. The alternative is two-tailed at a significance level of 5 % (a = 0.05).

Again, we have used SPSS to conduct the Wilcox on Signed Ranks Sum Test. The SPSS output is:

Ranks

		N	Mean Rank	Sum of Ranks
Calculated Option Price -Actual Option Price	Negative Ranks	75[a]	83.96	6297.00
	Positive Ranks	161[b]	134.59	21669.00
	Ties	0[c]		
	Total	236		

a. Calculated Option Price < Actual Option Price

b. Calculated Option Price > Actual Option Price

c. Actual Option Price = Calculated Option Price

Test Statistics[b]

	Calculated Option Price -Actual Option Price
Z	-7.321[a]
Asymp. Sig. (2-tailed)	.000

a. Based on negative ranks.

b. Wilcoxon Signed Ranks Test

In our case, the hypothesis is that the Median Difference for the two series of Actual option price and calculated option price of index do not differ significantly and are not statistically significant.

Now, the significance level against which the hypothesis is tested is 5 %. The corresponding criterion z statistic with a = 0.05 is ± 1.96. In other words, for 95 % Confidence Interval, the z value should be (-1.96 < z < + 1.96).

The significance level tells us that the probability that there is no difference between the two series is very small. From the output of SPSS we can conclude the value is less than 5%. Therefore our null hypothesis is rejected and alternate is selected. It means the difference between actual option price and calculated option price of NIFTY 50 is significantly different.

Hence, arbitrage opportunities are there in the Indian market.

RECOMMENDATIONS

- Before taking a particular view in the market, one should consider all the factors affecting the value of derivatives.
- One should not hedge entire amount of the liability at a particular moment. Hedging should be done in proportions.
- Derivative trading on basic necessities should not be allowed.

17

Case Study: Value at Risk

THE FORMULA

Measurement and management of something called RISK has today become the buzzword in the industry, especially in the Financial Services industry comprising Banks, Financial Institutions, Mutual Funds and the like. All financing and investment decisions in a business depend upon the riskiness of the money involved therein. As a result it becomes crucial to measure risk and decide upon the parameters to identify the same. An attempt has been made to identify the three types of risks involved in the Banking Industry, viz, Credit Risk, Liquidity Risk and Operational Risk. The Basel-I and Basel-II Regulations provide a good framework in helping banks in measuring and managing risk. One important tool to measure risk is Value At Risk Model, popularly known as VaR. Through this model, businesses galore have been able to better manage the risk involved in the businesses. The Derivatives market plays a very important role here in reducing VaR and thereby reducing risk as a whole. Hedging has now become a very popular method to manage risk. Investing money in Futures, Forwards, Options etc. enables diversification of the investment portfolio of any business, and hence reduce, if not eliminate, the uncertainties involved. There are a number of methods to calculate VaR, all of which provide a reasonable estimator of risk.

VALUE AT RISK (VaR)

While using VaR, an interesting statement is always heard in the following form:

"We are X% certain that we will not lose more than V rupees in the next N days"

The variable V is the VaR of the portfolio. It is a function of two parameters: N, the time horizon, and X, the confidence level. It is the loss over N days that the manager is X% certain will not be exceeded.

VaR is an attempt to provide a single number for senior management summarizing the total risk in a portfolio of financial assets. It has become widely used by corporate treasurers and fund managers as well as by financial institutions. Central bank regulators also use VaR in determining the capital a bank required to keep to reflect the market risks it is bearing.

VaR can be measured and described in two main approaches:

Historical Simulation Approach

It is one popular way of estimating VaR. It involves using past data in a very direct way as a guide to what might happen in future. First we need to identify the market variable(s) affecting the portfolio, and then we need to tabulate data for that variable over a certain suitable time horizon. All this is required so as to track volatilities for the concerned market variable(s).

Model Building Approach

The main alternative to historical simulation is the model-building approach (sometimes also called the variance-covariance approach). In this approach, we develop a model, either a Linear Model or a Quadratic Model, to estimate volatilities.

In our case, we have used the Historical Simulation approach to first estimate VaR and then to devise strategies to reduce VaR. The market variable used by us is the daily stock prices for the Equity Portfolio. A one-month time horizon has been taken into consideration to estimate the volatility of the entire portfolio.

CASE

To explain how VaR model can be used to calculate risk involved and to find ways to reduce VaR, we shall take up UTI Growth and Value Mutual Fund. We shall calculate VaR for the Portfolio Value as on 31st August 2006 and then suggest hedging strategies to reduce VaR of the portfolio.

It may strictly be noted that all calculations and analyses have been done, assuming the current date to be 31st August 2006.

We have adopted the following step-by-step approach in reaching to our conclusion:

Step 1: Portfolio Value(s) (Table 17.1)

Track daily stock prices for each of the Stocks in which the fund has invested money.

UTI-Growth & Value Fund (G) - Table 17.1(a) — Detailed Portfolio As on 31-Aug-2006

Type	Investment In	Industry	%	No. of shares	Value (Rs cr)
Equity	Grasim Inds.	Diversify-mega	6.79	49653	11.18
Others	Net CA & Others	-	6.09	-	10.03
Equity	Infosys Tech.	Computer-sw-larg	5.95	54274	9.8
Equity	Thermax	Engineering	5.55	310464	9.13
Equity	Bharti Airtel	Telecomm-service	5.49	219888	9.04
Equity	HCL Technologies	Computer-sw-larg	5.06	143350	8.34
Equity	St Bk of India	Banks-pub Sector	4.95	87462	8.14
Equity	Lupin	Pharm-ind-b Drug	4.92	161228	8.11
Equity	Tata Chemicals	Fertilizers	4.83	353845	7.95
Equity	O N G C	Oil Drill/allied	4.81	65000	7.91
Equity	Tata Tea	Tea	4.71	97000	7.75
Equity	Reliance Energy	Power Generation	4.37	164113	7.2
Equity	Guj. Mineral Dev	Mining/miner/met	4.18	200204	6.88
Equity	Gammon India	Construction	3.89	187469	6.41
Equity	Bharat EarthMove	Engineering	3.19	55034	5.25
Equity	ITC	Cigarettes	3.14	270000	5.17
Equity	Rallis India	Pest/agro-indian	3.06	177295	5.04
Equity	Zee Telefilms	Ent Etron Med Sw	2.87	170920	4.72
Equity	TV 18 India	Ent Etron Med Sw	2.8	77038	4.62
Equity	M & M	Auto-tractors	2.7	68714	4.44
Equity	Nicholas Piramal	Pharm-ind-bd&for	2.59	192241	4.27
Equity	Kohinoor Foods	Food-proc-indian	2.27	480751	3.73
Equity	Subros	Auto Ancillaries	1.54	120311	2.54
Equity	KSB Pumps	Pumps	1.51	48200	2.49
Equity	Patel Engg.	Construction	1.15	57509	1.9
Equity	Maruti Udyog	Auto-passeng.car	1.05	20000	1.72
Fixed Deposits	Allahabad Bank	Banks-pub Sector	0.55	-	0.9
Fixed Deposits	I L F S	Finance & Invest	0.01	-	0.01
Equity	Deldot Systems	-	N.A.	300000	-
Total			**100**		**164.7**

Table 17.1(b)

Date	NAV	Si/Si-1	ui=ln(Si/Si-1)	ui^2
3-Aug-06	46.42	1.00	0.0017	0.0000030
4-Aug-06	46.25	1.00	-0.0037	0.0000135
7-Aug-06	46.24	1.00	-0.0002	0.0000000
8-Aug-06	46.73	1.01	0.0105	0.0001111
9-Aug-06	47.56	1.02	0.0176	0.0003100
10-Aug-06	47.94	1.01	0.0080	0.0000633
11-Aug-06	48.35	1.01	0.0085	0.0000725
14-Aug-06	49.2	1.02	0.0174	0.0003037
16-Aug-06	49.75	1.01	0.0111	0.0001236
17-Aug-06	49.64	1.00	-0.0022	0.0000049
18-Aug-06	49.55	1.00	-0.0018	0.0000033
21-Aug-06	49.66	1.00	0.0022	0.0000049
22-Aug-06	49.65	1.00	-0.0002	0.0000000
23-Aug-06	48.99	0.99	-0.0134	0.0001791
24-Aug-06	49.17	1.00	0.0037	0.0000135
25-Aug-06	49.63	1.01	0.0093	0.0000867
28-Aug-06	49.72	1.00	0.0018	0.0000033
29-Aug-06	49.78	1.00	0.0012	0.0000015
30-Aug-06	49.62	1.00	-0.0032	0.0000104
31-Aug-06	49.27	0.99	-0.0071	0.0000501
	TOTALS		**0.0613099**	**0.0013583**
			0.0000099	0.0000715

Estimate of Standard Deviation of Daily NAVs = 0.007848464

Daily Volatility = 0.78%

1.207 crores

1-day 99% VaR = 2.81 crores

10-day 99% VaR = 8.89 crores

There are 29 items in the portfolio, of which 26 are equity investments, 2 are Fixed Deposits and 1 constitutes Other Items. For each of the 26 stocks, track daily market prices (closing) for each trading day of August 2006. (Note that we are tracking figures only for the month of August 2006 to calculate volatility.) Through this way, we calculate Portfolio values for all the trading days of August 2006.

Note that the number of shares in each category has been assumed to be the same for all the days of the month.

Step 2: Volatility (Table 17.2)

Now, to calculate daily volatility of the Total Portfolio Value, we first calculate Si/ Si-1 and then a take a natural logarithm of the same, naming it Ui. Then squares of Ui's are being calculated. Then using the following formula, we calculate the Daily Volatilty of UTI Fund as 0.89% or Rs. 1.471 crores:

$$\text{Daily Volatility} = \sqrt{\frac{\sum Ui^2}{(n-1)} - \frac{\sum (Ui)^2}{n(n-1)}}$$

Step 3: Estimating VaR (Table 17.2)

We calculate VaR as per following formula:

1-day VaR = (Daily Volatility) × (Portfolio Value) × (z-value for C.I.)
10-day VaR = (1-day VaR) × v10

Interpretation

1. 1-day 99% VaR of Rs. 3.43 crores shows that the there is 99% probability that not more than Rs. 3.43 crores out of total portfolio value of Rs. 164.68 crores would be lost over next one day, that is not more than Rs. 3.43 crores is risky.
2. 10-day 99% VaR of Rs. 10.84 crores shows that the there is 99% probability that not more than Rs. 10.84 crores out of total portfolio value of Rs. 164.68 crores would be lost over next ten days, that is not more than Rs. 10.84 crores is risky.

Now, the point in concern is to devise strategies to reduce the value of VaR. This can be achieved through selling some of the equity holdings and investing the proceeds in derivatives instruments like forward contracts, futures, option contracts etc. and hedge the position. In the next segment, we have tried to suggest a number of such hedging strategies.

UTI-Growth & Value Fund (G) - TABLE 17.2

Market Price	No. of shares	1-Aug-06	2-Aug-06	3-Aug-06	4-Aug-06	7-Aug-06	8-Aug-06	9-Aug-06	10-Aug-06
Grasim Industries	49653	2078.9	2080.25	2116.5	2141.25	2117.6	2133.3	2143.55	2152.85
Others (NA)	1	100300000	100300000	100300000	100300000	100300000	100300000	100300000	100300000
Infosys Techn.	54274	1658	1666.65	1672.95	1680.65	1673.6	1684.25	1702.05	1708.6
Thermax	310464	264.8	267.7	270.55	269.8	271.25	274.85	285.5	292.7
Bharti Airtel	219888	391.2	393.05	399.15	400.7	392.3	404.65	404	409.05
HCL Techn	143350	516.1	535.85	542.9	548.8	545.2	550.75	562.65	585.1
SBI	87462	811.75	826.35	830.6	807.8	810.55	831.7	865.05	862.85
Lupin	161228	444.925	449.15	445.575	448.125	462.025	467.55	460.75	466.125
Tata Chemicals	353845	201.05	204.9	202.95	201.25	202.95	204.35	209.95	215.05
ONGC	65000	1183.45	1192.15	1186.25	1181.05	1161.75	1190.45	1203	1192
Tata Tea	97000	827.1	847.95	835.75	815.2	833.6	830.65	847.95	873.35
Reliance Energy	164113	448.7	458.3	455.15	464.45	461.5	463.2	468.25	470.75
Gujarat Minerals	200204	288.5	289.9	290.4	285.2	285.5	285	291.3	281.9
Gammon India	187469	313.1	320.35	322.05	312.9	310.2	311.3	358.3	353.2
Bharat Earthmovers	55034	913.7	922.35	929.45	922.5	910.2	922.1	920.35	912
ITC	270000	169.25	173.4	171.95	168.2	168.4	172.25	178.8	176.3
Rallis India	177295	253.25	258.1	256.25	252.25	252	251.35	252.85	257.25
Zee Telefilms	170920	257.85	259.55	260.45	260.65	264.1	261.6	264.1	264.45
TV 18 India	77038	607.25	647.85	630.75	610.95	610.6	618.85	594.9	595.6
M&M	68714	584.6	597.75	593.05	585.75	590.2	601.25	614.65	614.25
Nicholas Piramal	192241	208.25	209.9	208.8	217.5	219.5	219.7	221.55	220.9
Kohinoor Foods	480751	0	0	0	0	0	0	0	0
Subros	120311	191.75	190.8	196.5	192.45	192.95	194.5	196.25	207.2
KSB Pumps	48200	469.6	473.55	470.6	476.75	484.35	484.15	500	503.55
Patel Engineering	57509	267.05	275.25	287.9	283.7	279.15	287.05	290.05	310.55
Maruti Udyog	20000	783.55	780.65	790.55	783.65	768.2	785.3	797.05	793.5
Allahabad Bank (FD)	1	9000000	9000000	9000000	9000000	9000000	9000000	9000000	9000000
ILFS (FD)	1	100000	100000	100000	100000	100000	100000	100000	100000
Value of Portfolio		1494614533.55	1515997830.25	1518259077.90	1512118785.35	1511773639.15	1526518861.45	1553239077.05	1564623514.35
Si/Si-1			1.014306897	1.00149159	0.995955702	0.999771747	1.009753591	1.017504019	1.007329482
ui=ln(Si/Si-1)			0.014205519	0.001490479	-0.004052499	-0.000228279	0.009706332	0.017352588	0.007302752
ui^2			0.000201797	0.0000022215	0.0000164227	0.000000052	0.000094213	0.000301112	0.000053330

UTI-Growth & Value Fund (G) - TABLE 17.2

Market Price	No. of shares	11-Aug-06	14-Aug-06	16-Aug-06	17-Aug-06	18-Aug-06	21-Aug-06	22-Aug-06	23-Aug-06
Grasim Industries	49653	2191.2	2197.35	2209.4	2209.8	2206.25	2239.85	2224.55	2195.45
Others (NA)	1	100300000	100300000	100300000	100300000	100300000	100300000	100300000	100300000
Infosys Techn.	54274	1742.2	1755.5	1752.3	1757.6	1762	1798.1	1781.15	1767.9
Thermax	310464	293.45	309.45	322.4	310.1	310.3	305.25	309.4	296.5
Bharti Airtel	219888	405.05	413	413.7	414.6	409.65	409.9	409.4	406
HCL Techn	143350	585.1	590	581.7	590.1	574.7	584.1	579.95	566.15
SBI	87462	859.5	871.45	888.5	881.65	879.1	883.35	878.45	863.15
Lupin	161228	475.3	490.15	505.35	531.3	538.7	529.55	524.35	513.25
Tata Chemicals	353845	215.1	215.15	215.75	212.1	212.25	213	215.95	216.25
ONGC	65000	1193.65	1215.3	1241.9	1211.1	1210.25	1190.7	1205.7	1198.45
Tata Tea	97000	868.1	869.25	856.35	841.25	844.8	845.75	846	828.15
Reliance Energy	164113	473.15	480.35	479.25	462.7	455.9	449	461.35	458.55
Gujarat Minerals	200204	295	327.35	324.85	342.75	343.15	340.2	333.15	321.15
Gammon India	187469	347.85	373.15	361.85	358.65	353.15	351.7	357.75	358.45
Bharat Earthmovers	55034	951.65	946.25	955.35	941.65	943.8	945.25	947.75	963.65
ITC	270000	175.25	178.55	180.9	181.1	179.75	180.75	181.9	178.8
Rallis India	177295	277.1	277.45	311.15	309.25	297.4	301.2	296.55	287.65
Zee Telefilms	170920	269.95	272.4	274.1	273.15	271.8	271.9	271.25	273.1
TV 18 India	77038	600.9	607.1	608.15	622.45	629.25	660.1	656.1	661.45
M&M	68714	612.95	620.2	634.6	644.8	644.85	663.9	659.75	632.8
Nicholas Piramal	192241	226.5	225.9	221.95	217.55	227	224.95	221.15	215.4
Kohinoor Foods	480751	0	0	0	0	82.5	81.6	81.9	79.75
Subros	120311	201.2	203.3	210.5	205.95	216.55	213.45	217.85	220.45
KSB Pumps	48200	504.65	510.5	548.05	537.75	551.9	556.4	546.55	538.25
Patel Engineering	57509	323.75	338.55	337.8	320.95	313.05	328.7	334.2	333
Maruti Udyog	20000	796.1	802.25	814.95	819.75	840.65	841.3	836.65	826
Allahabad Bank (FD)	1	9000000	9000000	9000000	9000000	9000000	9000000	9000000	9000000
ILFS (FD)	1	100000	100000	100000	100000	100000	100000	100000	100000
Value of Portfolio		1578415914.65	1607681998.50	1623522483.35	1618348090.85	1655771024.95	1659878143.55	1659918633.15	1637897049.05
Si/Si-1		1.007329482	1.018541427	1.009852996	0.996812861	1.023124156	1.002480487	1.000024393	0.986733335
ui=ln(Si/Si-1)		0.007302752	0.018371631	0.009804772	-0.003192229	0.022860844	0.002477416	2.43928E-05	-0.013355453
ui^2		0.000053330	0.000337517	0.0000961336	0.0000101903	0.000522618	0.0000061376	0.0000000006	0.000178368

UTI-Growth & Value Fund (G) - TABLE 17.2.

Market Price	No. of shares	24-Aug-06	25-Aug-06	28-Aug-06	29-Aug-06	30-Aug-06	31-Aug-06	Totals
Grasim Industries	49653	2200.2	2204.1	2229.25	2225.8	2264.75	2251.6	**48013.75**
Others (NA)	1	100300000	100300000	100300000	100300000	100300000	100300000	**2206600000**
Infosys Techn.	54274	1766.9	1766.7	1772.75	1805.8	1801.2	1806.4	**38283.25**
Thermax	310464	300.15	298.95	298.05	302.1	297.7	294.15	**6445.1**
Bharti Airtel	219888	415.3	417.55	416.7	415.25	413.8	411.05	**8965.05**
HCL Techn	143350	572.15	574.65	576.3	580.6	578.85	581.6	**12503.3**
SBI	87462	874.65	905.1	918.9	922.05	930.75	931.25	**19134.5**
Lupin	161228	502	525.25	514.2	513.25	507.9	502.8	**10817.575**
Tata Chemicals	353845	218.05	222.35	222.55	222.1	225.25	224.75	**4693.05**
ONGC	65000	1189.1	1193.45	1197.15	1221.6	1221.45	1217.6	**26397.5**
Tata Tea	97000	832.2	829.4	837.3	829.2	821.45	799.2	**18459.95**
Reliance Energy	164113	456.05	446.55	449.8	448.7	439.5	438.45	**10089.6**
Gujarat Minerals	200204	325.75	345.3	346.85	345.15	344.85	343.1	**6976.3**
Gammon India	187469	352.3	352.25	350.5	344.8	335.35	341.8	**7540.95**
Bharat Earthmovers	55034	984.2	995.45	1003.5	986.7	974.65	957	**20849.5**
ITC	270000	180.05	180.15	180.1	184.65	187.35	191.5	**3919.35**
Rallis India	177295	285.5	286.25	287.75	283.1	278.05	284.3	**6096**
Zee Telefilms	170920	279.2	291.4	287.65	287.75	289.6	276.1	**5982.1**
TV 18 India	77038	665.1	657.95	656.5	653.15	645.45	599.4	**13839.8**
M&M	68714	640.95	651.85	651.9	656.85	657.35	646.25	**13800.5**
Nicholas Piramal	192241	215.9	216.85	219.65	222.15	226.15	222.05	**4829.25**
Kohinoor Foods	480751	81.05	80.3	78.95	79.75	77.75	77.65	**801.2**
Subros	120311	215.4	217.35	219.35	215.6	213.45	211.05	**4543.85**
KSB Pumps	48200	531.1	526.9	520.2	517	522.85	516.7	**11291.35**
Patel Engineering	57509	328.9	342	336.65	329.35	329.85	329.55	**6907**
Maruti Udyog	20000	830.65	833.4	831.35	855.2	862.3	861.35	**17934.35**
Allahabad Bank (FD)	1	9000000	9000000	9000000	9000000	9000000	9000000	**198000000**
ILFS (FD)	1	100000	100000	100000	100000	100000	100000	**2200000**
Value of Portfolio		1643685812.95	1658364253.40	1660134693.65	1662384944.55	1657972890.10	**1646793902.40**	**35167915154.15**
Si/Si-1		1.003534266	1.008930198	1.001067582	1.001355463	0.997345949	0.993257436	**21.09798873**
ui=ln(Si/Si-1)		0.003528035	0.00889056	0.001067013	0.001354545	-0.002657579	-0.006765397	**0.096961972**
ui^2		0.000012447	0.000079042	0.000001139	0.000001835	0.000007063	0.000045771	**0.002044437**

Estimate of Standard Deviation of Daily NAVs =	**0.008935**	**0.000022385**
Daily Volatility =	**0.89%**	**0.000102222**
	1.471 crores	0.000079837
1-day 99% VaR =	**3.43 crores**	
10-day 99% VaR =	**10.84 crores**	

Step 4: Hedging Strategy

We have the following hedging opportunities available to minimise our risk:

1. Buy Put Options
2. Go Short on Futures

Note that the above contract can be entered into with respect to stocks as well as indices. Also, before deciding upon a particular hedging strategy, we need to first analyse the market trend and market expectation for the relevant stock or index.

Based on our study of the market, we propose the UTI MF Fund Managers to go for following investments:

1. Buy 55,000 2-month European Put Options Nifty Index @Rs. 57.80 with a Strike Price of Rs. 3,250. *(See TABLE 17.3)*
2. Short 2-month 55,000 Nifty Futures @Rs. 3,091.10. *(See TABLE 17.4)*
3. Buy 55,000 2-month European Put Options Nifty Index @Rs. 57.80 with a Strike Price of Rs. 3,250, and, Short 2-month 55,000 Nifty Futures @Rs. 3,091.10. *(See TABLE 5)*

Now, we have invested Rs. 31,79,000 in the Derivatives Market in Futures and Options. The required amount shall come from the available securities in the Portfolio. Now, to reduce VaR, we shall off-load those securities which have the highest volatilities. On examination, we see Patel Engineering has the highest volatility. Hence, the investment amount of Rs. 31,79,000 shall be funded by selling 9,646 shares @ Rs. 329.55 per share.

Step 5: Results of Hedging Strategy

Our main purpose to divert funds from the securities market to the derivatives market was to reduce the riskiness of the Portfolio by reducing VaR.

Through our strategy, we have been able to successfully reduce 10-day 99% VaR as well as 1-day VaR. The entire calculations have been done by repeating steps 1 to 3. (Tables 17.3, 17.4 and 17.5).

UTI-Growth & Value Fund (G) - TABLE 17.3.

Market Price	No. of shares	1-Aug-06	2-Aug-06	3-Aug-06	4-Aug-06	7-Aug-06	8-Aug-06	9-Aug-06	10-Aug-06
Grasim Industries	49653	2078.9	2080.25	2116.5	2141.25	2117.6	2133.3	2143.55	2152.85
Others (NA)	1	100300000	100300000	100300000	100300000	100300000	100300000	100300000	100300000
Infosys Techn.	54274	1658	1666.65	1672.95	1680.65	1673.6	1684.25	1702.05	1708.6
Thermax	310464	264.8	267.7	270.55	269.8	271.25	274.85	285.5	292.7
Bharti Airtel	219888	391.2	393.05	399.15	400.7	392.3	404.65	404	409.05
HCL Techn	143350	516.1	535.85	542.9	548.8	545.2	550.75	562.65	585.1
SBI	87462	811.75	826.35	830.6	807.8	810.55	831.7	865.05	862.85
Lupin	161228	444.925	449.15	445.575	448.125	462.025	467.55	460.75	466.125
Tata Chemicals	353845	201.05	204.9	202.95	201.25	202.95	204.35	209.95	215.05
ONGC	65000	1183.45	1192.15	1186.25	1181.05	1161.75	1190.45	1203	1192
Tata Tea	97000	827.1	847.95	835.75	815.2	833.6	830.65	847.95	873.35
Reliance Energy	164113	448.7	458.3	455.15	464.45	461.5	463.2	468.25	470.75
Gujarat Minerals	200204	288.5	289.9	290.4	285.2	285.5	285	291.3	281.9
Gammon India	187469	313.1	320.35	322.05	312.9	310.2	311.3	358.3	353.2
Bharat Earthmovers	55034	913.7	922.35	929.45	922.5	910.2	922.1	920.35	912
ITC	270000	169.25	173.4	171.95	168.2	168.4	172.25	178.8	176.3
Rallis India	177295	253.25	258.1	256.25	252.25	252	251.35	252.85	257.25
Zee Telefilms	170920	257.85	259.55	260.45	260.65	264.1	261.6	264.1	264.45
TV 18 India	77038	607.25	647.85	630.75	610.95	610.6	618.85	594.9	595.6
M&M	68714	584.6	597.75	593.05	585.75	590.2	601.25	614.65	614.25
Nicholas Piramal	192241	208.25	209.9	208.8	217.5	219.5	219.7	221.55	220.9
Kohinoor Foods	480751	0	0	0	0	0	0	0	0
Put Option (Nifty)	55000	272.85	249.90	237.80	236.20	240.45	210.10	187.00	177.15
Subros	120311	191.75	190.8	196.5	192.45	192.95	194.5	196.25	207.2
KSB Pumps	48200	469.6	473.55	470.6	476.75	484.35	484.15	500	503.55
Patel Engineering	47863	267.05	275.25	287.9	283.7	279.15	287.05	290.05	310.55
Maruti Udyog	20000	783.55	780.65	790.55	783.65	768.2	785.3	797.05	793.5
Allahabad Bank (FD)	1	9000000	9000000	9000000	9000000	9000000	9000000	9000000	9000000
ILFS (FD)	1	100000	100000	100000	100000	100000	100000	100000	100000
Value of Portfolio		1507045189.03	1527087134.53	1528560854.11	1522373076.81	1522305572.13	1535305337.17	1560726113.31	1571371047.62
Si/Si-1			1.013298835	1.000965053	0.995951893	0.999955658	1.008539524	1.016557473	1.006820501
ui=ln(Si/Si-1)			0.013211182	0.000964587	-0.004056322	-4.43427E-05	0.008503269	0.016421892	0.006797347
ui^2			0.000174535	0.0000009304	0.0000164538	0.000000002	0.000072306	0.000269679	0.000046204

UTI-Growth & Value Fund (G) - TABLE 17.3.

Market Price	No. of shares	11-Aug-06	14-Aug-06	16-Aug-06	17-Aug-06	18-Aug-06	21-Aug-06	22-Aug-06	23-Aug-06
Grasim Industries	49653	2191.2	2197.35	2209.4	2209.8	2206.25	2239.85	2224.55	2195.45
Others (NA)	1	100300000	100300000	100300000	100300000	100300000	100300000	100300000	100300000
Infosys Techn.	54274	1742.2	1755.5	1752.3	1757.6	1762	1798.1	1781.15	1767.9
Thermax	310464	293.45	309.45	322.4	310.1	310.3	305.25	309.4	296.5
Bharti Airtel	219888	405.05	413	413.7	414.6	409.65	409.9	409.4	406
HCL Techn	143350	585.1	590	581.7	590.1	574.7	584.1	579.95	566.15
SBI	87462	859.5	871.45	888.5	881.65	879.1	883.35	878.45	863.15
Lupin	161228	475.3	490.15	505.35	531.3	538.7	529.55	524.35	513.25
Tata Chemicals	353845	215.1	215.15	215.75	212.1	212.25	213	215.95	216.25
ONGC	65000	1193.65	1215.3	1241.9	1211.1	1210.25	1190.7	1205.7	1198.45
Tata Tea	97000	868.1	869.25	856.35	841.25	844.8	845.75	846	828.15
Reliance Energy	164113	473.15	480.35	479.25	462.7	455.9	449	461.35	458.55
Gujarat Minerals	200204	295	327.35	324.85	342.75	343.15	340.2	333.15	321.15
Gammon India	187469	347.85	373.15	361.85	358.65	353.15	351.7	357.75	358.45
Bharat Earthmovers	55034	951.65	946.25	955.35	941.65	943.8	945.25	947.75	963.65
ITC	270000	175.25	178.55	180.9	181.1	179.75	180.75	181.9	178.8
Rallis India	177295	277.1	277.45	311.15	309.25	297.4	301.2	296.55	287.65
Zee Telefilms	170920	269.95	272.4	274.1	273.15	271.8	271.9	271.25	273.1
TV 18 India	77038	600.9	607.1	608.15	622.45	629.25	660.1	656.1	661.45
M&M	68714	612.95	620.2	634.6	644.8	644.85	663.9	659.75	632.8
Nicholas Piramal	192241	226.5	225.9	221.95	217.55	227	224.95	221.15	215.4
Kohinoor Foods	480751	0	0	0	0	82.5	81.6	81.9	79.75
Put Option (Nifty)	55000	164.55	142.80	122.55	116.95	109.85	99.10	93.85	121.50
Subros	120311	201.2	203.3	210.5	205.95	216.55	213.45	217.85	220.45
KSB Pumps	48200	504.65	510.5	548.05	537.75	551.9	556.4	546.55	538.25
Patel Engineering	47863	323.75	338.55	337.8	320.95	313.05	328.7	334.2	333
Maruti Udyog	20000	796.1	802.25	814.95	819.75	840.65	841.3	836.65	826
Allahabad Bank (FD)	1	9000000	9000000	9000000	9000000	9000000	9000000	9000000	9000000
ILFS (FD)	1	100000	100000	100000	100000	100000	100000	100000	100000
Value of Portfolio		1584343114.28	1612270180.11	1627004149.83	1621684300.64	1658792942.00	1662157843.06	1661856526.98	1641367268.67
Si/Si-1		1.008255254	1.017626905	1.009138648	0.996730279	1.022882778	1.002028524	0.99981872	0.987670862
ui=ln(Si/Si-1)		0.008221365	0.017473353	0.009097143	-0.003275078	0.022624894	0.002026469	-0.000181296	-0.012405772
ui^2		6.75909E-05	0.000305318	0.0000827580	0.0000107261	0.000511886	0.0000041066	0.0000000329	0.000153903

UTI-Growth & Value Fund (G) - TABLE 17.3.

Market Price	No. of shares	24-Aug-06	25-Aug-06	28-Aug-06	29-Aug-06	30-Aug-06	31-Aug-06	Totals
Grasim Industries	49653	2200.2	2204.1	2229.25	2225.8	2264.75	2251.6	**48013.75**
Others (NA)	1	100300000	100300000	100300000	100300000	100300000	100300000	**2206600000**
Infosys Techn.	54274	1766.9	1766.7	1772.75	1805.8	1801.2	1806.4	**38283.25**
Thermax	310464	300.15	298.95	298.05	302.1	297.7	294.15	**6445.1**
Bharti Airtel	219888	415.3	417.55	416.7	415.25	413.8	411.05	**8965.05**
HCL Techn	143350	572.15	574.65	576.3	580.6	578.85	581.6	**12503.3**
SBI	87462	874.65	905.1	918.9	922.05	930.75	931.25	**19134.5**
Lupin	161228	502	525.25	514.2	513.25	507.9	502.8	**10817.575**
Tata Chemicals	353845	218.05	222.35	222.55	222.1	225.25	224.75	**4693.05**
ONGC	65000	1189.1	1193.45	1197.15	1221.6	1221.45	1217.6	**26397.5**
Tata Tea	97000	832.2	829.4	837.3	829.2	821.45	799.2	**18459.95**
Reliance Energy	164113	456.05	446.55	449.8	448.7	439.5	438.45	**10089.6**
Gujarat Minerals	200204	325.75	345.3	346.85	345.15	344.85	343.1	**6976.3**
Gammon India	187469	352.3	352.25	350.5	344.8	335.35	341.8	**7540.95**
Bharat Earthmovers	55034	984.2	995.45	1003.5	986.7	974.65	957	**20849.5**
ITC	270000	180.05	180.15	180.1	184.65	187.35	191.5	**3919.35**
Rallis India	177295	285.5	286.25	287.75	283.1	278.05	284.3	**6096**
Zee Telefilms	170920	279.2	291.4	287.65	287.75	289.6	276.1	**5982.1**
TV 18 India	77038	665.1	657.95	656.5	653.15	645.45	599.4	**13839.8**
M&M	68714	640.95	651.85	651.9	656.85	657.35	646.25	**13800.5**
Nicholas Piramal	192241	215.9	216.85	219.65	222.15	226.15	222.05	**4829.25**
Kohinoor Foods	480751	81.05	80.3	78.95	79.75	77.75	77.65	**801.2**
Put Option (Nifty)	55000	85.00	75.70	65.30	55.55	50.35	57.80	**3172.3**
Subros	120311	215.4	217.35	219.35	215.6	213.45	211.05	**4543.85**
KSB Pumps	48200	531.1	526.9	520.2	517	522.85	516.7	**11291.35**
Patel Engineering	47863	328.9	342	336.65	329.35	329.85	329.55	**6907**
Maruti Udyog	20000	830.65	833.4	831.35	855.2	862.3	861.35	**17934.35**
Allahabad Bank (FD)	1	9000000	9000000	9000000	9000000	9000000	9000000	**198000000**
ILFS (FD)	1	100000	100000	100000	100000	100000	100000	**2200000**
Value of Portfolio		1645188083.17	1659228654.63	1660478703.59	1662263123.85	1657560246.15	**1646793902.40**	**35275763364.06**
Si/Si-1		1.002327824	1.008534326	1.000753392	1.001074642	0.997170798	0.993504704	**21.08960659**
ui=ln(Si/Si-1)		0.002325119	0.008498115	0.000753108	0.001074065	-0.002833211	-0.006516482	**0.088679403**
ui^2		0.000005406	0.000072218	0.000000567	0.000001154	0.000008027	0.000042465	**0.001846268**

Amount invested in Options	3179000
Number of shares of Patel Eng. To be off-loaded	9646.487635

UTI-Growth & Value Fund (G) - TABLE 17.4.

Market Price	No. of shares	1-Aug-06	2-Aug-06	3-Aug-06	4-Aug-06	7-Aug-06	8-Aug-06	9-Aug-06	10-Aug-06
Grasim Industries	49653	2078.9	2080.25	2116.5	2141.25	2117.6	2133.3	2143.55	2152.85
Others (NA)	1	100300000	100300000	100300000	100300000	100300000	100300000	100300000	100300000
Infosys Techn.	54274	1658	1666.65	1672.95	1680.65	1673.6	1684.25	1702.05	1708.6
Thermax	310464	264.8	267.7	270.55	269.8	271.25	274.85	285.5	292.7
Bharti Airtel	219888	391.2	393.05	399.15	400.7	392.3	404.65	404	409.05
HCL Techn	143350	516.1	535.85	542.9	548.8	545.2	550.75	562.65	585.1
SBI	87462	811.75	826.35	830.6	807.8	810.55	831.7	865.05	862.85
Lupin	161228	444.925	449.15	445.575	448.125	462.025	467.55	460.75	466.125
Tata Chemicals	353845	201.05	204.9	202.95	201.25	202.95	204.35	209.95	215.05
ONGC	65000	1183.45	1192.15	1186.25	1181.05	1161.75	1190.45	1203	1192
Tata Tea	97000	827.1	847.95	835.75	815.2	833.6	830.65	847.95	873.35
Reliance Energy	164113	448.7	458.3	455.15	464.45	461.5	463.2	468.25	470.75
Gujarat Minerals	200204	288.5	289.9	290.4	285.2	285.5	285	291.3	281.9
Gammon India	187469	313.1	320.35	322.05	312.9	310.2	311.3	358.3	353.2
Bharat Earthmovers	55034	913.7	922.35	929.45	922.5	910.2	922.1	920.35	912
ITC	270000	169.25	173.4	171.95	168.2	168.4	172.25	178.8	176.3
Rallis India	177295	253.25	258.1	256.25	252.25	252	251.35	252.85	257.25
Zee Telefilms	170920	257.85	259.55	260.45	260.65	264.1	261.6	264.1	264.45
TV 18 India	77038	607.25	647.85	630.75	610.95	610.6	618.85	594.9	595.6
M&M	68714	584.6	597.75	593.05	585.75	590.2	601.25	614.65	614.25
Nicholas Piramal	192241	208.25	209.9	208.8	217.5	219.5	219.7	221.55	220.9
Kohinoor Foods	480751	0	0	0	0	0	0	0	0
Futures (Nifty)	55000	0.00	-41.32	-49.18	-39.14	1.22	-71.63	-114.02	-119.43
Subros	120311	191.75	190.8	196.5	192.45	192.95	194.5	196.25	207.2
KSB Pumps	48200	469.6	473.55	470.6	476.75	484.35	484.15	500	503.55
Patel Engineering	57509	267.05	275.25	287.9	283.7	279.15	287.05	290.05	310.55
Maruti Udyog	20000	783.55	780.65	790.55	783.65	768.2	785.3	797.05	793.5
Allahabad Bank (FD)	1	9000000	9000000	9000000	9000000	9000000	9000000	9000000	9000000
ILFS (FD)	1	100000	100000	100000	100000	100000	100000	100000	100000
Value of Portfolio		1494614533.55	1513725458.51	1515554016.43	1509965946.05	1511840803.55	1522579246.62	1546967811.81	1558054737.10
Si/Si-1		1.012786524	1.001207985	0.996312853	1.001241655	1.007102893	1.016017928	1.007166875	
ui=ln(Si/Si-1)		0.012705467	0.001207256	-0.003693961	0.001240885	0.007077786	0.015890995	0.007141315	
ui^2		0.000161429	0.0000014575	0.0000136453	0.000001540	0.000050095	0.000252524	0.000050998	

UTI-Growth & Value Fund (G) - TABLE 17.4.

Market Price	No. of shares	11-Aug-06	14-Aug-06	16-Aug-06	17-Aug-06	18-Aug-06	21-Aug-06	22-Aug-06	23-Aug-06
Grasim Industries	49653	2191.2	2197.35	2209.4	2209.8	2206.25	2239.85	2224.55	2195.45
Others (NA)	1	100300000	100300000	100300000	100300000	100300000	100300000	100300000	100300000
Infosys Techn.	54274	1742.2	1755.5	1752.3	1757.6	1762	1798.1	1781.15	1767.9
Thermax	310464	293.45	309.45	322.4	310.1	310.3	305.25	309.4	296.5
Bharti Airtel	219888	405.05	413	413.7	414.6	409.65	409.9	409.4	406
HCL Techn	143350	585.1	590	581.7	590.1	574.7	584.1	579.95	566.15
SBI	87462	859.5	871.45	888.5	881.65	879.1	883.35	878.45	863.15
Lupin	161228	475.3	490.15	505.35	531.3	538.7	529.55	524.35	513.25
Tata Chemicals	353845	215.1	215.15	215.75	212.1	212.25	213	215.95	216.25
ONGC	65000	1193.65	1215.3	1241.9	1211.1	1210.25	1190.7	1205.7	1198.45
Tata Tea	97000	868.1	869.25	856.35	841.25	844.8	845.75	846	828.15
Reliance Energy	164113	473.15	480.35	479.25	462.7	455.9	449	461.35	458.55
Gujarat Minerals	200204	295	327.35	324.85	342.75	343.15	340.2	333.15	321.15
Gammon India	187469	347.85	373.15	361.85	358.65	353.15	351.7	357.75	358.45
Bharat Earthmovers	55034	951.65	946.25	955.35	941.65	943.8	945.25	947.75	963.65
ITC	270000	175.25	178.55	180.9	181.1	179.75	180.75	181.9	178.8
Rallis India	177295	277.1	277.45	311.15	309.25	297.4	301.2	296.55	287.65
Zee Telefilms	170920	269.95	272.4	274.1	273.15	271.8	271.9	271.25	273.1
TV 18 India	77038	600.9	607.1	608.15	622.45	629.25	660.1	656.1	661.45
M&M	68714	612.95	620.2	634.6	644.8	644.85	663.9	659.75	632.8
Nicholas Piramal	192241	226.5	225.9	221.95	217.55	227	224.95	221.15	215.4
Kohinoor Foods	480751	0	0	0	0	82.5	81.6	81.9	79.75
Futures (Nifty)	55000	-129.44	-166.65	-212.48	-211.12	-217.69	-234.35	-237.90	-207.94
Subros	120311	201.2	203.3	210.5	205.95	216.55	213.45	217.85	220.45
KSB Pumps	48200	504.65	510.5	548.05	537.75	551.9	556.4	546.55	538.25
Patel Engineering	57509	323.75	338.55	337.8	320.95	313.05	328.7	334.2	333
Maruti Udyog	20000	796.1	802.25	814.95	819.75	840.65	841.3	836.65	826
Allahabad Bank (FD)	1	9000000	9000000	9000000	9000000	9000000	9000000	9000000	9000000
ILFS (FD)	1	100000	100000	100000	100000	100000	100000	100000	100000
Value of Portfolio		1571296641.66	15985164[illegible]2.01	1611836250.32	1606736738.62	1643798038.80	1646988968.87	1646834334.30	1626460623.53
Si/Si-1		1.008498998	1.017323[illegible]2	1.008332632	0.99683621	1.023066193	1.001941194	0.999906111	0.987628561
ui=ln(Si/Si-1)		0.008463085	0.017174[illegible]85	0.008298107	-0.003168806	0.02280419	0.001939312	-9.38937E-05	-0.012448602
ui^2		7.16238E-05	0.000294973	0.0000688586	0.0000100413	0.000520031	0.0000037609	0.0000000088	0.000154968

UTI-Growth & Value Fund (G) - TABLE 17.4.

Market Price	No. of shares	24-Aug-06	25-Aug-06	28-Aug-06	29-Aug-06	30-Aug-06	31-Aug-06	Totals
Grasim Industries	49653	2200.2	2204.1	2229.25	2225.8	2264.75	2251.6	**48013.75**
Others (NA)	1	100300000	100300000	100300000	100300000	100300000	100300000	**2206600000**
Infosys Techn.	54274	1766.9	1766.7	1772.75	1805.8	1801.2	1806.4	**38283.25**
Thermax	310464	300.15	298.95	298.05	302.1	297.7	294.15	**6445.1**
Bharti Airtel	219888	415.3	417.55	416.7	415.25	413.8	411.05	**8965.05**
HCL Techn	143350	572.15	574.65	576.3	580.6	578.85	581.6	**12503.3**
SBI	87462	874.65	905.1	918.9	922.05	930.75	931.25	**19134.5**
Lupin	161228	502	525.25	514.2	513.25	507.9	502.8	**10817.575**
Tata Chemicals	353845	218.05	222.35	222.55	222.1	225.25	224.75	**4693.05**
ONGC	65000	1189.1	1193.45	1197.15	1221.6	1221.45	1217.6	**26397.5**
Tata Tea	97000	832.2	829.4	837.3	829.2	821.45	799.2	**18459.95**
Reliance Energy	164113	456.05	446.55	449.8	448.7	439.5	438.45	**10089.6**
Gujarat Minerals	200204	325.75	345.3	346.85	345.15	344.85	343.1	**6976.3**
Gammon India	187469	352.3	352.25	350.5	344.8	335.35	341.8	**7540.95**
Bharat Earthmovers	55034	984.2	995.45	1003.5	986.7	974.65	957	**20849.5**
ITC	270000	180.05	180.15	180.1	184.65	187.35	191.5	**3919.35**
Rallis India	177295	285.5	286.25	287.75	283.1	278.05	284.3	**6096**
Zee Telefilms	170920	279.2	291.4	287.65	287.75	289.6	276.1	**5982.1**
TV 18 India	77038	665.1	657.95	656.5	653.15	645.45	599.4	**13839.8**
M&M	68714	640.95	651.85	651.9	656.85	657.35	646.25	**13800.5**
Nicholas Piramal	192241	215.9	216.85	219.65	222.15	226.15	222.05	**4829.25**
Kohinoor Foods	480751	81.05	80.3	78.95	79.75	77.75	77.65	**801.2**
Futures (Nifty)	55000	-253.78	-274.91	-288.65	-315.52	-325.00	-304.97	**-3813.896287**
Subros	120311	215.4	217.35	219.35	215.6	213.45	211.05	**4543.85**
KSB Pumps	48200	531.1	526.9	520.2	517	522.85	516.7	**11291.35**
Patel Engineering	57509	328.9	342	336.65	329.35	329.85	329.55	**6907**
Maruti Udyog	20000	830.65	833.4	831.35	855.2	862.3	861.35	**17934.35**
Allahabad Bank (FD)	1	9000000	9000000	9000000	9000000	9000000	9000000	**198000000**
ILFS (FD)	1	100000	100000	100000	100000	100000	100000	**2200000**
Value of Portfolio		1629727770.05	1643244014.42	1644258718.47	1645031399.57	1640098099.11	**1646793902.40**	**34974924455.76**
Si/Si-1		1.002008746	1.00829356	1.000617501	1.000469927	0.99700109	1.004082563	**21.09784312**
ui=ln(Si/Si-1)		0.002006731	0.008259357	0.00061731	0.000469816	-0.003003415	0.004074252	**0.096961972**
ui^2		0.000004027	0.000068217	0.000000381	0.000000221	0.000009021	0.000016600	**0.00175442**

Estimate of Standard Deviation of Daily NAVs	=	**0.008083**	**0.000022385**
Daily Volatility	=	**0.81%**	**0.000087721**
		1.331 crores	0.000065336
1-day 99% VaR	=	**3.10 crores**	
10-day 99% VaR	=	**9.81 crores**	

UTI-Growth & Value Fund (G) - TABLE 17.5.

Market Price	No. of shares	1-Aug-06	2-Aug-06	3-Aug-06	4-Aug-06	7-Aug-06	8-Aug-06	9-Aug-06	10-Aug-06
Grasim Industries	49653	2078.9	2080.25	2116.5	2141.25	2117.6	2133.3	2143.55	2152.85
Others (NA)	1	100300000	100300000	100300000	100300000	100300000	100300000	100300000	100300000
Infosys Techn.	54274	1658	1666.65	1672.95	1680.65	1673.6	1684.25	1702.05	1708.6
Thermax	310464	264.8	267.7	270.55	269.8	271.25	274.85	285.5	292.7
Bharti Airtel	219888	391.2	393.05	399.15	400.7	392.3	404.65	404	409.05
HCL Techn	143350	516.1	535.85	542.9	548.8	545.2	550.75	562.65	585.1
SBI	87462	811.75	826.35	830.6	807.8	810.55	831.7	865.05	862.85
Lupin	161228	444.925	449.15	445.575	448.125	462.025	467.55	460.75	466.125
Tata Chemicals	353845	201.05	204.9	202.95	201.25	202.95	204.35	209.95	215.05
ONGC	65000	1183.45	1192.15	1186.25	1181.05	1161.75	1190.45	1203	1192
Tata Tea	97000	827.1	847.95	835.75	815.2	833.6	830.65	847.95	873.35
Reliance Energy	164113	448.7	458.3	455.15	464.45	461.5	463.2	468.25	470.75
Gujarat Minerals	200204	288.5	289.9	290.4	285.2	285.5	285	291.3	281.9
Gammon India	187469	313.1	320.35	322.05	312.9	310.2	311.3	358.3	353.2
Bharat Earthmovers	55034	913.7	922.35	929.45	922.5	910.2	922.1	920.35	912
ITC	270000	169.25	173.4	171.95	168.2	168.4	172.25	178.8	176.3
Rallis India	177295	253.25	258.1	256.25	252.25	252	251.35	252.85	257.25
Zee Telefilms	170920	257.85	259.55	260.45	260.65	264.1	261.6	264.1	264.45
TV 18 India	77038	607.25	647.85	630.75	610.95	610.6	618.85	594.9	595.6
M&M	68714	584.6	597.75	593.05	585.75	590.2	601.25	614.65	614.25
Nicholas Piramal	192241	208.25	209.9	208.8	217.5	219.5	219.7	221.55	220.9
Kohinoor Foods	480751	0	0	0	0	0	0	0	0
Futures (Nifty)	55000	0.00	-41.32	-49.18	-39.14	1.22	-71.63	-114.02	-119.43
Put Option (Nifty)	55000	272.85	249.90	237.80	236.20	240.45	210.10	187.00	177.15
Subros	120311	191.75	190.8	196.5	192.45	192.95	194.5	196.25	207.2
KSB Pumps	48200	469.6	473.55	470.6	476.75	484.35	484.15	500	503.55
Patel Engineering	47863	267.05	275.25	287.9	283.7	279.15	287.05	290.05	310.55
Maruti Udyog	20000	783.55	780.65	790.55	783.65	768.2	785.3	797.05	793.5
Allahabad Bank (FD)	1	9000000	9000000	9000000	9000000	9000000	9000000	9000000	9000000
ILFS (FD)	1	100000	100000	100000	100000	100000	100000	100000	100000
Value of Portfolio		1507045189.03	1524814762.79	1525855792.64	1520220237.51	1522372736.53	1531365722.34	1554454848.07	1564802270.37
Si/Si-1			1.011791003	1.000682725	0.996306627	1.001415913	1.005907217	1.015077473	1.006656625
ui=ln(Si/Si-1)			0.01172203	0.000682493	-0.003700211	0.001414911	0.005889838	0.014964938	0.006634567
ui^2			0.000137406	0.0000004658	0.0000136916	0.000002002	0.000034690	0.000223949	0.000044017

UTI-Growth & Value Fund (G) - TABLE 17.5.

Market Price	No. of shares	11-Aug-06	14-Aug-06	16-Aug-06	17-Aug-06	18-Aug-06	21-Aug-06	22-Aug-06	23-Aug-06
Grasim Industries	49653	2191.2	2197.35	2209.4	2209.8	2206.25	2239.85	2224.55	2195.45
Others (NA)	1	100300000	100300000	100300000	100300000	100300000	100300000	100300000	100300000
Infosys Techn.	54274	1742.2	1755.5	1752.3	1757.6	1762	1798.1	1781.15	1767.9
Thermax	310464	293.45	309.45	322.4	310.1	310.3	305.25	309.4	296.5
Bharti Airtel	219888	405.05	413	413.7	414.6	409.65	409.9	409.4	406
HCL Techn	143350	585.1	590	581.7	590.1	574.7	584.1	579.95	566.15
SBI	87462	859.5	871.45	888.5	881.65	879.1	883.35	878.45	863.15
Lupin	161228	475.3	490.15	505.35	531.3	538.7	529.55	524.35	513.25
Tata Chemicals	353845	215.1	215.15	215.75	212.1	212.25	213	215.95	216.25
ONGC	65000	1193.65	1215.3	1241.9	1211.1	1210.25	1190.7	1205.7	1198.45
Tata Tea	97000	868.1	869.25	856.35	841.25	844.8	845.75	846	828.15
Reliance Energy	164113	473.15	480.35	479.25	462.7	455.9	449	461.35	458.55
Gujarat Minerals	200204	295	327.35	324.85	342.75	343.15	340.2	333.15	321.15
Gammon India	187469	347.85	373.15	361.85	358.65	353.15	351.7	357.75	358.45
Bharat Earthmovers	55034	951.65	946.25	955.35	941.65	943.8	945.25	947.75	963.65
ITC	270000	175.25	178.55	180.9	181.1	179.75	180.75	181.9	178.8
Rallis India	177295	277.1	277.45	311.15	309.25	297.4	301.2	296.55	287.65
Zee Telefilms	170920	269.95	272.4	274.1	273.15	271.8	271.9	271.25	273.1
TV 18 India	77038	600.9	607.1	608.15	622.45	629.25	660.1	656.1	661.45
M&M	68714	612.95	620.2	634.6	644.8	644.85	663.9	659.75	632.8
Nicholas Piramal	192241	226.5	225.9	221.95	217.55	227	224.95	221.15	215.4
Kohinoor Foods	480751	0	0	0	0	82.5	81.6	81.9	79.75
Futures (Nifty)	55000	-129.44	-166.65	-212.48	-211.12	-217.69	-234.35	-237.90	-207.94
Put Option (Nifty)	55000	164.55	142.80	122.55	116.95	109.85	99.10	93.85	121.50
Subros	120311	201.2	203.3	210.5	205.95	216.55	213.45	217.85	220.45
KSB Pumps	48200	504.65	510.5	548.05	537.75	551.9	556.4	546.55	538.25
Patel Engineering	47863	323.75	338.55	337.8	320.95	313.05	328.7	334.2	333
Maruti Udyog	20000	796.1	802.25	814.95	819.75	840.65	841.3	836.65	826
Allahabad Bank (FD)	1	9000000	9000000	9000000	9000000	9000000	9000000	9000000	9000000
ILFS (FD)	1	100000	100000	100000	100000	100000	100000	100000	100000
Value of Portfolio		1577223841.28	1603104583.62	1615317916.79	1610072948.41	1646819955.85	1649268668.39	1648772228.14	1629930843.15
Si/Si-1		1.007938109	1.016409048	1.00761855	0.996752981	1.022823194	1.001486934	0.999698994	0.988572476
ui=ln(Si/Si-1)		0.007906768	0.016275875	0.007589676	-0.003252302	0.022566641	0.00148583	-0.000301052	-0.01149332
ui^2		6.2517E-05	0.000264904	0.0000576032	0.0000105775	0.000509253	0.0000022077	0.0000000906	0.000132096

UTI-Growth & Value Fund (G) - TABLE 17.5

Market Price	No. of shares	24-Aug-06	25-Aug-06	28-Aug-06	29-Aug-06	30-Aug-06	31-Aug-06	Totals
Grasim Industries	49653	2200.2	2204.1	2229.25	2225.8	2264.75	2251.6	**48013.75**
Others (NA)	1	100300000	100300000	100300000	100300000	100300000	100300000	**2206600000**
Infosys Techn.	54274	1766.9	1766.7	1772.75	1805.8	1801.2	1806.4	**38283.25**
Thermax	310464	300.15	298.95	298.05	302.1	297.7	294.15	**6445.1**
Bharti Airtel	219888	415.3	417.55	416.7	415.25	413.8	411.05	**8965.05**
HCL Techn	143350	572.15	574.65	576.3	580.6	578.85	581.6	**12503.3**
SBI	87462	874.65	905.1	918.9	922.05	930.75	931.25	**19134.5**
Lupin	161228	502	525.25	514.2	513.25	507.9	502.8	**10817.575**
Tata Chemicals	353845	218.05	222.35	222.55	222.1	225.25	224.75	**4693.05**
ONGC	65000	1189.1	1193.45	1197.15	1221.6	1221.45	1217.6	**26397.5**
Tata Tea	97000	832.2	829.4	837.3	829.2	821.45	799.2	**18459.95**
Reliance Energy	164113	456.05	443.55	449.8	448.7	439.5	438.45	**10089.6**
Gujarat Minerals	200204	325.75	345.3	346.85	345.15	344.85	343.1	**6976.3**
Gammon India	187469	352.3	352.25	350.5	344.8	335.35	341.8	**7540.95**
Bharat Earthmovers	55034	984.2	995.45	1003.5	986.7	974.65	957	**20849.5**
ITC	270000	180.05	180.15	180.1	184.65	187.35	191.5	**3919.35**
Rallis India	177295	285.5	286.25	287.75	283.1	278.05	284.3	**6096**
Zee Telefilms	170920	279.2	291.4	287.65	287.75	289.6	276.1	**5982.1**
TV 18 India	77038	665.1	657.95	656.5	653.15	645.45	599.4	**13839.8**
M&M	68714	640.95	651.85	651.9	656.85	657.35	646.25	**13800.5**
Nicholas Piramal	192241	215.9	216.85	219.65	222.15	226.15	222.05	**4829.25**
Kohinoor Foods	480751	81.05	80.3	78.95	79.75	77.75	77.65	**801.2**
Futures (Nifty)	55000	-253.78	-274.91	-288.65	-315.52	-325.00	-304.97	**-3813.896287**
Put Option (Nifty)	55000	85.00	75.70	65.30	55.55	50.35	57.80	**3172.3**
Subros	120311	215.4	217.35	219.35	215.6	213.45	211.05	**4543.85**
KSB Pumps	48200	531.1	526.9	520.2	517	522.85	516.7	**11291.35**
Patel Engineering	47863	328.9	342	336.65	329.35	329.85	329.55	**6907**
Maruti Udyog	20000	830.65	833.4	831.35	855.2	862.3	861.35	**17934.35**
Allahabad Bank (FD)	1	9000000	9000000	9000000	9000000	9000000	9000000	**198000000**
ILFS (FD)	1	100000	100000	100000	100000	100000	100000	**2200000**
Value of Portfolio		1631230040.27	1644108415.65	1644602728.41	1644909578.87	1639685455.16	**1646793902.40**	**35082772665.67**
Si/Si-1		#REF!	1.007894886	1.000300657	1.00018658	0.996824066	1.004335251	**21.0894764**
ui=ln(Si/Si-1)		#REF!	0.007863885	0.000300612	0.000186563	-0.003180988	0.00432588	**0.088679403**
ui^2		#REF!	0.000061841	0.000000090	0.000000035	0.000010119	0.000018713	**0.001586905**

Estimate of Standard Deviation of Daily NAVs =		**0.007786**	**0.000018724**	Amount invested in Options	3179000
Daily Volatility	**=**	**0.78%**	**0.000079345**	Number of shares of Patel Eng. To be off-loaded	9646.487635
		1.282 crores	0.000060621		
1-day 99% VaR	**=**	**2.99 crores**			
10-day 99% VaR	**=**	**9.45 crores**			

Notes/Assumptions

1. For the Option Contracts, the data on Option Prices is readily available from the but the data for valuing a Futures Contract is not available. We are given only the Futures Prices and the Spot Prices. Hence, Value of Futures Contracts entered into, have been calculated in Table 17.6 – valuation of futures contracts.
   Now, to calculate the Number of Futures Contracts to be entered has been calculated by using the formula :
   (Calculated Beta – Target Beta) * (Current Value of Portfolio)
   (Current Value of stocks underlying one futures contract)
   It may be noted that Beta has been calculated using Regression.
   (See Table 17.7 – Calculation of Beta)
2. Since the Option Prices show higher volatilities as compared to Value pf Futures, substantial amount of money is recommended to be invested in Futures and relatively lesser in Option Contracts.
3. VaR has been calculated both for 1 day as well as 10 days, assuming the confidence interval to be 99%. Alternative intervals could also be taken, but the same shall have no effect on the hedging strategy taken.

Table 17.6. Valuation of Futures Contracts (Risk-Free Rate = 10%).

		Bank Nifty	
Date	k	Ft	f = (k-Ft) e^{-Rt}
1-Aug-06	3091.10	3091.1	0.00
2-Aug-06	3091.10	3133.45	-41.32
3-Aug-06	3091.10	3141.5	-49.18
4-Aug-06	3091.10	3131.2	-39.14
7-Aug-06	3091.10	3089.85	1.22
8-Aug-06	3091.10	3164.4	-71.63
9-Aug-06	3091.10	3207.75	-114.02
10-Aug-06	3091.10	3213.25	-119.43
11-Aug-06	3091.10	3223.45	-129.44
14-Aug-06	3091.10	3261.35	-166.65
16-Aug-06	3091.10	3308.05	-212.48
17-Aug-06	3091.10	3306.6	-211.12
18-Aug-06	3091.10	3313.25	-217.69
21-Aug-06	3091.10	3330.05	-234.35
22-Aug-06	3091.10	3333.6	-237.90
23-Aug-06	3091.10	3303	-207.94
24-Aug-06	3091.10	3349.65	-253.78
25-Aug-06	3091.10	3371.1	-274.91
28-Aug-06	3091.10	3384.85	-288.65
29-Aug-06	3091.10	3412.1	-315.52
30-Aug-06	3091.10	3421.65	-325.00
31-Aug-06	3091.10	3401.2	-304.97

So = Spot Price, Ft = Futures Price,Fo = Futures Price discounted,
f = Value of Futures,R = Risk-free rate (assumed as 10%), t = time to maturity

http://www.nseindia.com

Table 12.7 (a)

Date	Open	High	Low	Close
1-Aug-06	3128.2	3154.7	3113.6	3147.8
2-Aug-06	3129.45	3187.85	3127.9	3182.1
3-Aug-06	3182.55	3234.25	3175.15	3190
4-Aug-06	3189.7	3228.15	3161.8	3176.75
7-Aug-06	3176.7	3178.5	3142.55	3151.1
8-Aug-06	3151.55	3216.75	3151.55	3212.4
9-Aug-06	3211.55	3267.2	3187.85	3254.6
10-Aug-06	3254.6	3274.75	3229.45	3260.1
11-Aug-06	3260.05	3286.5	3236.95	3274.35
14-Aug-06	3274.95	3317.8	3269.15	3313.1
16-Aug-06	3314.75	3377.1	3314.75	3356.05
17-Aug-06	3359.7	3385.15	3328.6	3353.9
18-Aug-06	3354.5	3366.25	3332.2	3356.75
21-Aug-06	3356.8	3374.9	3332.9	3366
22-Aug-06	3369.6	3398.35	3351.5	3364.6
23-Aug-06	3363.6	3369.65	3325.1	3335.8
24-Aug-06	3336.65	3379.55	3304.85	3370.4
25-Aug 06	3368.55	3402.7	3368.55	3385.95
28-Aug-06	3386	3405.3	3377.75	3401.1
29-Aug-06	3405.05	3434.95	3396.1	3425.7
30-Aug-06	3425.8	3440.2	3407.75	3430.35
31-Aug-06	3404.5	3452.3	3403.65	3413.9

portfolio	**1-Aug-06**	**2-Aug-06**	**3-Aug-06**	**4-Aug-06**	**7-Aug-06**	**8-Aug-06**	**9-Aug-06**	**10-Aug-06**	**11-Aug-06**	**14-Aug-06**	**16-Aug-06**	**17-Aug-06**
	1.49E+09	1515997830	1.52E+09	1.51E+09	1511773639	1.527E+09	1553239077	1.565E+09	1.58E+09	1.61E+09	1.62E+09	1618348091
		1.0143069	1.001492	0.995956	0.99977175	1.0097536	1.017504019	1.0073295	1.008815	1.018541	1.009853	0.996812861
portfolio	**18-Aug-06**	**21-Aug-06**	**22-Aug-06**	**23-Aug-06**	**24-Aug-06**	**25-Aug-06**	**28-Aug-06**	**29-Aug-06**	**30-Aug-06**	**31-Aug-06**		
	1655771025	1.66E+09	1.66E+09	1.64E+09	1.64E+09	1.66E+09	1.66E+09	1.66E+09	1.66E+09	1.65E+09		
	1.023124156	1.00248	1.000024	0.986733	1.003534	1.00893	1.001068	1.001355	0.997346	0.993257		
		1-Aug-06	**2-Aug-06**	**3-Aug-06**	**4-Aug-06**	**7-Aug-06**	**8-Aug-06**	**9-Aug-06**	**10-Aug-06**	**11-Aug-06**	**14-Aug-06**	**16-Aug-06**
nifty	3147.8	3182.1	3190	3176.75	3151.1	3212.4	3254.6	3260.1	3274.35	3313.1	3356.05	3353.9
		1.0108965	1.002483	0.995846	0.99192571	1.0194535	1.013136596	1.0016899	1.004371	1.011834	1.012964	0.999359366
	17-Aug-06	**18-Aug-06**	**21-Aug-06**	**22-Aug-06**	**23-Aug-06**	**24-Aug-06**	**25-Aug-06**	**28-Aug-06**	**29-Aug-06**	**30-Aug-06**	**31-Aug-06**	
nifty	3356.75	3366	3364.6	3335.8	3370.4	3385.95	3401.1	3425.7	3430.35	3413.9		
	1.000849757	1.002756	0.999584	0.99144	1.010372	1.004614	1.004474	1.007233	1.001357	0.995205		

Calculation of Beta - Table 12.7(b)

portfolio	nifty
1.0143069	1.010896
1.00149159	1.002483
0.9959557	0.995846
0.99977175	0.991926
1.00975359	1.019454
1.01750402	1.013137
1.00732948	1.00169
1.00881516	1.004371
1.01854143	1.011834
1.009853	1.012964
0.99681286	0.999359
1.02312416	1.00085
1.00248049	1.002756
1.00002439	0.999584
0.98673334	0.99144
1.00353427	1.010372
1.00135546	1.007233
0.99734595	1.001357
0.99325744	0.995205

Regression Results

SUMMARY OUTPUT

Regression Statistics	
Multiple R	0.665103
R Square	0.442362
Adjusted R Square	0.4130126
Standard Error	0.006884
Observations	21

ANOVA

	df	*SS*	*MS*	*F*	*Significance F*
Regression	1	0.000714271	0.000714271	15.072284	0.00100252
Residual	19	0.000900404	4.73897E-05		
Total	20	0.001614675			

	Coefficients	*Standard Error*	*t Stat*	*P-value*	*Lower 95%*	*Upper 95%*	*Lower 95.0%*	*Upper 95.0%*
Intercept	0.1873688	0.210523992	0.890011681	0.3845907	-0.253262967	0.628000592	-0.253263	0.628000592
X Variable 1	**0.8141244**	0.209701348	3.882303941	0.0010025	0.375214406	1.253034336	0.3752144	1.253034336

No. of Contracts 275

The Multiplier taken for Nifty is 200

Target Beta 0.7

18

Commodity Derivatives

Ever since the dawn of civilization commodities trading have become an integral part in the lives of mankind. The very reason for this lies in the fact that commodities represent the fundamental elements of utility for human beings. The term commodity refers to any material, which can be bought and sold. Commodities in a market's context refer to any movable property other than actionable claims, money and securities. Over the years commodities markets have been experiencing tremendous progress, which is evident from the fact that the trade in this segment is standing as the boon for the global economy today. The promising nature of these markets has made them an attractive investment avenue for investors.

In the early days people followed a mechanism for trading called Barter System, which involves exchange of goods for goods. This was the first form of trade between individuals. The absence of commonly accepted medium of exchange has initiated the need for Barter System. People used to buy those commodities which they lacked and sell those commodities which were in excess with them. The commodities trade is believed to have its genesis in Sumeria. The early commodity contracts were carried out using clay tokens as medium of exchange. Animals are believed to be the first commodities, which were traded, between individuals. The internationalization of commodities trade can be better understood by observing the commodity market integration occurred after the European Voyages of Discovery. The development of international commodities trade is characterized by the increase in volumes of trade across the nations and the convergence and price related to the identical commodities at different markets. The major thrust for the commodities trade was provided by the changes in demand patterns, scarcity and the supply potential both within and across the nations.

COMMODITIES

Commodities actually offer immense potential to become a separate asset class for market-savvy investors, arbitrageurs and speculators. Retail investors, who claim to understand the equity markets, may find commodities an unfathomable market. But commodities are easy to understand as far as fundamentals of demand and supply are concerned. Retail investors should understand the risks and advantages of trading in commodities futures before taking a leap. Historically, pricing in commodities futures has been less volatile compared with equity and bonds, thus providing an efficient portfolio diversification option.

In fact, the size of the commodities markets in India is also quite significant. Of the country's GDP of Rs 13, 20,730 crore (Rs 13,207.3 billion), commodities related (and dependent) industries constitute about 58 per cent.

Currently, the various commodities across the country clock an annual turnover of Rs 1, 40,000 crore (Rs 1,400 billion). With the introduction of futures trading, the size of the commodities market grows manifold hereon.

INTERNATIONAL SCENARIO

Global Commodities Derivatives Industry

Globally commodities derivatives exchanges have existed for a long time. Table 18.1 gives a list of commodities exchanges across the world. The CBOT and CME are two of the oldest derivatives exchanges in the world. The CBOT was established in 1948 to bring farmers and merchants together. Initially its main task was to standardize the quantities and qualities of the grains that were traded. Within a few years the first futures-type contract was developed. It was known as the *to-arrive contract*. Speculators soon became interested in the contract and found trading in the contract to be an attractive alternative to trading the underlying grain itself. In 1919, another exchange, the CME was established. Now futures exchanges exist all over the world. On these exchanges, a wide range of commodities and financial assets form the underlying assets in various contracts. The commodities include pork bellies, live cattle, sugar, wool, lumber, copper, aluminium, gold and tin. We look at commodity exchanges in some developing countries.

Africa

Africa's most active and important commodity exchange is the South African Futures Exchange (SAFEX). It was informally launched in 1987. SAFEX only traded financial futures and gold futures for a long time, but the creation of the Agricultural Markets Division (as of 2002, the Agricultural Derivatives Division) led to the introduction of a range of agricultural futures contracts for commodities, in which trade was liberalized, namely, white and yellow maize, bread milling wheat and sunflower seeds.

Asia

China's first commodity exchange was established in 1990 and at least forty had appeared by 1993. The main commodities traded were agricultural staples such as wheat, corn and in particularly soybeans. In late 1994, more than half of China's exchanges were closed down or reverted to being wholesale markets, while only 15 restructured exchanges received formal government approval. At the beginning of 1999, the China Securities Regulatory Committee began a nationwide consolidation

Country	Exchange
United States of America	Chicago Board of Trade (CBOT)
	Chicago Mercantile Exchange
	Minneapolis Grain Exchange
	New York Cotton Exchange
	New York Mercantile Exchange
	Kanas Board of Trade
Canada	The Winnipeg Commodity Exchange
Brazil	Brazilian Futures Exchange Commodities and Futures Exchange
Australia	Sydney Futures Exchange Ltd.
Peoples Republic of China	Beijing Commodity Exchange Shanghai Metal Exchange
Hong Kong	Hong Kong Futures Exchange
Japan	Tokyo International Financial Futures Exchange
	Kansai Agricultural Commodities Exchange Tokyo Grain Exchange
Malaysia	Kuala Lumpur commodity Exchange
New Zealand	New Zealand Futures & Options Exchange Ltd.
Singapore	Singapore Commodity exchange Ltd.
France	Le Nouveau Marche MATIF
Italy	Italian Derivatives Market
Netherlands	Amsterdam Exchanges Option Traders
Russia	The Russian Exchange
	MICEX / Relis Online St. Petersburg Futures Exchange
Spain	The Spanish Options Exchange
	Citrus Fruit and Commodity Futures Market of Valencia
United Kingdom	The London International Financial Futures Options Exchange
	The London Metal Exchange

Source: cbot.com

Process which resulted in three commodity exchanges emerging; the Dalian Commodity Exchange (DCE), the Zhengzhou Commodity Exchange and the Shanghai futures Exchange, formed in 1999 after the merger of three exchanges: Shanghai Metal, Commodity, Cereals & Oils Exchanges. The Taiwan Futures Exchange was launched in 1998. Malaysia and Singapore have active commodity futures exchanges. Malaysia hosts one futures and options exchange. Singapore is home to the Singapore Exchange (SGX), which was formed in 1999 by the merger of two well-established exchanges, the Stock Exchange of Singapore (SES) and Singapore International Monetary Exchange (SIMEX).

Latin America

Latin America's largest commodity exchange is the Bolsa de Mercadorias & Futuros, (BM&F) in Brazil. Although this exchange was only created in 1985, it was the 8th largest exchange by 2001, with 98 million contracts traded. There are also many other commodity exchanges operating in Brazil, spread throughout the country. Argentina's futures market Mercado a Termino de Buenos Aires, founded in 1909, ranks as the world's 51st largest exchange. Mexico has only recently introduced a futures exchange to its markets. The Mercado Mexicano de Derivados (Mexder) was launched in 1998.

MAJOR INTERNATIONAL COMMODITY EXCHANGES

The following gives an overview of the most important commodity exchanges in the world (respectively exchanges dealing in commodities). A short description shows you the particular commodities traded in these markets, neglecting the trade of securities, stock index futures and options etc.

United Kingdom

International Petroleum Exchange (IPE)

A commodity market that deals in futures contracts (Brent and Dubai crude oil, gas oil, leaded and unleaded gasoline, naphtha and heavy fuel oil), as well as in options (Brent crude and gas oil). It offers the facilities for making an exchange of futures for physicals.

Futures and Options Exchange (London FOX)

This exchange, which includes the former ***London Commodity Exchange (LCE),*** is the leading exchange in Europe for soft commodities (e.g. cocoa, coffee, sugar, rubber, potatoes and grain).

London Metal Exchange (LME)

The LME is the London market for trade in metals and the world futures and cash market for trades in non-ferrous metals, such as aluminum, aluminum alloy, copper, lead, nickel, tin and zinc. There are also exchange-traded options, available on all futures contracts apart from aluminum alloy. The market is daily for cash and contracts up to three months, and weekly for contracts up to 15 months. The official prices of the LME are used by producers and consumers worldwide for their long-term contracts.

United States of America

Chicago Board of Trade (CBOT)

The CBOT is a trading centre for commodities and the largest futures exchange in the world. The market deals in futures and options on agricultural commodities, such as maize, soya beans, crude soya bean oil, soya bean meal, oats, and also in contracts on gold and silver.

Chicago Mercantile Exchange (CME)

The CME—the prime US futures and options market—trades a huge range of futures and options on commodities, above all futures contracts in livestock (live cattle, feeder cattle, live hogs, pork bellies). It is also the leader in exchange-traded financial derivatives.

Coffee, Sugar & Cocoa Exchange (CSCE)

The CSCE in New York is a major world commodity market dealing futures contracts and options on coffee, sugar, cocoa, cheddar cheese and non-fat dry milk. Together with London a main world market in cocoa.

Kansas City Board of Trade (KCBT)

This is the commodity market for grain, trading options and futures. Together with the exchanges of Chicago and Minneapolis, it sets the world price for grains. The KCBT's homepage will allow you access to contract specifications, daily price summary information and info on how to get started in trading commodities.

Mid America Commodity Exchange (MIDAM)

An exchange in Chicago that deals in futures and options contracts in a variety of commodities. It offers among others "mini" contracts in metals, meats and grains. The MIDAM is affiliated to the CBOT, and a number of its futures and options contracts are traded on the floor of the CBOT.

Minneapolis Grain Exchange (MGE)

A commodity market for grain, dealing in futures contracts for spring wheat and white wheat, and, on the cash market, for barley, maize, drum wheat, flaxseed, oats, rye, Soya beans, spring wheat and sunflower seeds. And it offers the world's only seafood futures contracts (White and Black Tiger shrimp).

New York Cotton Exchange (NYCE)

The oldest commodity exchange in New York (founded in 1870) and the world's prime market for cotton futures and options. The NYCE also trades in liquefied propane gas futures.

New York Mercantile Exchange (NYMEX)

The NYMEX in its current form was created in 1994 by the merger of the former New York Mercantile Exchange and the Commodity Exchange of New York (COMEX). Together they represent one of the world's largest markets in energy and precious metals. It deals in futures (and options) in oil products, such as crude oil, heating oil, leaded regular gasoline, natural gas, propane and in rare metals, such as platinum and palladium. It also deals in gold and silver, aluminum and copper, sharing with the London Metal Exchange a dominant role in the world metal trading. The trade of crack spread allows investors to construct their own spread combinations.

Australia

- **Sydney Futures Exchange (SFE)**
  The SFE trades commodity futures (wool and live cattle).

Brazil

- **Brazilian Futures Exchange (BBF)**

Canada

- **Winnipeg Commodity Exchange (WCE)**

France

- **Marche a Terme International de France (MATIF)**

Hong Kong

- **Hong Kong Futures Exchange (HKFE)**
  The HKFE (the former Hong Kong Commodity Exchange) trades in cotton, sugar, Soya bean and gold futures, and in other commodities.

Hungary

- **Budapest Commodity Exchange**
  This prime Commodity Exchange in Eastern Europe deals in futures and forward contracts in barley, maize and wheat. On the spot market it also trades beans, peas and other agricultural products.

Japan

- **Tokyo Commodity Exchange (TOCOM)**
- **Tokyo Grain Exchange (TGE)**
  One of the largest exchanges in Japan that actively trades in a range of agricultural products.

New Zealand

- **New Zealand Futures & Options Exchange (NZFOE)**
  The NZFOE is affiliated to the SFE. It trades wool.

Phillippines

- **Manila International Futures Exchange**

Russia

- **Russian Commodity and Raw Materials Exchange**

Singapore

- **Singapore International Monetary Exchange (SIMEX)**
  Deals in energy and commodity futures.

Slovenia

- **Commodity Exchange of Ljubljana**

South Africa

- **South African Futures Exchange (SAFEX)**
  Trades commodity futures, as well as options on futures.

EVOLUTION OF COMMODITIES MARKETS IN INDIA

Commodities Market

Commodity market is an important constituent of the financial markets of any country. It is the market where a wide range of products, viz., precious metals, base metals, crude oil, energy and soft commodities like palm oil, coffee etc. are traded. It is important to develop a vibrant, active and liquid commodity market. This would help investors hedge their commodity risk, take speculative positions in commodities and exploit arbitrage opportunities in the market.

In the context of the development of commodities markets, integration plays a pivotal role in surmounting the barriers of trade. The development of trading mechanisms in the commodities market segment largely helped the integration of commodities markets.

The major thrust for the integration of commodities trading was given by the European discoveries and the march of the world trade towards globalization. The commodities trade among different countries was originated much before the voyages of Columbus and Da Gama. During the first half of the second millennium India and China had trading arrangements with Southeast Asia, Eastern Europe, the Islamic countries and the Mediterranean. The advancements in shipping and other transport technologies had facilitated the growth of the trade in this segment. The unification of the Eurasian continent by the Mongols led to a wide transmission of people, ideas and goods. Later, the Black Death of 1340s, the killer plague that reduced the population of Europe and Middle East by one-third, has resulted in more per capita income for individuals and thus increased the demand for Eastern luxuries like precious stones, spices, ceramics and silks. This has augmented the supply of precious metals to the East. This entire scenario resulted in the increased reliance on Indian Ocean trade routes and stimulated the discovery of sea route to Asia.

Table 18.1. Turnover in Financial Markets and Commodities Market

Sr.No.	Market Segments	2002-03		2003-04		2004-05	
1.	Govt. Securities Markets	1,544,376	(63)	2,518,322	(91.2)	2,827,872	(91)
2.	Forex Markets	658,035	(27)	2,318,531	(84)	3,867,936	(124.4)
3.	Total Stock Market Turnover (I + II)	1,374,405	(56)	3,745,507	(136)	4,160,702	(133.8)
I	National Stock Exchange	1,057,854	(43)	3,230,002	(117)	3,641,672	(117.1)
	a) Cash	617,989		1,099,534		1,147,027	
	b) Derivatives	439,865		2,130,468		2,494,645	
II	Bombay Stock Exchange	316,551	(13)	515,505	(18.7)	519,030	(16.7)
	a) Cash	314,073		503,053		499,503	
	b) Derivatives	2,478		12,452		19,527	
4.	Commodities Market	N.A.		130,215	(4.7)	500,000	(16.1)

Note: Fig. in bracket represents percentage to GDP at market prices

Source: SEBI Bulletin

The second half of the second millennium is characterized by the connectivity of the markets related to the Old and the new worlds. In the year 1571, the city of Manila was found, which linked the trade between America, Asia, Africa ad Europe. During the initial stages, because of the high transportation costs, preference of trade was given to those commodities, which had high value to weight ratio. In the aftermath of the discoveries huge volumes of silver was pumped into world trade. With the discovery of the Cape route, the Venetian and Egyptian dominance of spice exports was diluted. The introduction of new world crops into China has led to the increased demand for silver and a growth in exports of tea and silk. Subsequently, Asia has become the prime trader of spices and silk and Americas became the prominent exporter of silver.

Earlier investors invested in those companies, which specialized in the production of commodities. This accounted for the indirect investments in commodity assets.

But with the establishment of commodity exchanges, a shift in the investment patterns of individuals has occurred as investors started recognizing commodity investments as an alternative investment avenue. The establishment of these exchanges has benefited both the producers and traders in terms of reaping high profits and rationalizing transaction costs. Commodity exchanges play a vital role in ensuring transparency in transactions and disseminating prices. The commodity exchanges ensured the standard of trading by maintaining settlement guarantee funds and implementing stringent capital adequacy norms for brokers. In the light of these developments, various commodity based investment products were created to facilitate trading and risk management. The commodity based products offer a huge array of benefits that include offering risk-return trade-offs to investors, providing information on market trends and assisting in framing asset allocation strategies. Commodity investments are always considered to be defensive because during the times of inflation, which adversely affects the performance of stocks and bonds, commodities provide a defense to investors, maintaining the performance of their portfolios.

The commodities trade in the 18th and 19th centuries was largely influenced by the shifts in macro economic patterns, the changes in government regulations, the advancement in technology, and other social and political transformations around the world. The 19th century has seen the establishment of various commodities exchanges, which paved the way for effective transportation, financing and warehousing facilities in this arena. In a new era of trading environment, commodities exchanges offer innumerable economic benefits by facilitating efficient price discovery mechanisms and competent risk transfer systems.

Evolution of Commodities Market in India

Organized futures market evolved in India by the setting up of "Bombay Cotton Trade Association Ltd." in 1875. In 1893, following widespread discontent amongst leading cotton mill owners and merchants over the functioning of the Bombay Cotton Trade Association, a separate association by the name "Bombay Cotton Exchange Ltd." was constituted. Futures trading in oilseeds were organized in India for the first time with the setting up of Gujarati Vyapari Mandali in 1900, which carried on futures trading in groundnut, castor seed and cotton. Before the Second World War broke out in 1939 several futures markets in oilseeds were functioning in Gujarat and Punjab.

Futures trading in Raw Jute and Jute Goods began in Calcutta with the establishment of the Calcutta Hessian Exchange Ltd., in 1919. Later East Indian Jute Association Ltd was set up in 1927 for organizing futures trading in Raw Jute. These two associations amalgamated in 1945 to form the present East India Jute & Hessian Ltd., to conduct organized trading in both Raw Jute and Jute goods. In case of wheat, futures markets were in existence at several centers at Punjab and U.P. The most notable amongst them was the Chamber of Commerce at Hapur, which was established in 1913. Other markets were located at Amritsar, Moga, Ludhiana,

Jalandhar, Fazilka, Dhuri, Barnala and Bhatinda in Punjab and Muzaffarnagar, Chandausi, Meerut, Saharanpur, Hathras, Gaziabad, Sikenderabad and Barielly in U.P.

Futures market in bullion began at Mumbai in 1920 and later similar markets came up at Rajkot, Jaipur, Jamnagar, Kanpur, Delhi and Calcutta. In due course several other exchanges were also created in the country to trade in such diverse commodities as pepper, turmeric, potato, sugar and gur (jaggery).

After independence, the Constitution of India brought the subject of "Stock Exchanges and futures markets" in the Union list. As a result, the responsibility for regulation of commodity futures markets devolved on Govt. of India. A Bill on forward contracts was referred to an expert committee headed by Prof. A.D.Shroff and Select Committees of two successive Parliaments and finally in December 1952 Forward Contracts (Regulation) Act, 1952, was enacted. The Act provided for 3-tier regulatory system:

a. An association recognized by the Government of India on the recommendation of Forward Markets Commission,
b. The Forward Markets Commission (it was set up in September 1953) and
c. The Central Government.

Forward Contracts (Regulation) Rules were notified by the Central Government in July, 1954. The Act divides the commodities into 3 categories with reference to extent of regulation, viz:

- The commodities in which futures trading can be organized under the auspices of recognized association.
- The Commodities in which futures trading is prohibited.
- Those commodities which have neither been regulated for being traded under the recognized association nor prohibited are referred as Free Commodities and the association organized in such free commodities is required to obtain the Certificate of Registration from the Forward Markets Commission.

In the seventies, most of the registered associations became inactive, as futures as well as forward trading in the commodities for which they were registered came to be either suspended or prohibited altogether.

The Khusro Committee (June 1980) had recommended reintroduction of futures trading in most of the major commodities , including cotton, kapas, raw jute and jute goods and suggested that steps may be taken for introducing futures trading in commodities, like potatoes, onions, etc. at appropriate time. The government, accordingly initiated futures trading in potato during the later half of 1980 in quite a few markets in Punjab and Uttar Pradesh.

The Kabra Committee Report

After the introduction of economic reforms since June 1991 and the consequent gradual trade and industry liberalization in both the domestic and external sectors, the Government of India appointed in June 1993 a committee on Forward Markets under chairmanship of Prof. K.N. Kabra. The committee was set up with the following objectives:

- To assess the working of the commodity exchanges and their trading practices in India and to make suitable recommendations with a view to making them compatible with those of other countries
  The role of the Forward Markets Commission and to make suitable recommendations with a view to making it compatible with similar regulatory agencies in other countries so as to see how effectively these agencies can cope up with the reality of the fast changing economic scenario.
- To review the role that forward trading has played in the Indian commodity markets during the last 10 years.
- To examine the extent to which forward trading has special role to play in promoting exports.
- To suggest amendments to the Forward Contracts (Regulation) Act, in the light of the recommendations, particularly with a view to effective enforcement of the Act to check illegal forward trading when such trading is prohibited under the Act.
- To suggest measures to ensure that forward trading in the commodities in which it is allowed to be operative remains constructive and helps in maintaining prices within reasonable limits.
- To assess the role that forward trading can play in marketing/ distribution system in the commodities in which forward trading is possible, particularly in commodities in which resumption of forward trading is generally demanded.

The committee submitted its report in September 1994. The recommendations of the committee were as follows:

- The Forward Markets Commission (FMC) and the Forward Contracts (Regulation) Act, 1952, would need to be strengthened.
  Due to the inadequate infrastructural facilities such as space and telecommunication facilities the commodities exchanges were not able to function effectively Enlisting more members, ensuring capital adequacy norms and encouraging computerization would enable these exchanges to place themselves on a better footing.
- In-built devices in commodity exchanges such as the vigilance committee and the panels of surveyors and arbitrators are strengthened further.
- The FMC which regulates forward/ futures trading in the country should continue to act a watchdog and continue to monitor the activities and operations of the commodity exchanges. Amendments to the rules, regulations and by-laws of the commodity exchanges should require the approval of the FMC only.
- In the context of globalization, commodity markets in India could not function effectively in an isolated manner. Therefore, some of the commodity exchanges, particularly the ones dealing in pepper and castor seed, are upgraded to the level of international futures markets.
- The majority of the committee recommended that futures trading be introduced in the following commodities:

- Basmati rice, Cotton and kapas, Raw jute and jute goods, Groundnut, rapeseed/mustard seed, cottonseed, sesame seed, sunflower seed, copra and soybean, and oils and oilcakes of all of them, Rice bran oil, Castor oil and its oilcake, Linseed, Silver, Onions.

The liberalized policy being followed by the government of India and the gradual withdrawal of the procurement and distribution channel necessitated setting in place a market mechanism to perform the economic functions of price discovery and risk management.

The national agriculture policy announced in July 2000 and the announcements in the budget speech for 2002.2003 were indicative of the government's resolve to put in place a mechanism of futures trade/market. As a follow-up, the government issued notifications on 1.4.2003 permitting futures trading in the commodities, with the issue of these notifications futures trading is not prohibited in any commodity. Options trading in commodities is, however presently prohibited.

Latest Developments

While the implementation of the Kabra committee recommendations was rather slow, today, the commodity derivative market in India seems poised for a transformation. National level commodity derivatives exchanges seem to be the new phenomenon.

The government has now allowed national commodity exchanges, similar to the BSE & NSE to come up and let them deal in commodity derivatives in an electronic trading environment. These exchanges are expected to offer a nationwide anonymous, order driven, screen based trading system for trading. The Forward Markets Commission (FMC) will regulate these exchanges. Consequently four commodity exchanges have been approved to commence business in this regard. They are:

- **Multi Commodity Exchange (MCX)** located at Mumbai.
- **National Commodity and Derivatives Exchange Ltd (NCDEX)** located at Mumbai.
- **National Board of Trade (NBOT)** located at Indore.
- **National Multi Commodity Exchange (NMCE)** located at Ahmedabad.

The increasing volumes on these exchanges suggest that commodity markets in India seem to be a promising game.

NATIONAL COMMODITY & DERIVATIVES EXCHANGE LIMITED (NCDEX)

National Commodity and Derivatives Exchange Ltd (NCDEX) is a technology driven commodity exchange. It is a public limited company registered under the Companies Act, 1956 with the Registrar of Companies, Maharashtra in Mumbai on April 23, 2003. It has an independent Board of Directors and professionals not having any vested interest in commodity markets. It has been launched to provide a world-class commodity exchange platform for market participants to trade in a wide spectrum of commodity derivatives driven by best global practices, professionalism and transparency.

NCDEX is regulated by Forward Markets Commission in respect of futures trading in commodities. Besides, NCDEX is subjected to various laws of the land like the Companies Act, Stamp Act, Contracts Act, Forward Commission (Regulation) Act and various other legislations, which impinge on its working. It is located in Mumbai and offers facilities to its members in about 91 cities throughout India at the moment.

Structure of NCDEX

NCDEX has been formed with the following objectives:

- To create a world class commodity exchange platform for the market participants.
- To bring professionalism and transparency into commodity trading.
- To inculcate best international practices like de-modularization, technology platforms, low cost solutions and information dissemination without noise etc. into the trade.
- To provide nation wide reach and consistent offering.
- To bring together the entities that the market can trust.

Promoters

NCDEX is promoted by a consortium of institutions. These include the ICICI Bank Limited (ICICI Bank), Life Insurance Corporation of India (LIC), National Bank for Agriculture and Rural Development (NABARD) and National Stock Exchange of India Limited (NSE). NCDEX is the only commodity exchange in the country promoted by national level institutions. This unique parentage enables it to offer a variety of benefits which are currently in short supply in the commodity market.

The four institutional promoters of NCDEX are prominent players in their respective fields and bring with them institution building experience, trust, nationwide reach, technology and risk management skills.

Governance

NCDEX is run by an independent Board of Directors. Promoters do not participate in the day-to-day activities of the exchange. The directors are appointed in accordance with the provisions of the Articles of Association of the company. The board is responsible for managing and regulating all the operations of the exchange and commodities transactions. It formulates the rules and regulations related to the operations of the exchange. Board appoints an executive committee and other committees for the purpose of managing activities of the exchange.

The executive committee consists of Managing Director of the exchange who would be acting as the Chief Executive of the exchange, and also other members appointed by the board. Apart from the executive committee the board constitutes committees like Membership committee, Audit Committee, Risk Committee, Nomination Committee, Compensation Committee and Business Strategy Committee, which, help the Board in policy formulation.

Exchange Membership

Membership of NCDEX is open to any person, association of persons, partnerships, co-operative societies, companies etc. that fulfills the eligibility criteria set by the exchange. All the members of the exchange have to register themselves with the competent authority before commencing their operations. The members of NCDEX fall into two categories, trading cum Clearing Members (TCM) and Professional Clearing Members (PCM).

Trading-cum-clearing members (TCMs)

NCDEX invites applications for Trading-cum-Clearing Members (TCMs) from persons who fulfill the specified eligibility criteria for trading in commodities. The TCM membership entitles the members to trade and clear, both for themselves and/ or on behalf of their clients. Applicants accepted for admission as TCM are required to pay the required fees/ deposits and also maintain net worth as given in Table 18.2.

Table 18.2. Fee/deposit structure and net worth requirement: TCM

Particulars	Rs. (in Lakhs)
Interest free cash security deposit	15.00
Collateral security deposit	15.00
Annual subscription charges	.50
Advance minimum transaction charges	.50
Net worth requirement	50.00

Source: *www. ncdex.com*

Professional clearing members (PCMs)

NCDEX also invites applications for Professional Clearing Memberships (PCMs) from persons who fulfill the specified eligibility criteria for trading in commodities. The PCM membership entitles the members to clear trades executed through Trading-cum-Clearing Members (TCMs), both for themselves and/ or on behalf of their clients. Applicants accepted for admission as PCMs are required to pay the following fee/ deposits and also maintain net worth as given in Table 18.3.

Table 18.3. Fee/deposit structure and net worth requirement: PCM

Particulars	Rs.(in Lakhs)
Interest free cash security deposit	25.00
Collateral security deposit	25.00
Annual subscription charges	1.00
Advance minimum transaction charges	1.00
Net worth requirement	5000.00

Source: *www.ncdex.com*

Capital Requirements

NCDEX has specified capital requirements for its members. On approval as a member of NCDEX, the member has to deposit Base Minimum Capital (BMC) with the exchange. Base Minimum Capital comprises the following:

1. Interest free cash security deposit
2. Collateral security deposit

All Members have to comply with the security deposit requirement before the activation of their trading terminal. Members can opt to meet the security deposit requirement by way of the following:

Cash

This can be deposited by issuing a cheque / demand draft payable at Mumbai in favor of National Commodity & Derivatives Exchange Limited.

Bank guarantee

Bank guarantee in favor of NCDEX as per the specified format from approved banks. The minimum term of the bank guarantee should be 12 months.

Fixed deposit receipt

Fixed deposit receipts (FDRs) issued by approved banks are accepted. The FDR should be issued for a minimum period of 36 months from any of the approved banks.

Government of India securities

National Securities Clearing Corporation Limited (NSCCL) is the approved custodian for acceptance of Government of India securities. The securities are valued on a daily basis and a haircut of 25% is levied.

Members are required to maintain minimum level of security deposit i.e. Rs.15 Lakh in case of TCM and Rs. 25 Lakh in case of PCM at any point of time. If the security deposit falls below the minimum required level, NCDEX may initiate suitable action including withdrawal of trading facilities as given below:

- If the security deposit shortage is equal to or greater than Rs. 5 Lakh, the trading facility would be withdrawn with immediate effect.
- If the securities deposit shortage is less than Rs.5 Lakh the member would be given one calendar weeks' time to replenish the shortages and if the same is not done within the specified time the trading facility would be withdrawn.

Members who wish to increase their limit can do so by bringing in additional capital in the form of cash, bank guarantee, fixed deposit receipts or Government of India securities.

THE NCDEX SYSTEM

Every market transaction consists of three components—trading, clearing and settlement. This section provides a brief overview of how transactions happen on the NCDEX's market.

Trading

The trading system on the NCDEX provides a fully automated screen-based trading for futures on commodities on a nationwide basis as well as an online monitoring and surveillance mechanism. It supports an order driven market and provides complete transparency of trading operations. The trade timings of the NCDEX are 10.00 a.m. to 4.00 p.m. After hours trading has also been proposed for implementation at a later stage.

The NCDEX system supports an order driven market, where orders match automatically. Order matching is essentially on the basis of commodity, its price, time and quantity. All quantity fields are in units and price in rupees. The exchange specifies the unit of trading and the delivery unit for futures contracts on various commodities. The exchange notifies the regular lot size and tick size for each of the contracts traded from time to time. When any order enters the trading system, it is an active order. It tries to find a match on the other side of the book. If it finds a match, a trade is generated. If it does not find a match, the order becomes passive and gets queued in the respective outstanding order book in the system. Time stamping is done for each trade and provides the possibility for a complete audit trail if required.

NCDEX trades commodity futures contracts having one-month, two month and three-month expiry cycles. All contracts expire on the 20th of the expiry month. Thus a January expiration contract would expire on the 20th of January and a February expiry contract would cease trading on the 20th of February. If the 20th of the expiry month is a trading holiday, the contracts shall expire on the previous trading day. New contracts will be introduced on the trading day following the expiry of the near month contract.

Clearing

National Securities Clearing Corporation Limited (NSCCL) undertakes clearing of trades executed on the NCDEX. The settlement guarantee fund is maintained and managed by NCDEX. Only clearing members including professional clearing members (PCMs) only are entitled to clear and settle contracts through the clearing house. At NCDEX, after the trading hours on the expiry date, based on the available information, the matching for deliveries takes place firstly, on the basis of locations and then randomly, keeping in view the factors such as available capacity of the vault/ warehouse, commodities already deposited and dematerialized and offered for delivery etc. Matching done by this process is binding on the clearing members. After completion of the matching process, clearing members are informed of the deliverable/ receivable positions and the unmatched positions. Unmatched positions have to be settled in cash. The cash settlement is only for the incremental gain/ loss as determined on the basis of final settlement price.

Settlement

Futures contracts have two types of settlements, the MTM settlement which happens on a continuous basis at the end of each day, and the final settlement which happens on the last trading day of the futures contract. On the NCDEX, daily MTM settlement and final MTM settlement in respect of admitted deals in futures contracts are cash settled by debiting/ crediting the clearing accounts of CMs with the respective clearing bank. All positions of a CM, either brought forward, created during the day or closed out during the day, are market to market at the daily settlement price or the final settlement price at the close of trading hours on a day. On the date of expiry, the final settlement price is the spot price on the expiry day. The responsibility of settlement is on a trading-cum-clearing member for all trades done on his own account and his client's trades. A professional clearing member is responsible for settling all the participants' trades which he has confirmed to the exchange. On the expiry date of a futures contract, members submit delivery information through delivery request window on the trader workstations provided by NCDEX for all open positions for a commodity for all constituents individually. NCDEX on receipt of such information matches the information and arrives at a delivery position for a member for a commodity.

The seller intending to make delivery takes the commodities to the designated warehouse. These commodities have to be assayed by the exchange specified assayer. The commodities have to meet the contract specifications with allowed variances. If the commodities meet the specifications, the warehouse accepts them. Warehouse then ensures that the receipts get updated in the depository system giving a credit in the depositor's electronic account. The seller then gives the invoice to his clearing member, who would courier the same to the buyer's clearing member. On an appointed date, the buyer goes to the warehouse and takes physical possession of the commodities.

Regulatory Framework

At present, there are three tiers of regulations of forward/futures trading system in India, namely, government of India, Forward Markets Commission (FMC) and commodity exchanges. The need for regulation arises on account of the fact that the benefits of futures markets accrue in competitive conditions. Proper regulation is needed to create competitive conditions. In the absence of regulation, unscrupulous participants could use these leveraged contracts for manipulating prices. This could have undesirable influence on the spot prices, thereby affecting interests of society at large. Regulation is also needed to ensure that the market has appropriate risk management system. In the absence of such a system, a major default could create a chain reaction. The resultant financial crisis in a futures market could create systematic risk. Regulation is also needed to ensure fairness and transparency in trading, clearing, settlement and management of the exchange so as to protect and promote the interest of various stakeholders, particularly non-member users of the market.

Rules Governing Commodity Exchanges

The trading of commodity derivatives on the NCDEX is regulated by Forward Markets Commission (FMC). Under the Forward Contracts (Regulation) Act, 1952, forward trading in commodities notified under section 15 of the Act can be conducted only on the exchanges, which are granted recognition by the central government (Department of Consumer Affairs, Ministry of Consumer Affairs, Food and Public Distribution). All the exchanges, which deal with forward contracts, are required to obtain certificate of registration from the FMC. Besides, they are subjected to various laws of the land like the Companies Act, Stamp Act, Contracts Act, Forward Commission (Regulation) Act and various other legislations, which impinge on their working.

Forward Markets Commission provides regulatory oversight in order to ensure financial integrity (i.e. to prevent systematic risk of default by one major operator or group of operators), market integrity (i.e. to ensure that futures prices are truly aligned with the prospective demand and supply conditions) and to protect and promote interest of customers/ non-members.

It prescribes the following regulatory measures:

1. Limit on net open position as on the close of the trading hours. Sometimes limit is also imposed on intra-day net open position. The limit is imposed operator-wise, and in some cases, also member-wise.
2. Circuit-filters or limit on price fluctuations to allow cooling of market in the event of abrupt upswing or downswing in prices.
3. Special margin deposit to be collected on outstanding purchases or sales when price moves up or down sharply above or below the previous day closing price. By making further purchases/sales relatively costly, the price rise or fall is sobered down. This measure is imposed only on the request of the exchange.

4. Circuit breakers or minimum/maximum prices: These are prescribed to prevent futures prices from falling below as rising above not warranted by prospective supply and demand factors. This measure is also imposed on the request of the exchanges.
5. Skipping trading in certain derivatives of the contract, closing the market for a specified period and even closing out the contract: These extreme measures are taken only in emergency situations.

Besides these regulatory measures, the FC(R) Act provides that a client's position cannot be appropriated by the member of the exchange, except when a written consent is taken within three day's time. The FMC is persuading increasing number of exchanges to switch over to electronic trading, clearing and settlement, which is more customer-friendly. The FMC has also prescribed simultaneous reporting system for the exchanges following open outcry system. These steps facilitate audit trail and make it difficult for the members to indulge in malpractices like trading ahead of clients, etc. The FMC has also mandated all the exchanges following open outcry system to display at a prominent place in exchange premises, the name, address, and telephone number of the officer of the commission who can be contacted for any grievance. The website of the commission also has a provision for the customers to make complaint and send comments and suggestions to the FMC. Officers of the FMC have been instructed to meet the members and clients on a random basis, whenever they visit exchanges, to ascertain the situation on the ground, instead of merely attending meetings of the board of directors and holding discussions with the office-bearers.

Rules Governing Intermediaries (NCDEX)

In addition to the provisions of the Forward Contracts (Regulation) Act 1952 and rules framed thereunder, exchanges are governed by its own rules and by- laws (approved by the FMC). In this section we have a brief look at the important regulations that govern NCDEX. For the sake of convenience, these have been divided into two main divisions pertaining to trading and clearing. The detailed by-laws, rules and regulations are available on the NCDEX home page.

Trading

The NCDEX provides an automated trading facility in all the commodities admitted for dealings on the spot market and derivative market. Trading on the exchange is allowed only through approved workstation(s) located at locations for the office(s) of a trading member as approved by the exchange. If LAN or any other way to

---

http://www.ncdex.com

other workstations at any place connects an approved workstation of a trading Member it shall require an approval of the exchange.

Each trading member is required to have a unique identification number which is provided by the exchange and which will be used to log on (sign on) to the trading system. A trading member has a non-exclusive permission to use the trading system as provided by the exchange in the ordinary course of business as trading member. He does not have any title rights or interest whatsoever with respect to trading system, its facilities, software and the information provided by the trading system.

For the purpose of accessing the trading system, the member will install and use equipment and software as specified by the exchange at his own cost. The exchange has the right to inspect equipment and software used for the purposes of accessing the trading system at any time. The cost of the equipment and software supplied by the exchange, installation and maintenance of the equipment is borne by the trading member.

Trading members and users

Trading members are entitled to appoint, (subject to such terms and conditions, as may be specified by the relevant authority) from time to time:

- Authorized persons
- Approved users

Trading members have to pass a certification program, which has been prescribed by the exchange. In case of trading members, other than individuals or sole proprietorships, such certification program has to be passed by at least one of their directors/ employees/ partners / members of governing body.

Each trading member is permitted to appoint a certain number of approved users as notified from time to time by the exchange. The appointment of approved users is subject to the terms and conditions prescribed by the exchange. Each approved user is given a unique identification number through which he will have access to the trading system. An approved user can access the trading system through a password and can change the password from time to time. The trading member or its approved users are required to maintain complete secrecy of its password. Any trade or transaction done by the use of password of any approved user of the trading member, will be binding on such trading member. Approved user shall be required to change his password at the end of the password expiry period.

Trading days

The exchange operates on all days except Saturday and Sunday and on holidays that it declares from time to time. Other than the regular trading hours, trading members are provided a facility to place orders off-line i.e. outside trading hours. These are stored by the system but get traded only once the market opens for trading on the following working day.

The types of order books, trade books, price limits, matching rules and other parameters pertaining to each or all of these sessions are specified by the exchange to the members via its circulars or notices issued from time to time. Members can place orders on the trading system during these sessions, within the regulations prescribed by the exchange as per these by-laws, rules and regulations, from time to time.

Trading hours and trading cycle

The exchange announces the normal trading hours/ open period in advance from time to time. In case necessary, the exchange can extend or reduce the trading hours by notifying the members. Trading cycle for each commodity/ derivative contract has a standard period, during which it will be available for trading.

Contract expiration

Derivatives contracts expire on a pre-determined date and time up to which the contract is available for trading. This is notified by the exchange in advance. The contract expiration period will not exceed twelve months or as the exchange may specify from time to time.

Trading parameters

The exchange from time to time specifies various trading parameters relating to the trading system. Every trading member is required to specify the buy or sell orders as either an open order or a close order for derivatives contracts. The exchange also prescribes different order books that shall be maintained on the trading system and also specifies various conditions on the order that will make it eligible to place it in those books.

The exchang specifies the minimum disclosed quantity for orders that will be allowed for each commodity/ derivatives contract. It also prescribes the number of days after which Good Till Cancelled orders will be cancelled by the system. It specifies parameters like lot size in which orders can be placed, price steps in which orders shall be entered on the trading system, position limits in respect of each commodity etc.

Failure of trading member terminal

In the event of failure of trading members workstation and/ or the loss of access to the trading system, the exchange can at its discretion undertake to carry out on behalf of the trading member the necessary functions which the trading member is eligible for. Only requests made in writing in a clear and precise manner by the trading member would be considered. The trading member is accountable for the functions executed by the exchange on its behalf and has to indemnify the exchange against any losses or costs incurred by the exchange.

Trade operations

Trading members have to ensure that appropriate confirmed order instructions are obtained from the constituents before placement of an order on the system. They have to keep relevant records or documents concerning the order and trading system order number and copies of the order confirmation slip/ modification slip must be made available to the constituents. The trading member has to disclose to the exchange at the time of order entry whether the order is on his own account or on behalf of constituents and also specify orders for buy or sell as open or close orders. Trading members are solely responsible for the accuracy of details of orders entered into the trading system including orders entered on behalf of their constituents.

Trades generated on the system are irrevocable and 'locked in'. The exchange specifies from time to time the market types and the manner if any, in which trade cancellation can be effected. Where a trade cancellation is permitted and trading member wishes to cancel a trade, it can be done only with the approval of the exchange.

Margin requirements

Subject to the provisions as contained in the exchange by-laws and such other regulations as may be in force, every clearing member, in respect of the trades in which he is party to, has to deposit a margin with exchange authorities.

The exchange prescribes from time to time the commodities/ derivative contracts, the settlement periods and trade types for which margin would be attracted. The exchange levies initial margin on derivatives contracts using the concept of Value at Risk (VaR) or any other concept as the exchange may decide from time to time. The margin is charged so as to cover one-day loss that can be encountered on the position on 99% of the days. Additional margins may be levied for deliverable positions, on the basis of VaR from the expiry of the contract till the actual settlement date plus a mark-up for default. The margin has to be deposited with the exchange within the time notified by the exchange. The exchange also prescribes categories of securities that would be eligible for a margin deposit, as well as the method of valuation and amount of securities that would be required to be deposited against the margin amount. The procedure for refund/ adjustment of margins is also specified by the exchange from time to time. The exchange can impose upon any particular trading member or category of trading member any special or other margin requirement. On failure to deposit margin/s as required under this clause, the exchange/clearing house can withdraw the trading facility of the trading member. After the pay-out, the clearing house releases all margins.

Unfair trading practices

No trading member should buy or sell, deal in derivatives contracts in a fraudulent manner, or indulge in any unfair trade practices including market manipulation.

This includes the following:

- Effect; take part either directly or indirectly in transactions, which are likely to have effect of artificially, raising or depressing the prices of spot/ derivatives contracts.
- Indulge in any act, which is calculated to create a false or misleading appearance of trading, resulting in reflection of prices, which are not genuine.
- Buy, sell commodities/ contracts on his own behalf or on behalf of a person associated with him pending the execution of the order of his constituent or of his company or director for the same contract.
- Delay the transfer of commodities in the name of the transferee.
- Indulge in falsification of his books, accounts and records for the purpose of market manipulation.
- When acting as an agent, execute a transaction with a constituent at a price other than the price at which it was executed on the exchange.
- Either take opposite position to an order of a constituent or execute opposite orders which he is holding in respect of two constituents except in the manner laid down by the exchange.

Clearing

National Securities Clearing Corporation Limited (NSCCL) undertakes clearing of trades executed on the NCDEX. All deals executed on the Exchange are cleared and settled by the trading members on the settlement date by the trading members themselves as clearing members or through other professional clearing members in accordance with these regulations, by-laws and rules of the exchange.

Last day of trading

Last trading day for a derivative contract in any commodity is the date as specified in the respective commodity contract. If the last trading day as specified in the respective commodity contract is a holiday, the last trading day is taken to be the previous working day of exchange.

On the expiry date of contracts, the trading members/ clearing members have to give delivery information as prescribed by the exchange from time to time. If a trading member/ clearing member fails to submit such information during the trading hours on the expiry date for the contract, the deals have to be settled as per the settlement calendar applicable for such deals, in cash together with penalty as stipulated by the exchange.

Delivery

Delivery can be done either through the clearing house or outside the clearing house. On the expiry date, during the trading hours, the exchange provides a window on the trading system to submit delivery information for all open positions.

After the trading hours on the expiry date, based on the available information, the matching for deliveries takes place. firstly, on the basis of locations and then randomly keeping in view the factors such as available capacity of the vault/ warehouse, commodities already deposited and dematerialized and offered for delivery and any other factor as may be specified by the exchange from time to time. Matching done is binding on the clearing members. After completion of the matching process, clearing members are informed of the deliverable/ receivable positions and the unmatched positions. Unmatched positions have to be settled in cash.

The cash settlement is only for the incremental gain/ loss as determined on the basis of the final settlement price. All matched and unmatched positions are settled in accordance with the applicable settlement calendar.

The exchange may allow an alternate mode of settlement between the constituents directly provided that both the constituents through their respective clearing members notify the exchange before the closing of trading hours on the expiry date. They have to mention their preferred identified counter-party and the deliverable quantity, along with other details required by the exchange. The exchange however, is not responsible or liable for such settlements or any consequence of such alternate mode of settlements. If the information provided by the buyer/ seller clearing members fails to match, then the open position would be settled in cash together with penalty as may be stipulated by the exchange.

The clearing members are allowed to deliver their obligations before the pay in date as per applicable settlement calendar, whereby the clearing house can reduce the margin requirement to that extent.

The exchange specifies the parameters and methodology for premium/ discount, as the case may be, from time to time for the quality/ quantity differential, sales tax, taxes, government levies/ fees if any. Pay in/ Pay out for such additional obligations is settled on the supplemental settlement date as specified in the settlement calendar.

Procedure for payment of sales tax/VAT

The exchange prescribes procedure for payment of sales tax/VAT or any other state/ local/central tax/fee applicable to the deals culminating into sale with physical delivery of commodities. All members have to ensure that their respective constituents, who intend to take or give delivery of commodity, are registered with sales tax authorities of all such states in which the exchange has a delivery center for a particular commodity in which constituent has or is expected to have open positions. Members have to maintain records/details of sales tax registration of each of such constituent and furnish the same to the exchange as and when required.

The seller is responsible for payment of sales tax/VAT, however the seller is entitled to recover from the buyer, the sales tax and other taxes levied under the local state sales tax law to the extent permitted by law. In no event is the exchange/ clearing house liable for payment of sales tax/VAT or any other local tax, fees, levies etc.

Penalties for defaults

In the event of a default by the seller or the buyer in delivery of commodities or payment of the price, the exchange closes out the derivatives contracts and imposes penalties on the defaulting buyer or seller, as the case may be. It can also use the margins deposited by such clearing member to recover the loss. The settlement for the defaults in delivery is to be done in cash within the period as prescribed by the exchange at the highest price from the last trading date till the final settlement date with a mark up thereon as may be decided from time to time.

Process of dematerialization

Dematerialization refers to the issue of an electronic credit, instead of a vault/ warehouse receipt, to the depositor against the deposit of commodity. Any person (a constituent) seeking to dematerialize a commodity has to open an account with an approved depository participant (DP). The exchange provides the list of approved DPs from time to time. In case of commodities (other than precious metals) the constituent delivers the commodity to the exchange-approved warehouses. The commodity brought by the constituent is checked for the quality by the exchange-approved assayers before the deposit of the same is accepted by the warehouse. If the quality of the commodity is as per the norms defined and notified by the exchange from time to time, the warehouse accepts the commodity and sends confirmation in the requisite format to the R & T agent who upon verification, confirms the deposit of such commodity to the depository for giving credit to the demat account of the said constituent.

In case of precious metals, the commodity must be accompanied with the assayers' certificate. The vault accepts the precious metal, after verifying the contents of assayers certificate with the precious metal being deposited. On acceptance, the vault issues an acknowledgement to the constituent and sends confirmation in the requisite format to the R & T agent who upon verification, confirms the deposit of such precious metal to the depository for giving credit to the demat account of the said constituent.

Validity date

In case of commodities having validity date assigned to it by the approved assayer, the delivery of the commodity upon expiry of validity date is not considered a good delivery. The clearing member has to ensure that his concerned constituent removes the commodities on or before the expiry of validity date for such commodities. For the depository, commodities, which have reached the trading validity date, are moved out of the electronic deliverable quantity. Such commodities are suspended from delivery. The constituent has to rematerialize such quantity and remove the same from the warehouse. Failure to remove deliveries after the validity date from warehouse is levied with penalty as specified by the relevant authority from time to time.

Process of dematerialization

Re-materialization refers to the issue of physical delivery against the credit in the demat account of the constituent. The constituent seeking to rematerialize his commodity holding has to make a request to his DP in the prescribed format and the DP then routes his request through the depository system to the R &T agent issues the authorization addressed to the vault/ warehouse to release physical delivery to the constituent. The vault/warehouse on receipt of such authorization releases the commodity to the constituent or constituent's authorized person upon verifying the identity.

Delivery through the depository clearing system

Delivery in respect of all deals for the clearing in commodities happens through the depository clearing system. The delivery through the depository clearing system into the account of the buyer with the depository participant is deemed to be delivery, notwithstanding that the commodities are located in the warehouse along with the commodities of other constituents.

Payment through the clearing bank

Payment in respect of all deals for the clearing has to be made through the clearing bank(s); Provided however that the deals of sales and purchase executed between different constituents of the same clearing member in the same settlement, shall be offset by process of netting to arrive at net obligations.

Clearing and Settlement Process

The relevant authority from time to time fixes the various clearing days, the pay-in and pay-out days and the scheduled time to be observed in connection with the clearing and settlement operations of deals in commodities/ futures contracts.

Settlement obligations statements for TCMs

The exchange generates and provides to each trading clearing member, settlement obligations statements showing the quantities of the different kinds of commodities for which delivery/ deliveries is/ are to be given and/ or taken and the funds payable or receivable by him in his capacity as clearing member and by professional clearing member for deals made by him for which the clearing Member has confirmed acceptance to settle. The obligations statement is deemed to be confirmed by the trading member for which deliveries are to be given and/ or taken and funds to be debited and/ or credited to his account as specified in the obligations statements and deemed instructions to the clearing banks/ institutions for the same.

Settlement obligations statements for PCMs

The exchange/ clearing house generates and provides to each professional clearing member, settlement obligations statements showing the quantities of the different kinds of commodities for which delivery/ deliveries is/ are to be given and/ or taken and the funds payable or receivable by him. The settlement obligation statement is deemed to have been confirmed by the said clearing member in respect of every and all obligations enlisted therein.

Delivery of Commodities

Based on the settlement obligations statements, the exchange generates delivery statement and receipt statement for each clearing member. The delivery and receipt statement contains details of commodities to be delivered to and received from other clearing members, the details of the corresponding buying/ selling constituent and such other details. The delivery and receipt statements are deemed to be confirmed by respective member to deliver and receive on account of his constituent, commodities as specified in the delivery and receipt statements.

On respective pay-in day, clearing members effect depository delivery in the depository clearing system as per delivery statement in respect of depository deals. Delivery has to be made in terms of the delivery units notified by the exchange. Commodities, which are to be received by a clearing member, are delivered to him in the depository clearing system in respect of depository deals on the respective pay-out day as per instructions of the exchange/ clearing house.

Delivery units

The exchange specifies from time to time the delivery units for all commodities admitted to dealings on the exchange. Electronic delivery is available for trading before expiry of the validity date. The exchange also specifies from time to time the variations permissible in delivery units as per those stated in contract specifications.

Depository clearing system

The exchange specifies depository(s) through which depository delivery can be effected and which shall act as agents for settlement of depository deals, for the collection of margins by way of securities for all deals entered into through the exchange, for any other commodities movement and transfer in a depository(s) between clearing members and the exchange and between clearing member to clearing member as may be directed by the relevant authority from time to time.

Every clearing member must have a clearing account with any of the Depository Participants of specified depositories. Clearing Members operate the clearing account only for the purpose of settlement of depository deals entered through the exchange, for the collection of margins by way of commodities for deals entered into through the exchange. The clearing member cannot operate the clearing account for any other purpose.

Clearing members are required to authorize the specified depositories and depository participants with whom they have a clearing account to access their clearing account for debiting and crediting their accounts as per instructions received from the exchange and to report balances and other credit information to the exchange.

Improving the Functioning of the Commodities Markets

India is rapidly doing away with its barriers on commodity imports and exports, opening up the country's commodity sector to foreign competition. In order for the domestic industry to be able to compete on an equal footing to its counterparts in other countries, India must develop commodity exchanges that meet international standards in the areas of market integrity, financial integrity and customer protection. Unless these standards are met, exchanges will make only minor contributions to the growth and stability of the Indian economy, and international firms and large domestic firms with significant hedging needs will not use these exchanges.

The thirty-year ban on futures exchanges has had an adverse repercussion on the growth and functioning of Indian commodity exchanges. It has forced people, skills and money to flow to other markets, leaving an older generation of traders in charge not in tune with the new market infrastructure and regulatory practices. While commodity exchanges have done remarkably well in the face of adverse conditions, these conditions have now changed. What was appropriate for the exchanges in the mid-1990s is no longer so today. The FMC has been trying to modernize the exchanges by regulating the functioning of the exchanges. Many of the commodity exchanges are now responding and have been making efforts to deal with their problems and imperfections.

India needs a more efficient, more comprehensive commodity futures industry. This futures industry should be organized in line with best international practice. That is to say, the system must rely to the extent possible on self-regulation (with powers vested in the exchanges and in the brokerage community, and the government's regulatory role limited to setting the general framework and ensuring that exchange- and broker-level self-regulation works properly); enable very low transaction costs; be financially secured; and be dynamic. This chapter discusses recommendations to exchanges on how they can modernize. It starts with a discussion of governance issues, and then moves into a discussion of market surveillance and clearing. Recommendations are given on contract design and delivery issues. The role of brokers, and how to modernize the brokerage community, is also discussed. The chapter concludes with other essential support functions that exchanges need to provide.

Management of Commodity Exchanges

One of the main issues in setting up effective exchanges is credible corporate governance. The current trend in the international markets is for ownership and access to exchanges to be separate issues, i.e. de-mutualization of Commodities Exchanges. Owners, i.e. shareholders, can have access to trading rights, but trading right holders need not be owners. In any case, the management of the exchange needs to be strictly independent of the brokers and end-users. Without this separation, the integrity of the exchange will be in question and it will be difficult or impossible to develop liquidity. In addition, in order to run the exchange efficiently, committees need to be set up to act as a sounding board for the management of the exchange, and to assist in the exchange's self-regulation and strategic planning.

The exchanges in India are all mutual organizations, like has traditionally been the case in the West. However, de-mutualization can have a number of advantages, as below:

- It provides the ability to respond and adapt to a fast-moving world, and to compete with new forms of electronic trade (such as Business-to-Business Internet exchanges);
- It can leverage the brand name of the exchange; and alliances can be created, for example with financial firms or technology providers.
- It enables the exchange to tap into equity capital, necessary for expansion.

Even though the vested interests of traders on an open-outcry, mutually owned exchange makes it very difficult to de-mutualize, most western exchanges have taken this step in recent years.

The exchange needs a Board, appointed executives, and independent committees. The Board is there to set exchange policy and to be the ultimate supervisors of the exchange as a business, but should delegate the running of the exchange and its administration to appointed executives. The constitution of the board should represent the trading members and broker representatives of the exchange together with the Chief Executive of the exchange, certain non-executive directors, some of whom may be lay-directors. This board will oversee the running of the exchange and will decide upon the delegation of certain aspects of the strategy to separate committees.

The appointed Executives and their staff are charged to act in compliance with its regulations. In their day-to-day functions, they should be strictly independent of the board, the members and the end-users. This will ensure the integrity of the exchange and will prevent trading interests from influencing decision-making.

Committees appointed by the Board should address issues such as business development and product design, legal and arbitration, marketing and other issues. Committees should comprise exchange staff and members as well as users to advise the board and to advise exchange staff on technical issues. Members of exchange committees need to be able to make decisions on the basis of rules and guidelines, rather than based on particular interests. Providing transparency (regular reporting) on the functioning of committees helps to ensure fair decision-making.

Cash Settlement System vs. Physical Settlement System

The Indian Commodities Exchanges are based on the system of physical delivery of the underlying commodities. Physical settlement involves the physical delivery of the underlying commodity, typically at an accredited warehouse. The seller intending to make delivery would have to take the commodities to the designated warehouse and the buyer intending to take delivery would have to go to the designated warehouse and pick up the commodity. The physical settlement of commodities is a complex process. The issues faced in physical settlement are enormous, such as:

Warehousing Problems

In case of physical settlement, the seller has to hand over the commodity and the buyer must take physical delivery of the underlying asset. This requires the exchange to make an arrangement with warehouses to handle the settlements. Thus, the efficacy of the commodities settlements depends on the warehousing system available. Most international commodity exchanges used certified warehouses (CWH) for the purpose of handling physical settlements. Such CWH are required to provide storage facilities for participants in the commodities markets and to certify the quantity and quality of the underlying commodity. The advantage of this system is that a warehouse receipt becomes a good collateral, not just for settlement of exchange trades but also for other purposes too. However, in India, the warehousing system is not as efficient as it is in some of the other developed markets. Central and state government controlled warehouses are the major providers of agri-produce storage facilities. Apart from these, there are a few private warehousing being maintained. However there is no clear regulatory oversight of warehousing services. Also, there are limits on storage facilities in different states.

Quality of Underlying Assets

The quality of the underlying asset is of prime importance. There may be quite some variation in the quality of what is available in the marketplace. Commodity derivatives demand good standards and quality assurance/ certification procedures. A good grading system is required for commodities to be traded. Currently there are various agencies that are responsible for specifying grades for commodities. For example, the Bureau of Indian Standards (BIS) under Ministry of Consumer Affairs specifies standards for processed agricultural commodities whereas AGMARK under the department of rural development under Ministry of Agriculture is responsible for promulgating standards for basic agricultural commodities. Apart from these, there are other agencies like EIA, which specify standards for export oriented commodities.

Transportation Related Issues

There are restrictions on interstate movement of commodities. Different states have their own rules and regulations' regarding movement of commodities within and outside their boundaries and this poses a great problem in smooth functioning of the commodities exchanges.

Besides state level octroi and duties have an impact on the cost of movement of goods across locations. These costs are not truly reflected in the futures and spot prices, thereby leaving a scope for arbitrage.

In light of the above problems being faced in the proper functioning of the commodities exchange, a shift from the physical settlement system of commodities to cash settlement system seems to be imminent. Cash settlement system does not involve any physical movement or transfer of any commodity. It involves paying up the differences in prices between the time the contract was entered into and the time the contract was closed. Under Cash settlement system, the problems of logistics of transportation, Quality, warehousing, taxes etc will be solved and the scope of arbitrage will be limited, thereby providing a level playing field for all the investors and making the market efficient.

Market Monitoring and Surveillance

The ability of a futures exchange to function properly depends in part upon the ability of the exchange and its regulators to ensure that prices of contracts traded on the exchange reflect supply and demand. In order to do this, the rules governing exchange operations must be price neutral and must be sufficient to detect and deter attempts to manipulate prices—market integrity should be impeccable.

Good market monitoring and surveillance is needed to ensure protection of market users and investors, which in turn should stimulate demand liquidity and turnover. The surveillance and monitoring environment should operate in parallel to and be proportionate with the commercial interests of the exchange. The conditions in Indian commodity exchanges have implications for the market surveillance function at the exchange level. Open outcry trading, which is recognized to be more difficult to human errors and intervention, is widely prevalent and preferred by market participants.

Proper market monitoring and surveillance has the following elements:

- A sound framework for regulation and compliance;
- Proper controls over floor trading practices;
- Properly enforced regulation for exchange members/brokers;

- A well-performing clearing system;
- A well-managed delivery system;
- The capacity to detect market manipulation attempts, and act in a timely manner.

Regulations and Compliance

The overall authority for regulation and compliance rests with the Board of the exchange and is performed via its executive. There should be a strict division between the commercial and marketing function of the exchange on the one hand and its regulatory and compliance disciplines on the other. The regulatory division should ensure that the confidentiality of any sensitive or commercial information required for regulatory and monitoring purposes is preserved and segregated. This may also require additional physical security measures, which would limit physical access to the regulatory and compliance areas within the exchange offices.

The exchange needs clear, written rules and procedures for regulation and compliance (and persons assigned to ensure that these rules and procedures are followed) in a number of areas:

- Market floor operations
- Electronic trading operations (where appropriate)
- Market surveillance (monitoring market activity)
- Member surveillance (to ascertain that members are acting in compliance with the exchange rules and that their procedures and systems promote a sound basis for their exchange activities)
- Investigation (into any breaches of exchange rules and regulations)
- Enforcement (where the exchange believes that there has been an identifiable breach of its rules, the matter might be referred to internal enforcement lawyers for consideration of formal disciplinary action as provided for within the exchange rules).

All modern exchanges whether screen-based or open outcry, rely on electronics technology to transmit orders, record trades, construct audit trails, and monitor surveillance. Through a reliable and sophisticated audit trail, the commodity exchange should be able to follow every stage of the transaction process. Exchange staff should focus on monitoring floor trading practices, review (through computer assistance) members' records and analyze trading data compiled through the clearing process. The exchange should also monitor the financial solvency of its members' firms (particularly during periods of volatile market activity).

Controlling Floor Trading

The procedures for order execution and floor trading should be recorded either in the rules of the exchange or in a separate procedural manual. They should be vigorously enforced by the exchange.

Exchanges need to guarantee that orders reaching the market floor and the price discovery mechanisms between trading members on the floor are conducted openly in accordance with the regulations. The resulting trades must be confirmed in a timely fashion thereafter and submitted to the clearing system.

Only licensed brokers/traders and exchange staff should have access to the trading floor during trading hours. Exchange officials need to monitor and control floor trading, to ensure that traders act within the rules of the exchange. Floor rules may range across the whole gamut of regulations—from banning eating on the floor and vandalizing booths to protection of customer orders. The exchange floor teams should blend in with the rest of the floor population. Individuals should be rotated in their jobs at regular intervals, say every six months, in order to keep fresh and to avoid any collusion with traders. Some exchanges use video and sound recording within the trading area, which can be used to review trading situations.

While exchange officials should be responsible for detecting abuses of the rules, a Floor Committee should be empowered to enforce discipline. Their roles may include resolution of minor disputes, decisions concerning the setting of end-of-day closing prices and of any disciplinary matter concerning conduct on the exchange floor. At a higher level the exchange should have the authority to impose strict controls which may include fines and restriction of members from trading. There should be a strict procedure governing the manner in which closing prices (daily or at delivery month expiry) are determined. This should not be left to the traders but must be an exchange official's decision. The accuracy of these prices must be guaranteed by the exchange.

Senior market operations employees should be members of any price quotations committee and floor disciplinary committee. The former would have the responsibility for determining official prices at the close of each day in each commodity. The latter would have the power to impose, on the spot, fines on individual dealers who have committed dealing offences, or to refer cases to a higher disciplinary body

Regulating Members: the Exchanges' Responsibilities Vetting Members/Brokers

Exchanges and their clearing corporations should have stringent rules as to the approval of and acceptance into membership of applicant companies. These rules should cover the financial integrity of the company concerned, its ownership, and the quality of its procedures and staff.

In order to verify the financial strength and compliance of member firms, the exchange should audit the financial books and records of the members. Their compliance with the rules should be strictly checked and enforced. The members must provide evidence of their financial status and that they have appropriate policies and procedures for providing accurate financial returns.

It will also be necessary for the exchange to satisfy themselves as to the expertise of the managers and the owners of the business and their rationale in wishing to use the exchange products. Why are they using these products? What are their intentions and how expert are they and what is their previous track record of activity in commodity markets?

Those applying to become member/broker must prove that they maintain effective operational and risk management procedures. Furthermore, they must be in compliance with exchange rules and standards of good practice. The company should have "fit and proper" staff, suitably qualified and experienced. Only individuals who have been trained and licensed, and have passed an examination set by the exchange should be permitted to trade on the floor. There should also be a time pėriod attached to this so that all traders are shown to have effectively served an apprenticeship and have the necessary experience to become qualified traders.

Protecting customers

The compliance officers of the exchange need to ensure that customers' orders are transmitted to the floor without any delay and that there should be no malpractice in respect of broker's front-running orders or withholding orders or failing to offer them to the market at the right time. If trading members are found to be colluding, doing pre-arranged deals, they should be fined or banned from trading.

This implies that it should be obligatory for brokers to maintain accurate records. The exchange should have the right to audit those records so that they are able to investigate cases of malpractice, under their overall responsibility for operating an orderly market.

Each exchange needs to have a risk-monitoring group to investigate any complaints from customers or members in connection with market trading. They should also conduct random checks. These may take various forms. One technique is to investigate particular deals, possibly market crosses for example, and establish precisely the whole audit trail for those deals. Sometimes they might also decide to undertake a complete audit into one firm's activity during one day.

Safeguarding the exchange's financial status

Any trading member has to have his or her trades guaranteed by himself or herself or by another member of the clearing organization, over and above his margin requirement. It may therefore be necessary from time to time for a clearing member to prevent a trading member from fulfilling any additional trades or stipulating then only trades can be carried out to reduce or close positions. The exchange needs to monitor these aspects and must have surveillance procedures in place to do so. Only with timely recording of trades and their entry into computer systems to check against the necessary limits under a risk management environment can this be successfully achieved.

Clearing

A strong and reliable clearing house is perhaps the single most important factor for instilling trust in an exchange among a wider public. Clearing houses or clearing departments play a major role in facilitating trade, and providing safety. They essentially perform the functions of trade clearing (the process of collecting trade information, matching trades, interposing the clearing house as a counterparty to each trade) and trade settlement (the process whereby clearing payments, margins and final payments are collected and distributed). While the clearing house does not deal directly with clients, it plays a crucial role in ensuring the financial integrity of the market and providing assurance to clients by providing strong margining and risk management procedures. The clearing house sets a range of measures in order to provide adequate protection to the clients of exchanges members.

The main set of measures concerns margining procedures and margin levels. The rules for contract margining in futures and options markets are fairly standard throughout the world. There are various systems and algorithms, which basically all perform the same crucial function – the margin called from the clearing members and from users of the market fairly represents the risk that the clearing corporation and the brokers are taking.

Margin rates must be reviewed continuously. Historical volatility and current market conditions are considered across all contracts in determining appropriate margin levels. Generally they would be set to cover a full day's price change. Sometimes a higher level of margin is employed on certain markets for speculative customer positions.

In addition to the above, the clearing house/department also needs to ensure that trades are within a firm's financial capacity by large position reporting. Action must be taken early to ensure that positions do not become too large for the members to manage and to ensure that customer positions do not become too unwieldy for the customers themselves to manage. Members must make daily notification to the exchange of all large positions above a certain declared threshold—for customers, non-customers and proprietary accounts. The exchange will analyze this information by comparing the financial exposure of a particular trader to the firm's capital. Furthermore, the exchange should have the ability within its risk management systems to forecast potential market exposures by conducting "what if?" scenarios on large trader positions. In this way, risk managers can estimate the impact of a particular set of positions if the market moves up or down by a designated amount.

Detecting, preventing and coping with market manipulation attempts

Exchanges and clearing houses should ensure that no problems are likely to occur as delivery approaches. The parties who hold long positions also need to be monitored, to ensure that they are able to take delivery, and pay the full contract value for the contracts upon delivery.

The clearing corporation should also employ strict margining procedures at the time of deliveries, which will ensure that additional margins are held from those trading members who are holding the short and long positions in the spot delivery month.

The exchange risk-monitoring group must monitor the spot position daily and physical (deliverable) stocks at least weekly. They maintain open interest figures for all members and record positions over a certain size (say 10 lots or 100 lots, depending on the market. They need to know what the intentions of large position holders are as the delivery month approaches (insisting to see evidence of physical positions held in the cash market, and verify this information). They must monitor any unusual positions or unusual trading activity, looking for concentration of positions and unusual sizes of positions. They should observe price differences and seasonal factors. They should compare between one delivery month and the next (asking – "Is this typically what happens with this member during a delivery period?"). For all this, they should use a computerized risk management system. This would combine details of positions held and of the financial strength of members, make comparisons and generate warnings. The clearing house, if separate, would conduct a similar exercise in parallel.

In the event that action needs to be taken to contain an undesirable situation in the market, such as a disorderly market, the board should be able to delegate full powers to a special committee. The members of the committee would not have any active commercial interest in the exchange markets. This will ensure that action can be taken on the basis of confidential regulatory information without any conflicts of interest arising. The constitution of such a committee should be drawn from non-executive members of the Board and would include the executive responsible for compliance and regulation. To further avoid suspicion on the acts of exchanges in the case of disorderly markets, FMC should require that decisions such as relaxation in daily/periodic price limits, or changes in net open position volume limits or special margin requirements, are approved by two-thirds or three-quarters of those Board members present and by all or larger number of the independent directors present at the meeting.

Failure to deliver should be punished severely, and delays in delivery should be fined. The clearing house will take the lead in managing such default situations.

Expanding the Role of Exchanges

An exchange that is to remain viable needs strong public relations, training, analysis and research departments,

a) To serve its members;
b) To expand its reach; and
c) To develop new contracts.

Even with credible exchange management – and implementation of (probably Internet-based) technology and adequate contract design – liquidity will not just come. The exchanges will have to be marketed aggressively to a wide range of potential users, from domestic traders and financial institutions to international traders and financial institutions to retail speculators (again, domestic and international) and, ultimately, commodity funds.

One easy way for the exchanges to make themselves more visible is to improve their price dissemination by:

1. Making prices available immediately after closing to all companies which ask for it.
2. Distributing these price data also to all newspapers.
3. Negotiating with one of the news vendors (Reuters, Knight Ridder, Dow Jones) that they distribute prices.
4. Actively exploring other possibilities for the dissemination of prices, e.g., a fax sheet exhibited at rural markets, or radio or television emissions.

As a further element in their marketing strategy, exchanges should prepare reports which explain the use of the exchange by various groups, e.g. farmers, processors, banks, pension funds, etc. In addition, accountants, auditors, tax officials, software providers, regulators and decision makers such as company directors also need to be aware of the role futures play in risk management and the impact of futures on the underlying industry. Given that these materials strongly overlap between exchanges, it would be most effective if these materials were developed in cooperation among the exchanges.

To better serve their members, exchanges should also prepare reports which analyze the relationship between the futures market and the underlying physical market, e.g., basis developments or seasonal tendencies.

Exchange should provide comprehensive training programmes to their staff, their members and end-users (the customers, the farmers, the producers and similar entities). The potential exists to develop these markets into the fund management communities, just as has been the case in more sophisticated Western markets.

Training for staff should encompass exchange executives as well as exchange members. One of its key functions should be to create a better understanding of the need for proper trade execution, reporting, etc., if exchanges are to expend their volumes. Exchanges should also train their staff in specialized skills, such as surveillance, so that they are able to detect threats to market integrity.

Exchange staff needs to be able to analyze possibilities to introduce new contracts, and if deemed feasible, elaborate contract specifications. This makes it possible that decisions on which commodity contract to trade are left to the exchange, and not taken by the FMC. The Exchange authorities will have an interest in coming up with the contract with the best liquidity potential. Competition among exchanges will be healthy as they seek to attract the greatest number of market participants as exchange members or non-members.

19

Case Study: Study of Selected Commodity Derivatives

The main objective of this case study is to comment upon the three key parameters of – Efficiency, Liquidity and Volatility – in the Commodities Market. Accordingly, this case study has been divided into four parts, each dealing with the specific aspect. These broad areas are:

1. Descriptive Statistics
2. Efficiency in Commodities Markets
3. Volatility in Future Prices
4. Liquidity levels in Commodities Markets

DESCRIPTION OF THE VARIABLES

A thorough analysis of the data has been done. The descriptive statistics of the variables can be classified into two broad areas—General Descriptives and Correlation Analysis.

General Descriptives

Descriptive Statistics describe patterns and general trends in a data set. They help us in finding out whether the distribution is symmetrical or not. In other words, descriptives help us in finding out whether the time-series of data we have form is a normal distribution or not. The major components of any descriptive series are Mean, Standard Deviation, Skewness and Kurtosis.

Mean is a measure of central tendency and gives a single description of the average or typical score in the distribution. Standard Deviation is a measure of dispersion. It is a measure of variability and quantifies how spreads out the scores are in the distribution. The last two measures, namely, Skewness and Kurtosis are also important descriptive measures which help us in commenting upon the symmetry of the distribution, whether they are normal or asymmetrical.

For a normal distribution, both Skewness and Kurtosis are zero and there is a perfect symmetrical distribution. However, if the distribution is asymmetric, it is either positively skewed or negatively skewed, thereby implying the concentration of the data towards the lower end of the scale or towards the upper end of the scale, respectively. Also, asymmetrical distribution is either Platykurtic or Leptokurtic, implying relative concentration of the data towards tails or peakedness at the centre, respectively. The basic descriptives for the time series of five commodities can be found in the following Tables 19.1 to 19.5.

Table 19.1. Descriptive Statistics of Brent Crude Oil Future Prices

	N	Mean		Std.	Skewness		Kurtosis
	Statistic	Statistic	Statistic	Ststistic	Std. Error	Statistic	Std. Error
Brent One	439	2882.9021	313.95345	.633	.117	-.650	.233
Brent Two	415	2941.8819	315.39121	.546	.120	-.847	.239
Brent Three	411	2988.3345	297.78685	.666	.120	-.837	.240
Valid N (listwise)	411						

Table 19.2. Descriptive Statistics of Chana Future Prices

	N	Mean		Std.	Skewness		Kurtosis
	Statistic	Statistic	Statistic	Ststistic	Std. Error	Statistic	Std. Error
Chana 1 month	870	1993.8414	495.04935	.834	.083	-.296	.166
Chana 2 month	870	1980.1241	488.91725	1.007	.083	-.029	.166
Chana 3 month	852	1956.2746	458.26708	1.002	.084	-.122	.167
Valid N (listwise)	852						

Table 19.3. Descriptive Statistics of Gold Future Prices

	N	Mean		Std.	Skewness		Kurtosis
	Statistic	Statistic	Statistic	Ststistic	Std. Error	Statistic	Std. Error
Gold 1 month	949	7364.0078	1428.027	.512	.079	-1.357	.159
Gold 2 month	931	7343.5816	1439.286	.594	.080	-1.248	.160
Gold 3 month	896	7326.7964	1448.429	.669	.082	-1.126	.163
Valid N (listwise)	896						

Table 19.4. Descriptive Statistics of Mustard Seed Future Prices

	N	Mean	Std.	Skewness		Kurtosis	
	Statistic	Statistic	Statistic	Ststistic	Std. Error	Statistic	Std. Error
Mustard 1 month	890	362.4688	23.70883	.883	.082	.464	.164
Mustard 2 month	878	363.6920	24.71683	.579	.083	-.079	.165
Mustard 3 month	927	365.0260	27.37349	.889	.080	.758	.160
Valid N (listwise)	878						

Table 19.5. Descriptive Statistics of Silver Future Prices

	N	Mean	Std.	Skewness		Kurtosis	
	Statistic	Statistic	Statistic	Ststistic	Std. Error	Statistic	Std. Error
Silver 1 month	974	13327.61	3819.875	.731	.078	-1.080	.157
Silver 2 month	958	13248.72	3810.145	.805	.079	-.940	.158
Silver 3 month	922	13169.66	3762.843	.877	.081	-.780	.161
Valid N (listwise)	922						

From the tables we can infer that the Skewness and Kurtosis levels are not very small, in either direction but somewhere it is. Now, we need to analyze whether the degrees of Skewness or Kurtosis for the different positions for the five commodities are significant or not.

This is found out by comparing the numerical value for Skewness/Kurtosis with twice the Standard Error of Skewness/Kurtosis and includes the range from minus twice the standard error to plus twice the standard error. If this value falls within this range, the Skewness/Kurtosis is considered insignificant and the distribution is normal. On the other hand, if it doesn't fall within this range, we conclude that the Skewness/Kurtosis is significant and the distribution is significantly non-normal.

From the results we have, we can say that the degrees of Skewness and Kurtosis for maximum positions of all commodities are significant and the distribution is non-normal, by the above rule. For example, for Gold One Month position, we can infer the following results:

1. Std. Error of Skewness is -0.158 to 0.158 ($\pm$ 2 $\times$ 0.079) and the value for Skewness is .512, which do not fall within this range. So the Skewness is not negligible.
2. Std. Error of Kurtosis is -0.318 to 0.318 (2 $\times$ 0.159) and the value for Kurtosis is -1.357, which also does not fall within this range. So the Kurtosis is also not negligible.

On the basis of the above, we can say that the distribution is non-symmetrical and does not approximate to normal distribution. This can also be verified by plotting the normal distribution graph.

From Fig. 19.1, it is clear that the distribution is not symmetrical on both the sides. So, we can conclude that the time series of future prices for one month position for gold forms a non-normal distribution.

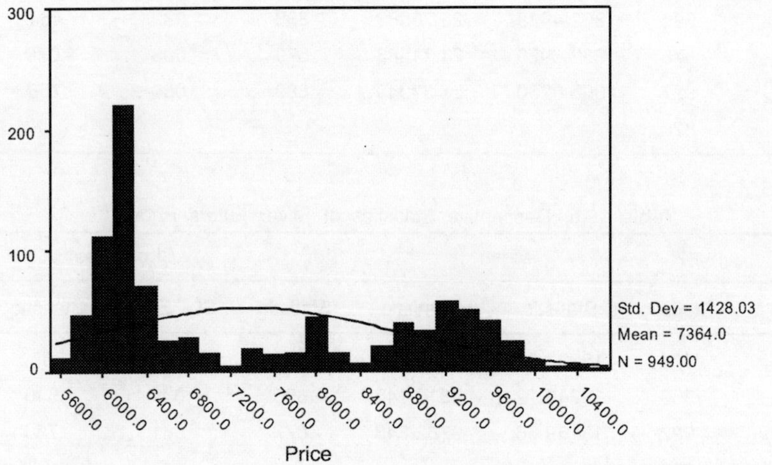

Fig. 19.1. Histogram of Gold 1-month Position (With Normal Distribution Curve)

Similarly, by using the same above rule, we can find out that the Skewness and Kurtosis levels for maximum positions for all commodities, are not normally distributed. In the following Figures (19.2 to 19.5), just the one month position for all the commodities has been plotted. All of them are not normally distributed.

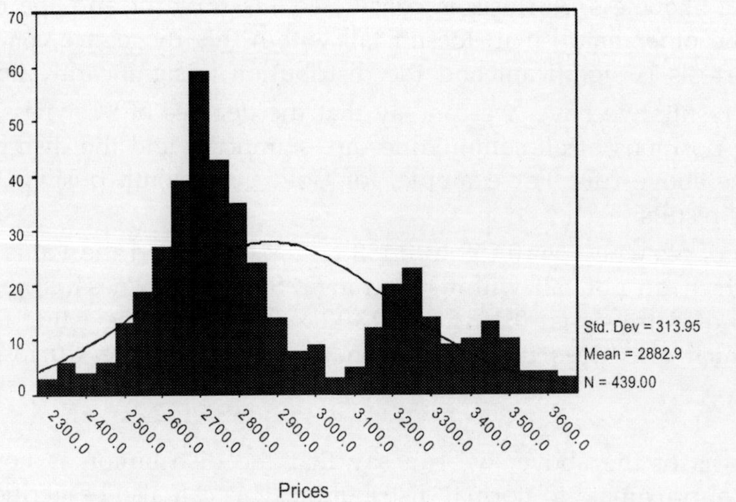

Fig. 19.2. Histogram of Brent Crude Oil 1-month Position (With Normal Distribution Curve)

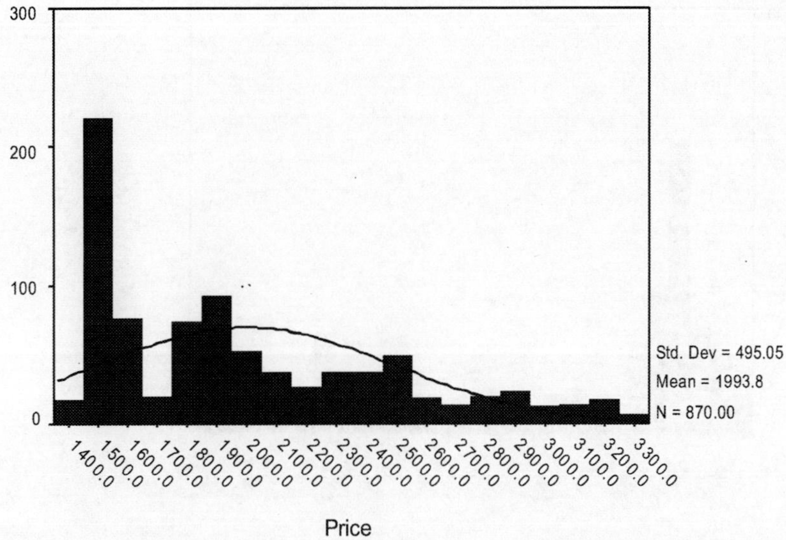

Fig. 19.3. Histogram of Chana 1-month Position (With Normal Distribution Curve)

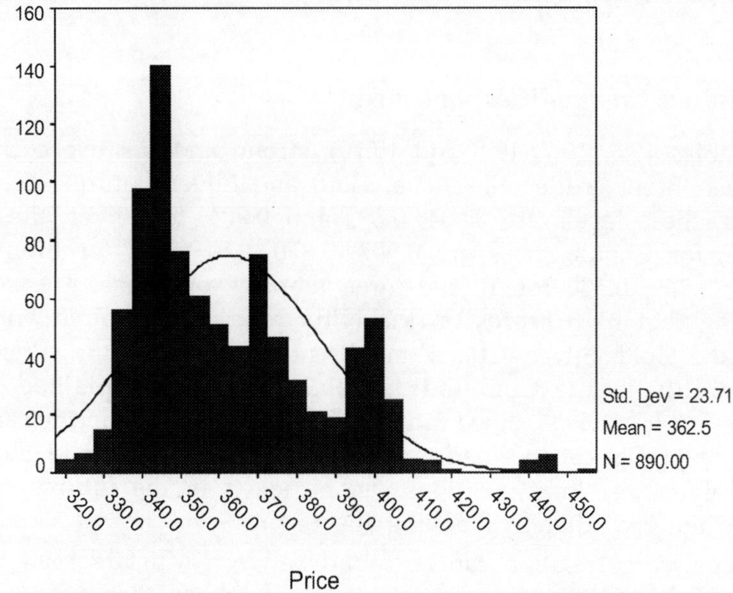

Fig. 19.4. Histogram of Mustard Seed 1-month Position (With Normal Distribution Curve)

Correlation Analysis

Correlation analysis is the statistical tool which helps to describe the degree to which one variable is linearly related to another. Since no analysis can be done in isolation from the various other variables, which directly or indirectly has an impact on it, therefore various correlations have been computed between the commodities and these other variables.

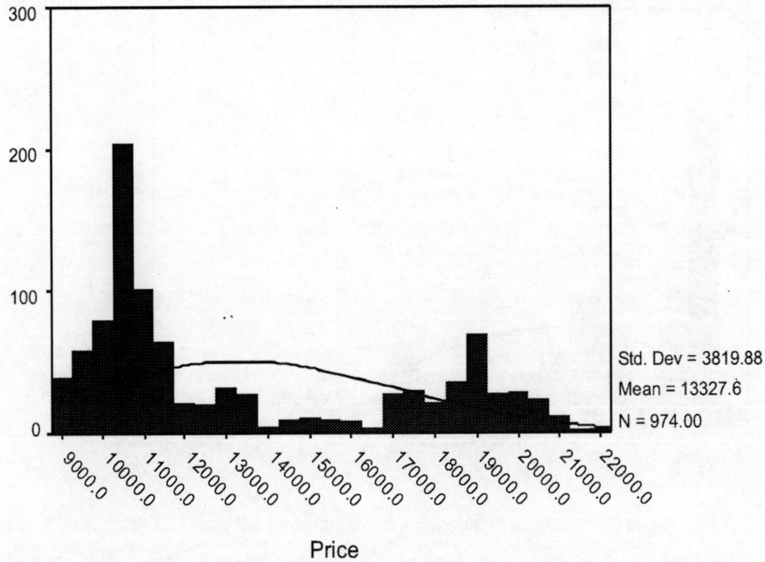

Fig. 19.5. Histogram of Silver 1-month Position (With Normal Distribution Curve)

Correlation between commodities and nifty

From Tables (Tables 19.6, 19.7, 19.8 and 19.10), strong and positive correlations can be found between Brent crude oil, Chana, Gold and Silver Future Prices and Nifty levels. For Gold, these levels are 0.904, 0.899 and 0.904, for Silver, these are 0.843, 0.845 and 0.852, for Chana, these are 0.907, 0.870, 0.819 and for Brent Crude oil, these are 0.213, 0.265, 0.500 for all the three month's positions. The correlation is positive, meaning that high scores on the Nifty tend to be paired with relatively high scores on the Gold, Silver, Chana and Brent Crude oil Future Prices, and vice versa. So, variability in the Commodities Market can be explained in terms of variability in the Stock Markets. Since future prices tend to move in the same direction as of Nifty, hence profits can be made by predicting the behavior of Stock Markets. In the periods of booms, long positions can be taken in the futures contract, and reversals can be entered, thereby booking the profits.

Similarly, negative correlation can be found between Mustard seed future prices and Nifty in Table 19.9, For Mustard seed these are -.585, -.508 and -.484 for all the three month's positions. Thus, future prices of this commodity tend to fall whenever Nifty rises. This can be used by the investors to hedge their risks, by entering into futures contract. For example, if the stock markets are expected to fall, the future prices are expected to rise. Thus, they can hedge their risk by taking short positions in the futures contract, so that at the expiry of the contract, they can buy the underlying commodity in the cash market at the low prices, and sell the same at higher prices to fulfill their obligation under future contract, the difference being their profit margin. Similar opposite strategy can be used, if markets are booming.

We have found out Correlation as a descriptor of the degree of linear association between Commodities and Nifty, thereby helping us to find out the key parameters of magnitude and direction. However, we need to know whether this correlation is sufficiently different to zero in order to assert that a real relationship exists. So, we need to conduct the Hypothesis testing to test the significance of correlations, whereby:

$$H_0 : \rho = 0$$
$$H_1 : \rho \neq 0$$

At a significance level of 5 % (a = 0.05)

From the SPSS Statistical Package output (Tables 19.6 to 19.10), we get the ρ levels for correlations between the five commodities and Nifty, for all the positions. For all the commodities, r $\rho < 0.05$. So, we determine that the correlation levels are significant at the .001 level. We infer that the null hypothesis is too unlikely to be correct and we accept the alternative as a more likely explanation of the finding.

Hence, we can say that there are significant correlation levels between the commodities future prices and nifty closing prices and all these correlations are statistically significant at 5 % level of significance.

Table 19.6. Correlation between Brent Crude Oil and Nifty
Brent Crude Oil - Nifty Correlation

		NIFTY
Nifty	Pearson Correlation	1
	Sig. (2-tailed)	
Brent 1 month	Pearson Correlation	.213**
	Sig. (2-tailed)	.000
Brent 2 month	Pearson Correlation	.265**
	Sig. (2-tailed)	.000
Brent 3 month	Pearson Correlation	.500**
	Sig. (2-tailed)	.000

Table 19.7. Correlation between Chana and Nifty
Chana - Fifty Correlation[a]

		NIFTY
Nifty	Pearson Correlation	1
	Sig. (2-tailed)	
Chana 1 month	Pearson Correlation	.907**
	Sig. (2-tailed)	.000
Chana 2 month	Pearson Correlation	.870**
	Sig. (2-tailed)	.000
Chana 3 month	Pearson Correlation	.819**
	Sig. (2-tailed)	.000

**Correlation is significance at the 0.01 level.
[a] Listwise N = 709

Table 19.8. Correlation between Gold and Nifty
Chana - Fifty Correlation[a]

		NIFTY
Nifty	Pearson Correlation	1
	Sig. (2-tailed)	
Gold 1 month	Pearson Correlation	.904**
	Sig. (2-tailed)	.000
Gold 2 month	Pearson Correlation	.899**
	Sig. (2-tailed)	.000
Gold 3 month	Pearson Correlation	.904**
	Sig. (2-tailed)	.000

**Correlation is significance at the 0.01 level.
[a] Listwise N = 790

Table 19.9. Correlation between Mustard Seed and Nifty
Mustard Seed - Nifty Correlation[a]

		NIFTY
Nifty	Pearson Correlation	1
	Sig. (2-tailed)	
Mustard 1 month	Pearson Correlation	.585**
	Sig. (2-tailed)	.000
Mustard 2 month	Pearson Correlation	.508**
	Sig. (2-tailed)	.000
Mustard 3 month	Pearson Correlation	.484**
	Sig. (2-tailed)	.000

**Correlation is significance at the 0.01 level.
[a] Listwise N = 744

Table 19.10. Correlation between Silver and Nifty
Silvor - Nifty Correlation[a]

		NIFTY
Nifty	Pearson Correlation	1
	Sig. (2-tailed)	
Silver 1 month	Pearson Correlation	.843**
	Sig. (2-tailed)	.000
Silver 2 month	Pearson Correlation	.845**
	Sig. (2-tailed)	.000
Silver 3 month	Pearson Correlation	.852**
	Sig. (2-tailed)	.000

**Correlation is significance at the 0.01 level.
[a] Listwise N = 815

Correlation between commodities and short-term interest rates

Relationship between Commodities and Short term interest rates has been studied by using 91-day T-Bills interest rates as a measurement for short term interest rates.

The monthly average interest rates for the 91-day T-Bills were taken as the short term interest rates and they are matched with monthly average future prices of the commodities.

Tables (19.11 to 19.15) show that as for relationship between Commodities Future Prices and Nifty, similar relationships can be found between future prices and short term interest rates. For Gold, Silver, Chana and Mustard Seed future prices, there are very strong positive correlations with short term interest rates. This again indicates that the future prices for these commodities tend to move in the same direction as that of interest rates. Whenever interest rates rise, they are accompanied by a rise in the future prices for these commodities. This indicates that the confidence of the commodities market goes hand in hand with the interest rate structure in the economy.

Table 19.11. Correlation between Brent Crude Oil and Short term Interest rate

Brent Crude Oil-Interest rate Correlation[a]

		Interest rate	Brent 1 month	Brent 2 month	Brent 3 month
Interest rate	Pearson Correlation	1	-.220	-.193	-.156
	Sig. (2-tailed)	.	.412	.473	.563
Brent 1 month	Pearson Correlation	.-.220	1	.997**	.990**
	Sig. (2-tailed)	.412	.	.000	.000
Brent 2 month	Pearson Correlation	-.193	.997**	1	.996**
	Sig. (2-tailed)	.473	.000	.	.000
Brent 3 month	Pearson Correlation	-.156	.990**	.996**	1
	Sig. (2-tailed)	.563	.000	.000	.

**Correlation is significance at the 0.01 level (2-tailed).

[a] Listwise N = 16

Table 19.12. Correlation between Chana and Short term Interest rate

Chana-Short term Interest rate Correlation[a]

		Short term Interest rate	Chana 1 month	Chana 2 month	Chana 3 month
Short term	Pearson Correlation	1	.433	.266	.102
Interest rate	Sig. (2-tailed)	.	.094	.320	.707
Chana 1 month	Pearson Correlation	.433	1	.970**	.843**
	Sig. (2-tailed)	.094	.	.000	.000
Chana 2 month	Pearson Correlation	.266	.970**	1	.932**
	Sig. (2-tailed)	.320	.000	.	.000
Chana 3 month	Pearson Correlation	.102	.843**	.932**	1
	Sig. (2-tailed)	.707	.000	.000	.

**Correlation is significance at the 0.01 level (2-tailed).

[a] Listwise N = 16

Table 19.13. Correlation between Gold and Short term Interest rate
Gold-Interest rate Correlation[a]

		Short term Interest rate	Gold 1 month	Gold 2 month	Gold 3 month
Short term	Pearson Correlation	1	.388	.391	.388
Interest rate	Sig. (2-tailed)	.	.137	.135	.137
Gold 1 month	Pearson Correlation	.388	1	1.000**	.999**
	Sig. (2-tailed)	.137	.	.000	.000
Gold 2 month	Pearson Correlation	.391	1.000**	1	1.000**
	Sig. (2-tailed)	.135	.000	.	.000
Gold 3 month	Pearson Correlation	.388	.999**	1.000**	1
	Sig. (2-tailed)	.137	.000	.000	.

**Correlation is significance at the 0.01 level (2-tailed).
[a] Listwise N = 16

Table 19.14. Correlation between Mustard Seed and Short term Interest rate
Mustard Seed-Short Interest rate Correlation[a]

		Short term Interest rate	Mustard seed 1 month	Mustard seed 2 month	Mustard seed 3 month
Short term	Pearson Correlation	1	.623*	.707**	.752**
Interest rate	Sig. (2-tailed)	.	.017	.005	.002
Mustard seed	Pearson Correlation	.623*	1	.765****	.622*
1 month	Sig. (2-tailed)	.017	.	.001	.017
Mustard seed	Pearson Correlation	.707**	.765**	1	.831**
2 month	Sig. (2-tailed)	.005	.001	.	.000
Mustard seed	Pearson Correlation	.752**	.622*	.831**	1
3 month	Sig. (2-tailed)	.002	.017	.000	.

*Correlation is significance at the 0.05 level (2-tailed).
**Correlation is significance at the 0.01 level (2-tailed).
[a] Listwise N = 14

Table 19.15. Correlation between Silver and Short term Interest rate
Silver-Interest rate Correlation[a]

		Short term Interest rate	Silver 1 month Position	Silver 2 month Position	Silver 3 month Position
Short term	Pearson Correlation	1	.424	.420	.416
Interest rate	Sig. (2-tailed)	.	.101	.105	.109
Silver 1 month	Pearson Correlation	.424	1	.999**	.998**
Position	Sig. (2-tailed)	.101	.	.000	.000
Silver 2 month	Pearson Correlation	.420	.999**	1	.999**
Position	Sig. (2-tailed)	.105	.000	.	.000
Silver 3 month	Pearson Correlation	.416	.998**	.999**	1
Position	Sig. (2-tailed)	.109	.000	.000	.

**Correlation is significance at the 0.01 level (2-tailed).
[a] Listwise N = 16

For Brent Crude Oil there is negative correlation, this implies that the future prices for Brent Crude Oil tend to move in the opposite direction to that of the interest rates. So, like in case of Nifty, hedging strategies can be used to hedge the risk. Whenever the interest rates are expected to rise or fall, accordingly, short or long position can be taken in the market and risk can be diluted.

By hypothesis testing, the significance of these correlations can also be tested for. Again, the Hypothesis can be set as follows:

$$H_0 : \rho = 0$$
$$H_1 : \rho \neq 0$$

at a significance level of 5 % ($\alpha = 0.05$)

From the tables, we can find out that for all; one, two and three months position for all the commodities (except one month position for Mustard Seed), $r < 0.01$, thereby implying that they are statistically significant at 1 % level of significance. For Mustard seed one month's position, $0.05 > r > 0.01$. So, it is significant at 5 % level of significance. Since our a level is 5 %, we can say that all the correlations are statistically significant and hence, these correlations are not random or by chance. So, real relationships exist between these commodities and short term interest rates.

So, from the above correlation analysis, we can say that significant correlations exist between the commodities and Nifty/Short term interest rates. India, being an agricultural economy, this analysis is of particular interest from the viewpoint of the farmers. It is interesting to note that the future prices of one agricultural commodity i.e. Mustard Seed and One Energy Commodity i.e. Brent Crude Oil in our analysis shows inverse relationship with the Nifty and the Interest rates respectively. So, it can be concluded that these commodities tend to react to news on the economic front and behave accordingly. This behavior of the Energy/agricultural commodity can be used by the oil companies/farmers to hedge themselves against the interest rate shocks or that of the booms and recessions in the economy as a whole. Again, both the precious metals, gold and silver, also show constant behavior with both the Nifty Index and short term interest rates. This reflects that the strong investor interest in these markets is directly linked with that of the performance of the financial sector. Good news for the stock market also brings confidence in the metals derivatives market and vice versa. Accordingly, suitable strategies can be adopted by all the three key players in the derivatives market, namely, arbitragers, speculators and hedgers.

EFFICIENCY IN COMMODITIES MARKET: EXPLORING THE ARBITRAGE OPPORTUNITIES

An efficient market is one in which trading takes place at the prices which reflect all the publicly available information. In an active futures markets the free flow of information is vital. Futures exchanges act as a focal point for the collection and dissemination of statistics on supplies, transportation, storage, purchases, exports, imports, currency values, interest rates and other pertinent information. Any significant change in this data is immediately re-elected in the trading pits as traders digest the new information and adjust their bids and offers accordingly. As a result of this free flow of information, the market determines the best estimate of today and tomorrow's prices and it is considered to be the accurate re-election of the supply and demand for the underlying commodity. Price discovery facilitates this free flow of information, which is vital to the effective functioning of futures market.

However, it may happen that the prices at which the trading takes place are not a proper indicator of all the parameters involved in an efficient price discovery mechanism. Many a times it happens that the future prices which are reflected in the market are either overvalued or undervalued. This is the area where the role of arbitragers comes into picture.

Arbitrage involves locking in a risk less profit by simultaneously entering into transactions in two or more markets. This arbitrage opportunity exists whenever the future price of an asset gets out of line with its cash price. This situation is explored by the arbitragers. They make use of cash-and-carry arbitrage, or reverse cash-and-carry arbitrage and make use of the price difference, which exists between the actual future prices which are reflected in the commodities market, and the theoretical future prices which must be there, taking into account all the background information into the analysis.

In this analysis, we have tried to fit an "Arbitrage free pricing model". This model attempts to find out the "No-arbitrage" future prices, which don't leave any scope for the arbitrage opportunities. The Arbitrage Free Pricing Model states that the buyer who needs an asset in the future has the choice between buying the underlying asset today in the spot market and holding it, or buying it in the forward market. If he buys it in the spot market today, it involves opportunity costs. He incurs the cash outlay for buying the asset and he also incurs costs for storing it. If instead he buys the asset in the forward market, he does not incur an initial outlay. However the costs of holding the asset are now incurred by the seller of the forward contract who charges the buyer a price that is higher than the price of the asset in the spot market. These costs consist of the following:

a. Financing Cost i.e. the cost of borrowing money from the market.
b. Transactions Cost
c. Storage Cost which involves warehousing costs for storage of commodities. Warehouse charges include a fixed charge per deposit of commodity into the warehouse, and per unit per week charge. The per unit charges include storage costs and insurance charges.

Thus, the "Arbitrage free pricing model" can be stated as below:

$$F_t = S_0 (1 + AFC + TC + SC)$$

Where,

F_t = Future Price of a commodity at time t

S_0 = Spot Price of a commodity at time 0

t = One Month, Two Months, Three Months
AFC = Average Financing Cost
TC = Transactions Cost
SC = Storage Costs

Whenever the future prices move away from the fair value, there would be opportunities for arbitrage. This may take place in the following two situations:

- $F_t > S_0$ (1 + AFC + TC + SC) – In this case, the future price is overvalued. The arbitragers can make use of this situation by borrowing an amount equal to S_0 from the short term money market. From the proceeds of the borrowing, they will buy the underlying asset from the market at the spot rate of S_0 and simultaneously they will enter into the futures contract and take short position in that asset, at a future price F_t, which is not fairly priced and is over valued. At the expiration date, they will sell the asset to fulfill the obligation under the futures contract. From the proceeds under the futures contract, they will pay a part of the money to repay the money borrowed, and the difference, which exist because of the future price not truly reflecting the mechanics, is their profit. This is technically referred to as Cash-and-Carry Arbitrage process of taking advantage of overly priced assets.
- $F_t < S_0$ (1 + AFC + TC + SC) – In this case, the future price is undervalued. In this situation, the arbitragers can make use by short selling the asset at the spot price S_0 (at present, short selling is not allowed in commodities market), and using the proceeds to lend the money at short term money market. Simultaneously, they will enter into futures contract and would take long position to buy the asset after the specified period, at an undervalued future price F_t. At the end of the expiry period, the money they had lent would be repaid back to them, and they will use this money to fulfill the obligation under the futures contract and would buy the asset at an under- valued price F_t. The difference shall be their profit margin. This is technically referred to as Reverse Cash-and-Carry Arbitrage process of taking advantage of under priced assets.

So, scope for arbitrage will always exist if the future prices do not reflect the true information. Any deviation from fair pricing of the assets would lead to participation by the arbitragers in the market and making use of the over or under pricing.

In our analysis, we have used the "Arbitrage Free Pricing Model" to find out the theoretical "No Arbitrage Future Prices" of the all the five commodities, for all the three different positions. Thereafter, these theoretical future prices have been compared with the "Actual Future Prices" on which trading took place during the analysis period. This comparison has allowed us to comment whether significant differences exist in the two time-series, and whether such differences are statistically significant. The following statistical tests have been used in this context:

1. The Paired Samples t-test.
2. Wilcoxon Signed Ranks Test.

The Paired Samples t-test

The Paired Samples t test is a hypothesis test of the difference between two population means based on the means of two paired samples. Under this test, the two samples are compared in such a way, that the elements in one sample are matched or paired with the elements or paired with the other sample, thereby helping in doing a precise analysis in finding out whether any significant difference exists in the two series.

In our analysis, under paired samples t-test, the two samples are:

1. Actual FP (Future Price)
2. Arbitrage Free FP (Future Price)

Thus, the Paired Sample t-test has been used to compare the means of the abovementioned two variables. As such, it helps in finding out if there is a statistically significant difference between the Actual FP at which trading took place and the theoretical Arbitrage Free FP, which has been computed by fitting an "Arbitrage Free Pricing Model" on the Spot Prices.

For the Paired Samples t-test, we state the null hypothesis that there is no significant Mean Difference between the two series and hence the two series do not statistically differ from each other. The alternate hypothesis is that the two series differ from each other significantly. So, the hypothesis can be stated as follows:

$$H_0 : m_d = 0$$
$$H_1 : m_d \neq 0$$

Where, m_d is the Mean Difference between the two series. The alternative is two-tailed at a significance level of 5 % ($\alpha = 0.05$).

We have used SPSS to conduct the Paired Samples t-test. The SPSS output (Tables 19.16 to 19.27) reports a t-statistic and degrees of freedom for all t-test procedures. Every unique value of the t-statistic and its associated degrees of freedom has a significance value. In our case, the hypothesis is that the two time-series of Actual FP and Arbitrage Free FP do not differ significantly and are not statistically significant. However, in all the cases, the t-statistic and its associated significance value indicate that this is not the case. In fact, the observed mean difference between the two time-series, in all the cases, for all the three different positions for all the commodities, would occur fewer than once in a thousand times if there really were no difference between the two series.

For instance, Gold 1 Month position has a t-statistic (19.647), and its associated significance level ($\rho < 0.000$). Similarly, Chana 2 Months position has a t-statistic (4.263), with a significance level ($\rho < 0.000$). Again, Silver 3 Months position has t statistic (9.106) and associated significance level ($\rho < 0.000$). Also, the 95% Confidence Interval values are also given. It indicates the range within which the true population mean lies, with a 95% probability. The significance level tells us that the probability that there is no difference between the two series is very small: specifically, less than one time in a thousand would we obtain a significant mean difference between these groups if there was really no

Table 19.16. Paired Samples t-test — Actual Future Prices and Arbitrage Free FP for Chana 1-month

Paired Samples Test

		Paired Differences							
					95% Confidence Interval of the Difference				
		Mean	Std. Deviation	Std. Error Mean	Lower	Upper	t	df	Fig. (2-Tailed)
Pair 1	Actual Future Price Arbitrage Free Future Price	6.9442	57.77494	2.02875	2.9619	0.0264	3.423	810	.001

Table 19.17. Paired Samples t-test — Actual Future Prices and Arbitrage Free FP for Chana 2-month

Paired Samples Test

		Paired Differences							
					95% Confidence Interval of the Difference				
		Mean	Std. Deviation	Std. Error Mean	Lower	Upper	t	df	Fig. (2-Tailed)
Pair 1	Actual Future Price Arbitrage Free Future Price	18.4423	123.20296	4.32624	9.9503	26.9343	4.263	810	.000

Table 19.18. Paired Samples t-test — Actual Future Prices and Arbitrage Free FP for Chana 3-month

Paired Samples Test

		Paired Differences							
					95% Confidence Interval of the Difference				
		Mean	Std. Deviation	Std. Error Mean	Lower	Upper	t	df	Fig. (2-Tailed)
Pair 1	Actual Future Price Arbitrage Free Future Price	1.4916	231.98689	8.14616	14.4984	17.4817	.183	810	.855

Table 19.19. Paired Samples t-test — Actual Future Prices and Arbitrage Free FP for Gold 1-month

Paired Samples Test

		Paired Differences							
					95% Confidence Interval of the Difference				
		Mean	Std. Deviation	Std. Error Mean	Lower	Upper	t	df	Fig. (2-Tailed)
Pair 1	Actual Future Price Arbitrage Free Future Price	48.0240	66.89639	2.44434	52.8226	43.2254	-19.647	748	.000

Table 19.20. Paired Samples t-test — Actual Future Prices and Arbitrage Free FP for Gold 2-month

Paired Samples Test

		Paired Differences							
					95% Confidence Interval of the Difference				
		Mean	Std. Deviation	Std. Error Mean	Lower	Upper	t	df	Fig. (2-Tailed)
Pair 1	Actual Future Price Arbitrage Free Future Price	12.2513	81.90858	2.99287	18.1267	-6.3759	-4.093	748	.000

Table 19.21. Paired Samples t-test — Actual Future Prices and Arbitrage Free FP for Gold 3-month

Paired Samples Test

		Paired Differences							
					95% Confidence Interval of the Difference				
		Mean	Std. Deviation	Std. Error Mean	Lower	Upper	t	df	Fig. (2-Tailed)
Pair 1	Actual Future Price Arbitrage Free Future Price	9.2942	96.87055	0.54431	2.3362	6.2522	5.444	746	.000

Table 19.22. Paired Samples t-test — Actual Future Prices and Arbitrage Free FP for Mustard seed 1-month

Paired Samples Test

		Paired Differences							
					95% Confidence Interval of the Difference				
		Mean	Std. Deviation	Std. Error Mean	Lower	Upper	t	df	Fig. (2-Tailed)
Pair 1	Actual Future Price Arbitrage Free Future Price	-2.8976	7.33526	.26929	-3.4262	-2.3689	-10.760	741	.000

Table 19.23. Paired Samples t-test — Actual Future Prices and Arbitrage Free FP for Mustard seed 2-month

Paired Samples Test

		Paired Differences							
					95% Confidence Interval of the Difference				
		Mean	Std. Deviation	Std. Error Mean	Lower	Upper	t	df	Fig. (2-Tailed)
Pair 1	Actual Future Price Arbitrage Free Future Price	-.4686	14.11607	.52175	1.4929	.5557	-.898	731	.369

Table 19.24. Paired Samples t-test — Actual Future Prices and Arbitrage Free FP for Mustard seed 3-month

Paired Samples Test

		Paired Differences							
					95% Confidence Interval of the Difference				
		Mean	Std. Deviation	Std. Error Mean	Lower	Upper	t	df	Fig. (2-Tailed)
Pair 1	Actual Future Price Arbitrage Free Future Price	1.2424	17.57056	.62712	.0114	2.4735	1.981	784	.048

Table 19.25. Paired Samples t test — Actual Future Prices and Arbitrage Free FP for Silver 1-month

Paired Samples Test

		Paired Differences							
					95% Confidence Interval of the Difference				
		Mean	Std. Deviation	Std. Error Mean	Lower	Upper	t	df	Fig. (2-Tailed)
Pair 1	Actual Future Price Arbitrage Free Future Price	66.7937	229.53002	8.21323	82.9164	50.6711	-8.132	780	.000

Table 19.26. Paired Samples t-test — Actual Future Prices and Arbitrage Free FP for Silver 2-month

Paired Samples Test

		Paired Differences							
					95% Confidence Interval of the Difference				
		Mean	Std. Deviation	Std. Error Mean	Lower	Upper	t	df	Fig. (2-Tailed)
Pair 1	Actual Future Price Arbitrage Free Future Price	8.5543	75.05478	82966	-.7413	7.8500	1.888	782	.059

Table 19.27. Paired Samples t-test — Actual Future Prices and Arbitrage Free FP for Silver 3-month

Paired Samples Test

		Paired Differences							
					95% Confidence Interval of the Difference				
		Mean	Std. Deviation	Std. Error Mean	Lower	Upper	t	df	Fig. (2-Tailed)
Pair 1	Actual Future Price Arbitrage Free Future Price	1.8353	81.49579	0.08563	2.0371	1.6336	9.106	778	.000

difference between the two series. Thus, for all the commodities, the null hypothesis (H_0: $m_d = 0$) is rejected in favor of the alternate hypothesis except for Chana 3-month position, Mustard 2-month position and Silver 2-month position where the alternate hypothesis is accepted because significance level is considerable and it is 85.5%, 36.9% and 5.9% respectively. The Actual FP differs significantly from the theoretical Arbitrage Free FP, and hence there is a scope for arbitrage taking place. The arbitragers can enter into cash-and-carry transactions, or reverse-cash-and-carry transactions, and can make profits.

Wilcoxon Signed Ranks Test

The Wilcoxon Matched-Pairs Ranks test is a non-parametric test that is often regarded as being similar to a matched pair t-test. The Wilcoxon Matched-Pairs Ranks test is used to determine differences between groups of paired data when the data do not meet the rigor associated with a parametric test.

Wilcoxon Signed Ranks test helps in the following purposes:

- The Wilcoxon test is used to determine the magnitude of difference between matched groups.
- The Wilcoxon test is used to determine more than only the direction of difference.

The name Wilcoxon signed ranks test comes from the fact that it is based on the direction (ranks) of a pair of observations. It helps in finding out whether there is a significant difference between the two series. This test follows the following procedure:

1. The null hypothesis is stated as the median difference, M, between the two series is equal to zero.
2. Paired differences, $d_i = x_i - y_i$, are calculated, where x_i, y_i are the pairs of observations.
3. The d_is are then ranked, ignoring the signs, in increasing order i.e. rank 1 is assigned to the smallest $|d_i|$, rank 2 to the next etc.
4. Each rank is then labeled with its sign, according to the sign of d_i.
5. The sum of the ranks of the positive d_is, W^+ and the sum of the ranks of the negative d_is, W^-, are calculated.

Under the null hypothesis, the distribution of the differences is hypothesized to be approximately symmetric around zero. Therefore the sum of the positive ranks is expected to be approximately equal to the sum of the negative ranks. Since the sum of all the ranks is equal to $\frac{n(n+1)}{2}$. Therefore, under the null hypothesis, both W^+ and W^- follow a binomial distribution with p = $\frac{1}{2}$ and n = $\frac{n(n+1)}{2}$. We therefore proceed as follows:

6. Choose W = max (W^-, W^+).
7. Tables of the binomial distribution are used to find the p-value or probability of observing a value of W or higher assuming $p = \frac{1}{2}$ and $n = \frac{n(n+1)}{2}$.

Thus, in our case, this test begins with finding out the paired differences in two series, namely, Actual FP series and theoretical Arbitrage Free FP series. The absolute differences are then ranked, starting from lowest to highest. Once the ranks are assigned, then original signs (of paired differences) are restored. After the sum of the positive and negative ranks is computed and a hypothesis testing is done to find out whether the distribution of differences is symmetric around the zero or not. Accordingly, the hypothesis can be stated as below:

$$H_0 : M_d = 0$$
$$H_1 : M_d \neq 0$$

Where, M_d is the Median Difference between the two series. The alternative is two-tailed at a significance level of 5% (α = 0.05).

Again, we have used SPSS to conduct the Wilcoxon Signed Ranks Sum Test. The SPSS output (Tables 19.28 to 19.39) reports in the first table for each commodities individual position, positive ranks, negative ranks, ties and total N. A corresponding to z statistic has also been found out. Every unique value of the z statistic has a significance value. In our case, the hypothesis is that the Median difference for the two time-series of Actual FP and Arbitrage Free FP do not differ significantly and are not statistically significant. However, in all the cases, the z statistic and its associated significance value indicate that this is not the case. In fact, the observed median difference between the two time-series, in all the cases, for all the three different positions for all the commodities, would occur fewer than once in a thousand times if there really were no difference between the two series.

Now, the significance level against which the hypothesis is tested is 5%. The corresponding criterion z statistic with α = 0.05 is ± 1.96. In other words, for 95% Confidence Interval, the z value should be = ($-1.96 < z < +1.96$).

From the Tables 19.20 to 19.39, we can see that the z value does not lie in the abovementioned range for any of the commodity. It is much lesser than1.96 level. So our null hypothesis is rejected in favor of alternate hypothesis, for all the commodities, for all the different positions.

Also, for all the commodities, for all the positions, the significance level, $\rho < 0.000$. It can also be observed that the calculated p value for all the commodities is less than the declared p value of .05 to determine the probability level of difference.

For instance, Gold 2-months position has a z statistic (-18.094), and its associated significance level ($\rho < 0.000$). Similarly, Mustard 3-month position has a z statistic (-4.523), with a significance level ($\rho < 0.000$). Again, Silver 2-months position has z statistic (-2.159) and associated significance level ($\rho < 0.000$). For Chana 1-month position, z statistic is (-6.634) and ($\rho < 0.000$).

The significance level tells us that the probability that there is no difference between the two series is very small: specifically, less than one time in a thousand would we obtain a significant Median Difference between these groups if there was really no difference between the two series. Thus, for all the commodities, the null hypothesis (H_0: $M_d = 0$) is rejected in favor of the alternate hypothesis. The Actual FP differs significantly from the theoretical Arbitrage Free FP, and hence there is a scope for arbitrage taking place.

Table 19.28. Wilcoxon signed ranks Sum test-Chana 1-month Position

		N	Mean Rank	Sum of Ranks
Arbitrage Free Future Price Actual Future Price	Negative Ranks	532[a]	392.68	208907.00
	Positive Ranks	279[b]	431.39	120359.00
	Ties	0[c]		
	Total	811		

a. Arbitrage Free Future Price < Actual Future Price
b. Arbitrage Free Future Price > Actual Future Price
c. Actual Future Price = Arbitrage Free Future Price

Test Statistics[b]

	Arbitrage Free Future Price Actual Future Price
Z	-6.634[a]
Asymp, Sig. (2-tailed)	.000

a. Based on positive ranks.
b. Wilcoxon Signed Ranks Test

Table 19.29. Wilcoxon signed ranks Sum test-Chana 2-month Position

		N	Mean Rank	Sum of Ranks
Arbitrage Free Future Price Actual Future Price	Negative Ranks	591[a]	378.14	223479.00
	Positive Ranks	220[b]	480.85	105787.00
	Ties	0[c]		
	Total	811		

a. Arbitrage Free Future Price < Actual Future Price
b. Arbitrage Free Future Price > Actual Future Price
c. Actual Future Price = Arbitrage Free Future Price

Test Statistics[b]

	Arbitrage Free Future Price Actual Future Price
Z	-8.818[a]
Asymp, Sig. (2-tailed)	.000

a. Based on positive ranks.
b. Wilcoxon Signed Ranks Test

Table 19.30. Wilcoxon signed ranks Sum test - Chana 3-month Position

		N	Mean Rank	Sum of Ranks
Arbitrage Free Future Price Actual Future Price	Negative Ranks	569[a]	361.83	205882.00
	Positive Ranks	242[b]	509.85	123384.00
	Ties	0[c]		
	Total	811		

a. Arbitrage Free Future Price < Actual Future Price
b. Arbitrage Free Future Price > Actual Future Price
c. Actual Future Price = Arbitrage Free Future Price

Test Statistics[b]

	Arbitrage Free Future Price Actual Future Price
Z	-6.181[a]
Asymp, Sig. (2-tailed)	.000

a. Based on positive ranks.
b. Wilcoxon Signed Ranks Test

Table 19.31. Wilcoxon signed ranks Sum test - Gold 1-month Position

		N	Mean Rank	Sum of Ranks
Arbitrage Free Future Price Actual Future Price	Negative Ranks	146[a]	227.79	33258.00
	Positive Ranks	603[b]	410.64	247617.00
	Ties	0[c]		
	Total	749		

a. Arbitrage Free Future Price < Actual Future Price
b. Arbitrage Free Future Price > Actual Future Price
c. Actual Future Price = Arbitrage Free Future Price

Test Statistics[b]

	Arbitrage Free Future Price Actual Future Price
Z	-18.094[a]
Asymp, Sig. (2-tailed)	.000

a. Based on positive ranks.
b. Wilcoxon Signed Ranks Test

Table 19.32. Wilcoxon signed ranks Sum test - Gold 2-month Position

		N	Mean Rank	Sum of Ranks
Arbitrage Free Future Price Actual Future Price	Negative Ranks	322[a]	342.77	110372.50
	Positive Ranks	427[b]	399.30	170502.50
	Ties	0[c]		
	Total	749		

a. Arbitrage Free Future Price < Actual Future Price
b. Arbitrage Free Future Price > Actual Future Price
c. Actual Future Price = Arbitrage Free Future Price

Test Statistics[b]

	Arbitrage Free Future Price Actual Future Price
Z	-5.076[a]
Asymp, Sig. (2-tailed)	.000

a. Based on positive ranks.
b. Wilcoxon Signed Ranks Test

Table 19.33. Wilcoxon signed ranks Sum test - Gold 3-month Position

		N	Mean Rank	Sum of Ranks
Arbitrage Free	Negative Ranks	418[a]	398.73	166669.50
Future Price	Positive Ranks	329[b]	342.58	112708.50
Actual Future	Ties	0[c]		
Price	Total	747		

a. Arbitrage Free Future Price < Actual Future Price
b. Arbitrage Free Future Price > Actual Future Price
c. Actual Future Price = Arbitrage Free Future Price

Test Statistics[b]

	Arbitrage Free Future Price Actual Future Price
Z	-4.573[a]
Asymp, Sig. (2-tailed)	.000

a. Based on positive ranks.
b. Wilcoxon Signed Ranks Test

Table 19.34. Wilcoxon signed ranks Sum test - Mustard seed 1-month Position

		N	Mean Rank	Sum of Ranks
Arbitrage Free	Negative Ranks	285[a]	288.62	82257.50
Future Price	Positive Ranks	457[b]	423.18	193395.50
Actual Future	Ties	0[c]		
Price	Total	742		

a. Arbitrage Free Future Price < Actual Future Price
b. Arbitrage Free Future Price > Actual Future Price
c. Actual Future Price = Arbitrage Free Future Price

Test Statistics[b]

	Arbitrage Free Future Price Actual Future Price
Z	-9.514[a]
Asymp, Sig. (2-tailed)	.000

a. Based on positive ranks.
b. Wilcoxon Signed Ranks Test

Table 19.35. Wilcoxon signed ranks Sum test - Mustard seed 2-month Position

		N	Mean Rank	Sum of Ranks
Arbitrage Free Future Price Actual Future Price	Negative Ranks	439[a]	333.56	146434.50
	Positive Ranks	293[b]	415.85	121844.50
	Ties	0[c]		
	Total	732		

a. Arbitrage Free Future Price < Actual Future Price
b. Arbitrage Free Future Price > Actual Future Price
c. Actual Future Price = Arbitrage Free Future Price

Test Statistics[b]

	Arbitrage Free Future Price Actual Future Price
Z	-2.148[a]
Asymp, Sig. (2-tailed)	.032

a. Based on positive ranks.
b. Wilcoxon Signed Ranks Test

Table 19.36. Wilcoxon signed ranks Sum test - Mustard seed 3-month Position

		N	Mean Rank	Sum of Ranks
Arbitrage Free Future Price Actual Future Price	Negative Ranks	482[a]	379.66	182995.00
	Positive Ranks	303[b]	414.22	125510.00
	Ties	0[c]		
	Total	785		

a. Arbitrage Free Future Price < Actual Future Price
b. Arbitrage Free Future Price > Actual Future Price
c. Actual Future Price = Arbitrage Free Future Price

Test Statistics[b]

	Arbitrage Free Future Price Actual Future Price
Z	-4.523[a]
Asymp, Sig. (2-tailed)	.000

a. Based on positive ranks.
b. Wilcoxon Signed Ranks Test

Table 19.37. Wilcoxon signed ranks Sum test - Silver 1-month Position

		N	Mean Rank	Sum of Ranks
Arbitrage Free Future Price Actual Future Price	Negative Ranks	286[a]	334.13	95560.00
	Positive Ranks	495[b]	423.86	209811.00
	Ties	0[c]		
	Total	781		

a. Arbitrage Free Future Price < Actual Future Price
b. Arbitrage Free Future Price > Actual Future Price
c. Actual Future Price = Arbitrage Free Future Price

Test Statistics[b]

	Arbitrage Free Future Price Actual Future Price
Z	-9.058[a]
Asymp, Sig. (2-tailed)	.000

a. Based on positive ranks.
b. Wilcoxon Signed Ranks Test

Table 19.38. Wilcoxon signed ranks Sum test - Silver 2-month Position

		N	Mean Rank	Sum of Ranks
Arbitrage Free Future Price Actual Future Price	Negative Ranks	430[a]	388.68	167134.00
	Positive Ranks	353[b]	396.04	139802.00
	Ties	0[c]		
	Total	783		

a. Arbitrage Free Future Price < Actual Future Price
b. Arbitrage Free Future Price > Actual Future Price
c. Actual Future Price = Arbitrage Free Future Price

Test Statistics[b]

	Arbitrage Free Future Price Actual Future Price
Z	-2.159[a]
Asymp, Sig. (2-tailed)	.031

a. Based on positive ranks.
b. Wilcoxon Signed Ranks Test

Table 19.39. Wilcoxon signed ranks Sum test - Silver 3-month Position

		N	Mean Rank	Sum of Ranks
Arbitrage Free Future Price Actual Future Price	Negative Ranks	505[a]	420.53	212368.00
	Positive Ranks	274[b]	333.73	91442.00
	Ties	0[c]		
	Total	779		

a. Arbitrage Free Future Price < Actual Future Price
b. Arbitrage Free Future Price > Actual Future Price
c. Actual Future Price = Arbitrage Free Future Price

Test Statistics[b]

	Arbitrage Free Future Price Actual Future Price
Z	-9.624[a]
Asymp, Sig. (2-tailed)	.000

a. Based on positive ranks.
b. Wilcoxon Signed Ranks Test

VOLATILITY IN FUTURE PRICES

Another important measure for any market is the volatility levels in the prices at which the trading takes place. A good and efficient market is one which reflects low levels of volatility. Volatility in itself is a negative measure. Higher volatility in prices is a signal of increasing role of speculators in the market. It is an indicator that artificial movements are being created by speculators and hence, small and genuine investors refrain from the markets. So, any good market is judged by a low level of volatility in the prices.

The volatility of Future Prices in commodities market, σ, is a measure of uncertainty about the returns provided by that commodity. For the purpose of our analysis, volatilities are expressed as percentages. And we have annualized the volatility levels, so as to make them more comparable. For example, a volatility level of 0.25 for One Month position for Gold future prices indicate that the volatility in future prices for that commodities about 25 % per annum and other values are also interpreted in the same way. Typical values of the volatility for any commodity are in the range 0.2 to 0.4 per annum, or in other words, about 20 to 40 percent per annum. If the volatility levels are above this range, then the future prices for the underlying commodity are said to be high on volatility and if they are below this range, they are said to be low on volatility.

Estimating Volatility for the Commodity Future Prices

In order to estimate the volatility for the future price movements for different positions for different commodities, the closing future prices for the various commodities, for different positions have been taken. The measures which are used to find out the volatilities are defined as below:

$n+1$: number of observation

C_i: Commodity future price at the end of ith Interval $(i = 0,1,2\ldots\ldots n)$

t : length of time interval in years *(a time interval of 250 trading days in a year have been used)*

And let

$$u_i : \ln\left(\frac{C_i}{C_{i-1}}\right)$$

An estimate, s , of the standard deviation of the u_i's is given by

$$s = \sqrt{\frac{1}{n-1}\sum_{i=1}^{n}\left(u_i - \bar{u}\right)^2}$$

As a rough approximation, $\sigma\sqrt{t}$ has been used as the standard deviation of the proportional change in the future price of the commodities in time *t*.

These values of $\sigma\sqrt{t}$ have been computed for all the commodities, for all the different three months positions and the information is presented in Table 19.40.

From the Table (19.40), a general inference we can draw about the volatilities is that volatility levels of different commodities are different and for some commodities it is decreasing keeping in mind the month wise position. They are showing a decreasing trend. For Gold, the volatilities levels are least. They are between the stipulated range of 20 to 40 %.This signifies stability in Gold future prices. The future prices remain more or less stable and there are not major fluctuations. So, Gold future prices tend to be low on volatility.

Table 19.40. Volatilities of all the Commodities Future Prices

Commodity	1 month	2 month	3 month
Brent Crude Oil	29.6486	26.2043	32.2593
Chana	52.0758	44.0274	43.7618
Gold	26.4621	25.6614	23.5481
Mustard Seed	37.1029	42.839	33.8508
Silver	48.4882	49.0923	46.118

For Silver, the story is altogether different; moreover it has crossed the stipulated range of 40%. For Chana, abnormal volatilities can be seen, and also that the volatilities tend to lower down, as per positions of different months are concerned.

Another interesting fact can be noticed for Mustard Volatility levels. From Table 19.40, it can be seen that the volatility levels of 1-month position was not very high in comparison to the 2-month position, also it is under the range of 20 to 40%, which signifies that volatility is quite normal. These were 37%, 42% and 33% for one month, two months and three months positions respectively. The value of 2-month position falls even outside our acceptable range of 0.2 to 0.4. This indicates significant fluctuations in future prices. For Brent Crude oil situation is favorable and it is under the stipulated range of 20 to 40% per annum. They are 29%, 26% and 32% for 1-month, 2-month and 3-month position respectively.

So, on the basis of these five commodities, we can comment that the volatilities in commodities future prices are not stable and they are different for every position. Barring Chana and Silver, the commodity volatility levels are acceptable, which is a good signal for the investors in particular and for the economic system of the country in general. More and more investor confidence is being generated by this, as investor feel safety of investment under such conditions.

LIQUIDITY LEVELS IN COMMODITIES MARKET

Liquidity in the market is one of the most important parameter. Liquidity in any market is measured on two parameters—width and depth. Depth in the market refers to the number of units of the underlying asset being traded in the market. On the other hand, width of the market refers to the number of investors trading in the market. For the purpose of liquidity, both are important. A highly liquid market is indicated by greater width and depth in the market.

The liquidity in the market is reflected by the trading volume of the underlying asset (in our case, it is the commodities) taking place in the market, the open interest (number of outstanding contracts on any day), the number of contracts being generated. A good commodities market depicts a high level of liquidity, in terms of higher trading volumes, both the rupee value of volumes as well as number of contracts generated. Higher liquidity levels are an indicator of more and more investors entering into the market. It is a signal of greater investor confidence in the market, which thereby leads to further higher volumes being generated. This is good news for the economy and helps in strengthening the overall economic system.

For our purposes, we have taken the Open Interest positions and the trading volume levels for the different commodities, for different positions and they have plotted on graphs so as to find out the behavior of these two parameters graphically. For open interest and the trading volume, the graphs have been plotted on the data readily available.

Figures 19.6 to 19.15 give the graphs for open interest positions and trading volume levels for different commodities, for all the positions. For Open Interest, markets began very confidently for Gold, Brent Crude oil and Silver. High levels of Open Interest can be seen, even at the beginning of the operations at NCDEX. This shows strong investor interest in the markets and large number of contracts being generated, for Mustard Seed the momentum has taken time to build and the trend has started from December, 2004 onwards, for Chana the development is slow but steady, for silver the path is full of highs and lows i.e, there was a sudden increase and then decline which is still continue. In the further periods, the level of Open Interest is constantly rising, and the peaks of Open Interest is forming higher highs, but in Gold the level is somewhat getting disappeared in near August, 2005, In Silver level is getting momentum in end the of 2006 and then started to decline; the same trend could be seen in Brent crude oil thereby signifying higher levels of liquidity in the market for Gold, Silver and Chana.

As far as Chana and Mustard seed are concerned, the markets at the beginning showed very lukewarm response with very small level of Open Interest, showing minimal number of contracts being generated. Even though Chana picked up the momentum after two quarters, trading in Mustard took jump only after 3 to 4 quarters. This shows poor investor interest in these commodities. However, in the middle stages, there has been some boost in the trading of these commodities with higher levels of Open Interest registered and the trend forming higher highs but suddenly the interest of the investors has declined in both these commodities. So, it can be concluded that the markets for these commodities have picked up the pace in 2006 but is losing investor's interest day-by-day.

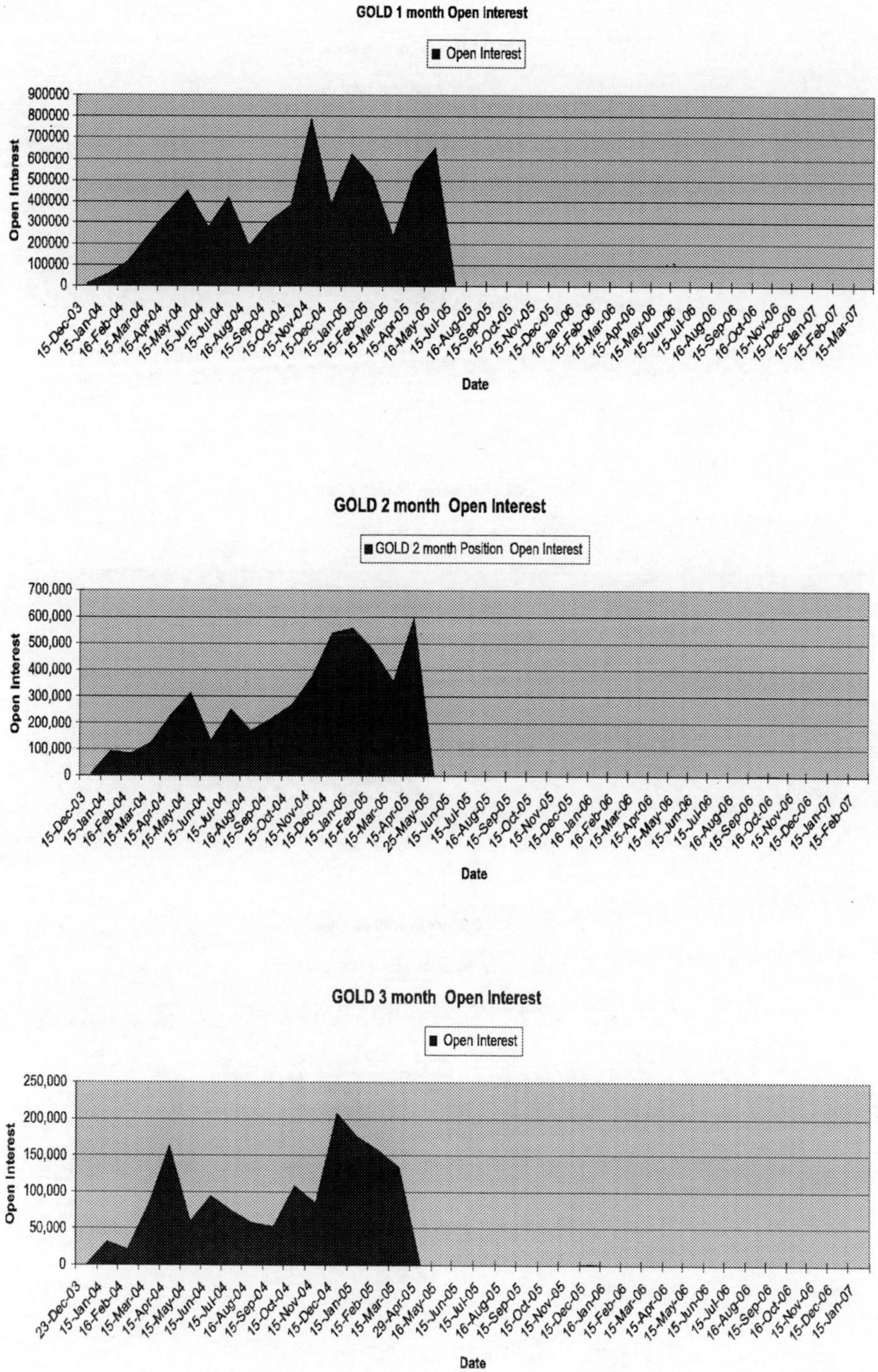

Fig. 19.6. Open Interest Chart - Gold.

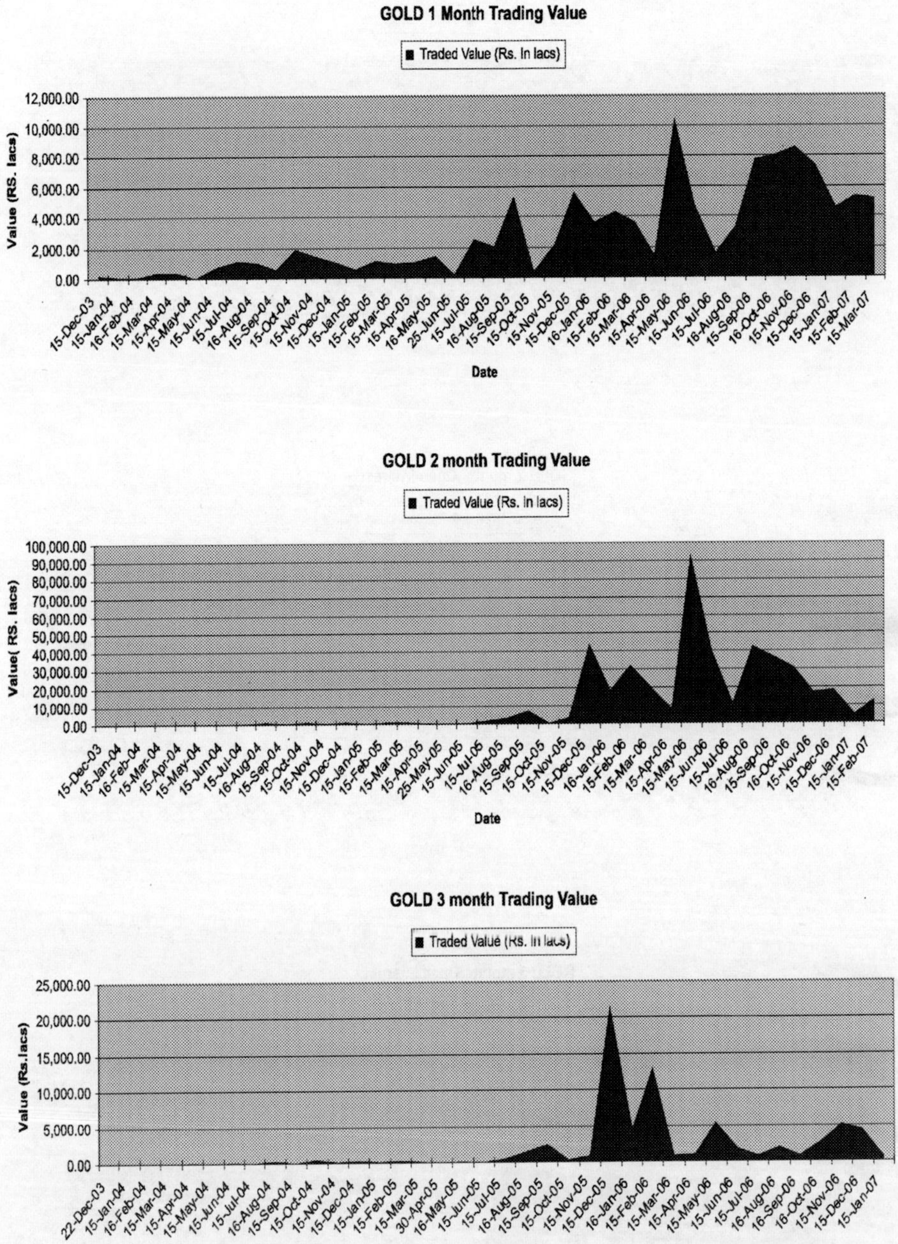

Fig. 19.7. Trading Volume Chart - Gold.

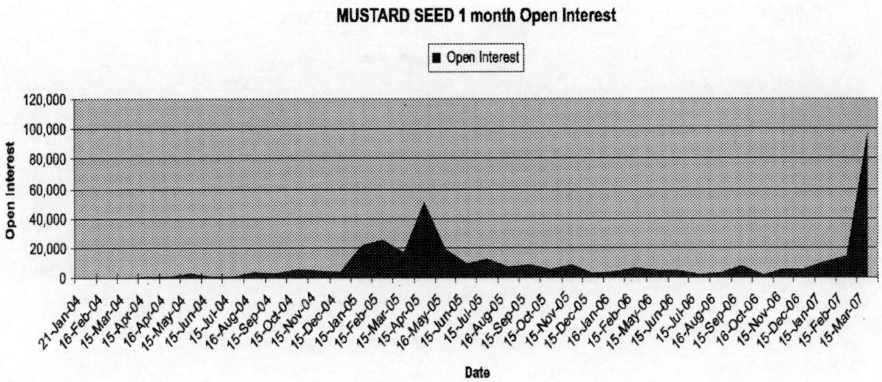

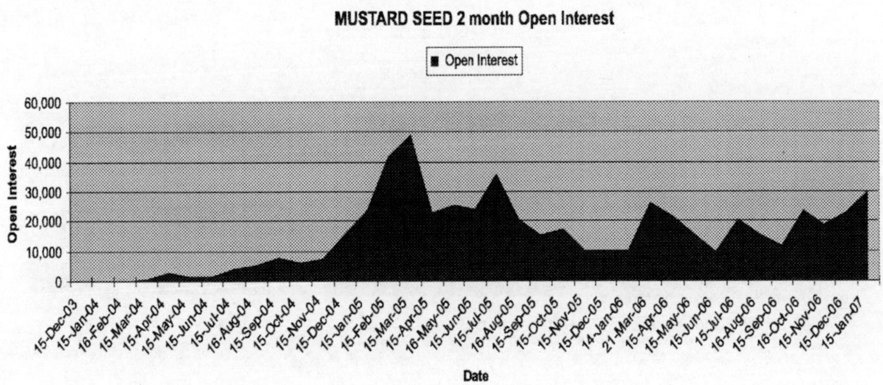

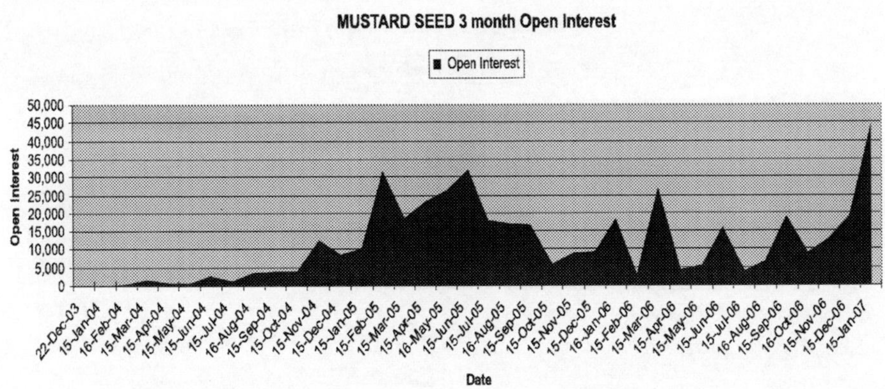

Fig. 19.8. Open Interest Chart - Mustard Seed.

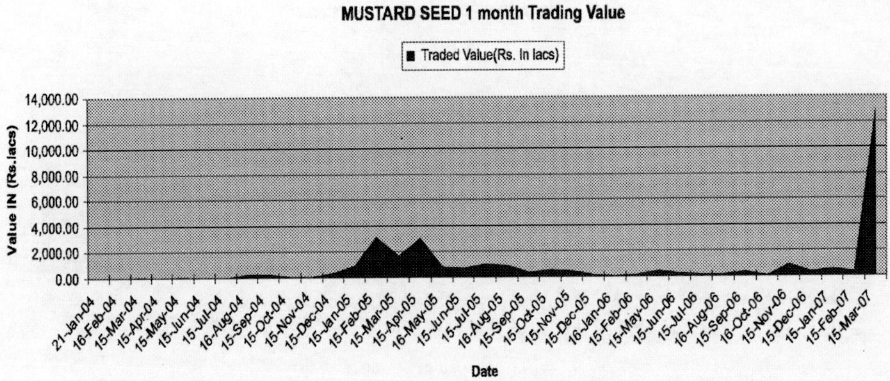

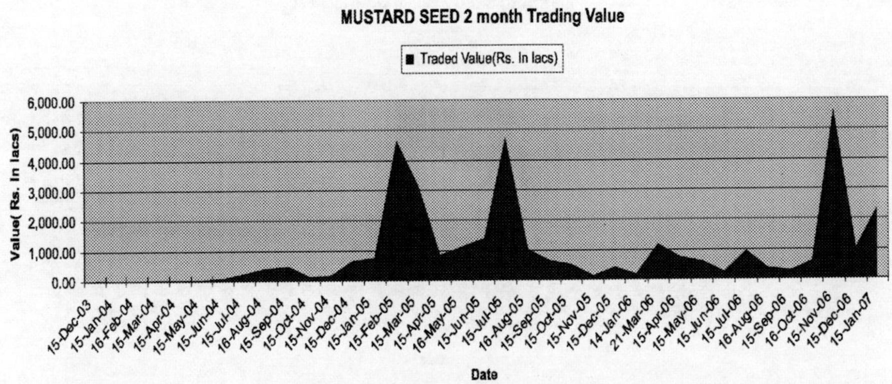

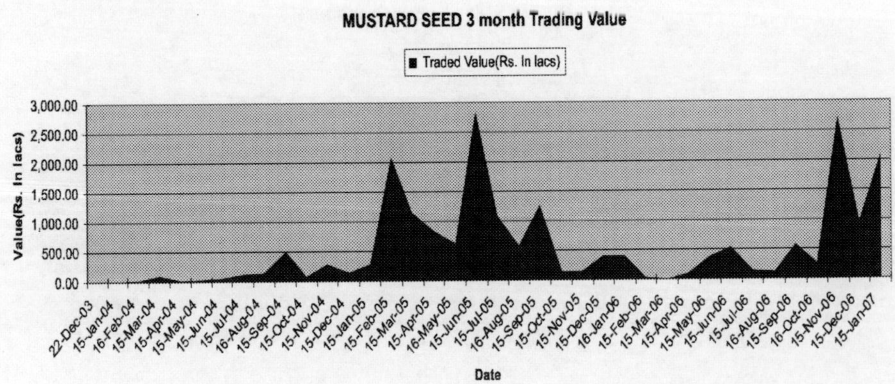

Fig. 19.9. Trading Volume Chart - Mustard Seed.

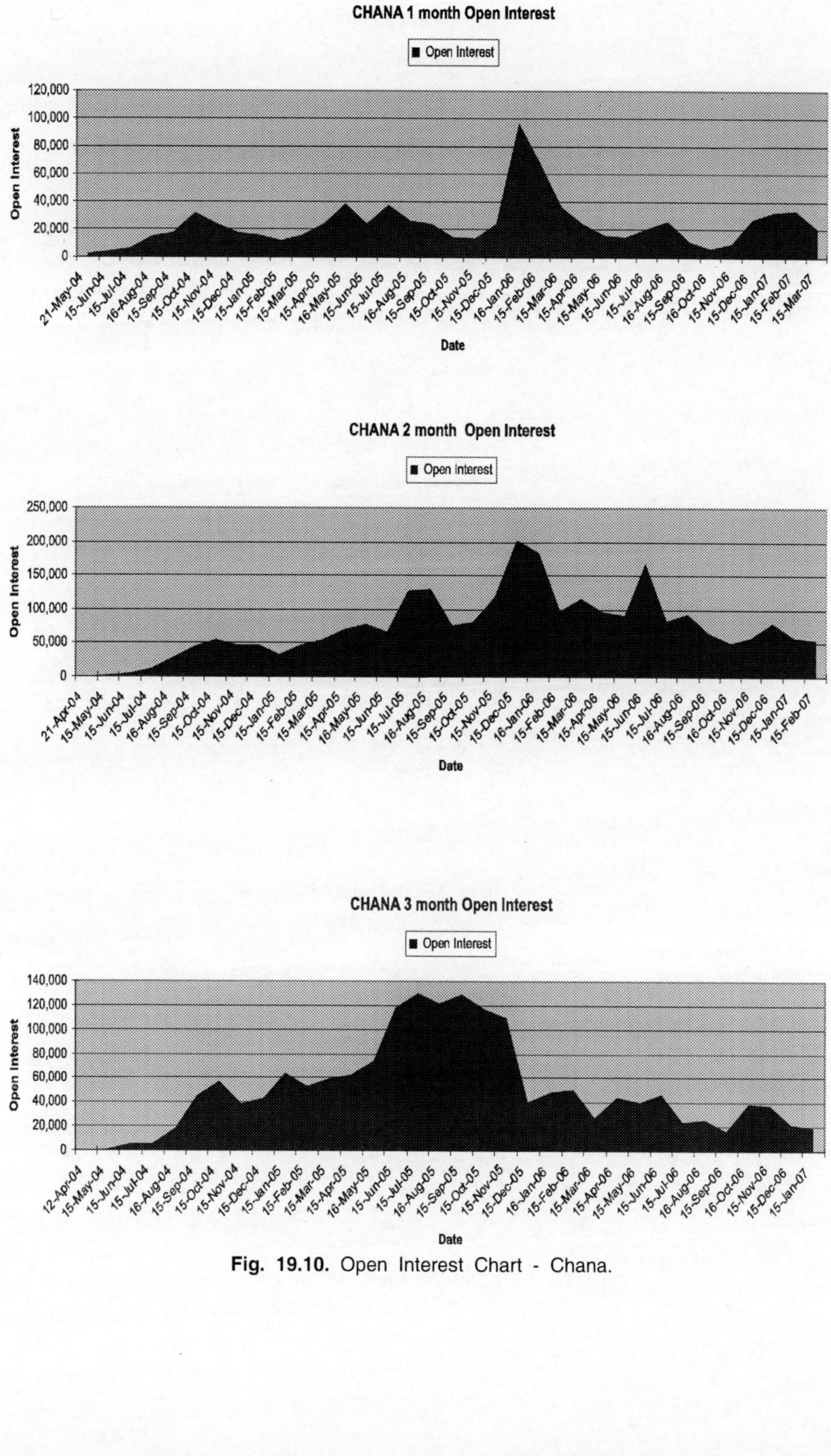

Fig. 19.10. Open Interest Chart - Chana.

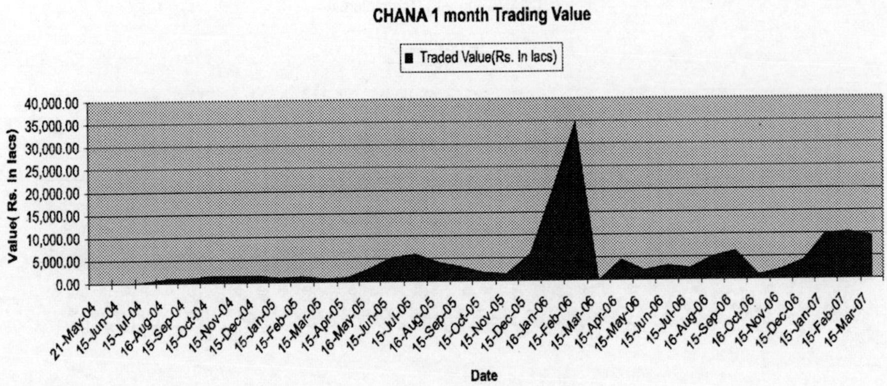

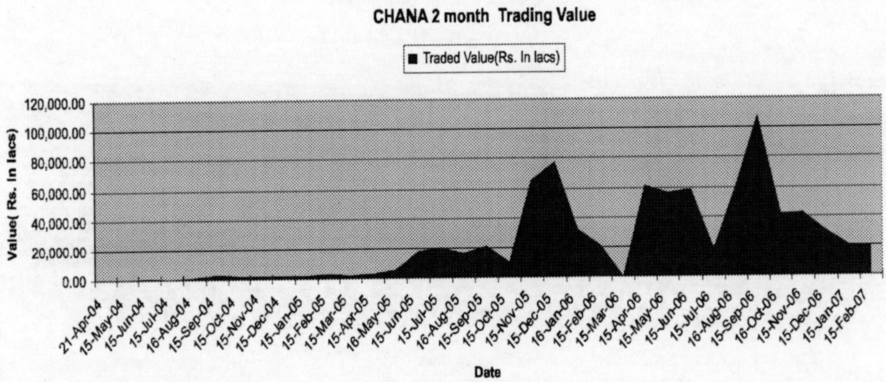

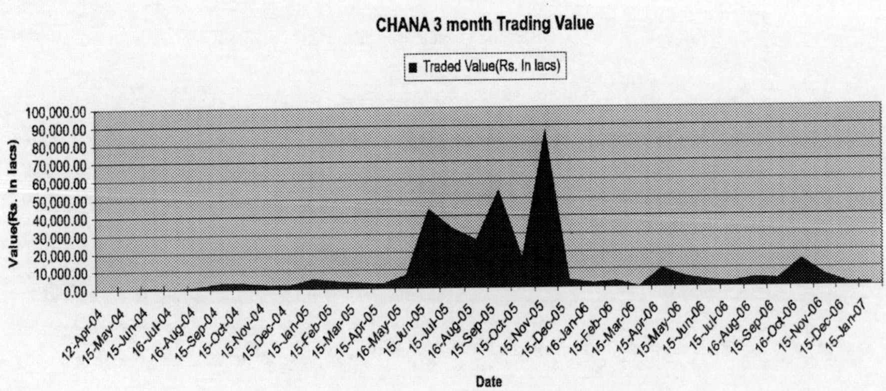

Fig. 19.11. Trading Volume Chart - Chana.

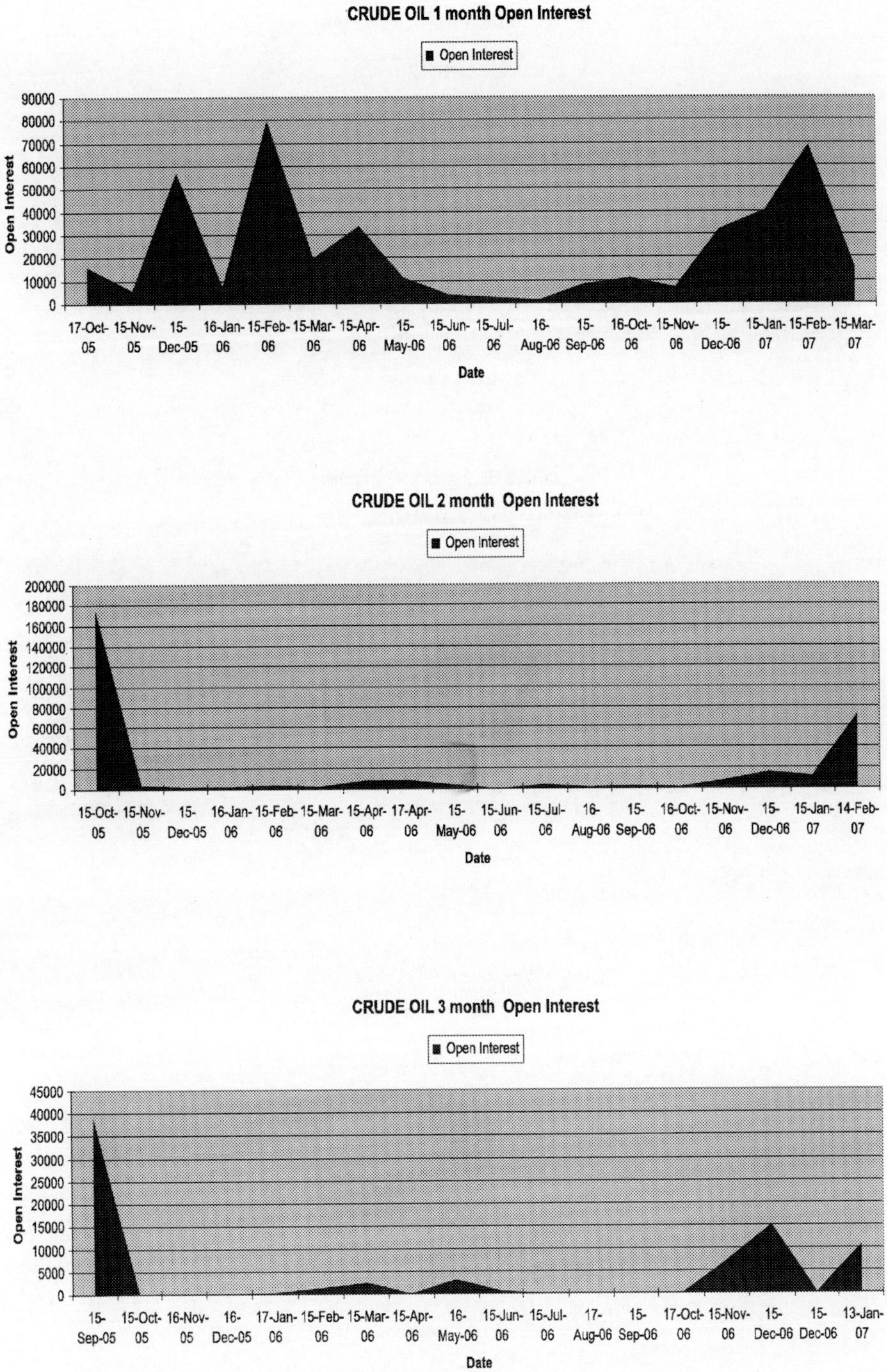

Fig. 19.12. Open Interest Chart - Brent Crude Oil.

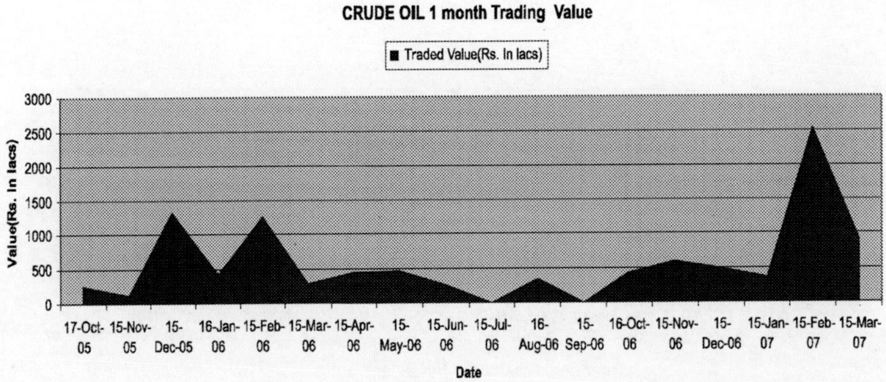

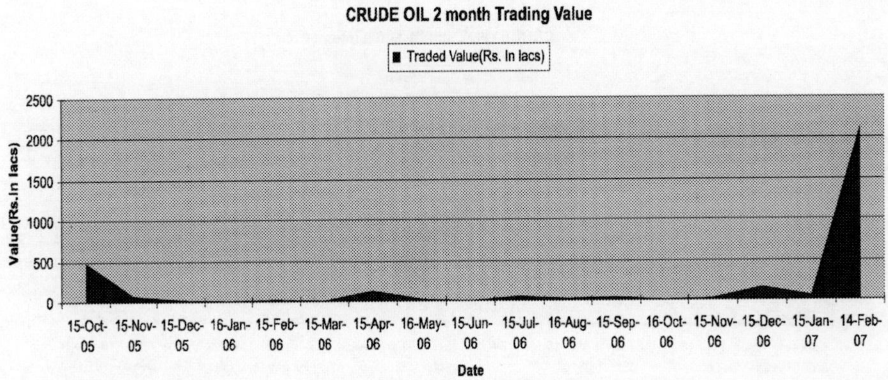

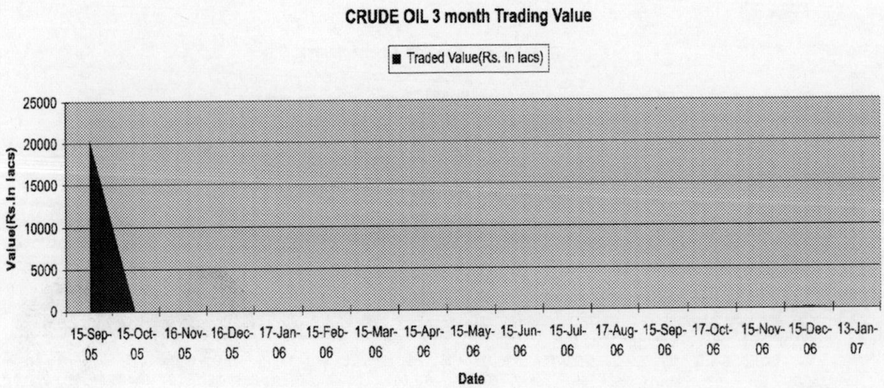

Fig. 19.13. Trading Volume Chart - Brent Crude Oil.

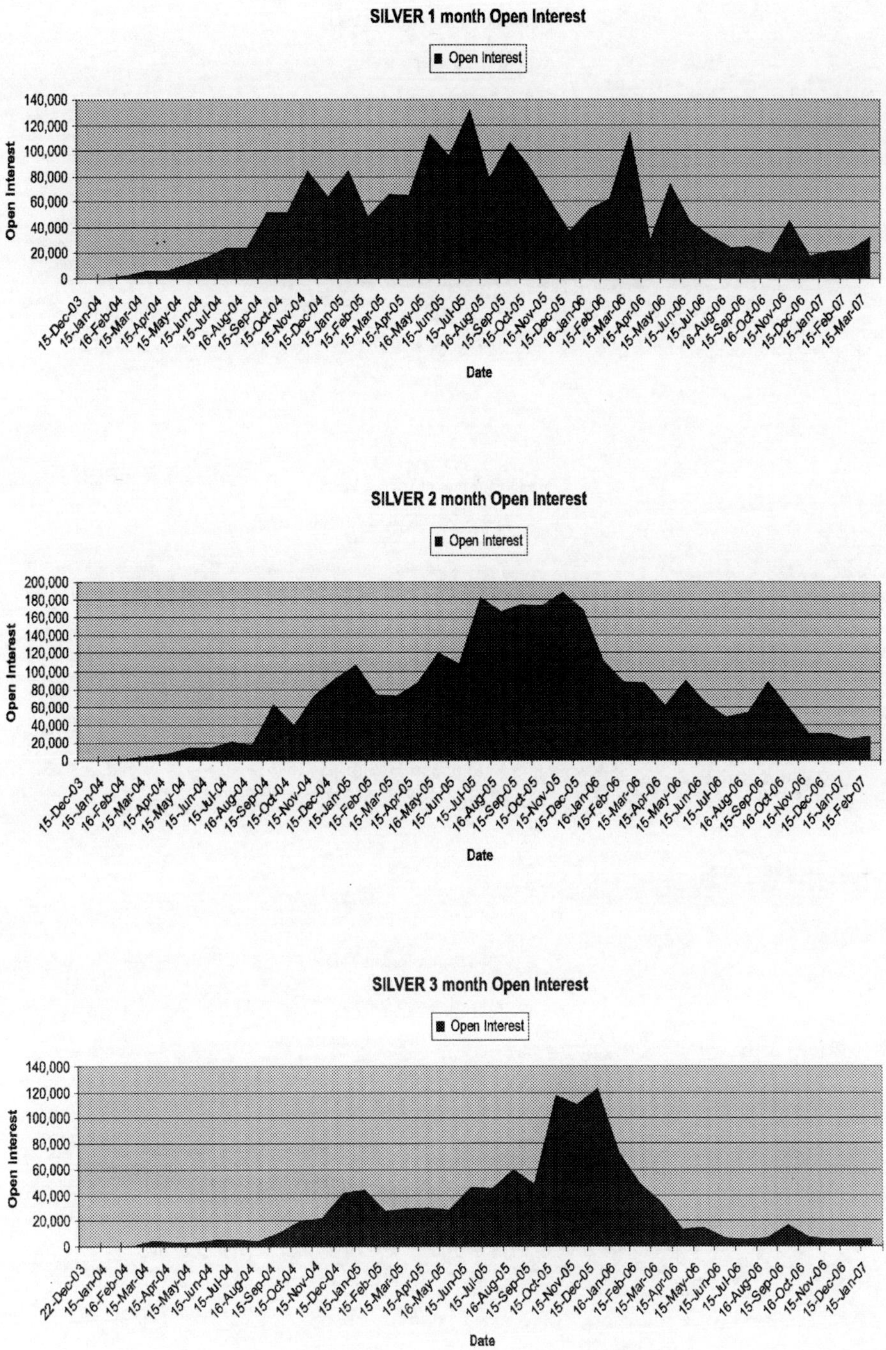

Fig. 19.14. Open Interest Chart - Silver.

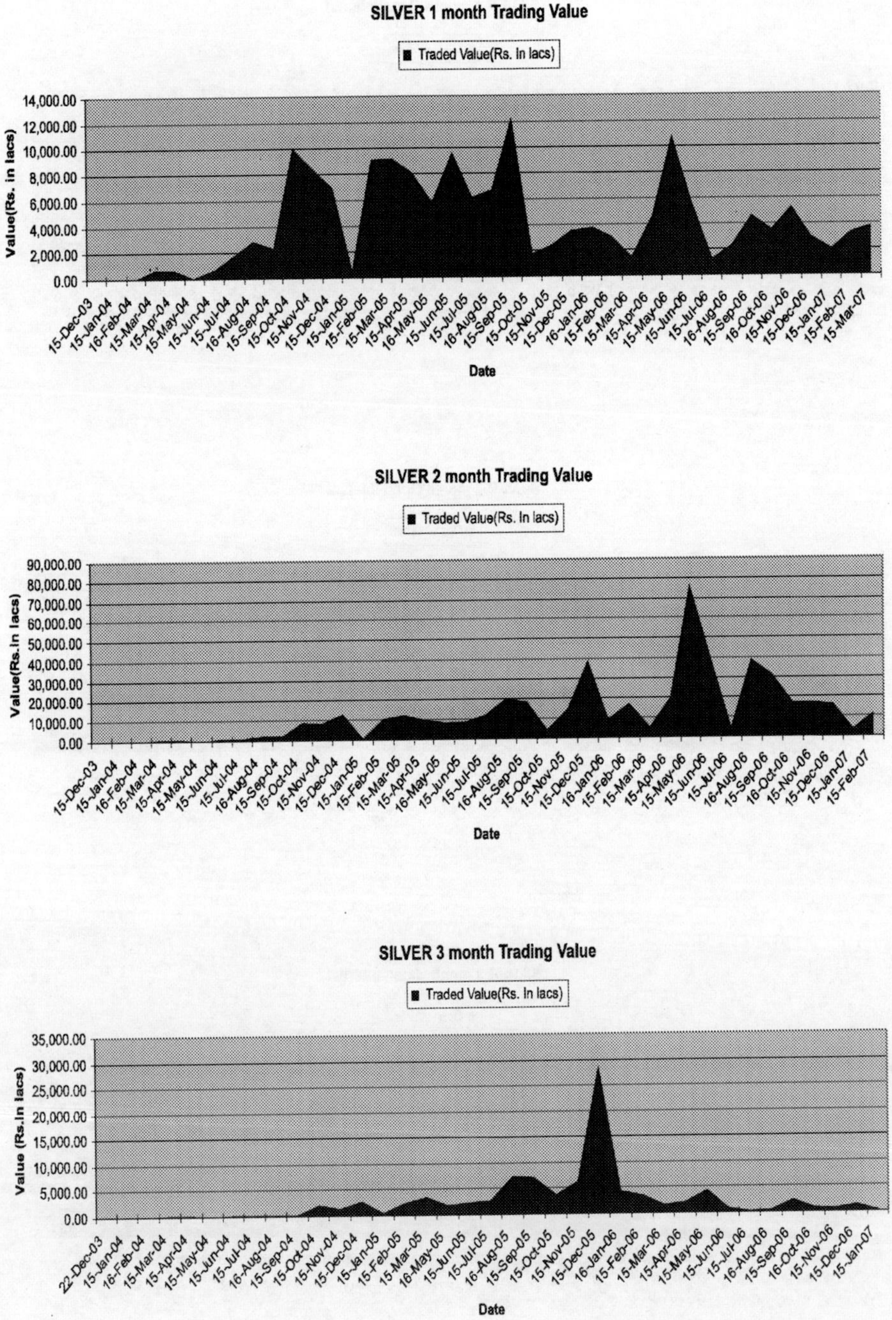

Fig. 19.15. Trading Volume Chart - Silver.

For trading volume of Chana and Mustard, it can be seen that they are also forming an increasing trend. Even though initially, the markets didn't do well in terms of lower trading volume levels, however, in the later phases, the trading volumes have been rising substantially, for Brent Crude oil market has taken some time to build up the momentum but now it is showing an increasing trend. For gold and silver, in the end of, 2006's the volumes were very high but suddenly they have started losing there shine and in the month of March, 2007 the volumes are abysmal. More and more investors are entering into the market and increasing number of contracts is being generated but overall liquidity is decreasing.

So, on the basis of the above liquidity analysis, it can be said that the liquidity in the market for the commodities is gaining momentum with time. Investors are gaining confidence in the markets. This is a good signal for the markets in particular, and for the entire economy in general.

INSIGHTS FROM FINDINGS

On the basis of empirical analysis, we have tried to evaluate the existing state of commodities market in terms of three parameters:

1. Efficiency in the commodities market.
2. Liquidity levels in the commodities market.
3. Volatility in the Future Prices.

By applying some statistical tools (parametric as well as non-parametric), we got the following results.

Returns Across the Markets

An analysis between the commodity future prices and Nifty Index as well as Short-term interest rates was done and the following results were found:

1. Strong and positive correlations between Metals and both Nifty and Short- term interest rates were found. Thus, future prices of the metals go hand in hand with both the Nifty Index as well as Short-term interest rates.
2. Strong and negative correlations between Agricultural /Energy commodity and both Nifty/Short-term interest rates were found. Thus, agricultural commodities behave in the opposite direction as compared with the Nifty Index and Energy Commodity behaves in the opposite direction as compared with the Short-term interest rates.

One thing we would like to point out is that since we had the limitation of data period (the data period being very small of about three and a half year, from Dec. 2003 to March, 2007), the results derived above may be said to be coincident. In other words, small sample size makes it difficult to derive conclusive results. But, in spite of this limitation, the consistent behavior of correlations over time, both for metals as well as agricultural commodities, makes us to believe that the relationship might not be coincidental or by chance. This information can be used by the investors to design their hedging strategies, in line with the behavior of the stock markets as well as the interest rates structure across the country.

Efficiency in the Commodities Market

An "Arbitrage Free Pricing Model" was fitted to find out the No-Arbitrage future prices. Then, a comparison was made between the actual future prices and the arbitrage free future prices to find out significant differences. Significant differences imply scope for arbitrage present in the market to make profits and hence, inefficiencies in the market. For this purpose, Paired Samples t-test and Wilcoxon Signed Ranks test were used.

It is found that there are wide differences in the actual future prices and arbitrage free future prices, for all the commodities, for all the different contracts. These differences are statistically significant, signifying thereby that there is a scope for arbitrage taking place. Hence, it can be said that there are inefficiencies in the market whereby all the publicly available information are incorporated in the future prices at which the trading takes place. The future prices are either overvalued or undervalued, thereby leaving a scope for the arbitragers to enter in the market and make profits.

Volatilities in Future Prices

The volatilities in future prices were found out by the measure propounded by John C. Hull in his book titled 'Options, Futures and Other Derivatives' for all the commodities, for all the different positions. An acceptable range for volatilities level was defined. The volatility levels which do not lie in this range were considered highly volatile (above the higher limit) or low on volatility (below the lower limit).

On the basis of the results we derived, we can say that the fluctuations in commodities future prices are showing a downward trend. For Gold, these levels are very low, signifying stability in the market but for Silver it is quite high which is a matter of concern. For agricultural commodities, even though at the beginning these commodities showed heavy fluctuations, but these fluctuations are being phased out in a gradual manner with time. More and more investor confidence is being generated by this, as investor feels safety of his funds. This is a good signal for the markets in particular, and the entire economy in general.

Liquidity Levels in the Market

Liquidity in any market is defined by its width and depth. We have tried to evaluate the liquidity in the commodities market on the basis of two parameters – Trading volume (rupee value) and Open Interest (No. of outstanding contracts on any day). Higher the trading volume and open interest, higher shall be the liquidity in the market and vice-versa.

A graphical plotting of the above parameters was done for all the commodities, for all the positions. It was found out that the liquidity in the market is gaining momentum with time. For metals, liquidity levels are high right from the very beginning and they are constantly showing a rising trend. For agricultural commodities, on the other hand, it was a clumsy behavior in the beginning. But, with time, higher and higher trading volumes are generated and more and more investors are entering into the market. These results are consistent with the fact that for metals the volatility levels are low throughout, whereas for agricultural commodities, these levels were high initially, but gradually they have fallen down.

CONCLUDING REMARKS

The dawn of the 21st century brought back the good times for commodity markets. With the end of a 20-year bear market for commodities, following the global economic recovery and increased demand from China and other developing nations, has revitalized the charisma of commodities markets. The Commodities Markets have rather emerged strongly after the intermediate ban on them. After the ban was lifted, the commodities that can be traded in the market were introduced slowly and gradually. At present, all the commodities have been allowed to be traded barring a few one. So the Commodities Markets are reviving slowly.

According to the forecasts given by experts commodities markets are likely to experience a bright future with the depreciation in the value of financial assets. Furthermore, increasing global consumption, declining U.S. Dollar value, rising factor-input costs and the recent recovery of the market from the clutches of bear trend are considered to be the positive symptoms, which contribute to the acceleration of growth in commodity markets segment.

20

Corporate Governance and SEBI Guidelines

The subject of corporate governance leapt to global business limelight after a string of collapses of high profile companies. Enron, Texas based energy giant, and WorldCom, the telecom behemoth, shocked the business world with both the scale and age of their unethical and illegal operations. Worse, they seemed to indicate only the tip of a dangerous iceberg. While corporate practices in the US companies came under attack, it appeared that the problem was far more widespread. Large and trusted companies from Parmalat in Italy to the multinational newspaper group Hollinger Inc., revealed significant and deep-rooted problems in their corporate governance. Even the prestigious New York Stock Exchange had to remove its director, Dick Grasso, amidst public outcry over excessive compensation. It was clear that something was amiss in the area of corporate governance all over the world.

DEFINITION

The central issue of corporate governance is the nature of the contract between shareholder representatives and professional managers, who are entrusted with the responsibility of managing the funds contributed by the shareholders. The main challenge comes from the fact that such contracts are necessarily "incomplete". It is not possible for the Board to fully instruct management on the desired course of action under every possible business situation. The list of possible situations is infinitely long. Consequently, no contract can be written between representatives of shareholders and the management that specifies the right course of action in every situation, so that the management can be held for violation of such a contract in the event it does something else under the circumstances. Because of this "incomplete contracts" situation, some "residual powers" over the funds of the company must be vested with either the financiers or the management. Clearly the former does not have the expertise or the inclination to run the business in the situations unspecified in the contract, so these residual powers must go to management. **The efficient limits to these powers** constitute much of the subject of corporate governance.

Summarised Definition: "Corporate governance is the system by which business corporations are directed and controlled. The corporate governance structure specifies the distribution of rights and responsibilities among different participants in the corporation, such as, the board, managers, shareholders and other stakeholders, and spells out the rules and procedures for making decisions on corporate affairs. By doing this, it also provides the structure through which the company objectives are set and the means of attaining those objectives and monitoring performance".

EVOLUTION AND GLOBAL SCENARIO

Before 1980, corporate governance was very different from today. Executives held modest amounts of stock options in their companies. Top executives and their incentives were more focused on traditional performance measures such as sales or earnings growth. Boards of directors were not particularly active and shareholders were relatively passive. In the 1980s, this began to change. The takeover wave of the 1980s appears to have been a capital market response to corporate governance deficiencies. During the years from 1968 to 1996, seven of the greatest amount of takeover activity occurred.

USA

The most convincing phenomenon in the 1980s, is that the rise of institutional shareholders and the greater availability of information to the capital markets placed more pressure on corporate managements to maximize shareholder value. This was the decade of confrontation. The governance and ownership structures of the 1960s and early 1970s were not sufficiently efficient for the financial markets of the 1980s. As of 1980, management was loyal to the corporation, not to the shareholder. This loyalty led to underutilised resources — organizational slack, operational slack, and mismatched product lines. The 1980s brought mechanisms for shareholders to rebel that had not existed before. The hypothesis that takeovers are more likely for firms with relatively low valuations is consistent with this explanation. In sum, the takeover and restructuring wave of the 1980s is best explained by an ascendancy of the capital markets over corporate managers. In some cases, the capital markets reversed ill-advised diversification; in others, the capital markets helped to eliminate excess capacity; in others, the capital markets disciplined managers who had ignored shareholders to benefit other stakeholders.

What Went Wrong?

Some of the things, which went wrong with corporate America in the 90 and early 00's, were:

- Executive compensation grossly disproportionate to corporate results;

- Stock promotion, such as initial public offerings (IPO), that has gone to an extreme in the creation of very questionable or unproven business concepts;
- Misuse of corporate funds;
- Trading on insider information, particularly by managers exercising stock options that have rewarded short-term thinking;
- Misrepresentation of the true earnings and financial condition of too many companies; and
- Obstruction of justice by concealing activities or destroying evidence.

The main transgressors were the rubber-stamping and passive Board of Directors, Non Accountable CEO's, Biased Investment Bankers, Non independent Public Accounting firms, Poor Regulators. The core of the problem is a breach of fiduciary duty by the trustees of the investors' interests: the board of directors and management. Management teams that place their personal interests above investor demand for value creation when conducting the affairs of the corporation incur a systemic conflict of interest. Breaches of fiduciary duty by management and boards of directors were condoned by non-independent auditors with limited capability and authority to challenge management. These problems were further exacerbated by investment bankers and market-makers focused exclusively on increasing their profits by enticing investors to invest in companies with unproven business models, giving rise to the tech bubble that burst in March 2000.

Recent Corporate scandals of ENRON & WorldCom have revealed how independence has been compromised by a cozy relationship between the CEO even with the so-called independent directors. However Independent directors are still the only hope to instill discipline in the murky world of corporate finance. It is necessary that greed does not play any part in their appointment. It is not necessary that independent directors should have high profiles. Branding is not essential as much as their competency to provide innovative and frank views without fear or favour.

The main benefits which independent director can bring to companies are:

- Counterbalance management weaknesses in a company.
- Ensure legal and ethical behaviour at the company, while strengthening accounting controls.
- Extend the "reach" of a company through contacts, expertise, and access to debt and equity capital.
- Be a source of well-conceived, binding, long-term decisions for a company.
- Help a company survive, grow, and prosper over time through improved succession planning through membership in the nomination committee etc.
- Independent directors have a direct role in reviewing performance of senior management in their functioning. Many corporate governing requirements stress on this by providing for their nomination on the remuneration committee, which involves review of their performance in relation to remuneration.

A Giant First Step in the Right Direction (2002)

Sarbanes-Oxley Act is designed to address the accounting scandals and was a quickly assembled, emergency legislation. The general notion is that the act was an expression of the view of the U.S. Congress that all the "watchdogs" (directors, auditors, ratings agencies, SEC and lawyers) over U.S. corporations had failed at the same time. Some of the principal provisions of the Sarbanes Oxley Act are the establishment of a new oversight body for auditors, called the Public Company Accounting Oversight Board (PCAOB), to exercise greater scrutiny. Since the main theme of the Act was that increased independence would improve the system, there were increased restrictions on the ability of audit firms to provide non-audit services to their clients. Other provisions include the internal control certification under Section 404. However it does not really address the issue of stock options, perhaps because it was too politically potent.

The Sarbanes-Oxley Act places considerable emphasis on correcting the most critical manifestations of lax corporate governance practices, including:

- Management dealing in an environment full of pervasive conflicts of interest;
- Lack of strict transparency, reliability, and accuracy standards in financial reporting;
- Lack of independence between the key players in corporate governance (the board of directors, management, and auditors);
- Lack of adequate enforcement tools at the disposal of regulators; and
- Widespread conflicts of interest influencing securities market transactions

UK

The evolution of Corporate Governance in UK started with the landmark Cadbury report and it had its logical extension in Myners Report. A cursory view of the important reports is outlined below:

Cadbury Report (1992)

The Cadbury Report was published in December 1992, following the recommendations of the Cadbury Committee. The establishment of the Committee in May 1991 by the Financial Reporting Council, the London Stock Exchange, and the accountancy profession arose in response to the occurrence of financial scandals in the 1980's involving UK listed companies, which led to a fall in investor confidence in the quality of company's financial reporting.

As such the Committee **addressed the financial aspects of corporate governance** and subsequently produced a **Code of Best Practice**, the provisions of which, in their belief, all boards of UK listed companies should comply with. Specifically, they recommended that listed companies should incorporate a formal *statement* into their Report and Accounts outlining whether or not they complied with each of the Code's provisions. In respect of areas of non-compliance an *explanation* of the reason was sought. Further to this, the Report recommended that auditors prior to release of the Annual Report review the compliance statements made by the companies.

Some of the main recommendations, which were made, are as follows:

- The majority of non-executive directors should be independent of management and free from any business or other relationship;
- Non-executive directors should be appointed for specified terms;
- Service contracts should not exceed three years;
- Executive remuneration should be subject to the recommendations of a Remuneration Committee made up entirely or mainly of non-executive directors; and
- An Audit Committee, comprising at least three non-executives, should be established.

Following publication of the Code, the London Stock Exchange introduced a requirement into the Listing Rules requesting all companies to include a statement of compliance, or non-compliance, with the provisions, in their annual Report and Accounts.

Greenbury Report (1995)

During the 1990's the issue of director's remuneration was becoming a primary concern for investors and the public at large. To address corporate Governance issue related to Directors Remuneration, Greenbury Committee was formed. However the only difference with its recommendation to those of Cadbury was that in terms of service contracts, a *maximum notice period of 12 months* rather than three years as suggested by Cadbury. The recommendation of Greenbury were incorporated in the UK listing rules but were not widely accepted as many believed the recommendations made did not sufficiently deal with the issue of linking directors pay to the Company's performance in the interests of shareholders.

Hampel Report (1998)

It emphasised principles of good governance rather than explicit rules in order to reduce the regulatory burden on companies and avoid 'box-ticking' so as to be flexible enough to be applicable to all companies.

Hampel viewed governance from a strict principal/agent perspective regarding corporate governance as an opportunity to enhance long-term shareholder value, which was asserted as the primary objective of the company. In particular, the report favoured greater shareholder involvement in company affairs. Another key advance was in the area of *accountability and audit*. The Board was identified as having responsibility to maintain a sound system of internal control, thereby safeguarding shareholders' investments Further, the Board was to be held accountable for *all aspects of risk management*, as opposed to just the financial controls as recommended by Cadbury.

Combined Code (1998)

The Combined Code consolidated the principles and recommendations of the Cadbury, Greenbury and Hampel reports.

The Code is divided in two sections. The first outlines principles of best practice and their supporting provisions for **companies**, while the second does the same for **shareholders**. While the compliance with this code was non-mandatory it was appended to listing rules and Companies have to give information regarding the extent of compliance with the code.

Higgs Report (2003)

The report recommended a number of changes to the Combined Code and a revision of the Code in July 2003 incorporated most of the Higgs recommendations.

The combined code did not explain how to assess independence. Higgs outlined a series of tests of independence such as length of service (10 years), associations to executive management, financial interest or significant shareholding. In particular cross-directorships were identified as compromising independence, the simplest case being where two directors act as executive directors and non-executive directors alternatively at two companies.

It called for all listed companies to establish a nomination committee, chaired by an independent Non Executive Director (not the Chairman) and comprising a majority of independent non-executive directors.

Other important recommendations of the Higgs report included:

- The Board should review its performance, the performance of its committees and individual directors at least once a year;
- The Company Secretary should be accountable to the Board through the Chairman on all governance matters; and
- The terms of reference of the remuneration committee should be published.

Revised Combined Code (2003)

The revised Combined Code, published in July 2003 was a direct result of the recommendations of the **Higgs** report outlined above and also the **Smith** review concerning Audit Committees. As with the 1998 Combined Code, companies are required to report on their compliance against the Code and should explain areas of non-compliance. The revised Combined Code is effective for Companies with financial years starting **on or after 1 November 2003**.

Myners Report (2004)

It states that the existing paper-based system of voting, which has a number of structural weaknesses, were to be, 'overhauled and upgraded,' it would lead to improvements being seen, the overriding conclusion is that, 'electronic voting remains the key to a more efficient voting system, and all parties – issuers, institutional investors and the intermediaries – need to make conscious efforts to introduce electronic voting capabilities in 2004.'

INDIAN SCENARIO

These potential problems of corporate governance are universal. The Indian financial sector is marked with a relatively unsophisticated equity market vulnerable to manipulation and with rudimentary analyst activity; a dominance of family firms; a history of managing agency system; and a generally high level of corruption. All these features make corporate governance a particularly important issue in India. Some of the issues of corporate governance of India are as follows:

- Concentrated ownership and family control
- Tunneling of funds within business groups in India.
- Absence of culture of Hostile Takeover
- Enforcement of laws and regulations
- Nominee directors of Financial Institutions (FI) as well as Board of Directors acting as rubber stamp of Management
- Poor Bankruptcy Laws
- Irregularities in share transfers and registrations – deliberate or unintentional.

The years since liberalization have witnessed wide-ranging changes in both laws and regulations driving corporate governance as well as general consciousness about it.

Perhaps the single most important development in the field of corporate governance and investor protection in India has been the establishment of the Securities and Exchange. Board of India (SEBI) in 1992 and its gradual emergence in regulating the stock market.

The concerns about corporate governance stemming from the scandals (such as Harshad Mehta scam, Preferential allotment of shares to promoter at discounted prices etc.) as well as opening up the capital market to the forces of competition and globalization. One of the first among such endeavors was the CII Code for Desirable Corporate Governance developed by a committee chaired by Rahul Bajaj. Later SEBI constituted two committees to look into the issue of corporate governance – the first chaired by Kumar Mangalam Birla that submitted its report in early 2000 and the second by Narayana Murthy three years later. However the latest Naresh Chandra committee report is the one that has taken care of most of the concerns of the earlier reports and the clause 49 of SEBI has been crafted on the basis of this report. The highlights of the reports in short are explained below.

CII Code Recommendations (1997)

Board of Directors

a) For a listed company with turnover exceeding Rs.100 crores, if the Chairman is also the MD, at least half of the board should be Independent directors, else at least 30%.
b) No single person should hold directorships in more than 10 listed companies.
c) Directors should be paid a commission not exceeding 1% or 3% of net profits for a company with or without an MD respectively over and above sitting fees.

Audit Committee

Listed companies with turnover over Rs. 100 crores or paid-up capital of Rs. 20 crores should have an audit committee at least three members, all non-executive, with clear terms of reference and access to all financial information in the company and should periodically interact with statutory auditors and internal auditors and assist the board in corporate accounting and reporting.

Disclosure and Transparency

a) Companies should inform their shareholders about the high and low monthly averages of their share prices and about share, performance and prospects of major business segments (exceeding 10% of turnover).
b) Stock exchanges should require compliance certificate from CEOs and CFOs on company accounts
c) For companies with paid-up capital exceeding Rs. 20 crore, disclosure norms for domestic issues should be same as those for GDR issues.

Birla Committee (SEBI Recommendations 2000)

Board of Directors

a) At least 50% non-executive members
b) For a company with an executive Chairman, at least half of the board should be independent directors, else at least one-third.
c) Non-executive Chairman should have an office and be paid for job related expenses.
d) Maximum of 10 directorships and 5 Chairmanships per person.

Audit Committee

A board must have an qualified and independent audit committee, of minimum 3 members, all non-executive, with at least one having financial and accounting knowledge. Its chairman should attend AGM to answer shareholder's queries. The committee should confer with key executives as necessary and the company secretary should be secretary of the committee. The committee should meet at least thrice a year — one before finalization of annual accounts and one necessarily every six months with the quorum being the higher of two members or one-third of members with at least two independent directors. It should have access to information from any employee and can investigate any matter within its TOR, can seek outside legal/ professional service as well as secure attendance of outside experts in meetings. It should act as the bridge between the board, statutory auditors and internal auditors with far ranging powers and responsibilities.

Remuneration Committee

The Remuneration committee should decide remuneration packages for executive directors. It should have at least 3 directors, all non-executive and be chaired by an independent director.

Disclosure and Transparency

Companies should provide consolidated accounts for subsidiaries where they have majority shareholding. A mandatory 'Management Discussion & Analysis' segment of annual report would be published to include discussion of industry structure and development, opportunities, threats, outlook, risks etc. as well as financial and operational performance and managerial developments in HR/IR front. Management should inform board of all potential conflict of interest situations. On appointment of directors, shareholders must be informed of their resume, expertise, and names of companies where they are directors.

Narayana Murthy committee (SEBI Recommendations 2003)

Board of Directors

a) There shall be no nominee directors. All Directors need to be elected by shareholders with same responsibilities and accountabilities.
b) Non-executive director compensation to be fixed by board and ratified by shareholders and reported. Stock options should be vested at least a year after their retirement. Independent directors should be treated the same way as non-executive directors.
c) The board should be informed every quarter of business risk and risk management strategies of the corporate.

Audit Committee

Audit Committee should comprise entirely of "financially literate" non-executive members with at least one member having accounting or related financial management expertise. It should review a mandatory list of documents including information relating to subsidiary companies. "Whistle blowers" should have direct access to it and all employees be informed of such policy (and this should be affirmed annually by management). Audit committee must approve all "related party" transactions. The committee should be responsible for the appointment, removal and remuneration of chief internal auditor.

Disclosure and Transparency

Management should explain and justify any deviation from accounting standards in Financial statements and companies should move towards a regime of unqualified financial statements. It was recommended that management should provide a clear description, followed by auditor's comments, of each material contingent liability and its risks.

Naresh Chandra Committee Recommendations (SEBI CLAUSE–49)

SEBI guidelines require all listed companies to follow the clause 49, which relate to corporate governance. A large portion of these guidelines has been adopted from the Naresh Chandra Committee Recommendations. As per the recommendations, companies shall annually affirm that they have not denied any personnel access to the audit committee of the company and that they have provided protection to "whistle blowers" from unfair or prejudicial practices. The appointment, removal and terms of remuneration of the chief internal auditor must be subject to review by the Audit Committee. Such affirmation shall form a part of the Board report on Corporate Governance that is required to be prepared and submitted together with the annual report.

NEW SEBI GUIDELINE: CLAUSE–49 (EFFECTIVE FROM 31.12.2005)

Mandatory Requirements

Compliances

The board shall periodically review legal compliance reports prepared by the company as well as steps taken the company to cure instances of non-compliances.

Code of Conduct

(i) The Board shall lay down a code of conduct for all Board members and senior Management of the company. The code of conduct shall be posted on the website of the company.

(ii) All Board members and senior management personnel shall affirm compliance with the code on an annual basis. The Annual Report of the company shall contain a declaration to this effect signed by the CEO.

Explanation: For this purpose, the term "senior management" shall mean personnel of the company who are members of its core management team excluding Board of Directors. Normally, this would comprise all members of management one level below the executive directors, including all functional heads.

Comments: Each Company is now required to draft and adopt a code of conduct of board members. In the interest of standardization and uniformity, SEBI has come out with the code of conduct, laying down at least the barest minimum norms but it is only a draft code and each company need to make necessary changes in it to make it relevant for them.

Review of Information by Audit Committee

The Audit Committee shall mandatory review the following information:

1. Management discussion and analysis of financial condition and results of operations;
2. Statement of significant related party transactions (as defined by the Audit Committee), submitted by management;
3. Management letters / letters of internal control weaknesses issued by the statutory Auditors;
4. Internal audit reports relating to internal control weaknesses; and
5. The appointment, removal and terms of remuneration of the Chief internal auditor shall be subject to review by the Audit Committee

Comments

What is a significant related party transaction is as defined by the audit committee and not as in management's view. This shows the lack of trust in management and overwhelming faith in audit committees which predominantly comprises independent Directors. In this din and bustle, it is of relief to note that the audit committee of the holding company is not required to review the consolidated accounts whose preparation is mandatory for listed companies. This has been inserted also with a view to give more powers as well as responsibility in the hands of the independent directors dominated Audit Committee. This will ensure greater independence of the internal auditors, as till now he was at the mercy of the management, now it will require the Audit Committee approval for any actions against them.

Disclosures

Board Disclosures: Risk Management

The company shall lay down procedures to inform Board members about the risk Assessment and minimization procedures. These procedures shall be periodically Reviewed to ensure that executive management controls risk through means of a properly defined framework.

Comments: Addition of this clause would require the following:

- Definition of risk
- Assessment of risk based on availability, reliability and relevance of information.
- Classification of risk.
- Time span involved
- Recurring measures to minimize the risk
- One time measure to minimize the risk
- Phase of trade cycle.
- Competitor strength and weakness.
- Passing of risk.

Business risks would include risk associated with litigation against company, criminal and civil and also risk associated with intellectual property rights (trade mark patent and design). This is expected to increase the paperwork of listed companies exponentially. This is in line with Section 404 of the Sarbanes-Oxley Act of USA, which provides for similar risk assessment requirements.

Proceeds from Public Issues, Rights Issues, Preferential, Issues etc.

When money is raised through an issue (public issues, rights issues, preferential issues etc.), it shall disclose to the Audit Committee, the uses / applications of funds by major category (capital expenditure, sales and marketing, working capital, etc), on a quarterly basis as a part of their quarterly declaration of financial results. Further, on an annual basis, the company shall prepare a statement of funds utilized for purposes other than those stated in the offer document/prospectus/notice and place it before the audit committee. Such disclosure shall be made only till such time that the full money raised through the issue has been fully spent. The statutory auditors of the company shall certify this statement. The audit committee shall make appropriate recommendations to the Board to take up steps in this matter.

Comments: This is in addition to clause 43, which requires the companies to furnish on a quarterly basis a statement showing the variations between projected and actual utilization of funds.

CEO/CFO Certification

The CEO, i.e. the Managing Director or Manager appointed in terms of the Companies Act, 1956 and the CFO i.e. the whole-time Finance Director or any other person heading the finance function discharging that function shall certify to the Board that:

(a) They have reviewed financial statements and the cash flow statement for the year and that to the best of their knowledge and belief :(i) these statements do not contain any materially untrue statement or omit any material fact or contain statements that might be misleading; (ii) These statements together present a true and fair view of the company's affairs and are in compliance with existing accounting standards, applicable laws and regulations.

(b) There are, to the best of their knowledge and belief, no transactions entered into by the company during the year that are fraudulent, illegal or violative of the company's code of conduct.

(c) They accept responsibility for establishing and maintaining internal controls and that they have evaluated the effectiveness of the internal control systems of the company and they have disclosed to the auditors and the Audit Committee, deficiencies in the design or operation of internal controls, if any, of which they are aware and the steps they have taken or propose to take to rectify these deficiencies.

(d) They have indicated to the auditors and the Audit committee
   (i) Significant changes in internal control during the year;
   (ii) Significant changes in accounting policies during the year and that the same have been disclosed in the notes to the financial statements; and
   (iii) Instances of significant fraud of which they have become aware and the involvement therein, if any, of the management or an employee having a significant role in the company's internal control system.

Comments: This certificate from the CEO/CFO would also enable the statutory auditor of the company to make his report regarding fraud under the new CARO regulations. However it has also put huge responsibilities on the part of CEO/CFO of the companies.

Whistle Blower Policy

The company may establish a mechanism for employees to report to the management concerns about unethical behaviour, actual or suspected fraud or violation of the company's code of conduct or ethics policy. This mechanism could also provide for adequate safeguards against victimization of employees who avail of the mechanism and also provide for direct access to the Chairman of the Audit committee in exceptional cases. Once established, the existence of the mechanism may be appropriately communicated within the organization.

Comments: The concept of whistle blowers may not work due to the following reasons.

Identity of the whistle blower and the information provided by him would be very difficult to guard due to leakages in the system. Ultimately it may end in harassment of the informant. The investigative mechanism may be unable to swiftly zero- in on the tip received. The whistle blower may become a victim of corruption.

At best whistle blowing may be confined to reporting of suspected or actual financial frauds otherwise disgruntled employees to make obnoxious complaints against their superiors especially under the cover of anonymity may misuse this mechanism.

Matters regarding industrial relations should be excluded from Whistle Blowing since there are other mechanisms under various labour laws to safeguard the interest of workers. However it may be necessary to have a whistle blowers Act as such a law exists in many developed countries.

Tenure of Independent Directors

Independent Directors may have a tenure not exceeding, in the aggregate, a period of nine years, on the Board of a company.

Comments: It is not understood how a person who serves on the board of the company as an independent non-executive director for a period of nine years can be deemed as non-independent non-executive director from the 10th year onwards. This provision will create a paucity of independent directors. It may also be noted that even Company Law does not restrict the term of office of a director (the maximum number of years for which one can serve as a director). So as it is non-mandatory directions NTPC should ignore it.

GOOD CORPORATE GOVERNANCE: CASES

Principles define and govern the very character of the governance of an organization and go a long way in ensuring effective and desired governance principles and practices. The core principles of corporate governance, according to the Committee of Sponsoring Organizations of the Treadway Commission (COSO) and as considered by **Standard & Poor's (S & P)** for assessing the corporate governance scores of corporate entities are:

- Fairness
- Transparency
- Accountability
- Responsibility

Infosys

The Corporate Governance philosophy of Infosys is based on the following principles:

- Satisfy the spirit of the law and not just the letter of the law. Corporate governance standards should go beyond the law.

- Be transparent and maintain high degree of disclosure levels. When in doubt, disclose.
- Make a clear distinction between personal conveniences and corporate resources.
- Communicate externally in a truthful manner, about how the company is run internally.
- Comply with the laws in all the countries in which it operates.
- Have a simple and transparent corporate structure driven solely by the business needs.
- Management is the trustee of the shareholders' capital and not the owner.

Board of Directors

The Principles call on company boards to act objectively and independently and to be accountable to shareholders. Importantly, the concept of board independence and objectivity also apply to situations characterized by block and controlling shareholders, and not just referring to independence from management. Also, the duties and responsibilities of the board are defined as fiduciary in nature, a clarification that is of particular importance in the case of conglomerates, or groups made up of a number of different corporate entities. Boards should monitor and manage potential conflicts of interest. They should also be responsible for corporate ethics, compliance with laws and standards and for overseeing internal control systems, such as accounting and financial reporting.

Selection and Composition

The composition and selection of the Board of Directors is a primary postulate for the practice of high corporate governance standards in any organization. They are the ones who direct, manage and operate the businesses by guiding the employees. The nature of significance of this calls for setting up of different criteria for the membership of the board, selection of Chairman and Chief Executive Officer, along with guidelines for orientation of directors and their continuing education.

General Motors (GM)

Board Membership Criteria

The Directors and Corporate Governance Committee are responsible for reviewing with the Board, on an annual basis, the appropriate skills and characteristics required of Board members in the context of the current make-up of the Board. In assessing potential new directors, the Committee considers individuals from various disciplines and diverse backgrounds. The selection of qualified directors is complex and crucial to GM's long-term success. Board candidates are considered based upon various criteria, such as their broad-based business skills and experiences, prominence and reputation in their profession, a global business and social perspective, concern for the long-term interests of the stockholders, and personal integrity and judgement — all in the context of an assessment of the perceived needs of the Board at that point in time. In addition, directors must have significant time available to devote to Board activities and to enhance their knowledge of the global automotive industry. Directors are expected to attend meetings of the Board, its Committees on which they serve and the Annual Meeting of Stockholders. The Directors and Corporate Governance Committee will annually review the membership criteria and modify them as appropriate.

Selection of New Directors

The Board itself should be responsible, in fact as well as procedure, for selecting its own members and in recommending them for election by the stockholders. The Board delegates the screening process involved to the Directors and Corporate Governance Committee with direct input from the Chairman and Chief Executive Officer.

Extending the Invitation to a Potential Director to Join the Board

The invitation to join the Board should be extended by the Board itself via the Chairman and Chief Executive Officer of the Corporation, together with an independent director, when appropriate.

Director Orientation and Continuing Education

The Board and Management will conduct a comprehensive orientation process for new Directors to become familiar with the Corporation's vision, strategic direction, core values including ethics, financial matters, corporate governance practices and other key policies and practices through a review of background material, meetings with senior management and visits to Corporation facilities. The Board also recognizes the importance of continuing education for its directors and is committed to provide such education in order to improve both Board and Committee performance. It is the responsibility of the Directors and Corporate Governance Committee to advise the independent directors about their continuing education, including leading-edge corporate governance issues. Directors are encouraged to participate in continuing director education programs.

Selection of Chairman and Chief Executive Officer

The Board should be free to make this choice any way that seems best for the Corporation at a given point in time. Therefore, the Board does not have a policy, one way or the other, on whether or not the role of the Chairman and Chief Executive Officer should be separate or combined and, if it is to be separate, whether the Chairman should be selected from the non-employee Directors or be an employee.

Chairman of the Directors and Corporate Governance Committee

The Chairman of the Directors and Corporate Governance Committee will be an independent Director and will act as the presiding director for the executive sessions of the independent Directors and in communicating the Board's annual evaluation of the Chairman and Chief Executive Officer. The Chairman of the Committee, together with the members of that Committee, will develop the agendas for those executive sessions and periodically review and propose revisions to the Board's procedures and the Corporate Governance Guidelines.

ONGC

Board Procedure

Institutionalized decision making process

With a view to institutionalize all corporate affairs and setting up systems and procedures for advance planning for matters requiring discussion/decisions by the Board, the Company has defined guidelines for the meetings of the Board of Directors and Committees thereof. These Guidelines seek to systematize the decision making process at the meetings of Board/Committees, in an informed and efficient manner.

Scheduling and selection of Agenda items for Board / Committee Meetings

(i) The meetings are being convened by giving appropriate notice after obtaining the approval of the Chairman of the Board/Committee. Detailed agenda, management reports and other explanatory statements are circulated in advance amongst the members for facilitating meaningful, informed and focused decisions at the meetings. To address specific urgent need, meetings are also being called at short notice. The Board is also authorized to pass Resolution by Circulation for all such matters which are of utmost urgent nature.

(ii) Where it is not practicable to attach any document or the agenda is of confidential nature, the same is placed on the table at the meeting with the approval of the C&MD. In special and exceptional circumstances, additional or supplemental item(s) on the agenda are permitted. Sensitive subject matters are discussed at the meeting without written material being circulated.

(iii) The agenda papers are prepared by the concerned officials and submitted to concerned functional Directors for obtaining approval of the Chairman and

Managing Director. Duly approved agenda papers are circulated amongst the Board members by the Company Secretary.

(iv) The meetings are usually held at the Company's Registered Office in New Delhi.

(v) Presentations are made at the Board/ Committees covering Finance, Operations & Business Segments, Human Resources, Marketing and Joint Venture Operations etc. of the Company before taking on record quarterly/annual financial results at the pre-scheduled Board/Committee Meetings.

(vi) The members of the Board have complete access to all information of the Company. The Board is also free to recommend inclusion of any matter in agenda for discussion. Senior management officials are called to provide additional inputs to the items being discussed by the Board, as and when necessary.

Recording minutes of proceedings at the Board Meeting

Minutes of the proceedings of each Board/Committee meeting are recorded. Draft minutes are circulated amongst all members of the Board/ Committee for their comments. The minutes of the proceedings of meetings are entered in the Minutes Book.

Follow-up mechanism

The guidelines for the Board and Committee Meetings facilitate an effective post meeting follow-up, review and reporting process for the action taken on decisions of the Board and Committee. Every functional Director submits follow-up Action Taken Report (ATR) on the areas of his responsibilities, once in a quarter, on the decisions/ instructions of the Board.

Compliance

Every functional Director while preparing the agenda notes is responsible for and is required to ensure adherence to all the applicable provisions of law, rules, guidelines etc. The Company Secretary has to ensure compliance to all the applicable provisions of the Companies Act, 1956, SEBI Guidelines, Listing Agreement, and other statutory requirements pertaining to capital market. A Quarterly Compliance Report confirming adherence to the applicable laws, rules, guidelines and on Corporate Governance is submitted to the Board of Directors for their review.

INDEPENDENT MONITORING

The role of independent directors has gained primary importance in the governance and functioning of an organization. They act as safeguards of the interests of the stakeholders in the company, be it the shareholders (including minority shareholders), the lenders, the government, the employees or the society. The Clause 49 of the

Listing Agreements of Indian stock exchanges explains the meaning of independent directors.

Infosys

It has eight independent directors and seven executive directors. The directors are not related to each other. It's not a family managed enterprise. The definition of independent director has been adopted as defined in (i) NASDAQ Rule 4200 and (ii) the rules of the SEC,. which satisfy the conditions of the Sarbanes-Oxley Act (SOX) and the Clause 49 of the listing agreements in Indian Stock Exchanges as prescribed by the SEBI. The company also has a lead independent director appointed by the board and is responsible:

- To preside over all the executive sessions of the board's independent directors;
- To work closely with the Chairman and the CEO to finalize the information flow, meeting agendas and meeting schedules;
- To liaise between the Chairman, CEO and the independent directors on the board; and
- Along with the Chairman take a lead role, in the board evaluation process.

GM

The Company defines the term "independent" as qualifying as independent under any definition or standard of "independence" adopted by the Securities and Exchange Commission (SEC) or the NYSE. Each independent director shall notify the Chairman of the Directors and Corporate Governance Committee, as soon as practicable, of any event, situation or condition that may affect the Board's evaluation of his or her independence.

General role and responsibilities

A strong and effective board should have a clear view of its role in relationship to management. The board's duty is to focus on guidance and strategic oversight, while it is management's duty to run the company's business, with the goal of increasing shareholder value for the long term. CEOs and management need to work with the board to establish the right kind of processes and communications to ensure that the company is running effectively and in accordance with the board's basic fiduciary oversight requirements. The ultimate responsibility for directing the company, however, lies with the board, since most state corporation statutes generally provide that the business of the company shall be managed under the direction of the board. The specifics of the board's role will vary with size, stage and strategy of the company, and talents and personalities of the CEO and the board.

Board: Role and responsibilities

A Corporate has been defined as a nexus of contracts among the stakeholders. The vital link of this nexus is a board of directors (referred also as the "board"). It is through this apparatus that the company acts. It is also known as the heart and mind of the company.

Essential functions of the board include,

(i) Providing strategic direction;
(ii) Ensuring compliance of laws;
(iii) Implementing adequate internal control and audit functions; and
(iv) Maintaining the highest standards of fairness in its relationship with other stakeholders.

Strategic direction

The board is expected to provide the strategic direction of the company. Members of the board are expected to bring the necessary professional expertise to analyze and anticipate future direction of the business. If the company prospers or sinks, it is the board that takes the credit or can be made accountable for the state of affairs of the company. Unfortunately, the board's responsibility in providing strategic direction has been conspicuously missing in the current debate of corporate governance. All other functions of the board mentioned above will be of no use, if a board fails to provide strategic direction to the company. Accountability to all the stakeholders, for example, social responsibility, employee welfare, etc. are subservient to this function.

Compliance

The board should create the necessary systems and processes by which it can ensure the compliance with laws of the land. The company needs to pay taxes, levies, salaries, debt servicing, etc. as and when they are due. The board also needs to be vigilant that the company is not damaging the environment and has all the necessary permissions for carrying out its given operations and activities. While doing so, the board needs to ensure that the company does not violate any provisions of the law. This compliance needs to be observed in spirit and not merely in the letter.

Internal control and systems

The board generally does not involve itself in the day-to-day business. It normally gets periodic reports from the management about company's routine operations. As a trustee of the shareholders' funds and public resources, the board is expected to put in place adequate internal control and audit systems to ensure fraud-free and corruption-free operations. Negligence in discharging this responsibility might lead to holding all the directors responsible for the loss to the company and its stakeholders. The Companies Act casts onerous responsibility on the board and the individual directors for not putting in place adequate and necessary internal controls and systems.

Fairness in dealing

The board is responsible for the dealings of the company with its stakeholders. Dealings of the company should be fair and should uphold the highest standards of ethical behavior. For ensuring fairness and ethical behavior, the board needs to clearly communicate up to the lowest level of the organization that only ethical means should be adopted to achieve the results and goals. The board needs to reinforce periodically the corporate philosophy related to code of conduct of its employees. It has to ensure that people in the organization uphold highest level of ethical and fairness standards while dealing inside the organization with their fellow members as well as interacting outside the organization with the environment.

To ensure maximum board effectiveness, *boards need to shift their entire emphasis—they can no longer be just "advisors" who wait for management to come to them.* Their new role requires they provide active oversight of the company's business to minimize corporate risk and promote creation of shareholder value. In the wake of the corporate scandals, the new challenge for boards will be to go beyond their traditional advisory role and increasingly focus on their oversight role. As fiduciaries, boards must be active monitors of management. Board dynamics need to be right for directors to add real value to the company. While boards need and value collegiality, this should not turn into complacency. Directors need to feel that they can raise objections and still be seen as team players. An effective board plays an integral role in the strategic planning process. Management develops the strategic plan, while the board reviews and approves it.

COMMITTEES

Number, Structure and Independence of Committees

Board committees are vital structural mechanisms that help the board to ensure adequacy and efficacy of internal controls and systems for objective decision making process. These committees report to the board on various important issues like audit, managerial remuneration, share-transfer, nomination of key positions in management etc.

ONGC

The Company has the following Committees of the Board:

- Audit & ethics committee
- Remuneration committee

- Shareholders'/Investors' grievance committee
- Human Resource Management committee
- Project Appraisal committee
- Share Transfer committee
- Health, Safety & Environment committee
- Policy & Planning committee

Audit & ethics committee

The scope of the committee includes:

1. Overseeing the Company's financial reporting process and the disclosure of financial information to ensure that the financial statement is correct sufficient and credible;
2. Recommending audit fees payable to Statutory Auditors appointed by C&AG and approving payments for any other services;
3. Reviewing with management the periodical financial statements before submission to the Board, focusing primarily on (i) changes in accounting policies and practices, (ii) major accounting adjustment based on management judgement, (iii) qualifications in draft audit report, (iv) significant adjustments arising out of the audit, (v) the going concern assumption, (vi) compliance with accounting standards, (vii) compliance with stock exchanges and legal requirements concerning financial statements, (viii) any related party transactions i.e. transactions of the company of material nature, with promoters or the management, their subsidiaries or relatives etc that may have potential conflict with the interest of the company at large;
4. Reviewing with the management, Reports of Internal, Statutory and the Government auditors, the adequacy of internal control systems and recommending improvements to the management;
5. Reviewing the adequacy of internal audit functions, including the structure of the internal audit department, staffing, reporting structure, coverage and frequency of internal audit;
6. Discussion with internal auditors any significant findings and follow-up thereon;
7. Reviewing the findings of any internal investigations by the internal auditors into the matters where there is suspected irregularity or a failure of internal control systems of a material nature and reporting the matter to the Board;
8. Discussion with the Statutory Auditors before the audit commences, the nature and scope of audit, as well as have post-audit discussion to ascertain any area of concern;
9. Reviewing the Company's financial and risk management policies; and
10. Review Ethical adherence and Corporate Governance principles.

Infosys

The board has six committees:

1. Audit Committee: the company has adopted a charter for the audit committee which elaborates on the various functions.
2. Compensation Committee
3. Nominations Committee
4. Investor Grievance Committee
5. Investment Committee
6. Share Transfer Committee

Compensation Committee

The compensation committee of Infosys consists entirely of non-executive, independent directors. The charter describes the purpose of the committee as, to discharge the Board's responsibilities relating to compensation of the Company's executive directors and senior management. The committee has overall responsibility for approving and evaluating the executive directors and senior management compensation plans, policies and programs of the Company. The compensation committee is also responsible for producing an annual report on executive compensation for inclusion in the Company's proxy statement.

GM

The current five committees are Audit, Directors and Corporate Governance, Executive Compensation, Investment Funds, and Public Policy. Committee membership on all the committees will consist only of independent Directors as defined in Bylaws. From time to time, the Board may want to form a new committee or disband a current Committee depending upon the circumstances, regulations or Bylaws. The Bylaws of GM define independent as a director who qualifies as independent director under any definition or standard of "independence" adopted by the SEC or NYSE.

The Board of Directors will assure that each Committee has a charter setting forth the purpose, authority and duties of each Committee. On an annual basis, each Committee will review its charter and will present any modifications to the Board for approval.

Information accessibility

The effectiveness of the board ultimately depends on the quality and timeliness of information directors have at their disposal. Information going to the board should be on the strategic monitoring level, which will help the board understand the big picture, and directors should ensure they have a thorough understanding of this information. Both formal and informal communication and information channels and cross-linkages need to be developed with the full support of the CEO.

The primary ways in which directors receive information about the state of the company are through:

Formal channels financial and other management reports, board and committee meetings, executive sessions, direct communication with management, technical means (raw data, intranet, etc.), factory and facility visits **Informal channels** phone or e-mail discussions among directors between meetings, conversations with managers, pre-meeting dinners, etc. The board needs to establish a solid information framework beginning with a thorough briefing of the annual plan and an overview of the significant risk/reward elements involved with the plan to actively monitor it continuously during the year. Boards should also set a calendar around board meetings where certain types of information such as quarterly results are required by the time the board meets. This serves to establish a routine whereby if information is late or is missing, members of the board realize it and a red flag is raised. Management must also adequately explain new developments to directors, such as key acquisitions, new products, etc. as the year progresses. To assure independence of thought and unvarnished perspectives, the board must have key information flowing from senior managers directly to the board, as well as to the CEO. For example, the heads of the legal, finance/accounting, human resources, and regulatory (if applicable) departments, and of any major business division, should regularly meet with the board (or a committee of the board). In this manner, the board receives information from those more directly responsible and intimately familiar with each major corporate center, and can obtain a more accurate overall picture of corporate performance, and, by the same token, the chief executive's performance, independently from the chief executive. This independent source of information is imperative for achieving an accurate assessment of performance and ultimately protecting shareholder value. Although directors receive, and should expect to receive, the bulk of their information from management, they need to be able to receive input from other sources, particularly when there is a lack of information or where the information is perceived as being overly-filtered.

CODE OF ETHICS

GM

The Board expects all directors, as well as officers and employees, to act ethically at all times and to adhere to GM's "Winning With Integrity: Our Values and Guidelines for Employee Conduct" guidelines. The Board will not permit any waiver of any ethics policy for any director or executive officer. If an actual or potential conflict of interest arises for a director, the director shall promptly inform the Chairman and the presiding director. If a significant conflict exists and cannot be resolved, the director should resign. All directors will recluse themselves from any discussion or decision affecting their business or personal interests.

Infosys

The company has a code of ethics for Principal Executive and Senior Financial Officers that help maintain the standards of business conduct for the company, and ensures compliance with legal requirements, specifically section 406 of the Sarbanes-Oxley Act, 2002, and the SEC rules promulgated thereunder. The purpose of the code is to promote ethical conduct and deter wrongdoing. The code lays down policies regarding honest & ethical conduct, conflicts of interest, compliance with laws and disclosures.

CODE OF BUSINESS CONDUCT

Infosys

The company's Code of Business Conduct and Ethics helps to ensure compliance with legal requirements and the standards of business conduct. All the employees and trainees of the company are expected to imbibe them in day-to-day activities and follow them in letter and spirit. It speaks about:

- Whistleblower policy
- Responsibilities of the personnel to the company and its shareholders: conflict of interest, related parties, confidentiality of information, insider trading, use of company's assets, etc.
- Responsibilities to customers and suppliers: customer relationships, payments or gifts from others, publications of others, confidential information of others, selection of suppliers, government relations, industrial espionage, etc.

Independence and Integrity

The audit committee should have the ultimate authority and responsibility to select, evaluate, and where appropriate, replace the independent auditors in accordance with law.

Keeping in view the need for the internal auditors' independence from management to remain objective, a formal mechanism should be created to facilitate confidential exchanges between the internal auditors and the Audit Committee, regardless of irregularities or problems. The work carried out by each of these auditors needs to be assessed and reviewed with the independent auditors and appropriate recommendations made to the Board.

Whistleblower Policy

A Whistleblower Policy is a true indicator of the extent of seriousness of the top management and involvement of the organization in its entirety, including all its personnel, in the ethical governance and operations of a company. In Indian laws, such a policy is non-mandatory, however, it is recommended that there should be documented policy in place and it should be followed in spirit in pursuit of high standards in ethics and governance. Companies like Infosys have well laid out policies in this regard which provide full protection to the whistleblower from any adverse treatment by the company's senior personnel, the board and the Chairman. An effective whistleblower policy should take care of **the 3C's**, namely

- **Categorical:** The policy should be unambiguous, clearly laying the procedures, options and access gateways available to the whistleblower. It should encourage the practice of following rules and ethics, and reporting any unethical action(s) or violation of rules/laws.
- **Communicated:** The policy should be communicated openly across the organization at all the hierarchy levels. Accessibility and approachability of the system and the audit committee should be ensured.
- **Culture:** The culture of the organization needs to be open and trusting. People should feel secure and should be ensured about getting some action done against any unethical practice.

The company has been globally acknowledged for its values and organizational culture. The company conducts workshops as a part of its induction programs and employee communication processes. The company has a written code of ethics and a whistle-blower policy, aimed at making all employees aware of the ethical requirements and providing avenues for reporting violations, if any.

The CEO and CFO of the company certify, apart from other things, that:

- They have not denied any personnel access to the audit committee of the company (in respect of matters involving alleged misconduct) and we have provided protection to "whistle blowers" from unfair termination and other unfair or prejudicial employment practices.
- That all board members and senior managerial personnel have affirmed compliance with the code of conduct for the year.

BENEFITS OF CORPORATE GOVERNANCE

Better Valuations

The expenditures on corporate governance (CG) will be judged not by CEOs, regulators or commentators but by the investor. The investor will give a higher valuation to those companies that embrace good governance and effective risk management — not because they have satisfied requirements, but because those that have turned this new era of compliance into a better tool for taking risks will turn out to be the winners in their markets."

Financing

Effective corporate governance (CG) enhances access to external financing by firms, leading to greater investment, as well as higher growth and employment. The proportion of private credit to GDP in countries in the highest quartile of creditor right enactment and enforcement is more than double that in the countries in the lowest quartile. As for equity financing, the ratio of stock market capitalization to GDP in the countries in the highest quartile of shareholder right enactment and enforcement is about *four* times as large as that for countries in the lowest quartile. Poor corporate governance also hinders the creation and development of new firms.

Lower Cost of Capital

Good corporate governance also lowers the cost of capital by reducing risk and creates higher firm valuation once again boosting real investments.

Higher Return On Assets

Effective corporate governance mechanisms ensure better resource allocation and management raising the return to capital. The return on assets (ROA) is about twice as high in the countries with the highest level of equity rights protection as in countries with the lowest protection.

Lower Macro Risks

Good corporate governance can significantly reduce the risk of nation-wide financial crises. There is a strong inverse relationship between the quality of corporate governance and currency depreciation.

Greater Trust

Finally, good corporate governance can remove mistrust between different stakeholders, reduce legal costs and improve social and labor relationships and external economies like environmental protection.

Index